THE
SOUTH

THE SOUTH

The Greenwood Encyclopedia of
American Regional Cultures

Edited by
Rebecca Mark and Rob Vaughan

Foreword by William Ferris, Consulting Editor

Paul S. Piper, Librarian Advisor

GREENWOOD PRESS
Westport, Connecticut • London

Library of Congress Cataloging-in-Publication Data

The South : the Greenwood encyclopedia of American regional cultures / edited by Rebecca Mark
    and Rob Vaughan ; foreword by William Ferris, consulting editor.
        p. cm.
    Includes bibliographical references and index.
    ISBN 0–313–33266–5 (set : alk. paper)—ISBN 0–313–32734–3 (alk. paper)
    1. Southern States—Civilization—Encyclopedias. 2. Southern States—History—Encyclopedias.
3. Southern States—Social conditions—Encyclopedias. 4. Popular culture—Southern States—Encyclopedias. 5. Regionalism—Southern States—Encyclopedias. I. Mark, Rebecca. II. Vaughan,
Robert. III. Series.
    F209.S68   2004
    975'.003—dc22   2004056057

British Library Cataloguing in Publication Data is available.

Library of Congress Catalog Card Number: 2004056057
ISBN: 0–313–33266–5 (set)
        0–313–32733–5 (The Great Plains Region)
        0–313–32954–0 (The Mid-Atlantic Region)
        0–313–32493–X (The Midwest)
        0–313–32753–X (New England)
        0–313–33043–3 (The Pacific Region)
        0–313–32817–X (The Rocky Mountain Region)
        0–313–32734–3 (The South)
        0–313–32805–6 (The Southwest)

First published in 2004

Greenwood Press, 88 Post Road West, Westport, CT 06881
An imprint of Greenwood Publishing Group, Inc.
www.greenwood.com

Printed in the United States of America

The paper used in this book complies with the
Permanent Paper Standard issued by the National
Information Standards Organization (Z39.48–1984).

10 9 8 7 6 5 4 3 2 1

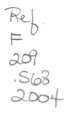

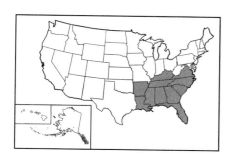

CONTENTS

Foreword
William Ferris   vii

Preface   xi

Introduction   xv

Architecture
Paula Mohr   1

Art
Barbara Rothermel   33

Ecology and Environment
Tasha Eichenseher   77

Ethnicity
Celeste Ray   111

Fashion
Maaja A. Stewart, with Bryce Reveley   161

Film and Theater
Thomas S. Hischak   193

Folklore
Jon Lohman   223

Contents

Food
Susan Tucker and Sharon Stallworth Nossiter   263

Language
Michael Montgomery   305

Literature
Susan V. Donaldson   325

Music
David Sanjek   375

Religion
Paul Harvey   407

Sports and Recreation
Bruce Adelson   439

Timeline   469

Notes   479

Bibliography   495

Index   499

About the Editors and Contributors   529

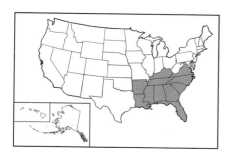

FOREWORD

Region inspires and grounds the American experience. Whether we are drawn to them or flee from them, the places in which we live etch themselves into our memory in powerful, enduring ways. For over three centuries Americans have crafted a collective memory of places that constitute our nation's distinctive regions. These regions are embedded in every aspect of American history and culture.

American places have inspired poets and writers from Walt Whitman and Henry David Thoreau to Mark Twain and William Faulkner. These writers grounded their work in the places where they lived. When asked why he never traveled, Thoreau replied, "I have traveled widely in Concord."

William Faulkner remarked that early in his career as a writer he realized that he could devote a lifetime to writing and never fully exhaust his "little postage stamp of native soil."

In each region American writers have framed their work with what Eudora Welty calls "sense of place." Through their writing we encounter the diverse, richly detailed regions of our nation.

In his ballads Woody Guthrie chronicles American places that stretch from "the great Atlantic Ocean to the wide Pacific shore," while Muddy Waters anchors his blues in the Mississippi Delta and his home on Stovall's Plantation.

American corporate worlds like the Bell system neatly organize their divisions by region. And government commissions like the Appalachian Regional Commission, the Mississippi River Commission, and the Delta Development Commission define their mission in terms of geographic places.

When we consider that artists and writers are inspired by place and that government and corporate worlds are similarly grounded in place, it is hardly surprising that we also identify political leaders in terms of their regional culture. We think of John Kennedy as a New Englander, of Ann Richards as a Texan, and of Jimmy Carter as a Georgian.

Because Americans are so deeply immersed in their sense of place, we use region like a compass to provide direction as we negotiate our lives. Through sense of place we find our bearings, our true north. When we meet people for the first time, we ask that familiar American question, "Where are you from?" By identifying others through a region, a city, a community, we frame them with a place and find the bearings with which we can engage them.

Sense of place operates at all levels of our society—from personal to corporate and government worlds. While the power of place has long been understood and integrated in meaningful ways with our institutions, Americans have been slow to seriously study their regions in a focused, thoughtful way. As a young nation, we have been reluctant to confront the places we are "from." As we mature as a nation, Americans are more engaged with the places in which they live and increasingly seek to understand the history and culture of their regions.

The growing importance of regional studies within the academy is an understandable and appropriate response to the need Americans feel to understand the places in which they live. Such study empowers the individual, their community, and their region through a deeper engagement with the American experience. Americans resent that their regions are considered "overfly zones" in America, and through regional studies they ground themselves in their community's history and culture.

The Greenwood Encyclopedia of American Regional Cultures provides an exciting, comprehensive view of our nation's regions. The set devotes volumes to New England, the Mid-Atlantic, the South, the Midwest, the Southwest, the Great Plains, the Rocky Mountains, and the Pacific. Together these volumes offer a refreshing new view of America's regions as they stretch from the Atlantic to the Pacific.

The sheer size of our nation makes it difficult to imagine its diverse worlds as a single country with a shared culture. Our landscapes, our speech patterns, and our foodways all change sharply from region to region. The synergy of different regional worlds bound together within a single nation is what defines the American character. These diverse worlds coexist with the knowledge that America will always be defined by its distinctly different places.

American Regional Cultures explores in exciting ways the history and culture of each American region. Its volumes allow us to savor individual regional traditions and to compare these traditions with those of other regions. Each volume features chapters on architecture, art, ecology and environment, ethnicity, fashion, film and theater, folklore, food, language, literature, music, religion, and sports and recreation. Together these chapters offer a rich portrait of each region. The series is an important teaching resource that will significantly enrich learning at secondary, college, and university levels.

Over the past forty years a growing number of colleges and universities have launched regional studies programs that today offer exciting courses and degrees for both American and international students. During this time the National Endowment for the Humanities (NEH) has funded regional studies initiatives that range from new curricula to the creation of museum exhibits, films, and encyclopedias that focus on American regions. Throughout the nation, universities with regional studies programs recently received NEH support to assist with the programs that they are building.

The National Endowment for the Arts (NEA) has similarly encouraged regional initiatives within the art world. NEA's state arts councils work together within regional organizations to fund arts projects that impact their region.

The growing study of region helps Americans see themselves and the places they come from in insightful ways. As we understand the places that nurture us, we build a stronger foundation for our life. When speaking of how she raised her children, my mother often uses the phrase "Give them their roots, and they will find their wings." Thanks to *American Regional Cultures*, these roots are now far more accessible for all Americans. This impressive set significantly advances our understanding of American regions and the mythic power these places hold for our nation.

William Ferris
University of North Carolina
at Chapel Hill

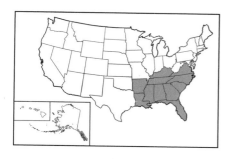

PREFACE

We are pleased to present *The Greenwood Encyclopedia of American Regional Cultures*, the first book project of any kind, reference or otherwise, to examine cultural regionalism throughout the United States.

The sense of place has an intrinsic role in American consciousness. Across its vast expanses, the United States varies dramatically in its geography and its people. Americans seem especially cognizant of the regions from which they hail. Whether one considers the indigenous American Indian tribes and their relationships to the land, the many waves of immigrants who settled in particular regions of the nation, or the subsequent generations who came to identify themselves as New Englanders or Southerners or Midwesterners, and so forth, the connection of American culture to the sense of regionalism has been a consistent pattern throughout the nation's history.

It can be said that behind every travelogue on television, behind every road novel, behind every cross-country journey, is the desire to grasp the identity of other regions. This project was conceived to fill a surprising gap in publishing on American regionalism and on the many vernacular expressions of culture that one finds throughout the country.

This reference set is designed so that it will be useful to high school and college researchers alike, as well as to the general reader and scholar. Toward this goal, we consulted several members of Greenwood's Library Advisory Board as we determined both the content and the format of this encyclopedia project. Furthermore, we used the *National Standards: United States History* and also the *Curriculum Standards for Social Studies* as guides in choosing a wealth of content that would help researchers gain historical comprehension of how people in, and from, all regions have helped shape American cultures.

American Regional Cultures is divided geographically into eight volumes: *The Great Plains Region*, *The Mid-Atlantic Region*, *The Midwest*, *New England*, *The Pacific Region*, *The Rocky Mountain Region*, *The South*, and *The Southwest*. To ensure that cultural elements from each state would be discussed, we assigned each state to a particular region as follows:

The Great Plains Region: Kansas, Nebraska, North Dakota, Oklahoma, South Dakota
The Mid-Atlantic Region: Delaware, District of Columbia, Maryland, New Jersey, New York, Pennsylvania, West Virginia
The Midwest: Illinois, Indiana, Iowa, Michigan, Minnesota, Missouri, Ohio, Wisconsin
New England: Connecticut, Maine, Massachusetts, New Hampshire, Rhode Island, Vermont
The Pacific Region: Alaska, California, Hawai'i, Oregon, Washington
The Rocky Mountain Region: Colorado, Idaho, Montana, Utah, Wyoming
The South: Alabama, Arkansas, Florida, Georgia, Kentucky, Louisiana, Mississippi, North Carolina, South Carolina, Tennessee, Virginia
The Southwest: Arizona, Nevada, New Mexico, Texas

Each regional volume consists of rigorous, detailed overviews on all elements of culture, with chapters on the following topics: architecture, art, ecology and environment, ethnicity, fashion, film and theater, folklore, food, language, literature, music, religion, and sports and recreation. These chapters examine the many significant elements of those particular aspects of regional culture as they have evolved over time, through the beginning of the twenty-first century. Each chapter seeks not to impose a homogenized identity upon each region but, rather, to develop a synthesis or thematically arranged discussion of the diverse elements of each region. For example, in turning to the chapter on music in *The Pacific Region*, a reader will discover information on Pacific regional music as it has manifested itself in such wide-ranging genres as American Indian tribal performances, Hawaiian stylings, Hispanic and Asian traditions, West Coast jazz, surf rock, folk scenes, San Francisco psychedelia, country rock, the L.A. hard-rock scene, Northwest "grunge" rock, West Coast hip-hop, and Northern California ska-punk. Multiply this by thirteen chapters and again by eight volumes, and you get a sense of the enormous wealth of information covered in this landmark set.

In addition, each chapter concludes with helpful references to further resources, including, in most cases, printed resources, Web sites, films or videos, recordings, festivals or events, organizations, and special collections. Photos, drawings, and maps illustrate each volume. A timeline of major events for the region provides context for understanding the cultural development of the region. A bibliography, primarily of general sources about the region, precedes the index.

We would not have been able to publish such an enormous reference set without the work of our volume editors and the more than one hundred contributors that they recruited for this project. It is their efforts that have made *American Regional Cultures* come to life. We also would like to single out two people for their help: William Ferris, former chairman of the National Endowment for the Humanities and currently Distinguished Professor of History and senior associate director for the Center for the Study of the American South, University of North Carolina at Chapel Hill, who served as consulting editor for and was instrumental in the planning of this set and in the recruitment of its volume editors; and Paul S. Piper, Reference Librarian at Western Washington University, who in his role as librar-

ian advisor, helped shape both content and format, with a particular focus on helping improve reader interface.

With their help, we present *The Greenwood Encyclopedia of American Regional
Cultures*.

Rob Kirkpatrick, Senior Acquisitions Editor
Anne Thompson, Senior Development Editor
Greenwood Publishing Group

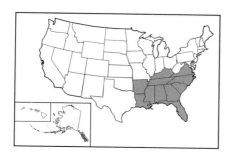

INTRODUCTION

Myths of the plantation, magnolia, and lost cause South have so frequently defined and confined our image of the southern United States that, while we cannot actually separate the mythological from the historical, we can, as this volume hopes to do, bring awareness to the intricate dance, the jazz sequence, played out in our multiple images and narratives of this region. While we often think of the region as a meeting place between European peoples, Native American peoples, and peoples of African descent, we find in these chapters the truly complex cultural mix the South has always been and continues to become. While reading these chapters our black and white South turns into many Souths with a multitude of different ethnicities, a land of people speaking a vast number of languages, bringing with them to this region diverse and multifaceted histories and cultures.

The confluence of cultures, like the many rivers emptying into the Mississippi River or the Chesapeake Bay, has at the same time produced terrible racial conflict and some of the richest cultural outpouring in the world, including intricate forms of music, an extraordinarily developed storytelling culture, folk art, architecture, rich language and religious traditions, and even sport. Each of these and other subjects is addressed in detail through the chapters of this volume, providing a survey of significant research and resources on each topic. Each subject is also set within the larger conceptual framework of the South, providing historical, social, and cultural perspectives for understanding this distinctive region in all its diversity.

The story of this region is the story of a rare meeting of peoples—not just Scottish, Irish, English, French, Spanish, Italian, German, Choctaw, and Cherokee, but also Cuban, Pakistani, Chinese, Vietnamese, Haitian, Honduran, Mexican, Colombian, Jamaican, Chickasaw, Creek, Natchez, Seminole, Powhatan, Algonquian, Tuscarora, and Shawnee. This volume is not about the homogeneity of southern culture but about its complexity. The accumulation of detail found in these chapters—the material artifacts, stories, and examples—questions the notion of a distinctive homogeneous geographical and cultural region known as "the U.S. South." At this moment southern studies scholars are redefining the geopolitical U.S. South as a global South, a Caribbean basin South, or an Atlantic world South.

Ironically, as we begin to taste, smell, and see the U.S. South in these chapters, when we understand the enormous variety of color and texture that makes up the art and fashion of these many Souths, when we are able to hear the differences in tone and rhythm from one song type to another, when we understand that the South exists on a temporal and spatial grid in a slow historical unfolding, juxtaposing cultures that gave birth to what we know as the blues and jazz, and when we understand the depth of cultural exchange that makes the people of the South who they are, then we can think and talk about a South that has not lost its cultural identity but gained it, which is not a cultural melting pot but a wonderful conglomeration of discordant and polymorphous cultural expressions, a meeting of peoples in an alchemical cultural cauldron. The more details we accumulate, the more connected this region becomes, so that the extremity of difference and variety of form actually create an identifiable place.

This place is not a known, loved, and longed-for *Gone with the Wind* Dixie, but instead a constantly fluctuating space which artists and scholars and thinkers of all types have tried both to re-create and rediscover and, on the flip side, violently and turbulently deconstruct. The stultifying impossibility of a lost world—one that did not and should not have existed in the first place, poisoned by slavery and race hatred—pervades and haunts our narratives of southern culture. This region we call the South is held together by a common unsettled history and a confluence of peoples unparalleled in other parts of the nation.

The South, settled initially by Europeans and Africans, is the South of the Atlantic world, the coastal states of Florida, Georgia, South Carolina, North Carolina, and Virginia. Geography defines this subregion. The Atlantic and the Appalachians set its east-west parameters, while the Chesapeake and Caribbean define the northern and southern boundaries. The Atlantic defines the long coastline that became a first place of landing for settlement and colony. It links the continent with the islands, and it set the stage for centuries of trade and migration between the two and with Europe, Africa, and Central and South America. The Appalachians, America's first frontier, link the South to the development of the continent as a new and expanding nation.

For the better part of 500 years, this South Atlantic region witnessed the continent's most profound and continuous contact among European, African, and native populations. Now Southeast Asian, Latin American, and African immigrants and refugees join these groups.

The South Atlantic region is home to the simultaneous beginning of African slavery in North America and the destruction of native peoples by Europeans. Slavery, Jim Crow, and subsequently the civil rights movement shaped not only minority identities in the South Atlantic region along lines of perseverance and resistance, but also white identities along dimensions of arrogance, fear, and hierarchy. The extent of historic Spanish influence is readily apparent in Florida and the surrounding Caribbean, but the rapid growth of the Latino population across the region gives the theme a contemporary region-wide focus.

The South Atlantic is a subregion of places, from Cold Mountain to Tinker Creek, from the Great Dismal Swamp to the Everglades, from Chesapeake Bay to the Sea Islands. It is Lee Smith's Appalachia, Pat Conroy's low country, Tennessee Williams' Key West, Flannery O'Connor's Georgia, Zora Neale Hurston's Florida, Reynolds Price's North Carolina, and Roberto Fernandez's Miami. It is a region of African American heritage trails, Civil War trails, the Appalachian Trail, the Blue Ridge Music Trail, and the new Cherokee Trail. Perhaps more than other parts of the United States, it is also a region of storefronts, churches, temples, and synagogues, of Pentecostals, Presbyterians, Jews, Episcopalians, Baptists, Catholics, Muslims, Hindus, and a growing number of other religious traditions and communities.

Beginning at least 4,500 years ago, maritime technology brought settlers to the South Atlantic; 4,000 years later Spanish ships and firearms enabled the conquest of America; and a mere 126 years later European shipping facilitated the enslavement of Africans and Native Americans in the region. Maritime trade and agricultural technology fueled the region's plantation economies. The first post windmill in North America ground grain by 1619 at Flowerdew Hundred on the James River. Today, sophisticated transportation systems, air conditioning, space travel and space centers, and new forms of communication and media have transformed the South Atlantic region.

The area most often identified as the "real South" includes Alabama, Arkansas, Louisiana, Mississippi, and Tennessee, delineated as the Deep South or Lower South, another subregion demanding recognition of both vastly disparate and intricately interdependent economic and cultural histories. We conventionally envision the mighty Mississippi flowing down into the Gulf taking goods, culture, and refuse in one direction, from north to south. But this ignores the migration of peoples, cultures, and goods upstream from New Orleans to Memphis and Chicago, and in an intricate web of trade, migration, industrial development, and cultural exchange throughout the Deep South, the Caribbean basin, and the Delta. This vibrant web has no single center, only a dynamic interchange among points of contact. The central stereotype in the study of southern culture is that a combination of a sense of place, a static dependence on local tradition, a connection to kin, an oral exchange from generation to generation, and an unbounded conservatism has created pockets of distinct folk culture resistant to the inroads of mass technology.

While there is some truth to this assumption, it is important to remember that economic and historical realities, including not only the slave trade, but also the fur trade, the cotton exchange, the freeing of slaves into poverty and illiteracy, and lack of economic growth, have undammed a flux of peoples, ideas, goods, prejudices, and insights. These peoples have moved not only up and down the Mississippi but also along the Natchez Trace; along the paths and dirt roads that are now such major thoroughfares as the Gulf Coast Highway, Highway 55, Highway 40 through Tennessee and Alabama, or Highway 20 crisscrossing Alabama, Mississippi, and Louisiana; along the Illinois Central Railway; and along the region's canals, bayous, and tributaries. By rethinking the basic dichotomy of static folk versus dynamic mass culture, we begin to question narratives that may imprison rather than define what we call "the South."

The web radiates not only from the urban centers of Memphis, Birmingham, Montgomery, Little Rock, Jackson, New Orleans, Knoxville, and Nashville, but more significantly into these centers from isolated rural enclaves and small towns. Like the waters of a swamp which look still but are stirred by constant currents, the small coal mining towns of Tennessee, the Delta shacks of Mississippi, the remote Ozark Mountain homes, have always thrived on cultural exchange. Movement across geographical ecosystems—from marshes and wetlands in Louisiana, to the great Piedmont that runs from the Blue Ridge Mountains through northern Alabama and Mississippi before slicing northward into Tennessee—allowed those living here to recognize and understand, if not always appreciate, difference. Southern Louisiana and Alabama have long been in international exchange with the Caribbean, Central America, Mexico, and South America. Mississippi, Alabama, and Tennessee join the region to the Midwest and the East. Arkansas and Louisiana open the South to the West through Texas and Oklahoma. Migration to such industrial cities as Detroit, Chicago, and Los Angeles has helped nationalize southern music, food, art, literature, and storytelling. Historical geography has made the region the crossroads for many cultures.

The natural environment is shaped by the unstable Mississippi, the shifting Gulf shores, and biblical extremes of weather. Southern literature, music, and art are odes to flux, transformation, and unpredictability. Viewing this region against the stereotype of conservatism, we also see the truth that this South came to cultural vibrancy in a context of debilitating poverty. Southern poets and writers, composers and musicians, bluesmen and photographers, all felt the weight of this poverty. The hard, dried hills of Alabama, the rasp of the coal miner, the stoop of the Mississippi sharecropper, the gnarled hands of the Arkansas farmer, made indelible impressions in our minds because of these artists.

This volume provides a resource guide for the cultural history of this region but can only hope to give the barest of outlines. Each author could have written a book, and each state could have provided an encyclopedia of material. Instead the authors have provided a guide and an educational tool, a jumping-off place for further research.

In the chapter on Architecture, Paula Mohr supports her thesis that although the southern United States helped create innovations in architecture unique to the climate and social demands of the region, the architecture of the South also borrowed forms from European and African sources: "The shotgun house, a typically southern form which emerged in the early nineteenth century, was an economical structure one room wide and several rooms deep. Its origins are unclear, but precedents appear in Africa, Haiti, and the West Indies." Mohr discusses not only material culture but the politics of preservation as well, which she claims originally promoted a nostalgic view of the past but has "matured into a serious effort to interpret a balanced view of history, material culture, and architecture." Mohr includes an interesting discussion on how early settlers' regulation of community and ordering of the landscape have created the public spaces, plazas, and grided streets that distinguish southern cities such as New Orleans and St. Augustine today.

In her chapter on Art, Barbara Rothermel observes that southern artists penetrate "the rituals and traditions of grace, strength, and 'southern hospitality,'" revealing the region's secrets and its precarious nature with resentment, celebration, and a lurking sense of ominous disquiet beneath the veneer." Rothermel takes us far beyond the three or four southern artists with whom everyone is familiar to introduce little-known figures such as "the Irish-born portraitist Henrietta Deering Johnston (c. 1670–c. 1728), who created pastel portraits of Huguenots in Charleston," or Bill Traylor, "a freed slave who began to draw at the age of eighty-three and in the remaining years of his life produced a wealth of pencil and charcoal drawings and paintings." Rothermel provides detailed analyses of southern arts from the utilitarian objects found in archaeological digs of Native American sites, to the complex embroidery found on bed linens and tablecloths, to the art of portrait painting. Her piercing awareness of variety in form and texture invites us to include in our understanding of southern art monuments, photographs, quilts, and Civil War paintings, the work of self-taught artists as well as the more traditional artistic expressions.

If anyone thinks they know the South topographically or that there is just one South, whether it is piney woods or the swamp, reading Tasha Eichenseher's account of the region's ecology and environment will convince them otherwise. Eichenseher divides the South into "six distinct geologic regions, represented by a series of stripes that run parallel to the Atlantic Ocean." This diversity carries over to the flora and fauna as well as the topography. One of the most beautiful passages in the book is Eichenseher's almost poetic list of birds: "Appalachian forests are a Mecca for birds. Red-breasted nuthatches, black-throated green warblers, golden-crowned warblers, golden-crowned kinglets, and northern juncos find solace in spruce and fir stands." It is with great sadness that we go on to read how in many areas we have destroyed this beauty or depleted our resources. Eichenseher reminds us that tobacco farming, though lucrative, ruined the land, and that "the mountaintop mining process begins by clearing forests, then removing the top layers of the mountain with explosives in order to extract the coal. . . . From the air, the remaining mountain slopes look like a Martian landscape, devoid of life." Eichenseher's chapter reveals the fragility of the region's natural environment.

Celeste Ray's exploration of southern ethnicity leaves us incredulous that such a mixture of peoples could ever have been reduced to a mere dichotomous duality of blackness and whiteness. Ray reminds us that, "as a region, the American South is not a cultural monolith, but a complex creole of multiple traditions." Ray takes issue with every ethnic category we think of as in any way stable or singular: "As Jeanette Keith has noted, Africans brought to America did not think of themselves as African, but as Hausa, Wolof, Fanti, Yoruba, Ewe, and Igbo." Within this cultural complex whiteness is clearly not a delineation that has any real meaning. Ray writes that "during Spanish control of Louisiana (1763–1800), settlers represented various Spanish ethnic groups, including Andalusians, Basques, Galicians, Catalans, and Canary Islanders. An estimated 2,000 Canary Islanders settled on Bayou Lafourche and at Galvestown, Valenzuela, and Barataria in the Louisiana parish of St. Bernard across the Mississippi River from New Orleans in the late 1770s and early 1780s." Her thorough reading of Irish and Scottish peoples and the many different cultural groups they represented makes the notion of even a Scotch-Irish hegemony impossible to maintain. She reminds us that this constant creolization of southern culture is not static and is still very much in evidence today.

Fashion has been a driving cultural force throughout history but regrettably is usually relegated to the society pages or to the unimportant annals of historical documentation. By not questioning what Maaja A. Stewart and Bryce Reveley in their groundbreaking chapter call "sartorial discriminations," we have failed to value the importance of cloth production, dye processes, the cultural exchange in textile and labor, and bodily adornment across distinctly ethnic social classes and groups. In a region in which cotton defined the economic and political development of the nation, one would think this would not have been such a neglected topic. Stewart reminds us that this discussion is the very foundation of an international system of trade based on material culture. "Raw materials for the fashioning of textiles moved from ports in New Orleans and Charleston to those in London, Paris, New York, and Boston." Stewart observes throughout the chapter that fashion was not an idle pastime but a violent means of keeping systems of oppression in place: "Booker T. Washington describes wearing a shirt made out of flax refuse as a 'most trying ordeal,' as torture, as equivalent to the pain of pulling a tooth, as having 'a dozen or more chestnut burrs, or a Hundred small pinpoints, to contact with his flesh.'"

In his tour of southern film and theater, Thomas Hischak states, "In fact, the designations 'southern play' and 'southern film' are of little use. The stage pieces *Uncle Tom's Cabin* and *A Streetcar Named Desire*, and the movies *The Birth of a Nation* and *Li'l Abner*, could not be further apart from each other, yet all four would be labeled southern." What is most surprising about this piece is how little film and theater was actually produced in the South until the 1950s and later. For this reason it is even more surprising that films such as *Gone with the Wind* and *The Birth of a Nation* and theatrical productions and adaptations of *Uncle Tom's Cabin* have been such culturally significant moments in American history. While reading Hischak it is impossible not to regret the films and theatrical productions that have been excluded from the canon, such as "*Deep Are the Roots* (1945), about an African American man who returns to his southern homestead and finds that the new freedoms offered him in the army are denied at home," or the film *Hearts in Dixie* (1929), considered the first all-black feature, an "episodic tale that follows the daily life of a Negro family who live on a plantation."

Exploring everything from folktales, legends, jokes, and folk beliefs to a select number of customs and ritualized events such as the celebration of holidays and folk festivals, Jon Lohman in his chapter on southern folklore reveals that "the development of folklore in the South is a story of diverse cultural communities constantly coming into contact with one another." By recording many stories and jokes that emerged from this human contact, Lohman gives teachers and researchers immediate access to some of the richest storytelling material in American letters. At the same time, he sets these tales in historical context by providing information on famous collectors, including James Mooney (1861–1921) and Horace Kephart (1862–1930), who "collected folktales, songs, customs, and other folklore from Cherokees in the late 1880s and [at] the turn of the century"; Vance Randolph (1892–1980), who "spent the majority of his time collecting in Arkansas and the greater Ozarks"; and urban legend scholar Jan Harold Brunvand, as well as more well known collectors like folklorist and novelist Zora Neale Hurston (1891–1960).

Susan Tucker and Sharon Stallworth Nossiter emphasize throughout their chapter that southern culinary history is a gumbo of spices from many different cultures: "In 1619 the first group of some twenty slaves arrived on a Dutch ship. With them and the millions more Africans who followed came foodstuffs, knowledge, and skills with okra, plantains, sweet potatoes and yams, [and] rice . . . that would form the bedrock of African American cooking traditions." Sitting in the position of greatest privilege and access to food, plantation cooking took on mythic proportions: "a dinner served at Monticello might have begun with consommé julienne and continued with a Virginia ham, corn pudding, celery with almonds, scalloped tomatoes, puréed cymlings, boeuf à la daube, damson plum preserves, Jerusalem artichoke pickles, and a wild turkey." However, as Tucker and Nossiter remind us, "The rest of the South, the enslaved themselves and the poor, did not eat so well. On one plantation, for example, slaves were allotted meal, rice, vegetables, salt, molasses, some sort of pork, and occasionally fish and coffee." In the 1930s and 1940s during sharecropper farming many of the South's whites and blacks went hungry. "The steady diet of the poor remained one of salt meat, cornbread, syrup or sorghum, and some sweet potatoes. Tooth decay, growth retardation in children, and even rickets were ever-present problems."

Michael Montgomery is absolutely accurate when he notes that "few traits identify southerners so readily as the way they speak English. It's what non-southerners often notice first, sometimes with ridicule but sometimes also with admiration." What is known as the southern accent has so affected the region that we forget that there are thousands of southern accents and that this part of the world has one of the richest linguistic heritages anywhere. Montgomery provides detailed analyses of several projects whose goal is to catalogue and verify language variety in the South, including *Annotated Bibliography of Southern American English* and *The Linguistic Atlas for the Middle and South Atlantic*. Montgomery's examples of language variety from many different cultures reveal that the notion of "a" southern accent is simply a fiction.

Susan V. Donaldson provides us with an introduction to southern literature, from its earliest sources—with such texts as "multiracial autobiographies, like *The Life and Adventures of James P. Beckwourth, Mountaineer Scout, and Pioneer, and Chief of the Crow Nation of Indians* (1856), written by a Virginia-born mixed-race slave who eventually married into the Crow Nation"—to new, little-known authors such as "a Baltimore writer named John Pendleton Kennedy [who] produced a novel titled *Swallow Barn* (1832), a congenial epistolary novel about life on a shabbily genteel Tidewater Virginia plantation" which defends slavery. Donaldson observes that "we need, in short, to read southern literature from the perspective of its earliest beginnings—as a borderlands culture in the sense defined by Latino/a writer-critics and specialists like Gloria Anzaldua and Mary Louise Pratt—as a 'contact zone,' in Pratt's words, where different cultures confront, intersect, and interpret one another's otherness." Her reading of the southern renaissance takes into account women writers and rereads canonical texts in the light of those that have been obscured or entirely left out of previous readings. Her chapter is so densely packed with factual material on new and little heard of literary texts that it could easily become required reading for southern literature courses.

In his discussion of music, David Sanjek justifiably asserts, "It is hard, in fact, to think of a single form of American music that does not bear some degree of southern influence," and enumerates "blues, jazz, gospel, country, rhythm and blues, rock and roll, funk, soul, and rap as well as such wholly regional variants as zydeco and swamp pop." Sanjek thinks that this music not only contributed enormously to the diversity of American musical forms but that the social interactions and connections brought about by the music in the South crossed difficult racial and economic barriers. Sanjek explains how the earliest recordings of New Orleans jazz, made in 1917, were by white musicians and that it was not until 1923 that "the preeminent black musicians from New Orleans . . . entered the recording studio." Sanjek includes a thorough history of the development of country music, noting the eagerness of marketers to pigeonhole the genre, belittling its performers as "hillbillies." Sanjek pays particular attention to individuals who helped shape and transform southern music, such as Alabama-born Sam Phillips (1923–2003), who "saw the city and the black neighborhood as a kind of promised land and spent a fabled career mining the unique talents he discovered there on his legendary Sun label."

Paul Harvey in his chapter on religion in the South demands that we think about the inherent contradiction between the teachings of Christianity, the South as the known Bible Belt, and the racism of the region. His discussion highlights "a paradox of southern, and American, religious history, namely, the deep contradiction between human spiritual equality in the eyes of God and divinely ordained social inequality in the everyday world." Harvey provides a thorough and insightful history of the evangelical South, its contradictions and its political power, as well as a remarkably full historiography of the existing literature in the field of southern religious studies. Harvey notices the spiritual and religious South in all its manifestations, and even though his strongest contribution is to the understanding of southern evangelicalism, he also discusses Native American, slave, Jewish, and other southern spiritual traditions. "Sometimes noticed (and often ridiculed) by whites, slave religion found its fullest expression in the brush arbors and secret places where enslaved Christians could express religious faith in the way they chose. In these private gatherings, the deepest desires for freedom found expression among people otherwise compelled to dissemble before old master."

In his discussion of sports and recreation, Bruce Adelson reminds us that the South was not always obsessed with only football, and that the ways in which sports developed in this region tell a story of class and racial distinction as well as challenges to these distinctions. "Indeed, in some parts of the South, such as Birmingham, Alabama, and the state of Louisiana, participating in integrated athletic and recreational activities was at one time a criminal offense, punishable by a jail term. Ironically, however, the region's, and the country's, first prominent athletes were slaves who, beginning in the eighteenth century, were paid to be jockeys." The history of sports in the region tells a story of exceptions to the rule, ways of defining and redefining privileged space, and how competitive sports tore down many of these demarcations. Such details as the fact that Jim Crow "resulted in the segregation of two of the South's newly created sporting extravaganzas—the Orange Bowl (1935, based in Miami) and the Sugar Bowl (1934, based in New Orleans)"; or that "during the war, Confederate prisoners watched their Union captors play baseball, a game they were largely unfamiliar with"; or that "Clara Baer of Sophie Newcomb College in New Orleans invented a version of [women's basketball] in 1895, six years before standard rules for women's basketball were adopted in 1901"; or that Big Bill France formed the National Association of Stock Car Racing in Daytona Beach on December 14, 1947," provide a fascinating glimpse into the ways in which sport both challenged and reified social structures in the South.

Though the South as a region is subdivided and its boundaries—both geographic and figurative—are hotly debated, it is unarguably one of the most fascinating and culturally rich sections of the United States. As these chapters reveal, southern music, art, literature, architecture, folklore, food, fashion, film and theater, and language have permeated every aspect of our national imagination. While the ghosts of the southern racial past continue to haunt us, the unparalleled diversity of cultural contact set forth in this volume questions the simplified narratives we have told about our history and challenges us to think in much more nuanced terms about the future.

ARCHITECTURE

Paula Mohr

For many of us, our perception and understanding of southern architecture is colored by evocative images drawn from popular culture. Margaret Mitchell's 1936 novel *Gone with the Wind* and the subsequent movie romanticized the plantation house for millions of readers and moviegoers. Tara—the centerpiece of Mitchell's story, with its majestic white columns, situated dramatically at the end of a long road lined with cedars—was for many the architectural embodiment of the moral superiority of the white planter class. Perhaps more real, but equally theatrical, is Elvis Presley's Graceland—filled with kitsch interiors that reinforced the stereotype of an unsophisticated southern culture populated with mobile homes, metal sheds, and barbeque joints. As powerful as these two icons are, neither image tells a complete or accurate story of southern architecture.

In 1941 the architectural critic Lewis Mumford was asked to address the meaning of regionalism in architecture. He observed that "regional forms are those which most closely meet the actual conditions of life and which most fully succeed in making people feel at home in their environment." In the same lecture, Mumford argued that all architecture, including that of the South, possesses universal characteristics—ideas which are shared in common with other cultures and geographical areas. Mumford's characterization of both the universality and the unique qualities of southern architecture mirrors the debate within the scholarly community today over the extent and ways in which southern architecture parallels—or differs from—that of the rest of the nation.

Some historians, including Jessie Poesch, who has written extensively on southern architecture, believe that the South was culturally isolated at least until the time of the Civil War. Accordingly, these historians argue that southerners built in response to cultural, functional, and environmental requirements unique to their region. African slaves appeared in the South during the first quarter of the seventeenth century and, indeed, until the Civil War the institution of slavery shaped the architectural environment in profound ways. The plantation landscape, including the interior plan of the master's house, was arranged to minimize contact between blacks and whites. During the Reconstruction period, segregation of whites from former slaves continued to influence the physical relationship of buildings within communities.

Eight of the eleven southern states covered in this volume are located along the Atlantic seaboard and the Gulf coast, resulting in the development of coastal areas for commerce, industry, defense, and tourism. This in turn has resulted in the introduction and dominance of specific types of buildings, construction technologies, and materials indigenous to coastal areas.

The balance between rural and urban development is also an important factor in the shaping of the built environment in the South. Compared with other regions of the country (especially the Northeast), the South throughout much of its history has characteristically been more rural, having a strong agrarian economy and being less dependent on the formation of towns and cities. This trend had a profound effect on settlement patterns as well as the development and form of individual building types.

One of the ways architecture in the South is distinguished from that in the rest of the country is in the use of building forms not common in other regions. Many of these forms are considered vernacular architecture, that is, architecture that is constructed with local materials and traditional building technology without the direct input of an architect. House plans including the single pen (one-room structures) and double pen (two-room structures) typify southern architecture. Other plans such as the dogtrot cabin—a two-room structure with an open passage in the center—and the T-shaped houses found in the Carolinas facilitated the movement of air throughout the house. Creole cottages (Creole refers to a person of European descent born in the West Indies or Spanish America) found in Alabama and Louisiana are typically structures which are elevated above the ground. Deep eaves and enveloping porches likewise were an architectural response to a warm and humid climate.

The shotgun house, a typically southern form which emerged in the early nineteenth century, was an economical structure one room wide and several rooms deep. Its origins are unclear, but precedents appear in Africa, Haiti, and the West Indies. Historians believe that the southern shotgun is most likely an amalgamation of all of these sources. Slave housing, made up of single-family and multifamily houses, similarly documents the influence of converging cultures. German migration into the South brought *fachwerk*—a distinctive method of timber framing with infill. This type of construction and a typical German floor plan composed of *küche* (kitchen), *stübe* (parlor), and *kammer* (chamber) can be seen in the architecture of the Moravians in North Carolina, although neither the construction nor the plan is unique to the South.

Similarly, scholars who argue that the South produced a distinctive architecture point to the impact of a warm climate on architectural form and the physical orientation of a building. In particular, the predominance of the porch in southern houses and the construction of buildings that are sufficiently permeable to allow for ventilation are tangible examples of the effect of climate on design.

Other trends in southern architecture include an interest in history that is expressed in the built environment. This phenomenon can be seen as an explanation for the popularity of classicism in the South, a topic that will be taken up in more

Special barns with open or slatted sides were constructed to facilitate the drying of tobacco before it was shipped to market. This photo dates from about 1926. Courtesy of the North Carolina State Archives.

detail below. Related to this interest in history, historians have noted a conservative tendency in southern architecture—a tendency to cling to old forms and eschew new ideas.

Moreover, agricultural buildings in the South reflect regional farming practices and dietary customs. The storage of grain was not a significant aspect of early agricultural practice in the South; accordingly, barns tended to be small. Tobacco, introduced to the South in the early seventeenth century, became an important cash crop. Special barns with open or slatted sides were constructed to facilitate the drying of tobacco before it was shipped to market. Other methods of drying tobacco developed in the eighteenth century, including the use of heat, necessitated further modifications to the tobacco barn. Buildings for the storage of cotton often housed a cotton gin as well. Rice plantations had winnowing houses and mills where the grain was cleaned of its chaff. Pigeonniers, especially popular in Louisiana, housed birds which were both ornamental and edible. Smokehouses, constructed of wood, stone, or brick, were critical to the drying and curing of pork, a staple of the southern diet. Kitchens were sometimes located in the basement of southern houses, but more commonly were located in a building separate from the house. Cooking in an outbuilding addressed concerns about the threat of fire, kept the main house cooler, and, importantly, segregated slaves from the family.

On the opposite side of the regional argument are scholars who believe that the architecture of the South follows national trends, albeit with a southern flavor. As evidence of this view, scholars point to the popularity of architectural books in the

South (many of which were published in England and the northern United States) which had the potential to standardize architectural taste. Evidence of the impact of these publications can be seen especially in the eighteenth century with the introduction of classicism and Palladianism, which enjoyed great popularity in the South among the gentry. Also important in understanding southern architecture as a part of a broader American culture is the influence of architects from other regions who worked in the South, a practice that persists to the present day. Examples include William Strickland, Alexander Jackson Davis, McKim, Mead and White, Frank Lloyd Wright, and Frank Gehry.

Whether or not one believes in the existence of a distinctly southern architecture, twentieth-century economic and political trends as well as technological developments have worked to diminish regional differences in the built environment. The national phenomenon of sprawling cities and commercial strips has had an impact on the South as it has the rest of the country. The dominance of chain stores, restaurants, and motels has resulted in a blurring of regional differences. The political influence exercised by elected officials at the national level has resulted in a more equitable distribution of federal dollars for road construction, public buildings, and infrastructure, and with this spending has come a certain level of standardization in execution of design. Finally, the widespread introduction of air conditioning after World War II has resulted in the lessening (but not complete elimination) of architectural features like porches, louvered doors, and elevated buildings that responded to the warm and humid climate of the southern states.

Yet, despite the more complete merging of the South's architectural character with that of the rest of the country, it is important to recognize the influence of southern architecture on the rest of the country. Perhaps the most important contribution was that made by Thomas Jefferson as architect. With his design of the Virginia State Capitol, Jefferson set the young nation on a course where classicism would be the language of choice for public buildings. His influence as an architect continues to be seen in the buildings constructed by federal, state, and local governments to the present time.

Another important contribution to the larger architectural discussion in this country was made with the onset of the Colonial Revival period when antiquarians rediscovered the architecture of the New England colonies as well as that of the southern colonies. This fascination with architecture of the colonial period led to the replication of southern-influenced houses in the Georgian and the giant columnar styles throughout the nation (a trend that continues to the present day). In particular, the research on and documentation of southern buildings undertaken by Colonial Revival architects such as Thomas Tileston Waterman, author of *Domestic Colonial Architecture of Tidewater Virginia* (1932), and Fiske Kimball, author of *Domestic Architecture of the American Colonies and Early Republic* (1922), contributed to the interest in and proliferation of southern-style buildings on the landscape. Books such as J. Frazer Smith's *White Pillars* (1941) and Frederick Nichols' *The Early Architecture of Georgia* are further expressions of the intense fascination with the historic architecture of the South.

A secondary but equally important outcome of the Colonial Revival was the emergence of the historic preservation movement, which had a strong and early presence in the South. Some of the first efforts to save historic structures took place in the South, notably the preservation of George Washington's Mount Vernon, begun in 1853. Other projects, such as the effort to preserve Jefferson Davis' White House of the Confederacy, were motivated by a desire to bolster the "Lost Cause" version of the Civil War. In the twentieth century, preservation in the South evolved beyond the promotion of white supremacy and a nostalgic view of the past and matured into a serious effort to interpret a balanced view of history, material culture, and architecture. Colonial Williamsburg, although criticized for offering a romanticized and antiseptic view of eighteenth-century life in Virginia, has inspired similar projects across the country. Citizen-organized neighborhood preservation projects, such as those undertaken in Charleston, South Carolina, Savannah, and New Orleans, have been lauded as successful efforts to preserve a local community's architectural character while making important contributions to quality of life and the local economy.

PRE-COLUMBIAN/NATIVE AMERICAN PERIOD

While the physical survival of pre-Columbian architecture is rare, archaeological excavations have provided some information about the complexity and development of architecture in the South prior to European contact. William Morgan has noted that until about 7000 B.C.E. the area that is now the eastern United States was sparsely populated. Settlements were typically located along waterways, which provided transportation and an important source of food. Around 700 C.E., with the introduction of agriculture, indigenous populations increased in number and became more sedentary. At least by the time of European contact, the scale of these

Chucalissa Mississippian Indian mound complex near Memphis, Tennessee, with chief's house on the top and shaman hut to the left. Mounds were used to support burial structures and the dwellings of important civic and spiritual leaders. Courtesy Chucalissa Museum.

settlements was large. For example, Talomico, near Augusta, Georgia, had 500 houses and a funerary temple that measured approximately 250 feet by 100 feet. Some settlements were surrounded by palisade enclosures, indicating a need to provide physical protection from neighboring tribes.

Among the earliest built structures in the pre-Columbian period were mounds, initially composed of refuse but later constructed out of earth. Along the southern Atlantic coast, shell eaters constructed monumental circular mounds out of discarded shells, for unknown purposes. Other mounds, either domed or pyramidal, were used to support burial structures and the dwellings of important civic and spiritual leaders. One of the earliest known examples is found on the Ouachita River in present-day Louisiana and dates to 5500–3000 B.C.E. These terraced pyramidal mounds were grouped around plazas, demonstrating a deliberate creation of public space. Iconography also played a role in the development of overall plans. Most notable is the site known as Ocmulgee Mounds, established c. 2000 B.C.E. near Macon, Georgia, which was constructed in the shape of an eagle.

Individual buildings in the pre-Columbian period were typically earthfast construction and were covered with mud, bark, woven mats, or hides. Tabby, a concrete building material made of shells, lime, and sand, was also in use as a mortar. Roofing materials included thatch, cane mats, mud plaster, bark, and tile. (Significantly, many of the building technologies and materials used by pre-Columbian cultures had been developed independently by European cultures and were employed by early European settlers in the New World.) Other building technologies and materials helped occupants to respond to the local climate. Notable examples include buildings constructed by Choctaw and Timucua tribes in

The Timucua tribes in present-day Florida used building technologies adapted to the local climate. The Great House/Menendez Fort, Saint Augustine, Florida. Florida Photographic Collection.

present-day Florida. These light framed structures sheathed with palm leaves were protected from the rain but were well ventilated in this humid climate.

Historians Peter Nabokov and Robert Easton estimate that at the time of European exploration in the early sixteenth century, the Native American population in the Southeast numbered 120,000. Post-Columbian structures built by Native Americans continued the building traditions developed earlier; however, increased exposure to the European population began to erode native building traditions. Conflicts over land between settlers and Native Americans resulted in the dislocation of tribes, severing Native Americans from their traditional building materials and interrupting the transmission of building customs to the next generation.

However, the elimination of Native American architectural traditions did not happen abruptly, and some tribes continued to build in traditional ways or adapted old forms to new circumstances. For example, the Creek tribe in Florida developed a residential building form called a *chickee* which borrowed the pre-Columbian technique of using palm leaves as a thatching material. The other distinguishing feature of the *chickee* was its floor, which was elevated as much as three feet above the ground—a significant response to the snake- and alligator-infested swamps of southern Florida. Nabokov and Easton note that the raised *chickee* may have also descended from a two-story structure that combined guest housing and storage.

More recently, Native American clients and architects have revived native building traditions and values in contemporary designs. The Museum of the Cherokee Indian in Cherokee, North Carolina (1976), designed by Six Associates of Asheville, North Carolina, draws upon traditional Cherokee materials including stone, wood, and copper. The form of this building also mimics the form of the nearby mountains, making the museum a symbolic expression of the Native American respect for nature.

EUROPEAN SETTLEMENT

In the sixteenth century, European exploration of the New World and the subsequent settlement of the present-day southern states introduced new cultural influences and a population motivated by economic expansion. Early explorers included Juan Ponce de León, who in 1513 explored the Atlantic and Gulf coastlines of Florida for Spain. Several decades later, Hernando de Soto expanded de León's discovery, traveling west from Florida to the southern part of the Mississippi River. These explorations inevitably led to efforts to lay physical claim to these lands. Spain and France had the earliest and most important outposts in the South, eventually creating permanent settlements. St. Augustine, the oldest European city in the United States, was established in 1565 by the Spanish, who retained control of it almost continuously until 1821. France, which claimed the mouth of the Mississippi River in the 1680s, laid out the city of New Orleans forty years later.

English settlement in the South followed in the early seventeenth century, and these settlements were culturally diverse as well. Architectural historian G. E. Kidder Smith noted that while colonists in New England came from a limited area in England, British colonists in the South were drawn from a broad geographical area. Like their Spanish and French counterparts, these English settlers were motivated by the possibilities offered in the New World for economic advancement and were therefore distinguished from the English Puritan and Pilgrim colonists in New England.

The multicultural occupation of the southern area of North America during the period of European settlement resulted in a number of robust cultural influences on the architecture of the South. The presence of African and Caribbean cultures during the period of early settlement, while without an official political basis, shaped what was built. In short, all of these competing cultural influences—English, Spanish, and French as well as others—made for the development of a rich and complex architecture in the southern states.

However, during initial settlement, the cultural expression of national identities was overshadowed by pragmatic concerns tied to survival. Not surprisingly, the most important priority was to construct rudimentary housing that would provide protection from the elements. Settlers combined building technology brought from their country of origin with local materials available in their new home to create shelter. Roofs were covered with wood, straw, or tile. Wood construction of varying types was the most common (and indeed would continue to dominate building well into the nineteenth century in the South). English settlers at Jamestown (1607) constructed houses using earthfast technology where the wood posts supporting the house were set directly into the ground and enclosed with wattle and daub, tar over straw, or wood cladding. Carl Lounsbury and other historians of southern architecture have noted that this rudimentary framing system was so pervasive in the Chesapeake region that it was known as a "Virginia house." After c. 1650 log and frame houses set on wooden blocks, rather than earthfast construction, became more common. Log construction was introduced on the coast of North Carolina in the late seventeenth century, and its use continued throughout the South through the end of the nineteenth century. Brick making became more widespread in the late seventeenth century, making the construction of more permanent and impressive dwellings possible for the elite. Two-room buildings with a central chimney were built in this early period, but most were single-room structures. As resources became available, these small structures were gradually expanded with an additional room or simply replaced with more permanent materials and construction techniques.

Related to the need for shelter was the need to provide defensive mechanisms to protect European settlements from hostile neighbors. The early settlement at Jamestown was surrounded by wooden palisades designed to provide protection from Native Americans. In Spanish Florida early fortifications were also built of wood. Later, the Spanish, drawing upon designs developed by European military engineers, constructed the stone fort of Castillo San Marcos (1672–1696) with star-shaped bastions to protect the residents of St. Augustine. Along the Gulf coast the French established forts at Mobile Bay, Natchitoches, and Natchez to defend themselves against encroachment by the Spanish.

Once shelter and a level of security were realized, a third priority was to establish a measure of order on the landscape. Scholars have observed that settlements in the South are notable for their planned quality. However, different cultures had different approaches to this problem. The Spanish were guided by the Law of the Indies, a legislative document that dictated the adoption of a gridded street pattern and a centralized plaza. St. Augustine, founded in 1565, was arranged in this manner with the plaza facing the ocean. The Seville Square area in Pensacola,

Florida, laid out in the early nineteenth century, is an important example of the lasting influence of this Spanish planning practice. In Louisiana, the French marked out narrow plots each with 1,500 feet of river frontage and extending back 8,000 feet—evidence of the importance of water transportation and the need for direct access to the river. Savannah's city plan was laid out and oriented to maximize the winter sun and the summer breezes. Savannah's plan is also notable for its provision of green space for common use in the form of public squares scattered throughout the city. Moreover, each settler received a garden plot outside of the city walls. In the rural areas of the English colonies of Virginia, the Carolinas, and Georgia, settlers imposed order on the land by creating individual plantations which divided up the countryside into units that could be managed as agricultural precincts.

During the period of early settlement, it is possible to discern discrete cultural expressions. The Mississippi Gulf coast offers an unparalleled opportunity to see these influences at work. In the early eighteenth century, French settlers from three different areas—France, French Canada, and the French West Indies—came to the region encompassing coastal Alabama, Mississippi, and Louisiana. The French from Canada and France adopted a type of timber frame construction practiced in their home countries and infilled with a mixture of mud and organic fiber used by Native Americans. The French called this timber and mud construction technique *bousillage entre poteaux* (mud between posts). The French from the West Indies contributed a number of distinctive floor plans for domestic architecture. For example, four-room raised cottages without interior circulation were a Creole influence from the West Indies. Circulation in the house was through a gallery that surrounded the building on all four sides. Multiple doors not only provided easy access to interior rooms, but also increased ventilation. Some galleries contained staircases leading to an upper level of the house. Other Creole features included roofs which extended over the sidewalk to provide shelter from the hot sun. These expansive roofs typically have two planes, each at a different angle. The highest part of the roof is sharply pitched, and approximately halfway down the roof the angle is less steep. This distinctive roof form sheds the rain and provides a broad area of shelter from the sun.

New Orleans, because of its strategic location at the mouth of the Mississippi River, drew a large population composed of many cultures. The Spanish made significant contributions to the range of building forms, materials, and construction techniques. The decorative wrought iron that adorns buildings inside and out, and for which New Orleans is famous, is Spanish in origin. The Cabildo (1795–1799) and its companion building the Presbytère (1791–1813) are examples of public build-

The Cabildo (1795–1799), New Orleans, Louisiana. Courtesy Louisiana Office of Tourism.

Wrought iron balconies adorn this building in the French Quarter, New Orleans. Courtesy Louisiana Office of Tourism.

ings with ornate ironwork, which soon was adopted for domestic and commercial buildings as well. The Spanish also introduced the multistory entresol house that relegated separate functions to different levels within the building. The term *entresol* refers to a short mezzanine level located between the ground and third stories. An important surviving example is the house at 517 Decatur Street (1785), which housed animals on the ground floor, grain and servants on the second or entresol level, and living quarters on the top floor.

COLONIAL PERIOD

By the end of seventeenth century, some of the early settlements, like Roanoke in North Carolina and Martin's Hundred in Virginia, had disappeared. Other towns, like Jamestown, which lost its status as the colonial capital of Virginia to Williamsburg, were superseded by new settlements further inland. In the eighteenth century, new settlers' quest for land holdings began to push the frontier west of the Appalachian Mountains.

Planning, which had been an important aspect of European settlement in the South, continued to be important in the colonial period. The capital city of Williamsburg (named in honor of the English monarch), established in 1699, is one example of this practice. Williamsburg's town plan is attributed to Lieutenant Governor Francis Nicholson, a well-educated gentleman fluent in architecture and city planning. A central focus of Nicholson's plan is the Duke of Gloucester Street—a ninety-nine-foot-wide avenue that runs from the College of William and Mary to the Capitol. A cross axis intersecting with the Duke of Gloucester Street places visual emphasis on the Governor's Palace. Nicholson's use of grand avenues to create dramatic sight lines demonstrates his knowledge of Baroque city planning and specifically his awareness of Christopher Wren's unrealized plan for rebuilding London after the devastating fire of 1666.

While English ideas dominated the way in which colonists arranged their towns, English architectural influences had an equally strong impact on the character of public buildings and domestic architecture in the southern colonies. In particular, Palladianism, the rediscovery of the architecture of the Italian Renaissance, dominated architecture in the southern colonies during much of the eighteenth century. Historian Kenneth Severens has argued that for southerners the aesthetic appeal of classical architecture was secondary to the recognition that ancient Greece and Rome shared in common a system of slave labor. Roger Kennedy has proposed a similar theory to explain the popularity of Palladianism in the South. He argues that the elite of the Veneto drew their wealth from the labors of black slaves, and thus the houses designed for them by the sixteenth-century architect

Andrea Palladio were appropriate forms for southern plantation owners to emulate.

Indeed, Palladio's influence in the colonies can be seen beginning with the second quarter of the eighteenth century. This timing is attributable to the growth of book publishing in this period, which made it possible for colonists to purchase copies of Palladio's works. William Salmon's *Palladio Londinensis* of 1734 was a popular edition, although Thomas Jefferson preferred the edition translated by the Italian Giacomo Leoni. Other books with a strong bias toward Palladian architecture were published by British architects Colen Campbell and Isaac Ware in the early and mid-eighteenth century. Importantly, the availability of these books made it possible for the southern elite, using local labor, to construct fashionable houses in the Palladian style. One of the most important examples to survive is Drayton Hall, located outside of Charleston, South Carolina. Of particular note is the two-story exterior portico, which can be traced to Palladio's work in the Veneto. Moreover, Palladio's influence stretched even further west. Jessie Poesch has argued that the classical plantation house model developed in Virginia and South Carolina was copied in the western regions of the South as settlers moved inland.

The Palladian style was also appropriated for public buildings where resources permitted. Charleston, because of its strong economic ties with England, was particularly known as a hotbed of English taste. The first statehouse in South Carolina (begun in 1753) and the Exchange (built in the 1770s) are excellent examples of Palladian buildings inspired by public architecture in England. Yet, at the same time, there was great diversity in architectural expression, suggesting that English tastemakers did not have a complete hold on the architecture. A view of Charleston from c. 1739 documents the existence of large buildings with curvilinear gables, indicating an explicit Dutch influence on the city's architecture.

The erection of religious buildings also became a greater priority in the colonial period, but, as with public buildings, their scale and ornamentation were somewhat limited by available resources. An exception is in Virginia, where the Church of England held great power; numerous parish churches were constructed there as symbols of the Church's reach and authority over the population. Bruton Parish Church in Williamsburg, with its cruciform plan, architectural embellishments, and tall tower, was a powerful expression of its prestigious location in the colony's capital city. More typical were churches such as St. John's in Suffolk, Virginia, which was rectangular in plan and modest in its ornamentation. In South Carolina, many churches such as St. Michael's in Charleston were brick coated with stucco to simulate stone—a practice attributable to the economic connection between Charleston and the sugar plantations in Barbados, where stuccoed buildings were common. Anglican churches in North Carolina were typically modest rectangular preaching halls.

Colleges in the colonial period were rare; however, there is one important example. The College of William and Mary in Williamsburg was chartered as an Anglican institution in 1693, making it second to Harvard University as the oldest institution of higher education in the country. The first college building at William and Mary was destroyed by fire and was replaced with a U-shaped building now known as the Wren Building (so named because of its attribution to the

English architect Christopher Wren) containing a lecture hall, living quarters, and a chapel. In the 1720s two additional buildings were constructed in front of and to the side of the main building, forming a forecourt. These buildings formed an important terminus for the Duke of Gloucester Street and were positioned on an axis with the Capitol at the opposite end.

Architects

Professional architects were rare in the colonial period, and those who practiced as architects were largely self-taught or had trained in an allied trade. William Buckland, who worked in Virginia as well as Maryland, is an example of a colonial architect who trained in England as a cabinetmaker and joiner through the apprenticeship system common at that time. He came to Virginia as an indentured servant to work on George Mason's Gunston Hall (1755–1760) in Fairfax County, Virginia. Both talented and successful, by the time of his death in 1774, Buckland referred to himself as an architect and owned a small but significant library of architectural books which aided him in his work.

Despite the dearth of professional architects, extant buildings document the high level of craftsmanship available in the colonies. For example, the interior woodwork of Drayton Hall near Charleston, South Carolina, is a testament to the degree of artistic refinement available locally. John Hemings (1776–1830+), an enslaved man owned by Thomas Jefferson in Virginia, was responsible for the interior woodwork in Jefferson's retreat, Poplar Forest, in Bedford County, Virginia. Hemings and Stewart Ellison, a slave who worked in Raleigh, North Carolina, in the mid-nineteenth century, are just two of the many African American craftsmen who were highly skilled artisans. Joiners, cabinetmakers, masons, and other craftsmen tied to the building industry were trained through the apprenticeship system. Familial ties were particularly important whereby a father passed his trade, skills, and tools on to his son.

By the end of the eighteenth century, professionally trained architects began to immigrate to the United States in greater numbers. In the late 1780s, Irish architect James Hoban immigrated to South Carolina, where he designed the Broad Street Theater in 1792. Benjamin Henry Latrobe emigrated from England and arrived in Norfolk, Virginia, in 1796. Trained in both architecture and engineering, Latrobe brought to America a fresh interpretation of neoclassicism, which continued to be the dominant architectural style. Moreover, Latrobe's training as an engineer gave him the technical knowledge needed to design fireproof buildings—an increasingly important skill as the new republic grew. In the South, most of Latrobe's work was done in Virginia, where he designed the Virginia State Penitentiary (1797–1806) in Richmond, one of his largest commissions. This monumental building, now demolished, shows the influence of London's Newgate Prison and a working knowledge of emerging ideas about prison reform. William Nichols, an architect and engineer who immigrated to North Carolina in 1800, was another English architect who put his mark on the state's public and domestic architecture in the first quarter of the nineteenth century. His design to remodel the statehouse in Raleigh into a more up-to-date interpretation of the Greek Ionic order was a compelling architectural statement for the state and a suitable setting for Italian sculptor Antonio Canova's sculpture of George Washington.

At the same time, native-born architects were emerging on the southern landscape. Robert Mills (1781–1855), who was born in Charleston, South Carolina, proudly boasted that he was the first architect born in this country. He reportedly trained with James Hoban for a brief time in Charleston, later studied with Thomas Jefferson, and apprenticed with Benjamin Latrobe in Philadelphia. Returning to South Carolina, he served as architect for the state of South Carolina from 1820 to 1830 and was responsible for designing courthouses, jails, and the state insane asylum. His Fireproof Building in Charleston, which Mills constructed of solid masonry, is considered among his most important structures because of its engineering and the way in which Mills treated the monolithic masonry sculpturally. The success of this building earned Mills a reputation for fireproof construction which helped him secure important federal commissions in Washington the following decade.

Plantation, Slave Quarter, and Residential Architecture

While city life had its own peculiar architectural challenges, the plantation was an important economic and social institution that shaped rural life. Historians John Michael Vlach and Dell Upton have written about the physical arrangement of plantations as both expressions of power and instruments of control over slaves. Beyond the master's house, plantations were a collection of buildings each with different purposes. Meat preservation, cooking, laundering, and storage of ice and dairy all took place in separate buildings. The architect Benjamin Henry Latrobe observed that, characteristically, the arrangement of these buildings vis-à-vis the main house was motivated by convenience and reminded him of "a litter of pigs around their mother." Jefferson's Monticello was arranged somewhat differently, with domestic activities housed in dependencies connected to the main house via an underground passageway. Industrial activities like blacksmithing and woodworking were housed in a 400-foot-long row of shops called Mulberry Row located adjacent to the house. Jefferson's use of underground passageways and his creation of a discrete work area represent his efforts to conceal from view the very institution that made his plantation function efficiently.

Slave quarters (the collection of buildings where slaves lived) were often organized rectilinearly so that they resembled small towns. Often, plantation owners prominently displayed the houses of their slaves as a boastful expression of the size of their holdings. In other cases, quarters for field slaves were located out of sight of the main house. Slave housing was constructed of a variety of material; log and frame were the most common, but brick, stone, and rammed earth were also employed, utilizing resources from the plantation. In Georgia, there is evidence that slaves built houses using branches woven in a basketweave construction and coated with mud. Floor plans for slave housing included single and double pen houses, three-room cabins containing a hall and two sleeping rooms, and double-tenement house plans. Barrack-style housing for slaves was rare in the South.

In the colonial period, most free and enslaved people continued to live in single-room houses; however, for affluent families more elaborate plans became popular. Hall and parlor plans (two rooms) became more common. Center passage plans featured a centrally placed passage for circulation and ventilation, with parlor and dining room on either side. Center passages with two rooms (double pile) on ei-

These tabby ruins are part of an antebellum plantation on Sapelo Island, Georgia, that was deserted following the Civil War. Courtesy Sapelo Island National Estuarine Research Reserve.

ther side allowed even more differentiation of space. Sleeping chambers were usually, but not always, located on the second floor.

Timber frame construction remained pervasive throughout much of the South in the colonial period. This frame joined with mortise and tenon joints was sometimes infilled with brick, as was done by the Moravians in Salem, North Carolina, but more commonly covered with weatherboard. Brick construction was more permanent, costly, and prestigious. Stone was commonly used for foundations and chimneys, but less commonly for the construction of walls. Plantation owners also began to experiment with other materials for agricultural buildings. *Pisè* (rammed earth) and tabby, a concrete mixture with crushed oyster shells, were employed during the period.

Gardens

Finally, the establishment of elaborate gardens was an important way for southern gentry in the seventeenth and eighteenth centuries to display their wealth and taste. As with architecture, much of this taste in landscape design was shaped by books published in England. An example is Philip Miller's *The Gardeners Dictionary* (1731), which landscape historian Allan Brown notes was a popular reference work in eighteenth-century Virginia. Yet, while many of these ideas came to the colonies from English publications, their original source was Italy. Gentry in Virginia, among the wealthiest of the colonists, had elaborate formal gardens reminiscent of Italy. Boxwood, bowling greens, allees, and graveled walks were among the features arranged symmetrically around the house. Terraces connected the main house to the river, as at Sabine Hall along the Rappahannock River. At Gunston Hall a double row of evergreens formed an axis between the Potomac River and the house, effectively focusing the view for visitors arriving via water. Mt. Airy, the Palladian house of John Tayloe II constructed in the 1750s in Richmond County, Virginia, had numerous features including marble statues, a conservatory, a bowling green, and a deer park.

South Carolina, also a wealthy colony, had gardens to rival those in Virginia. Of particular note is the garden at Middleton Place near Charleston. Historian Jessie Poesch has described the garden as a series of intimate and open rooms which offered the visitor a variety of spatial and sensory experiences. The strict symmetry of the garden was designed to heighten the effect from the river, and its scale was a conspicuous display of the wealth required to create and maintain this landscape.

By the late eighteenth century, however, taste in landscape design had shifted to the picturesque style, and some of the most important political figures of the time were among its early practitioners. By the 1780s, George Washington had transformed the landscape around Mount Vernon from a rectilinear plan to a naturalistic landscape with curvilinear roads winding through the planted "wilderness," as Washington described it. Thomas Jefferson also reworked the landscape around his mountaintop home, Monticello, altering the landscape to a naturalistic one after he returned from his diplomatic post in France.

PERIOD TO THE CIVIL WAR

Transportation

In the period leading up to the Civil War, the development of the railroad in the South shifted the focus from water transportation and made new areas of the region desirable for settlement. North Carolina, for example, received its first railroad in the 1830s, and in 1849 construction was begun on a line from Wilmington to points west. In 1836 the state of Georgia approved construction of the railroad that gave birth to Atlanta (originally called Terminus). Railways led to the construction of train stations like the Georgia Railroad Freight Depot (1869) and the Union Passenger Depot (1870) constructed in Atlanta.

Travel, either by water or by rail, also gave rise to large hotels in the South. A notable example, the St. Charles Hotel (1835–1838) in New Orleans by James Gallier and Charles Dakin, had 350 rooms. With its impressive dome and classical portico, this commercial building connoted its status within the city by appropriating the monumental scale and grandeur of a public building. The Charleston Hotel, designed in the late 1830s by Charles Reichardt, is another southern hotel that symbolized the greater frequency and ease of travel in the second quarter of the nineteenth century. In 1853 inventor James Bogardus added a cast-iron exchange fifty feet in diameter to the hotel. This exchange was inspired by the Crystal Palace exhibition building in New York of the previous year and is an example of the growing interest in cast-iron construction, which offered some degree of fire protection, had great potential for spanning large spaces, and allowed for an expansive use of glass.

Educational Institutions

The establishment of public institutions also characterized the period prior to the Civil War. The number of educational institutions increased, making it possible for male students to receive their education closer to home rather than in New England. Thomas Jefferson's University of Virginia is perhaps the best known of all the southern campuses, and much has been written about the influence Jefferson's university has had on the development of the American campus. The focal point for Jefferson's design is a rotunda (modeled on the Pantheon) containing the library. Arranged in two parallel rows in front of the Rotunda are ten pavilions containing classrooms and living quarters for faculty. The pavilions were Jefferson's most important way to display a variety of architectural expressions, and these facades are modeled after ancient and modern classical examples admired by Jefferson. Interspersed between the pavilions are the student rooms. Two additional rows of student rooms with dining halls were located behind the pavilions. All of Jefferson's buildings are connected with a covered colonnade providing shelter from the elements.

Historian Paul Venable Turner has argued that the success of Jefferson's academical village is due to the fact that it "seems to embody perfectly the ideal of an intimate and enlightened dialogue between students and teachers." Indeed, the spatial arrangement of Jefferson's academical village established public space in which students and faculty could interact, as well as private space for each. Jefferson's plan also displays in architectural form an important hierarchy. The Rotunda, housing the library, was the university's most important building, and accordingly the most prominent and elevated one. The pavilions where faculty lived and learning took place were second in importance. Finally, student rooms were less important and appropriately were fronted with columns in the Tuscan order, the simplest and least refined of the classical orders.

The establishment of Jefferson's university was quickly followed by that of the University of Alabama in Tuscaloosa, designed by William Nichols in 1828. The organization of this campus, with its centrally located rotunda containing the library, and with classrooms and residences for students and teachers on the periphery, resembles Jefferson's academical village. Other colleges and universities founded in the South before the Civil War adopted the classical idiom for their buildings. The College of Charleston, in South Carolina, and the University of Georgia, in Athens, are just two of the many educational institutions that chose to appropriate the temple form for their buildings. For Davidson College, Alexander Jackson Davis prepared a square quadrangle plan containing student residences and fronted with a classical portico.

Public Buildings

Classical architecture continued to be the preferred idiom for public buildings, and to a lesser extent for domestic buildings in the period up to the Civil War. William Strickland's Tennessee State Capitol, topped with a lantern modeled on the Choragic Monument of Lysicrates in Athens, is considered to be one of the most original interpretations of the Greek Revival in the country. The popularity of classical forms was further fueled by the increased availability of architectural style books in the nineteenth century—many of them written by Americans. Asher Benjamin's *American Builder's Companion* (1806) and Minard Lafever's *The Beauties of Modern Architecture* (1835) are just two of a number of works published in the North and available in the South. These books were valuable references for the builder and client alike for the design of residences, institutional buildings, and public buildings.

Religious Structures

The period leading up to the Civil War brought profound changes in religious practice in the South. Following the American Revolution, the position of the Anglican Church was considerably weakened in the South. In the period leading up to the Civil War, the South became home to a greater variety of religious traditions than during the colonial period. For example, the Shakers, while primarily associated with the northeastern United States, had a presence in Kentucky during the early nineteenth century. Pleasant Hill (today a restored village) located in central Kentucky, had a population of nearly 500 believers within twenty years of the community's founding. Many of the buildings at Pleasant Hill were designed and constructed by Micajah Burnett, a skilled Shaker craftsman. The frame and clapboard meetinghouse by Burnett, with its separate entrances for men and women, is typical of Shaker religious structures. The Center Family house is built of stone, and its interior is outfitted with simple trim, white plaster walls, and bare floors typical of Shaker aesthetic and religious sensibilities.

Popular Architectural Styles

Also in the antebellum period, a number of picturesque architectural styles vied for popularity and challenged the primacy of classical architecture. The popularity of these revival styles was also due to the proliferation of books by a new generation of tastemakers including Andrew Jackson Downing (1815–1852) and Samuel Sloan (1815–1884), who both published their designs and architectural theories in books and periodicals. The Italianate style had great currency because its features were thought to address the southern climate. The deep eaves of an Italianate building provided welcome shade, and Tuscan towers helped ventilate the building, making it particularly suitable for the hot and humid climate of the South. An extreme example of the Italianate style rendered in a fanciful manner is Longwood in Natchez, Mississippi. This octagonal house, topped with an observatory and onion dome, was designed by Samuel Sloan, a Philadelphia architect. Construction began on the house in 1860, but the impending war and then the death of the client in 1864 halted construction. Today, the house in its unfinished state is a museum. Other stylistic expressions such as the Egyptian Revival had a more limited impact in the South; important examples include Thomas Stewart's Medical College of Richmond (1844–1845) and the First Presbyterian Church (1849–1851) in Nashville by William Strickland.

The Gothic Revival had certain appeal for churches but a more limited appeal for residences and public buildings in the South. In certain circumstances, however, the use of Gothic Revival reinforced southern ideas about chivalry, honor, and paternalism. A notable example of the use of Gothic Revival to project the ideals of the "cavalier of the South" is Belmead, a castellated plantation house in Powhatan County, Virginia, designed in 1849 by the New York architect Alexander Jackson Davis. Slave housing and outbuildings were sometimes cloaked in the Gothic Revival style, such as at the Aiken-Rhett House located in Charleston, South Carolina. Finally, the state capitols of Georgia and Louisiana were constructed in the Gothic style.

Materials

Cast iron as a building material enjoyed increasing popularity before and after the Civil War. This material was appealing for two reasons. First, it lent itself to mass production and was an economical way to imitate a more expensive material such as stone and to execute elaborate ornamentation. Second, architects and builders were interested in new technologies for constructing noncombustible buildings, and the application of cast iron appeared to have great potential. (The threat of fire was a concern for all American cities. Savannah, for example, was devastated by fires in 1796 and 1820.) Robert Mills had used cast iron in the 1820s in his Fireproof Building in Charleston for door and window frames. However, in the late 1850s architects and builders began using cast iron more extensively for storefronts in densely built cities like New Orleans and Richmond. Iron was also commonly used in the early nineteenth century for ornamental detail, fencing, and railings. In the mid-1850s, the state of Tennessee installed an ornate cast-iron library in William Strickland's classical state capitol. James Dakin's use of cast iron in the Baton Rouge state capitol to create an elaborate Gothic-inspired interior is another example of the application of ornamental cast iron in the mid-nineteenth century.

PERIOD TO WORLD WAR I

After the Civil War, the South was transformed politically, culturally, economically, and architecturally—but not without significant resistance. The rebuilding of urban fabric and infrastructure following the Civil War was accomplished relatively quickly using federal funds. However, problems stemming from the social upheaval and unresolved tensions between whites and former slaves lingered far longer. Jim Crow laws legalizing racial segregation emerged in the late nineteenth century and led to the establishment of all-black neighborhoods, institutions, and public facilities. The "New South," a term coined by Henry Grady, editor of the *Atlanta Constitution*, represented the belief that the South should abandon its agrarian past and become more commercial and industrial, like the North. Indeed, after the war there was a significant migration from rural areas as people searched for alternative jobs. Existing cities like Atlanta exploded. Others, like Birmingham, Alabama, established in 1871, were created new. An important aspect of developing an alternative economy was the establishment of new factories and warehouses. To the extent that capital resources and materials were available, many of these buildings were indistinguishable from their northern counterparts, with rusticated and crenellated buildings being common. Fireproof construction continued to be desirable, and brick or stone was used when possible. Efficient floor plans, made possible by a system of regularly placed supports and large glazed areas letting natural light into the interior, were also characteristic of these buildings.

Air Conditioning

Other technological advances included the introduction of air conditioning, a term coined by Stuart Cramer, a textile mill engineer who worked in Charlotte, North Carolina. While Cramer did not invent air conditioning technology, his own experiments to humidify textile mills in North Carolina were motivated by the realization that when cotton and wool fibers contained moisture, a factory's efficiency was improved. The tobacco industry also had an interest in technologies that would condition air. In 1913 the Carrier Air Conditioning Company installed an air filtering system in the American Tobacco Company plant in Richmond, Virginia. Theaters were another important application for air conditioning where customer comfort was desirable. In 1917 the New Empire Theater in Montgomery, Alabama, was equipped with a refrigeration unit designed to cool air, making it the first theater with air conditioning.

Office Buildings

Office buildings in the South began to appear in the late nineteenth century. These structures often resembled buildings being constructed in Chicago, New York, and other northern cities. The Equitable Building in Atlanta was the first skyscraper in Georgia. Designed by the prominent Chicago architect and Georgia native John Wellborn Root (1850–1891), this building stood eight stories tall and symbolized the growing economic importance of Atlanta. Birmingham, Alabama, because of its local steel industry, was another important southern city to have skyscrapers.

Expositions

Atlanta and other southern cities acquired economic clout by hosting a series of international expositions. Atlanta's Cotton States and International Exposition (1895), the South Carolina Interstate and West Indian Exposition (1901–1902), and the Jamestown Tercentenary Exposition (1907) are three of a number of fairs held in the South before World War I. The construction of monumental temporary and permanent exhibition buildings served as a powerful vehicle to promote the idea of the New South, showcase southern products, and celebrate southern history—real or imagined. For the Tennessee Centennial Exposition of 1897, organizers chose to construct a full-size replica of the Parthenon—an explicit and symbolic architectural expression of the state's desire to be known as the "Athens of the West."

Domestic Architecture

It was perhaps in the realm of domestic architecture that southern architects made their most significant contributions and received the most national attention. Knoxville architect George Barber began a successful mail order business for his house plans in the late 1880s. With customers throughout the United States, Barber was committed to filling customer needs by offering a broad selection of plans for houses at various prices and in different materials, even addressing regional climate in his designs. The Georgia Classicists were an influential school of architects whose work revived eighteenth- and nineteenth-century classical southern architecture. Members of this school included Philip Trammell Shutze, Neel Reid, Edward Vason Jones, Lewis Edmund Crook, and Jimmy Means, many of whom received their architectural training at the Georgia Institute of Technology. Best known are their residential commissions for affluent southern clients; however, the Georgia Classicists also designed schools, synagogues, churches, and other building types in the South and elsewhere. The Georgia Classicists began practicing in the 1910s, and their influence continues today.

Architectural Professionalism in the South

Other manifestations of the desire to extend the influence of southern architecture beyond the boundaries of the region can be seen in the late nineteenth century. *Southern Architect* (later renamed *Southern Architect and Building News*), a monthly architectural journal published from 1889 to 1932, promoted the work of southern architects and likewise kept southern architects informed of work their peers were undertaking. Efforts to legitimatize southern architectural practice were also critical in this period. Historian Charlotte V. Brown has noted that the American Institute of Architects, a national organization, established a southern chapter in Atlanta in 1892 which had members in Alabama, Georgia, Kentucky, Louisiana, Mississippi, South Carolina, Tennessee, and Virginia. This organizational effort was an important step in merging architectural practice in the South with national practice.

Tourism and Development

Meanwhile, other trends led to more commissions for architects in the South. In the late nineteenth century, the South began to develop as a vacation destination. In the early nineteenth century resorts were built at natural springs in Kentucky. Hot Springs, Arkansas, designated a federal reservation in 1832, has drawn people in search of a therapeutic cure for more than two centuries. The Crescent Hotel, constructed in 1886 in Eureka Springs, Arkansas, is yet another architectural example inspired by the craze for mineral water. Jekyll Island in Georgia became a winter retreat in the 1880s and was particularly popular with wealthy clients from the North. Other northerners acquired historic properties or large tracts of land on which to develop their southern retreats. William du Pont purchased President James Madison's Montpelier in 1900 and immediately began expanding the house. Du Pont's daughter would later develop the property into a premier facility for training horses. At approximately the same time, George W. Vanderbilt was developing Biltmore, his estate in Asheville, North Carolina. New York architect Richard Morris Hunt designed the house in the style of a French chateau, and Frederick Law Olmsted & Co. was hired to design the extensive arboretum featuring plant material appropriate for the South.

It was in Florida, however, where perhaps the most intensive and concentrated development occurred, made possible by the extension of the railroad in the late nineteenth century. Developers sought to bring northern tourists to new vacation spots in Florida. Henry Flagler was among the first of these developers; he constructed a number of hotels including the exotic Spanish-style Ponce de Leon in St. Augustine. Notable as the first large cast concrete building in the country, it was designed by the young New York firm of Carrèe and Hastings. Bernard Maybeck, who was employed by the firm, assisted in developing the historical symbolism used to underscore the building's Spanish association. Developer Henry Bradley Plant followed with the Tampa Bay Hotel (1891)—a fanciful Moorish Mediterranean style building. Architect Addison Mizner was one of the most successful and well-known practitioners in the design of these elaborate resort hotels, and his career coincided with the period of great land development in Florida following World War I. Drawing upon Venetian, Spanish, and Latin American ar-

George W. Vanderbilt contracted with New York architect Richard Morris Hunt to design the Biltmore in Asheville, North Carolina, in the style of a French chateau. Frederick Law Olmsted & Co. was hired to design the extensive arboretum featuring plant material appropriate for the South. Courtesy of the North Carolina State Archives.

chitecture, Mizner created fantastical designs for projects throughout the country, but most notably in Florida, where his work was particularly in keeping with the local landscape, climate, and culture. Mizner's house for Leonard Thomas, Casa de Leoni in Palm Beach (1921), was the architect's first use of the Venetian palazzo as design inspiration. Situated directly on a lake, the design included a portal for the gondola, as well as balconies and tall Venetian arched windows. Beginning in 1925, Mizner launched his own development company to undertake the construction of a resort hotel and housing development in Boca Raton. While the project ultimately collapsed under financial strain and the land bust, Mizner succeeded in shaping the city plan and image of Boca Raton with the construction of his Cloister Inn, city buildings, and housing developments Old Floresta and Spanish Village.

In the twentieth century, other wealthy clients challenged their architects to design modern interpretations of the southern plantation house. For publisher Henry R. Luce, architect Edward Durell Stone designed Mepkin Plantation in South Carolina and incorporated a number of ideas from nineteenth-century southern sources into this International style residence. The guest houses at Mepkin are grouped so that on three sides they form a space which the architect intended to recall a Charleston garden. The fourth side is closed by a brick serpentine wall—a respectful nod to Thomas Jefferson and his garden walls at the University of Virginia. However, Stone's wall is not a literal copy, as the wall is perforated—a detail he used regularly. Auldbrass (1939), designed by Frank Lloyd Wright in South

Carolina, was also envisioned as a modern interpretation of the antebellum plantation.

Educational Institutions

After the Civil War, a number of educational institutions were founded to address the educational needs of newly freed slaves. Hampton University in Hampton, Virginia, was founded in 1868 as Hampton Normal and Agricultural Institute. Tuskegee, founded in Alabama in 1881 by Booker T. Washington and Olivia A. Davidson, was a secondary school designed to train rural African Americans and Native Americans in a range of skills including architectural design and building trades. New York architect Richard Morris Hunt was hired to design the school's first permanent buildings.

The slow emergence of architectural education in the South is perhaps one reason for the conservative nature of architecture in the region. As early as 1814, Thomas Jefferson advocated that architecture be taught at the higher education institution he was working to establish (later named the University of Virginia). However, it was not until 1919 that Jefferson's dream of a formal architectural curriculum was finally realized at the university. Other southern colleges and universities were nearly as slow to establish their own programs. In 1893, Tuskegee Institute founded an architecture program, making it the first southern school to do so. This program, which symbolized Tuskegee founder Booker T. Washington's belief in the power of architecture to inspire, emphasized practical experience. Accordingly, students and faculty designed many of the buildings on campus. Construction experience was also part of the curriculum, and students made the bricks with which these early buildings were constructed. Tulane University followed with its own program in 1894. Georgia Institute of Technology, Alabama Polytechnic, and Clemson all established architecture programs in the first two decades of the twentieth century. The University of Arkansas, which graduated native southerners Edward Durell Stone (1902–1978) and E. Fay Jones (1921–), included architecture in its engineering program until 1946, at which point a separate program for architecture was created.

African American architects, wherever they received their training, had few opportunities to work in the South, and most moved north, where employment opportunities were marginally better. One notable exception is William Sidney Pittman (1875–1958). An African American architect born in Alabama, Pittman was an early graduate of the Tuskegee Institute, where he later returned to teach. In 1907 Pittman received national attention when he won the competition for the Negro Building at the Jamestown Ter-Centennial, making him the first African American to design such a building. Robert R. Taylor (1868–1942), an African American architect who trained at the Massachusetts Institute of Technology, designed many of the buildings at the Tuskegee Institute.

College education for women in the South also became more widely available, and the design of many women's college campuses continued the southern preference for classical architecture. The red brick campus of Sweet Briar College in Sweet Briar, Virginia, established in 1901, was designed by the Boston firm Cram, Goodhue and Ferguson in the Georgian style. Newcomb College in New Orleans was founded in 1886. The present campus was designed in 1911–1917 by architect James Gamble Rogers, who used a southern colonial style, reportedly to distinguish it from the campus of the all-male Tulane University, located nearby.

Agricultural Buildings

Despite significant changes in the southern economy, agriculture continued to be an important aspect of culture and life in the South. Accordingly, farmers continued to build agricultural buildings that reflected not only current farming practices but also ethnic traditions. An important example is the cantilever barn—a distinct form documented by historians Henry Glassie, Marian Moffett, and Lawrence Wodehouse in eastern Tennessee, western North Carolina, and eastern Kentucky. This form, usually placed on a flat stone foundation, has a two-part elevation, with the upper part of the building projecting out over the lower part. This enabled wagons to pull up under the overhang for loading protected from the elements. Historians have proposed a number of possible sources for this form, including Pennsylvania German barns and the military blockhouses built in the eighteenth century in the southern backcountry.

PERIOD TO WORLD WAR II

Public Works

In the period between the two world wars, the New Deal had a significant impact on the built environment of the South. Projects sponsored by the Public Works Administration (PWA), the Tennessee Valley Authority (TWA), and the Civilian Conservation Corps (CCC) were among the most important federal programs to result in the construction of buildings, engineering projects, and parks. These initiatives had the added benefit of putting southerners to work on construction projects during the Great Depression. The PWA and the Treasury Department designed and erected federal buildings, often in a modern style labeled "stripped or modernized classicism." The Tennessee State Office Building (1937–1940) in Nashville and the United States Post Office and Courthouse in Baton Rouge, Louisiana (1931–1933), with their pared down columns and volumetric massing, are two examples of federally sponsored projects in the 1930s. The Federal Art Project (FAP) and a succession of Treasury Department programs sponsored the creation of art for public buildings such as post offices and federal courthouses.

The federal government was also involved in the creation of new housing during this period. Techwood, constructed beginning in 1935 near Atlanta, has the distinction of being the first federally funded public housing project in the country. Administered by the Public Works Administration and designed by the Atlanta architectural firm Burge and Stevens, the apartment buildings and townhouses are brick veneer in a Georgian Revival style. By the following decade, the war had created significant demand for worker housing at key defense manufacturing centers and military bases. Levitt and Sons helped fill this vacuum by building Oakdale Farms in Norfolk, Virginia, to house naval officers and their families. Like Techwood, this development drew its architectural inspiration from the past, but in the case of Oakdale Farms the homes were modeled after New England Cape Cod–style houses.

The Tennessee Valley Authority (TVA), created in 1933, had a number of goals, among them flood control, energy generation, improved navigation, and economic development. TVA created the new model town of Norris, Tennessee, which had federally constructed houses, a library, a school, and several demonstration projects including a creamery and a ceramics lab. Designed by the TVA landscape architect Tracy B. Auger, Norris was inspired by Garden City planning theories such as those espoused by Ebenezer Howard. Other communities created for TVA construction workers were temporary and could be relocated as necessary. This housing was prefabricated, demountable, and low cost.

Tennessee was also home to the Manhattan Project, a secret initiative to develop the atom bomb located in Oak Ridge. Oak Ridge grew to a population of 82,000 just prior to the bombing of Hiroshima, Japan, in August 1945. This project also made extensive use of prefabricated units for housing to meet demand quickly. More than seventy manufacturing buildings were constructed as well. One of the largest was the gaseous diffusion plant, which covered forty-four acres. Skidmore, Owings & Merrill planned and designed Oak Ridge, and their master plan would have a significant influence on the development of postwar town planning in the United States.

Preservation

Amid the efforts to modernize and construct buildings in step with the twentieth century, the southern interest in the past continued. In the 1920s John D. Rockefeller, Jr., and the Reverend Dr. D.A.R. Goodwin collaborated on a project to preserve and re-create the colonial city of Williamsburg, Virginia. Motivated by patriotism and a concern that surviving eighteenth-century buildings would be lost, this project, overseen by the Boston firm Perry, Shaw, and Hepburn, captivated the public's imagination and has been extremely influential by inspiring other restoration projects around the country. Women's garden clubs were a major force in the preservation movement. According to garden historian Hubert B. Owens, the first garden club in the world was established in Athens, Georgia, in 1891. Similar clubs were founded throughout the South, and many of these organizations worked to restore eighteenth- and nineteenth-century gardens.

College Architecture

Georgian remained a popular style for campuses in this period, but was complemented by an interest in Gothic Revival. Horace Trumbauer's design for Duke University was composed of medieval-style buildings arranged in a symmetrical and balanced plan. Despite the pervasiveness of revival styles, there were notable exceptions. Frank Lloyd Wright's design for Florida Southern College in Lakeland was a significant departure from the norm. Historian Paul Venable Turner has noted that in his master plan, Wright drew upon his plan for the utopian Broadacre City. As in Broadacre City, individual buildings took on a number of different shapes—rectangular, square, and circular. Yet there was a sense of unity to the master plan, achieved in part by a covered passageway that connected the campus and provided shelter from the sun. Other bold modernist designs include Black Mountain College in North Carolina, which hired Walter Gropius and Marcel Breuer to design a new campus. Their plan, although modified by a local architect to reduce the cost, is a powerful sculptural design in the International style situated in a rural setting.

Travel

Following World War I, Americans became increasingly mobile. The construction of roads like the Dixie Highway (a 5,700-mile highway system begun in 1915 stretching from Ontario, Canada, to Miami) made long-distance travel easier. Not surprisingly, tourist destinations targeted at these travelers became prominent features on the southern landscape. One attraction located along the Dixie Highway, Renfro Valley in Rockcastle County, Kentucky, was established in 1939 and is believed to be the first auto tourism site devoted to country music. In the following decades, live radio programs broadcast from Renfro Valley drew large numbers of visitors to the site. Tourist amenities including tourist cabins constructed in log—a local vernacular—were built. In the 1930s, the federal government established the Great Smoky Mountains National Park spanning Tennessee and North Carolina. Shelters, fire towers, and other park buildings were constructed by CCC workers out of local stone and timber.

POST–WORLD WAR II

Following World War II, the South experienced many of the urban trends seen throughout the rest of the United States. The construction of the Eisenhower Interstate System has facilitated travel between cities and regions of the country. Interstate 95 links Miami to Boston. Moreover, the impact of the automobile and the increasing availability of air travel have led to the dramatic expansion of southern cities like Atlanta and Miami.

Southern Architectural Forms

After World War II the South more enthusiastically embraced modernism, and architects began to explore southern forms and construction techniques in their own work. The Sarasota school of the 1940s and 1950s is an important example of this practice. This school, named after the work of Paul Rudolph and Ralph Twitchell, demonstrated a commitment to regional references using new and experimental methods of construction. Drawing upon the raised cottage idiom and open-sided buildings common in the South for their inspiration, Rudolph and Twitchell executed their designs using concrete, steel, and wood in a modernist language. For example, Rudolph's Cocoon House (1950) in Siesta Key, Florida, which is elevated on short stilts, has a tentlike roof and walls that are glazed or louvered. New York architect Edward Durell Stone also designed a number of buildings in the South, including the library at the University of South Carolina and the Legislative Building for North Carolina. In both of these projects, Stone employed his trademark pierced screen walls on the exterior, effectively filtering the sun.

Miami Beach, which had become known for its Art Deco hotels in the period after World War I, continued to be a popular tourist destination. Architects in the

Charles Moore's Piazza d'Italia fountain. Courtesy Louisiana Office of Tourism.

1950s, fueled by the economic prosperity following World War II, designed exotic settings where vacationers could relax and spend money. The Fontainebleau Hotel by Morris Lapidus (1953) is a notable example of resort architecture built during the decade following the end of World War II. The hotel is sleek and modern on the exterior, and historian Alice T. Friedman has described the interior as a "highly theatrical, period revival décor intended to overwhelm the visitor with color, texture, and opulence."

Other urban statements that either originated in the South or have important examples in the South should also be noted. Out of Atlanta emerged a new architectural concept for the hotel with John C. Portman's design for the Hyatt-Regency Hotel. Portman, a developer and architect, transformed the design of urban hotels with his soaring twenty-three-story lobby ringed with balconies and glass elevators that whisk people up through the lobby. Postmodernism, which plays an important role in a number of the Disney projects from the 1980s and 1990s discussed below, made an earlier appearance in New Orleans with Charles Moore's Piazza d'Italia (1975–1978). This urban folly/fountain is a humorous tribute to the local Italian community in New Orleans. The focal point is a fountain shaped like the country of Italy. Classical elements rendered in modern materials and finished with brilliant colors are outlined with neon tubing. Sculptures of the architect's face squirt water.

Entertainment

Florida became a popular destination for tourists drawn to its amusement parks. Disney World opened in Orlando in 1971, followed by Sea World, also located in Orlando, in 1973. EPCOT (an acronym for Experimental Prototype Community of Tomorrow), Disney's exhibition park of the future, opened in 1982. The focal points include the monumental geodesic dome, based on the designs pioneered by Buckminster Fuller, and the World Showcase—national pavilions highlighting an architectural icon of each country. The United States is represented by a facsimile of Independence Hall, and a copy of the Eiffel Tower is the exhibition building for France. Expansion of the Disney presence in Florida in the late 1980s included construction of the fantastical Swan and Dolphin hotels (1989–1990) by postmodern celebrity architect Michael Graves.

The central part of the southern region initiated its own tourist attractions, many of them centered around country music. The Grand Ole Opry, which began broadcasting in 1925 from an office building in Nashville, moved to Opryland, a music theme park with a 4,400-seat theater in 1974. Dolly Parton, a country music star, established Dollywood, a 400-acre theme park in Gatlinburg, Tennessee, in 1985. This park interprets the culture of Appalachia and the life of Dolly Parton, and includes a re-creation of her Appalachian childhood home.

Trends

New Urbanism, a planning approach that emerged in the late twentieth century, has had a strong impact on the southern landscape. This movement sought to address the problems caused by decentralization and suburbanization by replicating the spatial organization and quality of life in a small town. The early theorists and practioners of New Urbanism were Andres Duany and Elizabeth Plater-Zyberk, architects and planners on the architecture faculty at the University of Miami. Their project, Seaside, Florida, is an important southern example and was modeled after nineteenth-century towns. Even the town's slogan—"The New Town—The Old Ways"—signified its debt to the past. The town was designed to be a pedestrian-friendly community built on human scale with attention paid to public space. The architects involved in Seaside were inspired by architectural forms, details, and materials indigenous to the area. Familiar southern forms like the dogtrot house and sharecropper houses are adapted and used liberally throughout the community. Porches are also a ubiquitous detail in this affluent community. The town of Celebration, another New Urbanism community near Orlando, Florida, was created by the Disney Corporation and opened in 1996. Cooper Robertson & Partners and Robert A.M. Stern Architects provided the master plan. Internationally renowned architects including Venturi, Scott Brown & Associates Inc., Philip Johnson, Cesar Pelli & Associates, and Aldo Rossi Architects were commissioned to design individual buildings.

At the other end of the economic spectrum are the architects working to create quality buildings for people of low and modest incomes in the South. Architect Samuel Mockbee (1944–2001) founded the Rural Studio in the early 1990s to design and build houses for poor people in Alabama. Using recycled and donated materials, architecture students from Auburn University draw upon vernacular sheds and barns, trailers, and other forms typical in the South to construct housing and community buildings. An example of Rural Studio's work is the "Butterfly House" designed and constructed for Ora and Anderson Harris in Hale County, Alabama. The sharply pitched inverted roof that gives the house its name directs rainwater into a cistern. Other environmentally conscious features make this house inexpensive to heat.

Arkansas architect E. Fay Jones was also known for his interest in adapting local forms and materials in his designs. Trained by Frank Lloyd Wright, throughout his career Jones continued to be guided by the organic principles he was taught at Taliesin. His most famous building is Thorncrown Chapel near Eureka Springs, Arkansas. This building, constructed predominantly of wood and glass, is set into a wooded slope and recalls the sacred quality of the forest.

As is the case throughout the country, the historic preservation movement in the South has continued to professionalize and gain more legitimacy. The passage of the National Historic Preservation Act in 1966 resulted in the creation of preservation and documentation programs at state and local levels. These programs have made great strides in recording southern architecture and increasing public awareness of its importance. Research centers such as the architectural research and archaeological research departments at Colonial Williamsburg, as well as research projects undertaken by the Museum of Early Southern Decorative Arts in Salem, North Carolina, have resulted in the publication and dissemination of information relating to architecture in the South. As a testament to the interest in southern architecture, a number of historic preservation programs have been founded within southern universities. The architectural history program at the University of Virginia is the oldest in the country, having been founded in 1958 as an undergraduate program. The Georgia Institute of Technology began a graduate program in the history of architecture in the mid-1980s.

With the rising popularity of spectator sports in the twentieth century, the South has followed national trends by erecting large stadiums and other sports facilities. For example, college football bowl games such as the Sugar Bowl, Orange Bowl, and Gator Bowl have historically been held in warm climates. To meet the public's growing interest in these bowl games and other sporting events, a number of southern cities constructed increasingly larger stadiums which benefited from new building technologies developed in the twentieth century. The Louisiana Superdome, erected in New Orleans (1971–1975), is one example; it claims to be the largest interior space constructed of steel and unobstructed by posts. In 1996 Atlanta hosted the Centennial Olympic Games, resulting in the construction of an extensive purpose-built sports and residential facility. The Atlanta firm Sizemore, Floyd Architects was responsible for planning this facility, which included thirty-one sports venues and housing for more than 16,000 athletes and related personnel.

While southern architecture has in many ways merged with national trends, the idea of a unique style of southern architecture persists in the public's imagination. The popularity of "shelter" magazines like *Southern Living*, which had 3 million subscribers in 2000, and *Southern Accents* suggests that the public not only accepts the notion of southern regionalism in architecture but is willing to pay for it. Whether these readers are drawn by aesthetics, are motivated by nostalgia, or see southern architecture as the stage where the stereotype of gracious and easy living, good music, and home cooking is played out is difficult to tell. Perhaps what is most important is that the public believes in the survival of a southern way of life—whether it exists or not.

The Superdome in New Orleans. Courtesy Louisiana Office of Tourism.

RESOURCE GUIDE

Printed Sources

The scholarship on southern architecture is somewhat uneven in coverage and depth from state to state. Historians working in Louisiana, North Carolina, and Virginia have made significant progress documenting and analyzing the built environment within their states. Other states have been dealt with less comprehensively, although studies for individual cities and selected regions are available. The Society of Architectural Historians has undertaken a publication project titled the Buildings of the United States; completed volumes for Virginia and Louisiana are listed below. Volumes for the states of Alabama, Arkansas, Florida, Georgia, and South Carolina are currently under way.

Andrews, Wayne. *Pride of the South: A Social History of Southern Architecture*. New York: Athenaeum, 1979.

Bishir, Catherine W. *North Carolina Architecture*. Chapel Hill: University of North Carolina Press for the Historic Preservation Foundation of North Carolina, 1990.

Bishir, Catherine, Charlotte V. Brown, Carl Lounsbury, and Ernest H. Wood III. *Architects and Builders in North Carolina: A History of the Practice of Building*. Chapel Hill: University of North Carolina Press, 1990.

Brownell, Charles, et al. *The Making of Virginia Architecture*. Richmond: Virginia Museum of Fine Arts, 1992.

Carson, Cary, Norman F. Barka, William M. Kelso, Garry Wheeler Stone, and Dell Upton. "Impermanent Architecture in the Southern American Colonies." *Winterthur Portfolio* 16, no. 2/3 (Summer-Autumn 1981): 135–196.

Glassie, Henry H. *Folk Housing in Middle Virginia: A Structural Analysis of Historic Artifacts*. Knoxville: University of Tennessee Press, 1975.

Kingsley, Karen. *Buildings of Louisiana*. New York: Oxford University Press for the Society of Architectural Historians, 2003.

Lane, Mills. *Architecture of the Old South*. 10 vols. New York: Abbeville Press, 1993. (This multivolume series includes Alabama, Georgia, Kentucky, Louisiana, Mississippi, North Carolina, South Carolina, Tennessee, and Virginia. Two additional volumes are concerned with colonial, federal, Greek Revival, and romantic architectural styles in the South.)

Lanier, Gabrielle M., and Bernard L. Herman. *Everyday Architecture of the Mid-Atlantic: Looking at Buildings and Landscapes*. Baltimore: Johns Hopkins University Press, 1997.

Lee, Anne Carter. *Buildings of Virginia: The Valley, South, and West*. New York: Oxford University Press for the Society of Architectural Historians. In press.

Lounsbury, Carl R., ed. *An Illustrated Glossary of Early Southern Architecture and Landscape*. New York: Oxford University Press, 1994.

Mumford, Lewis. *The South in Architecture*. 1941. Reprint, New York: Da Capo Press, 1967.

Perspectives in Vernacular Architecture. Annapolis, MD: Vernacular Architecture Forum, 1982–2003. Multivolume collection of essays on vernacular architecture topics often about southern architecture.

Poesch, Jessie J. *The Art of the Old South: Painting, Sculpture, Architecture, and the Products of Craftsmen, 1560–1860*. New York: Knopf, 1983.

Reps, John W. *Tidewater Towns: City Planning in Colonial Virginia and Maryland*. Williamsburg, VA: Colonial Williamsburg Foundation. Distributed by the University Press of Virginia, Charlottesville, 1972.

Severens, Kenneth. *Southern Architecture: 350 Years of Distinctive American Buildings*. New York: E. P. Dutton, 1981.

Turner, Paul Venable. *Campus: An American Planning Tradition*. 2nd ed. New York: Architectural History Foundation; Cambridge, MA: MIT Press, 1994.

Upton, Dell, ed. *America's Architectural Roots: Ethnic Groups that Built America.* Washington, DC: Preservation Press, 1986.

Vlach, John Michael. *Back of the Big House: The Architecture of Plantation Slavery.* Chapel Hill: University of North Carolina Press, 1993.

Weiss, Ellen. *An Annotated Bibliography on African-American Architects and Builders.* Teaching Materials in Architectural History, No. 1. Philadelphia: Society of Architectural Historians, 1993.

Wilson, Richard Guy, ed. *Buildings of Virginia.* Vol. 1, *Tidewater and Piedmont.* New York: Oxford University Press for the Society of Architectural Historians, 2002.

Web Sites

State historic preservation offices (most of which have Web sites) are an excellent source of information for architecture in a particular state. Other Web sites of interest include:

The Architecture of Thomas Jefferson
http://jefferson.village.virginia.edu/wilson/home.html

Center for the Study of Southern Culture, University of Mississippi
http://www.olemiss.edu/depts/south/

The Colonial Revival in America: Annotated Bibliography
http://etext.lib.virginia.edu/colonial/

Southeast Chapter of the Society of Architectural Historians
http://www.sesah.org/

Vernacular Architecture Forum
http://www.vernaculararchitectureforum.org/

Videos/Films

An American Legacy: The Sarasota School of Architecture. Dir. Heather Dunhill and Bill Wagy. Heather Dunhill in association with the Fine Arts Society of Sarasota, 2001.

America's Castles. A&E, 1994–1999. This series includes episodes titled "The Confederacy," "The Biltmore Estate," "Bayou Estates," "The Winter Castles," and "Savannah," as well as other episodes of general interest which include historic southern residences.

Far Fetched and Dear Bought: Four Architects Who Changed North Carolina. Preservation North Carolina and Mark Spano Communications, in association with UNC-TV, 1997.

The Rural Studio Film. Dir. Chuck Schultz. Alabama Public Television and Independent Television Service, 2002.

Organizations, Museums, Special Collections

Association for the Preservation of Tennessee Antiquities, Nashville, Tennessee
http://www.mtsu.edu/~histpres/APTA/index.html

This organization owns a number of historic properties throughout the state of Tennessee that are open to the public.

Association for the Preservation of Virginia Antiquities, Richmond, Virginia
http://www.apva.org

The association operates a number of historic properties throughout Virginia as museums.

Auburn University Special Collections and Archives; Southern Architecture
http://www.lib.auburn.edu/sca/manuscripts.html

Carnegie Survey of the Architecture of the South by Frances Benjamin Johnston Collection; Library of Congress
http://lcweb.loc.gov/rr/print/coll/039.html

Colonial Williamsburg, Williamsburg, Virginia
http://www.history.org/history/

Frontier Culture Museum of Virginia, Staunton, Virginia
http://www.frontiermuseum.org/

Grand Village of the Natchez Indians, Natchez, Mississippi
http://www.mdah.state.ms.us/hprop/gvni.html

Historic American Building Survey (HABS)/Historic American Engineering Record (HAER) at the Library of Congress
http://memory.loc.gov/ammem/hhhtml/hhhome.html

Historic Bethabara Park, Winston-Salem, North Carolina
http://www.bethabarapark.org

Museum of Early Southern Decorative Arts, Salem, North Carolina
http://mesda.org/

National Trust for Historic Preservation, Washington, DC
http://www.nationaltrust.org/

The National Trust owns a number of historic properties including several in the South.

New Orleans Notarial Archives
http://www.notarialarchives.org/

Measured drawings and plans for 5,500 properties in New Orleans and some nearby plantations from 1802 to 1903.

Ocmulgee National Monument, Macon, Georgia
http://www.nps.gov/ocmu/

The Pictorial Archives of Early American Architecture (PAEAA); Library of Congress
http://lcweb.loc.gov/rr/print/coll/186.html

Rural Life Museum, Baton Rouge, Louisiana
http://rurallife.lsu.edu/

ART

Barbara Rothermel

The search for a common aesthetic in southern art is one of contradiction that often leads to cultural clichés and stereotypes in a region that is complex and diverse; a region that, despite contemporary homogenization, remains distinctive. When searching for commonality or consistency in southern art, the search must examine how the South and its people have perceived themselves throughout their history. In the colonial and antebellum eras, southern art was one of pride, social ambition, and a sense of personal and community honor. Emphasis was placed on portraiture, with its implications of inherited name, land, and social status, with portraits valued both for their decorative quality and as emblems of prosperity. In the era following the Civil War, southern art became more introspective, seeking answers to the meaning of the New South. The established social order had been shattered, and with it the social significance of portraits. The land itself, however, had not been lost. Rather than depicting domestic genre scenes, artists turned to the land, which represented the "glorious cause" and a lost way of life. Consideration was first given to sentimental and often stereotypical genre scenes, but soon artistic attention turned to the examination of landscape itself, enduring and evolving.

The bonds of place are integral to southern culture, and the commonality in post–Civil War southern art is itself found in the land. Scarlett O'Hara, the heroine of Margaret Mitchell's classic novel of the South, *Gone with the Wind*, comes to recognize, as her father stresses, that the South is the land. So, too, is the art of the South about the land, and its many places and people. The land of southern art, at once lush and ravaged, gentle and cruel, seems to have always been old.

The past is ingrained in southern art. Yet, while the art of the South may be rooted in the antebellum past, it is not art of simple nostalgia or glorification. It is art that pays homage to the past, remains haunted by it, fatalistically accepts its bygone splendor, and despairs its wounds. Remnants of the past are ever present in southern art—a reverence for place, emblems of myth and history, unresolved prejudices and fears, and a pervasive sense of mystery and self-absorption. There is a dark, sultry, brooding quality to much of the art of the South, a visceral and evocative presence of the air—hot and humid; the light—glaring and shadowed; the sounds—quiet and biting; the smells—fragrant and decaying; and the sights—languid, fertile, and deeply scarred. The rituals and traditions of grace, strength, and southern hospitality are penetrated by the artists of the South to reveal the region's secrets and its precarious nature with resentment, celebration, and a lurking sense of ominous disquiet beneath the veneer. It is art that is, above all, ambiguous.

The question remains: Is there a southern aesthetic? Is southern art different from art in other regions of the United States? The danger in seeking a commonality in any art form is that of oversimplification. Many artists from the South defy generalization. In the mid-twentieth century, southern artists such as Jasper Johns, like other artists throughout America, migrated to New York City in search of new forms of artistic expression. And artists from other regions of America have explored the South and, especially, the violence of racial injustices. Yet the ambiance of the South as personified by its native artists seduces us, intrigues us, and defies us to see beyond the superficiality of the ghostly beauty of the land to the steely resolve of its people and the enduring force that reverberates in its art.

NATIVE AMERICAN ART IN THE SOUTH

The art of native cultures in the South, as elsewhere in America, is inseparable from both myth and everyday life. The artifacts and relics of the past are both art and documentation of life. The art expresses a bond to the spiritual world, especially animals that were regarded as ancestors. Art from the earliest stages features supernatural spirits—symbols and patterns in carved, painted, woven, and sewn form. This includes rock paintings, carved masks used for magico-religious purposes, weaving, pottery vessels and effigy pipes, basketry, body ornaments, beadwork, and stone sculpture. Wood, although easy to carve, is rarely preserved due to the environment, and few pre-European contact examples (figurines, knife handles, ladles, bowls, clubs, speaker's staffs, and loom heddles) survive.

The first sign of settled society in the South was the mound culture that flourished between c. 200 B.C.E. and 400 C.E. and spread from the Ohio River valley along the Mississippi River. The sites of important mounds in Alabama and eastern Arkansas are home to the descendant tribes, including the Chickasaw and Chocktaw. Objects discovered in these mounds were made from shells, obsidian, copper, clay, and stone. Artifacts found in the lower Mississippi include figurines, pipes, and ceremonial pottery jars and effigy vessels with bands of crosshatched lines and curvilinear, geometric, or bird motifs. Bird motifs have also been found on stone, bone, copper, and shell objects. Clay figurines are the earliest known sculptural forms and are generally rudimentary in nature. Mounds of the Caddoan culture of western Arkansas contained distinctive ceramics with heavy curvilinear and crosshatch engraving.

The Mississippian culture emerged and flourished from c. 800 to 1500 C.E. The South Appalachian Mississippian culture, ancestors of the Creek and Cherokee, was found in parts of Georgia, northern Alabama, and western North Carolina. The Fort Walton Mississippian culture, whose inhabitants were the ancestors of the Apalachee, was found in western Florida. The Mississippian culture had extensive trade, hierarchical political and social organization, and large population centers with earthen mounds and temples. Artifacts including gorgets and jewelry made of mica from North Carolina, black chert from Arkansas, shell from the Gulf of Mexico, wood, and other materials are characterized by technical and aesthetic development. Incised pottery, shell, bone, horn, and metal are naturalistic, with dynamic movement and attention to detail. Destruction and looting have long hindered preservation of archaeological evidence from these sites.

By the time of the earliest European explorations of the sixteenth century, beginning with the Spanish expedition led by Hernando de Soto in 1539, Native American societies were established throughout the South, with tribes ranging from the Appalachian Mountains to Florida and the Gulf of Mexico. Among the earliest contacts were the Calusa of the Florida Keys. The polychrome masks and figurines recovered archaeologically are evidence of traditions annihilated by European contact. Other prominent tribes that survived contact were the Cherokee, Chickasaw, Choctaw, Creek, Natchez, and Seminole. The Powhatan, Algonquian, Tuscarora, and Shawnee, although considered northeastern tribes, were also living in present-day Virginia and Kentucky.

The Cherokee, Chickasaw, Creek, Choctaw, and Seminoles were referred to by Europeans as the Five Civilized Tribes, because of their affluence and adaptability in the face of European encroachment. Accommodation of whites did not prevent the eventual displacement of these people to the Indian territories of the West, present-day Kansas and Oklahoma, by the 1830s. With

Chucalissa Mississippian Rhodes incised jar with arcaded handles (top); Hunchback effigy bottle (bottom). Courtesy Chucalissa Museum.

westward expansion by whites in search of land and natural resources, relations with the Five Civilized Tribes became increasingly tense, with numerous treaties made and broken until 1838, when the Cherokee were forcibly removed to Oklahoma along what became known as the Trail of Tears. Only fractions of the Chero-

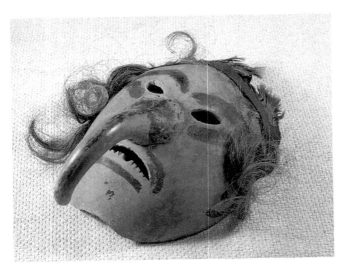

Cherokee Indian "Booger" mask. Courtesy of the North Carolina State Archives.

kee, Choctaw, Creek, Chickasaw, and Seminole remained in their homes in North Carolina, Mississippi, Georgia, Alabama, and Florida. Their art, in the form of baskets, pottery, beaded adornment and clothing, as well as their creation myths and legends of ancestors and migrations, whether produced by those who remained in the traditional homelands in the South or by those who were forced westward, retained a connection to their homelands.

Evidence exists of the Native American inhabitation of the southern Appalachian Mountains as long as 12,000 years ago, and this region eventually became the homeland of the Cherokee. Stone human and animal effigy pipes with conventionalized features date from the Mississippian culture. The Mississippian tradition continued into historic times with Cherokee pipemakers, including pipes illustrating human sexuality. By the eighteenth century, pipemaking was on the decline. Cherokee "Booger" masks were carved of wood and were somewhat similar to Iroquois false face masks with distorted, exaggerated facial features and expressions. These masks ridicule strangers who do not behave with human decency.

Basketry is a form of art long made by Native Americans, and the design of indigenous basketry in the South reached its epitome among the Cherokee. Cherokee baskets were traditionally made of split river cane, white oak, and honeysuckle. The primary technique is plaiting, with split river cane used for single and double woven baskets. Undyed, red, black, and (more rarely) orange and yellow cane splits were twilled to produce geometric designs. Wood split basketry developed after European contact, as iron implements are needed to make thin regular hardwood splints. Basketry figures of humans and animals made of coiled pine needles are of fairly recent origin.

Mats, belts, bag straps, garters, sashes, and bags were also made by plaiting and braiding techniques. Indigenous materials such as vegetal fibers and animal wool were the original materials, with glass beads and commercial yarns added by the end of the eighteenth century as a result of trade with whites. Earlier preference was for plain backgrounds with narrow borders or central stripes; however, geometric designs created by white glass beads threaded on yarn, and polychrome horizontal, V, W, and zigzag designs became more popular as commercial yarn became available.

Quill and beadwork were traditionally used for adornment on clothing and on necklaces and other ornaments, and patterns were often related. Dyed and flattened porcupine quills were threaded and woven to achieve a polychrome pattern. Beads used for appliqué were primarily shell, with design based on line rather than color. With the arrival of trade goods, shell beads were replaced by glass beads.

The earliest preference for glass beads was white and blue, probably because of the traditional monochromatic motifs. White beadwork in scroll-pattern sashes continued to be preferred by the Choctaw, while the Potawatomi filled forms with parallel lines. Polychrome motifs developed in the later nineteenth century. Large opaque beads known as "pony beads" were the first to be introduced, and from c. 1840 smaller opaque seed beads became standard.

Leather, textile, and feather appliqué designs were traditionally used by a number of tribes, and silk ribbon appliqué became important with trade in the eighteenth century. Ribbon appliqué consisted of simple decorative borders, except by the Seminole of Florida. Ribbon appliqué among the Seminole started as rectilinear borders and bands of triangles, but became increasingly elaborate. By the second half of the nineteenth century, designs of male and female clothing included horizontal stripes of various widths, with triangles, crosses, square frames, meanders, and several superimposed layers of fabric. Quilts were also introduced in the nineteenth century, and the patchwork tradition of the Seminole replaced appliqué beginning c. 1915, although the patterns retained their rectilinearity.[1]

Native American art in the South, like elsewhere in America, is combined with the traditions of storytelling and dance. Tribal knowledge and heritage are steeped in ancient beliefs in superior powers and a dominant Great Spirit, ancestral spirits, elaborate social structures and laws, and a dependency on the natural world—all of which are evident in the rich and diverse forms of visual expression.

REGIONAL AND ETHNIC CONSIDERATIONS

With the earliest European settlements in America came cultural diversity, regionalism, and the religious, social, and racial division which continue to characterize the South: French Catholic settlements in the Mississippi River basin and New Orleans; a French Protestant (Huguenot) colony in present-day South Carolina; Spanish colonies in Florida; English Protestant colonies in Virginia and the Carolinas, beginning with Jamestown in 1607; Scots-Irish in the Appalachian Mountains; Cajun and Creole in Louisiana; and Native Americans and African slaves throughout America. More recently, the influence of Cuban culture has been felt in the Florida Keys and the Tampa region, beginning in the late nineteenth century with the influx of the cigar industry, and since the 1950s in Miami and South Florida. Yet while there are distinctions of history and culture, preferences in art, especially in painting, are not prevalent. With the exception of Native Americans, the earliest inhabitants of the South, both artists and patrons, were transplanted Europeans who brought with them prevailing European tastes. As such, the influence of cultural,

Mardi Gras masks. Courtesy Louisiana Office of Tourism.

religious, and ethnic diversity is seen primarily in iconological use of symbols and traditional motifs.

ART IN THE SOUTHERN COLONIES

Early European explorer artists had little interest in the landscape itself, but did record Native American culture and appearances in an attempt to depict the world they encountered. These early drawings and watercolors provide visual documentation of Native American life before the invasive influence of European culture. Jacques LeMoyne de Morgues (c. 1533–1588) is considered to be the first European explorer-artist to record native life in the South on French expeditions to Georgia, Florida, and the Carolinas in 1564. John White, a member of England's Roanoke expedition of 1585, painted detailed watercolors of Native American villages, ceremonies, and fishing in what is now North Carolina. These watercolors are now in the collection of the British Museum, London.

The southern colonies were populated by transplanted Europeans whose tastes were consistent with their homelands, and few distinctions are evident. The portrait was most prevalent; the landscape, which was to become all-important in later southern art, serves only as a backdrop. Those artists who did depict the land were concerned with the natural environment. The self-taught artist-naturalist Mark Catesby (c. 1679–1749) arrived in Virginia in 1712 and began to make sketches and drawings of the flora and fauna of the region. A subsequent trip to the Carolinas, Georgia, and Florida ultimately resulted in the two-volume *The Natural History of Carolina, Florida and the Bahama Islands* and his election to England's Royal Society in 1733.

Although religious freedom was an important consideration in immigration to the colonies, there was no widespread interest in religious subjects in art. Compared with the North, there are relatively few portraits from the South in the seventeenth century, due in part to the climate, which was not conducive to the long-term preservation of material goods, and to the low number of women who immigrated to the southern settlements, with the consequent lack of emphasis on household management.[2]

England's southern colonies in the seventeenth century were predominantly royalist and affiliated with the Church of England. Protestantism in general condemned the visual arts in the context of religious services, particularly images of God. As such, the focus of art in the English colonies became the worldly life rather than the spiritual life. The plantation lifestyle of the South supported an aristocratic social and political structure. The wealthy elite lived in country manors and a favored portrait painting. Portrait painting in the English colonies in the South was carried out first by European-trained painters such as Charles Bridges (English, 1670–1747), who practiced in Virginia from 1735 to 1740, and Jeremiah Theüs (Swiss, c. 1719–1774), who worked in Charleston, South Carolina, where he became the city's principal artist, painting portraits and advertising his services to paint landscapes and coats of arms for coaches.

By the 1750s, the new stylistic changes referred to as Rococo were evident in southern colonial portraits. This style included pastel colors, curving lines, emphasis on the decorative, and the incorporation of leisurely pursuits such as grand dances. The English painter John Wollaston (c. 1710–after 1775), the son of a portrait painter, who probably studied with his father, was one of the first to introduce the Rococo style to the colonies.[3] He traveled from New York to Maryland and then to Virginia, where he painted more than sixty-five portraits. He then moved on to St. Kitts and Charleston, South Carolina, before returning to England. Wollaston is considered to have had significant influence on American painters of the time, including Benjamin West.

Similar to the portraits of English colonists, the portraits of French colonists show them in the fashions of French court society. This includes portraits of Huguenot colonists of Charleston, South Carolina, despite their having fled the religious and political restrictions of France. Irish-born portraitist Henrietta Deering Johnston (c. 1670–c. 1728), who created pastel portraits of Huguenots in Charleston, is credited with being the first woman to work as a professional artist in America.[4]

Throughout the seventeenth and eighteenth centuries, America's colonial period, and prior to the Industrial Rev-

Colonial Needlework

Portrait painter Henrietta Deering Johnston, like most women artists of the day, also created needlework. The character of the art created by American women from the earliest colonial settlements was largely determined by the prevailing attitudes about women, which were shaped by ideas defining the nature and place of women in society. The needle arts were the most socially acceptable and therefore the most popular arts for a woman. Due to a shortage of imported goods, the needle and sewing box were at the core of the colonial woman's domestic chores. The needle arts also provided the opportunity for socialization and offered an outlet for creativity. Textiles and needlework commonly include handmade bedcovers, samplers and needlework pictures, hooked and braided rag rugs, as well as a variety of miscellaneous handcrafts that were used to cover tables, windows, floors, and, sometimes, the human form. Education for women outside of the home was limited to reading, writing, and simple arithmetic, providing knowledge necessary for their domestic role. Samplers, containing the alphabet, numbers, virtuous sayings, and pastoral or religiously based scenes, served as a confirmation of the lessons learned. Sewing was a tool of all classes, and plain sewing was a knowledge that no woman could be without. Only those with some leisure time and disposable income, however, could indulge in more ornamental or nonutilitarian needlework.

olution, life in America revolved around the home, especially in the South with its agrarian society and economy. One of the few pieces of furniture to be mentioned in many early household inventories was the bed. The size of the hearth and the predominance of the bed indicate the two most important centers of activity. Of all the textiles extant from colonial times, those related to the bed form the largest category. A bed might be the major piece of furniture in the house, and it was often the focus of the room, especially when the house consisted of only one or two rooms. What was on the bed was displayed, and what was displayed was important. In keeping with this prominence, the bed was covered by one of the few items of textile decoration in the home, and that decoration came in great variety.[5] These bed coverings included crewel-worked coverlets of embroidered patterns on a base of linen homespun, stenciled bedcovers with floral patterns, hand-embroidered or loomed candlewick spreads, and block-printed coverlets called palampore, in which the design was printed by hand from wooden blocks and often overpainted to bring out the color in certain areas. These bedcovers were originally from the East Indies and became especially popular in the warm climate of the southern colonies.

ART OF THE AMERICAN REVOLUTION AND THE EARLY REPUBLIC

In the years of the American Revolution and the consolidation of the new United States under the Constitution, ratified in 1787, portrait painting continued to dominate. Artists and sitters alike sought to show their allegiance in portraits defined by emblems of the new nation. Itinerant limners who made their living traveling from place to place painting portraits were obviously knowledgeable about contemporary artistic trends, although their work lacked the grand manner and technical proficiency of their European predecessors. The tastes of the southern patron remained conservative, and portraits emphasized every biographical detail of background, costume, and face. They are characterized by the elegantly clothed subject, posed in a courtly manner and in a palatial setting, surrounded by the elaborate and expensive accoutrements representative of the sitter's social position. The pretension of these compositions indicates a preoccupation with social status and a domestic sphere of affectation and refinement.

As some larger cities such as Richmond and Charleston grew and the demand for portraits of wealthy merchants and prominent politicians increased, amenities such as art academies and museums were established. Major portrait painters of the day, including Thomas Sully (1783–1872) and Samuel F.B. Morse (1791–1872), also visited the South, while native-born artists such as Matthew Harris Jouett (1788–1827) gained popularity and financial success.

Thomas Sully was a leading American portrait painter of the early Republic who completed more than 2,000 portraits as well as history paintings and landscapes. The son of a family of actors, he arrived in Charleston as a child in 1792 to begin his studies. At the age of sixteen, he moved to Richmond to study with an older brother who specialized in miniatures, and then to Norfolk. In 1805 he went to New York and Boston, and from time to time studied with Gilbert Stuart. He later settled in Philadelphia before traveling to England, where he met Pennsylvania-born Benjamin West (1738–1820) and Sir Thomas Lawrence, and visited the Royal Academy. The influence of Lawrence and the Romantic movement is evident in Sully's work, which is characterized by fluid brushwork, elegant composition, and dramatic use of light. Sully made many trips to Washington, Richmond, and Charleston, where his portraits of southern patrons, especially women and children, his gracious manner, and his support of young artists made him a favorite.

Morse, although best known as an inventor, was also a painter of considerable reputation in the North who found eager patrons in Charleston, South Carolina. After studying with Benjamin West in London, he made a number of trips to Charleston to complete commissions, including a full-length portrait of President James Monroe for the City Council of Charleston in 1820. Together with Thomas Cole and Rembrandt Peale, he founded the National Academy of Design in 1826 and served as its first president.

Matthew Harris Jouett was a native of Kentucky who studied law before moving to Boston in 1816 to study with Gilbert Stuart. The influence of Stuart is evident in Jouett's use of composition and color, but he became best known for his controlled brushstrokes and emphasis on architectural detail. In his later years, the influence of Sully is revealed in Jouett's romanticizing of his subjects.

Historical, battle, and narrative subjects and cityscapes also gained in popularity as records of independence, expansion, and unification. The landscape also gained importance as subject matter with the influence of Europe's Romantic movement and the academic tradition, with its emphasis on harmony, beauty, and truth. Early landscapes in the South included estate portraits that served as a record of plantation life and topographical records that document the growth of cities, such as *The North Carolina State House at Raleigh* (1830) by Jacob Marling (1774–1833). Among the early landscape painters of the South was George Cooke (1793–1849). A native of Maryland, he worked as a portraitist in Richmond before traveling to Europe to broaden his horizons. In the 1840s, he traveled to Georgia and New Orleans, where he painted landscapes such as *Tallulah Falls* (1834–1849) in the Romantic tradition with idealization, drama, and strong use of light that show the influence of the Hudson River school.

Naturalist painters continued the work of their European predecessors in recording the natural environment, animals, and Native Americans. The naturalist John James Audubon (1785–1851) devoted his life to depicting the birds and mammals of North America. He was born in Haiti and raised in post-Revolutionary France, then immigrated to the United States in 1806. His brief stint as a storeowner in Kentucky failed and he turned to painting, beginning his career as a portrait painter. He turned his attention to nature and native wildlife and developed a portfolio of hand-colored aquatint bird studies. His life's work, *The Birds of America*, with subjects from throughout the South from Virginia and Kentucky to the Florida Keys, depicts more than 1,000 birds with precision and detail. Unable to find an interested American publisher, he moved to England, where the folio was published between 1826 and 1838.

Engraving of *Richmond, from the Hill above the Waterworks*, a painting by George Cooke (1793–1844). Courtesy Library of Congress.

Southern art during the early years of the Republic is similar to all American art of the time, especially in the influence of European Romanticism. While historical and genre subjects and a sense of place gained importance over time, the interest in portraiture remained dominant, and itinerant folk artists helped fill this need.

EARLY NINETEENTH-CENTURY FOLK ART

In the simplest terms, American folk art consists of paintings, sculpture, and decorations of various kinds, characterized by an artistic innocence that distinguishes them from works by those academically trained in fine art or the formal decorative arts. This folk art is characterized by the qualities of vigor, honesty, inventiveness, imagination, and a strong sense of design. While it may show imperfect technical mastery on the part of the artist, it makes effective use of color and pattern in line and form. Most practitioners were not trained as artists in the academic sense, but were self-taught or trained in craftsmanship and use of traditional imagery through apprenticeship.[6]

Like their counterparts working in the academic tradition, American folk artists of the early nineteenth century were influenced by the art of Europe. All forms of painting, including portraits, commonly considered in the American folk art tradition can be traced to Old World predecessors as sources of inspiration and for the conventions of pose and scene. In the South, where the plantation and its accompanying self-contained agrarian lifestyle remained predominant until the Civil War, the taste for English styles and wares lingered far later than in other regions. Folk artists, either born in England or influenced by English styles, earned a living by painting portraits, signs, fireplace overmantels, and other utilitarian wares. In the South, especially popular were wooden overmantels, painted with scenes reminiscent of England, which showed the southern landowners' regard for painted decoration as a status symbol. Paintings of exterior domestic scenes further documented plantation life, with emphasis on the manor house, the land, its crops, and auxiliary buildings that supported its self-sufficiency.

The first portraits by folk painters in America were produced in New England, but folk artists emigrating from England soon found their way to the South. They were predominantly itinerants, moving from place to place plying their trade, and partially preparing the portraits in advance, then filling in the details of their patron. As such, portraits relied on stock formulas, poses, and personal effects such as swords for a military man, a flower for a lady, or a toy for a child. Among the earliest portrait painters in the folk tradition was the unidentified artist known as the Payne Limner, so-called because of his group of portraits of the Archer Payne family of Goochland County, Virginia, c. 1791. John Frymire (1765/74–1822) was born in Pennsylvania and may have trained for a time in Philadelphia. He worked from New Jersey to northern Virginia and Kentucky. His work is characteristic of the naïve style, strong linearity, and flattened forms of folk portraits.

Although southern folk art has English roots, Europe's influence extended beyond England. German immigrants who settled first in Pennsylvania before moving south through the Shenandoah Valley of Virginia, then to the Carolinas, brought *fraktur*, pottery, and elaborate ornamental ironwork. African motifs and sources, brought to the South with the slave trade, also found their way into southern folk traditions.

Folk art is directly affected by the environment—natural and social—from which form, style, and material emerge. This is evident in the dwelling and its furnishings, tools and implements of the day's work, everyday and festive costume, all the appurtenances of home devotions and religious observance, recreational objects, and equipment for the chief events of life—birth, marriage, death, and disposition of the corpse. These objects are functional, yet they are also decorative, art that is a reminder of the need for beauty and the human impulse for creativity, the need to endow even the most utilitarian of objects with beauty and creativity.

Utilitarian objects were an integral component of the development of the economy in the South, both urban and rural, and in the self-sufficiency of the plantation or farm, but the hot and humid southern climate has destroyed many of the painted objects carved from wood. Examples are shop signs using literal and symbolic imagery that told of the services or wares provided within; whirligigs, with human and animal representations, that gave information on wind direction and speed; and ship ornaments with images of the ship's namesake and home port. Cigar store signs, used by businesses selling tobacco, were primarily in the form of sculpture-in-the-round intended to be placed on the sidewalk outside the store, with many representations of Pocahontas, thus paying tribute to the Native American role in the early tobacco industry.

Other utilitarian objects that developed in the South were in the form of pottery. Most prevalent was the pottery of the Seagrove, North Carolina, region that developed in the eighteenth century and continues to this day, and potteries in Georgia. The earthenware and stoneware pottery of these regions has a distinctive dark glaze and forms that were handed down through generations of potter families. They were made on a kick wheel, glazed, and fired in a ground hog kiln. The earliest wares were functional, including plates, bowls, food storage jars, crocks, churns, and whiskey jugs that were sold from wagons traveling throughout the region. Also popular were face, effigy, or grotesque jugs, sometimes whimsical but often with biting, sardonic portraits. Although they were found in many potteries in America, most seem to be associated with southern potteries.

Folk art for the home was created by women, including mourning pictures, theorem paintings, and needlework. Fancy needlework became prized in the South, where the virtues of womanhood and social graces were all-important. Mourning pictures, inspired by the nation's mourning of the death of its first president, George Washington, were made by women as expressions of grief and as a memorial for the deceased. Neoclassical motifs such as weeping willows, urns, and women with bowed heads dominated the standard formula scenes, rendered first in embroidered form and later as paintings or combinations of paintings and embroidery.

Jugtown crock, Seagrove, North Carolina. Courtesy of the North Carolina State Archives.

These memorials also had a practical function in an age of few public records, as they recorded the vital statistics of the deceased. Theorem painting, a technique popular in England, where it was introduced from China, was taught in ladies' finishing schools, academies, and seminary schools beginning c. 1812, with later instruction available in books. The process used several stencil sheets and water-colors, and was used as a way to demonstrate proficiency in painting. A wide range of subjects including landscapes, historical scenes, and biblical images were created, but still lifes were the favorite subject.

Quilts

Needlework remained an integral part of every woman's education and life in America until well into the nineteenth century, when the progress of the Industrial Revolution finally made it possible to buy many of the necessities of everyday life that once had to be produced in the home. The rate of change brought by the Industrial Revolution varied regionally, with change first coming to the Northeast, the industrial hub of America, and arriving later in the South, which remained primarily agrarian.

Of all the needlework produced, no form has been as important as the quilt. Making quilts may have been a necessity, but it was also an area of creativity that was fully appreciated by makers, users, and viewers alike. Quilts may, in fact, be considered one of America's great indigenous art forms. Although the earliest quilt designs may have originated in Europe, they reached full bloom in America.

The earliest references to quilts in America are found in the estate and household inventories of the late seventeenth century; these quilts probably came from

Stately Oaks Quilt Show. Courtesy Georgia Department of Economic Development.

England. The first quilts made in America were utilitarian, as in the early years of the colonies there was little time for creating decorative quilts, even among the wealthy. Girls were taught the art of quilting at an early age. As soon as they were old enough to cut cloth into squares and sew them together, they began to make quilts, simple at first but increasingly complex. Tradition says that every young girl aspired to have a "baker's dozen"—thirteen quilts for her dowry—stored in her dower chest by the time she married. Often, the young bride-to-be pieced and quilted these herself, and then a special bee would be held to finish either all the quilts, or just the special thirteenth and more elaborate Bride's Quilt, which her friends joined in finishing.[7]

Regional differences in quilts began to appear quite early. Those made in New England were more likely to be made of homespun and created for warmth. They were usually constructed of strips of whole cloth or simple geometric pieces. In the South, with its warmer climate, large plantations, and slave labor to handle much of the basic textile work, the women of the house could create fancier work, although slave women who were skilled with a needle also contributed to these more elaborate pieces. *Broderie perse*, or Persian embroidery, a technique in which the forms of flowers, birds, animals, and foliage were cut from pieces of printed cotton and chintz and then stitched to a plain ground fabric, was especially popular in the South. But although some styles remained prevalent in certain regions for many years, designs and techniques spread quickly, and often it is difficult to pinpoint their origins.

Quilted bedcovers, made from any and all available scraps of material, were made in abundance, and are generally divided into three main groups: whole-cloth quilts, pieced quilts, and appliqué quilts. Both pieced and appliqué quilts are frequently referred to as patchwork. Some theories consider pieced quilts as the predecessor of appliqué quilts, but equally convincing is evidence that appliqué quilts predate pieced quilts. It seems likely that both types developed about the same time and have coexisted through the years. Whole-cloth quilts are usually made from several lengths of one or two fabrics only, the lengths of one sewn together and used as the top, and lengths of the other, usually a lesser or coarser fabric, used as the backing, with the front and back held together with extensive and elaborate quilting. The plain white background was an effective backdrop for decorative stitching, and these quilts became popular as trousseaux and wedding gifts. Pieced quilts were time-consuming but economical in times when fabric was expensive. The earliest pieced quilts were made from remnants. It was not until the nineteenth century that fabric began to be bought just for the purpose of making quilts. Pieced quilts were, for the most part, considered utilitarian and were used as an everyday bedcover. However, piecework produced stunning, even astonishing, geometric designs, in infinite varieties and patterns. The remnants used in pieced quilts often tell their own story—pieces from a favorite dress, a remnant of a dead relative's favorite fabric, men's ties, and so on—making the quilt not only an object for warmth but an artifact of one's life or one's heritage. Appliqué quilts involved cut-out shapes stitched to a ground fabric. In essence, an appliqué quilt is made of a double layer of fabric, and thus is more expensive to make than a pieced quilt. The blank spaces between the appliqué designs, however, provide an ideal place to showcase elaborate quilting. Appliqué quilts came into common use in the mid- to late eighteenth century, when factory-made fabrics were more easily obtained.

Despite the cost, many women preferred the greater freedom of design in appliqué quilts, whether realistic, narrative, or abstract. The South had a particularly strong appliqué tradition, and some of the finest examples originated in and around Baltimore, Maryland, distinguishable by elaborate and identifiable stitching. Fine, intricate stitching was always considered one of the most important elements of a quilt.

Album quilts, on which names were often stitched or written, were popular products of quilting bees, made particularly as gifts by the women of the community or church parish for a friend moving to a new home, often on the western frontier. There are great similarities between bride's quilts and album quilts, and the terms are sometimes used interchangeably. They are both forms of friendship quilts, where patches of a specified size were made by friends, and were either stitched together by the bride or by the group all sewing together. Motifs used for bride's quilts were frequently symbolic images representing love, fidelity, and fertility, while album quilts might be more general, or even simple patchwork designs. Whether called presentation, album, bride's, autograph, or friendship quilts, these works were steeped in sentiment, and were often lovingly stored in chests, becoming heirlooms handed down from mother to daughter. They are more than just personal treasures, however, as they also provide information on families, such as marriage names and dates, and on emigration, population, and cultural heritage. These quilts are often considered to be more important as documents than as works of art.

The inspirations for quilt patterns are innumerable and reflect regional folklore, religious belief, and personal history, often with names derived from the Bible. Whatever the inspiration for naming the pattern, it was meaningful to the maker. Once a pattern name was established, it might be handed down from one generation to the next, but just as often it was changed to reflect the views of the woman using it. And sometimes a quilt pattern called by one name in the South might be known by an entirely different name in the frontier West.

Sooner or later, almost every significant historical event or movement of the day showed up in quilts—centennials, war, elections, temperance, suffrage, emancipation, the environment, civil rights, and so on. Numerous quilts contained visible or veiled references to contemporary political and social events through both the design and the names assigned to them. The use of patriotic themes and politically inspired designs such as Sherman's March (also known as Lincoln's Platform in the North) gave the quiltmaker an opportunity to express her views on patriotism, politics, wars, and issues such as slavery.

Various ethnic, religious, and social groups also created their own quilting traditions. A strong appliqué tradition is also seen in many pieces by African American quilters from the South. The quilts of African Americans are thought to represent a unique style and a continuation of the textile traditions of West Africa, with strip techniques, strong color contrasts, asymmetry, large designs, and multiple patterning. Recent research has focused on the use of quilt patterns and their placement on fences or windows as guides and maps for the slaves escaping the South on the Underground Railroad.[8]

MONUMENTS TO THE CIVIL WAR

The Civil War renewed interest in historical painting in America in general, and for the first time history became a significant subject of painting in the South. One of the few painters in the South with experience in history painting was Enoch Wood Perry of Louisiana (1831–1915), who painted the Louisiana Legislature on its adoption of secession in 1861. But with the outbreak of civil war, artists found fertile new ground for social commentary, propaganda, and subtle persuasion in the images rendered with pen and paint. For the first time in history, news reports were illustrated, and many artists, south and north, sought work as war correspondents.[9]

William Ludwell Sheppard (1833–1912), in *Equipment 61*, depicted a soldier, standing proudly in uniform, with his headgear being adjusted by one who will soon be left behind. His *In the Hospital* (1861) showed a neatly dressed woman reading a letter to a wounded soldier, and *News from Home* featured a Confederate cavalryman by a campfire, reading a letter from home. Sheppard offered romanticized, sentimentalized scenes that served to glorify the southern soldier while ignoring the grim reality of the war.

Conrad Wise Chapman (1842–1910) was one of the most talented and tormented of the Confederate soldier-artists. The son of Virginia portrait and landscape artist John Gadsby Chapman, he was raised in Rome but always claimed himself as a native son of Virginia. In 1861 he returned home to serve the Confederacy by enlisting in the Third Kentucky Infantry, but was disastrous as a soldier. After accidentally and unexplainably shooting himself, he was transferred to a Virginia regiment that was assigned to Charleston. During that time, he made numerous sketches of life in camp that became the basis for a series of oil paintings, including *Battery, Laurens Street, Charleston, February 7, 1864*, in which a sentry stands guard over the harbor.

Richard Norris Brook (1847–1920), on the other hand, depicted the all-too-human cost of war in his paintings *Dead Drummer Boy* (c. 1870) and *Furling the Flag* (1872). Although painted after the war ended, they vividly show, skillfully but sentimentally, the conflict's continued impact on the South. Brook was born in Warrenton, Virginia, and was educated in private schools before entering the Pennsylvania Academy of Fine Arts in Philadelphia in 1865. In 1871 he was appointed professor of drawing at the Virginia Military Academy. He was subsequently named U.S. Consul to France by President U. S. Grant. Later he settled in Washington, D.C., where he worked in portraiture and art instruction.

Paintings of the Civil War also inspired engraved adaptation. Engravings, with their easy transfer to publications and multiplicity of copies, became increasingly important due to their accessibility to the masses. Among the most notable southern engravers was William D. Washington (1833–1870), a Virginia-born artist who started his career as a draftsman in the U.S. Patent Office. Washington turned his attention to panoramic landscape paintings such as *Jackson Entering Winchester* (c. 1862–1865), which shows General Stonewall Jackson in the pose of an equestrian statue and bears obvious evidence of the influence of Albert Bierstadt and Emmanuel Leutze, with whom Washington studied at the Dusseldorf Academy in Germany.

Portraiture remained an important art form, with subjects including military heroes and political leaders, most notably Robert E. Lee and Stonewall Jackson. Portraits by John Adams Elder (1833–1895), who studied in Dusseldorf with Emmanuel Leutze before returning home to Fredericksburg, Virginia, and enlisting as an aide in the Confederate Army; William Ludwell Sheppard; and many others show the leaders of the Confederacy in traditional poses with attributes of their military rank. Portraits of Lee, who did not welcome posing for artists, often reveal a world-weary visage and a dignified, resolved posture.

The art of the Civil War and the Reconstruction period soon reflected both localized events and noteworthy individuals, as well as the universality of the impact of war on the human condition. It further served to reinforce and drive the collective memory of the events that decimated the southern way of life and devastated its land. The role of the artist in war, whether on the battlefield, on the homefront, as reporter, or as historian, was to bring to life the human side of the conflict. Through the face of the hero and the anonymous soldier, the artist documents and interprets the fighting spirit and abject misery of battles, army campsites, and those left behind.

African Americans in Art

The Civil War also brought about a reconsideration of how artists depicted black Americans. African slave labor had enabled the plantation economy of the South to flourish in the seventeenth, eighteenth, and early nineteenth centuries. Justification of slavery took many avenues, including visual depictions of Africans as savages, simpletons, or childlike in nature. Prior to the Civil War, black men and women were shown as working cheerfully in the field or the house with exaggerated, stereotypical features, happy to serve their masters. In the North, paintings of African Americans focused on the plight of slaves and the involvement with the Union Army, albeit shown on a superficial level that continued to be stereotypical and often focused on humor. In the South, however, resistance to the new order was widespread and confrontational, and imagery of emancipation was virtually nonexistent. An exception to this was Kentucky artist Thomas Satterwhite Noble (1835–1907), a supporter of abolition, who created a series of paintings on the inhumanity of the slave trade. *The Price of Blood: A Planter Selling His Son* is a disturbing depiction of a wealthy landowner arranging for the sale of his mulatto son. The cruelty of the scene is accentuated by the father's arrogantly casual pose and confrontational stare at the viewer; the son's pose is filled with tension and resolve as he angrily looks away from the bargain, refusing to acknowledge it.[10]

Emancipation, likewise, did not feature in the sculpture of the South following the Civil War, which instead focused on the protection of states' rights. Among the most famous monumental sculptures of the era is an equestrian statue of General Robert E. Lee by the French sculptor Antonin Mercié (1845–1916) that stands along Monument Avenue in Richmond, Virginia, the capital of the Confederacy. Nobility is also at the fore of the Confederate monuments by Moses Ezekiel (1844–1917). Born in Richmond to Sephardic Jews of Dutch ancestry, Ezekiel entered the Virginia Military Academy in 1862, the first Jewish cadet in VMI history. In 1864, as a corporal in the color guard, he fought alongside his classmates at the Battle of New Market. In 1869, after one year of medical school, where he studied anatomy, he gained entry to the Royal Academy of Art in Berlin. Among his most notable commissions are *Virginia Mourning Her Dead* (1903), a cast bronze sculpture at VMI dedicated to the cadets who died in the Battle of New Market, and *New South*, the Confederate monument at Arlington National Cemetery (1912).

Realism and Naturalism

In the early post–Civil War years, many artists turned away from both the decorative portraiture of prosperity and the emotional response brought forth by the war itself, and found creative expression in the rationality of realism and naturalism. Richard Clague, Jr. (1821–1873), the son of a Louisiana family of French descent, was one such artist who turned away from the Romantic aesthetic of the past. A man of some sophistication, he studied at the École des Beaux Arts in Paris, where he was exposed to the newest art theories and aesthetic considerations before returning to New Orleans. Clague began his career as a mural and portrait painter, but after duty in the Louisiana Infantry during the Civil War, turned to detailed and rustic landscapes of Louisiana, Alabama, and Mississippi, and is considered to be the first artist to make the Mississippi Delta a recurring theme in his art.[11]

During Reconstruction, southern artists, like all people, sought answers amid the changing social and political tides. Concurrent with the movement toward realism and naturalism was an antithetical movement toward sentimental or heroic genre paintings. This often took the form of depicting genteel behavior, sentimentality, and idealization of the mementos of the Old South. William Aiken Walker (1838–1921), a native of Charleston, South Carolina, reinforced the division of the races with genre paintings showing a lack of change in the lives of freed slaves in the South. Blacks are depicted as still subservient and menial. His paintings are now seen as condescending and almost caricature-like in their lack of expression, while also revealing a basic interdependence among all strata of southern society.[12] Like Walker, John Beaufain Irving (1825–1877), the son of a Charleston family financially ruined by the war, painted scenes of black life following Emancipation that are sweetly formulaic but found popular favor with his audience.

The expectation of the audience for art in the South in the late nineteenth century was for refinement and the inviolate sense of social and moral responsibility. Art was expected to be a force for cohesive social ideals. It was expected to elevate and fill the individual with higher aspirations, and to embody divine moral truth and spiritual values. And it was expected to impose a sense of order on the turmoil of everyday life. The end of the nineteenth century and beginning of the twentieth was a time of departure from the elite-centered culture of the past. The familiar world was threatened by scientific advancements that challenged existing values, and the attendant art forms were subjected to a discourse among naturalism, realism, and abstraction. Some artists looked inward, searching for self-fulfillment through introspection and a mood of nostalgia. Others entered the cultural debate, sometimes rancorous, sometimes shaken to their foundations, and southern art moved into the twentieth century.

EARLY PHOTOGRAPHY AND SOCIAL CONSCIENCE

The interest in portraits took a new turn in the 1840s with the advent of photography. The daguerreotype, an early form of photography, was developed in France in the 1830s by Louis Daguerre (1789–1851) and introduced in the United States by Samuel F. B. Morse. The daguerreotype used light-sensitized metal plates.

Almost simultaneously William Henry Fox developed another process called the calotype, in which the exposure produced a reversed, or negative, image that could then be made into unlimited prints on treated paper. This process was surpassed in the 1850s by the wet collodion process, in which a glass plate was used instead of a paper one, allowing for a sharper image and the further production of photographic portraiture.

Before the development of photography, painters and sculptors were the ones who visually recorded people and events. The popularity of photography, however, soon exploded as an inexpensive means of portraiture, surpassing the folk portrait as the most prevalent form of personal documentation.

The impact of the Civil War on photography, and of photography on the Civil War, cannot be overemphasized. Photographers such as Mathew Brady and George P. Barnard brought the war to the homefront in new and dramatic ways. While historical paintings of the glorious armies and monuments of noble generals kept alive the lore of war in past ages, photography, with its immediacy and sense of commentary, found its way into the consciousness of the victorious and the defeated alike. Visions of battlefield atrocities and grueling camp life in photographic form brought home the human side of war as no art before had done. Through these images, battles were memorialized, public opinion was shaped, and history was recorded.

The devastation of the Great Depression (1929–1940) in the South was also recorded in photographs. The Farm Security Administration (FSA) photography project was organized in 1935 by Roy Stryker, the result of the influence on the public of photographs of child labor and urban squalor in the early twentieth century. The goal of the FSA photography project was to record rural conditions and the sociological and economic impact of the Depression on farms, especially those in the Midwest and the South. Among the most prominent photographers of the project was Walker Evans (1903–1975), a native of Missouri, who, like the others involved with the project, saw it as one of documentation rather than art. Evans was an anomaly among the FSA photographers, as he considered himself an artist with social concerns rather than a photojournalist. By using a large plate camera that demanded the careful posing of his subjects and closer scrutiny of his compositions, his photographs of farm families in Hale County, Alabama, 1936, for example, elicit a power and sense of integrity that go far beyond documentation. These photographs were published in the book *Let Us Now Praise Famous*

The First Full-Color Photography

The development of full color photography in America came at the hands of Michael Miley (1841–1918). Miley was raised on a farm in Rockbridge County, Virginia, near the city of Lexington, and at the age of nineteen he joined General Thomas J. Jackson's "Stonewall Brigade." Following the Civil War, he worked in a photography studio in the Shenandoah region, where he learned the collodion wet-plate process, and then worked for an itinerant photographer. By the late 1860s, he had opened his own commercial studio where he featured his photographic portraits of General Robert E. Lee, Confederate President Jefferson Davis, and others. Miley was, however, more interested in the highly stylized, idealized images showing women draped in classical clothing and printed in softly muted tones that were popular at the time. His continued experimentation led to an investigation of the carbon printing process that allowed for one-color prints in fifteen colors, and ultimately to the superimposing of primary-colored carbon images. Miley is now considered the first photographer in America to successfully produce full-color photographs on paper, a process he patented in 1902.

Men, published by Evans and James Agee in 1941. His objectivity, precision, and attention to detail demanded that the viewer respond to the image itself and not the maker of the image. Evans' work has continued to influence each succeeding generation of photographers. During his travels for the FSA, he also photographed pre–Civil War architecture, laying a foundation of introspection and examination of the landscape of the South as influenced by the past for contemporary photographers from the South.

Eudora Welty (1909–2001), best known as a writer, also worked for the Works Progress Administration (WPA) in the 1930s and 1940s in her native state of Mississippi. Her work as a publicist resulted in photographs that were spontaneous in nature, rather than carefully composed like those of Evans, but that reveal her intimate knowledge of the social structure of the Deep South. She is a storyteller, and her photographic images of a bygone era are marked by the same sensitivity to the regional dialect found in her writings. William Hollingsworth, Jr. (1910–1944), also from Mississippi, was interested primarily in images of African American culture in the South. Hollingsworth's photographs are influenced by the American Scene and Regionalist movements, with their focus on themes of national identity.

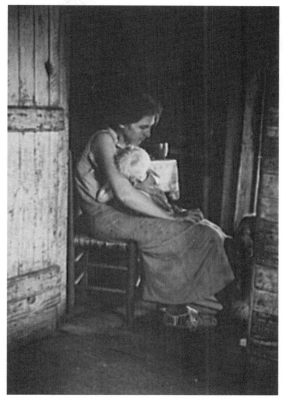

Walker Evans considered himself an artist with social concerns rather than a photojournalist. His photographs of farm families elicit a power and sense of integrity. Photo of Lily Rogers Fields and children, Hale County, Alabama, 1936. Courtesy Library of Congress.

SELF-TAUGHT ARTISTS OF THE TWENTIETH CENTURY

Outsider Artists and Folk Art

Twentieth- and early twenty-first century folk art in the South is dominated by outsiders, that is, those whose work developed outside of the conventional art world of schools, galleries, and museums. They may work within the cultural mainstream with concepts and imagery drawn from tradition, or they may be psychologically, emotionally, or physically isolated from the outside world, either by circumstance or by choice. Their work is individualistic, distinctive, and occasionally indecipherable or visionary. Their skill and articulation may vary, and, although their work is outside of the realm of academic discourse, they, like other contemporary artists, seek to master the qualities that are considered inherent in modern art, including attention to formal qualities of shape and color and an interest in abstract reasoning to resolve design problems. The commonality of outsider art resides in its creation by untrained artists who, although far more exposed to the world than their folk art predecessors, still seek to find their own visual solutions and express their own personal perceptions of their world, whether grounded in the community or intensely private.[13]

Bill Traylor (1856–1949) lived and worked in Alabama. He was a freed slave who began to draw at the age of eighty-three and in the remaining years of his life produced a wealth of pencil and charcoal drawings and paintings of poster paint on cardboard, intimate in scale but overwhelming in their power. His imagery was drawn from personal memory, full of action, and characterized by a curved delineation of form, emphasis on animals and humans shown in profile, lack of attention to scale, and without background. Edgar William Edmondson (c. 1870–1951), a stone carver from Tennessee, resourcefully made tools from old railroad nails and acquired stone from local quarries. His sculpture is distinguished by simplification of form that is as spare, geometric, and abstracted as early modern sculpture. He believed his images, derived from both nature and biblical stories, were an expression of God's will and that he was doing God's work.

Alexander McKillop (1879–1950) got his inspiration from the mountains of North Carolina, with their rich tradition of folk carvings derived from Native American, Scots-Irish, German, and African American sources. He first worked on his parents' farm and later worked at a cotton mill. He began experimenting with wood carving, using black walnut, and developed an inventive style that is roughly carved with a chisel or a knife and then finely finished to a smooth surface. His carved animal and human figures were often depicted in a struggle, both real and metaphysical. Edgar Tolson (1904–1984), from the southern Appalachians of Kentucky, was also a woodcarver. Using traditional whittling, he carved wooden dolls, human and animal figures, and narrative scenes from the book of Genesis. In 1973 his work was included in the Biennial Exhibition at the Whitney Museum of American Art in New York City, a commendation of the qualities and sensibilities of modernism found in twentieth-century self-taught artists.

It may be that Sister Gertrude Morgan (1900–1980) never entered a religious order. What is known is that she was an African American woman raised in Alabama who was often homeless and was, upon her death, buried in an unmarked grave in New Orleans. She had a deep faith in Christian teachings, with resolute belief in the final judgment that, as a street preacher, she shared with anyone who would listen. In the late 1950s, she received what she considered divine revelations and began to make simple crayon drawings that told forcefully of faith and salvation. She ceased to work several years before her death when, in another revelation, she was told to stop making graven images.

Nellie Mae Rowe (1900–1982) created images from memories that revealed both her dream world and the temporal world of everyday experiences. She first drew as a small child, but did not engage herself as an artist until after the death of her second husband in 1948. Her scenes are full of energy, sophisticated and complex, with detailed patterns and strong colors, and often incorporate found objects and photographs. She was intrigued with popular culture and often included personalities such as Elvis Presley in her compositions. Yet her work is also spiritual, with evidence of her strong religious convictions and empathy for those who suffered melded into a realm that is both earthly and heavenly.

Thornton Dial, Sr. (born in Alabama, 1928), is a painter and sculptor whose work has demanded the reconsideration of self-taught folk art in the twentieth century. In his work, he confronts the social ills of the day, including racism and unemployment. He worked a variety of jobs near Birmingham, including constructing railroad boxcars. He also worked odd jobs, such as making wooden crosses for cemeteries and planting gardens. His first art was on metal, including patio furniture. And he began to make mixed-media constructions using found objects that, over the years, he related to the blues music he heard in local juke joints that, like his art, articulated his observations and feelings about his life and the world in which he lived.

Reverend Howard Finster (1916–2001) is one of the twentieth century's most famous outsider artists. A Baptist preacher in Georgia, Finster created thousands of painted objects and a persona as a visionary whose sermons and paintings alike were urgent messages from God. Replete with mysterious cosmological worlds, invective soliloquy, and images derived from popular culture, Finster's art is confrontational, chaotic, and often commercial, as evidenced by his 1961 construction of Paradise Gardens and Museum, near Atlanta.

Like Finster and so many other outsider artists from the South, James Hampton (1909–1964) was guided by his religious faith. An African American and son of a Baptist preacher from South Carolina, he worked as a night janitor in federal buildings in Washington, D.C. In 1950 he began construction of his massive sculpture, *The Throne of the Third Heaven of the Nations Millennium General Assembly*. He continued to work on the sculpture, which he believed was guided by heavenly forces, until his death. It contains myriad pieces of furniture and other found objects, all covered with silver and gold foil, along with text, and was intended, upon completion, for his church. It remains a testament to his religious dedication and fervor. Although created entirely from personal vision, *The Throne of Heaven* recalls the colossal and ornate liturgical sculpture of Europe's great cathedrals.

Twentieth- and early twenty-first century folk artists have also lived and worked in the cultural mainstream, producing work that recalls the past as it was specific to their community. Such memory painters are Clementine Hunter (1886/87–1988), Queena Stovall (1887–1980), and Mario Sanchez (b. 1908). Clementine Hunter is now considered one of the most important African American women artists. She was born in rural Louisiana, in a region reputed to be the inspiration for Harriet Beecher Stowe's *Uncle Tom's Cabin*.[14] After moving with her family to Melrose Plantation, Louisiana, she went to work in the fields and later as a house servant and cook. She took up painting in the 1940s when she acquired some paints left over from a visit by New Orleans artist Alberta Kinsey. Hunter, who painted and quilted into her 100th year, considered her work to be memory paintings, as they show scenes of everyday life around the plantation and her church, depicting a community from which she rarely ventured.

Queena Stovall painted the rural life and traditional values of the foothills of the Blue Ridge Mountains of Virginia. With meticulous detail, she created perceptive documents of the life-sustaining chores of the country farm, the joys of family at home, at work, and at prayer, and the people, customs, and events of her community. Stovall is frequently included at the forefront of women folk artists, whose ranks include Anna Mary Robertson Moses ("Grandma Moses") and Clementine Hunter. After leaving high school in her senior year, Queena took a job as a secretary in a buggy business, and at the age of eighteen married its owner. When Stovall's family was young she expressed her creativity through sewing and by painting

Clementine Hunter, *Saturday Night*, oil on board, n.d., New Orleans Museum of Art. Gift of Dr. and Mrs. Robert F. Ryan in memory of Sally F. and William W. Arnoult, 74.332.

floral and fruit designs on trays, plates, and chairs. Not until her children were mostly grown and her life slowed down did she begin to paint scenes in oils. At the age of sixty-two, she completed her first painting, a scene of slaughtered hogs hanging on a tree limb, their meat curing for the Christmas feast. She eventually painted all forty-eight of her known works within the following two years. Stovall's paintings are peopled with family and neighbors going about their agricultural or domestic chores, simple tasks, as in *Toting Water from the Spring*. Stovall had a great capacity for portraiture, with faces drawn from her personal relationships, or from photographs, frequently from newspapers, revealing characteristic personalities and postures. She favored black people as subjects and their traditional activities as themes for her paintings. Still, Stovall painted the life she knew, that of a white farm woman and her neighbors. These neighbors, whether black or white, are rendered with compassion and an understanding of both day-to-day life and the wider social mores of the rural South from the late nineteenth to the mid-twentieth century.

Cuban American artist Mario Sanchez, the son of a reader in a Key West, Florida, cigar factory, is, likewise, a memory painter whose carved and painted compositions recall infinitesimal details of the people and places of his community. He began his career as an artist during the Great Depression by carving and painting replicas of the fish found in the Gulf waters that he sold at a local hardware store. His mother-in-law suggested he carve scenes of life in Key West on

Folk artist Mario Sanchez's carved and painted works recall infinitesimal details of life in Key West. Courtesy Florida Photographic Collection/Dale M. McDonald Collection.

discarded boards of tobacco leaf crates, and his work soon began to sell in local art galleries. Over more than fifty years, he produced a large body of work based on the people and history of Key West, and his life there. His nostalgic scenes are part sculpture and part painting, with pencil drawings transferred to wood that is then carved and painted. As is typical of untrained artists, Sanchez does not always adhere to artistic principles of perspective, proportion, or even shape and color. Buildings are seen only from the front; people are seen in profile and appear almost puppet-like; forms are stylized and repeated; and shading is absent.[15] His memories are positive ones, without poverty or tragedy, but imbued with humor and a gentle prodding of the viewer to enjoy life.

AFRICAN AMERICAN ARTISTS OBSERVE THE SOUTH

African American art in the South forms an intersection of artistic forms and images from the traditions of both Africa and the West. Despite the oppressive measures of the eighteenth- and nineteenth-century slave trade, manifestations of African culture persisted in the South. This is most prevalent in the traditions of dance, storytelling, celebrations, and burial practices, but is also found in symbolic, rhythmic, decorative motifs used in art. Contemporary African American artists have sought to illustrate the African American experience through paintings, woodcarvings, and other forms of art, in keeping with the tradition of storytelling that has traditionally kept culture alive. African American art in the South cannot be classified or simplified in terms of aesthetic considerations any more than the art of the South in general. It is derived from diverse cultures that have both influenced and been influenced by prevailing artistic forms.

African American art in the twentieth and early twenty-first centuries has responded to the need for representations of spiritual and substantive lives of African Americans. One of the first organized efforts was the New Negro Arts movement, which focused on scenes of Harlem life. Later organizations included the Harlem-based Urban League, founded in 1910 to aid African Americans moving from a rural environment to an urban community, and, in the 1930s, the WPA Harlem Art Workshop. Many of the artists working in Harlem in the first half of the twentieth century, although not from the South, searched for an understanding of the African American place in American society through an examination of the social, cultural, and historical role of blacks in the South. Foremost among these artists was Jacob Lawrence (1917–2000). Lawrence was born in Harlem and moved to Philadelphia in 1930, where he became aware of the debates of African American intellectuals, including the writer Langston Hughes and the artist Aaron Douglas (1899–1979), well known for his illustrations for authors of the Harlem Renaissance. During this time, Lawrence set his sights on the subject matter that would consume his artistic career: the history of African Americans and, especially, the realities and brutality of slavery. This included a series of paintings depicting the migration of African Americans from the agrarian South to the industrialized North in the years following the Civil War, and of narrative paintings of African Americans who had escaped slavery and worked to free others, including Frederick Douglass and Harriet Tubman, all of which are characterized by a rawness, immediacy, and simplification of form.[16]

African American artists from the South also found success. Richmond Barthé (1901–1989), a native of Bay St. Louis, Mississippi, became well known for his lyrical, sensual, figurative sculptures based on African dance. Alma Thomas (1891–1978), born in Columbus, Georgia, became the first student to graduate from Howard University's art department, in 1924, and the first African American woman to be given a solo exhibition at the Whitney Museum of American Art. And Ellis Wilson (1899–1977), a native of Mayfield, Kentucky, graduated from the Art Institute of Chicago. He traveled throughout Georgia and South Carolina, painting scenes of everyday life, and made numerous trips to Haiti. His painting *Funeral Procession*, c. 1950s, from the collection of the Amistad Research Center, is widely recognizable to American audiences, as a reproduction of the painting was used on the living room set of *The Cosby Show* in the 1980s.

Sowing by William H. Johnson. Courtesy Smithsonian American Art Museum, Washington, D.C./Art Resource, New York.

The civil rights movement of the 1960s, like the Harlem Renaissance, spurred the artistic interpretation of African American history. Romare Bearden (1914–1988) was born in Charlotte, North Carolina, and studied at the Art Students' League in New York and the Sorbonne in Paris. After settling in New York, he received mainstream recognition and is credited with co-founding the Spiral Group, which concerned itself with civil rights and African American identity. Bearden's roots remained in the South, and his series of narrative collages of memories and heritage recall the flattened, abstract forms of African masks, rhythms of African dance, and appliquéd quilts made by generations of African American women.[17] William H. Johnson (1901–1970) was born in Florence, South Carolina, and moved to New York in 1918 to attend the Art Students' League. In the early 1930s, he worked and traveled in Denmark and Norway, then returned to America in 1938 to work for the WPA and the Harlem Community Center. Johnson's painting *Chain Gang* (1939–1940), which was exhibited at the New York World's Fair in 1940, is a semi-autobiographical account of his arrest for vagrancy in Florence in 1930, when he was in the act of painting outdoors.[18] More recently, Benny Andrews (b. 1930), the son of sharecroppers from Plainview, Georgia, has received widespread recognition for his collages, sculpture, and illustrations, and for his advocacy for the inclusion of African American artists in American museums. The figures in his compositions are isolated and imbued with spiritual and physical suffering of the individual within the restrictions of society.

The work of twentieth-century African American artists is shaped by the experiences of African Americans in the South, yet it has far broader implications of the questioning of humanity and inhuman actions, of social graces and human civility, of the noble character and human dignity. The South is not so much a place for African American artists as it is an act of storytelling, an ambiance, sometimes subtle and sometimes intense, but always present.

MODERN PAINTING IN THE SOUTH

The South continues to be a place of imagination and introspection for contemporary artists, disquieting in its complexities and contradictions, precarious in its ironies and misconceptions. The artists of today's South recognize the negative preconceptions of the region as provincial and racist.[19] Yet they seek the elusive essence of the South in its light, its legends, and its popular culture.

Southern art in the twentieth century has three distinct periods: (1) the early years of the century when many artists received their training outside the South but later returned to their roots, bringing with them new styles and aesthetic considerations; (2) the years of the Great Depression and World War II, when artists explored new creative avenues; and (3) the post–World War II years, when artists acknowledged their roots but allowed their work to rise above them.[20] Throughout, the examination of the landscape and the search for a southern ethos persevered.

Many of the southern painters of the early twentieth century were grounded in the academic tradition. Artists such as Elliott Daingerfield (1859–1923) embraced the Tonalist movement, a group of American landscape painters of the last decades of the nineteenth century who were influenced by the French Barbizon school. Their paintings were executed with limited hues, soft contours, and a dark, moody quality that reflected the overriding mood of the South. Others with financial means studied at the École des Beaux Arts and the Académie Julien in Paris, or at the Art Students' League in New York, where they encountered myriad avant-garde movements of Modernism, influenced in part by scientific breakthroughs that called into question the way in which the world is seen.

They took their first steps into nonrepresentational art through emotionally expressive color and the abandonment of realistic imagery. Representative of artists studying in Paris were Georgia Morgan (1869–1951) and John Kelly Fitzpatrick (1888–1953). Georgia Morgan was born in rural Campbell County, Virginia, and began her art studies with German-born artist Bernhard Gutmann in Lynchburg. She received a scholarship to study in Paris at the Académie Julien, where she concentrated on the study of miniatures. After her return to Virginia, she worked in portraiture, landscapes, genre scenes, and still lifes, all of which exhibit evidence of the influence of Impressionistic brushstrokes, color, and light. John Kelly Fitzpatrick hailed from Alabama. After military service in France during World War I, he, like Morgan, studied at the Académie Julien. After returning to Alabama, he painted colorful narrative scenes, and co-founded the Alabama Art League and the Poka-Hutchi Art Colony, a summer residency that attracted many important artists of the day. Elliott Daingerfield and Alexander Drysdale (1870–1934) both studied at the Art Students' League in New York. Daingerfield was raised in North Carolina. He settled in New York, where he was influenced by George Inness (1825–1894), but continued to visit and paint mountain landscapes of his native state. Drysdale, a native of Georgia, studied first in New Orleans before attending the Art Students' League. After returning to Louisiana, he painted landscapes of the bayous that were strongly influenced by the Symbolists. Both Daingerfield and Drysdale were concerned with the mystical, atmospheric effects of light and color on their environments.

During the Great Depression and World War II, art was increasingly and effectively used as a vehicle for public policy. Many southern artists, along with photographers, took advantage of the federal WPA projects by working for the Section of Painting and Sculpture of the Treasury Department. Most believed that the WPA art projects had a practical use and felt a responsibility to reach out to as many people as possible, while also promoting American art and culture. A significant aspect of the program was funding for art in federal buildings such as libraries, post offices, and courthouses. Most effective were murals that portrayed their subjects with the recurring theme of strength and dignity in the face of difficult circumstances. Subjects were carefully controlled by the Treasury Department, and included history, local industry, agriculture, and landscapes. Ethnic, religious, and racial distinction was discouraged, and references to the hardships of slavery were not allowed, although content concerning the Underground Railroad was approved.[21] Although concerned with everyday activities such as harvesting crops or going to market, both historical and of the time, many of these murals are now seen as discriminatory. Many of the artists who painted murals in the South were from the Midwest or the North. H. Amiard Oberteuffer's *Vicksburg—Its Character and Industries* (1939) in the Vicksburg, Mississippi, post office and courthouse, shows a panoramic view of the city in which the races are clearly divided.[22] Virginia artist Scaisbrooke Langhorne Abbot's *Going Down to Lynchburg* (1934) takes its title and theme from a nineteenth-century song with the refrain "going down to the Lynchburg Town, to take my tobacco down." The painting, mounted in Lynchburg, Virginia's former city hall (now the Juvenile and Domestic Relations Court), depicts a white planter and his black servant, who walks a step behind, bringing tobacco to market.

Many artists from the South became politically and socially active in the years during and after World War II. For Robert Gwathmey (1903–1988), social criticism was expressed through abstract composition. Gwathmey was born in Virginia and studied at the Pennsylvania Academy of Fine Arts before securing a position as a mural painter with the WPA. He was deeply concerned with human rights and depicted the bleak environment of southern sharecroppers, both black and white. He was angered and felt guilt regarding the ongoing debate over the role of African American southerners in the Civil War. However, in the catalogue to a 1946 exhibition at the ACA Galleries in New York, the African American singer and activist Paul Robeson praised his "responsibility to exploited people of the South."[23]

Robert Rauschenberg (b. 1925), Kenneth Noland (b. 1924), and Cy Twombly (b. 1928) all entered Black Mountain College in North Carolina as students. Rauschenberg was born in Port Arthur, Texas, enrolled in a pharmacy program at the University of Texas, and was drafted into the U.S. Navy before he turned to art. He first studied at the Kansas City Art Institute, then at the

Black Mountain College

At a time when many southern artists were moving to established art centers such as New York City, the pull of the South and its land drew an important group of Modernists to rural North Carolina. Black Mountain College, near Asheville, was founded in 1933 as a reaction to more traditional schools. Revolutionary for its time, its philosophy was one of liberal and fine arts education, developing and experimenting simultaneously inside and outside the classroom, with informal class settings, continuous discussions outside of class settings, and examinations without grades. Among the first art professors was Josef Albers (1888–1976), who had fled Nazi Germany with his artist wife Anni with the closing of the Bauhaus, the groundbreaking school of design, in 1933. While at Black Mountain College, Albers began his explorations of color perception and illusion through his series *Homage to the Square*. Albers' color theories were innovative in contemporary art education, while his work brought modern art to the South. By the 1940s, Black Mountain College brought some of the greatest mainstream modern artists of the time to the South, including Jacob Lawrence, Willem de Kooning, and Robert Motherwell. Low enrollment and dwindling funds forced the closure of the college in 1956, but not before it brought an emerging awareness of Modernism to the South.

Académie Julien in Paris, before enrolling at Black Mountain College, where he studied with Albers, who instilled in him both a work ethic and a fascination with found objects. In the 1950s, he also worked with fellow southerners Cy Twombly and Jasper Johns. Rauschenberg has remained a southerner, living in Florida and working primarily in printmaking and mixed media, always seeking to combine life, art, media, and place. Kenneth Noland is a native of Asheville, North Carolina, who also studied with Albers and Ilya Bolotowsky, a member of the American Abstract Artists group of the 1930s. Noland, like Albers and Bolotowsky, focused on geometric abstraction (most important of which are his circle paintings of the late 1950s) and juxtaposition of color, while also being influenced by the mountains of North Carolina and the jazz music of the South. Cy Twombly began painting early in his childhood in Lexington, Virginia, taking private lessons from the Catalan American Modernist Pierre Daura. He went on to study at the Art Students' League in New York, where he met Rauschenberg, and then at Black Mountain College. With Rauschenberg, he traveled through Italy, North Africa, and Spain in the early 1950s, and in 1957 moved to Rome. His work is intensely personal, with vestiges of the South apparent in his use of the forms of neoclassical antebellum architecture, warm white light, emblems and images of military tradition, cultural artifacts, music, and literature. In the 1980s and 1990s, Twombly's collage-like images turned to pastoral subjects and the changing seasons in which he refers to the landscape of the South.[24]

Jasper Johns (b. 1930) is, like Rauschenberg, Noland, and Twombly, at the forefront of Modernism in America, as well as in the South, and one whose work most exemplifies the South. Born in Augusta, Georgia, and raised in South Carolina, he has worked in both the Abstract Expressionism and Pop art movements, the latter of which he is often credited with initiating with his series of flags and targets. His work is an amalgam of images and objects, personal and impersonal, which offer a glimpse into his heritage, and both entice the viewer to reflect on history and question illusion versus reality.[25] His paintings of flags, created during the Cold War, expressed his questioning of the function of art and his interest in the iconography of America. They are an intellectual and aesthetic exercise that also served his creative desire to work with something transcendently familiar, something that is both physical matter and an abstract concept, and to then rethink it, reexamine it, and, like art itself, question its purpose.

Red Grooms (b. 1937), like Johns, looks to popular culture for inspiration. Born in Nashville, Tennessee, he decided to become an artist while in high school. He attended the Art Institute of Chicago, which he found to be too academic for his taste, and then studied briefly with Hans Hofmann. His work is figurative, rendered with satirical humor, but ultimately humanist, as in his color lithograph *Elvis* (1987). Louisiana native Douglas Bourgeois (b. 1953) is the following generation's exponent of popular culture. His detailed paintings and sculptural assemblages are memories of his life, filled with both everyday people and rock-and-roll stars. Bourgeois' work lacks the cynicism of Grooms', instead incorporating cultural symbols and treating both his common and iconic subjects with compassion and concern for the social ills of poverty, abuse, crime, and racism.

CONTEMPORARY PHOTOGRAPHY

Photographers have long been interested in the relationship of photography to the other visual arts, and see photographic images with the same aesthetic interests found in other art forms. Photographers of the New South such as Shelby Lee Adams, William Christenberry, Birney Imes, Maude Schuyler Clay, Tom Rankin, Carrie Mae Weems, Sally Mann, and others use a diversity of processes and approaches, yet all portray the cultural presence and southern environment in which nature and the land prevail. Perhaps more than any other artistic medium, photography is the means by which the southern ethos becomes manifest.

The influence of Walker Evans and other WPA photographers is unmistakable in the work of Shelby Lee Adams (b. 1950). Adams's images of the rural, isolated world of the people of Kentucky's Appalachian Mountains, taken over a period of years, are straightforward and respectful documentations of an unchanging way of life. William Christenberry (b. 1936) is from a family of artists from Tuscaloosa, Alabama. Christenberry freely acknowledges his debt to Walker Evans. His landscapes of sites are documented over time, revealing the layers of change in the sites themselves and the human relationships within them. Birney Imes (b. 1951) depicts the land and people of his rural Mississippi home. His carefully composed images are intense examinations of how both land and people are influenced and informed by artifacts discarded and forgotten, but still present. Maude Schuyler Clay (b. 1953) depicts the land and culture of Tallahatchie County, Mississippi, where her family has lived for generations. Her photographic project Delta Land, published in 1999, records the indigenous structures of the Mississippi Delta with the intimate eye of an insider. Churches, stores, fences, and barns are all abandoned, fading into the past in the subtle hues of Clay's black-and-white film. Tom Rankin, like Clay, explores the culture of the Mississippi Delta. Rankin's photographs document the African American church, its music and dance traditions, its symbols and spirituality, and its social function within the larger context of a working community. The photography of Carrie Mae Weems (b. 1953) bears evidence of the African American experience in the South, with images depicting the continuation of folk beliefs of the descendants of African slaves inhabiting the Gullah Islands of coastal South Carolina and Georgia that combine West African and Christian iconography and practices.

Perhaps no contemporary photographer in the South is better known than Sally Mann (b. 1951), whose photographs evoke the South's past in both imagery and process. Mann utilizes large format bellows cameras with brass-rimmed lenses from the nineteenth century, and then develops the images in large scale with collodion and ether. Her hauntingly beautiful landscapes of Virginia, Georgia, Louisiana, and Mississippi exemplify the paradox of the frailty and endurance of the South. Her book *Immediate Family*, published in 1992, caused immediate controversy for its depictions of her unselfconscious, nude children taken on the family farm near Lexington, Virginia. Her recent work *What Remains*, published in 2003, examines Civil War battlefields imbued with the spirit of the past.

CONCLUSION

Artists from the South have been involved in the major art movements from the nineteenth century to the present, from the Tonalists whose contemplative mood echoed the mood of southern society and the expatriate American impressionists working in Paris to the artists of the Harlem Renaissance and the Abstract Expressionists who dominated the art world of New York in the 1950s. But curiously, despite common patterns of creativity and artistry that evolved within the regions of the South, there have been no art movements contained within the South. Rather, the story of the art of the South is one of legacy, tradition, and history as interpreted by its artists. It is art that is rich in memories of family, community, and the land itself that have shaped the southern identity. It is art that is fatalistic, that acknowledges defeat and predestines survival. It is art that at once is distinctive and evocative of its environment, and unwavering from the prevailing tastes of art and artistic concerns established throughout America and in Europe. It is art that is intriguing and frustrating in its complexity. It is art that is bound inextricably with yesteryear, consumed by continuity and reluctant to relinquish its past. It is art that is dynamic, but slow to change. Yet it is also art that is willing to confront new realities and artistic challenges. Southern art is not a technique or a single style; it is inexplicably just "southern" in its sensibility.

RESOURCE GUIDE

Printed Sources

Adams, Shelby Lee. *Appalachian Legacy*. Jackson: University Press of Mississippi, 1998.
Alexander, Edward. *Museums in Motion: An Introduction to the History and Function of Museums*. Nashville: American Association for State and Local History, 1979.

Bishop, Robert, and Jacqueline Atkins. *Folk Art in American Life*. New York: Viking Studio Books, 1995.

Blackard, David M. *Patchwork and Palmettos: Seminole-Miccosukee Folk Art Since 1920*. Fort Lauderdale: Fort Lauderdale Historical Society, 1990.

Bundy, David S., et al. *Painting in the South, 1564–1980*. Richmond: Virginia Museum, 1983.

Clay, Maude Schuyler. *Delta Land*. Introduction by Lewis Nordan. Jackson: University Press of Mississippi, 1999.

Delehanty, Randolph. *Art in the American South: Works from the Ogden Collection*. Baton Rouge: Louisiana State University Press, 1996.

Dewhurst, C. Kurt, Betty MacDowell, and Marsha MacDowell. *Artists in Aprons: Folk Art by American Women*. New York: E. P. Dutton, 1979.

Downs, Dorothy. *Art of the Florida Seminole and Miccosukee Indians*. Gainesville: University Press of Florida, 1997.

Elliott, Susan Sipple, ed. *The South by Its Photographers*. Birmingham, AL: Birmingham Museum of Art, 1996.

Feest, Christian F. *Native Arts of North America*. New York: Thames and Hudson, 1992.

Hanzal, Carla, curator. *Southern Exposure*. Virginia Beach: Contemporary Art Center of Virginia, 2000.

Haskell, Barbara. *The American Century: Art and Culture, 1900–1950*. New York: Whitney Museum of American Art in association with W. W. Norton, 1999.

Holzer, Harold, and Mark E. Neely, Jr. *Mine Eyes Have Seen the Glory: The Civil War in Art*. New York: Orion Books, 1993.

Hughes, Robert. *American Visions: The Epic History of Art in America*. New York: Alfred A. Knopf, 1997.

Imes, Birney. *Whispering Pines*. Introduction by Trudy Wilner Stack. Jackson: University Press of Mississippi, 1994.

Kuspit, Donald. *Homeland of the Imagination: The Southern Presence in Twentieth Century Art*. Atlanta: NationsBank, 1996.

Law, Rachel Nash, and Cynthia W. Taylor. *Appalachian White Oak Basketmaking: Handing Down the Basket*. Knoxville: University of Tennessee Press, 1991.

Longhauser, Elsa, and Harald Szeeman, curators. *Self-Taught Artists of the Twentieth Century: An American Anthology*. New York: Museum of American Folk Art, 1998.

Lowenstein, Tom, and Piers Vitebsky. *Mother Earth, Father Sky: Native American Myth*. London: Duncan Baird Publishers, 1997.

Moses, Kathy. *Outsider Art of the South*. Lancaster, PA: Schiffer Publishing Ltd., 1999.

Pennington, Estill Curtis. *Look Away: Reality and Sentiment in Southern Art*. Spartanburg, SC: Saraland Press, 1989.

Pohl, Frances K. *Framing America: A Social History of American Art*. New York: Thames and Hudson, 2002.

Rankin, Tom. *Sacred Space: Photographs from the Mississippi Delta*. Foreword by Charles Reagan Wilson. Jackson: University Press of Mississippi, 1990.

Rothermel, Barbara. "I Paint What I Remember: The Art of Mario Sanchez." In *Folk Art*. New York: Museum of American Folk Art, Fall 1996.

Tobin, Jacqueline L., and Raymond G. Dobard. *Hidden in Plain View: A Secret Story of Quilts and the Underground Railroad*. New York: Anchor Books, 1999.

Weatherford, Claudine. *The Art of Queena Stovall: Images of Country Life*. Ann Arbor, MI: UMI Research Press, 1986.

Organizations, Museums, Special Collections

Museums in the South, like museums throughout the United States, are social instruments for preservation, interpretation, and education, with collections, exhibitions, and programs that sustain the art and heritage of the region. Museums developed in the American South beginning in the late colonial era. The first museums were dedicated to natural history, including the Charleston, South Carolina, Museum, founded by the Charleston Library Society in 1773, whose early accessions were Native American artifacts. By the nineteenth century, history museums featured panoramas or cycloramas, where visitors sat in the center of huge circular paintings such as the *Battle of Atlanta* at the Cyclorama in Atlanta. Living history museums, such as Colonial Williamsburg, the restored capital of eighteenth-century Virginia, and Old Salem, a restored Moravian community in North Carolina, provide a glimpse into life, work, and craftsmanship in the early South. Arts centers also continue regional and cultural traditions through the teaching of traditional crafts. The High Museum of Art in Atlanta has been an innovator of educational programs for children, while the Virginia Museum of Fine Arts in Richmond, with its extensive collection of world art, including the art of the South, has long been at the forefront of public service through its educational and outreach programs, including a statewide affiliates program. Many museums, such as the Morris Museum of Art in Augusta, Georgia, and the Ogden Museum of Southern Art at the University of New Orleans, now focus specifically on southern art.

The following list includes non-profit institutions and other arts organizations that identify their collections or missions as southern art, specific southern artists, or regional southern art. It does not include historic house museums with period furnishings that may or may not include art, nor does it include commercial galleries or stores selling southern arts and crafts. Any exclusion is unintentional.

Alabama

Alabama Constitution Village, Huntsville
Alabama Department of Archives & History, Montgomery
American Sport Art Museum, Daphne
Anniston Museum of Natural History, Anniston
Birmingham Civil Rights Institute
Birmingham Museum of Art
Burritt Museum & Park, Huntsville
Eastern Shore Art Center, Fairhope
Fayette Art Museum
Gadsden Museum of Fine Arts
George Washington Carver Museum, Tuskegee Institute
Huntsville Museum of Art
Kennedy-Douglass Center for the Arts, Florence
Mobile Museum of Art
Montgomery Museum of Fine Arts
Museum of Mobile
Russell Cave National Monument, Bridgeport
Sarah Moody Gallery of Art, University of Alabama, Tuscaloosa
Tennessee Valley Art Center, Tuscumbia
Visual Arts Gallery, University of Alabama at Birmingham
Wiregrass Museum of Art, Dothan

Arkansas

Arkansas Arts Center, Little Rock
Arkansas Museum of Science and History, Little Rock
Arkansas State University Museum, Jonesboro
Arts & Science Center for Southeast Arkansas, Pine Bluff
Baum Gallery of Fine Art, University of Central Arkansas, Conway
Fort Smith Art Center
Henderson State University Museum, Arkadelphia
Hot Spring National Park
Ka-Do-Ha Indian Village Museum, Murfreesboro
Old State House, Little Rock
Ozark Folk Center, Mountain View
Shiloh Museum of Ozark History, Springdale
South Arkansas Art Center, El Dorado

Toltec Mounds Archeological State Park,
  Scott
University of Arkansas at Little Rock Art
  Galleries

University of Arkansas Museum,
  Fayetteville

Florida

Bass Museum of Art, Miami Beach
Brevard Museum of Art and Science,
  Melbourne
Charles Hosmer Morse Museum of
  American Art, Winter Park
Cornell Museum of Art and History,
  Delray Beach
Cummer Museum of Art & Gardens,
  Jacksonville
Deland Museum of Art
Florida International University Art
  Museum
Florida State University Museum of Art,
  Tallahassee
Jay I. Kislak Foundation, Miami Lakes
Key West Art & Historical Society
Latin American Art Museum, Coral
  Gables
Lightner Museum, Saint Augustine
Lowe Art Museum, University of Florida,
  Coral Gables
Maitland Art Center
Miami Art Museum
Museum of Art, Fort Lauderdale

Museum of Arts and Sciences & Center
  for Florida History, Daytona Beach
Museum of Fine Arts, Saint Petersburg
Museum of Florida Art and Culture,
  South Florida Community College,
  Avon Park
Norton Museum of Art, West Palm Beach
Orlando Museum of Art
Pensacola Museum of Art
Polk Museum of Art, Lakeland
Samuel P. Harn Museum of Art,
  University of Florida, Gainesville
Southeast Museum of Photography,
  Daytona Beach Community College
Tampa Museum of Art
University of South Florida Contemporary
  Art Museum, Tampa
University of West Florida Art Gallery
Vero Beach Center for the Arts
Visual Arts Center of Northwest Florida,
  Panama City
Wolfsonian, Florida International
  University, Miami Beach

Georgia

Chattahoochee Valley Art Musuem,
  LaGrange
Clark Atlanta University Art Gallery,
  Atlanta
Columbus Museum
Foxfire Museum & Center, Mountain City
Gallery 303, Georgia Southern University,
  Statesboro
Georgia Museum of Art, University of
  Georgia, Athens
Hammonds House Galleries and Resource
  Center, Atlanta
High Museum of Art, Atlanta

High Museum of Art, Folk Art and
  Photography Galleries, Atlanta
Marrietta/Cobb Museum of Art
Michael C. Carlos Museum, Emory
  University, Atlanta
Morris Museum of Art, Augusta
Oglethorpe University Museum, Atlanta
Okefenokee Heritage Center Art Gallery,
  Waycross
Telfair Museum of Art, Savannah
Tubman African-American Museum,
  Macon

Kentucky

Allen R. Hite Art Institute Galleries,
  University of Louisville

Behringer-Crawford Museum, Covington
Berea College, Berea

Central Bank and Trust Company,
Lexington
Hopewell Museum, Paris
John James Audubon Museum, Henderson
Kentucky Art and Craft Gallery, Louisville
Kentucky Folk Art Center, Morehead State
University
Kentucky Museum, Western Kentucky
University, Bowling Green
Museum of the American Quilter's Society,
Paducah

Owensboro Museum of Fine Art
Speed Art Museum, Louisville
University Art Galleries, Murray State
University
University of Kentucky Art Museum,
Lexington
University of Louisville Photographic
Archives
Yeiser Art Center, Paducah

Louisiana

Alexandria Museum of Art
Amistad Research Center, New Orleans
Clark Hall Gallery, Southeastern Louisiana
University, Hammond
Contemporary Arts Center, New Orleans
Crowley Art Association and Gallery
Goldring/Woldenberg Institute for the
Advancement of Southern Art and
Culture, University of New Orleans
Historic New Orleans Collection
Louisiana Arts and Sciences Center, Baton
Rouge

Louisiana State Museum, New Orleans
New Orleans Museum of Art
Newcomb Arts Complex, Tulane
University, New Orleans
Ogden Museum of Southern Art,
University of New Orleans
R. W. Norton Art Gallery, Shreveport
University Art Museum, University of
Louisiana at Lafayette
Zigler Museum, Jennings

Mississippi

Art Gallery, Mississippi University for
Women, Columbus
Lauren Rogers Museum of Art, Laurel
Meridian Museum of Art
Mississippi Museum of Art, Jackson
Ohr-O'Keefe Museum of Art, Biloxi

University of Mississippi Museums, Oxford
University of Mississippi Museums,
University
Walter Anderson Museum of Art, Ocean
Springs

North Carolina

Ackland Art Museum, University of North
Carolina at Chapel Hill
Afro-American Cultural Center,
Charlotte
Appalachian Heritage Museum, Blowing
Rock
Art Galleries, North Carolina Wesleyan
College, Rocky Mount
Asheville Art Museum
Barton Museum, Barton College, Wilson
Black Mountain College Museum and Arts
Center, Asheville
Blount-Bridgers House/Hobson Pittman
Memorial Gallery, Tarboro

Catherine J. Smith Gallery, Appalachian
State University, Boone
Chapel Hill Museum
Diggs Gallery, Winston-Salem State
University
Fayetteville Museum of Art
Gallery of Art & Design, North Carolina
State University, Raleigh
Green Hill Center for North Carolina Art,
Greensboro
Greenville Museum of Art
Guilford College Art Gallery, Greensboro
Hickory Museum of Art
Mint Museum of Art, Charlotte

Mint Museum of Craft and Design, Charlotte
Mountain Heritage Center, Western Carolina University, Cullowhee
Museum of American Pottery, Creedmoor
Museum of Early Southern Decorative Arts, Winston-Salem
Museum of the Cherokee Indian, Cherokee
Museum of the Native American, Pembroke State University
North Carolina Central University Art Museum, Durham
North Carolina Museum of Art, Raleigh
Oconaluftee Indian Village, Cherokee

Rankin Museum of American Heritage, Ellerbe
Reynolda House Museum of American Art, Winston-Salem
St. James Place Museum, Roberson
St. John's Museum of Art, Wilmington
Southern Highland Craft Guild & Blue Ridge Parkway's Folk Art Center, Asheville
Spiers Gallery, Brevard College
Tryon Palace Historic Site and Gardens, New Bern
University of North Carolina Charlotte Galleries
Weatherspoon Art Gallery, University of North Carolina at Greensboro

South Carolina

Brookgreen Gardens, Murrells Inlet
City Hall Council Chamber Gallery, Charleston
Columbia Museum of Art
Florence Museum of Art, Science and History
Gibbs Museum of Art, Charleston
Greenville County Museum of Art, Greenville
McKissick Museum, University of South Carolina, Columbia

Museum of York County, Rock Hill
Pickens County Museum, Pickens
Rudolph E. Lee Gallery, Clemson University
South Carolina Artisans Center, Walterboro
South Carolina State Museum
Spartanburg County Museum of Art, Spartanburg
Sumter Gallery of Art

Tennessee

Arrowmont School of Arts and Crafts Gallery, Gatlinburg
B. Carroll Reece Memorial Museum, East Tennessee State University, Johnson City
Baldwin Photographic Gallery, Middle Tennessee State University, Murfreesboro
C. Kermit Ewing Gallery of Art & Architecture, University of Tennessee, Knoxville
Center for Appalachian Studies and Services, Johnson City
Creekwood Botanical Garden and Museum of Art, Nashville
Dixon Gallery and Gardens, Memphis
Fisk University Galleries, Nashville
Frank H. McClung Museum, Knoxville

George Cress Gallery of Art, University of Tennessee at Chattanooga
Hunter Museum of American Art, Chattanooga
Joe L. Evans Appalachian Center for Crafts, Tennessee Technological University, Smithville
Knoxville Museum of Art
Memphis Brooks Museum of Art, Memphis
The Parthenon, Nashville
Tennessee State Museum, Nashville
Trahern Gallery, Austin Peay State University, Clarksville
Vanderbilt University Fine Arts Gallery, Nashville
Watkins Institute College of Art and Design, Nashville

Virginia

Abby Aldrich Rockefeller Folk Art
Museum, Williamsburg
Anderson Gallery, Virginia
Commonwealth University, Richmond
Armory Art Gallery, Virginia Polytechnic
Institute, Blacksburg
Art Museum of Western Virginia,
Roanoke
Artisans Center of Virginia, Waynesboro
Belmont, the Gari Melchers Estate and
Memorial Gallery, Fredericksburg
Chrysler Museum of Art, Norfolk
Contemporary Art Center of Virginia,
Virginia Beach
Danville Museum of Fine Art and History
Daura Gallery, Lynchburg College
Fine Arts Center for the New River Valley,
Pulaski
Folk Art Center, Ferrum College, Ferrum
Hampton University Museum
Hollins University Art Gallery, Hollins
Hunt Gallery, Mary Baldwin College,
Staunton
James Madison University Art Galleries,
Harrisonburg
Longwood Center for the Visual Arts,
Longwood College, Farmville
Lynchburg Museum System

Maier Museum of Art, Randolph-Macon
Woman's College, Lynchburg
Mariners' Museum, Newport News
Marsh Art Museum, University of
Richmond
Mary Washington College Galleries,
Fredericksburg
Muscarelle Museum of Art, Williamsburg
Museum of the Confederacy, Richmond
Olin Hall Galleries, Roanoke College,
Salem
Peninsula Fine Arts Center, Newport
News
Radford University Art Museum, Radford
Reeves Center, Washington and Lee
University, Lexington
Second Street Gallery, Charlottesville
Suffolk Museum
Sweet Briar College Art Galleries, Sweet
Briar
University of Virginia Museum of Art,
Charlottesville
Valentine Museum, Richmond
Virginia Historical Society, Richmond
Virginia Museum of Fine Arts, Richmond
Virginia Quilt Museum, Harrisonburg
William King Regional Arts Center,
Abingdon

Other Important Museums with Collections of Southern Art

American Folk Art Museum, New York,
NY
National Gallery of Art, Washington, DC
National Museum of American Art,
Smithsonian Institution, Washington,
DC

National Museum of American History,
Smithsonian Institution, Washington, DC
National Museum of Natural History,
Smithsonian Institution, Washington, DC
National Museum of the American Indian,
Smithsonian Institution, Washington, DC

State Arts Commissions
Alabama

Alabama State Council on the Arts
201 Monroe Street
Montgomery, AL 36130-1800
http://www.arts.state.al.us

Arkansas

Arkansas Arts Council
1500 Tower Building

323 Center Street
Little Rock, AR 72201
http://www.arkansasarts.com

Florida

Division of Cultural Affairs, Florida Arts
1001 DeSoto Park Drive
Tallahassee, FL 32301
http://www.florida-arts.org

Georgia

Georgia Council for the Arts
260 14th Street, Suite 401
Atlanta, GA 30318
http://www.gaarts.org

Kentucky

Kentucky Arts Council
Old Capitol Annex
300 West Broadway
Frankfort, KY 40601-1980
http://www.kyarts.org

Louisiana

Louisiana Division of the Arts
P.O. Box 44247
Baton Rouge, LA 70804-4247
http://www.crt.state.la.us/arts

Mississippi

Mississippi Arts Commission
239 North Lamar Street, Suite 207
Jackson, MS 39201
http://www.arts.state.ms.us

North Carolina

North Carolina Arts Council
Department of Cultural Resources
Raleigh, NC 27699-4632
http://www.ncarts.org

South Carolina

South Carolina Arts Commission
1800 Gervais Street
Columbia, SC 29201
http://www.state.sc.us/arts

Tennessee

Tennessee Arts Commission
Citizens Plaza Building
401 Charlotte Avenue
Nashville, TN 37243-0780
http://www.arts.state.tn.us

Virginia

Virginia Commission for the Arts
Lewis House
223 Governor Street
Richmond, VA 23219
http://www.arts.state.va.us

Art Festivals

The following list includes art festivals, folklife celebrations, and craft shows. Events are listed alphabetically by state. Any exclusion is unintentional.

Alabama

Arts Alive Festival, Florence
Bloomin' Festival Arts and Crafts Fair, Cullman
Bluff Park Art Show, Hoover
Chalaka Arts and Crafts Show, Sylacauga
Cotton Pickin Celebration, Harpersville
Cullman Day in the Park, Cullman
Fairhope Arts and Crafts Show, Fairhope
Gadsden's Art and Craft Show, Gadsden
Grand Festival of Art, Fairhope
Guntersville Art on the Lake, Guntersville
Helen Keller Art Festival, Tuscumbia
Homespun Arts and Crafts Show, Athens
Homestead Hollow's Spring Festival, Springville
Jubilee Arts and Crafts Festival, Daphne
Jubilee CityFest, Montgomery
Magic City Art Connection, Birmingham
Moundville Native American Festival, Moundville
NEACA Spring Craft Show, Huntsville
Panoply Arts Festival, Huntsville
Piney Woods Arts Festival, Enterprise
Port City Craftsmen Spring Craft Show, Mobile
Southern Wildlife Festival, Decatur
Tuscaloosa International CityFest, Tuscaloosa

Arkansas

Arkansas Folk Festival, Mountain View
Arkansas Valley Arts and Crafts Fair, Russellville
Bella Vista Arts and Crafts Festival, Bella Vista
Clarion Convention Center Spring Arts & Crafts Show, Bentonville
Fayetteville Fine Arts Festival, Fayetteville
FolkFest, Mountain View
Hillbilly Corner Arts, Crafts & Antiques Fair, Hindsville
Hot Springs Arts and Crafts Fair, Hot Springs
Lit'l Bita Christmas Arts and Crafts Show, Jonesboro
Little Rock Worldfest, Little Rock
Mountainfest, Mena
Old Hardy Town Spring Arts and Crafts Show, Hardy
Old Timer's Day, Van Buren
Ole Applegate Place Spring Arts & Crafts Festival, Bentonville

Ozark Mountain Christmas Arts & Crafts
Festival, Fort Smith
Pioneer Craft Festival, Rison
Portfest Rollin' on the River, Newport

Quartz, Quiltz and Craftz Festival, Mount
Ida
Springfest, Heber Springs
War Eagle Fair, Hindsville

Florida

Anna Maria Island Fest Arts & Crafts
Show, Holmes Beach
Art at the Mission, Saint Augustine
Art Fest by the Sea, Jupiter
Art Festival in the Pines, Pembroke
Pines
ArtFest Fort Myers, Fort Myers
Arts and Crafts Show at the Depot,
Naples
Aventura Arts & Crafts Festival,
Aventura
Beaux Arts Festival, Coral Gables
Boca Fest, Boca Raton
Boca Raton Museum of Art Festival, Boca
Raton
Bonita Springs National Art Festival,
Bonita Springs
Cape Coral Festival of the Arts, Cape
Coral
Celebration Art Festival, Orlando
Chain of Parks Art Festival, Tallahassee
Country Folk Art, Miami
Country Folk Art, Tampa
Daytona Riverfront Artfaire, Daytona
Beach
Deerfield Beach Festival of the Arts,
Deerfield Beach
Downtown Delray Festival of the Arts,
Delray Beach
Downtown Dunedin Street Art Festival,
Dunedin
Downtown Lake Worth Craft Festival,
Lake Worth
Downtown Stuart Art Festival, Stuart
Downtown Venice Art Classic, Venice
Festival at Five Points Park Arts &
Crafts Show, Sarasota
Fiesta of Arts, Boca Raton
Florida Folk Festival, White Springs
Florida Keys Art Guild Art Festival,
Islamorada & Key West
Fort Myers Winterfest Arts and Crafts
Show, Fort Myers
Gasparilla Festival of the Arts, Tampa
Indialantic Art Festival, Indialantic

Indian River Festival Arts and Crafts
Show, Titusville
Jupiter Island Hobe Sound Art Festival,
Jupiter Island
Key Biscayne Arts Festival, Key Biscayne
Key West Art Fest, Key West
Lake Placid Art League Show, Sebring
Las Olas Art Fair, Fort Lauderdale
Lido Key Beach Arts and Crafts Show,
Lido Key
Mandarin Art Festival, Jacksonville
Marco Island Invitational, Marco Island
Mount Dora Arts Festival, Mount Dora
Naples Invitational Art Festival, Naples
Naples National Art Festival, Naples
Old Hyde Park Village Festival, Tampa
On the Green Art Festival, Fort Pierce
Osceola County Fair Arts & Crafts Show,
Kissimmee
Panama City Spring Festival of the Arts,
Panama City
Paradise City Arts Festival, Fort
Lauderdale
Pigeon Key Art Festival, Marathon
Ponte Vedra Art Festival, Ponte Vedra
Punta Gorda Arts and Crafts Show, Punta
Gorda
Saint Pete Beach Art Fest, Saint Pete
Beach
Saint Petersburg Art Festival, Saint
Petersburg
San Pablo Art Festival, Marathon
Sarasota Arts Day, Sarasota
Sarasota Festival of the Arts, Sarasota
Siesta Key Arts and Crafts Show, Siesta
Key
South Miami Arts and Crafts Festival,
South Miami
Snowbird Arts and Crafts Show, Punta
Gorda
Tarpon Springs Arts and Crafts Festival,
Tarpon Springs
Under the Oaks Art Show, Vero Beach
Venice Area Art Festival, Venice
The Village Craft Fair, The Village

Willington Art Festival, Wellington
Winter Craft Fair, Bradenton
Winter Craft Fair, Melbourne

Winterfest at the Mansion, Sarasota
Ybor City Main Street Arts & Craft Series, Tampa

Georgia

Adventures in the Arts, Cornelia
American Craft Council, Atlanta
Art in the Garden Festival, Dawsonville
Arts in the Heart of Augusta, Augusta
Atlanta Dogwood Festival, Atlanta
Atlanta Regional Juried Art Exhibition, Atlanta
Augusta Spring Art and Crafts Show, Augusta
Augusta Summer Arts and Crafts Show, Augusta
Blue Ridge Arts in the Park Festival, Blue Ridge
Calico Spring Art and Crafts Show, Moultrie
Cane Grinding and Crafts Festival, Savannah
Canton Festival of the Arts, Canton
Cedar Valley Arts Festival, Cedartown
Cornelia Fine Art, Crafts & Antiques Show, Cornelia
Decatur Arts Festival, Decatur
Fine Art Mecca Festival, Carrollton
Fireside Craft and Art Show, Helen
First Saturday Art and Crafts Festival, Savannah
Golden Isles Arts Festival, Saint Simons Island
Heritage Festival, Ailey
Hiawassee Festival of Arts, Hiawassee
Jonesboro Juried Art Show, Jonesboro
Jubilee Art in the Gardens, Atlanta
Mable House Artfest, Mableton
Marietta Art in the Park, Marietta
Mulberry Street Festival, Macon
National Black Arts Festival, Atlanta
New Salem Mountain Festival, Rising Fawn
North Georgia Wildlife Art Festival, Blue Ridge
Old Courthouse Art Show, Fayetteville
Pine Log Arts and Crafts Fair, Rydal
Riverfest Weekend, Columbus
Southland Jubilee, Greensboro
Spring Fine Art & Craft Show, Saint Simons Island
Stone Mountain Village Arts and Crafts Festival, Stone Mountain
Stonecrest Arts Festival, Lithonia
Telfair Art Fair, Savannah
Traditions Arts and Crafts Show, Dalton
Virginia Highland Summerfest, Atlanta
Wildflower Festival of the Arts, Dahlonega
Winter Art Show, Monroe

Kentucky

American Quilter's Society Quilt Show and Contest, Paducah
Art in the Arbor Festival, Louisville
Autumn Arts Fest, Crittenden
Bardstown Arts, Crafts, and Antiques Fair, Bardstown
Berea Craft Festival, Berea
Buffalo Crossing Fall Craft Show, Shelbyville
Capital Expo Festival, Frankfort
Country Peddler Craft Show, Lexington
Creative Arts Festival, Henderson
Daniel Boone Pioneer Festival, Winchester
Forkland Heritage Festival & Revue, Danville
Hatfield-McCoy Festival, Pikeville
Hillbilly Days Festival, Pikeville
Kentucky Crafted: The Market, Louisville
Kentucky Guild Fall Fair, Berea
Kentucky Guild Spring Fair, Berea
LaGrange Arts on the Green, LaGrange
Lower Town Fine Arts Festival, Paducah
Mainstrasse Village Maifest, Covington
Mayfest, Lexington
Pleasant Hill Craft Fair, Harrodsburg
Saint James Court Art Show, Louisville
Summer Motion Arts & Crafts, Ashland
Ursuline Campus Art Fair, Louisville
Woodland Art Fair, Lexington

Louisiana

Cottontails Trail Arts and Crafts Show, Kenner

Covington Three Rivers Art Festival, Covington

Fest for All, Baton Rouge

Festival International de Louisiane, Lafayette

Louisiana Swamp Festival, New Orleans

New Orleans Fresh Art Festival, New Orleans

New Orleans Jazz and Heritage Festival, New Orleans

Oak Alley Plantation Arts and Crafts Festival, Vacherie

Red River Revel Arts Festival, Shreveport

Saint Luke Courtyard Craft Fair, Slidell

Shadows-on-the-Teche Art & Craft Festival, New Iberia

Southdown Fall Marketplace, Houma

Southdown Spring Marketplace, Houma

Spring Fling, Lafayette

Spring Fling Arts and Craft Show, Lake Charles

Mississippi

Brick Street Festival, Clinton

Canton Flea Market Arts and Crafts Show, Canton

Country Peddler Show, Jackson

Crosstie Arts and Jazz Festival, Cleveland

Gum Tree Festival, Tupelo

Holiday Fest, Greenville

Mississippi Kudzu Festival, Holly Springs

Oxford Double Decker Arts Festival, Oxford

Picayune Fall Street Fair, Picayune

Prairie Arts Festival, West Point

Tallahatchie Riverfest, New Albany

North Carolina

Airlie Arts Festival, Wilmington

Apple Festival Arts and Crafts Fair, Hendersonville

ArtFest of Matthews, Matthews

Arts and Crafts at Sapphire Valley, Cashiers

Arts by the Sea and Storytelling Festival, Swansboro

Artsplosure Spring Arts Festival, Raleigh

Banner Elk Fine Art and Master Crafts Show, Banner Elk

Bele Chere, Asheville

Black Mountain Arts & Crafts Show, Black Mountain

Blooming Arts Festival, Monroe

Blowing Rock Art in the Park, Blowing Rock

Buxton Spring Arts & Craft Show, Buxton

Carolina Spring Arts and Crafts Show, Wilmington

Centennial Arts and Crafts Show, Maggie Valley

Centerfest, Durham

Charlotte Festival in the Park, Charlotte

Concord Winter Celebration of Arts and Crafts, Concord

Craft Fair of the Southern Highlands, Asheville

Dimensions National Juried Art Exhibition, Winston-Salem

Durham Art Guild Annual Juried Art Show, Durham

Durham Native American Pow Wow, Durham

East Carolina Wildlife Arts Festival & NC Decoy Carving, Washington

Eastern Carolina Craftsmen's Spring Festival, Fayetteville

Fall Celebration of Arts, Spruce Pine

Festival for the Eno, Durham

Fine Arts and Crafts Showcase, Brevard

Fine Arts Festival, Southern Pines

Folkmoot USA, Waynesville

Frank Stick Memorial Art Show, Nags Head

Kernersville Spring Folly, Kernersville

Lake Eden Arts Festival, Black Mountain

Lazy Daze Arts and Crafts Festival, Cary

Madison County Heritage Festival, Mars Hill

Mollie Fearing Memorial Art Show, Manteo

Mount Mitchell Crafts Fair, Burnsville
National Juried Art Exhibition, Rocky Mount
New World Festival of the Arts, Manteo
Oak Island Arts and Crafts Festival, Oak Island
On the Square Arts and Crafts Festival, Newland
Patchwork Craft Group Show & Sale, Brevard
Piedmont Crafts Fair, Winston-Salem
Pilot Mountain Mayfest, Pilot Mountain
Raleigh International Festival, Raleigh
Riverwalk Festival, Jacksonville

Rosen Outdoor Sculpture Competition and Exhibition, Boone
Rumba on the Lumber Arts & Crafts Festival, Lumberton
Smoky Mountain Arts & Crafts Fest, Franklin
Sparta Mountain Heritage Festival, Sparta
Spring Daze Arts and Crafts Show, Cary
Summer Magick Craft Fair, Asheville
Taste of Charlotte, Charlotte
Urban Trail Arts Fest, Asheville
Wilmington Art Association Spring Art Show, Wilmington

South Carolina

Abbeville Spring Festival on the Square, Abbeville
Atalaya Arts and Crafts Festival, Murrells Inlet
Charleston Fall Arts and Crafts Show, Charleston
Charleston International Antique Show, Charleston
Charleston Summer Fun Art and Crafts Festival, Charleston
Clariant Fine Art Exhibit, Allendale
Coastal Discovery Museum's Art Market, Hilton Head Island
Columbia Place, Columbia
The Craftsmen Classic Arts & Crafts Festival, Columbia
Edisto Riverfest, Canadys
Fall Arts and Crafts Show, Anderson
Florence Arts and Crafts Shows, Florence
Jubilee Arts Festival, Bennettsville
Jubilee Festival of Heritage, Columbia

Jubilee: Harvest of the Arts, Rock Hill
MOJA Arts Festival, Charleston
Moncks Corner Juried Fine Art Show, Moncks Corner
Moving Sculpture: The Art of the Motorcycle World, Spartanburg
Myrtle Beach Art in the Park, Myrtle Beach
North Charleston Arts Festival, North Charleston
Olde Towne Artisans' Fair, North Augusta
Piccolo Spoleto Crafts, Charleston
Piccolo Spoleto Festival, Charleston
Piedmont Interstate Fair, Spartanburg
Sculpture in the South, Summerville
South Carolina Quilt Show, Aiken
Spartanburg Juried Sidewalk Art Show, Spartanburg
Spartanburg's Spring Fling, Spartanburg
Sumter Arts and Crafts Show, Sumter
Waccamaw Arts and Crafts Guild Art Show, Myrtle Beach

Tennessee

American Artisan Festival, Nashville
American Quilter's Society Quilt Exposition, Nashville
Artist Market Show & Sale, Memphis
Blue Plum Arts and Music Festival, Johnson City
Celebration of Fine Craft, Chattanooga
Cordova Arts and Crafts Festival, Cordova
Dollywood's Harvest Celebration, Pigeon Forge

Elk Valley Crafters Association Spring Craft Show, Fayetteville
Fayetteville-Lincoln County Arts and Craft Show, Fayetteville
Festival of British & Appalachian Culture, Rugby
Foothills Country Fair, Cleveland
Four Bridges Arts Festival, Chattanooga
Franklin Main Street Festival, Franklin
Gatlinburg Craftsmen's Fair, Gatlinburg

Goodlettsville Colonial Fair, Goodlettsville
Ketner's Mill Country Art Fair, Whitwell
Knoxville Dogwood Arts Festival,
Knoxville
Lenoir City Arts and Crafts Festival,
Lenoir City
Maryville Spring Arts and Crafts Show,
Maryville
Morristown International Festival,
Morristown
Mountain Makins Festival, Morristown
Mountain Quiltfest, Pigeon Forge
Murfreesboro Pioneer Day, Murfreesboro
New Midland Plaza Spring Arts & Crafts
Fair, Alcoa
Nillie Bipper Outdoor Arts & Crafts
Festival, Cleveland

Pilot Club Arts and Crafts Fair, Oak
Ridge
Pink Palace Crafts Fair, Memphis
Rogersville Heritage Days, Rogersville
Sequoyah Arts and Crafts Festival, Vonore
Shelbyville Spring Fun Show, Shelbyville
Smithville Fiddlers' Jamboree and Crafts
Festival, Smithville
TACA Fall Crafts Fair, Nashville
Tennessee Crafts Fair, Nashville
Townsend in the Smokies Spring Festival,
Townsend
Tullahoma Fine Arts & Crafts Festival,
Tullahoma
Webb School Arts and Crafts Festival, Bell
Buckle
White Oak Crafts Fair, Woodbury

Virginia

Aldie Mill Art Show & Sale, Aldie
Alexandria Festival of Arts, Alexandria
American Indian Pow Wow, Virginia
Beach
Apple Days Craft Show, Waynesboro
Arlington Arts Center State of the Art,
Arlington
Art on the Green, Chesapeake
Art on the Halfshell Fine Arts & Crafts
Festival, Urbanna
Arts on the Lawn, Richmond
Bedford Centerfest Art Show, Bedford
Blackstone Arts and Crafts Festival,
Blackstone
Blue Ridge Folklife Festival, Ferrum
Boardwalk Art Show & Festival, Virginia
Beach
Chautauqua Festival, Wytheville
Chesapeake Fine Arts and Crafts Festival,
Chesapeake
Craftsmen's Classic Arts & Crafts Festival,
Richmond
Danville Festival in the Park, Danville
Easter Decoy Art Festival and Auction,
Chincoteague
Floyd Fest, Floyd
Fort Clifton Music, Arts and Crafts
Festival, Colonial Heights
Forty-Third Street Festival, Richmond
Fredericksburg Art Festival,
Fredericksburg

Fredericksburg Fine Arts Exhibit,
Fredericksburg
Gosport Arts Festival, Portsmouth
Hampton Bay Days, Hampton
Hand Workshop Art Center Craft and
Design Show, Richmond
Hungry Mother Arts and Crafts Festival,
Marion
Jasmine Plantation Fine Art and Craft
Festival, Providence Forge
Lynchburg Art Club Art Festival,
Lynchburg
Mid-Atlantic Art Exhibition, Norfolk
National Arts and Crafts Extravaganza,
Richmond
New Market Heritage Days Fall Festival,
New Market
Newport News Fall Festival of Folklife,
Newport News
Northern Virginia Fine Arts Festival,
Reston
An Occasion for the Arts, Williamsburg
Occoquan Spring Arts and Crafts Show,
Occoquan
Old Town Arts and Crafts Fair, Alexandria
Princess Anne Park Art and Craft Festival,
Virginia Beach
Richmond Arts in the Park, Richmond
Roanoke City Art Show, Roanoke
Roanoke Sidewalk Art Show, Roanoke
Seawall Art Show, Portsmouth

Shenandoah Valley Arts & Crafts Shows, Orkney Springs

Shenandoah Valley Powwow, Quicksburg

Spring Craft Show, Berryville

Staunton Art in the Park, Staunton

Stockley Gardens Spring Arts Festival, Norfolk

Sugarloaf Crafts Festival, Chantilly

Summer Kickoff Art & Craft Show, Nellysford

Virginia Beach Junior Women's Art and Craft Show, Virginia Beach

Virginia Beach Spring Craft Market, Virginia Beach

Virginia Center Commons Arts & Crafts Show, Glen Allen

Virginia Craft and Folk Art Festival, Annandale

Virginia Fall Craft Show, Salem

Virginia Highlands Festival, Abingdon

Virginia Lake Festival, Clarksville

Virginia Wine and Craft Festival, Front Royal

Wildlife Arts Festival, Newport News

Williamsburg Festival Week, Williamsburg

Woodlawn Plantation Needlework Exhibition, Mount Vernon

ECOLOGY AND ENVIRONMENT

Tasha Eichenseher

While the rugged American West may have captured the imaginations of well-known adventurers and pioneers, it was the mucky shores of the southeastern corner of this country that colonists first settled. What ensued were bloody colonial battles, grandiose cotton plantations, rustic coal mining towns, New Orleans jazz, Elvis, and tourists looking for sand and sun. The history, culture, and economy of the southern United States are inextricably tied to its ecological landscape. The dark, rich soils of the Mississippi River floodplain created what was once the most lucrative agricultural land in the country; the forests on the Piedmont Plateau, between the Atlantic coast and the southern Appalachian Mountains, today produce one of the country's largest timber harvests; ancient geologic activity resulted in valuable reserves of coal and offshore oil; and fierce tropical storms, sea level rise, and coastal erosion wreak havoc on the southeastern seaboard, regularly causing millions of dollars worth of damage to oceanfront property. From the barrier islands off North Carolina to the banks of the Mississippi River, the South is one of the oldest settings in the United States for the continual struggle between humans and nature. Historically exploited for its natural resources, the region has, quite remarkably, remained a hub of astonishing ecological and agricultural productivity and diversity, and is now the target of the nation's most expensive environmental restoration projects.

DEFINING A REGION

The South as defined in this volume stretches more than 1,200 miles from its most eastern point at Cape Hatteras on the North Carolina coast across the coastal plain and over the rocky foothills and weathered peaks of the southern Appalachian Mountains, then through the Mississippi River Valley before reaching the mountainous Ouachita area of western Arkansas. From one of its most southern cities, Miami, Florida, to one of its most northern, Richmond, Virginia, the region is just over 1,000 miles long. The south end is framed by the Gulf of Mexico, and the northern boundary approximates the extent of the last ice age, more than 50,000 years ago. Glaciers moving south across the continent stopped advancing just north of the Kentucky and Virginia borders.

Historically, the South has been defined by the Mason-Dixon Line, which runs along the Maryland-Pennsylvania border and used to separate the southern Confederates from the northern Yankees. However, ecology and environmental landscapes are not bound by political borders. Instead, ecological regions, or ecosystems, are determined by geology and soils, climate and weather, and plants and animals.

Ecological Zones

A topographic map of the American South reveals six distinct geologic regions, represented by a series of stripes that run parallel to the Atlantic Ocean. Starting at the shore is the flat, sandy, and marshy coastal plain; farther inland the rocky undulating Piedmont Plateau—the second region—rises slowly up to the southern Appalachian Mountains—the third obvious division. West of the southern Appalachians is another rolling plateau region to the north and the sunken Mississippi River basin to the south. The land rises again west of the Mississippi River in Arkansas to form the Ouachita Mountains—the southern extension of the Ozark Mountains.

The South has been divided by ecologists into even smaller zones. According to Robert G. Bailey, the pioneering mapper of the world's ecosystems and an employee of the U.S. Forest Service in Fort Collins, Colorado, there are eight distinct ecological "provinces," or ecosystems, in the southern United States, most of which are warm and wet, making them part of the humid temperate domain, with subtropical characteristics near the Atlantic and Gulf coasts and Mississippi River Valley, and relatively drier and more seasonal "hot continental" characteristics farther inland.

The Coastal Plain

The Outer Coastal Plain Mixed Forest Province

The coastal plain is a subtropical region that technically runs from the Rio Grande in Texas around the Atlantic shore north to Long Island in New York, covering at least a third of Arkansas, Louisiana, Mississippi, Alabama, and Georgia, and all but the very southern tip of Florida before it sweeps around through South Carolina, North Carolina, Tennessee, and Virginia, narrowing as it climbs north.

Estuaries, salt marshes, swamps, and the occasional beach fringe much of the coastline. Streams move at the speed of molasses, and water lingers in this generally flat region, which slopes only slightly toward the Atlantic Ocean. Along most of the eastern Gulf coast and parts of the Atlantic coast, the often-foggy transition area from sea level to higher elevations is host to eerie bald cypress swamps, where trees draped in long Spanish moss, like derelict spider webs, steep in shallow and still, black waters. This moss is an epiphyte, meaning it has a symbiotic relationship with its host tree and can live on water and air without soil. Farther inland at higher elevations, swamps and marshes transition into pine forests or temperate rainforest, also called temperate evergreen or laurel forest. Laurel forests are named for the laurel species of trees there, which have durable leathery leaves and burst with large pink or white flowers in the spring. Lush evergreen oaks, magnolia trees, ferns, and liana fill these forests. Temperate rainforests, found where soils are wet and acidic, are neither as dense nor as diverse as tropical rainforests, but are characterized by wet conditions. This region of the American South experiences between forty and sixty inches of rainfall a year, and is

Spanish moss has a symbiotic relationship with its host tree and can live without soil. Courtesy Louisiana Office of Tourism.

characterized by average annual temperatures between 60 and 70 degrees Fahrenheit. Along the Atlantic coast, upland forested areas are dominated by evergreens that grow well in sandy soils, such as loblolly pine. Under the treetop canopy, the ground is covered in savanna-like grasses. This landscape is punctuated by small depressions filled with water called bogs or pocosins.

Much of the wildlife that once lived and fed in coastal swamps and forests has been hunted away or squeezed out as the human population exploded and developed the land. Whitetail deer, popular for trading during the colonial period, remain the most common large native mammal. Small, isolated populations of black bear and the endangered Florida panther still survive. Common small mammals include raccoons, opossums, flying squirrels, rabbits, and many different types of rodents. The American alligator remains the largest reptile in the region. Bobwhite quail and turkey are hunted for game, and hundreds of migratory bird species make their way south during winter months on the Atlantic flyway. The red-cockaded woodpecker, which has barely visible red spots on its face, is a longtime resident of coastal woodlands and on the verge of extinction, as it nests only in old pines and is easily disturbed by logging activity.

Everglades Province

The southern tip of Florida is so different from the rest of the coastal plain that it warrants its own ecosystem classification. This is the only tropical region in the continental United States, with average annual temperatures of 70 to 75 degrees Fahrenheit, and fifty to sixty-five inches of rainfall a year, most falling in late spring and mid-autumn. This tiny area is home to two unique and important conservation reserves: Everglades National Park, which has been designated a World Heritage Site and an International Biosphere Reserve because of its tremendous ecological value; and Biscayne Bay National Park, the largest marine park in the country—95 percent of which is under water.

In general the landscape is flat, rising from sea level to twenty-five feet, and wet, with broad streams and channels crisscrossing through thousands of acres of shockingly green marsh grasses, reminiscent of midwestern prairies, before reaching the ocean. In most areas, several feet of muck and sand cover the limestone bedrock, with occasional low beach ridges and dunes. Swamp and mangrove areas again are dominated by bald cypress, with mahogany and palmetto species. The Everglades is host to both temperate and tropical plants, including prairie saw grasses, mangrove trees, and pines. The park is famous for its fascinating mélange of diverse flora. There are at least twenty-five types of orchids, and 1,000 other plant species.

The 1.5 million acre estuary, under management by the National Parks Service, and its associated wooded areas are home to more than thirty-six threatened or endangered species of animals, including the American alligator and American crocodile, the Florida panther, and the West Indian manatee, a slow-moving marine mammal that often falls victim to motorboats. More than 300 species of birds have been recorded in the park. And it is the only place in the world where alligators live next to crocodiles.

The other ecological treasure found in this province, Biscayne Bay National Park, has also drawn considerable attention from conservationists. The world's third longest coral reef begins in Biscayne Bay. Coral reefs are one of the most fragile ecosystems. A glimpse through the turquoise water over this primeval sculpture garden reveals an intricate and colorful underwater world thousands of years in the making. More than 200 species of tropical fish, representing every color of the rainbow, swim around and through coral blooms and flowing strands of sea fans, while octopi and nurse sharks float past. The reef was formed by coral polyps, which are tiny creatures that use calcium found in seawater to produce a limestone shell. Over time colonies of these miniature shells join to create a reef. Exceptionally sensitive to pollution and disease, and vulnerable to destruction by motorboat blades and the fins of careless divers, this reef is threatened by human development and rising global temperatures. As the oceans warm, coral is subject to bleaching, which can disrupt the functions of the polyps and kill the reef.

The American alligator remains the largest reptile in the region. Courtesy Louisiana Office of Tourism.

A small portion of Biscayne Bay protects the longest remaining stretch of mangrove forest in eastern Florida. Mangrove trees appear to have dozens of legs supporting their trunks above shallow, salty coastal waters. In some species, this dense network of aboveground roots can block out the salt—which would otherwise kill the tree—and absorb only freshwater. Other species absorb the salt, but then excrete it through their leaves. The complex root system helps to protect the water quality of the bay by collecting sediments. It also serves as a nursery and feeding ground for fish and other aquatic organisms, which in turn serve as a tasty food source for the pelicans and other birds nesting in the tree

Spanish hogfish at the Florida Keys National Marine Sanctuary. Courtesy Florida Keys National Marine Sanctuary.

canopy, and for larger fish, shrimp, and lobster. Without the mangrove forest, populations of these commercially fished species would dwindle.

The Piedmont Plateau

Southern Mixed Forest Province

This ecosystem is a transition area from coastal habitat to the higher foothills of the Appalachian Mountains. It runs to the west of the outer coastal plain, working its way around the Mississippi River Delta, and covering most of Mississippi, Arkansas, and western Louisiana, where it reaches the Gulf coast. The path it takes through the Gulf coast states coincides with the famous cotton black belt, named for the dark, fertile soils found there that support intensive agricultural production of this fuzzy crop.

Mild winters and hot, humid summers, with average annual temperatures from 60 to 70 degrees Fahrenheit, create a long growing season (200 to 300 days). Midsummer and early spring thunderstorms contribute to an average of forty to sixty inches of rainfall each year. Snow is rare, but frosts prohibit year-round growing of cotton, rice, and sugar, among other crops. Typically clayish soils support loblolly pine and shortleaf pine, mixed with broadleaf deciduous species such as oak, hickory, sweetgum, blackgum, red maple, and winged elm. The groundcover is a mosaic of different grasses interspersed with other species, including dogwood, viburnum, blueberry, and woody vines. Salt marsh grass species, predominantly spartina, line the shores of Louisiana.

Whitetail deer and cottontail rabbits are scattered throughout the forests, sometimes accompanied by the fox squirrel in deciduous areas. Other small mammals in this region include the gray squirrel, raccoon, fox, and the nine-banded armadillo. The latter, a curious cat-size creature protected with bony, scaled armor, can live only where soils are soft enough for burrowing. Eastern wild turkey, bobwhite quail, and mourning dove are popular game birds with hunters. Other common bird species include the pine warbler, cardinal, summer tanager, Carolina wren, ruby-throated hummingbird, blue jay, hooded warbler, eastern towhee, and tufted titmouse. The red-cockaded woodpecker also lives here in mature forests. Snakes, lizards, and salamanders abound.

The Southern Appalachian Mountains

Central Appalachian Broadleaf Forest—Coniferous Forest—Meadow Province

The Appalachian Mountains run from Maine to northeastern Alabama and sever the rich soils of the Piedmont Plateau from the equally fertile Mississippi River valley and the western plateaus. Peaks and ridges cut into the northwest corner of Georgia, and also form the boundary between Kentucky and Virginia, as well as the border between North Carolina and Tennessee. Nearly 600 miles from the Atlantic coast, this ecosystem is commonly called the Appalachian Highlands, where mountains reach up to 6,684 feet—at Mount Mitchell in North Carolina.

Unlike the relatively new and sharply dramatic mountains in the Rockies and other western ranges, the Appalachians have been worn down and rounded out by the elements—rain, snow, ice, and wind—since before the breakup of the supercontinent Pangaea. Known as the Smokies in Tennessee, the Blue Ridge in North Carolina and Georgia, the Red Mountains in Alabama, and the Allegheny in western Virginia, these highly eroded mountains create some of the most spectacular scenery and one of the longest intermittent stretches of national forest in the eastern United States. For example, just a small segment of this corridor, Shenandoah National Park, includes 101 miles of the famous Appalachian Trail, which runs the length of the entire range, and 190,000 acres of the Blue Ridge Mountains, which get their name from the water vapor haze lingering over the dense forests, a result of photosynthetic processes and climatic conditions. Not until the last several decades has this haze also been the result of human activity—automobile exhaust and other industrial pollution.

Because the Appalachians reach higher elevations, temperatures are cooler, ranging from 50 to 64 degrees Fahrenheit. The growing season, or frost-free period, in the southern Appalachians generally runs about 220 days, and thirty-five to eighty inches of precipitation falls annually off the mountain peaks, tending to flow east through valleys, across the Piedmont to the Atlantic. The Great Smoky Mountains see more than thirty inches of snow a year. Because south-facing Appalachian slopes are warmer and drier than north-facing slopes, forest fires are more of a problem on south-facing slopes.

On the mountain peaks, spruce stands and meadows create an alpine-like environment. At lower elevations, evergreen forest transitions into northeastern hardwood forest—a mix of birch, beech, maple, elm, basswood, and oak combined with hemlock and white pine. Lower valleys are populated with oak-pine forests, much like the ones on the coastal plain. Higher areas are predominantly oak forests. Under the tree canopy, dramatically lush and brilliantly hued rhododendrons and azaleas provide shelter for birds and small mammals.

The forests of the southern Appalachian are reminiscent of how much of the Northern Hemisphere looked thousands, if not millions, of years ago, and are crucial habitat for the remaining wildlife, such as black bear and whitetail deer. As forests die of disease or are cleared for timber or development, species are being forced farther up the slopes. The eastern cougar, an elusive predator, may be extinct or near extinction due to habitat loss. Appalachian forests are a Mecca for birds. Red-breasted nuthatches, black-throated green warblers, golden-crowned warblers, golden-crowned kinglets, and northern juncos find solace in spruce and fir stands. A large variety of woodpeckers, including pileated, downy, hairy, and red-bellied, feed in the hardwood stands. The passenger pigeon, which was abundant when settlers arrived in North America, composing 25 to 40 percent of the total bird population, was hunted to extinction. Most impressive, however, may be what lies closest to the ground. The wet ground conditions in the valleys and on the mountainsides of the southern Appalachians support the most diverse population of salamanders, more than twenty-seven species, in North America.

The Mississippi Valley

Lower Mississippi Riverine Forest Province

The lower portion of Mississippi River begins in St. Louis, Missouri, and runs to the swampy shores of Louisiana's Gulf coast. The river's floodplain valley extends for miles past the riverbed west into Louisiana and Arkansas and east into Mississippi, Tennessee, and Kentucky. The Mississippi River has left an indelible mark in the minds of millions of people who have navigated its waters, have been displaced by its floods, and have read Mark Twain's *The Adventures of Tom Sawyer*. The Mississippi floodplain and valley ecosystem, created by the river, has had a powerful influence on the history, culture, and economy of the United States. A subtropical region, the valley is filled with rich alluvial soils, deposited by the river, that have created prime agricultural conditions.

Summer temperatures range from 70 to 80 degrees Fahrenheit, while winter temperatures range from 50 to 60 degrees Fahrenheit. The farther south you travel, the warmer it gets, and the wetter. Average annual precipitation for the region is fifty-five inches. Generally flat, or gently sloping toward the Gulf of Mexico, the landscape is decorated with ribbons of oxbow lakes, created as the Mississippi changed course over time and sections settled into their own basins and were separated from their source. The only elevation in this area is found in the natural, and man-made, levees built along river and stream banks. Levees, while created naturally when a river deposits sediments during a flood, are often built up even higher by engineers and local residents to protect property from flood damage. Much of the forested land in this region has been cleared for agriculture, leaving only pockets of deciduous ash, elm, cottonwood, pecan, and other water-loving species. Riverbanks are entangled in several vine species.

The abundant water resources and natural river path support a well-traveled migratory route for hundreds of bird species. Called the Mississippi Flyway, this avian

An Indian mound in Arkansas serves as a refuge during a spring flood. From *The Floods of the Spring of 1903 in the Mississippi Watershed*, by H. C. Frankenfield (1904). Courtesy NOAA, Historic NWS Collection. Archival photograph by Mr. Sean Linehan.

superhighway attracts the most diverse and largest migratory flock in all of North America. Among the year-round residents are the prothonotary warbler, white-eyed vireo, wood duck, yellow-billed cuckoo, and Louisiana waterthrush. The artist and naturalist John James Audubon, for whom the Audubon Society was named, lived near the area and often observed and wrote about birds during migration.

Western Plateaus

Eastern Broadleaf Forest (Oceanic) Province

This is a diverse area that extends to parts of the western foothills of the Appalachians, New England lowlands, and mid-Atlantic coastal plain. It covers both eastern Kentucky and eastern Tennessee. An inland ecosystem, it experiences typical continental weather, with cold winters and warm summers. Average annual temperatures range from 40 to 65 degrees Fahrenheit, and snow and rainfall average thirty-five to sixty inches per year, with more rain in summer. Most is (or once was) forested with tall broadleaf species, such as oak, and evergreen pines, which form a dense canopy in the summer. West of the Appalachians, American beech, tulip tree or yellow poplar, basswood, sugar maple, sweet buckeye, red oak, white oak, and eastern hemlock dominate. Chestnut trees used to be part of the mix, until they were wiped out by the chestnut blight, a fungus from Asia that was introduced in this country in the early 1900s. Pine-oak forest stands, or pine barrens, are found on dry sandy soils and are subject to frequent fires.

The usual suspects can be found making a home in the forests: whitetail deer, black bear, bobcat, gray fox, raccoon, gray squirrel, and other small mammals, as well as bobwhite and mourning dove. Box turtles, garter snakes, and timber rattlesnakes shuffle and slither across the forest floor.

Eastern Broadleaf Forest (Continental) Province

This ecosystem province has a huge range, extending north from the lower Mississippi River valley through the midwestern United States to the Canadian border, and west from the foothills of the Appalachians and the Eastern Broadleaf Forest Oceanic Province to the prairie lands in middle America. The portion of this ecosystem found in central and western Tennessee and western Kentucky is characterized by low rolling hills, dissected plateaus, and small basins.

This area is similar to the Eastern Broadleaf Forest Oceanic Province, but drier, averaging about fifty inches of precipitation in the south. Average annual temperatures are around 65 degrees Fahrenheit. Drought-resistant deciduous oak-hickory forests find the conditions here favorable. Flowering dogwood and wildflowers add color during spring and summer. And grasses, such as Kentucky bluegrass, found in the central and northern part of the state, blanket the hills. The oak and hickory species provide acorns and hickory nuts for foragers such as the gray squirrel, eastern chipmunk, and blue jay.

Ouachita Mountains

Ouachita Mixed Forest—Meadow Province

Isolated primarily in Arkansas just west of the Mississippi River valley, with ramparts in eastern Oklahoma, the Ouachita Mountains reach up to 2,600 feet. With typical subtropical weather—warm winters and hot summers, with an average annual temperature around 63 degrees Fahrenheit and annual precipitation measured at forty-one inches—this mountainous area is distinguished by drier summers and dry sandstone ridges. Oak-hickory-pine forests provide habitat for the same bird and mammal species found in the Southern Mixed Forest Province. The Ouachita dusky salamander is endemic to the region's rocky streams, meaning that it is found nowhere else in the country. It is an ecological indicator species sensitive to water pollution and siltation; the health of the entire ecosystem can be monitored through this salamander.

Environmental groups such as the Sierra Club have used Robert Bailey's approach to identify broader ecoregions, showing that dividing a continent, nation, or region based on ecology is just as complicated as drawing a political boundary. The southern United States fall into four Sierra Club ecoregion classifications: the Atlantic coast shoreline, including the barrier islands off the Carolinas and the mangrove swamps of Florida; the Gulf coast; the Mississippi basin; and the southern Appalachian Highlands.

HOW WAS THE NATURAL LANDSCAPE CREATED?

The coral reefs, mountain ridges, and floodplains that support today's southern flora and fauna, including humans, and help determine current weather patterns are the result of millions of years of pressure and heat that have fused the sediments left on ancient ocean floors and folded and moved the tectonic plates composing the earth's crust. The landscape has been carved by water as sea levels have fallen and risen with glacial formation and melting over the course of planetary evolution. The geology of the region has also manufactured huge reserves of oil off the Gulf coast and coal in the southern Appalachians, and has created some of the world's oldest mountains and soils and largest limestone caves.

The Coasts

Pangaea began to split apart about 150 million years ago, eventually creating the seven continents we know today. The first step in this million-year process was the breakup of the north, called the Laurasia landmass, and the south, called the Gondwanaland landmass. The subsequent rift flooded with ocean waters to create the Tethys Seaway. As organic material from dead sealife and ocean bed sediments built up over time, pressure converted the carbon contained in organic matter into oil, and rocks formed from the sediments encased this valuable liquid resource. The shores of the Gulf of Mexico were once the shores of the western end of the Tethys; across the Atlantic Ocean, the Persian Gulf, Black Sea, and North African Mediterranean Sea were all part of the eastern end of the same seaway. When the Tethys evaporated, the salt residue above its sedimentary rock base was covered with limestone, creating a geological layer cake. This limestone shelf extends past the Gulf coast and is the base of the Florida peninsula. The Florida Keys, an island chain off the tip of Florida, were shaped by a similar process. The limestone-laden islands were once ancient coral reefs formed during periods of higher sea levels.

The weight of Mississippi River sediment that has accumulated on this shelf (discussed in the next section) has produced enough heat to essentially liquefy the salt layer, allowing it to escape through fissures in the limestone and rise up in columns of large, cooling crystals toward Gulf surface waters. These salt domes can grow up to six and a half feet wide and are usually capped with limestone that has come along for the ride. This upward growth disturbs the sedimentary layers, and oil is released into the salt, where it is trapped in new reservoirs and is more accessible.

The Atlantic coastline was also part of the primeval Tethys Seaway and has retreated and advanced with fluctuating sea levels over time. We are now at a time of relatively low sea levels. Many of the barrier islands that serve as the first line of defense against the raging winds and waters of Atlantic storms, such as those found in the Outer Banks of North Carolina, were formed when the last glacial period ended and icy meltwaters found their way to the Atlantic, covering the exposed continental shelf that once extended far beyond the current eastern shoreline. Violent waves approaching from the opposite direction pummeled these new shallow shores and pushed enough sand westward to produce long, narrow sandbars tall enough to remain above water. These barrier islands are constantly shifting, often retreating inland as ocean currents and storms exert power. The islands create a calmer environment to the west, where freshwater now flows from the Appalachian Mountains and across the Piedmont Plateau to mix with salty tidal waters from the Atlantic in estuaries and salt marshes.

The Mississippi River Delta

During one of many ice ages, the weight of the Laurentide ice sheet created a depression in the middle of the continent, causing the landscape to slope down toward the Gulf of Mexico. This depression became the enormous Mississippi River basin. When the glacier retreated, it left a network of rivers that all drained into the Mississippi and its outlet on the coast of Louisiana. The waters that run east off the Rocky Mountains pass through highly erodable land, collecting sediment and silt as they make their way south to drain into the Mississippi River. At the same time, some rainwater runoff from the older, less erodable Appalachians flows west to join waters from as far away as Montana and Canada. This mighty confluence begins to slow once it passes through a narrow passage near the shared corners of Missouri, Arkansas, Kentucky, and Tennessee. The southern section of the river is known as the Mississippi Embayment. As the river makes its way from the constriction 640 miles south along the Louisiana/Mississippi border to the Gulf of Mexico, sediment that has traveled hundreds of miles settles in the embayment, which has grown to more than twenty miles wide at the Mississippi's mouth at the Gulf. The building blocks of coastal marshes and the delta landscape, sediments have also been pushed out miles beyond the coastline onto the limestone bedrock shelf that is the foundation of the Gulf states. More than 60 million years of this accretion at the river outlet has created a sediment base up to seven miles thick that is heavy enough to dent tectonic plates. During the last 5,000 years, the Mississippi River has changed points of discharge into the Gulf at least seven distinct times, creating multiple subdelta extensions. The main one terminates in Atchafalaya Bay, west of New Orleans and the current course of the Mississippi River. The Mississippi River Delta, at the southern end of Louisiana, is the only portion of this delta formation above water. The depression, called a geosyncline, creates the shores of the Gulf states and Florida. The entire depression and its river sediment accumulation, running from New Madrid in Missouri to the Gulf, is so severe that it may have buried the southern extensions of the Ouachita Mountains to the west and the Appalachians to the east.

Appalachia

The Appalachian Mountains are the result of a 475-million-year-old mountain-building process. During the formation of Pangaea, the continental plates that eventually became North American and Africa continually collided with one another before creating one landmass, causing enough force to compress and then fold and stack sheets of harder metamorphic rock over more easily erodable sedimentary rock. Before erosion took its toll, the Appalachians may have been as grandiose as the Himalaya Mountains. The now exposed cap of metamorphic rock prevents the mountains from being eroded to the ground. During this mountain-making period, one tectonic plate was lifted by the subduction of another, causing the present-day drainage systems of rivers flowing to the Atlantic. Because of their extended history, the Appalachians have been the classroom where many geologic discoveries about mountain-chain development have been made. When Appalachian bedrock was under construction, decomposing prehistoric sea life, including plants, was deposited on ancient ocean floors, similar to the phenomenon that created offshore oil reserves along the Gulf coast. The accumulation of these decaying sediments is called peat. Over time old peat was buried under newer peat. The heat and pressure from the accumulation morphed the old peat into coal, trapped underneath the more recent peat-turned-rock layer. These layers were then folded upward. Erosion of the top layer in some sections of the mountain range has left coal seams near the surface.

West of the Appalachian Mountains are sedimentary plateau formations, such as the Cumberland Plateau, that are more elevated and severely dissected than typical plateaus. The Mississipian Plateau underlies most of central-western Kentucky, where more than 4,000 caves have been carved by underground streams as they dissolve limestone bedrock over time—referred to as karst topography. Mammoth Cave in Mammoth Cave National Park has been declared a World Heritage Site; it is possibly the world's largest cave, with nearly 400 miles of discovered passageways. Spacious caverns have nicknames that allude to their enormity, including "Grand Central Station." Some geologists believe that the Ouachita Mountains, farther southwest, are a detached and displaced extension of the Appalachians.

The Fall Line

There is an obvious geological feature that separates the coastal plain from the Piedmont Plateau and Appalachian foothills called the fall line, named for the waterfalls and rocky rapids it creates as rivers running from the mountains to the sea pass over its distinct ledge. The fall line runs almost 650 miles north-south and indicates the western reaches of ancient oceans that existed when sea levels were much higher. Ocean waves have eroded the continental shelf up to the fall line, and have left sedimentary layers of coastal sediment on the eroded part of the shelf to the east, referred to as the coastal plain.

HOW HAVE HUMANS RELATED TO AND SHAPED THE SOUTHERN LANDSCAPE?

People and mother nature have historically had a tenuous and complicated relationship. We live off the land; timber harvests provide siding for home construction; soils, the eroded remains of once unscalable mountains and prehistoric forests, now deliver nutrients to the food we eat and support crops such as cotton, which we depend on for the production of T-shirts and underwear. But the forces of nature do not always cooperate with human needs, nor do they necessarily obey human manipulations. Life in the South has always been about finding a balance between harnessing the power of nature and rolling with its punches.

A Native Stronghold

The First Southerners

From the Cherokee, who inhabited the Appalachian Highlands, to the Apalaches of North Florida and Arkansas tribes of the Mississippi River valley, Native American subsistence in the southern United States depended on a healthy natural resource base. When the last ice age ended and sea levels began to rise, many large mammals became extinct, forcing Native American populations to switch from a nomadic hunting existence to a more sedentary life. From 8,000 to 7,000 B.C.E., primitive communities hunted and foraged from settlements close to wetlands, where fish and oysters were abundant. Eventually tools were fashioned from shell, bone, stone, and wood. Tribes of the woodland tradition, from 700 to 1,000 C.E., had larger, more permanent villages and were increasingly dependent on agricultural crops, such as barley, sunflower, and squash.

Different southern ecological zones supported different native lifestyles. The mountain people of Appalachia combined farming with hunting, as did tribes on the Piedmont Plateau, who were able to take advantage of rich alluvial soils and game-filled forests that could support larger populations and more complex settlements. The Mississippi River valley experienced the highest population density. Cognizant of Mississippi flooding, tribes such as the Natchez built their homes on stilts. The coastal plain nurtured fishing and gathering communities, as its sandy soils had minimal agricultural value. Communities in southern Florida were able to subsist on fishing alone.

The shift to agriculture in the Mississippi River valley may have caused the largest Native American population increases. But this growth backfired when societies were unable to manage resources for future use. The great Cahokia ceremonial villages along the Mississippi began to deteriorate as natural resources were depleted or degraded. Drought, soil nutrient depletion, and unsustainable timber extraction in the early thirteenth century helped to contribute to the dispersal of the population. Families began to move into the mountains toward new farmland.

Then the Colonists Arrived

By the time European settlers arrived in the sixteenth century, however, most Native American tribes in the southeastern United States had developed powerful chiefdoms, and stable towns and agricultural practices, making them less mobile and more determined to hold on to their land. Even as late as 1760, there were twice as many Indians as European and African residents combined in southern Virginia and the Carolinas. By trading deerskins with the Europeans, the Native Americans were able to participate in the new Atlantic economy. Males hunted deer while female tribe members processed hides into leather. Unfortunately, as colonists established large agricultural plantations, cotton became a more valuable internationally traded commodity than deerskins, and Native Americans lost some of the footing they had found within colonial culture. Tribes slowly became indebted to the colonists and began to lose their land—a phenomenon credited with causing political upheaval among chiefdoms. Tribal populations also fell victim to smallpox, introduced in North America by the colonists. The almost 200,000 Native Americans living between the south Atlantic coast and the Mississippi were reduced to nearly 55,000 by 1775. However, it was not until the Louisiana Purchase of 1803 and then the Removal Act of 1830 that a westward exodus began.

Colonization: Not What They Bargained For

First Exposure

The patterns of southern exploration, and the exploration of the United States by Europeans in general, were set by weather, water, and chance. The Gulf Stream, first discovered in 1513 by Juan Ponce de León on the same trip in which he was looking for the mythical fountain of youth and claimed Florida for Spain, helped to direct European explorers who were looking to expand their countries' resource bases and economies toward the Atlantic coast from the Caribbean. The Gulf Stream is a warm ocean current that originates in the Caribbean Sea and the Gulf of Mexico and runs around the tip of Florida and up the eastern seaboard to Cape Hatteras, where it veers east across the Atlantic. It was often used to propel ships leaving North America for the Straits of Gibraltar.

In the 1530s and 1540s, Spanish explorer Hernando de Soto made excursions inland from the Gulf of Mexico and discovered the Mississippi River. In 1565 the first permanent European settlement was established at St. Augustine, Florida. And since 1513, explorers had been continually bumping into the Atlantic shore and landing, but not sticking around long enough to build homes or establish farming plots. In 1524 the French landed in North Carolina, but it was not until 1858 that Queen Elizabeth I sent Sir Walter Raleigh to claim the outer banks and establish a British colony on Roanoke Island in the Pamilico Sound. The area in general, adjacent to a rough shoreline, was hard to access and had already claimed many ships and lives. Colonists must have originally found their way into the more tranquil sound through well-hidden outlets. The ill-fated settlement is often called the lost Virginia colony. The British, unfortunately, chose a geographically and ecologically inhospitable home. Camped on unhealthy salt marsh, settlers were plagued by disease and exposed to unforgiving Atlantic storms, as well as defensive natives. When Raleigh returned three years later after the second colony attempt there were no signs of the colonists. Their disappearance remains a mystery to this day.

While Roanoke was a failure, Jamestown was not, and became the first permanent Atlantic coast settlement. When George Percy, from England, landed in Jamestown, Virginia, in 1607, he described it as a paradise. He was impressed by the raw beauty of the meadows, tall trees, freshwater woodland streams, and the blanket of colorful wildflowers that covered the ground. He wrote about the productivity of the soil, which yielded "fine and beautifull Strawberries, foure times bigger and better than ours in England," and "excellent good Timber." The ocean was also a source of life: "mussels and oysters . . . lay upon the ground as thicke as stones." But life in Jamestown was not all roses. There were frequent battles with Native American tribes, and horrible diseases, such as typhoid from contaminated water. The original 105 settlers of Jamestown were at the mercy of the weather. The first winter left only 38 survivors who had to depend on the Powhatan natives for food, particularly corn.

What drew Europeans to the "new world" was land. There was an abundance of it, and it did not take long for visions of lucrative farms to come to fruition and for the plantation era to begin. Settlers in Jamestown received fifty acres for every person they convinced to cross the Atlantic. Towns were established in South Carolina, where swamps were filled so they could be settled, and the population grew steadily during the 1600s. In order to settle Georgia, the English had to offer a bigger incentive—500 acres per person. It seems that St. Augustine had been forgotten. Florida became a place known for poor soils, hurricanes, and pirates. However, Spanish land grants lured colonists to the Mississippi River valley, and settlements began to spring up there, but it was not until 1718 that New Orleans was built. The valley then grew slowly into a hodgepodge hangout for hunters, farmers, herders, commercial traders, and subsistence gatherers, all united by river transportation, before becoming a serious industrial and political center.

Moving Inland

As settlements grew along the coast, explorers continued inland and west in search of more agricultural land, for which they often had to fight the natives. Before the construction of roads, rivers served as main transportation corridors and delivered colonists farther inland to establish farming and trade communities. The boating method of travel and exploration had its limitations, however. From the coastal plain, an explorer or entrepreneur could navigate waterways only as far as the fall line and the Piedmont Plateau. It was impossible to continue upstream over waterfalls and rapids. Early explorations often led to the development of major commercial centers at the intersection of east-west rivers and the north-south fall line. For example, a 1607 journey up the James River ended at present-day Richmond, Virginia.

The waterfalls that mark the fall line were actually a welcome sight, as they represented a potential source of power for the traditional waterwheel, which was used for energy generation before the discovery of steam power. Harnessed energy from the waterwheel was used to produce flour from wheat, tools from iron, and boards from timber. Plus, these inland riverside towns provided a respite from the humid, stagnant, and disease-ridden swamps colonists had settled on the coasts. Once trails, primitive roads, and railroads opened up farther west of the fall line, colonists were pleased to discover fertile soils and productive forests, and eventually coal and other sought-after mineral resources. Famous explorer Daniel Boone said of Kentucky in the mid-1700s: "so rich a soil, covered in clover in full bloom, the woods alive in wild game . . . it appeared that nature in the profusion of her bounties had spread a feast for all that lives." By the late eighteenth century, western Virginia and Tennessee were thriving.

Agriculture: Tobacco, Cotton, Rice, Sugar

All along the Atlantic coast, agriculture supported the growth of towns, and plantations became the economic base of many settlements, bringing in unimaginable wealth. Four main crops—tobacco, cotton, rice, and sugar—dominated the landscape and economy, with a few other interesting plants scattered here and there, including hemp in central Kentucky; wheat and corn in nearly every state; indigo in South Carolina; and mulberry trees for silk production and wine grapes in Georgia. Livestock also played an important role in farming communities. Pork was a popular meat, and at least one hog was raised annually on most farms. The mule, used in fields and for transporting goods, has been referred to as "a southern animal." In 1860 southerners owned nearly 90 percent of the nation's mules. Both agricultural and livestock practices continue to present economic solutions and environmental problems for the South (discussed later in this chapter).

Tobacco

The overall popularity of tobacco was due to the fact that it could be grown on small farms or large plantations. In fact, the average farm size in the nineteenth century was around eight acres. Virginia did, however, set the model for plantation, or large commercial, farming. Colonists depended heavily on African slaves, who were brought to Virginia as early as 1619, to clear the land for agriculture and maintain labor-intensive production and harvesting. Virginia's primary crop was tobacco, referred to as the "golden weed." The tobacco that Virginia colonists marketed to Europe was not a native crop—the native variety was too bitter, so they cultivated a West Indian species instead. By the mid-1700s tobacco production had moved onto the Piedmont Plateau, where production practices were often more humble, and by the late nineteenth century, tobacco leaves could be found on drying racks in North Carolina, Kentucky, and Tennessee.

Before the technological revolution, tobacco was one of the most labor-intensive crops grown in the South. It required unmechanized plowing, weeding, pest removal, suckering, and topping after seedlings were transferred to fields and before harvested leaves were cured, dried, and sent to wholesalers or stores. Suckering meant pulling off smaller leaves to encourage the growth of larger leaves that were more valuable. Topping was necessary to prevent the plant from going to seed and acquiring a bitter taste. Slash and burn techniques were used to clean and stimulate the soil before plantings.

Early tobacco production peaked in the 1850s when 124 million pounds were produced in Virginia alone. Tobacco farmers were able to avoid slow sales when prices jumped by marketing a new, more aesthetically pleasing variety called Bright Yellow. Tobacco was five times more valuable than wheat in the 1800s, but more environmentally devastating. After three or four years of planting tobacco, the soil was almost entirely depleted of nutrients and farmers moved on to new land—which was often cheaper than employing more sustainable farming techniques, such as crop rotation.

Cotton

Cotton, which became the economic pillar of the South, was not a popular crop with early colonists. However, it soon caught on. The "Cotton Kingdom," as the South was called, started in the late 1790s in South Carolina and Georgia. By the mid-1800s, the gauzy plant was blanketing fields from North Carolina to Texas, up to Tennessee and down to Florida. By the mid-nineteenth century, production was dominated by Alabama, Mississippi, Louisiana, and Arkansas, where rich alluvial blackbelt soils created the best growing conditions. Conditions only got better with each Mississippi flood, as new nutrient-packed sediments were deposited on the floodplain.

It was the invention of the cotton gin in 1793 that made the crop such an economic sensation. Cotton production exploded with the gin: at the beginning of the nineteenth century only 73,000 bales were produced in the South, increasing to 4.5 million bales by 1860. The demand for cotton continued to grow with the Industrial Revolution and the construction of an increasing number of textile mills, where cotton was fashioned into cloth and garments. It was a cash crop that required much less input than tobacco. Cotton was picked by hand, but required only one laborer for each six- to nine-acre plot. The boll weevil, a tiny cotton-eating insect with a big bite, came to the southern United States in 1892 from Mexico. After it destroyed nearly 10 percent of cotton crops in the South, farmers began to diversify their fields. Since its arrival, it has caused the cotton industry an estimated loss of $14 billion. Eventually, larger-scale growers, who generally had the most fertile land, began to use more fertilizers and pesticides, improved or modified seeds, and more efficient cultivation practices. Heavy pesticide use on cotton continues to plague the South and its waterways today, and the introduction of new, genetically engineered seeds is a source of controversy among farmers, seed and agricultural corporations, and environmentalists.

Rice

In South Carolina, deerskins and livestock were the economic base until the introduction of rice in the late 1600s by slaves from western Africa. Rice was grown primarily in coastal South Carolina and Georgia, where conditions were ideal—wet and warm. Southwestern Louisiana experienced a brief pulse of rice production when cotton fields were devastated by the boll weevil. Early rice cultivation and irrigation were complicated, requiring fields to be located in tidal flood zones, but elevated enough so as not to be inundated with salt water—poison to most plants. Rice plantations were built along tidal rivers and employed more slave labor than any other type of southern agriculture. Workers were busy engineering and constructing water control structures such as dikes, levees, canals, and sluice gates, as well as leveling fields. Because rice was so labor-intensive and needed to be done on a large scale, it did not become as popular as tobacco and cotton, but did alter the landscape. Today rice is grown primarily in the Mississippi River Delta and coastal Florida and Louisiana. While southern rice farmers worry less than California and Texas rice growers, about potential future water shortages, they have to guard against rice diseases that thrive in subtropical climates, such as the sheath blight, and be aware of potential water quality impairments from pesticide and fertilizer runoff into surface and ground water and the public drinking water supply.

Sugar

Like rice, sugar cane can only grow in very specific conditions. Given that it requires a growing season of at least eight months and ample rain, sugar production found a home in the United States on the east coast of central Florida, in parts of southern North Carolina, and in coastal and west central Louisiana. First introduced in Louisiana in the 1790s, sugar cane became a successful crop when producers began turning it into juice that could be dried to form sugar granules. During the nineteenth century, it became the most lucrative crop in southern Louisiana. Mississippi soils gave the bamboo-like sugar cane stamina, but close proximity to the river also made flood protection necessary. Elaborate networks of ditches, bridges, and levees were built to drain, guard, and travel across fields. The introduction of steam power in 1822 helped to speed up sugar cane juicing and milling, of which molasses is a by-product. Eventually mechanized harvesting replaced hand picking, and sugar now grows in abundance where salt marsh used to purify water and nurture fish. A fourth of the sugar consumed in the United States is grown in the Everglades Agricultural Area. Florida attracted sugar cane growers by offering low taxes on land and water. Unfortunately sugar cane seasons conflict with Everglades wet and dry seasons—as a result of sugar cane production, remaining marshes are drained during the wet season and irrigated in the dry season, throwing this fragile wetland ecosystem off balance and putting the health of the Everglades at risk.

Southern Farming Today

Tobacco and cotton helped build the South. But since the mid-twentieth century, agriculture has undergone dramatic changes, and industry, primarily banking and shipping, eventually overtook agriculture as the most profitable industries. At the onset of World War II, more than 40 percent of southerners were farmers and there were 2.9 million farms; today less than 5 percent of southerners depend on farming as their primary source of income and there are fewer than 1 million farms. This rate of loss is the highest in the nation. The change in southern livelihoods, in which more than 14 million southerners left farming for city life between 1940 and 1980, has been described as one of the greatest migrations of people to take place within a moment in history. Despite this, the average size of a farm and its productivity have increased due to corporate farming and biotechnology, including extensive pesticide and fertilizer use. Tobacco remains a profitable venture, but soybeans, fruits and nuts, cattle (which are now a substitute for deer as a source of leather), and poultry have replaced much of the cotton, rice, and sugar, adding new environmental considerations and concerns to the old.

Forest and Mountain Resources: Sustainable Extraction?

Exploration of the forests and mountains uncovered valuable animal, food, timber, and mineral resources. Unfortunately, the stands of pine, oak, and hickory trees that shade the coastal plain, Piedmont Plateau, and southern Appalachians were often wasted, as they were cut or burned down in a frenzy to clear more land for agriculture and grazing. This caused severe erosion and water quality problems, as streams and rivers clogged with sediments and the remains of dead trees. Decades later, after wolves and woodpeckers had lost their homes, and valuable deer and timber resources were waning, settlers began to worry about their own futures, and started to pay attention to long-term resource protection and sustainable forest management.

Non-Timber Forest Resources

Southern settlers were entrepreneurs, taking seemingly simple and useless plants and turning them into industries. Such was the case with the Spanish moss that hung from cypress trees in coastal swamps. Colonists collected clumps, up to a ton a year, dried them, and then marketed the moss as stuffing for mattresses and furniture. Other endeavors were not as creative, and were generally demanded by the motherland. During the 1800s, turpentine, pitch, and rosin, extracted from pine trees, were a significant part of the southern economy, particularly in North Carolina. These sticky products were requested by the navy and other shipping crews, but amateur harvesting techniques could and did kill hundreds of pines. On the eve of the Revolutionary War, the Carolinas were producing about 200,000 barrels of pitch, tar, and turpentine. Other non-timber forest ventures included hunting. Deerskins provided the economic base for trade before agriculture took over, and deer meat was an important source of protein. In the mid-1700s, Louisiana alone exported an average of 50,000 deer skins each year.

Timber

Although not as popular as tobacco and rice, timber was a main export crop during the colonial period. Wood was also used extensively in the colonies to build cities and stoke steamships. Much of the wood needed for these activities was harvested near the riverbanks on the Piedmont, as forests elsewhere were hard to access and the timber nearly impossible to transport. Large-scale commercial logging took a while to come to the South. As late as the mid-1800s, the timber industry was focused on the northern United States. The first sawmill in Virginia's Alleghenies wasn't established until 1776.

But things progressed quickly, and by the end of the eighteenth century the government began to notice that resources were thinning. To ensure that the navy would have shipbuilding material far into the future, the government set aside 250,000 acres of protected forest in Georgia, Alabama, Florida, and Louisiana. These became designated naval resources, but were hard to defend against trespassers. Pine, already overharvested in Europe, proved to be the best material for ship masts. Coastal cypress was valuable for naval vessels and homes in Louisiana because of its resistance to moisture. The commercial timber industry in the South, ironically, evolved from government policy designed to protect public lands and prevent flooding. For example, the Swamp Land Acts of 1849–1850 allowed Louisiana, Arkansas, Mississippi, and Alabama to reclaim any uncultivated land so that it could serve

Coastal cypress was valued as a building material because of its resistance to moisture. Courtesy Louisiana Office of Tourism.

as a buffer. Forested areas, considered ripe for cultivation, then ended up in the hands of private companies, often non-southern companies, instead of under government control. Despite local clearing for agricultural land and timber extraction for homes and fences, there was still more timber, especially pine, in the South in the mid-1800s than in most of the rest of the country. In Appalachia, logging peaked in the late 1800s under the unfortunate philosophy of "cut and get out."

In the tension between forests and humans, one battle stands out. The pine borer infestation during 1848–1849 killed thousands of trees, causing the industry to panic. To address new diseases, fire, and deforestation, the scientific study of forests, including sustainable and efficient harvesting and management, started at Yale University in the 1870s and reached North Carolina, one of the primary timber states in the South, by the 1880s. Under more academic guidance, forestry continued to grow in the South. By the end of the twentieth century, private timber companies, including big names such as Weyerhaeuser, owned nearly 130 million acres of southern forest and were producing pulpwood for two-thirds of the paper manufactured in the United States and a fourth of the nation's yearly lumber output.

Appalachian Gold

Before 1900 iron and coal were the most lucrative exports in the South. Iron ore, used in the production of iron and steel, could be found in nearly every southern state, and by 1860 most towns had blast furnaces and forges to convert ore into usable iron for tools and railways. Iron converted Birmingham, Alabama, from marshes and muddy roads to the southern U.S. iron capital. After the Civil War ended, population and economic growth created a demand for bituminous coal, one of several coal mineral resources historically used to generate steam electrical power. Because of geological activity millions of years ago, coal is abundant in the southern Appalachians, primarily in West Virginia and western Kentucky. Coal mining intensified even more in eastern Tennessee and Kentucky and western Virginia when advanced transportation networks were established after 1900. Production in the south rose from 7 million tons in 1880 to 52.8 million tons in 1900 (one-fifth of U.S. production), creating dozens of coal-mining towns along the way. Coal has not brought prosperity to the area; it remains one of the poorest in the country, and for generations coal miners have faced hazardous conditions just to put food on the table, while "coal barons" have claimed mineral rights and reap rewards from a distance.

The coal found in this region is low in sulfur and has been in high demand since the 1990 Clean Air Act required coal-fired power plants to lower their sulfur dioxide (SO_2) emissions. SO_2 is a cause of acid rain that has been responsible for the degradation of southern Appalachian forests. Today destructive strip-mining techniques threaten the temperate forests of eastern Kentucky, considered by some ecologists and the World Wildlife Fund to be the most biologically diverse on earth. Mountaintop removal/valley fill coal mining is a type of strip mining that is able to access thin seams of low-sulfur coal that are impossible to reach with traditional underground mining. The mountaintop mining process begins by clearing forests, then removing the top layers of the mountain with explosives in order to extract the coal. The waste, millions of tons of soil and rock, is dumped into the valleys. From the air, the remaining mountain slopes look like a Martian landscape, devoid of life.

During the first coal boom, petroleum was discovered. The first oil well in Kentucky was drilled accidentally in 1818 by a salt-making company probing for brine. The oil in Appalachia, extracted primarily from limestone and sandstone, was abundant, and companies began to ship wooden barrels full of it on barges down the Cumberland River. Since then more than 156,000 wells have perforated Kentucky rock in search of oil and natural gas. Oil was discovered first off the Gulf coast of Texas in 1894 and then off Louisiana in 1899, and offshore production began in 1947. Currently 18 percent of U.S. oil, worth nearly $6.3 billion annually, and 24 percent of U.S. natural gas, worth $10.3 billion a year, is produced off the coast of or transported through coastal Louisiana, drawing again upon ancient geologic activity, and threatening priceless marine habitat. The region has experienced oil spills, and some identify the expansive canal systems required by the industry as a cause of wetland disruption and loss.

Control of the Mississippi

West of the Appalachians, the Mississippi River controls life. With the third largest drainage basin in the world, behind the Amazon and Congo rivers, the Mississippi drains 41 percent of the continental United States and parts of two Canadian provinces. Water from thirty-one states flows into this powerful river, which starts in Minnesota and runs for more than 2,400 miles, uniting the North and the South—commercially and environmentally.

The river has been flooding for centuries, reaching levels of biblical proportions beyond the natural, and now man-made, levees once every 100 years. This was not a problem until humans settled on the banks, not knowing what they could expect from the river. Settlements were often well established before they experienced a flood. Once they did, Europeans, like the Natchez, built their homes on stilts. The next step was to construct artificial levees that raised the riverbank to protect increasingly large towns and farms. However, now being deprived of the option to deposit silt along its banks, the Mississippi River grew taller instead of wider. Higher levees needed to be constructed, and on and on went this cycle of construction and increased flood risks. Not only did the river get higher, the delta and the mouth of the Mississippi became artificially elongated as they received more than their normal share of sediment.

The first recorded flood of the Mississippi, witnessed by de Soto in 1543, was described as severe and prolonged, taking more than two months to run its full course. The devastating floods of 1849 and 1850 sparked a national interest in controlling the river. According to the U.S. Army Corps of Engineers, the Mississippi River Commission, established in 1879, embraced the mission to devise "a plan or plans and estimates as will correct, permanently locate, and deepen the channel and protect the banks of the Mississippi River, improve and give safety and ease to navigation thereof, prevent destructive floods, promote and facilitate commerce, trade, and the postal service."[1] Then in 1881 the U.S. Army Corps of Engineers assumed responsibility for engineering and maintenance of the river—a task the agency is still charged with. The next disastrous flood, in 1882, was a foreshadowing of what was to come in 1927. During a summer rainstorm that year, a levee burst on the Arkansas River, causing a chain of events that made their way down the Mississippi, breaching levees, inundating 16.6 million acres, and destroying buildings, crops, and commercial transportation, to the detriment of industry. Property damage amounted to about $1.5 billion at today's prices, and more than 200 lives were lost and 600,000 people displaced. River policy changed after that: the 1927 flood was the catalyst for the federal flood-control policy in place to this day—the Flood Control Act of 1928. The Flood Control Act authorized the nation's premier flood control and navigation program, called the Mississippi River and Tributaries Project.

The Army Corps now made efforts to redirect floodwater through artificial floodways into reservoirs such as Lake Pontchartrain near New Orleans. A complex system of levees and flood routes covering at least four major drainage basins and including five flood control reservoirs, complemented by channel stabilization and tributary basin improvement projects, is continually being improved upon and added to. Natural pools, referred to as backwater areas, and artificial floodways or channels cut through marshlands capture some of the river's overflow. Channel stabilization increases the "flood-carrying capacity" of the river and reinforces the levee systems. Dams, pumping stations, and reservoirs are expensive "basin improvements" that channel water through a highly engineered course, directing it into safe areas, while still maintaining important transportation routes along the river. The current main levee and floodwall system is 2,203 miles long, with 1,607 miles along the Mississippi and the rest along the southern banks of the Arkansas and Red rivers and in the Atchafalaya basin. The river channel has essentially undergone surgery: cutoffs shorten the river; revetments control the river's natural meandering tendencies; dikes direct the river flow; and dredging helps to realign the channel when it starts to slip out of the hands of the Corps.

If the Mississippi were not controlled this way, it would run into Atchafalaya Bay to the west, leaving New Orleans void of industrial transport options. If the river had been allowed to take its natural course from the beginning, New Orleans would be a saltwater estuary today. The Atchafalaya River still diverts 30 percent of the Mississippi's flow through a salt marsh channel to the Atchafalaya Bay. The current highly engineered system of levees, canals, and reservoirs, designed by the U.S. Army Corps of Engineers, is built to withstand a flood of greater magnitude than the devastating flood of 1927, but despite elaborate control efforts, some people feel that nature will eventually revolt, and that a deadly flood is imminent.

It has always been a risky river; it is likely Mark Twain named his famous character Tom Sawyer after the dangerous trees that would "saw" surface waters, bobbing up and down spelling danger for ship captains and steam engines. One of the primary reasons the Mississippi is so highly controlled, besides protecting New Orleans from sinking, is its enduring economic importance for industry and transportation, which blossomed after the introduction of the steamboat. Before highway systems created cement transportation networks across the continent, rivers were the primary means of transporting goods and supporting trade and commercial and industrial development. For this reason, the Mississippi has been the backbone of much of the nation's economic growth. The first cargo shipment, 15,000 bear and deer hides from Indiana and Ohio, was sent downstream on its way to France in 1705. Today millions of tons of cargo move down the Mississippi each year, but because of flood tendencies, the river is as much an asset as it is a potential liability.

CURRENT ENVIRONMENTAL CHALLENGES AND CONSERVATION STRATEGIES IN THE SOUTH

Since it was first inhabited, the natural landscape of the South has been exploited and manipulated to meet human needs, but when lives, lifestyles, and livelihoods are threatened—from the dramatic loss of farmland and the near-extinction of the Florida panther to the increased pollution of water and air—southerners respond, often from the grassroots level, with concern. Recently, the endangered ecosystems and the large industry interests associated with these areas have received national attention, particularly threats to the Everglades from sugar, other agriculture, and development in general; threats to coastal Louisiana from offshore oil exploration and the reengineering of the Mississippi River; and threats to the Appalachian Mountains from mountaintop mining.

These environmental crises aside, two of the biggest overarching environmental challenges facing the South in the twenty-first century are climate change and population growth. Both of these will affect ecosystem health, agricultural production, and quality of life in the South, requiring adaptations to accommodate rising sea levels, changing growing seasons, access to freshwater resources, and the increased demands for food, housing, and transportation infrastructure that accompany a growing southern population.

Greenhill oil spill. Oiled marsh plants, salicornia, mangroves, and *Spartina alterniflora*. East Timbalier Island, Lafourche Parish, Louisiana, September 1992. Courtesy NOAA Restoration Center.

The United Nations Intergovernmental Panel on Climate Change (IPCC) predicts up to a three-foot rise in sea levels over the next 200 years due to increased concentrations of carbon dioxide and other greenhouse gases in the atmosphere that will warm global temperatures and melt polar ice caps once again. Atlantic and Gulf coast wetlands, agriculture in the Southeast, and estuarine beaches in developed areas will be among the areas in the United States most sensitive to climate change. As the South gets even warmer and wetter, other consequences of climate change include increased risk of forest diseases, increased rainfall and flooding, lower water levels on the Mississippi River and the subsequent disruption in river transportation, a possible increase in severe storm events, and species migration northward in both terrestrial and aquatic habitats. (A 39 degree Fahrenheit increase in southern Appalachian temperatures is expected to eliminate more than 50 percent of brook trout habitat.) Climate change will have some positive effects as well: a doubling of CO_2 inputs may actually increase crop yields of cotton, soybeans, and wheat by 30 percent. Much discussion about climate change has to do with the economic and social costs of adapting to environmental changes. It is almost impossible to predict how climate change will play out on a local scale and how the South will respond.

The concerns revolving around climate change and a landscape in flux are exacerbated in the face of population growth. The last U.S. Census, in 2000, indicated that the South is the second fastest growing region after the West, ballooning by 17 percent, or 14.8 million people, from 1990 to 2000. Georgia and Florida experienced the most intense increases.

A Return to the Coasts

According to research done by the Pew Oceans Commission, coastal cities are experiencing the greatest population increases. This nonprofit policy institute estimates that an additional 27 million people will populate the coasts between 2005 and 2020. Already more than half of the country's population lives near the ocean. This trend is in direct conflict with rising sea levels and increased coastal storms and erosion. Plus, coastal development increases pollution from garbage, fertilizers, oil, gas, and other toxic substances that run off impervious surfaces, such as roads and parking lots, into coastal estuaries and fisheries. The Pew Commission and other planning organizations, including state government agencies, have developed guidelines for urban development that minimize impervious surfaces and encourage mixed-use construction that incorporates stores, offices, and homes in small clusters so that commuting and automobile use are reduced. Nitrogen, from fertilizers and nitrous oxide emissions from cars, is already impairing the functions of coastal estuaries.

Sea Level Rise and Coastal Erosion

As more people move to coastal cities or buy beachfront vacation homes, coastal erosion and storms become a larger problem, capable of destroying millions of dollars worth of property. Erosion is a natural geologic process in many of these areas, but often homes have not been designed to adapt to the rate of change along the coast, including rising sea levels and an increase in severe storm events.

Because sea level rise and fall has been ongoing for thousands of years, the effects of climate change on coastal systems are understood better than they are for many other ecosystems. The IPCC warns that over the next 100 years, seawater could inundate approximately 50 percent of North American coastal wetlands—a predicted twenty-inch rise in sea levels equates to a 17 to 43 percent loss of U.S. coastal wetlands, as well as beaches, which can not migrate inland as they normally would in order to survive because of artificial structures such as seawalls. With this in mind, several states have issued regulations that prohibit construction of such structures and other developments too close to the shore. Another alarming consequence of sea level rise is saltwater intrusion. Ocean waters may contaminate freshwater drinking and irrigation supplies as they move inland and upstream.

Many scientists believe that climate change has an effect on the formation, intensity, and lifespan of tropical storms. Climate change is associated with rising ocean surface temperatures (the same phenomenon that causes coral reef bleaching) and a likely increase in the overall atmospheric energy flux over the Caribbean and Atlantic. Relatively new computer models of climate change and storm intensity have indicated that a 36 degree Fahrenheit change in surface temperatures increases wind speed by 3 to 10 percent and can result in a 20 to 30 percent increase in hurricane-level rain, which leads to more flooding in an area already plagued with some of the country's worst weather.

According to research done by the National Oceanic and Atmospheric Association (NOAA), hurricane events generally begin with an area of low atmospheric pressure near the Caribbean islands, called a "tropical disturbance." During late summer and early fall ocean water heats up, causing thunderstorms and adding to the pre-hurricane energy. Thunderstorms become tropical storms and acquire

A view of the Pinewoods Villa area of Miami in the aftermath of Hurricane Andrew. Courtesy NOAA, Historic NWS Collection.

names from the National Hurricane Center (from a list that is recycled every six years) when wind speeds reach up to 40 miles per hour. If the tropical storm speeds up to 74 miles per hour, and many do not, it becomes a hurricane, fueled by the accumulation of warm, humid air from above the ocean and the upward release of cool, dry air, a by-product of the condensation of water vapor. NOAA states that the amount of heat energy released by an average hurricane is equivalent to the amount of electric energy produced by the United States in an entire year. Hurricanes are rated by the National Weather Service on the Saffir-Simpson scale based on wind speed and their potential to cause damage. There are five ratings. Category Five has sustained winds of 155 miles per hour or more.

These often deadly storms can be up to 300 miles wide, travel at a rate of 15–20 miles per hour or faster, and take unpredictable paths. They usually fizzle out as they glide over cooler water or dry areas. During an El Niño period, when Pacific Ocean temperatures are warmer than usual, there seem to be fewer hurricanes coming out of the tropical Atlantic. La Niña periods bring opposite conditions, as decreased wind resistance in the tropical southern Atlantic allows hurricanes to grow unchecked. After devastating events, such as Hurricane Andrew in 1992, which swept over southern Florida and south-central Louisiana, causing $25 billion in damage, massive evacuations, and the loss of more than 60 lives and 125,000 homes, state and federal agencies are now prepared for serious storm events and evacuation plans are in place in most threatened areas.

People in these regions live with the constant threat of hurricanes. Prediction technology has improved significantly, however, and areas can usually be evacuated before lives are lost. Andrew's path and intensity were fairly well known before the hurricane arrived, but it arrived faster than expected. The U.S. Geological Survey started its severe storm project in 1996 to "assess coastal erosion from severe storms by acquiring pre- and post-storm aerial data" from research stations located in the Caribbean and along the Gulf coast.[2] Aerial photos using advanced radar technology, including the National Aeronautics and Space Administration's (NASA) Airborne Topographic Mapper, are now being used to analyze hurricane and severe storm formation and travel.

Barrier islands can help dampen the effects of severe storm events. Because of this, there are several large-scale barrier island restoration projects along the Atlantic and Gulf coasts that focus on planting native grasses in an attempt to minimize erosion of these exposed sandbars.

As more people move to coastal cities, and shorelines are fortified with resorts and expensive homes, the economic consequences of coastal erosion and severe storms have rapidly increased. Many researchers and planners feel that property owners who develop land in hazardous areas, and then use tax dollars during emergency planning and disaster recovery, should pay more, or be denied flood and storm insurance.

Coastal dwellers are going to great extremes to battle erosion, including building seawalls and jetties, and importing sand, called beach nourishment. Scientists at Sea Grant, a research institution for coastal issues, are skeptical of such engineering solutions and recommend simply planning for erosion and building farther inland.

Wetland Loss

As described above, sea level rise will cause severe coastal wetland loss, particularly in Louisiana and southern Florida. Louisiana is already losing 16,000 to 22,000 acres of wetlands a year because sediment levels in coastal marshes can't keep up with sea level rise. This is a function of altered delta and floodplain environments, 1928 flood control legislation, and oil infrastructure: the highly engineered Mississippi River channel now diverts sediments away from marshes that need them. Land in much of coastal Louisiana is sinking up to two feet every 100 years. The loss of coastal wetlands in the area would mean the loss of nearly 30,000 oil wells, 3,000 miles of transportation channels, fifteen of the nation's largest ports, a $3.5 billion commercial and recreational fishing industry, added hurricane protection, and wildlife and waterfowl habitat. In an attempt to prevent these losses, the Louisiana Coastal Wetlands Planning, Protection and Restoration Act, passed by Congress in 1990, allocated $50 million a year for restoration projects, which may include river diversions, barrier shoreline restoration, and smaller-scale projects.

Sea levels around Florida are rising up to ten times faster than the average rate for that area over the past 3,000 years, and are likely to rise by twenty inches in the next 100 years. Many of the same consequences are likely. Plus, the freshwater Everglades, currently separated from the sea by mangroves, may be subject to saltwater intrusion and a change in species composition to more saltwater-tolerant plants if the mangroves can't keep up with sea level rise. A Comprehensive Everglades Restoration Plan focuses on data collection, land acquisition, and outreach to prevent ecosystem destruction. The part of the Everglades designated as a na-

ACE Basin National Estuarine Research Reserve. Interior wetlands on ACE Basin island, 45 miles south of Charleston, South Carolina. Courtesy NOAA National Estuarine Research Reserve Collection.

A great blue heron wading along the mangrove shoreline in the Florida Everglades. Photo by Alison G. Delaplaine. Courtesy NOAA.

tional park has the best chance of survival, but is also affected by the health of the surrounding marshes and upstream uses, such as the water diversions and chemical processing needed for sugar production. Protection of wading birds from commercial exploitation and encroachments was the prime reason for setting the park aside in 1947. Now manatees and the Florida panther are at risk. The USGS, National Parks Service, and several local non-profit conservation organizations have undertaken restoration efforts on their behalf. Part of the Everglades is also a National Estuarine Research Reserve System, referred to as a living laboratory where scientists can investigate coastal habitat changes.

Freshwater Resources

While the southern region we look at in this book escaped glaciation, it was still inundated with water as glaciers melted and sea levels rose. The southern United States is a land carved by streams and rivers—Kentucky alone has 90,000 miles of streams—and one of the wettest areas in the country, with southern Florida, the Gulf coast, and the Appalachian Mountains in northern Georgian and southern Tennessee blessed with more precipitation than anywhere else in the United States except the Pacific Northwest and northern California. But these freshwater resources are often taken for granted and subjected to pollution from industry and agriculture.

Water Pollution

Agriculture and animal husbandry pose some of the greatest threats to water quality. To combat the boll weevil, southern agricultural agencies decided twenty-five years ago to embark on a comprehensive eradication programs to prevent the insect from causing any more damage. While this was great news for farmers and advocates of an agricultural economy, it has also encouraged the heavy use of pesticides. Cotton is one of the most chemical-intensive crops, and nonorganic or traditional cultivation methods threaten local water quality as pesticides are washed off by rain or irrigation and drain into lakes, rivers, estuaries, and the public drinking water supply. It is estimated that up to 10 percent of all agricultural chemicals used in the United States are applied to cotton, which is grown today on less than 1 percent of land in this country. Pesticide use has been reduced somewhat with the introduction of genetically modified species that are resistant to the boll weevil and other harmful insects. However, genetically modified organisms (GMOs) have come under fire by environmental advocates who say they have not been studied thoroughly enough and may threaten ecological diversity and human health.

Other agricultural pollutants, particularly nitrogen from farms and lawns upstream as far north as Minnesota, have caused severe problems in the Gulf. These nutrients encourage overzealous algal blooms, a phenomenon called eutrophication. Dead algae sinks to the bottom, and significant oxygen resources are required to decompose it, starving other species of oxygen. This condition, referred to as hypoxia, has created a "dead zone" off the coast of Louisiana at the foot of the Mississippi that spans nearly 4.5 million acres in the middle of one of the most important fisheries in the United States. Research and outreach are under way to uncover solutions and discourage excessive fertilizer use.

An issue of recent concern and the subject of public education campaigns by national environmental organizations such as Environmental Defense is industrial hog farming in North Carolina and its crippling effects on water quality. The hog population in the state, concentrated on the ecologically sensitive coastal plain, has grown from 2.6 million to 10 million in less than twenty years. Hog rearing in North Carolina produces 19 million tons of feces and urine a year. According to Environmental Defense, that's more waste in one year than the entire human population of Charlotte, North Carolina, would produce in fifty-eight years. More effective waste management strategies and legislation are in the works. Other pollutants include other non–point source pollutants, such as oil and gas, heavy metals—which often bioaccummulate in commercially harvested marine species, such as shellfish, and are eaten by humans—sediments and silt from deforestation, and the waste from strip and mountaintop mining, which is being fought against in courts for the damage it costs to land and water resources.

Flooding, Dams, Dredging, and Draining

"Whenever you try to control nature, you've got one strike against you," said legendary environmental writer John McPhee in his book about the Mississippi River, *The Control of Nature*. But policymakers have not taken heed. From the Everglades to the Mississippi, water engineering is changing the course of nature and setting humans up for possible failure. American Rivers, a nonprofit advocacy group, named the Big Sunflower River in Mississippi the nation's Most Endangered River in 2003. The U.S. Army Corps of Engineers will drain 200,000 acres of wetlands and dredge the river bottom in an attempt to improve agricultural conditions. A $181 million pump system, called the Yazoo Pumps, was approved by Congress in 2002. Dredging, which would accelerate drainage, would also ruin mussel beds and other river habitat, potentially increase flooding downstream, and expose buried toxins, pesticides, and heavy metals that have been stored in the sediment and immobile for decades.

Perhaps the most dramatic example of how delicate engineering solutions are is the sinking city of New Orleans, built on unconsolidated and unstable river delta sediments and swamplands, protected now only by controlling the Mississippi. However, increased flood risk may be on the way with climate change. Higher sea levels will provide a higher base for storm surges and increase the floodplains of many coastal rivers. Sea-level rises of twelve to thirty-five inches would increase the size of the 100-year floodplain on the Mississippi from approximately 12.5 million acres to 17.2 million acres. Increased development and population growth exacerbate the problem, and property damage is expected to increase by up to 58 percent.

Land Resources

As populations explode, the South must address land use issues. While the colonial period was not an era of great conservation efforts, it was a start. Land preservation for recreation and parks has always been important in the South. In 1899 the Appalachian National Park Association was established to protect the scenery in Asheville, North Carolina. Subsequently, the parks movement adopted thousands of acres, but could not prevent the loss of farmland or the exploitation of private land.

Loss of Farmland

The American Farmland Trust serves as a voice for farmers who are concerned about the loss of cropland due to encroaching urban settlements. It identifies the Everglades region and Nashville basin in Tennessee as the most threatened agricultural areas, and advocates for improved urban planning and local, state, and federal legislation, such as the federal Farmland Protection Policy Act. It also promotes revised tax structures to keep agricultural lands in the hands of families instead of corporations.

In an effort to minimize erosion and protect valuable soil nutrients, most states have soil conservation commissions or districts that recommend sustainable farming and soil management strategies and provide technical assistance to local farmers. The Soil and Water Conservation District in Jackson County Mississippi, for example, states its goals as follows: "control and prevention of soil erosion, improve water quality, flood control, prevent impairment of dams and reservoirs, preserve wildlife, protect public lands and wetlands, develop private lands and waters for recreational purposes, promote economic welfare, and provide leadership in the promotion of the conservation of land, water and related resources."

Disappearing Forests

The U.S. Department of Agriculture is now heavily involved in monitoring and protecting southern forests. A recent study by this agency in cooperation with the U.S. Environmental Protection Agency, the Tennessee Valley Authority, and the U.S. Fish and Wildlife Service determined that southern forests are once again sustainable, meaning that if managed properly into the future they will remain diverse and productive and continue to provide economic benefits. The chief threats to this sustainability are sprawl and increased urbanization, which are eating up land at an alarming rate. Before 2020 nearly 6 percent of the forests on the Piedmont Plateau and the coastal plain could be lost, and habitat severely fragmented, often isolating animals in inadequate areas or forcing them to cross busy roads or developments.

Almost 90 percent of forested land in the South belongs to private landowners, a result of earlier policy, and therefore conservation efforts are aimed at educating nearly the region's 5 million landowners.

Urbanization, Industry, Smart Growth, and Environmental Justice

The 2000 U.S. Census showed Georgia to be the fastest growing state. Its population was up 26.4 percent from the 1990 Census, with much of that increase centered in the suburbs of Atlanta, often cited as the best example of unsustainable and unpleasant urban sprawl in the country. On the other hand, Chattanooga, Tennessee, is often called one of the greenest cities in the country and is often recognized for its efficient and environmentally friendly electric-hybrid public transportation systems, parks and trail network, and air and water quality improvements.

Air pollution is a serious problem in the South and the child of population growth, industrial and government irresponsibility, and poor urban planning. The National Parks Conservation Association (NPCA), a nonprofit watchdog organization, has listed Shenandoah and the Great Smokies National Park as two of the country's most endangered national parks due to their air pollution problems. (Everglades and Biscayne Bay also made the list for other reasons.) Unregulated power plant pollution and increased vehicular traffic have created an unhealthy haze above the Appalachians. According to NPCA, from 1991 to 2001 ozone exposure at levels harmful to vegetation was higher at Shenandoah than in Washington, D.C., Atlanta, and other cities. The park is also plagued by acid rain, mercury deposition, and an invasive insect called the woolly adelgid that snacks on Shenandoah's eastern hemlock forests.

Lastly, environmental racism is prevalent in the South. In his book *Dumping in Dixie*, Robert Bullard makes the connection between the disposal of toxic waste and communities of color. An example that is often cited is Convent, Louisiana, where industry dominates in a small area and residents, primarily of color, suffer from the cumulative effects of emissions. Some parts of the South, particularly Mississippi, Alabama, Georgia, Arkansas, South Carolina, and eastern Kentucky, are the poorest in the country, with 25 percent or more of the population below the poverty line. It is often in these areas, such as the destitute coal-mining towns of the southern Appalachians, that grassroots public health and social justice campaigns adopt environmental values.

CONCLUSION

Native Americans established the paths that connect present-day urban centers such as Montgomery, Alabama, and Chattanooga, Tennessee. Today southerners are struggling to reconnect with nature before climate change and population growth destroy their chances of an economically stable and healthy future. The story of Chattanooga, Tennessee, is a perfect example of what is possible. Before turning "green," Chattanooga was so polluted that residents who spent time outdoors would return to work or home with soot covering their clothing. Urban rivers and creeks were highly polluted. Now a celebrated trail system along the Chattanooga River not only brings people together, but also reconnects them with the natural world. According to City Councilman David Crockett, a distant relative of the famous adventurer Davy Crockett, it has helped to create awareness of the importance of water quality and environmental preservation. Chattanooga's green development slogan—"It takes us all; it takes forever"—can be extended to hog farmers in North Carolina, foresters in Virginia, coal executives in Kentucky, environmentalists in the Everglades, river engineers in Mississippi, and factory workers in Louisiana. These are the people who hold the key to the South's environmental future.

RESOURCE GUIDE

Printed Sources

Barry, John M. *Rising Tide: The Great Mississippi Flood of 1927 and How It Changed America*. New York: Simon and Schuster, 1997.

Boles, John B., ed. *A Companion to the American South*. Malden, MA: Blackwell, 2002.

Bottcher, A. B., and F. T. Izuno, eds. *Everglades Agricultural Area (EAA): Water, Soil, Crop, and Environmental Management*. Gainesville: University Press of Florida, 1994.

Bullard, Robert D. *Dumping in Dixie: Race, Class, and Environmental Quality*. 3rd ed. Boulder, CO: Westview Press, 2000.

Clark, Thomas D. *The Greening of the South: The Recovery of Land and Forest*. Lexington: University Press of Kentucky, 1984.

Colten, Craig E., ed. *Transforming New Orleans and Its Environs: Centuries of Change*. Pittsburgh: University of Pittsburgh Press, 2000.

Cook, Samuel R. *Monacans and Miners: Native American and Coal Mining Communities in Appalachia*. Lincoln: University of Nebraska Press, 2000.

Cooper, William J., Jr., and Thomas E. Terrill. *The American South: A History*. 2nd ed. New York: McGraw-Hill, 1996.

Cowdrey, Albert E. *This Land, This South: An Environmental History*. Lexington: University Press of Kentucky, 1983.

Dao, James. "Rule Change May Alter Strip-Mine Fight." *New York Times*, January 26, 2004.

Davis, Donald Edward. *Where There Are Mountains: An Environmental History of the Southern Appalachians*. Athens: University of Georgia Press, 2000.

Fisher, Stephen L., ed. *Fighting Back in Appalachia: Traditions of Resistance and Change*. Philadelphia: Temple University Press, 1993.

Hopkins, Bruce. *The Smithsonian Guides to Natural America: Parks, Wilderness Preserves, Nature Sanctuaries, and Scenic Wonders: Central Appalachia: West Virginia, Kentucky, Tennessee*. Washington, DC: Smithsonian Books, 1996.

Howell, Benita J., ed. *Culture, Environment, and Conservation in the Appalachian South*. Urbana: University of Illinois Press, 2002.

McPhee, John. *The Control of Nature*. New York: Noonday Press; Farrar, Straus and Giroux, 1989.

Myers, Ronald L., and John J. Ewel, eds. *Ecosystems of Florida*. Orlando: University of Central Florida Press, 1990.

National Research Council: Committee on Coastal Erosion Zone Management, Water Science and Technology Board, Marine Board, Commission on Engineering and Technology Systems. *Managing Coastal Erosion*. Washington, DC: National Academies Press, 1990.

Otto, John Solomon. *The Final Frontiers, 1880–1930: Settling the Southern Bottomlands*. Westport, CT: Greenwood Press, 1999.

————. *Southern Agriculture During the Civil War Era, 1860–1880*. Westport, CT: Greenwood Press, 1994.

Redfern, Ron. *The Making of a Continent*. New York: Times Books, 1983.

Robson, George L., Jr., and Roy V. Scott, eds. *Southern Agriculture since the Civil War: A Symposium*. Santa Barbara: McNally and Loftin, West and Washington (The Agricultural History Society), 1979.

Ross, John. *The Smithsonian Guides to Natural America: Parks, Wilderness Preserves, Nature Sanctuaries, and Scenic Wonders: The Atlantic Coast and Blue Ridge: Maryland, District of Columbia, Delaware, Virginia, North Carolina*. Washington, DC: Smithsonian Books, 1995.

Strutin, Michele and Harry Middleton. *The Smithsonian Guides to Natural America: Parks, Wilderness Preserves, Nature Sanctuaries, and Scenic Wonders: The Southeast: South Carolina, Georgia, Alabama, Florida*. Washington, DC: Smithsonian Books, 1997.

White, Mel. *The Smithsonian Guides to Natural America: Parks, Wilderness Preserves, Nature Sanctuaries, and Scenic Wonders: The South-Central States: Texas, Oklahoma, Arkansas, Louisiana, Mississippi*. Washington, DC: Smithsonian Books, 1996.

Yarnell, Susan L. *The Southern Appalachians: A History of the Landscape*. Asheville, NC: U.S. Dept. of Agriculture, Forest Service, Southern Research Station, 1998.

Web Sites

Alabama Department of Conservation and Natural Resources
www.dcnr.state.al.us/

Alabama Department of Environmental Management
www.adem.state.al.us/

American Farmland Trust. Farming on the Edge.
www.aftresearch.org/researchresource/foe2/report/foe_exec.html

American Rivers. America's Most Endangered Rivers.
http://www.amrivers.org/index.php?module=HyperContent&func=displayview&shortname=endangered

Arkansas Department of Enrivonmental Quality
www.adeq.state.ar.us/

Bailey, Robert G. Ecoregions of the United States. U.S. Forest Service, USDA, March 1995.
www.fs.fed.us/land/ecosysmgmt/ecoreg1_home.html.

Beach, Dana. Coastal Sprawl: The Effects of Urban Design on Aquatic Ecosystems in the United States. Prepared for the Pew Oceans Commission.
www.pewoceans.org/oceanfacts/2002/04/12/fact_25649.asp

Biscayne Bay National Park
www.nps.gov/bisc/index.htm

Everglades National Park
www.nps.gov/ever/index.htm

Florida Department of Environmental Protection
www.dep.state.fl.us/

Georgia Department of Natural Resources
www.gadnr.org

Great Smoky Mountains National Park
www.nps.gov/grsm/index.htm

Kentucky Department for Environmental Protection
www.dep.ky.gov/default.htm

Kentucky Department for Natural Resources
www.naturalresources.ky.gov/default.htm

LACoast
www.lacoast.gov

Louisiana Department of Environmental Quality
www.deq.state.la.us/

Mississippi Department of Environmental Quality
www.deq.state.ms.us/MDEQ.nsf/page/main_home?opendocument

National Oceanic and Atmospheric Administration's National Weather Service Tropical Prediction Center and National Hurricane Center
www.nhc.noaa.gov

National Parks Conservation Association. *Ten Most Endangered National Parks Across the
Nation.*
www.npca.org/across_the_nation/ten_most_endangered/shenandoah.asp

North Carolina Department of Environment, Health and Natural Resources
www.enr.state.nc.us/

Shenandoah National Park
www.nps.gov/shen/index.htm

Sierra Club. *Ecoregions.*
www.sierraclub.org/ecoregions/

South Carolina Department of Natural Resources
http://water.dnr.state.sc.us/

Tennessee Department of Environment and Conservation
www.state.tn.us/environment

United Nations Intergovernmental Panel on Climate Change. *The Regional Impacts of
Climate Change.* Chapter 8: North America.
www.grida.no/climate/ipcc/regional/173.htm

United States Army Corps of Engineers, New Orleans District. *The Mississippi River
and Tributaries Project.*
www.mvn.usace.army.mil/pao/bro/misstrib.htm

United States Forest Service's Southern Research Station. *Southern Forest Resource Assessment.*
www.srs.fs.usda.gov/sustain

Virginia Department of Conservation & Recreation
www.dcr.state.va.us/index.htm

Virginia Department of Environmental Quality
www.deq.state.va.us/

Virginia Department of Forestry
www.vdof.org/index.html

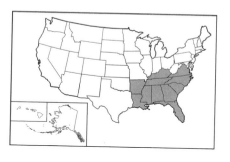

ETHNICITY

Celeste Ray

As a region, the American South is not a cultural monolith, but a complex creole of multiple traditions. Creolization simply means a blending of cultures after long exposure, coexistence, and interaction of two or more social groups. Southern folklore, foodways, and material culture are a synthesis of African, European, and Native American cultures. What we think of as typically southern often reveals the hybridity of cultural patterning. Bluegrass music, for example, is really a mix of Celtic fiddle and African banjo. Howlin' Wolf (Chester Burnett), of the Mississippi Delta Blues tradition, earned his name by imitating the "blue yodels" of the father of country music, Jimmie Rodgers (who had derived his new sound in the 1920s by combining black field hollers and Swiss yodeling).[1] All regions of America have diversity; it is the patterns of cultural blending that define the southern region as unique. The whole is greater than the sum of its parts. Through desegregation and dramatic changes in politics, economics, and the ways in which southerners interact with each other, cultural constants remain—certainly a feeling of cultural identity and distinctiveness remains.

What is southern in any given period continues to evolve, but since the 1700s there has always been the notion that the region is distinct. The South is a product of a unique quilting of union and disunion, inclusion and exclusion, prejudice and tolerance. In discussing southern culture as a creole we can talk about shared cultural traditions without necessarily implying that the contributing ethnic groups also shared egalitarian communities. The idea, especially popular since the 1960s, that the long and intimate coexistence of African Americans and European Americans in the South can enable the region to have the most harmonious "race relations" in the nation is what Charles Reagan Wilson calls "the Myth of the Biracial South."[2] Martin Luther King Jr.'s "Dream" drew on the redemptive power of such an idea for evangelical southerners. Elvis Presley's provocative appeal was in his blend of blues with black and white gospel sounds. The popular media has touted Bill Clinton as "America's first black president." In many southern towns Martin

Luther King Day and Robert E. Lee's birthday are celebrated together, which Wilson says is "surely a ritual triumph of the myth of the biracial South."[3] Whether or not southerners who celebrate one birthday would celebrate the other, such combinations acknowledge the need/desire for both accommodation and distinctiveness. According to historian Charles Joyner, "every white southerner has an African heritage as well as a British one, and every black southerner has a European heritage as well as an African one."[4] Many southern scholars prefer to say "black and white southerners" rather than "southern blacks and whites" to emphasize what the two groups share through regional culture. Ralph Ellison remarked that "you can't be Southern without being black and you can't be a black Southerner without being white," but as historian James Cobb notes, "Such sentiments are heartfelt and appealing, but they also [are] more wishful than specific."[5]

THE SOUTHERN REGION AND ETHNIC GROUPS

For the purposes of this volume we include the following twelve states as "southern": Alabama, Arkansas, Florida, Georgia, Kentucky, Louisiana, Mississippi, North Carolina, South Carolina, Tennessee, Texas, and Virginia, recognizing the ambivalence of Texans in defining themselves as part of the South or as part of the Southwest, and recognizing that residents in parts of Oklahoma also define themselves as southerners. In Florida, the northern portion of the state is culturally "southern," while the southernmost portion is often considered "northern" due to northern "emigration." We also note a number of enduring subregions within the South, including the Sun Belt, the Carolina Piedmont, the Kentucky Bluegrass Country, the Mississippi Delta, the Ozarks, the Deep South (Alabama, Georgia, Louisiana, Mississippi, and South Carolina), the Uplands of southern Appalachia (making a distinction between the Cumberland Plateau and the Blue Ridge), Wiregrass Country (from southeastern Alabama and the panhandle of Florida across the southwestern coastal plain of Georgia to the east coast of Savannah), and the flatlands of the Black Belt (named for the rich soils across Mississippi, Alabama, Georgia, and South Carolina, the prime areas for cotton farming, though the "Cotton Belt" also extends into the Piedmont and the Delta).

Each subregion is home to multiple ethnic groups so that, as W. J. Cash observed in 1941, "there are many Souths and many cultural traditions among them."[6] The blending of these cultures over time has forged *the* South and a southern identity that is ethnic within the United States.

After the devastation of the Civil War, the South did not experience the dramatic influx of immigrants that arrived in industrial urban areas of the Northeast and both the urban areas and vast farmlands of the Midwest in the late nineteenth and early twentieth centuries. Despite the active efforts of southern state governments to recruit European immigrants to replace ex-slaves, only Arkansas and Louisiana received a significant number of Italians to work the sugar cane and strawberry fields, and Chinese workers came only to the cotton fields of Mississippi, Texas, and to some extent Louisiana. Some Swiss, Irish, and Czechs, for example, trickled into the South in the nineteenth century, but the largest numbers of new immigrants to arrive since the colonial period have come to the dynamic and economically sound South of the late twentieth and early twenty-first centuries. Because the South received fewer immigrants than the rest of the country after the

Civil War, creolized southern identities are some of the oldest American identities. On the 2000 Census, southern states had the highest numbers of persons reporting their ancestry as "United States" or "American," rather than any of the three groups most frequently self-reported for ancestral origins (German, Irish, or English, in that order). Along with California, the states of Florida, Georgia, North Carolina, and Texas were the only ones in the country in which more than 1 million people reported their ancestry as American. Perhaps because of the Texan border with Mexico, the influx of Mexican immigrants, and the accompanying emphasis on national identity, over 1,554,000 Texans claimed American ancestry alone on the 2000 Census (more than in any other state). That said, the South has an abundance of ethnic groups (new and old). On the 1990 Census, 47 percent of those self-identifying as "Scots-Irish" were from the South. Of the four states whose largest ancestry groups were Irish on the 2000 Census, two were in the South (Arkansas and Tennessee). Nationally, the highest percentages of African Americans were in the Deep South. In the 2000 Census, 26 percent of Alabama's population was African American; in Georgia the figure was 28.7 percent; in Louisiana, 32.5 percent; in South Carolina, 29.5 percent; and in Mississippi, 36 percent. The South has 69 percent of the nation's Cuban Americans, 91 percent of Acadian/Cajuns, 40 percent of Hondurans, and over 40 percent of Haitian immigrants and Haitian Americans.

That Americans could check more than one ethnic identity in the 2000 Census made the news, but increasingly Americans are identifying themselves not only as ethnic, but as multiethnic. Scottish Americans not only celebrate Scottish roots, but may also claim to be German American, Italian American, African American, or Mexican-Scottish American. Southerners may also simultaneously feel southern *and* Chinese or southern *and* Italian and sometimes conflate the two. This is most obvious in expressive culture and at festivals, which are superb indicators of the evolution of ethnicities. Beverly Stoeltje notes that festivals enable the expression of group or community identity through "memorialization, the performance of highly valued skills and talents, or the articulation of the group's heritage." When those in attendance are primarily observers or consumers, festivals "relate more to commercial or political purposes of self-interested authorities or entrepreneurs" than to community social life.[7] Yet ethnic festivals in the South relate to indigenous and transnational developments, to religious and historical experience, and to community and familial ties.

The deeper south one travels, the more unusual the festivals become, making Virginia seem rather tame. The South has fewer "Old World" ethnic festivals (such as Octoberfest, or St. Joseph's Day celebrations) than elsewhere in the United States and more ethnic festivals related to identities forged through the creolization of the southern region. Celebrations that have become standard across the nation take on new foci in the South. The highlight of the Shamrock, Texas, St. Patrick's Day celebration is its beard-growing contest. The popularity of the St. Patrick's Day parade in Jackson, Mississippi (introduced only in 1982), is due to the "Sweet Potato Queens." Self-described "fallen belles," wearing flowing red wigs, majorette boots, and sequined green dresses overstuffed to emphasize particular parts of the anatomy, the Queens occupy the featured float in the parade and toss sweet potatoes rather than doubloons to the tens of thousands of spectators. In the South, even saints' days in the most Catholic state, Louisiana, layer on southern themes;

for example, the Festival of Lights in honor of St. Lucy (patroness of eyes) in St. Martinville features a barbecue dinner. Such syncretism of discrete cultural practices with those characteristic of the southern region continues with the arrival of new immigrants.

AMERICAN INDIANS

From the eighth century C.E. until European contact, Native Americans across the Southeast lived predominantly in pre-states and chiefdoms.[8] Chiefs generally had military, political, spiritual, and economic authority over several villages or towns, and entered into shifting alliances with other chiefs. Most of the major southeastern tribes are descendants of the Mississippian peoples who inhabited the area from Florida, Georgia, and Alabama into the Mississippi Valley. The groups we call collectively "Mississippian" were hunters and also practiced agriculture, growing mostly beans, corn, gourds, melons, and squash. They are especially known for constructing earthen mounds on which they built temples and residences for their chiefs. These flat-topped mounds served as political, social, economic, and religious centers, as at Etowah in Georgia and at Town Creek in North Carolina. Sometimes a group of mounds was enclosed with wooden palisades, as at Moundville, Alabama.

Members of the Powhatan tribes of Virginia eased the first English settlers' hardships at Jamestown, Virginia. They met over pork, corn, and roasted oysters, but in subsequent winters it was corn, or the lack thereof, over which they fought. First contact between the two peoples also brought typhoid and smallpox to Native Americans, decimating populations and social organization. Many Native Americans were enslaved during the seventeenth century. The new settlers' desire for land led to "Indian Wars" and the Removal Period, best remembered by the Cherokee Trail of Tears in 1838–1839, but also experienced by the Creek, Seminoles, Choctaw, Chickasaw, and the bulk of tribes whose national status the federal or state governments recognized at the time. Thomas Jefferson had advocated creating a buffer zone settled by eastern American Indians between the United States and lands occupied by European powers in the western continent early in the 1800s. In the first four decades of the nineteenth century, the Cherokees, Chickasaws, Choctaws, Creeks, and Seminoles signed treaties ceding lands to the United States. When Andrew Jackson became president (1829), he advocated an even more aggressive policy to relocate eastern Native Americans, and Congress passed the 1830 Indian Removal Act to force them west of the Mississippi River. Over 3,000 Alabama Creeks and 4,000 Cherokee died en route to "Indian Territory" or what would become Oklahoma. This land, set aside for Native Americans in 1834, was opened to white settlers in 1889. The (1887) Dawes Act reallocated the lands of the Five Civilized Tribes (the Cherokee, Choctaw, Chickasaw, Creek, and Seminole) to non-Indians under the pretense of attempting to "better assimilate" Native Americans and inviting them to become United States citizens. The survival of any "Indian Territory" outside U.S. government control ended when Oklahoma became the forty-sixth state in 1907.

Many southeastern tribes share cultural traditions and games such as stickball or the oldest game in the United States, chunkey, in which players throw greased, eight-foot-long sticks in an attempt to hit a smooth quartz (or granite) disk rolled along the ground. Stomp dances, religious dances performed on ceremonial grounds (or stomp grounds), are also common to southeastern tribes. A "fire-keeper" begins the Cherokee stomp dance by lighting a fire from the innermost part of an oak tree at dawn. The female counterpart to the lead male dancer-singer is the shell-shaker. The "first woman" leading the others into a dance shuffles her feet to create a beat with the box tortoise shells strapped to her lower legs (though tortoise shells are often replaced by other materials today). Many southeastern tribes had clan systems. Some, like the Chickasaw, have largely forgotten their clan systems. Most clan systems are exogamous and, among the Cherokee, endogamous marriage may still be frowned upon. Clans are matrilineal, so if one's mother is not a daughter of a woman from one of the seven clans, one does not have a clan. Many do not know what their clan is, but a cultural revival in the last decade (related to a general emphasis on identity in America's multicultural age) has inspired efforts among cultural nationalists to "return" to their clans.[9] Many Native American tribes have adopted the Plains-style powwows fostered by Pan-Indianism, yet fuse this tradition with their own southeastern songs, clothing, and tribe-specific dances and rituals.[10] The development and meaning of powwows in the claiming of identity relate to Native Americans' efforts to regain control of their own representations and the interpretation of their own heritage. As Elizabeth Bird notes, authenticity can be "less a matter of historic accuracy and more a matter of power."[11]

Patterns of cultural interactions in the South were much more obvious between Africans and Europeans than between either group and Native Americans. Part of the reason we find less cultural creolization with Native Americans, yet a cultural exchange that transformed both Europeans and Africans in the South, is of course due to slavery and simple demographics. By 1860 European and enslaved African population numbers were very close in several southern states (for example, Alabama's population was 54 percent "white" to 45 percent slave; Florida, 55 percent to 44 percent; Georgia 56 percent to 43 percent; Louisiana 50 percent to 46 percent), and in two states the percentage of the enslaved population was well above the figure for Europeans: Mississippi 44 percent to 55 percent; South Carolina 41 percent to 57 percent.[12] Yet the Native American population decreased in relation to the European and African population. Peter Wood tells us that in 1685, Native Americans constituted four of every five inhabitants in the region, but due to Old World diseases and warfare, by 1790 scarcely three persons among every one hundred were Native Americans.[13]

Tribes in the South Today

Today Native Americans constitute just under 1 percent of the U.S. population. Several of the largest Native American groups are in the South, including the Chickasaw, the Seminole, the Lumbee (not a federally recognized tribe), and the Cherokee. The Cherokee is the largest group in the South according to the U.S. Census, which includes Oklahoma in the South. In their original homeland, the Eastern Band of Cherokee Indians in North Carolina has 13,000 tribal citizens. The Cherokee lived in log homes, had many métis chiefs (of mixed European and Native American ancestry), and were one of the most assimilated tribes after 1800 (even fighting with Andrew Jackson in the Creek War of 1813–1814). In 1821 Sequoyah invented the Cherokee syllabary (in which each character represents a syllable), so rapidly enabling literacy that a Cherokee newspaper was published just seven years later. While the Eastern Band strictly requires one-sixteenth Cherokee ancestry for membership, one need only trace an ancestor listed as Cherokee on the Dawes rolls of the Five Civilized Tribes for membership, so that descendants of those removed to Indian Territory far outnumber the Eastern Cherokee. The Cherokee tribal government recognizes close to 260,000 citizens, with approximately 90,000 of these living within the jurisdictional boundaries of the Cherokee Nation of Oklahoma, and the United Keetoowah Band of Cherokee Indians, also in Oklahoma, has approximately 16,000 citizens. However, hundreds of thousands more consider themselves of Cherokee descent or acknowledge a Cherokee ancestor—usually too far removed to qualify for tribal membership.[14]

Southerners are more likely to claim Native American ancestry than Americans in other regions, and as sociologist John Shelton Reed has noted, the most common mythic claim is to have a "Cherokee princess" in the family tree. In the late 1990s, only 2 percent of southerners identified themselves as Indian, but 40 percent claimed some native ancestry—almost double the number (22 percent) who claimed descent from a Confederate soldier.[15]

Of the 562 federally recognized Native American nations in the United States, only 13 are in the South (not including Oklahoma). Of the over 230 non-federally recognized tribes, about 60 are in the South. Federal recognition of tribal status depends on a tribe demonstrating its existence as a distinct community since first contact with Europeans. In the case of combined tribes, descent from historic tribes must be demonstrated. For example, the Tunica and the Biloxi of Auoyelles Parish, Louisiana, merged with remnants of neighboring tribes—the Avoyel, Ofo, and Choctaw—over the centuries to form a new group with identifiable traditions, and gained recognition as the Tunica-Biloxi in 1981. Federal recognition is required to receive services from the Bureau of Indian Affairs; it connotes status to non-Indian neighbors and to other Native American nations, and gives a nation sovereignty. The only southern tribes to have recognition and government-to-government relations with the United States before 1970 were the Chitamachas, Coushattas, Alabama-Coushattas, Eastern Band of Cherokees, Mississippi Choctaws, Florida Seminoles, and the Miccosukees and the Catawbas.[16] Today this group also includes the Jena Band Choctaws of Louisiana, the Poarch Band of Creek Indians of Alabama, and the Kickapoo Traditional Tribe and Yselta Del Sur Pueblo—both of Texas.

Self-determination allows recognized Native American tribes to make and enforce their own laws, to collect their own taxes, and to be exempt from state taxes. The latter has allowed the growth of Florida Seminole "smoke shops," which sell tobacco goods without a state excise tax, and has led to the opening of casinos by the Chitimacha, Coushatta, and Tunica-Biloxi, all of Louisiana, the Mississippi Choctaws, and the Eastern Band of Cherokees, among others.[17]

Louisiana

Defining the South in historical rather than Census boundaries, the largest concentration of recognized Native American nations in the Southeast is in Louisiana. Only the Attakapas, Chitimacha, Houma, Tunica-Biloxi, and Caddo are documented in Louisiana from the European contact period, but other groups have arrived since. Numbering close to 3,000 at the beginning of the eighteenth century, the Caddo left Louisiana for the pine forests of northeast Texas, where the Kadohadache Caddo are probably the paramount chiefdom over a confederacy of close to a dozen tribes. Today's federally recognized tribes, collectively called Louisiana's Four Nations, include the Tunica-Biloxi (mentioned above), the Chitimacha, the Coushatta (Koasati), and the Jena Band Choctaw.[18]

Not subject to removals, the Chitimacha are thought to be descendants of Native Americans who lived in Louisiana 6,000 years ago. In the 1700s, they also lived on the northern Gulf coast of Florida and entered the historical record for prolonged war with the French, who enslaved them. Receiving federal recognition in 1919, the Chitimacha are particularly proud of their long connection to the land and their basket-making traditions. They number about 1,000 persons.

The Coushatta, or Koasati in their own Muskogean language, originally lived in the Tennessee River valley, especially Upper Alabama, and encountered de Soto there in 1540. In the eighteenth century, the Coushatta had affiliated with the Creek Confederacy and lived in what is now Alabama. Relocating many times to maintain their neutrality in the power shifts among Spanish, French, British, and American governments, the Coushatta now have three federally recognized tribes: that in Louisiana; the Alabama-Coushatta Tribe of Texas; and the Alabama-Quassarte Tribe of Oklahoma, which was a product of the removal period.[19] Temporarily losing federal recognition in 1953, the Coushatta Tribe of Louisiana regained sovereignty in 1973. As with so many tribes, the church and the Indian schools played an important role in maintaining identity and the primacy of the Koasati language. Each October, the Coushatta hold a tribal powwow in Kinder, Louisiana, and throughout the year tribal members travel to intertribal powwows across the nation. They opened a casino in 1995 and continue to expand their reservation holdings near the community of Elton.

Choctaw

Most numerous of Louisiana's four sovereign nations is the Choctaw. At the end of the nineteenth century, "Choctaw" was synonymous with "Indian" in the state. Among the Choctaw moving west to Indian Territory (what would later become Oklahoma) were five Choctaw families who stopped their travels to settle along Trout Creek in what became LaSalle Parish. Growing from these few families, the Jena Band Choctaw were first mentioned on the 1880 Census and interviewed by linguist Albert Gatschet in 1886. They worked in the timber industry, as domestics for the local European American community, or as sharecroppers. They maintained traditional tribal leadership, adopted a constitutional form of government in the 1970s, and in 1995 became the fourth federally recognized sovereign nation in Louisiana. As do many tribes, the Choctaw have a "princess contest," and the winner is seen as an ambassador for the tribe (as with the Cherokee and the Waccamaw-Sioux).

In 2000, a total of 87,349 people across the country claimed a Choctaw ethnicity alone (not in conjunction with any other identity). Most of these, of course, are part of the Choctaw Nation in Oklahoma, and there are other, unrecognized, Choctaws in the state, collectively giving Louisiana a Choctaw population of just under 2,000. Jena Band Choctaw number under 200. South Alabama is home to another contested group, the Mowa Choctaw. Having hidden their identity to avoid removal and Jim Crow legislation, the Mowa revived their community in the 1960s. In 2004 they held their twenty-fifth annual powwow.

Oklahoma is now home to over forty Native American nations, many of which were removed there from elsewhere. The few mentioned below had their roots in southern states. Originally claiming a territory from northern Alabama to Tennessee, Mississippi, and western Kentucky, the Chickasaw had customs similar to those of the Choctaw, Natchez, Cherokee, and Creek. The estimated 40,000 Chickasaw are quite assimilated into American culture, yet they do maintain expressive cultural traditions (dancing, music) and encourage the young to take classes in their Muskogean language, which is a dialect quite similar to that spoken by the Choctaws. Gradually losing their land through a series of treaties with federal officials, the Chickasaw signed the Treaty of Doaksville in 1837, through which the Chickasaw came to reside with the Choctaw in Oklahoma. In 1856 the Chickasaw established their first constitution, giving them geographic and legal separation from the hospitable Choctaws. Farmers and ranchers, Chickasaws owned slaves, and the nation joined the Confederacy in 1861. Losing sovereignty in 1906, the Chickasaw regained a native-elected governor in 1971 and ratified a second constitution in 1983. The seat of the tribal government is now Ada, Oklahoma.[20]

The eponymous homeland of the Natchez lies in Mississippi, where they first encountered Europeans in the late seventeenth century. Through the French their numbers were decimated by disease, enslavement, and war. By the middle of the eighteenth century the Natchez were mostly dispersed and had settled with tribes who were allies of the English (the Chickasaw, Creek, and Cherokee). The Natchez language was spoken into the twentieth century, and "Notchee" identity is still recognized, but those who embrace it today live among the Creek or Cherokee with whom they were removed to Oklahoma.

Shawnee

The name Shawnee means "person of the South." At the time of European contact, the Shawnee, who speak an Algonquian language, were settled across the Ohio River valley (mostly in Ohio and Kentucky), but by the eighteenth century they had also settled in what is now the Midwest and Alabama, Georgia, and South Carolina, where they participated in the fur trade. Many of these Shawnee moved to Arkansas, Texas, and Oklahoma during the nineteenth-century removal period. As with many other southeastern tribes, their ritual year related to a village economy based on hunting and corn-growing, the latter done by women. In the spring, Shawnee celebrated planting time with the bread dance, and the ripening of the crops with the green corn dance, followed by the autumn bread dance at harvest. Today many are Protestants or belong to the Native American Church in addition to maintaining indigenous religious rituals (originally related to a belief in a grandmotherly deity). The largest group are now in Oklahoma, known as "the Loyal Shawnee." After over 130 years of being part of the Cherokee Nation, the Loyal Shawnee received federal recognition in 2001.

Creek

A total of 40,223 people claimed a Creek identity on the 2000 Census. While the Muskogean (Creek) Nation now resides in Oklahoma, Muskogean-language speakers include a number of related southeastern tribes.[21] The Creek Nation ceded the last of its homelands to the United States by treaty in 1832. By the mid-twentieth century, those remaining in traditional homelands were anglicized Christians with very little of their native Muskogean language or customs surviving. Yet, in 1984, the Poarch Band of Creeks became the only Creek group east of the Mississippi to receive acknowledgment as a sovereign Native American tribe under federal law, and the only federally recognized tribe in Alabama.[22] Other Muskogean speakers include the Kusso-Natchez (also called Edisto—after their traditional territory near the Edisto River in South Carolina). The Kusso-Natchez (two distinct groups prior to the mid-1700s) now number under 800 members. Like most southeastern tribes they had a green corn ceremony; grew corn, beans, squash, sunflowers, and gourds; and lived in villages that usually had a council house for meetings.

The Yuchi are also part of the Creek Confederacy and now part of the Muscogee (Creek) Nation of Oklahoma despite not speaking a Muskogean language. They originally lived in Georgia (a few bands were in South Carolina), but were forcibly removed in the nineteenth century to Indian Territory. The Chattahoochee Indian Heritage Association in Eufaula, Alabama, and Columbus College in Columbus, Georgia, sponsor annual homecomings near old Yuchi village sites featuring stomp dances.

In the mid-eighteenth century, Creeks began settling in Florida on lands depopulated through the introduction of European diseases by successive waves of Spanish, French, and English invaders and through slave raids from the Carolina coasts. Eventually establishing their own identity and political autonomy from the Creek Confederacy, they became known as the Seminoles from the Spanish word *cimmarone* (runaway). Even before the United States gained the territory of Florida in 1821, it had begun one of three wars against the Seminoles. The Second Seminole War (1835–1842) resulted in the removal of over 3,000 Seminoles to Indian Territory (Oklahoma). On the 2000 Census, 12,450 Oklahomans identified themselves as Seminoles. Floridian Seminoles include close to 3,000 members and reside primarily on or around five reservations near Hollywood, Tampa, and Fort Pierce. Rural residents are mostly involved in cattle, citrus, and vegetable industries and maintain an active awareness of clan identity. The Seminoles have had federal recognition since 1957. The 550 Miccosukees are also descended from the Seminoles, but organized separately to receive recognition in 1962. Living on three reservations near Miami, they run a resort and gaming business.[23]

Virginia

Native Americans maintaining their identities and communities in Virginia, against dramatic pressures to assimilate, have only recently received recognition. When the English arrived at Jamestown in 1607, a chiefdom of close to thirty Algonquian-speaking tribes occupied Virginia's coastal plain under the leadership of Chief Powhatan. The horticulturalist Virginia tribes were among the first native groups to be assigned reservation lands—some of which the Mattaponi and Pamunkey tribes still hold. Many converted to Christianity during the Great Awakening, and today Native American Baptist churches remain a focus of native communities. Being smaller in number than any of the so-called Five Civilized Tribes, these groups maintained a lower profile, intermarried with non–Native Americans, and avoided the nineteenth-century removals. In the 1980s, the commonwealth of Virginia granted state recognition to eight Virginia tribes, seven of which are descendants of the original Powhatan tribes (the Mattaponi, Pamunkey, Chickahominy, Chickahominy Eastern Division, Nansemond, Upper Mattaponi, and Rappahannock).[24]

Siouan-Speaking Groups

Also receiving recognition were the non-Powhatan Monacans who were a confederacy, or alliance, of Siouan-speaking tribes in western and Piedmont Virginia. Groups such as the Tutelos and Manahoacs may also have been part of this alliance, sharing a common language and matrilineal clan system. Today only one family lives on the 200-acre tribal land base, but there are just over 1,000 enrolled tribal members.[25]

Descendants of other Siouan-speaking groups remain throughout the Carolinas. Siouan speakers, but sharing cultural traditions with the Cherokee, the Catawbas of South Carolina were nearly wiped out by one smallpox epidemic in 1759 (the population dropped by 60 percent in that year alone). The Catawbas resisted removal and by the 1890s remained in South Carolina, but most had converted to Mormonism.[26] The Mormons had such success among them as they believed them to be descended from one of the "lost tribes of Israel" and, as such, to be among God's chosen people. Such an identity no doubt had appeal as Native Americans were assimilating to American culture, yet being increasingly marginalized as "non-whites" by Jim Crow laws. The Catawbas regained federal recognition in 1993 and were given funds to expand land holdings around their reservation near the town of Rock Hill on the Catawba River. Also Siouan are the Chicora of coastal South Carolina. The Chicora reestablished a chiefship in 1993 under the leadership of Chief Gene Martin (Igmu Tanka Sutanaji) and, while lacking state and federal recognition, over 450 people claim a Chicoran identity.

Migrating between the Carolinas during the colonial period, the Waccamaw-Sioux today live mostly in Bladen and Columbus counties in North Carolina's coastal plain. From the 1880s, the Waccamaw-Siouans ran their own "all-Indian" schools that helped maintain their traditions and identity in the Jim Crow era. They were some of the first North Carolinians to import the idea of a powwow, as anthropologist Patricia Lerch has argued, to express their Indian identity in post-desegregation public venues.[27] Having received state recognition in 1971, the Waccamaw-Siouans have not yet obtained federal recognition. Other Siouan speakers include the Haliwa-Saponi and the Occaneechi Band of the Saponi Indians. The Haliwa-Saponi (state recognized since 1965) include over 3,000 residents of Halifax and Warren counties in northern North Carolina. Protestant churches (mostly Methodist and Baptist), social and geographical isolation, and segregated schools contributed to the maintenance of Native American identity through the nineteenth century and the first half of the twentieth.[28] Some of the most common surnames today are Richardson, Lynch, Harris, and Hedgepeth. The Haliwa-Saponi are descendants of the Saponi, Tuscarora, and Nansemond.

Other Saponi descendants include the 600 members of the Occaneechi Band of the Saponi Indians who live mostly in Alamance County in North Carolina. A German physician, John Lederer, visited the Occaneechis in 1670, at which time they controlled trade through the North Carolinian and Virginian Piedmont. In response to European settlement and the accompanying disempowerment of many native groups, the Occaneechis formed the Saponi Confederation with other Siouan-speaking tribes such as the Saponis, the Cheraws, the Enos, and the Tutelos. Today, tribal members sponsor an annual powwow near Mebane, North Carolina, and have reconstructed an Occaneechi village for educational purposes and for tourists at the nearby colonial town of Hillsboro. The North Carolina Commission of Indian Affairs granted the tribe state recognition in 2002.

Tribes with Contested Identities

Various tribes in Virginia and the Carolinas are romantically cast as descendants of Sir Walter Raleigh's failed colony at Roanoake. The favored tribes change over the decades, but most persistently include the Coharie and the Lumbee. Located primarily in Hartnett and Sampson counties in southeastern North Carolina, the Coharie number about 1,700 and are also thought to perhaps be descended from Tuscaroras or Waccamaws who lived in the coastal plain region. As with many other Carolinian Native Americans, the Coharie retained a strong sense of ethnicity and community through Protestant churches and their schooling system. The tribe has had state recognition since 1971 and holds an annual harvest-season powwow in the town of Clinton, which is also home to tribal headquarters.

Having one of the most contested tribal identities in the Carolinas, the Lumbee are also one of the largest of the South's native populations without federal recognition. On the 2000 Census, almost 52,000 persons self-identified as Lumbee. They are mostly concentrated in North Carolina's Robeson County near the Lumber River. Their "particularly obscure origins have led some to claim descent from the 'Croatan' Indians" and survivors of Sir Walter Raleigh's Lost Colony.[29] Others suggest that the Lumbees descend from the Cheraws, or Sauras who migrated from southwestern Virginia to South Carolina in the 1700s. While quite active in the American Indian Movement, Lumbee have often lacked a collective voice and internal unity.[30] The lack of a historically documented name has hindered recognition, and in frustration over their lack of political status, about 2,500 Lumbee began to call themselves Tuscarora in the early 1970s.[31] Anthropologist Gerald Sider notes that families were often split over ethnonyms, with full siblings identifying differently as Lumbee or Tuscarora (1993). While the historic Tuscarora are thought to have left North Carolina two centuries ago, several hundred consider themselves part of the Tuscarora Nation today and live particularly around Maxton, North Carolina.

Internal divisions mean that not only do Lumbees and Tuscaroras not agree on a shared American Indian identity, but other American Indians offer varying levels of support for their recognition process. Making any definition of this group additionally problematic are the numbers of people with mixed African, Native

American, and European American identities who claim to be Lumbee. Like the Creoles, Melungeons, and Hispanics (discussed below), the Lumbee offer another example of how ethnicity can cross so-called racial categories.

EUROPEANS

Spanish Settlers

Although the Spanish were the first Europeans to settle in what is now the South, on the 2000 Census, "Spanish" does not appear on the ancestry sections of the state-by-state social characteristics profiles. Ponce de León discovered La Florida in 1513. Spanish explorer Hernando de Soto followed him, only to die on the banks of the Mississippi River in 1542. Spaniards founded America's first city in 1565 at St. Augustine and developed a quite ethnically heterogeneous society in Florida.[32] Gaining Louisiana in 1763, Spain lost it back to France in 1800, but not without adding to the cultural mix of that territory. After three centuries of colonial endeavors, Spain ceded Florida to the United States in 1821. The largest Spanish American enclave for late nineteenth-century and twentieth-century Spaniards was Tampa, Florida, portions of which the U.S. military occupied during the 1898 Spanish-American War.

One enduring Spanish group are the Canary Islanders (Los Isleños) of Louisiana. During Spanish control of Louisiana (1763–1800), settlers represented various Spanish ethnic groups including Andalusians, Basques, Galicians, Catalans, and Canary Islanders. The colonial administration especially encouraged Spanish soldiers and their families to settle in the colony. An estimated 2,000 Canary Islanders settled on Bayou Lafourche and at Galvestown, Valenzuela, and Barataria in the Louisiana parish of St. Bernard across the Mississippi River from New Orleans in the late 1770s and early 1780s.[33] They became shrimpers, crabbers, and fisher folk (supplying New Orleans restaurants throughout the nineteenth and twentieth centuries) or small farmers and ranchers, and also supplemented their incomes through trapping (mink and muskrat) and hunting (both for the table and, in the case of duck, commercially). While some continue to fish, many contemporary Isleños work in the industrial and chemical plants surrounding New Orleans. Surnames still common in the area include Alleman, Caballero, Falcon, Fernandez, and Molero. Living among Acadians, African Americans, and Anglo-Americans, the Islanders nevertheless maintained the use of their Spanish dialect in their homes and communities well into the twentieth century. They often married out of their communities, and today few of those who claim Canary Island ancestry can do so through both their parents' lineages. Members of the Los Isleños Heritage and Cultural Society (formed in 1976) have encouraged Isleños cultural traditions, bilingualism, and foodways, and have organized an annual fiesta with flamenco dancing and heritage pilgrimages "back" to the Canary Islands. The Canary Islanders Heritage Society of Louisiana developed in 1996 to promote friendship and cultural exchanges between Louisiana and the Canary Islands.

Another eighteenth-century Spanish ethnic group that maintains a sense of identity and community today is the Minorcans of St. Augustine, Florida. In 1768 close to 1,500 immigrants came to British East Florida as indentured servants from the island of Menorca (Minorca) in the Balearic Islands off the Spanish coast. Over a third of their number died within two years due to inadequate housing, hunger, and disease. Revolting against the harsh conditions of their indenture, Minorcans deserted their British settlement for Spanish St. Augustine. The Minorcan Quarter of that city exhibits vernacular architectural styles, with west-facing loggias and upstairs balconies overhanging the quarter's narrow streets. Minorcan fishing traditions, religious festivals, and foodways still influence St. Augustine life, and close to 10,000 Minorcan descendants still call St. Augustine home.[34]

French Settlers

The French influence on southern foodways, linguistics, architecture, and religion was greatest in Charleston, South Carolina, and in Louisiana. Cajuns or Creoles compose the majority of Louisiana residents who reported speaking French in the home on the 1990 Census. To have fostered such an ethnically diverse colony in Louisiana, the French settlers in the South were less ethnically diverse than the Spanish. Walloons (French-speaking Belgians) settled in Louisiana in the eighteenth century, but the Protestant Huguenots (Calvinists) were one of the largest French groups to settle outside of French territory. The Huguenots initially made a disastrous attempt to colonize Florida in the 1560s. Protestantism was tolerated in France under the Edict of Nantes (1598), but the edict's revocation in 1685 by Louis XIV further spurred emigration. Huguenots had arrived in Virginia as early as 1619, but after 1685 immigration increased as persecution in France accelerated. Huguenots requested a refuge in the English Carolinas from Charles I as early as 1629, but it was his son, Charles II, who made settlement possible with a grant of lands in 1663. The first Huguenots arrived in 1670, and after 1685 Charles Town (Charleston, South Carolina) became a favored destination. Many others settled at Goose Creek, twenty miles inland from Charleston, and at Santee, about forty miles north of Charleston, where they built plantations producing silk, olive oil, wine, and naval supplies; still others moved on to the tideland areas, where they developed rice plantations.

Charleston's Huguenot Church is the oldest continuously active Huguenot congregation in America. The town is also home to the Huguenot Society of South Carolina (established in 1885), which holds an annual service in honor of the Edict of Nantes. Typical surnames include Chastain, Du Val, Gourdine, Fuion, Fuqua, Lemay, LaRue, Martin, and Rambout. Descendants of these settlers take pride in wearing the Huguenot cross (a Maltese cross with a dove attached), which is believed to have identified French Protestants to one another in public places as early as the 1600s.[35]

Europeans Fleeing Religious Persecution

As with the Huguenots, many European groups came to the South seeking freedom from religious persecution. About 200 of the 19,000 Protestants expelled from the Austrian Archbishopric at Salzburg in 1731 came to settle in the colony of Georgia. The Georgia Trustees began the last of Britain's thirteen American colonies "to provide a home for impoverished Englishmen and persecuted foreign Protestants."[36] Salzburgers settling northwest of Savannah in 1734 named their community Ebenezer, where Jerusalem Evangelical Lutheran Church, built between 1761 and 1769 from local clay, still stand on the banks of the Savannah River. They were later joined by Swiss and Palatine settlers. These German-speaking Georgians engaged in silk production and lumber processing. Surnames such as Arnsdorff, Gnann, Lastinger, Rahn, and Zittrauer are still common in the area, and the Georgia Salzburger Society, formed in 1925, still flourishes with a membership of over 1,700.

Waldenses from the Cottian Alps of northern Italy settled Valdese, North Carolina, in 1893. The Waldensian Church is the oldest evangelical Protestant church in existence, predating the Reformation. Persecuted over several centuries in Italy and France, the group eventually obtained a haven in Switzerland until their return to the Cottian Alps in 1689. This return from exile is celebrated in Valdese on the second Saturday of August with the annual Waldensian Festival (first held in 1976). Since 1967 they have recounted their story in a summertime outdoor drama called *From This Day Forward*. The Waldenses were quick to organize bakeries, a mutual assistance society (called Le Phare des Alpes), and a hosiery mill, while continuing to make Waldensian wines and ciders, play bocce ball, preserve their architectural traditions, and speak their original language (French, not Italian). Many Waldensians are now Presbyterians and Methodists.

The Protestant Moravians also settled in North Carolina. They were persecuted for their faith in Bohemia and Moravia (what eventually became the Czech Republic). Sponsored by the Saxon Count Nicholas Ludwig von Zinzendorf, they briefly formed an unsuccessful settlement near Savannah, Georgia, in 1733–1740. By 1753 they had settled near what is today Winston-Salem, North Carolina. They called their new home Wachovia (now the name of a banking company headquartered in the city) in honor of the Zinzendorf family estate in the Austrian Wachau Valley. Their first communities were at Bethabara and Bethania, but the central town, founded in 1766, was Salem.[37] Old Salem is home to a girls' boarding school, a women's college, and a living history museum that interprets the eighteenth- and nineteenth-century Moravian lifestyle. Several blocks of the settlement preserve the architectural style of their homeland, employing *fachwerk* (half-timbering, or timber-framed buildings infilled with brick or wattle and daub and often covered with plaster). Moravian spiced cookies and sugar cakes are marketed across the state and beyond. The Moravian tradition of a post-worship "love feast" with sweet buns and coffee still follows the meetings of some congregations. Residents of Winston-Salem decorate for the Christmas holidays with the Moravian multipointed star, which appears on porches and in hallways from the first Sunday of Advent through January 7 (Old Christmas).

Jewish Settlers

Jews also came to the South in the colonial period. The first Jewish immigrants to the South were Sephardic (descendants of Jews expelled from Portugal and Spain in the late 1400s). Two of the oldest Jewish communities in America were established in the 1730s in Charleston and Savannah. By the late eighteenth century, nearly one-quarter of America's Jewish population had settled in these cities. By the mid-nineteenth century, Jewish congregations in both Charleston and Savannah had become predominantly composed of Ashkenazi (Yiddish-speaking Jews from eastern and central Europe). The first Jewish governor in America was David

Emanuel, elected governor of Georgia in 1801. Jews held political office in the Confederacy, including secretary of state and surgeon general, and fought in the Civil War. While Jewish women joined southern organizations such as the United Daughters of the Confederacy, exclusion of Jews from country clubs and New Orleanian Mardi Gras krewes persisted well into the twentieth century. Today Jews constitute about 2.2 percent of the U.S. population. Twenty-one percent live in the South, and about 10 percent of all Jews in America live in Florida.[38] Some of the largest concentrations of Jewish populations are in Fort Lauderdale (215,000), Miami (135,000), South Palm Beach County, West Palm Beach, and Atlanta (at least 80,000).[39]

German Settlers

Thousands of German Lutherans, Anabaptists, and members of other Protestant sects also immigrated to the South in the early 1700s. The first Germans had come to Virginia in 1608, the year after the founding of Jamestown, but some of these first arrivals left the English settlement to join Chief Powhatan. Later arrivals seeking religious tolerance came mostly from the Palatinate of southern Germany along the Rhine (today's state of Rhineland-Pfalz). They were called Palatines or Palatinates, and by the beginning of the 1800s they had established Lutheran, German Reformed, Mennonite, Dunker, and United Brethren congregations in Virginia and South Carolina.[40] Along with Palatines, Swiss and German-speakers from Alsace in France also settled in the Piedmont in the first half of the eighteenth century at places called Germantown, Frankford, and Germania. With the Scots-Irish they were the predominant settlers on the Virginia frontier and in the Blue Ridge Mountains. The culture shaped in the Virginia frontier by Scots-Irish, German, and English settlers spread across the backcountry and into the Midwest. In southern Appalachia, the Germans were often referred as "Dutch," so that Melungeons in eastern Tennessee and western North Carolina, where many Germans had settled, were also called "Black Dutch."

So many Germans came to eighteenth-century Louisiana that the area on the Mississippi River in today's St. John and St. Charles parishes was called "the German Coast." Most came from the German Rhineland, but some also came from Switzerland. Near places such as Bayou des Allemands (Germans Bayou) they intermarried with Acadians, which explains why some German surnames (such as Toups, Himel, Folse, and Stelly) are now considered Cajun. Louisiana was home to new German arrivals in the 1850s, but by the 1890s many Germans were once again going to Virginia, where they were the largest immigrant group at that time. These new Germans settled across the state, but had their strongest presence in Richmond. Many were second and third generation Americans who moved to Virginia from Maryland, Pennsylvania, or New York, but still spoke German.[41] A German-American Association formed in 1890 in Richmond and sponsored an annual German Day.

Germans are the largest ethnic group in the country (23 percent of the population reported German ancestry in the 1990 Census), but only a few of the twenty-nine states in which German was the largest ancestry group were in the South (Virginia, West Virginia, Kentucky, and Florida). In Virginia, 828,664 claimed German ancestry on the 2000 Census. While the nation's largest ethnic group, few

German Americans exhibit ethnic boundary markers these days, excepting, perhaps, the Amish and Mennonites, who have also settled throughout the South in the last century. Amish and Mennonites moved to Punta Gorda and Sarasota, Florida, originally to grow celery in the 1930s. Today, their original community of Pinecraft is a neighborhood within the Sarasota city limits and, in addition to a Saturday farmers' market, they operate at least five "Amish" restaurants in the city (Dutch Oven, Sugar & Spice, Yoder's, Dutch Haus, and Der Dutchman) offering shoofly pie and spaetzle (noodles). Beginning in the 1960s, Amish and Mennonites also began settling in the Ozarks and in Tennessee in small rural communities like Belvedere where they still maintain a distinctive style of religious faith, "plain clothing," and foodways and are endogamous. As elsewhere in the country, the South also has its own German fakelore in the town of Helen, Georgia. In an effort to revive the community's flagging economy, residents of Helen redesigned their town on an Alpine theme. German inns and restaurants in a Bavarian architectural style have proved a successful draw for tourists seeking oompah-pah music in the north Georgian foothills.

Dutch and Swiss Settlers

The Dutch and the Swiss have also had an impact on southern states in their formative periods. The Dutch first arrived in Kentucky in the early 1780s from Pennsylvania and built meetinghouses in the tradition of the Dutch Reform Church. "The Old Mud Meeting House" of timber framework with wattle and daub still stands near Harrodsburg in Mercer County, Kentucky. Swiss and German settlers led by Baron Christoph von Graffenried settled the second oldest town in North Carolina, New Bern, at the confluence of the Trent and Neuse rivers, in 1709–1710. Over 12,000 North Carolinians claim Swiss descent today. Swiss settled the Kentucky frontier, remembered by a Swiss Descendants' Club in the town of London. In 1869 the Tennessee Colonization Agency recruited close to 100 Swiss families to settle the Cumberland Plateau. Finding the proffered land unimproved and remote from railroad access, half of the would-be colonists left. Those who remained settled in the area around Beersheba Springs and formed communities such as Gruetli-Lager, where Baggenstoss and Banholzer are still common surnames. Swiss opened the Dutch Maid Bakery in Grundy County just over a century ago and still import traditional Swiss candies. Descendants of these Swiss settlers also founded the Marugg Company, which produces traditional scythes with wooden handles for haying and now also exports these to the old country. A little over 10,000 Tennesseans reported Swiss ancestry on the 2000 Census.

Irish Settlers

The experience of the Irish in the South is a good example of how ethnic, rather than racial, politics have been largely ignored in studies of antebellum southern life. David Gleeson notes that the Irish are some of "the forgotten people of the Old South."[42] A significant escalation of Catholic Irish immigration to America began in the second decade of the nineteenth century. Much has been written about their negative experiences in the Northeast, but those 10 percent who settled south of the Mason-Dixon Line have received less attention. Settling largely in urban areas, the Irish helped maintain urban growth rates in the South during the two decades prior to the Civil War, with 65 percent of South Carolina's Irish living in Charleston and 58 percent of the Irish in Alabama living in Mobile. In Georgia, Augusta and Atlanta had sizable Irish populations and Savannah was home to almost 5 percent of the South's antebellum Irish-born. Common surnames of Irish settlers in Georgia included Thompson, Ryan, O'Neill, Griffin, Luckett, and Darden.

The most Catholic of states, Louisiana, attracted the most southbound Irish, 60 percent of whom lived in New Orleans by 1860.[43] Many Irish came to New Orleans on ships used to transport cotton to Liverpool (the Irish passengers made the return trip more lucrative for shipping merchants) and continued to work in the shipyards or worked digging canals from the Mississippi River. Although they never had a "quarter" in New Orleans (they never lived in a segregated neighborhood), their cultural and occupational solidarity fostered the notion of an "Irish Channel" which still references their unique New Orleans Irish identity.

In the Northeast, social conditions caused Irish immigrants to turn inward and refuse to assimilate. Irish immigrants to the South, never seriously threatening the status quo or dominating the population of any city, had a greater opportunity for acceptance and, in some cases, social mobility despite a rigid class system. They also met with greater acceptance in the South due to their contributions to the urban workforce (depleted by demands for rural slave labor) and their willingness to take on potentially high-mortality occupations deemed too dangerous for slaves. Hibernian Societies and other immigrant-aid organizations were organized in At-

Savannah's St. Patrick's Day Parade. First organized in 1824, the parade is now over four hours in length. Courtesy Georgia Department of Economic Development.

lanta, Charleston, New Orleans, and Savannah. In each city, Irish communities also found a focus in church life. New Orleans saw the erection in 1833 of St. Patrick's Church to offer support to the growing number of Irish immigrants to that city. Savannahans began the Cathedral of St. John the Baptist in 1799 and rebuilt the church to accommodate a growing congregation in 1835.

The Civil War hastened the decline of ethnic distinctiveness among nineteenth-century immigrants, including the Irish, as regional loyalties reshaped ethnic as southern identities. Irish immigrants often sought parallels between their southern experience and their Irish history, and their ethnic activities in the nineteenth century (parades, fundraisers, and other celebrations) made them proud of their Irishness, while placing it firmly in a southern context.[44] Contemporary celebrations of Irishness tend to blend with southern themes. Today, Savannah is home to the second largest St. Patrick's Day parade in the country, after New York City. First organized in 1824, the parade is now over four hours in length. Close to 400,000 visitors swamp the city to watch the parade wind through its historic leafy squares. Irish and "Celtic" festivals featuring Irish folk music and Irish step-dancing competitions take place annually throughout the South. The economic growth of the South in the last few decades has attracted many new Irish immigrants, so that Irish pubs, fraternal organizations, and athletic groups (playing hurling or Gaelic football) have become more common on the southern cultural landscape.

Italian Settlers

Those groups arriving in the South after the Civil War retain some of the most distinctive European communities. As elsewhere in the country, the late nineteenth century saw the arrival of southern and eastern Europeans. While the first Italians (Venetian glassblowers) came to Jamestown in 1622, the South had very few Italians until after the Civil War. Arkansas had a few rural settlements of northern Italians. Several hundred Genoese settled Tonitown, Arkansas, where there is still an annual Grape Festival in honor of the community's best known product, and where surnames such as Ardemagni, Bariola, Ceola, Maestri, Morsani, Pianalto, Sbanotto, Taldo, and Zulpo remain common. By the first decade of the 1900s, Italians also lived at Daphne and Lambeth, Alabama, and Valdese, North Carolina. In Texas they farmed cotton and rice; and in Louisiana and Mississippi they worked on sugar and cotton plantations—often displacing African American workers there.[45] Predominantly Catholic Louisiana was particularly preferred by Sicilians, almost 16,000 of whom had taken on farm work in the state by the beginning of World War I.

Louisiana Italians often sponsored St. Joseph's Day altars, also once popular in Tampa, Florida, where Italians (particularly Sicilians) had come to work in the cigar industry. Communities might hold processions on St. Joseph's Day (March 19), and families might construct an altar in anticipation of St. Joseph's intervention in a particular family crisis or in thanksgiving for a particular blessing (an ill family member's return to health or a difficult teenager's completion of high school). Baked goods (cookies and breads) and other foods are displayed on the altar to be consumed by the neighborhood poor. (St. Joseph's Day altars are more rare today, and food is more often taken to homeless shelters.) Ethnic organizations such as the

Sons of Italy and local branches of the National Italian American Foundation remain popular across the South, as do heritage societies such as the Italian Cultural Association of Greater Austin, Texas, and the Italian-American Club of Venice, Florida, which sponsor annual festivals. In Tampa's neighboring Ybor City, historic Italian social clubs such as L'Unione Italiana (1917) remain, as does the Latin American Fiesta (of which Elvis Presley was honorary king in 1961). (When the fiesta began in 1927, "Latin" meant Spanish, Cuban, or Italian, not Central or South American as "Latino" means today.) Italian American men are also particularly involved in Catholic fraternities such as the Knights of Columbus.

Czech Settlers

Since the early 1800s, non-Moravian Czechs have formed small communities in Georgia, Alabama, and Mississippi, and over 250 communities in Texas. Almost 200,000 people in Texas claim Czech ancestry today. In 2004 Caldwell, Texas, held the twentieth annual Kolache Festival (celebrating Czech heritage and Texans' favorite stuffed pastry). Many Czechs in the South have joined southern Protestant denominations, although some in Texas and Louisiana are Catholic. The strongest Czech communities in Louisiana today are in the twin towns of Libuse and Kolin, where annual festivals celebrate Czech dancing, foodways, music, and needlework. Of the more than 5,000 who claim predominantly Czech ancestry in the state today, only the elders of the Czech communities can speak the Czech language.

Romani (Gypsy) and Irish Traveler Settlers

Romani people, or Gypsies (also called Rom), first came to the South from Spain on the third voyage of Christopher Columbus.[46] The Romani people have traveled across Europe since the Middle Ages; their more distant origins were in India. There are several different "tribes," the largest in the American South being the Romanichals, numbering perhaps as many as 75,000. While many have occupations that involve seasonal migration, many others are settled. Their ethnicity is not often obvious to outsiders, unless played upon to end or enhance relations with outsiders. The supposed "King and Queen" of the Gypsies, Emil (d. 1942) and Kelly Mitchell (d. 1915), are buried at Rose Hill Cemetery in Meridian, Mississippi. (Gypsies may confer such invented titles on community members to impress outsiders ["Gaje" or "Gadjo"], and this status may have assisted in securing cemetery plots.) Nevertheless, visitors to the gravesite regularly deposit Nehi sodas, watermelons, vanilla wafers, and candy bars. While Mitchell is often an Irish name, the Irish Travelers are quite different from the Gypsies.

The Irish Travelers maintain an endogamous, quite closed society in the South, with concentrated communities in South Carolina and Texas. They often choose a distinctive architectural style for their houses, are frequently in the news as scam artists (most commonly posing as pavers or roofers who receive payment in advance of construction jobs which are never done), and are particularly talented at evading legal authorities. Most young women leave school in the eighth grade and may still have arranged marriages. Some of the older community members may have retained a dialect of Gaelic. Some theories suggest that the Irish Travelers are descended from Irish "spalpeens," seasonal migrant laborers who took to the road permanently during famine times and came to America in the nineteenth century.

Greek Settlers

Greeks first arrived at St. Augustine, Florida, in 1768. Greek merchants and sailors also settled in New Orleans in the 1700s and founded the first Greek Orthodox church in America there in 1864. While Greeks settled in south Alabama and coastal Mississippi, one of the largest Greek settlements in America began north of Tampa at Tarpon Springs in 1895. The sponge harvesting industry on the Gulf of Mexico had attracted well over 2,000 Greeks by the first decade of the twentieth century. Floridian Greek communities also exist in Miami, West Palm Beach, Orlando, and Jacksonville. Today, over 18 percent of Greek Americans live in the South with population concentrations in Atlanta, Birmingham, Charlotte, Houston, Richmond, and Norfolk. Ethnic identification and organization remain strong.[47]

More recent immigrants maintain the use of the Greek language and Greek foodways in the home. Traditional instrumentation is declining at community events, but the Greek bagpipe (the *tsabouna*) may occasionally be heard at social events. The Greek Orthodox Church offers a focus for Greek communities across the South. Churches display icons and hold Epiphany services on January 6. At Tarpon Springs, businesses and schools close for festivities at the local St. Nicholas Cathedral. Each year the archbishop visits and tosses a white cross into a bayou which is then retrieved by one of several dozen teenage boys who wait poised on the edges of their boats to make the dive. The young man who gets the cross is blessed in the cathedral, and the event is followed by the *glendi*, a day of Greek food, dancing, and music.

Hungarian Settlers

Livingston Parish, Louisiana, is home to the largest rural Hungarian settlement in the United States. Three Hungarian men arrived in 1896 to work in a local lumber mill and encouraged the gradual settlement of almost 200 Hungarian families by 1935. Their community, now known as Hungarian Settlement, was originally known as Arpadhon after the legendary ninth-century leader of the Magyar tribes. Socially isolated and largely endogamous through the first half of the twentieth century, the Hungarians of Livingston Parish were assimilated Hungarian Americans by the nation's bicentennial year. Since that time, the Arpadhon Hungarian Settlement Cultural Association has sponsored an annual Hungarian Heritage Day.[48]

English Ancestry

As newer immigrant groups reshape southern culture, how many southerners continue to identify with those most numerous in settling the colonial South? With the romanticized notions of "southern cavaliers," one might expect the South to be the most English of regions, yet today more residents of the Northeast (Maine, New Hampshire, and Vermont) claim English ancestry than do southerners. The state with the most residents claiming English ancestry is Texas with 1,462,984, followed by Virginia (788,849) and North Carolina (almost 768,000). In contrast, only 211,226 claimed English ancestry in Arkansas and just under 345,000 persons self-identified English descent in Alabama. Rather, the most common ethnic identity in the South is Scots-Irish, one of three Scottish ethnic groups arriving in the colonial period.

Scottish Settlers

Close to one hundred communities across the South host annual Scottish Highland Games with their accompanying clan gatherings and *céilidhs*, and dancing, bagpiping, harp, and fiddle competitions. These events draw thousands of participants; one weekend games event at Grandfather Mountain in North Carolina sees over 30,000 participants annually. Southern Scottish Americans also celebrate national Tartan Day on April 6 each year and have active Scottish Country Dance groups or Scottish Clan or heritage societies.[49] While southerners claiming a Scottish ethnicity today generally claim a Highland Scottish identity, Scottish immigrants to the South were members of three distinct ethnic groups: Highland Scots, Lowland Scots, and the Scots-Irish or Ulster Scots (who had settled in Northern Ireland before immigrating to America).

On America's first census in 1790, people of Scottish birth or descent represented 8.3 percent of the population. The South had the highest percentage of Scottish settlers: 10.2 percent of Virginia's population was of Scots origin as well as 14.8 percent in North Carolina, 15.1 percent in South Carolina, and 15.5 percent in Georgia. David Dobson claims that the Register of Emigrants for the period 1773 to 1775 indicates that two-thirds of those who migrated directly from Great Britain to Georgia had been born in Scotland. Some of the first St. Andrew's Societies, Scottish immigrant aid societies, formed in Charleston (1729—the first in North America), Savannah (c. 1750), and Alexandria, Virginia (c. 1760). Solicited by the Trustees for Establishing the Colony of Georgia, hundreds of Highlander families immigrated to the pine barrens of the Georgia coast beginning in January 1736, to settle and protect the new British colony under military governor James Oglethorpe. In his study of the settlement, Antony Parker notes that "Scottish names are to be found throughout Georgia's continuing history in the ranks of politics and place-names. . . . These Highlanders may scarcely have been missed in the glens and mountains of Scotland, but in Georgia they made a difference." One of the community's leaders was John Mohr Mackintosh, for whom a competitive bagpipe band based in Atlanta is now named. A living history unit called the Oglethorpe Highlanders (set about 1742) encamps at local schools and at Highland Games across the South.

North Carolina became such a popular destination for Highlanders that it became known as "the land of the God-blessed Macs." Highlander immigration increased about the late 1760s and peaked in the mid-1770s. By the 1770s, the Highlanders accounted for almost a fifth of all immigration to British North America. Impelled by bad harvests and the oppressive social and political climate following the failed Jacobite Risings, whole communities immigrated together, especially from the Western Highlands and Isles. The Highlander settlement along the Cape Fear River in North Carolina received new immigrants in 1884 when

Close to one hundred communities across the South host annual Scottish Highland Games, such as the Virginia Highlands Festival, with their accompanying clan gatherings and *céilidhs*, as well as dancing, bagpiping, harp, and fiddle competitions. Courtesy Virginia Tourism Corporation.

the British Napier Commission financed the immigration of Highlanders there. Not finding the "Highland," predominantly Gaelic-speaking community they would have found a century earlier, or the prosperity that the commission had promised, many returned to Scotland. Descendants of Cape Fear Valley Highlanders pioneered settlement in Alabama, Tennessee, Mississippi, and Texas. Others, beginning with Neill McLendon and Daniel Douglas Campbell, settled "Argyle" in Florida's panhandle (near DeFuniak Springs in Walton county). They brought family and friends to form a satellite of the Cape Fear community in the 1820s when the county was established. By 1850 the census notes over 1,200 settlers. The first settlement was Eucheeanna, named after the twelve-mile-wide and twenty-five-mile-long Euchee Valley and the Native American tribe who seemed happily ensconced before the Scots pushed them out. A signer of the Florida Constitution, Col. John McKinnon, was among them, as were McLeans, McCaskills, Gunns, and MacBrooms, several of whom have memorials in the Euchee Valley Presbyterian Church Cemetery.[50]

The first Lowland Scots were transported to Charleston, South Carolina, in 1682–1683 for being Covenanters (Presbyterians seeking political and religious liberty in Scotland). Many Lowland Scots immigrants were often transported minor criminals or homeless paupers, or military or political prisoners, and even among those of the landed and professional classes, arriving as indentured servants was not uncommon. Yet, of the three Scottish ethnic groups, the Lowlanders were less distinctive culturally and assimilated most rapidly. Lowlanders did not as often settle in groups and moved away from Scots settlements more readily. Linguistics also played a part in their acculturation within English communities. Highlanders often retained Gaelic for several generations, while the Lowland Broad Scots often gave way within a generation to more American, upwardly mobile accents and dialects.

From the late 1600s through the early 1800s, most emigrants from Ireland to America came from Northern Ireland, and the majority of these were the Scots-Irish Presbyterians. The Scots-Irish were Lowland Scots who in the early seventeenth century began settling in the area of Ireland most problematic for British rule, Ulster, where they are known as Ulster Scots. The Scots-Irish so named themselves in America to convey their distinctiveness from the Scots Highlanders, whose Loyalist reputation survived long after the Revolution.[51] Later the name served to distinguish them from "Celtic" or native Catholic Irish, who came to America in the hundreds of thousands with the famines of the 1840s and 1860s.

The Scots-Irish remained a separate group in America through religion, politics, a tendency to settle on the frontier, and choice, rather than by any continuing affinity with Ulster, where they had always been in some way marginal (even among other Protestants). They more readily relinquished cultural ties with Ulster than the Gaelic-speaking Highlanders did with their homeland. Letters sent home by Scots-Irish immigrants were riddled with homesickness, but emphasized the freedom and independence to be found in America and encouraged others to follow. Historians Tyler Blethen and Curtis Wood refer to the Scots-Irish as "a people practiced in abandoning their past." While they famously brought folklore, musical, and architectural traditions, they did not bring a material culture as distinctly representative of their identity as the Highlanders' unique fabrics and style of dress.

Due in part to repressive trade laws, famine, and a decline in the linen industry, close to 150,000 Ulster Scots came to the colonies between 1710 and about 1760.[52] Figures vary, but Leonard Dinnerstein, Roger Nichols, and David Reimers note that the Scots-Irish comprised the largest number of non-English Europeans coming to the colonies during the eighteenth century. By the time of Independence, nearly a quarter of a million Scots-Irish had entered the colonies and "numbered between 7 and 10 percent of the white population." Scots-Irish settlements across the Ozarks and Appalachia contrasted with those of Lowland and Highland Scots elsewhere in the Scots-Irish preference for relatively isolated, individual family homesteads and their focus on a mixed economy of animal husbandry and diversified crops. Kerby Miller has estimated that 50 percent or more of the settlers west of Appalachia by 1790 had emigrated from Ulster or were descendants of immigrants from Ulster. Along with the Germans, the Scots-Irish were the largest ethnic group to enter America in colonial times and remain the largest ethnic group in the South today.

AFRICANS AND CREOLE POPULATIONS

Scholarship is now developing on the African ethnicities that survived for a few generations in the South before being displaced by a racial identity through slavery.[53] While distinct national identities from Africa did not endure to the present, they did shape new cultural groups that formed in the South, and southern identity itself. The first Africans to come to America were twenty-one indentured servants who arrived in Jamestown in 1619. Some historians contend that these Africans' children were born free and when their indentures were up they were eligible for free land as were indentured deportees from England, Ireland, and Scotland.[54] They, and later arrivals, were free before 1661 when the Virginia legislature passed laws making blacks slaves for life and began the phase of American history in which persons were brought involuntarily to this country without the choice to pursue "liberty or happiness." English colonists brought some indentured servants and slaves to Charlestown from Barbados (already an established colony in 1670 at the time of the first permanent English settlement in South Carolina). John Thornton notes that only about 6 percent of people transported in the eighteenth-century Atlantic slave trade went to North America. Thornton figures that by 1700 there were 13,000 persons of African descent living in the Chesapeake Bay region, with an annual arrival rate of about 1,000 Africans per year. However, the numbers brought to the colonies quintupled by 1760 the African population in that year was 327,000. Peter Wood notes that by 1790 Africans composed 35 percent of the population of the South. Slaves came predominantly from the nations between Ghana (the Gold Coast) and Angola, but also from Senegal, the Gambia (Senegambia), Sierra Leone, and Igbo country.[55]

As Jeanette Keith has noted, Africans brought to America did not think of themselves as African, but as Hausa, Wolof, Fanti, Yoruba, Ewe, and Igbo, "just as newly arrived indentured servants thought of themselves as Scots, Irish, Welsh and English. Moreover, the 'saltwater Negroes' who had been the first slaves in British North America tended to look down on newcomers from Africa, with whom they had little in common."[56] Racially based identities replaced older tribal, national, and cultural affiliations over the course of several generations. Plantations were not ethnically homogeneous, but were home to people of different nations. Those with shared cultures of course gathered to share religious beliefs, storytelling, songs, and dance, and "slaves chose their spouses or other domestic partners from their home nation or closely related ones." As Thornton notes, plantation "masters were not always willing or able to restrict cultural life, group meetings, or networks of friendship. Within the space that the slave regime allowed, the Africans re-created an African culture in America." Archaeologists are uncovering artifacts of material culture that reveal the continuation of homeland traditions in a new land, including "Mandinga motifs on clay pipes from Virginia and distinctively central African motifs on pottery from South Carolina."[57]

In the Chesapeake and in North Carolina, slaves and European Americans interacted on a regular basis and the slave population was more Anglicized than that of the low country and Sea Island district to the south.[58] In the South Carolina low country, most planters spent their time in Charleston and left their rice plantations to overseers, meaning that slaves had less interaction with European Americans there and retained greater cultural distinctiveness. Nowhere was this more true than in the islands off the coast of South Carolina.

These islanders, known as Gullah and Geechi today, are a creole of several different ethnic groups (including the Mende, Temmne, Limba, and others). Their language, though related to Krio, which is still spoken in Sierra Leone, is not an African language but an African American language. In Gullah-speaking communities, some members still have African nicknames, called basket names, such as Jilo, Jah, or Bala. Burial customs draw on African origins, such as drumming to

Cherokee African Americans, Greene County, Georgia, 1941. Courtesy Library of Congress.

announce a death, breaking bottles on the grave to ensure the health of the deceased's family, and leaving food on a porch for the spirit of a deceased person. Carved grave markers also exhibit African roots, as do walking sticks, calabash containers, and the basketry now marketed to tourists.

In the late 1700s, some Africans escaped plantations in what are now Gullah communities and went to Florida, where they were beyond the reach of the British colonial administrators. There they adopted the clothing styles, material culture, and, to some extent, the language of the Seminoles. Their descendants became known as the Black Seminoles. After the United States acquired Florida from Spain in 1819, attempts to force the Black Seminoles back into slavery failed, and they were forced to move to Indian Territory after the Seminole Wars. In the 1850s, some Black Seminoles moved to Mexico and were hired by the Mexican government to fight Comanche and Apache raiders from Texas. In the 1870s, the U.S. Calvary invited them to join the American army and fight the Comanches; they were known as the Seminole Negro Indian Scouts. Descendants of the Cavalry Scouts live in Brackettville, Texas; descendants of those who remained in Mexico reside in the state of Coahuilla; and around 2,000 still live near the Seminoles in Oklahoma.[59]

Enslaved Africans and African Americans were sometimes freed, especially when they were children of their mother's master. They occupied an ambivalent position, frequently owning slaves, but at risk of being captured and returned to slavery themselves if they traveled or moved out of areas in which they were known.[60] By 1800 over 100,000 free people of color lived in the United States, 61,000 of whom resided in the South.[61] By 1861 their numbers had grown to 488,000 and the majority (262,000) still lived in the South. In the nineteenth century, free persons of color (the *gens de couleur libre*) began intentionally calling themselves Creoles of color.[62] They maintained their identity and communities through the Jim Crow period in New Orleans, in Spanish Mobile, in Pensacola, Florida, and in smaller enclaves along the Gulf coast.

People of mixed ancestry had more freedoms in South Carolina and Louisiana than they did in the rest of the South.[63] Louisiana has often been called the Latin South—a separate cultural world in which ethnicities developed differently. Most Africans coming to New Orleans came from French-speaking West Africa. While Senegambia never furnished more than 10 percent of the Atlantic slave trade after 1640, "two-thirds of the slaves brought to Louisiana by the French" were Senegambians. Among them were the Bambara, who allied with Indian nations to revolt against the French and played "a preponderant role in the formation of the colony's Afro-Creole culture.[64]

We most commonly think of creoles in terms of language. Serving all the functions of a language, a creole replaces a pidgin, the form of communication in first contact between two or more groups speaking different languages. "Creole" has also denoted a person descended from the original French or Spanish settlers of the southern states or a person of African or Caribbean *and* European ancestry who speaks a creolized language, especially one based on the Romance languages. "Creole" might also specifically refer to the francophone dialect native to southern Louisiana.[65] We might also speak of creole cuisine, with a New Orleans style tomato, onion, and pepper sauce or a dish like filé gumbo (a union of West African and Choctaw cooking styles). Although "Creole" is variously applied to people of European or African descent, we might also use the term to refer to African Americans of French-speaking Louisiana as opposed to their European American "Cajun" neighbors.[66] As early as the eighteenth century in Louisiana, "Creole" described descendants of French and Spanish settlers. It eventually came to refer also to people of French, Spanish, and African descent who were known as "free people of color" and also to light-skinned immigrants from the Caribbean, including those who immigrated to Louisiana after the revolution in the French colony of Saint-Domingue (1791–1803), which became Haiti. Definitions of the term "Creole" vary and remain contentious. Most simply and inclusively put, the category of Creole may refer to anyone with African or European, but not Anglo-American, ancestry who was born in the Americas.[67]

James Dorman notes that throughout the colonial period in Louisiana (1699–1803) "Creole" also referred to any children of mixed African and Native American parentage, who were particularly termed "Grifs."[68] As Gwendolyn Midlo Hall notes, however, Indian slavery was prohibited during Spanish rule, so that Creole slaves of Native American parentage were rarely acknowledged on slave lists. Elsewhere in the South a mix of Native American and black was called "Mustee" (occasionally this referred to combined Native American and European ancestries, also called "mestizo" or "métis").[69] Creoles provide another example of the complexity of ethnicity and how ethnic identities can cross and confuse social conceptions of racial categories. The use of the term has varied through time, but the ethnonym "Creole" refers to a genetic and cultural mixing unknown before the colonial experience in the Western Hemisphere.

Creole Culture

One of the best-known exports of Creole culture, itself a cultural creole, is zydeco music. Traditionally sung in French with improvised lyrics, zydeco mixes "Afro-Caribbean rhythms, blues, and Cajun music (zydeco's white counterpart)."[70] Ethnomusicologist Jeff Todd Titon suggests that zydeco makes use of "Cajun melodies, Afro-Caribbean rhythms, and Afro-American performance styles, but the cross-fertilization is so effective that analytical generalizations tend to fly apart in the face of specific features."[71] Creole cuisine and culture have long been staples of the Louisiana tourism industry, but also engage the interest of local preservation societies and scholars. In addition to the numerous Creole historical and heritage societies flourishing today, there is also a Creole Heritage Center at Northwestern State University in Louisiana, and that university in conjunction with the Deep South Regional Humanities Center at Tulane University has initiated a Creole Studies Consortium.

The most thoroughly creolized urban culture in America is found in the city of New Orleans, which celebrated Creole Heritage Day on October 24, 2003.[72] While north Louisiana has some French-influenced enclaves, Scots-Irish and English Protestants predominantly settled the area. South Louisiana is a blend of American Indian, French, Spanish, African, Irish, and German cultures, but is also the most Acadian (Cajun) area of the state.[73]

Cajuns

Immortalized in Henry Wadsworth Longfellow's poem *Evangeline*, Cajuns are descendants of Catholic French Acadians who settled in Nova Scotia. After being expelled by the British in the mid-eighteenth century, they settled in French Louisiana. "Cajun" generally refers to European American residents of French-speaking Louisiana as distinct from their African American "Creole" neighbors, although some people of African descent self-identify as Cajun. Estimates of the Cajun population vary radically, from several hundred thousand to 85,000 across the United States, often depending on how individuals with multiple ancestries prioritize that portion of their identity. After centuries of mixing with other ethnic groups, Cajun surnames now include the Spanish Castille and Romero; the Scots-Irish McGee, and the German Hymel and Schexnider.[74]

In the nineteenth century, the ethnonym "Genteel Acadians" referred to Cajuns who, becoming prosperous through sugar plantations, had joined the elite Anglo-American or French Creole society. After the Civil War, some married into poorer Cajun families, but many remained prominent in society well into the twentieth century. At the end of the twentieth century a quite different Cajun self-ascriptive arose that is anything but genteel: the "Coonass." Pejorative if used by a non-Coonass, the term distinguishes working-class Cajuns from commodified Cajunness. One suggested origin for the appellation comes from Cajuns' experience in World War II, during which French soldiers referred to individual Francophone Americans by the term *Conasse*, meaning a stupid person. Coonasses or "Coonies" speak some French, have a Cajun accent in English, generally enjoy fishing, hunting, or other outdoor activities, and may excel in Cajun music or foodways. The

Acadian cabin at LSU Rural Life Museum, Baton Rouge, Louisiana. Courtesy Louisiana Office of Tourism.

term is more commonly applied to men than to women. Coonasses consider themselves "real Cajuns."

Multiracial Groups

Living in the traditionally Francophone areas of Terrebonne and Lafourche parishes, the Houma are one of many populations across the South that were "neither black nor white" during the Jim Crow era and are denied recognition by state and federal governments as Native Americans today. The original Houma in Louisiana were displaced by the Tunica and "probably incorporated members of the Byogoula, Acolapissa, Chitimacha, Washa and Chawasha."[75] Over the centuries they intermarried with whites and blacks. Their ethnic identity now defies racial categorization.[76] In the 2000 Census almost 7,000 people self-identified as Houma.

Across America, children of mixed unions are assigned the identity of the socially and economically more disadvantaged group—a practice called hypodescent. Categorized as "colored" by the Louisiana Bureau of Vital Statistics because her great-great-great-great-grandmother was black, Susie Phipps garnered international attention in 1982 by trying to have herself declared "white."[77] According to America's "one drop rule," having one black ancestor makes one black, but having one white ancestor does not make one white. In the biracial classification schemes of the Jim Crow era (a period of racial segregation across twenty-nine states after the Civil War, lasting until the mid-1960s passage of federal civil rights legislation), Native Americans and those of mixed ancestry were variously unacknowledged, self-segregated, or classed with African Americans. Some of the most interesting and contested identities in the South are those of mixed Native American, European, and African heritage such as Melungeons, Brass Ankles, Redbones, Turks, Guineas, Ahoskie Blues, Santees, and Houma. Formerly called "Pardos" or "tri-racial isolates," communities with triple-mixed ancestries survive in pockets across the South. Neither black nor white nor Indian, they often found themselves disdained by all three groups. Some "passed" as "white," and sometimes as "black," and left their communities. Many communities have long denied their ethnicity. However, in an age of multiculturalism, some members (usually those whose parents or grandparents had moved away from the original settlement areas) have begun to embrace a resurgent ethnicity and to claim a once-stigmatizing ethnonym as their own rather than as an imposed category.

Now identifying themselves as having Native American, African American, and English, Scots-Irish, Tunisian, Portuguese, or other Mediterranean ancestry, Melungeons problematize the usual binary categorization of "race." They populate areas from southeastern Kentucky to east Tennessee and southwest Virginia in unknown numbers. John Shelton Reed cited those who dared to advance any population figure, however imprecise, as estimating the Melungeon population at 5,000 to 15,000. Christopher Everett notes that there have been other, more sensational, estimates as high as 200,000.[78] The 1990s saw the development of Melungeon family reunions, cookbooks, historic preservation efforts, and heritage tourism to Turkey (another possible ancestral homeland).[79] In Barbour and Taylor counties of West Virginia, those of mixed African, Native American, and European ancestry are called "Guineas." The Melungeons of Louisiana have been called "Redbones," and number perhaps 20,000.

Brass Ankles is a term, still considered derogatory by some, specific to South Carolinians and often included those once called "mulatto" (half black, half white). Brass Ankle communities are predominantly located in Berkeley, Colleton, Dorchester, and Orangeburg counties. Some of those who focus on their Native American roots call themselves Santees. Gary Mills notes that the "Turks" or "Free Moors" of South Carolina's up-country are thought to have been the mixed offspring of Joseph Benenhaley, "a Caucasian of 'Arab' descent who fought with General Thomas Sumter during the American Revolution and then settled on Sumter's plantation."[80] In northeastern North Carolina's Hertford County, persons with a triple-mixed ancestry have a community at Ahoskie, giving them the name "Ahoskie Blues."

Cuban Beginnings in the South

While the Melungeons and Redbones are new creole populations formed in the South, some "multiracial" immigrant groups, such as the Cubans, found themselves divided into separate categories in the South despite a shared nationality. Cubans and Afro-Cubans first came to Ybor City and West Tampa in the 1880s to work in cigar factories. More black and white Cubans arrived as exiles from the 1895 War for Independence from Spain. When organizing the revolution (in which he died), Cuban writer José Martí had recruited support in Ybor City, where his life-sized statue now stands in José Martí Park. Cuban immigrants founded the Martí-Maceo Society (a mutual aid, social, and Cuban independence group) over a century ago in honor of both white Cuban Martí and an Afro-Cuban hero—the

Cubans working in a Tampa cigar factory, c. 1920. As early as 1831, Cubans were making cigars in Florida. Courtesy Florida Photographic Collection.

revolutionary General Antonio Maceo. About 15 percent of the Tampa Cuban community at the time was black. In Florida, black Cubans found a society in which they were separated from white Cubans by Jim Crow laws and from African Americans by culture, language, and religion. As anthropologist Susan Greenbaum notes in her book on the Tampa Afro-Cuban community, they were "black with Cubans and Cuban when with blacks."[81] When the cigar industry collapsed in the 1930s during the Great Depression, many Afro-Cubans moved away, but began returning in the 1970s and 1980s and rejuvenated the membership of the century-old Martí-Maceo Society.

OTHER CULTURAL GROUPS

Conchs

Other cultural groups that have evolved in the South include the Conchs, who are natives of the Florida Keys. Named for the marine gastropod mollusk, the original Conchs were British, Irish, and African Bahamians who moved to the Florida Keys in the early nineteenth century. They maintained a unique accent well into the twentieth century. Mostly fishers and spongers, Conchs also worked in wrecking crews for which the Keys were famous. Tourism and popular culture promote the Keys as "the Conch Republic" and nineteenth-century architecture as "Conch vernacular." Restaurants serve conch fritters and conch stew, and new residents of the Keys are humorously called "freshwater conchs." Traditional Conch surnames include Albury, Carey, Curry, Kemp, Knowles, Roberts, and Sawyer.

Appalachians

As a subregion of the South, the Appalachian South has forged its own unique identities. Novelist Lee Smith expressed the cultural dissimilarities between the South and southern Appalachia when she described her mountain home as "far from the white columns and marble generals." In terms of outsiders' perceptions, she notes: "Appalachia is to the South what the

The original Conchs were British, Irish, and African Bahamians who moved to the Florida Keys in the early nineteenth century. Tourism and popular culture promote the Keys as the "Conch Republic." Courtesy Florida Photographic Collection.

South is to the rest of the country. That is: lesser than, backward, marginal. Other."[82] The three bands of southern Appalachia—the Allegheny-Cumberland (part of West Virginia, Kentucky, Tennessee, and Alabama), the Blue Ridge (parts of Maryland, Virginia, North Carolina, and Georgia), and the Great Appalachian Valley (parts of Maryland, Virginia, Tennessee, Georgia, and Alabama) have been the subject of their own extensive mythology disconnected from that of the Old South.[83] Beginning with the introduction of outside interests cutting timber, mining coal, and establishing manufacturing industries in the 1880s, "local color writers" and missionaries have popularized images of Appalachia which still shape stereotypes of the region and the ways in which "mountain people" see themselves. From "uplift literature" portraying the region as a "social problem," to romantic and fanciful theses about residents' feuding, supposed "Elizabethan dialects," and fallacious status as the most "Anglo-Saxon" of all American populations, Appalachia has been created and re-created by outsiders. The resulting stereotypes have engendered a particular self-consciousness among mountain people.

Scholars have only recently begun to address the ethnic diversity of the mountain population.[84] The two predominant ethnic groups displacing Cherokees were the Scots-Irish and the Germans. African Americans arrived in the mountains first as slaves. Richard Drake notes that while the majority of antislavery societies in the United States prior to 1830 were in the mountain South, a slave-owning elite existed in many Appalachian counties.[85] He further notes that the mountain South had smaller populations of slaves, with multi-county areas having populations of less than 1 percent black, and that "Madison County, Alabama was the only Appalachian county with a more than 50 percent black population in 1860."[86] At the end of the nineteenth century, newly freed slaves came in search of work in the coal mines. Today African Americans comprise approximately 12 percent of the population of southern Appalachia (as compared with 2 percent in central Appalachia and 3 percent in northern Appalachia). A group of Appalachian poets have coined a new ethnonym, "Affrilachian," to describe African American mountain people.

Ozarkers

The South's other mountain people are the Ozarkers. European American settlement of the Ozark hill country began only in the nineteenth century, principally by Scots-Irish from Kentucky and Tennessee. The incursion of missionaries, logging companies, and tourists began in the 1920s, at least four decades later than their arrival in southern Appalachia. Often deemed more "backward" than southern Appalachia, the Ozarks, unlike Appalachia, have largely been neglected by scholars. Only in 2002 did a native scholar, Brooks Blevins, write about the history, folk life, and expressive culture of the section of the Ozarks in northern Arkansas.[87]

TWENTIETH-CENTURY NEW SOUTHERNERS

New immigrants to the South reflect the increasingly globalized political and economic context in which we live. Greeks and Irish continue to immigrate to the South, and Sudanese immigrants fleeing the ongoing civil war in their homeland are establishing communities in Nashville and Atlanta. However, the bulk of the new southerners are from Central and South America, the Middle East, and Asia, rather than from Europe or Africa. The 1965 Immigration Reform Bill abolished the national origins quota system and particularly favored Latin American and Asian immigration. Between 1961 and 1979, 39 percent of immigrants were from Latin America and 24 percent were from Asia. Between 1981 and 1996, 47 percent of immigrants were from Latin America and 34 percent were from Asia.[88]

Haitians now have burgeoning populations in South Florida and the Carolinas; Hmong from Thailand also have settled across the rural South in places like Mt. Airy, North Carolina, and South Asians have become a significant presence in the medical professions and as hoteliers.[89] Most of these immigrant groups arrived after World War II. Muslim Arab Americans have also become more visible in the South since that period, but Christian Arab and Middle Eastern Americans have been a part of southern communities since the late nineteenth century.

Arab Immigrants

While Arab Americans have more commonly settled in urban areas of California, New York, and Michigan, three southern states have attracted large Arab American populations: Florida foremost, followed by Texas and Virginia. Florida and Texas are home to Syrian and Lebanese Americans whose ancestors immigrated between the 1880s and the 1940s. During that period most immigrants called themselves Syrian (Lebanon only achieved independence in 1946) and came to the rural South for farmwork or to establish businesses in Atlanta, Birmingham, New Orleans, and eventually Miami. Now called Lebanese Americans, the descendants of these original immigrants constitute a large proportion of Arab Americans living across the country. Ten percent are from a variety of Muslim sects, and the majority are Christian. Their churches include the Chaldean Catholic, Eastern Orthodox, Maronite, and Melktine. In the South, many have joined Roman Catholic congregations as well as Baptist and Methodist denominations. Arab Americans place a strong emphasis on education; 40 percent obtain a bachelor's degree compared with the national average for Americans as a whole of 24 percent.

In Florida, Jacksonville, Miami, Palm Beach, and Tampa have some of the largest communities. In Texas, Dallas, Houston, and San Antonio are home to Syrian and Lebanese communities. In Vicksburg, Mississippi, the Lebanese community centers around St. George Antiochan Orthodox Church.[90] In Mobile, Alabama, some of the best known Lebanese surnames include Kahalley, Kalifeh, Saad, Sudeiha, Naman, and Zoghby. The Arab American populations of Florida and Texas have more than doubled since the 1980 Census in part due to a growing presence of Egyptians, Jordanians, and Palestinians. Virginia's Arab American population, though smaller than those of Florida and Texas, has nonetheless quadrupled since 1980, largely due to the immigration of North Africans. Most Arab Americans live in the northern suburbs of Virginia, although many Lebanese Americans live in Richmond or the Tidewater area.

Asian Immigrants

In the second half of the twentieth century, the Asian population of the South grew dramatically. The "Asian" category on the U.S. Census is too broad to relate to ethnicity as it includes Asian Indians as well as Chinese, Filipinos as well as people from Nepal, and Japanese as well as Samoans and other Pacific Islanders. The reductionistic category "Asian American" unfortunately racializes what are very distinct ethnic identities, and most of the groups discussed below have not yet entered the census "ancestry" questionnaire, so that census figures for Asians can mask the quite distinct communities that, for example, Indians and Filipinos form within America. While Asians more commonly settled in California and Hawaii, since the 1970s Filipinos, Koreans, Vietnamese, Hmong, and Asian Indians have been immigrating or migrating to the South so rapidly that close to 20 percent of Asian Americans now reside in the region. (This is almost double the percentage in the Midwest and about the same as the percentage in the Northeast. Asian Americans now constitute approximately 4.2 percent of the U.S. population. This national average was exceeded in one southern state (Virginia has 4.3 percent). However, in only nine states did Asians represent less than 1 percent of the total population, and four of those were in the South (Alabama, Kentucky, Mississippi, and West Virginia).[91]

Chinese

The Chinese were the first Asian immigrants to come to the South, and headed first to Texas to build railroads. Less than 1,000 Chinese had come to Texas before federal passage of the Chinese Exclusion Act of 1882. Once this was repealed in 1943, the Chinese communities in Mississippi attracted new arrivals, and concentrations of Chinese began forming in Houston and San Antonio, where they operated a separate school during the Jim Crow period. By 1900 El Paso had a small Chinatown. In Texas, cultural distinctions still separate the "old" and "new" Chinese immigrants. The Cantonese-speaking nineteenth-century immigrants were mostly from southern China, while twentieth-century arrivals were from various other locations in China and predominantly Mandarin-speaking. The older immigrants came mostly from peasant backgrounds, were upwardly mobile, and have succeeded in business. The newer immigrants were of China's elite and have focused on the professions. Descendants of the older immigrants long maintained a focus on clan or family association (defined by surname). Today Chinese New Year may still be celebrated and a Confucian emphasis on family obligations remains strong.[92] Many are now Baptists.

In the nineteenth century the Chinese also came to Louisiana, where Chinese men replaced slave labor at the sugar plantations in Jefferson Parish and where they often intermarried with African Americans or Native Americans. As they did in Texas and Louisiana, Chinese also went to Mississippi as sojourners, but eventually settled. By 1950 about 10,000 Chinese called the South home. Most arriving in the Delta came from Guangdong Province in southern China. Unhappy with the work situation on plantations, some left to labor in restaurants and laundries in more urban areas. Many opened small, family-operated grocery stores in African American communities—where there had not previously existed any alternative to the planters' supply store.[93] The Mississippi Chinese formed an enduring community, though not Chinatowns. Their social life focused on their local Baptist communities and evenings of mahjong (a popular Chinese game played with tiles instead of cards). Seeking a lower cost of living and a more rural Chinese community, Chinese from urban areas elsewhere in the United States continue to migrate there, and to operate small businesses.

Koreans

Some of the first Korean immigrants to the South in the 1950s were Korean war brides and adopted war orphans. Most Koreans who have come to the South arrived after the passage of the 1965 Immigration Act and settled in urban areas, where they own small businesses or work in manufacturing or in professional and technical fields. Between the 1990 and 2000 censuses the Korean population of the South grew by 36 percent. Today Korean southerners represent 12 percent of the total Korean population in the United States. Virginia is home to the largest number, followed by Georgia and Florida. While many arrive straight from Korea, many others are moving from the American West. Korean Baptists churches are increasing in number, while Korean Presbyterians constitute one of the fastest growing Protestant denominations in the South.

Vietnamese

The war in Vietnam also spurred Vietnamese immigration to the United States. After California and Texas, Louisiana, with its Catholic-French heritage, was a particularly attractive destination for immigrants from a former French colony. One of the largest Vietnamese enclaves in the United States is the Versailles community in New Orleans, with its Buddhist temples and Vietnamese groceries. Approximately 12,000 Vietnamese live in New Orleans today. Many Vietnamese also settled along the Gulf coast of Mississippi in the early 1980s to work as fishers and in seafood plants. Many of the estimated 10,000 Vietnamese in the area have opened successful restaurants and coffeehouses.[94]

Cambodians

Cambodian immigrants to the South are almost exclusively Khmer, the largest ethnic group of the Southeast Asian nation. Spurred by the Vietnamese takeover of their country, now called Kampuchea, 300,000 Cambodians have resettled in the United States since 1979. Cambodian communities with their own Buddhist temples may now be found across the South, primarily in Texas and Virginia, but smaller communities also exist in North Carolina, Georgia, and Florida. Many of these new southerners find employment in agricultural and fishing industries or in furniture factories and textile mills. Cambodians may particularly display Khmer expressive culture (dancing, music, foodways) on Chol Chnam (New Year around mid-April), on which children give gifts to their parents and receive a blessing in return. Another religious holiday is Pchum Ben (the Feast of the Ancestors), celebrated in mid-September.

Japanese

The Japanese have come south quite slowly. By 1940 a few hundred Japanese were living as rice farmers in Texas, but no other concentrated communities were noted in the census of that year. Two of the World War II internment camps for Japanese Americans were located in Arkansas, incarcerating over 15,000 people until 1945, but the vast majority of those interned left the South at the war's end. The 1950 Census recorded only 3,000. Today, North Carolina alone is home to over 5,600 Japanese Americans, almost twice as many Filipinos, 12,600 Koreans, 15,600 Vietnamese, almost 19,000 Chinese, and over 25,000 Asian Indians.[95]

Transnationalism

As immigrants do around the world, new immigrants to the South often maintain links with their homelands. They frequently foster the immigration of friends and relations to join them in their new home and establish societies for the financial support of newly arrived fellow nationals. They may also import religious practitioners, educators, and performers of the expressive arts to teach their children their own cultural traditions and to create a focus for a community of their nationals. In many cases, immigrants save money to send to relatives in the homeland and to make return visits. This process is often referred to as transnationalism (when people maintain a cultural identity and social, economic, and political links to their homeland, but establish a new home abroad). Of the many groups now establishing transnational communities in the South, the Guatemalan Maya offer an excellent case study.

Guatemalan Mayans

Leaving their homeland during the civil war of the 1980s and 1990s, Guatemalan Mayans have immigrated particularly to South Florida in the tens of thousands. Near West Palm Beach, the settlement of Indiantown is known as a Mayan community. Guatemalan Mayans have also moved to the Carolinas, Georgia, and Alabama, settling together with others from their home villages. After an initial immigration period, spouses and relatives, schoolteachers, and practitioners of tra-

Leaving their homeland during the civil war of the 1980s and 1990s, many Guatemalan Maya immigrated to South Florida, the Carolinas, Georgia, and Alabama. Photograph by Merri Belland. Courtesy Florida Photographic Collection.

ditional arts soon followed. Many younger male Mayans are engaged in farmwork, including the nursery or poultry industries, or work for resort communities. With other Latino immigrants, Guatemalan Mayans are renting and buying houses in small southern towns that had previously experienced depopulation.[96]

Cuban Immigrants

Before the recent surge of Mexican immigrants, Cubans were one of the largest, and oldest, Latin American groups in the South. Florida has become a new home to more Cubans than any other state.[97] As early as 1831, Cubans were making cigars in Key West. Vicente Martínez Ybor brought Cuban cigar manufacturing to Tampa in the 1880s, where cigar-making flourished until about the time of World War I. Cubans who came to work in Tampa founded Ybor City (today Ybor is within the metropolitan area of Tampa). Ybor remains home to Cuban social clubs, Catholic churches, grocery stores and bakeries, and Cuban restaurants such as the Columbia. Opened in 1905, the restaurant seats 1,200, features flamenco dancing some weekends, and serves favorite Cuban dishes such as yellow rice and chicken, *boliche*, and flan. The Silver Ring sandwich shop is still known for serving the best "Cuban sandwiches." Ybor retains a residential area, but the main shopping area is now an art district and a popular venue for weekend nightlife. A statue of an immigrant family stands in Ybor's Centennial Park, and a museum dedicated to cigar factory workers is located near preserved workers' cottages. Many Cuban Social and Mutual Aid Society buildings remain (El Pasaje [Cherokee Club], 1896; El Centro Asturiano, formed in 1886 as a medical and social society for both Italians and Cubans; and the Cuban Club, 1916).

Descendants of these early Cuban immigrants to Tampa remain engaged in ethnic organizations, but were quickly upwardly mobile and are quite distinct from newer Cuban communities in and around Miami (now "a Cuban city"). After the Cuban Revolution of 1959 and until the mid-1970s, approximately 16,000 Cubans risked their lives to come to Florida as *balseros* (on homemade rafts) without permission from the Cuban or U.S. governments. Many more came in the famous 1980 Mariel sealift. The last large influx of Cubans came in 1994 when Fidel Castro announced that anyone wanting to leave Cuba was free to do so. Faced with assimilating the over 35,000 Cubans who did, the U.S. government returned to Cuba the rafters picked up by the U.S. Coast Guard. The South Florida Cubans remain deeply committed to political goals for their homeland and to bringing relatives to the United States, as sadly demonstrated by the notorious case of Elian Gonzalez, a six-year-old boy whose mother drowned on their flight to Florida; the child was returned to his father in Cuba.

Latino Immigrants

Demographic changes in the South make discussion of a biracial South out-moded. After the Southwest, the South has the highest proportion of Hispanics in the nation. The Census Bureau considers "Hispanic" to mean a person of Latin American descent (including persons of Cuban, Mexican, or Puerto Rican origin) living in the United States who may be of any "race" (which the Bureau oddly phrases as "white, black, Asian, etc."). Across the nation in the 1990s, the Hispanic population increased by 57.9 percent to 35.3 million (at a time when the U.S. population as a whole saw an increase of 13.2 percent). Hispanics now comprise the same proportion of the American population as African Americans. In the 2000 Census, Hispanics comprised 12.5 percent of the population while African Americans made up 12.3 percent.[98]

While the South's population grew 17.3 percent in the 1990s, to 100 million, and the area is now home to 36 percent of Americans, it is also home to 33.2 percent of Hispanics in America. Many recent Hispanic immigrants settled in north Georgia, contributing to Georgia's status as the fastest growing state in the region in the 1990s, with population growth of 26 percent. (The 1990s was the only decade in the twentieth century when Florida was not the South's fastest growing state.)[99] Georgia is home to two of the five U.S. counties that more than doubled their populations in the 1990s. In addition to Georgia, other nontraditional Hispanic states (North Carolina and Tennessee) experienced significant growth in Hispanic population.

North Carolina experienced a 400 percent rise in its Hispanic population from 1994 to 2004—largely due to the North Carolina Growers Association and other employers recruiting thousands of workers through the federal H2A guest worker program. Neither expecting nor demanding benefits, Mexican laborers have accepted such low wages that the average farmworker in North Carolina now earns less than $8,000 a year. In addition to documented guest worker program recruits, perhaps 50 percent of migrant laborers in North Carolina are working illegally. Their numbers are much more difficult to confirm, as are the percentages of such "guest" workers who make the South their permanent home.

Immigrants from Central and South America are forming new ethnic groups in the South, both with members of their own nations and through assimilation with southern ethnic groups. The next few decades will see the emergence of new creoles and mestizo cultures. From the Spanish *mestizaje*, "mestizo" refers to the social and reproductive blending between indigenous peoples, Africans, and/or Europeans. How will the increasing numbers of children born to parents of Latino and European or African backgrounds, whom Marcos Villatoro calls the new *Mestizaje*, define themselves?[100] What will demographic changes mean for the South culturally?

The 1970s saw some of the first Spanish-speaking Protestant churches in the South. Just thirty years later, Latino evangelicals outnumber Episcopalians and Presbyterians in the South.[101] Fiestas and *quinceaneras* (coming-of-age celebrations for fifteen-year-old girls) with hoop-skirted *quinceanera* dresses are becoming as common on the southern cultural landscape as hollerin' contests, swamp cabbage festivals, and bluegrass jamborees. Across the South, annual Hispanic festivals—like that in Augusta, Georgia; the Gran Fiesta de Fort Worth; the Fiesta Latina in Asheville, North Carolina; and the Festival Hispano in North Charleston, South

Carolina—are also increasingly appealing to non-Hispanic participants. The shape of such festivals demonstrates how immigrant communities assimilate not just to America, but to the southern region.[102] As Fredrik Barth asserted, the characteristics of a culture may change though its boundaries with other cultures remain.[103] The various new immigrants to the South may reshape what it means to be southern, but thus far new immigrants to the region have continued to express their identity in a southern style.

RESOURCE GUIDE

Printed Sources

Alba, Richard. *Ethnic Identity: The Transformation of White America*. New Haven: Yale University Press, 1990.

Ancelet, Barry Jean, Jay Edwards, and Glen Pitre. *Cajun Country*. Jackson: University Press of Mississippi, 1991.

Anderson, Benedict. *Imagined Communities*. London: Verso, 1983.

Appadurai, Arjun. "Theory in Anthropology: Center and Periphery." *Comparative Studies in Society and History* 28, no. 1 (1986): 356–361.

Ardener, Edwin. "The Construction of History: Vestiges of Creation." In *History and Ethnicity*, ed. Elizabeth Tonkin et al., 22–33. London: Routledge, 1989.

Axtell, James. *The Indians' New South: Cultural Change in the Colonial Southeast*. Baton Rouge: Louisiana State University Press, 1997.

Baird, W. David. *The Quapaw Indians: A History of the Downstream People*. Norman: University of Oklahoma Press, 1980.

Baker, Lee. *From Savage to Negro: Anthropology and the Construction of Race, 1896–1954*. Berkeley: University of California Press, 1998.

Banks, Marcus. *Ethnicity: Anthropological Constructions*. London: Routledge, 1996.

Barnes, Jessica, and Claudette Bennett. *The Asian Population, 2000*. Washington, DC: U.S. Census Bureau, 2002.

Barth, Fredrik, ed. *Ethnic Groups and Boundaries: The Social Organization of Cultural Differences*. Boston: Little, Brown, 1969.

Beaver, Patricia, and Helen Lewis. "Uncovering the Trail of Ethnic Denial: Ethnicity in Appalachia." In *Cultural Diversity in the U.S. South*, ed. Carole E. Hill and Patricia Beaver, 51–68. Athens: University of Georgia Press, 1998.

Belfiglio, Valentine. *The Italian Experience in Texas: A Closer Look*. Austin: Eakin Press, 1994.

Bender, Margaret. *Signs of Cherokee Culture: Sequoyah's Syllabary in Eastern Cherokee Life*. Chapel Hill: University of North Carolina Press, 2002.

Bendix, Regina. "Heredity, Hybridity and Heritage from One *Fin de Siècle* to the Next." In *Folklore, Heritage Politics and Ethnic Diversity*, ed. Pertti J. Anttonen. Botkyrka, Sweden: Multicultural Centre, 2000.

———. *In Search of Authenticity: The Formation of Folklore Studies*. Madison: University of Wisconsin Press, 1997.

Bernard, Shane. *The Cajuns: Americanization of a People*. Jackson: University of Mississippi Press, 2003.

———. *Swamp Pop: Cajun and Creole Rhythm and Blues*. Jackson: University of Mississippi Press, 1996.

Berry, Jason. *The Spirit of Black Hawk: A Mystery of Africans and Indians*. Jackson: University Press of Mississippi, 1995.

Bhabha, Homi K. *The Location of Culture*. London: Routledge, 1994.

Bird, Elizabeth, ed. *Dressing in Feathers: The Construction of the Indian in American Popular Culture*. Boulder, CO: Westview Press, 1996.

Blevins, Brooks. *Hill Folks: A History of Arkansas Ozarkers and Their Image*. Chapel Hill: University of North Carolina Press, 2002.

Blu, Karen. *The Lumbee Problem: The Making of an American Indian People*. Cambridge: Cambridge University Press, 1980.

———. "Region and Recognition: Southern Indians, Anthropologists, and Presumed Biology." In *Indians of the Southeastern United States in the Late Twentieth Century*, ed. J. Anthony Paredes, 71–85. Tuscaloosa: University of Alabama Press, 2001.

Boles, John. *The South Through Time: A History of an American Region*. Vol. 1. Upper Saddle River, NJ: Prentice-Hall, 1999.

Bonney, Rachel, and Anthony Paredes. *Anthropologists and Indians in the New South*. Tuscaloosa: University of Alabama Press, 2001.

Boswell, Thomas. "Cuban Americans." In *Ethnicity in Contemporary America: A Geographical Appraisal*, ed. Jesse McKee, 139–180. Lanham, MD: Rowman and Littlefield, 2000.

Brasseaux, Carl. *Acadian to Cajun: Transformation of a People, 1803–1877*. Jackson: University Press of Mississippi, 1992.

Bucuvalas, Tina. "Epiphany in Tarpon Springs." *Florida Heritage Magazine* 7, no. 4 (Fall 1999).

Burns, Allan. *Maya in Exile: Guatemalans in Florida*. Philadelphia: Temple University Press, 1993.

———. "The Newest Indians in the South: The Maya of Florida." In *Anthropologists and Indians in the New South*, ed. Rachel Bonney and Anthony Paredes, 108–125. Tuscaloosa: University of Alabama Press, 2001.

Carter, Cecile. *Caddo Indians: Where We Come From*. Norman: University of Oklahoma Press, 1995.

Cobb, James, *Redefining Southern Culture: Mind and Identity in the Modern South*. Athens: University of Georgia Press, 1999.

Coe, Joffre. *Town Creek Indian Mound: A Native American Legacy*. Chapel Hill: University of North Carolina Press, 1995.

Cohen, Ronald. 1978. "Ethnicity: Problem and Focus in Anthropology." *Annual Review of Anthropology* 7 (1978): 379–403.

Cook, Samuel. *Monacans and Miners: Native American and Coal Mining Communities in Appalachia*. Lincoln: University of Nebraska Press, 2000.

Crumley, Carole. "Heterarchy and the Analysis of Complex Societies." In *Heterarchy and the Analysis of Complex Societies*, ed. Robert Ehrenreich, Carole Crumley, and Janet Levy. Arlington, VA: Archaeological Papers of the American Anthropological Association, 1995.

———. "Three Locational Models: An Epistemological Assessment for Anthropology and Archaeology." In *Advances in Archaeological Method and Theory*, ed. Michael Schiffer, 141–173. New York: Academic Press, 1979.

De Vos, George, and Lola Romanucci-Ross, eds. *Ethnic Identity: Cultural Continuities and Change*. Palo Alto, CA: Mayfield, 1975.

Din, Gilbert. *The Canary Islanders of Louisiana*. Baton Rouge: Louisiana State University Press, 1988.

Domínguez, Virginia. *White by Definition: Social Classification in Creole Louisiana*. New Brunswick, NJ: Rutgers University Press, 1986.

Dorman, James, ed. *Creoles of Color of the Gulf South*. Knoxville: University of Tennessee Press, 1996.

Drake, Richard. *A History of Appalachia*. Lexington: University Press of Kentucky, 2001.

Dunaway, Wilma. *Slavery in the American Mountain South*. Cambridge: Cambridge University Press, 2003.

Early, Ann. "The Caddos of the Trans-Mississippi South." In *Indians of the Greater Southeast: Historical Archaeology and Ethnohistory*, ed. Bonnie McEwan, 122–141. Gainesville: University Press of Florida, 2000.

Elliott, Rita, and Daniel Elliott. "Guten Tag Bubba: Germans in the Colonial South." In *Another's Country: Archaeological and Historical Perspectives on Cultural Interactions in the Southern Colonies*, ed. J. W. Joseph and Martha Zierden, 79–92. Tuscaloosa: University of Alabama Press, 2002.

Ellis, Clyde. "'There's a Dance Every Weekend': Powwow Culture in Southeast North Carolina." In *Southern Heritage on Display: Public Ritual and Ethnic Diversity Within Southern Regionalism*, ed. Celeste Ray, 79–105. Tuscaloosa: University of Alabama Press, 2003.

Ethridge, Robbie. *Creek Country: The Creek Indians and Their World*. Chapel Hill: University of North Carolina Press, 2003.

Everett, C. S. "Melungeon History and Myth." *Appalachian Journal: A Regional Studies Review* 26, no. 4 (1999): 358–409.

Everett, C. S., and Marvin Richardson. "Ethnicity Affirmed: The Haliwa-Saponi and the Dance, Culture, and Meaning of North Carolina Powwows." In *Signifying Serpents and Mardi Gras Runners: Representing Identity in Selected Souths*, ed. Celeste Ray and Luke Eric Lassiter, 51–71. Athens: University of Georgia Press.

Finger, John. *Cherokee Americans: The Eastern Band of Cherokees in the Twentieth Century*. Lincoln: University of Nebraska Press, 1991.

———. *The Eastern Band of Cherokees, 1819–1900*. Knoxville: University of Tennessee Press, 1984.

Fink, Leon, and Alvis E. Dunn. *The Maya of Morganton: Work and Community in the Nuevo New South*. Chapel Hill, NC: University of North Carolina Press, 2003.

Forbes, Jack. *Africans and Native Americans: The Language of Race and the Evolution of Red-Black Peoples*. Urbana: University of Illinois Press, 1993.

Gannon, Peter Steven. *Huguenot Refugees in the Settling of Colonial America*. New York: Huguenot Society of America, 1985.

Gans, Herbert. "Symbolic Ethnicity: The Future of Ethnic Groups and Culture in America." *Ethnic and Racial Studies* 2 (January 1979): 1–20.

Gerster, Patrick. "Religion and Mythology." In *The Encyclopedia of Southern Culture*, ed. Charles Reagan Wilson and William Ferris, 488–491. Chapel Hill: University of North Carolina Press, 1989.

———. "Stereotypes." In *The Encyclopedia of Southern Culture*, ed. Charles Reagan Wilson and William Ferris, 494–496. Chapel Hill: University of North Carolina Press, 1989.

Gibson, Arrell. *The Chickasaws*. Lincoln: University of Nebraska Press, 1971.

Glazer, Nathan, and David Moynihan. *Beyond the Melting Pot: The Negroes, Puerto Ricans, Jews, Italians, and Irish of New York City*. Cambridge: MIT Press, 1963.

Gleeson, David T. *The Irish in the South, 1815–1877*. Chapel Hill: University of North Carolina Press, 2001.

Goldfield, David. *Black, White, and Southern: Race Relations and Southern Culture, 1940 to the Present*. Baton Rouge: Louisiana State University Press, 1990.

Gossett, Thomas. *Race: The History of an Idea in America*. Dallas: Southern Methodist University Press, 1963.

Granthan, Bill. *Creation Myths and Legends of the Creek Indians*. Gainesville: University of Florida Press, 2002.

Greenbaum, Susan. *More than Black: Afro-Cubans in Tampa*. Gainesville: University Press of Florida, 2002.

Grieco, Elizabeth, and Rachel Cassidy. "Overview of Race and Hispanic Origin." *Census 2000 Brief*. Washington, D.C.: U.S. Census Bureau, 2001.

Griffin, Patricia. *Mullet on the Beach: The Minorcans of Florida, 1768–1788*. Jacksonville: University of North Florida Press, 1991.

Guzmán, Betsy. "The Hispanic Population." *Census 2000 Brief*. Washington, D.C.: U.S. Census Bureau, 2001.

Hall, Gwendolyn Midlo. *Africans in Colonial Louisiana: The Development of Afro-Creole Culture in the Eighteenth Century*. Baton Rouge: Louisiana State University Press, 1995.

Hall, Jonathan. *Ethnic Identity in Greek Antiquity*. Cambridge: Cambridge University Press, 1997.

Hall, Stuart. "Cultural Identity and Diaspora." In *Identity: Community, Culture, Difference*, ed. J. Rutherford, 222–238. London: Lawrence and Wishart, 1990.

Halter, Marilyn. *Shopping for Identity: The Marketing of Ethnicity*. New York: Schocken Books, 2000.

Hancock, Ian. "Gypsies." In *Encyclopedia of Southern Culture*, ed. Charles Reagan Wilson and William Ferris, 57–58. Chapel Hill: University of North Carolina Press, 1989.

Harrison, Faye. "The Persistent Power of 'Race' in the Cultural and Political Economy of Racism." *Annual Review of Anthropology* 24 (1995): 47–74.

Hartley, Michael. "Bethania: A Colonial Moravian Adaptation." In *Another's Country: Archaeological and Historical Perspectives on Cultural Interactions in the Southern Colonies*, ed. J. W. Joseph and Martha Zierden, 111–132. Tuscaloosa: University of Alabama Press, 2002.

Hill, Carole E. "Contemporary Issues in Anthropological Studies of the American South." In *Cultural Diversity in the U.S. South: Anthropological Contributions to a Region in Transition*, ed. Carole E. Hill and Patricia D. Beaver, 12–33. Southern Anthropological Society Proceedings, No. 31. Athens: University of Georgia Press, 1998.

Hirsch, Arnold, and Joseph Logsdon, eds. *Creole New Orleans: Race and Americanization*. Baton Rouge: Louisiana State University Press, 1992.

Hook, Jonathan. *The Alabama-Coushatta Indians*. College Station: Texas A&M University Press, 1997.

Hudson, Charles. *The Catawba Nation*. Athens: University of Georgia Press, 1970.

———. Introduction to *Red, White and Black: Symposium on Indians in the Old South*, ed. Charles Hudson, 1–11. Athens: University of Georgia Press, 1971.

Hyde, Samuel. "Introduction: Perspectives on the Common South." In *Plain Folk of the South Revisited*, ed. Samuel Hyde, 1–20. Baton Rouge: Louisiana State University Press, 1997.

Inscoe, John. *Appalachians and Race: The Mountain South from Slavery to Segregation*. Lexington: University Press of Kentucky, 2001.

———. *Mountain Masters, Slavery, and the Sectional Crisis in Western North Carolina*. Knoxville: University of Tennessee Press, 1989.

Jones, George, and Renate Wilson. *Detailed Reports on the Salzburger Emigrants Who Settled in America*. Volume 18, 1744–1745. Camden, ME: Picton Press, 1995.

Jones, Loyal. *Faith and Meaning in the Southern Uplands*. Urbana: University of Illinois Press, 1999.

Joyner, Charles Winston. *Shared Traditions: Southern History and Folk Culture*. Urbana: University of Illinois Press, 1999.

———. "A Single Southern Culture: Cultural Interaction in the Old South." In *Black and White: Cultural Interaction in the Antebellum South*, ed. Ted Ownby, 3–22. Jackson: University Press of Mississippi, 1993.

———. "The South as a Folk Culture: David Potter and the Southern Enigma." In *The Southern Enigma: Essays on Race, Class and Folk Culture*, ed. Walter J. Fraser and Winfred B. Moore, 157–167. Westport, CT: Greenwood Press, 1983.

Kehoe, Alice. *Land of Prehistory: A Critical History of American Archaeology*. New York: Routledge, 1998.

Kein, Sybil, ed. *Creole: The History and Legacy of Louisiana's Free People of Color*. Baton Rouge: Louisiana State University Press, 2000.

Keith, Jeanette. *The South: A Concise History*. Vol. 1. Upper Saddle River, NJ: Prentice-Hall, 2002.

Landers, Jane. *Black Society in Spanish Florida.* Urbana: University of Illinois Press, 1999.

Lavere, David. *Contrary Neighbors: Southern Plains and Removed Indians in Indian Territory.* Norman: University of Oklahoma Press, 2000.

Lefler, Lisa. "Stress and Coping among Chickasaw Indian Fathers: Lessons for Indian Adolescents and Their Counselors in Treatment or Substance Abuse." In *Southern Indians and Anthropologists: Culture, Politics, and Identity*, ed. Lisa Lefler and Frederic Gleach, 115–123. Athens: University of Georgia Press, 2002.

Leitch, J. Wright. "The Original Southerners." In *Major Problems in the History of the American South*, ed. Paul Escott and David Goldfield, 50–66. Lexington, MA: D. C. Heath, 1990.

Lerch, Patricia. "Powwows, Parades and Social Drama among the Waccamaw Sioux." *Museum Anthropology* 16, no. 2 (1993).

Loewen, James. *The Mississippi Chinese: Between Black and White.* Prospect Heights, IL: Waveland Press, 1988.

Malcolmson, Scott. *One Drop of Blood: The American Misadventure of Race.* New York: Farrar Straus Giroux, 2000.

McEwan, Bonnie, ed. *Indians of the Greater Southeast: Historical Archaeology and Ethnohistory.* Gainesville: University Press of Florida, 2000.

McGuire, James Patrick. *The Hungarian Texans.* San Antonio: University of Texas at San Antonio, Institute of Texan Cultures, 1994.

McKee, Jesse. "Humanity on the Move." In *Ethnicity in Contemporary America: A Geographical Appraisal*, ed. Jesse McKee, 19–48. Lanham, MD: Rowman and Littlefield, 2000.

Mills, Gary. *The Forgotten People: Cane River's Creoles of Color.* Baton Rouge: Louisiana State University Press, n.d.

———. "Tracing Free People of Color in the Antebellum South: Methods, Sources, and Perspectives." *National Genealogical Society Quarterly* 78, no. 4 (1990): 262–278.

Moore, Angela. "Latinos and Southern Religion." Paper presented at the annual meeting of the Southern Anthropological Society, Atlanta, Georgia, 2004.

Moretti-Langholtz. *We're Still Here: Contemporary Virginia Indians Tell Their Stories.* Richmond: Palari Press, 2000.

Nagel, Joane. "Constructing Ethnicity: Creating and Recreating Ethnic Identity and Culture." In *New Tribalisms: The Resurgence of Race and Ethnicity*, ed. Michael Hughey, 237–272. New York: New York University Press, 1998.

Niehaus, Earl. *The Irish in New Orleans.* Baton Rouge: Louisiana State University Press, 1965.

Paredes, Anthony. "Federal Recognition and the Poarch Creek Indians." In *Indians of the Southeastern United States in the Late Twentieth Century*, ed. J. Anthony Paredes, 120–139. Tuscaloosa: University of Alabama Press, 1992.

Perdue, Theda, and Michael Green. *The Columbia Guide to American Indians of the Southeast.* New York: Columbia University, 2001.

Perry, Marc J., and Paul J. Mackun. "Population Change and Distribution." *Census 2000 Brief.* Washington, DC: U.S. Census Bureau, 2001.

Perttula, Timothy. *The Caddo Nation.* Austin: University of Texas Press, 1992.

Porter, Kenneth. *The Black Seminoles: History of a Freedom-Seeking People.* Rev. and ed. Alcione Amos and Thomas Senter. Gainesville: University Press of Florida, 1996.

Puckett, Anita. "The Melungeon Identity Movement and the Construction of Appalachian Whiteness." *Journal of Linguistic Anthropology* 11, no. 1 (2001): 131–146.

Quan, Robert Seto. *Lotus among the Magnolias: The Mississippi Chinese.* Jackson: University Press of Mississippi, 1982.

Ray, Celeste. *Highland Heritage: Scottish Americans in the American South.* Chapel Hill: University of North Carolina Press, 2001.

———. Introduction to *Southern Heritage on Display: Public Ritual and Ethnic Diversity Within*

Southern Regionalism, ed. Celeste Ray, 1–37. Tuscaloosa: University of Alabama Press, 2003.

Reed, John Shelton. "The Cherokee Princess in the Family Tree." *Southern Cultures* 3 (Spring 1997): 111–113.

———. Mixing in the Mountains. *Southern Cultures* 3, no. 4 (1997): 25–36.

———. *One South: An Ethnic Approach to Regional Culture*. Baton Rouge: Louisiana State University Press, 1982.

———. *Southern Folk, Plain and Fancy: Native White Social Types*. Athens: University of Georgia Press, 1986.

Rhoads, Edward. "The Chinese in Texas." *Southwestern Historical Quarterly* 81 (July 1977): 1–36.

Roberts, John Storm. *Black Music of Two Worlds: African, Caribbean, Latin, and African-American Traditions*. New York: Schirmer Books, 1998.

Ross, Thomas. *American Indians in North Carolina: Geographic Interpretations*. Southern Pines, NC: Karo Hollow Press, 1999.

Roth, George. "Federal Tribal Recognition in the South." In *Anthropologists and Indians in the New South*, ed. Rachel Bonney and Anthony Paredes, 49–70. Tuscaloosa: University of Alabama Press, 2001.

Rountree, Helen. "Indian Virginians on the Move." In *Indians of the Southeastern United States in the Late Twentieth Century*, ed. Anthony Paredes, 9–28. Tuscaloosa: University of Alabama Press, 1992.

———. *Pocahontas's People: The Powhatan Indians of Virginia Through Four Centuries*. Norman: University of Oklahoma Press, 1990.

Sabo, George. "Reordering Their World: A Caddoan Ethnohistory." In *Visions and Revisions: Ethnohistoric Perspectives on Southern Cultures*, ed. G. Sabo and W.M. Schneider, 25–47. Athens: University of Georgia Press, 1987.

Sandmel, Ben, and Rick Olivier. *Zydeco!* Jackson: University Press of Mississippi, 1999.

Schrift, Melissa. "Melungeons and the Politics of Heritage." In *Southern Heritage on Display: Public Rituals and Ethnic Diversity Within Southern Regionalism*, ed. Celeste Ray, 106–129. Tuscaloosa: University of Alabama Press, 2003.

Sheskin, Ira. "American Jews." In *Ethnicity in Contemporary America: A Geographical Appraisal*. ed. Jesse McKee. Lanham, MD: Rowman and Littlefield, 2000.

Shlasko, Ellen. "Frenchmen and Africans in South Carolina: Cultural Interaction on the Eighteenth-Century Frontier." In *Another's Country: Archaeological and Historical Perspectives on Cultural Interactions in the Southern Colonies*, ed. J.W. Joseph and Martha Zierden, 133–144. Tuscaloosa: University of Alabama Press, 2002.

Sider, Gerald. *Living Indian Histories: Lumbee and Tuscarora People in North Carolina*. Chapel Hill: University of North Carolina Press, 2003.

———. *Lumbee Indian Histories: Race, Ethnicity, and Indian Identity in the Southern United States*. Cambridge: Cambridge University Press, 1993.

Smith, Lee. "The Forgotten South: Far from the White Columns and Marble Generals." *Charlotte Observer*, August 4, 1996, Q3.

Smith, Todd. *The Caddos, the Wichitas, and the United States, 1846–1901*. College Station: Texas A&M University Press, 1996.

Sollers, Werner. *Beyond Ethnicity: Consent and Descent in American Culture*. Oxford: Oxford University Press, 1986.

Stanton, Max. "A Remnant Indian Community: The Houma of Southern Louisiana." In *The Not So Solid South: Anthropological Studies in a Regional Subculture*, ed. Kenneth Morland, 82–92. Athens: University of Georgia Press, 1971.

Stoeltje, Beverly J. "Festival." In *Folklore, Cultural Performances, and Popular Entertainments*, ed. Richard Bauman. Oxford: Oxford University Press, 1992.

Swanton, John. *The Indians of the Southeastern United States*. Washington, DC: Smithsonian Institution Press, 1988.

Therrien, Melissa, and Roberto R. Ramirez. "The Hispanic Population in the United States." Census 2000 Brief. Washington, DC: U.S. Census Bureau, 2001.

Thornton, John. *Africa and Africans in the Making of the Atlantic World, 1400–1800*. 2nd ed. Cambridge: Cambridge University Press, 1998.

Tindall, George Brown. *Natives and Newcomers: Ethnic Southerners and Southern Ethnics*. Athens: University of Georgia Press, 1995.

Titon, Jeff Todd. "Zydeco: A Musical Hybrid." *Journal of American Folklore* 94, no. 373 (July–September 1981): 403–405.

Turner, Randolph. "Socio-political Organization Within the Powhatan Chiefdom and the Effects of European Contact, A.D. 1607–1646." In *Cultures in Contact: The Impact of European Contacts on Native American Cultural Institutions, A.D. 1000–1800*, ed. William Fitzhugh, 193–224. Washington, DC: Smithsonian Institution Press, 1985.

Turner, William, and Edward Cabbell, eds. *Blacks in Appalachia*. Lexington: University Press of Kentucky, 1985.

Twyman, Bruce. *The Black Seminole Legacy and North American Politics, 1693–1845*. Washington, DC: Howard University Press, 1999.

VanSpanckeren, Kathryn. "The Mardi Gras Indian Song Cycle: A Heroic Tradition." In *Southern Heritage on Display: Public Ritual and Ethnic Diversity Within Southern Regionalism*, ed. Celeste Ray, 57–78. Tuscaloosa: University of Alabama Press, 2003.

Villatoro, Marcos McPeek. "Latino Southerners: A New Form of *Mestizaje*." In *Cultural Diversity in the U.S. South*, ed. Carole E. Hill and Patricia D. Beaver, 104–114. Athens: University of Georgia Press, 1998.

Walls, Thomas. *The Japanese Texans*. San Antonio: University of Texas at San Antonio, Institute of Texan Cultures, 1996.

Walton, Shana. "Louisiana's Coonasses: Choosing Race and Class over Ethnicity." In *Signifying Serpents and Mardi Gras Runners: Representing Identity in Selected Souths*, ed. Celeste Ray and Luke Eric Lassiter, 38–50. Athens: University of Georgia Press, 2003.

Weisman, Brent Richards. *Unconquered People: Florida's Seminole and Miccosukee Indians*. Gainesville: University Press of Florida, 1999.

Wikramanayake, Marina. *A World in Shadow: The Free Black in Antebellum South Carolina*. Columbia: University of South Carolina Press, 1973.

Willis, John. *Forgotten Time: The Yazoo-Mississippi Delta after the Civil War*. Charlottesville: University of Virginia Press, 2000.

Wilson, Charles Reagan. "The Myth of the Biracial South." In *The Southern State of Mind*, ed. Jan Nordby Gretlund, 3–22. Columbia: University of South Carolina Press, 1999.

———. *The New Regionalism: Essays and Commentaries*. Jackson: University Press of Mississippi, 1998.

Wood, Peter. "Re-Counting the Past: Revolutionary Changes in the Early South." *Southern Exposure* 16, no. 2 (Summer 1988): 30–37.

Wright, Muriel. *A Guide to the Indian Tribes of Oklahoma*. Norman: University of Oklahoma Press, 1986.

Wust, Klaus. *The Virginia Germans*. Charlottesville: University of Virginia Press, 1969.

Young, D. C., and Stephen Young. "Ethnic Mississippi 1992." In *Ethnic Heritage in Mississippi*, ed. Barbara Carpenter, 157–198. Jackson: University Press of Mississippi, 1992.

Young, Gloria, and Michael Hoffman. "Quapaw." In *Handbook of North American Indians*, vol. 1, *The Plains*, ed. Raymond DeMallie. Washington, DC: Smithsonian Institution, 2002.

Web Sites

Alabama-Coushatta Tribe of Texas
http://www.alabama-coushatta.com

Alabama Folklife Program
http://www.arts.state.al.us/folklife/folklife.htm

Black Seminoles (The University of Texas Institute of Texan Cultures [ITC] at San Antonio)
http://www.texancultures.utsa.edu/seminole/blackseminoleintro.htm

Catawba Tribe of South Carolina
http://www.catawba-nation.nsn.us

Center for the Study of Southern Culture, University of Mississippi
http://www.olemiss.edu/depts/south/

Center for the Study of the American South, University of North Carolina at Chapel Hill
http://www.unc.edu/depts/csas/archives_resources/

Chattahoochee Folklife Project
http://www.hcc-al-ga.org/folk_index.cfm

Chickasaw Nation
http://www.chickasaw.net/index.html

Chitimacha Nation
http://chitimacha.com/

Council for the Development of French in Louisiana (CODOFIL)
http://www.codofil.org/

Coushatta Tribe of Louisiana
http://www.coushattatribela.org/

Creole Studies Consortium at Tulane University's Deep South Regional Humanities Center
http://deepsouth.tulane.edu/programs/creole.html

Florida Folklife Program
http://dhr.dos.state.fl.us/folklife/

Jena Band of Choctaw Indians
http://www.jenachoctaw.org/

Louisiana's Living Traditions
http://www.louisianafolklife.org/LT/creole_articles.html
A collection of detailed and diverse articles on Louisiana's ethnic groups.

Low Country Gullah Geechee Culture
http://www.nps.gov/sero/ggsrs/gg_res.htm

Miccosukee Tribe of Florida
http://www.miccosukeeseminolenation.com/

Mississippi Band of Choctaw Indians
http://www.choctaw.org/

Official Homepage of the Eastern Band of Cherokee
http://www.cherokee-nc.com/

Poarch Band Creek
http://www.poarchcreekindians-nsn.gov

Seminole Tribe of Florida
http://www.seminoletribe.com/

Texas State Historical Association's Handbook of Texas Online
http://www.tsha.utexas.edu/handbook/online/
A multidisciplinary encyclopedia of Texas history, geography, and culture.

Tunica-Biloxi
http://www.tunica.org/

Virginia Folklife Program
http://www.virginiafolklife.org/

Videos/Films

Documentaries

Black Indians: An American Story. 2000. VHS (60 min.). Dallas: Rich-Heape Films. Explores interactions between Native Americans and African Americans.

Black Warriors of the Seminole. 1990. PBS documentary on the relationship between African Americans and Florida Seminole.

Borders and Identity. 1996. VHS (57 min.). This video considers complex notions of identity connected to occupational traditions and expressive culture along the United States/Mexico border. Grades 6–12. Smithsonian Center for Folklife and Cultural Heritage.

Cajun Crossroads. 1987. Produced by WLAE-TV, New Orleans; directed by Karen Snyder. This documentary explores Cajun communities from the bayou and the prairie to the city, examining the lives of oil rig workers, professionals, and fisherfolk.

Catawba: The River People. 1987. VHS (18 min.). Charlotte, NC: Charlotte-Mecklenburg schools. A history of the Native American tribe indigenous to North and South Carolina.

The Corn Lady. 1991. VHS. Tallahassee: AIMM Video Productions. Betty Mae Jumper, former tribal chairperson of the Seminoles, tells folk stories.

Cultural Contributions of German-Speaking Settlers [in South Carolina]. 1996. VHS (c. 20 min.). Helene M. Kastinger Riley. Documents an exhibit at Clemson University, Clemson, SC, October 1–November 30, 1996. The exhibit documents early settlements of Germans in South Carolina and contributions of Germans and German Americans in the state in art, architecture, religion, music, politics, and religion.

Dance for a Chicken: The Prairie Cajun Mardi Gras. 1993. VHS (60 min.). Directed by Patrick Mire; produced by Liberty Cultural Association. This documentary examines rural Cajun Mardi Gras traditions, focusing on the "gumbo run" in which masked participants go door to door in search of ingredients for a communal Fat Tuesday feast.

Dancing the Shrimp. 1992. (60 min.). Produced by Magic Lantern Films for Louisiana Public Broadcast. Directed by James and Isabel Kenny. This documentary tells the story of Filipino immigrants to Louisiana and focuses on those who lived in Little Manila, on Barataria Bay, where they made a living by shrimping and fishing.

Delta Jews: Jews in the Land of the Blues. 1999. VHS (57 min.). Produced and directed by

Mike DeWitt and Alfred Uhry. Oxford: Mississippi Educational Television. This documentary considers the relationship between the Delta's Jewish community and its white and black Christian neighbors. While individuals exhibit southern accents and attitudes, they have maintained Jewish traditions.

Family Across the Sea. 1990. VHS (56 min.). Produced and directed by Domino Boulware, Tim Carrier, and Augusta Baker. San Francisco: California Newsreel. Members of a Gullah community travel to Sierra Leone on a heritage pilgrimage.

Finding Refuge in Alabama. 1992. VHS (26 min.). Alabama is home to close to 4,000 refugees. This documentary considers the Cambodian settlement in 1985 at Irvington, Alabama, the Laos community at Opelika, and the Vietnamese setters of Bayou La Batre.

From China to Louisiana. 2003. Tina Soong and Mackie Blanton (Rusty Nail Productions) created this three-part historical documentary on the Chinese in Louisiana featuring oral histories and interviews for Louisiana's WVUE-TV Fox 8.

Good for What Ails You: Healing Secrets of the Creoles and Bayou Indians. 1998. VHS (60 min.). Directed by Glen Pitre. This documentary considers ethnic faith healing, folk remedies, and ritual magic through interviews with one Cajun, one Creole, and one Houma Indian.

Hidden Nation: The Story of the Houmas, Louisiana's Largest Native American Tribe. 1993. VHS (57 min.). Directed by Barbara Sillery and Bill Yeager. This documentary tells the story of the United Houma Nation of south Louisiana and their quest to gain federal recognition.

Island of Saints and Souls. 1990. VHS (29 min.). Directed and produced by Neil Alexander. This documentary examines ethnic expressions of Catholicism in New Orleans; the traditions of throwing cabbages on St. Patrick's Day, building St. Joseph's Day altars, and tending family graves on All Saints' Day; and the story of the city's own saint, St. Expedite.

Italian New Orleans. 2001. Produced by Terry Landry. Directed by Dave Landry. VHS (60 min.). Beginning in the 1700s, this video explores the contributions of Italian Americans to New Orleans.

Miss India Georgia. 1997. VHS (56 min.). Produced and directed by Daniel Friedman and Sharon Grimberg. Yellow Springs, OH: Urban Life Productions. The experience of first-generation Native Americans in Georgia.

The Native Americans: The Southeast. 1994. Turner Broadcasting System production; part of a series.

Old Salem. 1990. VHS (Video tour; 30 min.). Glastonbury, CT: VideoTours. This video gives a brief history of the Moravians in North Carolina and a tour of their settlement at Old Salem.

The People. 1993. University of Alabama Center for Public TV and Radio. Produced by George Smith Alabama Experience Series. Conversations with Cherokee, Creek, Shawnee, and Choctaw tribal members at the 1993 Native American Festival in Moundville and the Southeastern Native American Celebration at the Red Mountain Museum in Birmingham.

Pushcarts and Plantations: Jewish Life in Louisiana. 1999. VHS (54 min.). Produced by Carousel Films (New York); directed by Brian Cohen. This documentary examines three centuries of Jewish history in Louisiana from the French colonial period to the present and considers the cultural exchanges among Jews, Cajuns, and Creoles.

Scots-Irish Heritage: Thomas "Kanawha" Spratt. 1990. VHS (28 min.). Series director Mary Long. Columbia: South Carolina Educational Television Network. Story of the Scots-Irish pioneers in South Carolina, concentrating on Thomas Spratt, the first settler in York County.

A Singing Stream: A Black Family Chronicle. 1987 (57 min.). This film tells the story of the musically gifted Landis family from Granville County, North Carolina. The documentary uses interviews, scenes from daily life, and footage of the Landis family performing at reunions, gospel concerts, and church services to explore African American life in the rural South. Directed by Tom Davenport and produced by Davenport Films and the Curriculum in Folklore at UNC, Chapel Hill with Daniel Patterson and Allen Tullos.

The Snowbird Cherokees. 1995. VHS (approx. 60 min.). Columbia, SC: South Carolina ETV. Narrated by Fred Bradley. History and folklore of the Eastern Band of the Cherokee. Interviews with Cherokee consider creation myths, stories of fairies ("little people"), family life, continuing native and Christian rituals, ceremonial dances, and folk music.

Strangers and Kin: A History of the Hillbilly Image. 1984. VHS (58 min.). Whitesburg, KY: Appalshop. This video explores prejudices and misconceptions about Appalachian people and their identity.

For a wide range of films on Appalachian culture see the Web site for Appalshop, http://www.appalshop.org/film/.

You can learn more about the Isleño community through a documentary by St. Bernard's Parish Historian Emeritus Frank Fernandez in conjunction with New Orleans Public Television Station WYES entitled *Louisiana's Disappearing Spanish Legacy* (1975). The documentary includes interviews with septuagenarian and octogenarian oral history informants from the mid-1970s.

Films

The Blood Is Strong: The Gaelic Scots Abroad. 1988. VHS (approx. 60 min.). Aberdeen, Scotland: Grampian Television PCL. Narrated by Angus Peter Campbell, directed by Bernd Shulze, and produced by Ted Brocklebank. Tape 2 of the three-part series considers Highland Scots who came to North and South Carolina.

Every Island Has Its Own Song: The Tsimouris Family. 1988. VHS (27 min.). WEDU (St. Petersburg Public Television); Florida Folklife. The Tsimouris family of Tarpon Springs, Florida, describe their life as Floridians and their retention of Greek traditions.

Grandfather Mountain Highland Games. 2001. VHS (55 min.). Dumfriesshire, Scotland: Border Heritage Ltd. This video discusses several of the activities that shape the annual Scottish Highland Games in Linville, North Carolina.

Land of Promise: The Jews of South Carolina. 2002. VHS (57 min.). Big Pictures; Jewish Historical Society of South Carolina.

Living in America: One Hundred Years of Ybor City. 1992. VHS (52 min.). New York: Modern Educational Video Network. This documentary relates the history of Cuban, Spanish, and Italian immigrants to Tampa to work in the cigar industry and how their community has changed in recent decades.

Miami-Havana. 1992. VHS (52 min.). New York: Cinema Guild. This documentary discusses the identity of Cubans in Florida and their politically induced separation from family members in Cuba.

Sea Island Journey. 1992. Film (30 min.). National Geographic Society Educational Services. This documentary considers conflicts between development in the South Carolina Atlantic coast islands and the traditional way of life for the Gullah.

Organizations, Museums, Special Collections
Museums/Archaeological Sites Connected to Native Americans

Alabama-Coushatta Indian Museum on Alabama-Coushatta Reservation near Livingston, Texas
http://www.alabama-coushatta.com

Caddoan Mounds State Historical Site, near Alto, Texas
http://www.tpwd.state.tx.us/park/caddoan/caddoan.htm

Cherokee Chief Joseph Vann's House, Chatsworth, Georgia
http://ngeorgia.com/parks/chief.html and http://home.alltel.net/vannhouse/

Chieftains Museum, Rome, Georgia
http://www.chieftainsmuseum.org/

Chucalissa Indian Town and Museum, Memphis, Tennessee
http://cas.memphis.edu/chucalissa

Colonial National Historical Park, Jamestown Visitor Center, Virginia
http://www.nps.gov/colo

Cumberland Gap National Historic Park, near Harrogate, Tennessee
http://www.nps.gov/cuga/index.htm

Emerald Mound, Natchez Trace Parkway, Mississippi
http://www.cr.nps.gov/aad/feature/emerald.htm

Etowah Mounds State Park, Cartersville, Georgia
http://ngeorgia.com/parks/etowah.html

Five Civilized Tribes Museum (located in Oklahoma)
http://www.fivetribes.org/

Fort Matanzas National Monument, near St. Augustine, Florida
http://www.nps.gov/foma/home/home.htm

Grand Village of the Natchez Indians
http://www.mdah.state.ms.us/hprop/gvni.html
Administered by the Mississippi Department of Archives and History in Natchez (a native ceremonial mound center during the French colonial period).

Kings Mounds (Ancient Buried City), near Wickliffe, Kentucky
http://www.uky.edu/OtherOrgs/KMNH/pages/areamus.htm#wickliffe

Madira Bickel Mound, near Bradenton, Florida
http://www.floridastateparks.org/madirabickelmound/default.asp

McClung Museum, University of Tennessee, Knoxville
http://mcclungmuseum.utk.edu

Monacan Ancestral Museum
http://www.monacannation.com/museum.shtml

Moundville (Alabama)
http://www.ua.edu/academic/museums/moundville/sketch.html

Oconaluftee Indian Village, Cherokee, North Carolina
http://www.oconalufteevillage.com

Old Stone Fort State Park, Manchester, Tennessee
http://www.state.tn.us/environment/parks/parks/OldStoneFort

Pamunkey Indian Museum, King William, Virginia
http://home.earthlink.net/~pamunkey/museum.htm

Pinson Mounds State Archaeological Area, near Jackson, Tennessee
http://www.state.tn.us/environment/parks/parks/PinsonMounds

Poverty Point State Commemorative Area (Archaic), near Epps, Louisiana
http://www.crt.state.la.us/crt/parks/poverty/pvertypt.htm

Santee Indian Mound, near Santee, South Carolina

Thunderbird Museum and Archaeological Park, Front Royal, Virginia

Toltec Mounds State Park, near Little Rock, Arkansas
http://www.cast.uark.edu/parkin/toltecvisitpg.html

Town Creek Indian Mound, State Historic Site, near Mount Gilead, North Carolina
http://www.ah.dcr.state.nc.us/sections/hs/town/town.htm

Tunica-Biloxi Tribal Museum
http://www.tunica.org/museum.htm

Other Museums of Interest

Acadian Museum
http://www.tourlouisiana.com/acadian_museum.htm

Appalachian Cultural Museum at Appalachian State University
http://www.museum.appstate.edu/

Beth Ahabah Museum and Archives Museum of Richmond, Virginia's Jewish History
http://www.bethahabah.org/museum/museum.html

Black History Museum and Cultural Center, Richmond, Virginia
http://www.blackhistorymuseum.org

Cajun Village, Sorrento, Louisiana
http://www.tourlouisiana.com/cajun_village.htm

Chattanooga African American Museum
http://www.caamhistory.com/

Frontier Culture Museum, Staunton, Virginia
http://www.frontiermuseum.org/
Examines the life of German, Irish, and English immigrants before emigration and after settlement in the Virginia frontier and backcountry.

Louisiana State University Rural Life Museum
http://www.tourlouisiana.com/rural_life_museum.htm

Mountain Heritage Center at Western North Carolina University, Cullowhee
http://www.wcu.edu/mhc/

Ozarks Afro-American Heritage Museum
http://www.oaahm.org/

St. Bernard Parish's Los Isleños Museum Complex
http://www.losislenos.org/complex.htm
Features vernacular architecture.

Scottish Tartan Museum and Heritage Center in Franklin, North Carolina
http://www.scottishtartans.org/

FASHION

*Maaja A. Stewart,
with Bryce Reveley*

The uniqueness of the American South becomes instantly recognizable in stereo-typical clothing in the narratives of popular culture, if not in reality. The images are memorable: Scarlett O'Hara creating her wasplike waist with the help of a bed-post and a mammy; the grinning, broad-faced Aunt Jemima with her headscarf tied into rabbit ears offering food and unconditional nurture; Li'l Abner's Daisy Mae with her bare feet and lush body bursting out of ragged seams; the aged, elegant Colonel Sanders with the immaculate whiteness of his hair, mustache, and suit. As currency in movies and advertisements, these images of instantly recognizably southern uniqueness multiply: Miss Daisy, the quintessential aging southern lady whose accessories—high heels, gloves, hat, and black chauffeur—signify her leisure as well as protections against dust, sun, and movement; the stylish riverboat gam-bler; the free mulatto woman of color of New Orleans with her elaborate head-dress and flamboyant clothing, both suggesting voodoo connections; the redneck with a Confederate flag on his baseball cap; southern belles sweeping their way across spacious lawns in front of white colonnaded houses in diaphanous dresses and shawls. These can be difficult images, as are any stereotypes of culture. They can also be read as an elaborately coded vision of sartorial discriminations and hi-erarchies (distinctions signaled through clothing) that remains a heritage of a pe-culiar culture of slavery. The unique climate necessary for growing many southern crops, including those essential to the cloth trade so lucrative in the global econ-omy, remains the context of such cultural images.

CLIMATE VS. CULTURAL HIERARCHIES

The climate of the South, which ranges from moderate to semitropical, invites the comfort of light, loose clothing of fine cottons and linens. In a culture in which distinctions between those who live in leisure and those who labor must become naturalized, however, comfort is often secondary to the need to reinforce

161

Close-fitting, heavily layered clothing styles of European origin proved uncomfortable in the hot and humid southern climate. Jane Sabate-Newman and Juanita Huici, descendants of the original indentured Minorcans, model eighteenth-century fashions, Florida, 1959. Photo by Merri Belland. Courtesy Florida Photographic Collection.

through clothing the differences in skin. The climate can emphasize sacrifices made by the body to maintain such distinctions in hierarchy and entitlement: the body encased in hoopskirts, crinolines, bustles, corsets, tight pantaloons, high cravats, and gloves in a semitropical environment—and this without perspiring—becomes distinctly different from the body of the laboring slave in loose-fitting, unadorned, rough, work- and sweat-stained clothing. The need to add marks of difference in addition to those of skin color then becomes embodied in the form, material, and details of southern sartorial practices. Various attempts in the eighteenth and nineteenth centuries to reinforce such distinctions by laws emphasize their cultural importance. Instances of violence directed against those who flaunted these distinctions reveal how thoroughly sartorial practices in a society involve sometimes desperately internalized images of identity and values. Clothing, therefore, becomes one site where social order seeks to stabilize authority and prestige, and where, inevitably, authority and prestige will be contested.

The African slaves and their European masters came from opposed textile traditions. The Europeans, in their form-fitting, tailored clothing, were heirs of the ancient Mongol/Gaul tradition designated "humanity sewn" by Philippe Perrot in his brilliant book *Fashioning the Bourgeoisie*, whereas the West Africans wore clothing made of uncut cloth. This tradition of "humanity draped"[1] was one they shared with southeastern American Indians, whose men resisted replacing their breechcloths and loose capes with trousers and jackets into the nineteenth and even the twentieth century. Southern fashions represent the meeting of these disparate cultures in new contexts of labor and authority, a meeting that complicates any simple reading of southern fashions. What E. P. Thompson has said about class is preeminently true of fashion: fashion, like class, is defined by relationships, and is never a thing in itself.

SOUTHERN FASHIONS IN GLOBAL ECONOMY

The hoopskirts, corsets, pantaloons, and gloves were themselves, of course, not unique to the South, but had developed and been refined in European and American fashion centers. While the clothing men, women, and children wore in the American South in the eighteenth and nineteenth centuries reflected its own unique climate and social structure, it also reflected the complex Atlantic economy that circulated raw materials, finished textiles, fashion plates, people, and desires from the interconnected ports of Paris, London, Lagos, Kingston, New Orleans, Richmond, and Charleston. Raw materials for the fashioning of textiles moved from ports in New Orleans and Charleston to those in London, Paris, New York, and Boston. Finished textiles, in turn, arrived down the rivers and across the ocean, bringing cloth from faraway parts of the world to southern ports. The leisured classes wore silk woven in Lyons, France, or in London's Spittalfields, where skilled Huguenot weavers settled to escape religious persecution in continental Europe. The flax of the fine linens of the southern ladies and gentlemen was exported from Belgium, Flanders, France, and Germany, their superfine woolens from England, and their silky cottons from Egypt. On the other extreme, the enslaved Africans wore bandannas and, in the eighteenth century, cotton cloth specifically designated as "Negro cloth" from India and the coarse linen *osnaburgs* from Germany. Cloth trade was central to the circum-Atlantic economy, and part of the reason the English settled in South Carolina, the Spanish in Florida, and the French in Louisiana. All colonies tried to grow crops for the textile export trade: they experimented, unsuccessfully, with silkworms, but succeeded with their lucrative fields of indigo, flax, and, later, cotton.

In the eighteenth century, settlers—whether from France, Great Britain, Africa, or Spain—remembered their homelands through their fashions. The English in South Carolina and the French in Louisiana consciously attempted to duplicate the life of the upper classes in Europe by adopting close-fitting, heavily layered, and decorated fashions that would prove most uncomfortable in the hot and humid southern climates with long summers and damp winters.[2] Similarly, the enslaved Africans remembered the aesthetic preferences of West Africa in spite of the very strenuous realities of their labor;[3] the clothes the enslaved wore on Sundays—the day marked as "theirs"—stood in often-remarked-upon contrast to workclothes provided by their masters.

SLAVE CLOTHING

Sunday Wear for Slaves

Researching slave clothing is especially difficult because most of the accounts that have survived are by European Americans, accounts that range from hostile to sympathetic, but always remain outside the tradition on which they are commenting. As Shane White and Graham White point out in *Stylin': African American Expressive Culture*, interpretation of slave clothing has to confront the ambivalent and difficult relationship between African Americans and the dominant culture and deal with sources that are "one-sided and fragmentary."[4] The two major scholarly books on slave clothing, the Whites' *Stylin'* and Helen Bradley Foster's *"New Raiments of Self,"* have supplemented the above sources by reading slave narratives, runaway ads, and, in particular, *The American Slave*, a nineteen-volume set of interviews edited by George Rawick with former slaves and their direct descendants conducted between 1936 and 1938, sponsored by the Federal

Writers' Project. These sources help us to understand the history of the most distinctive part of southern textile tradition, one that grew out of the fusion of African and European modes of bodily adornment and cloth work. Recently, this tradition has once again asserted its vivid presence in various African American quilts, the most widely publicized being the exhibit of quilts from Gee's Bend, Alabama, in a touring show that reached New York's Whitney Museum of American Art in 2002. As Mensie Lee Pettway, one of the artists, states, "We got a tradition of the old peoples' ways." For her, a quilt is not merely a covering, but "represents safekeeping. It represents beauty, and you could say it represents family history."[5] And as Blake Gopnik argues in the *Washington Post*, "The complexities and irregularities of what these women turned out can make the work of the country's most famous abstract artists seem simple-minded and predictable."[6] Traces of this kind of achievement and cultural uniqueness are present in accounts of slave clothing in spite of the partiality, even hostility, of some of the observers.

As scholars working in various locations of the African diaspora have made clear, African American textile tradition derives from the same aesthetic choices that have created radical innovations in music.[7] This tradition values improvisation rather than the symmetries of European textile choices; it prefers "visual elaboration" of "flexible patterning" to repetition.[8] From the earliest contact between the two cultures, this textile tradition has been available to European Americans, whose fascinated commentary is filled with obsessive misreadings of that part of slave clothing where the slaves exercised some choice—in their Sunday wear. Thus, the fashionable British actress Frances Kemble was invariably sympathetic to the slaves on her husband's Georgia plantation, but this sympathy did not extend to their dress, a lack of sympathy shared by most white observers:

> Their Sabbath toilet really presents the most ludicrous combination of incongruities that you can conceive—frills, flounces, ribbons; combs stuck in their wooly heads, as if they held up any portion of the stiff and ungovernable hair; filthy finery, every color in the rainbow, and the deepest possible shades blended in fierce companionship round one dusky visage; head handkerchiefs, that put one's very eye's out from a mile off; chintzes with sprawling patterns . . . ; beads, bugles, flaring sashes, and above all, little fanciful aprons, which finish these incongruous toilets with a sort of airy grace.[9]

Kemble's dismay at what the Whites designate a "vivid, visual presence" of the slaves' Sunday clothes centers on strong and contrasting colors, hair arrangements that seem to counter the very nature of the "stiff and ungovernable . . . hair," and decorations—the ribbons, flounces, and frills; the beads, bugles, flaring sashes, and little fanciful aprons—all familiar in European clothing, but assembled in ways that disconcertingly defamiliarize them. African Americans not only appropriated the clothing and decorations of their masters, but, argue the Whites, reassembled them according to a different aesthetic code.[10] The "sort of airy grace" Kemble grants to the aprons, which clearly do not here function as the kind of aprons that marked women as workers, but seems rather to recall ceremonial breechcloths, indicates a momentary recognition of a ritual use of clothing in an alien culture which she quickly dismisses by reverting to ridicule: a young man comes "to pay respects" dressed in "magnificent black satin waistcoat, shirt gills which absolutely engulfed his black visage, and neither shoes nor stockings on his feet."[11] The image of labor meeting leisure in the bare feet and satin waistcoat threatens to disorder hierarchies and suggests multiple meanings. Kemble, however, can respond only with mockery. The enslaved, she implies, try to imitate their masters, but will inevitably fail because they are savage or ignorant in their excessive love of "finery." This finery contrasts strangely with the "dusky" or "black visage" that signifies their allotted role on the American continent. Kemble fails to consider economic necessity, the "making-do," in spite of the unavailability of shoes, in the boy's get-up. She also fails to see various other ways the boy's clothes could be read: fascination with costuming, a mockery of the masters' assumptions of superiority, even the presence of the trickster mode in the reassembled clothing, a mode so prevalent in the slaves' reassembled stories and songs. To Kemble's words, *ludicrous* and *incongruous*, which register her incomprehension, can be added *savage*, *bizarre*, and *outlandish*, which reverberate similarly in European American accounts of African American clothing and of music and dance. The ridicule directed against the African Americans is almost always touched with an "edginess," argue the Whites, a sense that somehow their masters' authority is being challenged in ways that cannot quite be pinpointed. bell hooks similarly argues for such a reading: "Living and working in a racially segregated environment where domination of black folks via dramas of humiliation and disregard were the norm, dressing up, expressing one's style, was a declaration of independence."[12]

Kemble's description of the Georgia sea-island slaves in their Sunday wear in the early nineteenth century finds a parallel in a description of Mardi Gras Indians in New Orleans in 1940: "The regalia consists of a large and resplendent crown of feathers, a wig, an apron, a jacket, a shirt, trousers and moccasins. They vie with each other . . . as to richness and elaborateness. Materials used include satins, velvet, silver and gold lame and various furs. The trims are sequins, crystal, colored and pearl beads, sparkling imitation jewels, rhinestones, spangles and gold clips put to extravagant use. Color is used without restraint. (Flame, scarlet and orange are possibly the preferred shades)."[13] In choosing to name themselves "Indians," these twentieth-century African Americans emphasize their centuries-long alliances, intermarriages, and shared heritages with the indigenous peoples of the area. For southern Indians, as for the African Americans, dominant aesthetic energy of their culture focused on clothing and the ornamentation of the body. Neither culture made the distinction between art and craft that marks modernity among Europeans. Both developed sophisticated traditions of finger-weaving, beading, and other surface manipulations of draped cloth, traditions European Americans alternately dismissed and desired.

Elizabeth Botume, working with groups of freed Gullah-Geegee people after the Civil War in South Carolina sea islands, is as troubled as was Kemble by what the Whites call "a different aesthetic code." Describing the attempts of the former slaves to wear black to honor President Lincoln in a memorial service, she consciously pulls back from ridicule: "A man turned his coat and wore it inside out because it had a 'mourning lining,' and a woman begged us for some strips of black cambric, which she basted around the bottom of her gown, and up and down the front with white cotton. Their appearance would have been ludicrous had it not been so sad."[14] Botume's assumption that these people aimed at but failed to achieve black mourning clothes ignores the different funeral practices of Africans.

Black as a color of mourning is reserved for European practices. These former slaves were only partially adopting the mode of their former masters, as is suggested by later accounts. For example, Mamie Fields in *Lemon Grass* states that the nineteenth-century African American middle class in Charleston defined a family as "the ones you knew would wear black after you were gone," and thereby emphasizes their adoption of white fashions. Her father's family, however, from a sea island, wore red at funerals into the 1920s.[15] The strong contrasts created by the black strips of cloth sewn with white thread, observed by Botume, similarly allude to non-European mourning customs. Bright colors and startling juxtapositions can still be seen in jazz funerals in New Orleans.

Earlier Botume expresses a greater awareness when she admires the cloth work of a skillful spinner and knitter, or describes alterations made to dresses: "They pieced them out, often with most unsuitable material, putting old cloth with the new, and a cotton frill to a worsted skirt." Singling out one, she comments, "It looked, when done, like a modern 'crazy quilt.' It was very odd, but really not ugly." Another woman darned with "coarse yarn she had spun herself. The coat was black and the thread white, but it made no difference. On the contrary, I think she liked it better so. It looked like coarse embroidery to her." These women, Botume concludes, "seemed to delight more in an old garment than a new. They felt at liberty to cut and alter and patch it *ad libitum*."[16] The ability to transform drab reality by masterful patching, weaving, and dyeing forms a part of the slaves' own memory of their clothing many years later, as does their love of contrast and color.

African American Textile Production

Behind this love and mastery is a sophisticated textile tradition of dyeing, weaving, and appliqué patching brought from West Africa and developed in the most hostile conditions in the American South. In the eighteenth century, Europeans acknowledged West Africans' skills in dyeing, skills that brought high returns on the global commodity market hungry for color. The need for indigo was especially intense: the Europeans dressed their servants and armies in cloth dyed with this difficult purple-blue color. In indigo-growing regions of South Carolina and Louisiana, it is clear that a number of West Africans were targeted for slavery because of their expertise with growing the plant and processing the dye.[17] Large-scale indigo production polluted the land and poisoned the slaves. In 1806 an English traveler, Thomas Ashe, confronted a wasteland left by one of these plantations in Natchez, Mississippi. For Ashe the ghostly presence of the African captives is rendered only too visible in memory: "The culture of indigo is nearly renounced. After several years of sad experience, the planters at length found out, that, on an average, it killed every Negro employed in the culture in a short space of five years."[18] Similarly, Bernard Romans, after his visit to indigo fields in Florida, describes the pollution created by dye works: the smell and the flies around the area where indigo is processed make it "scarce possible to keep any animal on an indigo plantation . . . even poultry scarce thrive but little where indigo is made." Discounting the bodies of the workers who are needed for all stages of indigo processing, Romans concludes that the poisoned atmosphere, which neither animals nor poultry can endure, represents the single "inconvenience . . . this profitable business is subject to."[19] This dismissal of suffering by rendering it invisible makes dependence on African knowledge even more painfully ironic. It also adds poignancy to the continuing love for indigo expressed in the African American textile tradition.

The enslaved were skillful with the processing not only of indigo, but also of other dyes because they came from a tradition that invited an attentiveness to and a reciprocal relationship with their biological environment. They were particularly knowledgeable about the uses of plants for dyes: "Folks them days knowed how to mix pretty colors," states a former Mississippi slave.[20] Millie Evans, born in 1849, recounts in detail not only what plants produce what color, but also which mordants are necessary to fix the color: "I'll tell yo' how to dye. A little beech bark dyes slate color set with copperas. Hickory bark and bay leaves dye yellow set with chamber lye; bamboo dyes turkey red, set color wid copperas. Pine straw dyes purple, set color with chamber lye. To dye cloth brown we would take de cloth and put it in the water where leather had been tanned an let it soak then set the color with apple vinegar. An we dyed blue wid indigo an set the color wid alum." Other accounts tell us that walnut bark produced brown; a mixture of cedar and sweet gum produced purple; queen's delight produced black; and cedar moss out of canebrake produced yellow. The enlaved also knew what "roots, bark an' stuff" to add to the dye pot to create particularly rich and lasting colors. "An' when she hang dem up on de line in de sun, dey was every color of de rainbow," remembers one slave with pleasure. Another former slave describes a "lively . . . spectacle" in South Carolina: "The women were dressed in gay colors, with handkerchiefs uniting all the colors of the rainbow, around their temples."[21] Besides dyeing plain cloth, slaves also dyed yarn that they wove into "pretty streaks" in cloth. These rainbow colors and "pretty streaks" were systematically dismissed by the dominant culture as simply bad, vulgar taste, as does Kemble in her ridicule of "the most ludicrous combination of incongruities that you can conceive . . . every color in the rainbow, and the deepest possible shades blended in fierce competition."[22] Similarly, *Harper's Magazine* of 1853 describes Louisiana peddlers at Christmas selling the slaves "ribbons and nick-nacks, that have no other recommendation than the possession of staring colors in the most glaring contrasts."[23] The love for strong colors contrasted and juxtaposed—of colors "hitting each other"—is present not only in the American South, but also throughout the African diaspora.

European American Appropriation of Slave Knowledge

The interest in dyes and textile production in slave narratives is duplicated in white narratives only during the Civil War after blockades rendered lack of cloth a daily concern. Access to the global marketplace was closed; the few cotton mills proved inadequate to supply "our vast need for clothing of every kind. Every household now became a miniature factory in itself, with its cotton, cards, spinning-wheels, warping frames, looms," states Parthenia Antoniette Hague in a memoir about life in southern Alabama.[24] She spends half of her book describing the making not only of dyes, but of cloth of various kinds, thread, buttons, hats, and shoes—all activities familiar to the antebellum slaves. "Great trouble was experienced, in the beginning," she states, "to find dyes with which to color our stuffs; but in the course of time . . . barks, leaves, roots, and berries were found containing coloring properties."[25] It is difficult not to insert the well-developed

African American as well as Indian knowledge of all aspects of cloth-work into Hague's narrative of how "the course of time" solved the problems. As Elizabeth Fox-Genovese points out in *Within the Plantation Household*, it was common for white women to appropriate the labor and knowledge of their slaves almost unthinkingly.[26] Thus Hague's detailed account of how a people who have to "depend on our own ingenuity to supply the necessities of existence."[27] could be read as the masters' discovery of what the slaves always knew.

This knowledge that turned the woods into "the great storehouse for all our dye-stuffs"; that found a "variety enough of material to make hats for both men and women" out of straw of oats or wheat, corn husks, pine-straw, squash; that became "skilled in making designs of palmetto and straw braiding"; that valued carefully hoarded and exchanged scraps of fabric for decorations—this knowledge did not come from the poor whites in the area.[28] Many travelers commented that the slaves in their Sunday wear dressed better than "crackers."[29] The latter are frequently described as dirty, bare-footed, bare-headed, and seen regularly in "undress" in their linen shifts.[30] They wore clothing only "to cover their nakedness" and to keep warm, states Frederick Olmsted.[31] In contrast, West African as well as Indian cultures traditionally valued cloth-wealth, using it to mark status and to communicate important symbols and stories, and as currency. The finger-weaving that Hague gleefully enumerates becomes an unstated homage to the well-developed tradition among the local Creek people of weaving all kinds of local materials—grasses, barks, feathers—into wearable textiles. This tradition they shared with all Indian peoples. During their initial contact, their skill, argues Pamela V. Ulrich, was as sophisticated as European textile tradition of spinning wool and flax.[32]

Cultural Meanings of Colors

Some colors cultivated by the enslaved retain their West African meanings. Indigo, in particular, was a sacred color in West Africa and remains a protection against evil throughout South Carolina sea islands as well as in Louisiana, in spite of the brutality of large-scale indigo processing. Love of red emerges together with its prominence in diasporic religions such as voodoo in Louisiana. Solomon Northrup, enslaved for twelve years in a Red River cotton plantation until his rescue in 1853, describes feast-days with an emphasis on the importance of red: "As a general thing, the women wear handkerchiefs tied about their heads, but if chance has thrown in their way a fiery red ribbon, or a cast-off bonnet of their mistress' grandmother, it is sure to be worn on such occasions. Red—the deep blood red— is decidedly the favorite color among the enslaved. . . . If a red ribbon does not encircle the neck, you will be certain to find all the hair of their woolly heads tied up with red strings of one sort or another."[33] Northrup, identifying with the dominant cultural values, tries to dismiss red by allying it with an old-fashioned bonnet, but the color—"fiery" and "deep blood red"—vibrates with unstated meaning in his text. Even the red petticoat that Rhett Butler brings Mammy from New Orleans in *Gone with the Wind* may carry meaning beyond Margaret Mitchell's amused account of the blacks' outrageously inappropriate tastes. George Washington Cable, a more sensitive observer of cultural meanings, adds vivid red to the dress of his voodoo priestess, Palmyra, in *The Grandissimes*, whereas indigo blue is strikingly present in her house to emphasize her connection with spiritual powers. Such deep cultural resonance of colors informs the fictions of contemporary African American writers like Toni Morrison and Gloria Naylor. In *Beloved*, both Baby Suggs's last attachment to life and Sethe's coming back to life are marked by the characters' concentration on bright batches of dyed cloth.

Among former slaves, even necessity is transformed into the joy of artistry as "ol' plain white cloth" achieved interest only after it had been torn and "patched fum de legs to de waist, some so patched 'till dey looked like a quilt." To warmth is added beauty, as patching that Botume noticed is remembered by the slaves themselves as art: "My mother used to quilt my skirts from way up here 'round the thigh down to the bottom." Even the fields on which the textile plants were grown could be converted from the pain of labor to beauty, as in a memory that transforms flax into silk: "The long shoots, no thicker than a pencil, would bloom—the purtiest little pink and white flowers—and when the wind would sweep over the field it would ripple and wave like silk."[34]

The slaves' production of vividly assembled, colored, and patched garments took place in a context of extreme hard work and deprivation. During the colonial period when the British restricted local cloth production, the majority of cloth for slaves was imported, as it would be later on some plantations. However, flax patches developed early on plantations as an alternative to English wool and were processed by slaves who were familiar with working with a similar bast fiber—that of West African raffia palm.[35] After the American Revolution, most of the slave clothing was produced on the more diversified plantations that kept sheep for wool and developed extensive cotton fields. By the 1840s and 1850s, according to Fox-Genovese, much of the manufacture of slave clothing was in the hands of female slaves, work that took place in dimly lighted cabins after a day in the fields or in the big house.[36] White mistresses tended to keep the annual cutting-out of the slave clothing in their own hands, thus assuring that the cuts not be too generous. Otherwise, the slaves produced most of their own clothing as well as that of their masters. Numerous former slaves testify that slave women's "spare time from labor" was spent in spinning, knitting, and sewing. Foster details the various steps it took for a slave to produce cloth from cotton[37] to emphasize the lengthening of the workday from the standard sunup to sundown to "from can to can't."[38] Furthermore, as Botume becomes aware after a skilled cloth worker proves "shy" about showing her work, access to textile goods was decidedly difficult for these workers on the cotton fields: "The colored people were prohibited by law from appropriating even a singe boll of cotton to their own use. But it was a very common thing for each woman to secret a few handfuls of the cotton she had picked when she left the field . . . [thus] helping themselves to a fraction of the products of their labor."[39] While cotton helped to revolutionize European fashions in the eighteenth and nineteenth centuries by making affordable, comfortable, and washable fabric available to men and women of all classes, it could criminalize the workers who helped to clothe peoples of the global marketplace.

Slave Clothing Allotment

Inadequate clothing allotment constitutes a major theme in slave narratives, as "nakedness" rivals hunger in the memory of those who were enslaved to embody the pain of chattel slavery. Olmsted reports a 1846 government survey that clearly shows some planters saving money on slave clothing: the expenses of forty-eight sugar planters in Louisiana were $30 per year for workingmen's clothing, but only $15 per year for slaves.[40] He describes field workers as "very ragged and slovenly" in striking contrast to their vivid Sunday appearance. The standard for field workers seems to be that enumerated by Frederick Douglass: for summer the male workers were allotted two shirts and one pair of trousers out of a blend of coarse cotton and flax. For winter, they were allotted "a woolen jacket, with one pair of yarn stockings and a pair of shoes of the coarsest description," together with a heavier shirt, trousers, and hat.[41] Louis Hughes lists two dresses and two chemises for each woman in the summer, whereas in the winter their dresses were made of heavier wool cloth. Undergarments, generally worn only in the winter, were variously fashioned by the slaves themselves. According to Hughes, *pantalets* were common; these were cut up from old clothes and made up like a pant leg tied just above the knee.[42] For more warmth in the winter, the enslaved people engaged in "making do" in other ways: cotton petticoats quilted with layers from the knee down, old dress-coats, warm wraps called sacks, or large shawls functioned as extra layers against the cold.[43] Children, both boys and girls, writes Douglass, were allotted "two coarse linen shirts a year. When these failed them, they went naked until the next allowance day."[44] In urban centers, slave-owners faced pressure to clothe their slaves decently, whereas in rural areas the mistress sometimes revolted against the nakedness that was so abhorrent to her own moral upbringing. However, as Foster speculates, the ungendered clothing for children, as well as the nakedness of some, may have served to emphasize the difference between the slaves and their masters in an ideologically powerful way: "Unlike the way in which extremes in forms of clothing highlighted the sexual differences between white men and women, asexual forms of clothing perhaps were meant to downplay the sexuality and physical appeal of Black girls and women."[45] Linda Brent's reaction suggests how much the clothes themselves became a badge of slavery as she remembers the hated "linsey-woolsey dress given me every winter."[46] Even this dress was granted grudgingly; her grandmother, a free woman, provided most of the other clothing for her still enslaved grandchildren.

Slave clothing emphasizes how fully the slave body constituted a contested site in discourse as well as in flesh. Clothing in all societies creates a cultural skin that can be more important than the biological one. Controlling this surface of the body reinforced authority and created difference. Clothes not only represented economic deprivation but also attempted to dehumanize the workers, as clothing allotments helped to create interchangeable uniform bodies, reducing individuals to "hands" to do the field work.[47] Throughout the period of slavery, specific cloth was set aside for the enslaved: in 1736 Hill and Guerard Company of Charlestown, for instance, listed imported "white welsh plains" as "Negro Cloth," an often used designation referring to numerous coarse textiles like plain cottons, fustian (a cotton and linen blend), linsey-woolsey (a blend of wool and flax), or flax. That slave clothing had ideological as well as utilitarian rationale in the minds of the masters is further emphasized by various pieces of unenforceable legislation passed in slave states that attempted to keep the distinctions between the elite and the laborers rigid by specifying what kinds of fabrics could be used for the enslaved. South Carolina's 1735 "Negro Act" restricted these to "Negro cloth, duffels, course [*sic*] kearsies, osnabrigs, blue linnen or scotch plaids."[48] The same act specifically forbade slaves to wear the cast-off clothing of their owners. Such extreme laws written to enforce difference through controlling the body surface never work in human interaction where clothing functions centrally to define and test power and authority. Between the masters and their slaves, exchange of clothing created obligation and submission: the house-slaves wore the master's cast-off clothing and could develop a tendency to identify with the master. On the other hand, successful stealing or borrowing of the master's clothing could reinforce a slave's feeling of independence. Among the enslaved themselves, clothing served as currency: they were bought and sold, bartered, traded, and gambled in an underground economy that developed extensively in urban areas.[49]

Slave work-clothing denied individuality: garments were loose, often ill-fitting, made to very general measures with little consideration for unusual body types. Women's aprons with pockets and scarves or handkerchiefs for covering heads defined them as workers. For men, at least for men with the standard body type, generous cut around the armholes freed the arms for physical labor, whereas the short jackets left the lower part of the body unencumbered. Secondhand coats were often shortened when passed on to the slaves. Breeches were similarly loose, made of coarse materials that would take many washings to becomes bearable next to the skin. Booker T. Washington describes wearing a shirt made out of flax refuse as a "most trying ordeal," as torture, as equivalent to the pain of pulling a tooth, as having "a dozen or more chestnut burrs, or a Hundred small pinpoints, to contact with his flesh." His obsessive search for metaphors to vivify the general designation of "coarse" serves to emphasize the body literally suffering its covering. In the next sentence, however, he uses the description to bring to the forefront the strength of the community some slaves were able to forge out of the suffering itself: "One of the most generous acts that I ever heard of one slave relative doing for another" was enacted by his elder brother, John, who wore Booker's new flax shirt for him for several days until it was "broken in."[50]

Former slaves' accounts of shoes induce a similar vivid, even obsessive memory of pain.[51] Washington remembers his as made of cowhide, with an inch-thick wooden sole, neither fitted nor yielding to the pressure of his feet once worn. Another account evokes the desperate choice between going barefoot and attempting to wear such shoes: "Sey was so hard we would have to warm dem by de fire and grease dem wid tallow to ever wear dem 'tall."[52] At the other extreme were hog-skin shoes that spread out flat after a few days' wear because this leather was "very extensible."[53] Shoes provided for the slaves were an extreme version of the general discomfort of European shoes. The far superior Indian moccasins were adopted by all classes for their comfort. Not until dominant culture developed tennis shoes—which the Indians gleefully appropriated as "the new moccasins"—did the feet of most people cease to suffer.

Among the enslaved peoples, the memories of achievement—of the rainbow colors, the beauty of patching, the comfort of keeping warm, the community created by sharing skills and pain—always appear in the context created by coarse clothing that was stiff and painful against the skin and shoes that never conformed to the shape of individual feet.

FASHION FOR PEOPLE OF COLOR IN THE NINETEENTH CENTURY

While dress could be used to enforce racial differences or to celebrate cultural heritages, it could also contest them. Olmsted observed "remarkably well dressed Negroes" on Sundays in Richmond, one of the earliest fashion centers on the American continent: "Finest French cloths, embroidered waistcoats, patent-leather shoes, resplendent brooches, silk hats, kid gloves and *eau de mille fleurs*, were quite common." The ladies, he adds, show "good taste and effect, after the latest Parisian mode."[54] In such urban settings, pressure to wear only what was deemed proper became more intense as well as more unsuccessful than in rural areas. One observer notes the difference between country slaves who are generally dressed as is *"suitable* to their Condition," and Charleston slaves whose dressing above their station represents their immorality. The latter are *"rude, unmannerly, insolent, and shameless,"* he concludes. The well-dressed female slave, in particular, stands as a clear sign of "scandalous Intimacy."[55] To be well dressed reflected badly on a slave's character in the minds of a number of observers who wanted clothes to reinforce absolute difference between slaves and masters. Such a line was, however, difficult to maintain either with skin or with cloth.

In the 1830s, an anonymous observer describes a New Orleans free woman of color whose liminal position between black and white disturbs him. His description emphasizes how lightened skin color, reinforced by marks of leisure woven into the clothing and revealed by the body, could threaten the boundary between the ideologically constructed category of difference. His mocking tone attempts to maintain such a boundary even as it dissolves:

> Directly in front of me sat a handsome yellow "lady," her head surmounted by an orange and scarlet plaid handkerchief, bound about in Turkish-turban fashion; a style that prevails here among Creole servants. . . . upon her neck was a richly worked black lace scarf; her dress was plain colored silk made in the most costliest manner. Her olive hands, which had very tapering fingers and remarkably oval nails, were covered with rings, chiefly plain gold ones. In one hand she held a handsome parasol and in the other fondled a snow white French poodle upon her lap, said poodle having the tips of its ears tied with knots of pink ribbon, and a collar of pink silk quilled, and made like a ruff, while the end of its tail was adorned with a bow of blue ribbon, in the tastiest style; and as if his poodleship were not sufficiently decorated to be taken to the city to visit his town cousins, it had a nice bow of red satin tied about each of its four ankles.[56]

The ironic tone allies this passage with numerous criticisms of people of color—both during slavery and after, both of African or American Indian heritages—for "dressing above themselves" and for loving elaborate ornamentation. As Booker T. Washington stated in 1902, "No white American ever thinks that any other race is wholly civilized until he wears the white man's clothes."[57] However, those who adopted Western clothing needed to do so with the humility and restraint that clearly allied them with the laboring classes. Members of the black middle class, which began to develop among craftsmen and women as well as professionals such as doctors and lawyers, were conscious how much sartorial practices mattered: being well dressed had to do with self-respect, and, sometimes, a denial of the heritage of slavery. Fields, in her memoir, emphasizes this throughout her description of black middle-class life in Charleston in the decades after slavery. Public appearance was carefully maintained even in the most adverse circumstances. Her community always dressed in their best clothes for traveling although the dust, cinders, and smoke in the "colored cars" placed near the locomotive soiled the clothing. On arrival, "everybody would get up and commence to shake and brush and turn around, ask their neighbor to look over the coat, try not to offend anybody by shaking dust on them."[58] She also insists on restraint in style, ornamentation, and color. "Fashion articulated class position,"

African American men and women posed for portrait on steps, Georgia, c. 1899–1900. Courtesy Library of Congress.

states Fox-Genovese, "extravagance defied it. A lady had to know the difference."[59]

Thus Fields instantly dismisses a black man described as "dressed in nice clothes but really with too much on. . . . He will do and overdo." In contrast, she remembers with pleasure her grandmother from St. Kitts: "With her jewelry and hats and carrying herself the way she did, she could look like some of those women who lived on the Battery, except for her color. Yes, indeed, the way 'Miss Mary' walked and stood, she seemed to us like one of those 'aristocratic' whites."[60] Fields stresses the importance of accessories as well as movements of the body. The way a person stands and walks, as much as dress, signifies social class. Whether to white eyes Miss Mary had indeed gotten all the vestimentary signs right, in Fields's memory she represents "good dress," which was a close ally to both "good conduct" and "good morality." Middle-class African Americans openly emulated white styles and practiced restraint in choice of colors and styles. As Perrot states, "Tracking down signs that betrayed social positions that were either usurped or recently acquired, mercilessly flushing out, unmasking, and excluding the ignorant person who violated the new sumptuary laws of 'proper comportment,' became a compulsive preoccupation of the dominant classes" whether these were, in the case of the American South, white or black.[61]

Hair and Headgear

The New Orleans free woman of color described by the anonymous observer resembles "Miss Mary" more than the "fast" young men and women whom Fields identifies as not respectable—those who will "do and overdo." The only startling aspect of the New Orleans woman's clothing is the "orange and scarlet plaid" headdress: the colors create a juxtaposition strange to European eyes. Her head scarf

Women's hats, c. 1890. Courtesy Florida Photographic Collection, MOSAIC Collection.

in the New Orleans setting recalls the sumptuary laws imposed specifically on free women of color by the Spanish government of Louisiana in 1786. These women were forbidden to wear silks, gold, silver, pearls, mantillas, and elaborate hair-dressing. Henceforth, their hair was to be covered by a *tignon*, a headwrap that would identify them with women slaves in spite of their freed condition and some-times lives of leisure and wealth.[62] However, the headgear of this free woman of color, in its guise of an intricately twisted turban of the latest oriental fashion and its violent juxtaposition of colors, denies such associations with slaves and servants. Rather, it recalls the elaborate hair designs in West African cultures, designs that carried deep social meanings and achieved complicated patterns impossible to Eu-ropean hair-types. As the Whites point out, eighteenth-century runaway ads fre-quently described the slaves' hair, suggesting that the Africans carried the rituals of dressing their hair in a great variety of styles into the plantations. When Euro-peans first met Africans in the fifteenth century, they invariably commented on their hair: "Various combinations of braids, plaits (often with shells, beads, or strips of material woven in), shaved areas cut in different lengths to make patterns adorned heads of people, creating a stunning effect."[63] By the nineteenth century, however, most slave women's hair was covered by handkerchiefs (sometimes intri-cately wrapped) and African hair was devalued by the designation "wool," used so regularly that even African Americans like Northrup used it unthinkingly. The as-sociation with animals attempted to deny the unique quality of such hair: in Kem-ble's view, it becomes "stiff and unmanageable" rather than being open to cultural manipulation into elaborate designs not possible for Caucasian hair. The red and orange turban described by the anonymous observer also looks forward to the flamboyant Sunday hats worn by African American middle-class women into the twenty-first century, hats celebrated stunningly by Michael Cunningham and Graig Marberry in *Crowns: Portraits of Black Women in Church Hats*. As Charlene Graves, one of the hat-wearers, states, "When a . . . woman walks with a hat [on], she walks in with an attitude. . . . Some of us think there's going to be a section in heaven just for us and our hats."[64] Skillfully fashioned West African hair, the variously wrapped *tignons*, and the contemporary church hats all celebrate the top of the head as a place of spiritual connections as well as a sign of status. The hat, even for middle-class African Americans who worked to emulate white styles, never lost connection with its heritage.

Clothing as a Sign of Status

The free woman of color described above wears no apron and her *tignon* is fashionable, not a badge of service. The rest of the description of her dress also characterizes leisured classes. Excessive expenditure of both material and construction is foregrounded with the "richly worked black silk scarf" and the "plain colored silk" of the dress, as well as the expensive way the dress is made "in the most costliest manner." Silk with its soft texture constituted a fabric of status well into the twentieth century. That it is "plain colored" also asserts its status and would do so increasingly as the century progressed. When bright-colored chemical dyes were developed later in the nineteenth century, making colors widely available to the lower classes for the first time in the history of dress, discrimination and restraint in the use of color began to be the mark of a lady. The dress also signifies status by being fitted closely to the individual body rather than to a standard measure, a fit that requires that the fabric be cut into many small, uneven pieces by an expert dressmaker. This cutting of yardage wastes more fabric than the straight-cut large square or rectangular piece construction of slave clothing; it also makes it more difficult to reuse the fabric once the dress is no longer worn.

Various body parts further reinforce these signs of status written into the clothing in the portrait of the New Orleans woman of color. The "remarkably oval nails" and tapering hands signify hands that have been protected against dirt and work; for the observer these leisured fingers are juxtaposed incongruously with their color, "olive," which to him signifies laboring hands, not being the "magnolia white" of the "real" southern lady. Women's small white hands were a particularly powerful sign of leisure and status in the American South: nineteenth-century paintings tend to diminish ladies' hands to child size, while gloves or mitts constitute an essential fashion accessory for the well-born. Multiplication of other accessories—the lace shawl, parasol, rings, and lapdog—is also characteristic of the leisured classes. Parasols helped to keep skin white by protecting it from the sun. Furthermore, like fans, they were useful in flirtations, as coded meanings were attached to their movements. A parasol, like a fan, a cane, or an umbrella, could also function as protection of personal space in public. Fields describes her white teacher employing her accessory just this way: "She used that parasol to make sure you didn't come too near her. Stretch out her arm with the parasol in her hand. When you reached the end of the parasol, which was at the end of her arm, then she would say 'Halt! Right there!' "[65] Whether for flirtation or aggression, the parasol formed a useful appendage to the body and thus signified social power, representing one of the accessories, argues Perrot, that lend grace to gesture.[66] The major function of the shawl worn by the New Orleans free woman of color is decorative and not functional, whereas a parasol as well as the rings would be an encumbrance to laboring hands. Lapdogs begin to make their appearance as fashion accessories for ladies in seventeenth-century European paintings: the more fully distinguished from working dogs, the more status they grant. The observer reads the dog as an extension of the woman holding it. Whereas there is little in her own dress that is easily open to ridicule, the excessive decorations on this small dog become his major focus of mockery, taking up almost half of his description. This mockery could be somewhat misguided since the woman may be doing some gentle mocking of her own. The whiteness of the dog is suggestive, as is its breed as a "French" poodle. Also suggestive is the marked contrast between the restraint shown by the lady's apparel and the decorative exuberance that overwhelms the animal.

Attention to hair and clothing could translate into professions for free blacks. Nineteenth-century New Orleans quadroon hairdressers were famous: one traveler described them as representing a "refinement in which the richest ladies in Boston would not think of indulging."[67] Marie Laveau, the "voodoo queen," worked as a hairdresser, going house to house with many regular white clients. Eliza Ripley in solidly middle-class white New Orleans before the Civil War describes another such hairdresser as a normal part of a festive day: "Monday morning Mme. Casmir or Mam'zelle Victorine comes to sew all day like wild for seventy-five cents. . . . Later, dusky Henriette Blondeau comes, with her *tignon* stuck full of pins and the deep pockets of her apron bulging with sticks of bandoline, pots of pomade, hairpins and a bandeau comb, to dress the hair of mademoiselle."[68] Henriette's *tignon* functions as it was meant to function when the Spanish imposed their codes on free women of color: like the apron, it serves her in her work as she dresses European hair. The headwrap remained a central part of a working black woman's outfit into the twentieth century. Its history, the various ways it could be wrapped, and its often startling colors make it the most commented on fashion item in African American sartorial practices.

Although the observer attempts to associate the free woman of color with such Creole servants because of her *tignon*, she refuses to be clearly placed either in the class with Ripley's Henriette or in the leisured class. African American tailors and milliners did at times use their expertise to threaten clear distinction between the races, a distinction that the clothing they made for their white clients helped to maintain. Fields's uncle, a tailor at Charleston's exclusive Rubinheimer's, copied the clothing he made for white clients: "After making the newest style for the customers, Thaddeus made his own." Fields's own attempt to copy almost lost her a job with a mulatto dressmaker in Charleston: "The white people would take their work away from me if they found colored people wearing those dresses," warned Florence Bryant.[69] The intimate relationship created by fittings could blur the color line between the races in a different way, as Mary Lincoln's friendship with her White House dressmaker, Elizabeth Keckly, a former slave, testifies. Thus the free woman of color described by the anonymous observer remains in indeterminate space, as, indeed, did women like Keckly, an indeterminacy she documents in her own memoirs, which form the major source for Jennifer Fleischner's recent *Mrs. Lincoln and Mrs. Keckly.*

If the distinctions between the races could be blurred when the African Americans assumed the clothes of white ruling classes, increasingly radical distinction between genders became more deeply marked. According to a number of scholars, this characterizes the growing dominance of the bourgeoisie in Western societies. As always, the dominant fashions in the American South followed the trends set in New York, London, and Paris. The loss of easy access to the centers of fashions created a deprivation often mentioned by the ladies of the Confederacy during the Civil War. In *Gone with the Wind* among the most valued contraband goods that Rhett Butler smuggles through the blockade and brings to Atlanta are rich fabrics and fashion news. Less lucky, Hague laments the lack of fashion plates and ladies' magazines during the blockade. Later in the nineteenth century, Fields's evaluation of her city would fit any southern city, even the fashionable Richmond or the cosmopolitan New Orleans, often mentioned in diaries and letters as sources of fashions for the hinterlands: "Charleston was backward when it came to fashions. I am talking about 'the latest from New York.'"[70] Later, the "latest Parisian fashions," which she copied as a dressmaker for the middle-class black community, became her standard. Thus, the South followed the cycles and trends of the rest of the Western world and participated in the revolution in men's clothing, a revolution that emphasized asymmetrical access to power between the genders.

GENDER: UNEVEN DEVELOPMENTS

Eliza Ripley, writing about her youth in antebellum New Orleans, evokes her former image as representing an enduring vision of an ideal lady, an image her female descendants would do well to emulate: "I have a stiff, wooden corset board that I sometimes take out to show to my granddaughter when I find her 'stooping,' that she may see the instrument that made grandma so straight."[71] The "straightness" that came at the expense of flexibility is a price Ripley does not question. She is amused, however, by male fashions of the past that similarly constricted the body:

> The men of that day wore skin-tight pantaloons (we did not call them trousers), often made of light-colored materials. I clearly remember a pea green pair that my brother wore, flickering like a chameleon in and out of open street doors. Those tight-fitting pantaloons were drawn taut over the shoe, a strong leather strap extending under the foot buckled the garment down good and tight, giving the wearer as mincing a gait as the girl in the present-day hobble skirt. The narrow clawhapper coat with tails that hung almost to the knees behind and were scarcely visible in front, had to have the corner of a white handkerchief flutter from the tail pocket.[72]

Ripley's asymmetrical evaluation of female and male clothing of an earlier age emphasizes how little women's fashions had responded to the revolution in men's clothing. The fashionable outfits for both the ladies and the gentlemen of the 1840s constricted free movement of arms and legs.[73]

The light-colored materials further marked the wearers as people who did not work with their bodies, whereas, in a culture where dyes were expensive and scarce, bright colors among the ruling classes proclaimed their easy access to the luxuries of the world. Forty years later, the clothes Ripley's brother wore in her youth seem to feminize him: she remembers with amusement how he was forced to walk like a girl. Not only the tight cut, but the colors of his outfit are clearly "old-fashioned" and therefore ridiculous: "the light-colored material," especially the "pea green" pantaloons, which flicker "in and out of open street doors" like chameleons, would be reserved for women's clothes in Ripley's old age, as would the tight fit. Thus she accepts without question the hobble skirts that still discipline the female form at the same time that she reflects on the enduring value of the wooden corset board that has become an old-fashioned curiosity.

Uniforms

Ripley's pride in her disciplined body reinforced the image of the southern lady in popular culture. Anne Hollander in *Sex and Suits* suggestively argues that such disciplining by clothing can infuse people wearing them "with the aura of power and triumph, not with the sense of submission to burdens." In Hollander's view, nineteenth-century women shared men's "sartorial heroism" by wearing clothing that "reached extremes of rigidity and display"; female clothing of the period shared qualities with military officers' dress uniforms, which required "masculine corseting" with a history going back "to the strict girding of fighting men's loins in ancient cultures."[74] Indeed, Ripley describes just such a military uniform with a detailed interest in its construction and an awareness of the power bodily discomfort can confer: "All such who could sport a military record wore stiff stocks about their long necks. Those stocks made the necks appear abnormally long. They were made of buckram (or sheet iron?), so broad that three straps were required to buckle them at the back, covered with black satin, tiny satin bows in front which were utterly superfluous, for they tied nothing and were not large enough to be ornamental." The wearers "could not turn their heads when they were buckled up, and, like a little boy with the broad collar, could not spit over them. However they did impart a military air of rigidity and stiffness, as though on dress parade all the time."[75] The "rigidity and stiffness" required of a proper "military air" are impressive. However, these uniforms also remind Ripley of "little boys" dressing up and thereby unable to indulge in their natural impulse of spitting over obstructions. Ladies, finally, in their rigidity and stiffness represent the truly civilized and disciplined beings in the American South.

The love of dress uniforms in the American South lends this account poignancy. Indeed, at the beginning of the Civil War, this love invited flamboyant displays: Louisiana Zouaves were the most extreme, going to fight in "scarlet bloomers, blue shirts, brocaded jackets, wide sashes, white gaiters, and gaudy fezzes worn at a jaunty angle."[76] Instead of the regulation, if not real, uniforms consisting of "gray tunics, sky-blue trousers, double-breasted gray overcoats fitted with capes, French-style caps with havelocks of canvas or oilcloth to protect neck, black leather cravats, and Jefferson-style boots." Other groups, according to Wiley, "arrived at the front in uniforms of green, yellow, flaming red," with the Orleans Guard Battalion unthinkingly choosing flashy blue for theirs, a color that made them targets to their fellow southerners at Shiloh until they turned their coats inside out and presented the white lining. Clearly, the love of display, along with the power this conferred, was a trait shared by the South's military men and its ladies until practicality intervened. Uniforms were also popular with African Americans. Olmsted describes those from the Mexican War used as slave clothing after they came on sale in auction houses in New Orleans. The "negroes," he records, "were greatly pleased with it."[77] Army jackets, dating from Civil War, worn by black rural laborers were a common sight in the early years of the twentieth century. Male house slaves sometimes describe their outfits, if particularly "fine," as "uniforms." Southern Indian men copied European military uniforms with their elaborate decorations, believing such clothing signified masculine power.[78]

Working classes also wore "uniforms," but these functioned not to assert individuality, as did flamboyantly decorated ones, but to identify them by their trade and reassuringly assert their alliance with a larger group. Mamie Fields designates clothes of Charleston black craftsmen as such. In yearly parades, "each group of men wore the uniform of their trade; the bakers were in white hats and aprons, the carpenters in blue overalls, the bricklayers in white overalls."[79] New Orleans Irish Channel dockworkers in the nineteenth century wore red flannel underwear. "We always wore our shirt sleeves rolled up to show the red flannel beneath," states an imitator of this practice, which was associated with the manliness of hard work and sweat of real longshoremen.[80] Such imitations of working-class uniforms have, of course, become common in the whole Western Hemisphere as overalls, jeans, baseball caps and jerseys, cowboy hats and boots, tennis shoes, and basketball hightops constitute leisure wear of all classes. Uniforms worn by African Americans could, however, assert group identities that made the wearer particularly vulnerable to violence. After World Wars I and II, African Americans appearing in military uniforms in the South began to represent the struggle between the power of the government in Washington and that of the states, becoming, therefore, a symbol of both black pride and white aggression.

Men's Suits

In the course of the nineteenth century the male body was freed from the extreme constriction of fashionable clothing or dress uniforms. Display was also discouraged as the new uniform for middle-class men developed into the modern suit. Henceforth the display endemic to the southern "leisure ethic" centered increasingly on ladies' clothing. Men visibly asserted their status through their wives' clothing, which continued to display wealth through rich, colorful fabrics, elaborately ornamented and manipulated with pleats, tucks, and ruffles. The frequent active participation by a husband in choosing such fashions reinforced his own position in society through the richness and showiness of his women's and servants' clothing. Men traveling to fashion centers considered it a part of their task to observe the latest fashions carefully: through verbal accounts by Mary Todd Lincoln's father, the women of the Todd family in Lexington could adjust their own outfits according to the styles of New Orleans after his numerous business trips down the Mississippi.[81]

The deep revolution of man's fashions originated in London. This revolution depended on new tailoring techniques that developed out of the British tradition

Man's walking suit, c. 1925. Courtesy Library of Congress.

of manipulating the particularly flexible woolen cloth. The cut, construction, highly visible seams, sections padded and curved with pressure and steam—all these techniques combined to fashion the suit coat so as to create a good approximation of the ideal shape for even the least promising body.[82] The suit reaffirmed, states Perrot, "the concepts of modesty, effort, propriety, reserve, and 'self-control,' which were the basis of bourgeois 'respectability.'" It did so by disguising and effacing the body, allowing the wearer "to distance [oneself] from it, abandon it, and forget its embarrassing or inopportune presence." His discussion of the cultural meanings of the suit is one of many excellent studies of this important moment in nineteenth-century social history and in the European tailoring tradition which so centrally affected the fashions of the American South.[83]

Woolens, and, especially in the summer months in the American South, linens replaced the richly colored and decorated brocades, silks, velvets, and laces that characterized men's clothing in earlier ages. Fabrics as well as the rich colors that still signified wealth in women's, children's, and servants' clothes were now hidden under collars, coattails, and lapels as linings for the austere clothing in "black, white, and grey" that represented, according to Jean Baudrillard, "the very negation of colors" and therefore constituted "the paradigm of dignity, control, and morality."[84] Vests, hidden under coats, and dressing gowns, worn in privacy, constituted the only play for fabrics, colors, and ornamentation left in men's garments. Other luxuries were confined to the most intimate wear. For instance, trousseau underwear made of silk and including socks was probably passed down to others in the family as a special indulgence. Meanwhile, "lace, jewels, ruffles, snuffboxes, swords, garter belts, and shoe buckles" disappeared. Hats, canes, and gloves worn on the street could still be used effectively to mark hierarchies and status and to add power to gesture. Inside buildings, however, the body had to speak for itself.[85] But this was the body carefully tailored. Hollander describes this masterfully: "The subtle lines of the coat formed an abstract design based on the underlying curves of human bone and muscle, and the matte texture suggested the smoothness of skin. The careful modeling allowed the actual body to assert itself only at certain places when the wearer moved, to create a vital interaction between costume and person. . . . The discreet padding in the upper chest and shoulders was carefully thinned out over the chest and back and disappeared in the lower half of the coat, so the effect was of a wholly unpadded garment, an apparently natural covering."[86] The white linen suit worn by the most fashionable southern gentlemen in the summer retained in a small measure the tendency to display leisure with clothing.

Ladies' Clothing

After the development of this "natural" shape of the man's suit, *fashion* increasingly became "the outward sign of distinctively female superficiality and moral weakness" as the shapes of ladies' dresses continued to move through cycles, alternating among the tubular, bell-shaped, and bustled outlines between 1830 and 1914.[87] The small waist, the source of Scarlett O'Hara's considerable pride as well as anxiety, remained the anchoring center of female beauty throughout the period, and it was this that determined the contour of the rest of the dress as well as the kinds of undergarments ladies wore. The cut of the dress helped to foster the illusion of the smallness of the waist by adding width to contrasting parts of the body. The full skirt—whether bell-shaped or bustled—covered the ankle throughout of the period, sometimes reaching the floor, and provided a contrast to the tightly fitted bodice, where the balancing width was achieved through a sloping shoulder line, wide sleeves, or widening neck ornamentation. In the 1860s, for instance, shoulders were given a sloping, wide appearance with trims or sleeve caps on tops of the sleeves. Trims tended to be horizontal or diagonal. Stays in the corset made from whalebone, metal, or wood further strangled the waist. The body was literally re-formed in response to the canon of beauty.

Excessive material and decorative effects were marks of a lady's dress throughout the period. The basic dress in 1865, for instance, required twenty-five yards of 30" wide material in contrast to the two or three yards of 45" wide material consumed by contemporary dresses. This Civil War dress had approximately twenty-eight buttonholes, with other, nonfunctional buttons sometimes added for good measure since buttons—sometimes made of real

Sources for historical fashions include the popular periodical *Godey's Lady's Book*, first published in the 1830s. Courtesy Library of Congress.

mother of pearl, hand-stamped, and hand-carved—signified luxury. This dress also had a lining, a pleated bodice, and elaborate trimming, and was able to attain its heady proportions in width with the aid of the crinoline, an iron cage supporting the heavy skirt. This reduced the petticoats from as many as seven to two or three, and required the wearing of pantaloons, hitherto looked at with suspicion. By 1868 the wide skirt shrank to a bustle. Whether bell-shaped or bustled, such skirts represented, according to Perrot, "textile exuberance" and "radical impracticality."[88] They could also put a woman at risk when working in kitchens with open fireplaces. Burning was cited as a cause of death among southern women in the nineteenth century in numerous oral testimonies.

Such a dress could not be made by amateurs: cutting the fabric and fitting the upper part of the dress close to the body required an expert dressmaker who worked with the individual client. Cleaning was difficult: the dress could not be washed and boiled in lye soap made on the plantations for work clothing.[89] Petrol-based spirits used for dry cleaning that were developed between 1850 and 1875 created fire hazards and serious pollutants. In the early twentieth century when this technology led to the development of dry-cleaning businesses, cancer deaths among the workers in these shops were notably high. Sometimes the dress was taken apart so that individual sections could be cleaned. As a rule, detachable parts for easier cleaning were common, especially hem-tapes, collars, and cuffs. Fields describes making numerous changeable embroidered, lacy, and crocheted collars for her midi blouses in 1905. She also describes detachable guards on her domestic science class uniforms: the gathered apron with bib front, of yellow homespun, had matching sleeve guards that covered the arm from wrist to elbow, each with four buttons.[90] Throughout the period, ladies had full aprons that covered the dress they wore for domestic labors. These were often made of wool, as was the clothing of anyone who worked around fire.

Because ladies and gentlemen changed their clothing a number of times a day, even dressing and undressing involved time and labor. They started with a morning dress, proceeded to a walking dress, and ended with an evening gown, each progressively more "complicated and richer as the hours passed," with each requiring its own accessories and revealing different parts of the body.[91] The erotic energy of seduction scenes in contemporary movies representing the earlier period would move in slow motion if the real steps of undressing a lady were shown. According to the owner of the textile conservation company Gentle Arts in New Orleans, in 1875 a daytime disrobing would require a lady's total concentration for at least fourteen minutes as she undid her various fasteners and stepped out of numerous layers. She would first remove her gloves, then her hat after she took out the hatpins. The next item would be the bodice. She would first need both hands to unhook the collar around her neck. Then she would begin to unhook or unbutton the fastenings across the shoulder seam, fasteners of an average size of about half an inch. More buttons extended diagonally across the chest area or down the front, numbering at least eighteen on the bodice as a whole. The waistband inside the bodice would have to be unhooked in the back, as would the anchoring hook and eye that secured the bodice to the skirt in the center back. This done, she could loosen the hook and eye of the waistband and loosen the drawstring that held the fabric-bustled train to the skirt. She would then release the drawstring waistbands of at least three petticoats and, finally, she could remove her shoes, steady herself, and step out of the skirt, bustle, and petticoats. All this unhooking and loosening would require patience; having assistance at this stage of undressing would not necessarily help. Her lingerie, yet to be removed, consisted of a corset cover buttoned up the center back with a drawstring at the neckline. She could not unlace and unhook herself out of this garment, marking her daily dependence on someone else. Her camisole, pantaloons (also known as knickers), and stockings and garters were the last items taken off. It has been estimated that fourteen minutes would be required to remove twenty items, including pairs of shoes, garters, stockings, and gloves. Then there was the jewelry—earrings, finger-rings, a pair of bracelets, and a necklace if the scene took place at night. The bodice-ripping scenes in sensational novels emphasize the erotic frustration such cloth-armory would invite.

By 1914, in the midst of World War I, a nighttime seduction scene would find both the quantity of clothes and the time invested greatly reduced. A woman could now dress and undress without assistance. First to come off would be the hair ornament, held in place with a hairpin. Next she could remove her bodice by unbuttoning fewer than ten buttons (zippers were already used for men's attire, but would not be introduced into women's clothes until the 1930s). She would unbutton her skirt and release the drawstring of one slip. Her lingerie would be composed of a corset cover, a soft corset that could hook in the front, and a camisole, which to the modern voyeur looks like a baby-doll pajama top. The garment was pulled over the head after one or two buttons were undone in the crotch area. In contrast to the fourteen minutes of 1875, Reveley estimates that the time required in the early twentieth century was reduced to five.

Such dresses could prove awkward not only to remove, but to wear. Fields describes playing musical chairs in a full-skirted one after the styles had been considerably simplified from their heyday: the skirts "would jump up in front if you sat down forcefully, or they would want to spread over the chair beside yours." A girl in the neighboring chair would create more difficulty: "And here you both are, each of you struggling to pull the skirt in so it won't be sat on. In the process, maybe you would sit on your own long ribbon and pull down your hair with it." These dresses were, however, made for dancing: "If we went to the right, the skirt switched to the left. If Bob turned me out under his arm, the skirt floated up in a little circle. I often wore my hair in a 'psyche knot' on the back of my head, with the long ribbon around it. The ends would fly out behind me. After a while, I would seem to come up the ground and fly myself."[92] The femininity gained by such a dress in motion characterizes for Fields the energy of her youth.

The second decade of the twentieth century saw radical changes in women's fashions as the hemline rose, revealing women's legs and the contours of the lower part of her body for the first time in centuries. The corset ceased to emphasize the waist, moving down to rearrange and constrict the rear and stomach around the hips. The first brassiere was patented in 1914. The movement of women into the labor market required simplified clothing. Sports, such as bicycling, popular by 1894, made bifurcated culottes a necessity. However, cultural myths about ladies of the South—both white and black—made it difficult for them to relinquish their disciplined bodies. According to oral history, students at Newcomb College in New Orleans wore hats and gloves to football games well into the 1940s. Middle-class black college women at Bennett in Greensboro were required to wear hats, gloves, and stockings to any off-campus outings, which included all football and basketball games at A & T State University as late as 1958.[93]

COMMERCIALIZATION: TWENTIETH- AND TWENTY-FIRST-CENTURY DEVELOPMENTS

Commercialization: Twentieth-Century Developments

Increasing commercialization of all aspects of the fashion industry throughout the Western Hemisphere transformed sartorial practices in the American South, changing as well the relationships between classes and genders such practices reflected. These changes tended to be slower in the South than in other regions. For instance, factory-made fabrics replaced homespuns in the South years later than in the North: Olmsted estimates that "half the white population in Mississippi wore homespuns with a wheel and loom appearing in every second house" just before the Civil War.[94] According to Tallant, isolated groups like the Cajuns in Louisiana bayous wove their own cloth into the twentieth century and resisted wearing any kind of shoes. As late as 1945 they went to church in starched and ironed white dresses with their bare feet scrubbed clean for the occasion.[95] Similarly, ready-made clothing was slow in coming to parts of the South. Shirley Abbott, a descendant of southern hill people, describes her mother, a young woman in 1930, as the first generation "in farming south to look toward town, to break the terrible old rule of utter self-sufficiency, to dare to cross the bridge into civilization." This "look toward town" significantly involved not only the technologies of electricity, radios, and automobiles, but new kinds of clothing: "She and her sister were the first of their line to buy readymade dresses."[96] Sartorial practices of other groups reflected an even more complex relationship to the dominant culture. Notable among these are the Florida Seminolas: they developed their distinctively patterned cloth when they acquired sewing machines in the second decade of the twentieth century. This twentieth-century emergence forms one of the most admired and influential American Indian textile traditions. Their practice of sewing together strips of fabric and then cutting them in various angles to achieve often enormously complex geometric patterns helped to revolutionize quilting traditions in the dominant culture in the 1990s.

The Florida Seminolas developed their distinctively patterned cloth by sewing together strips of fabric and then cutting them at various angles to achieve complex geometric patterns. Photo by Merri Belland. Courtesy Florida Photographic Collection.

Seminola Textiles and Fashion

The story of Seminola textile work forms a particularly powerful example of the complexities interpreters face when decoding ethnic clothing, an issue important to the American South as new groups immigrated to the area to escape wars, revolutions, and poverty from Asia, the Caribbean islands, and South America in the twentieth century. Terms connected in the popular mind with ethnic clothing, such as *authenticity* and *cultural continuity*, have become problematic.

Complex cultural exchanges and disruptions, as well as self-conscious invention of tradition, mark all groups whose very survival has been threatened in various historical disasters and pressures to assimilate.[97] That the Seminola women invented their distinctive tradition at a time when Indian nations were at their weakest in all ways emphasizes complex cultural exchanges that involved appropriating materials and technologies from another culture. To what extent Seminola patchwork revives aesthetic preferences of their Creek ancestors remains problematic. William Bartram in his 1791 description of Creek practices emphasizes the looseness of the clothing and the skillful surface decorations: the words *curious* and *ingenious* repeatedly express his recognition that he is encountering a sophisticated alien textile tradition: the waist is "encircled by a curious belt of sash," soft deerskin moccasins are "curiously ornamented," the "curious diadems" on their heads are "ingeniously wrought or woven, and curiously decorated with stones, beads, wampum, porcupine quills."[98] One could argue that the effects achieved by Creek finger-weaving, which so fascinated Bartram, have been duplicated in the complex surface texture and design of Seminola patchwork. Other interpreters have seen influences of African strip-weaving or European quilting behind its development. Whatever complex cultural exchanges have converged to create the twentieth-century Seminola patchwork, the results remain as "curious" and "ingenious" as

the finger-weaving observed by Bartram. Contemporary Seminola patchwork designs, furthermore, often refer self-consciously to earlier myths of the culture about turtles, rattlesnakes, and alligators. These designs also pay tribute to nature's power with images that evoke fire, rain, lightning, storms, and waves.

Some Seminola clothing styles also refer to earlier modes. Seminola men still wear the kind of long shirts that Creek men refused to relinquish for trousers. The men's eighteen-inch breechcloth, states Bartram, is "usually plaited and indented at the ends, and ornamented with beads, tinsel lace, etc. . . . The shirt hangs loose about the waist, like a frock, or split down before, resembling a gown, and is sometimes wrapped close."[99] In this clothing style they resembled Scottish Highlanders, with whom eighteenth-century southeastern Indians felt a kinship: for both groups manliness was defined by garments the Europeans read as effeminate skirts. In turn, the Indians considered European trousers indecent. Many other southern Indian communities, especially ones newly enriched with casino money, have begun to revive or reinvent earlier clothing traditions, especially for ceremonial occasions.

Young Coushatta brave in native dress. Courtesy Louisiana Office of Tourism.

Commercial Fashion

Seminola patchwork remains a unique development, supported by the modern technology of sewing machines and the modern economy of tourism. Throughout the South, ready-made clothing began to replace the work of milliners and tailors as department stores were opened in all the southern cities by 1870s, with large window displays of the latest fashions available to stir desire in all classes. After their appearance in the 1870s, the Montgomery Ward and Sears, Roebucks catalogues provided news about styles as well as clothing for the most isolated rural areas of the South.

Before the advent of ready-made clothing, Sears catalogues, and department stores, every woman was involved in all aspects of her dress, while her clothing was designed and made by other women. A lady picked out the style of her new dress from fashion periodicals, shopped in specialty stores for fabrics and trims, and decided what looked best in the various fittings. Every woman thus knew precisely how clothes were constructed; the end result of her clothing reflected her own choices as much as the skill of the milliner. She was also an expert about luxury: she was familiar with a wide assortment of fabrics and the cost of various trims and dyes, and she knew how much time was consumed in various fabric manipulations. Ripley enumerates long lists of imported French cloth available to her in an antebellum specialty shops: "Woodlief's was the leading store on Chartres Street and Barriere's on Royal, where could be found all the French *nouveautes* of the day, beautiful *bareges*, Marcelines and chine silks, organdies stamped in gorgeous designs, to be made up with wreathed and bouquet flounces, but, above and beyond all for utility and beauty, were the imported French calicoes, fine textures, fast colors." She also has an eye on reusability of the fabrics. Before aniline dyes, "blues were indigo, reds were cochineal pure and unadulterated; so those lovely goods, printed in rich designs—often the graceful palm-leaf pattern—could be 'made over,' turned upside down and hindpart before, indefinitely, for they never wore out or lost color, and were cheap at fifty cents a yard."[100] This kind of expert knowledge was not a normal characteristic of shoppers in the New Orleans department stores that opened on the newly fashionable Canal Street later in the century.

The contrast offered by factory-made clothes is drawn by Fields, who not only describes the workers who made them but also imagines the new kind of customers who bought them as she recounts the transition from a milliner's establishment in Charleston to a garment factory in Boston.[101] At the milliner's, seamstresses were ladies, neat and silent as they worked in rooms decorated with "a finished piece of work hanging for you to admire until the customer claimed it, an embroidered Scripture verse, pictures of dresses you could make." In a garment factory, in contrast, rows of machines were running at the same time as "the girls drove those treadle machines like locomotives. Zzt, zzzt, zzzzt, and a seam was done. Since everybody's 'zzzt' was at a different time, you never heard such a racket. Zzzt, zzzt, zzzt, *clackity-clackity*, incessant." She was given only sleeves to do: "The walls were dirty, and bare except for a clock and maybe a calendar. . . . Why the room wasn't even kept neat. Whatever work was finished sat in piles. As a girl got through with a piece, she just threw it on the pile carelessly." Once Fields put sleeves into bodices backwards. Although the supervisor assured her "nobody will know," Fields imagined a scene at the department story where a saleslady convinces the customer that she needs to buy a better corset to make the garment fit. "When it was sleeves, I made big ones and little ones but had no idea what type of arm would have to fit in them, big arms like Miss Green's or small ones like mine. That was the difference. You didn't know and couldn't care who would be wearing the ladies' clothing we made . . . or how they would look."[102] The dresses she made for her African American clients followed Parisian styles adjusted to the contours of individual bodies. Even the very fat Mrs. Green went away feeling elegant after Fields covered the mirrors during her fittings to keep her interference at a minimum.

Fields's personal experience places in focus the large-scale loss of control by women of the production of women's apparel. New business forms created by commercialization reconfigured gender: the new spaces where clothing was fashioned, sold, and bought were ones in which women exercised less skill and less control. Access to capital and credit needed for mass production in factories and large-scale retailing was in men's hands. As Wendy Gamber sums it up in *The Female Economy: The Millinery and Dressmaking Trades, 1860–1930*, "Female economy of fashion by 1930 was all but supplanted by the ladies' garment trade."[103] This meant that women lost one source of economic independence. Ladies' garment trades were controlled by men; women's garments were often designed by men; the clothing was made by lower-class women in sweatshops.

The relationship between the producer and her client ceased to be an intimate one conducted around the privacies of the body. Women became full-fledged consumers in spaces like the department stores where excessive displays and reflecting surfaces offered dreams of excess. African Americans were excluded from such stores, allowed to try on neither shoes nor clothing until after the civil rights movement in the twentieth century. The displays of sartorial discrimination that defined southern fashions reflected more than ever the global marketplace in which economic exclusions marked both the production and consumption of clothing. However, the changes in the economy of clothing made it possible for more and more people to afford to challenge clear class distinctions through their dress. In the age of consumer capitalism, more and more people could also express their individual aesthetic preferences with skillful shopping that increasingly replaced skillful creation of what they wore.

RESOURCE GUIDE

Printed Sources

Abbott, Shirley. *Womenfolks: Growing Up Down South*. New York: Ticknor and Fields, 1983.

Ashe, Thomas. *Travels in America*. 3 vols. London: William Sawyer and Co., 1808.

Barthes, Roland. *The Fashion System*, trans. Matthew Ward and Richard Howard. Berkeley: University of California Press, 1983.

Bartram, William. *Travels of William Bartram*. New York: Dover Publications, 1955.

Beardsley, John, and William Arnett, et al. *The Quilts of Gee's Bend*. Atlanta: Tinwood Books, 2002.

Botume, Elizabeth-Hyde. *First Days among the Contrabands*. New York: Arno Press, 1968.

Brent, Linda. *Incidents in the Life of a Slave Girl*. New York: Harcourt, Brace, 1973.

Burman, Barbara, ed. *The Culture of Sewing: Gender, Consumption and Home Dressmaking*. New York: Berg, 1999.

Clifford, James. *The Predicament of Culture: Twentieth-Century Ethnography, Literature, and Art*. Cambridge: Harvard University Press, 1988.

Cocuzza, Dominique. "The Dress of Free Women of Color in New Orleans, 1780–1840." *Dress: The Annual Journal of the Costume Society of America* 27 (2000): 78–87.

Cunningham, Michael, and Craig Marberry. *Crowns: Portraits of Black Women in Church Hats*. New York: Doubleday, 2000.

De Marley, Diana. *Dress in North America: The New World, 1492–1800*. New York: Holmes and Meier, 1991.

Douglass, Frederick. *Narrative of the Life of Frederick Douglass, an American Slave*. New York: Signet, 1968.

Downs, Dorothy. *Art of the Florida Seminole and Miccosukee Indians*. Gainsville: University Press of Florida, 1995.

Farrell-Beck, Jane. "Nineteenth-Century Construction Techniques: Practice and Purpose." *Dress: The Annual Journal of the Costume Society of America* 13 (1987): 11–20.

Fernandez, Nancy Page. "Pattern Diagrams and Fashion Periodicals, 1840–1900." *Dress: The Annual Journal of the Costume Society of America* 13 (1987): 5–10.

Fields, Mamie Garvin. *Lemon Swamp and Other Places: A Carolina Memoir*. New York: The Free Press, 1983.

Fleischner, Jennifer. *Mrs. Lincoln and Mrs. Keckly*. New York: Broadway Press, 2003.

Foster, Helen Bradley. *"New Raiments of Self": African American Clothing in the Antebellum South*. New York: Berg, 1997.

Fox-Genovese, Elizabeth. *Within the Plantation Household: Black and White Women in the Old South*. Chapel Hill: University of North Carolina Press, 1988.

Fry, Gladys-Marie. *Stitched from the Soul: Slave Quilts from the Antebellum South*. Chapel Hill: University of North Carolina Press, 1990.

Gamber, Wendy. *The Female Economy: The Millinery and Dressmaking Trades, 1860–1930*. Urbana and Chicago: University of Illinois Press, 1997.

Hague, Parthenia Antoinette. *A Blockaded Family: Life in Southern Alabama During the Civil War*. Boston: Houghton Mifflin, 1888.

Hall, Gwendolyn Midlo. *Africans in Colonial Louisiana: The Development of Afro-Creole Culture in the Eighteenth Century*. Baton Rouge: Louisiana State University Press, 1992.

Harvey, John. *Men in Black*. Chicago: University of Chicago Press, 1995.

Hollander, Anne. *Sex and Suits: The Evolution of Modern Dress*. New York: Kodansha International, 1995.

hooks, bell. "My Style Ain't No Fashion." *Z Magazine* (May 1992): 27–29.

Hughes, Louis. *Thirty Years a Slave: From Bondage to Freedom*. New York: Negro University Press, 1969.

Hunt, Patricia. "Swathed in Cloth: The Headwrap of Some African American Women in Georgia and South Carolina During Late Nineteenth and Early Twentieth Century." *Dress: The Annual Journal of the Costume Society of America* 21 (1994): 30–38.

Kemble, Frances Anne. *Journal of a Residence on a Georgia Plantation in 1838–39*. New York: Harper and Brothers, 1863.

Leon, Eli. *Who'd a Thought It: Improvisation in African-American Quiltmaking*. San Francisco: San Francisco Craft and Folk Art Museum, 1987.

Littlefield, Daniel C. *Rice and Slaves: Ethnicity and Slave Trade in Colonial Carolina*. Baton Rouge: Louisiana State University Press, 1981.

Masson, Ann, and Bryce Reveley. "When Life's Brief Sun Was Set: Portraits of Southern Women in Mourning—1830–1860." *Southern Quarterly: Journal of the Arts of the South* 27 (1988): 33–56.

McWhiney, Grady. *Cracker Culture: Celtic Ways in the Old South*. Tuscaloosa: University of Alabama Press, 1988.

Northrup, Solomon. *Twelve Years a Slave*, ed. Sue Eakin and Joseph Logsdon. Baton Rouge: Louisiana State University Press, 1996.

Olmsted, Frederick Law. *The Cotton Kingdom: A Traveller's Observations on Cotton and Slavery in the American Slave States*. New York: Alfred A. Knopf, 1953.

Perrot, Philippe. *Fashioning the Bourgeoisie: A History of Clothing in the Nineteenth Century*, trans. Richard Bienvenu. Princeton, NJ: Princeton University Press, 1994.

Price, Richard, and Sally Price. *Maroon Arts: Cultural Vitality in the African Diaspora*. Boston: Beacon Press, 1999.

Reveley, Bryce. "The Black Trade in New Orleans, 1840–1880." *Southern Quarterly* 31 (1993): 119–122.

Ripley, Eliza. *Social Life in Old New Orleans*. Gretna, LA: Pelican Publishing Co., 1998.

Romans, Bernard. *A Concise Natural History of East and West Florida*. New York, 1775. Reprint, New Orleans: Pelican Publishing Co., 1961.

Severa, Joan L. *Dressed for the Photographer: Ordinary Americans and Fashion, 1840–1900*. Kent, Ohio: Kent State University Press, 1995.

Shep, R. L. *Corsets: A Visual History*. Mendocino, CA: R. L. Shep, 1993.

Starke, Barbara M. "Nineteenth-Century African-American Dress." In *Dress in American Culture*, ed. Patricia A. Cunningham and Susan Voso Lab, 66–79. Bowling Green, OH: Bowling Green University Popular Press, 1993.

Tallant, Robert. *Gumbo Ya-Ya: A Collection of Louisiana Folk Tales*. Gretna, LA: Pelican Publishing Co., 1998.

Tandberg, Gerilyn. "Decoration and Decorum: Accessories of Nineteenth-Century Louisiana Women." *Southern Quarterly: Journal of the Arts of the South* 27 (1988): 9–32.

Thompson, Robert Farris. *Flash of the Spirit: African and Afro-American Art and Philosophy*. New York: Random House, 1983.

Ulrich, Pamela V. "Promoting the South: Rhetoric and Textiles in Columbus, Georgia, 1850–1880." *Dress: The Annual Journal of the Costume Society of America* 11 (1985): 31–46.

Volo, Dorothy Denneen, and James M. Volo. *Daily Life in Civil War America*. Westport, CT: Greenwood Press, 1998. 237–270.

Wahlman, Maude Southwell. *Signs and Symbols: African Images in African-American Quilts*. New York: Studio Books, 1993.

Warwick, Alexander, and Dani Cavallaro. *Fashioning the Frame: Boundaries, Dress and the Body*. Oxford: Berg, 1998.

Washington, Booker. *Up from Slavery*. New York: Penguin Books, 1901.

White, Shane, and Graham White. *Stylin': African American Expressive Culture from Its Beginnings to the Zoot Suit*. Ithaca, NY: Cornell University Press, 1998.

Wiley, Bell Irvin. *Plain People of the Confederacy*. Chicago: Quadrangle Books, 1943.

Windley, Lathan A., comp. *Runaway Slave Advertisements: A Documentary History from the 1730s to 1790*. 4 vols. Westport, CT: Greenwood Press, 1983.

Zakim, Michael. "Sartorial Ideologies: From Homespun to Ready-Made." *American Historical Review* 106 (2001): 1–30.

Organizations, Museums, Special Collections

Alabama

Birmingham Museum of Art
http://www.artsbma.org/showglry.asp?I=D&G=Decorative-Arts:-American&A=0

As described on its Web site, "The museum's collection of American decorative arts permits a closer view of American craftsmen as artists, businessmen, and interpreters of style and culture. The collection stems primarily from the nineteenth and early twentieth centuries, and is particularly strong in examples of Alabama decorative arts. Included in the collection are a number of objects from the Arts and Crafts and Art Nouveau period. The collection of American textiles includes costumes, coverlets, and needlework, as well as over 300 Alabama-made quilts containing a variety of traditional patterns, crazy quilts, art quilts by contemporary studio quilt makers as well as traditional quilts made by women and men working today."

Arkansas

Old State House Museum, Little Rock
http://www.oldstatehouse.com/collections/

The Old State House Museum offers a collection of quilts made by African Americans from Arkansas from 1880 to the present, a collection of Civil War battle flags, and a collection of Arkansas First Ladies' gowns from 1889 to the present. All of the museum's collections will soon be available for viewing online.

Florida

Museum of Florida History, Tallahassee
http://dhr.dos.state.fl.us/museum/

The Museum of Florida History has holdings that include a collection of First Ladies' gowns and a Florida quilt collection.

Georgia

Atlanta History Center
http://www.atlantahistorycenter.com/exhibitions/html/museum_collections.htm

The Atlanta History Center has holdings including a Textiles and Social History Collection. This large and regionally significant collection of clothing for men, women, and children also includes quilts, coverlets, and other flat textiles.

Newnan County Male Academy Museum
http://newnan.com/mam/

This museum in Newnan, Georgia, describes itself as having "received recognition and wide acclaim for its extensive collection of period clothing from the nineteenth and early twentieth centuries. Many prominent families from the area have donated exquisite items of attire from bygone years, which textile experts have carefully reworked and preserved. Select exhibits from this vast collection are mounted throughout the year. Story boards identify the origin, fabric, style and donor of the article." The museum's costume gallery, according to the Web site, exhibits items selected from "the best textile collection in the Southeast."

Kentucky

Kentucky Museum
http://www.wku.edu/Library/kylm/collections/inhouse/km/clothing.html

The Kentucky Museum is located in Bowling Green. Its Web site states: "The Clothing & Textiles collection includes more than 7,000 examples of nineteenth and twentieth century textiles. Major components include historic costume, clothing accessories, and quilts and coverlets. Other examples of household linens and fine needlework are present as well. The majority of historical clothing dates between 1870 and 1960, although there are examples from every decade between 1810 and 1980."

Louisiana

Louisiana State Museum, New Orleans
http://lsm.crt.state.la.us/site/collections/costumes.htm

This museum at the Cabildo in New Orleans holds a costume/textile/carnival collection. The Web site states: "The Louisiana State Museum has one of the largest and finest costume and textile collections in the United States. Overall the museum's collection ranges from late 18th century to the present with the majority of objects having a Louisiana provenance. Of the approximately 15,000 objects in the collection, one third is the costumes and accessories collection, one third is the textile collection, and one third is the Carnival collection." The collection includes bedding; floor, window, and furniture coverings; Acadian textiles; ladies' costumes and accessories; menswear; uniforms; religious and ceremonial artifacts; infants' and children's clothing; textile art (needlework); flags and banners; fashion plates and magazines, as well as patterns to document the objects; and an array of Carnival costumes and formal wear.

Mississippi

Manship House, Jackson
http://www.mdah.state.ms.us/admin/news/manship_wedding.html

The Mississippi Department of Archives and History's Manship House includes an exhibit on nineteenth-century wedding attire and customs and an exhibit on nineteenth-century mourning customs, particularly mourning dress customs.

North Carolina

Mint Museum of Art, Charlotte
http://www.mintmuseum.org/collections.php

The Mint Museum of Art offers historic costumes and accessories.

Museum of Early Southern Decorative Arts, Winston-Salem
http://www.oldsalem.org/mesda.html

The museum's Web site states: "The Museum of Early Southern Decorative Arts (MESDA) is the only museum dedicated to exhibiting and researching the regional decorative arts of the early South. With its 24 period rooms and seven galleries, MESDA showcases the furniture, paintings, textiles, ceramics, silver, and other metalwares made and used in Maryland, Virginia, the Carolinas, Georgia, Kentucky, and Tennessee through 1820."

South Carolina

South Carolina State Museum, Columbia
http://www.museum.state.sc.us/main/exhibits.html

The museum, housed in a 1893 textile mill building, features a permanent exhibit on the textile industry in South Carolina.

Tennessee

Englewood Textile Museum, Englewood

This museum recounts the history of the textile industry in Englewood and the important role women played in the development of this unique southern textile town.

Memphis Brooks Museum of Art

http://www.brooksmuseum.org/public/exhibitions/default.asp?id=10000059

The museum has collections of beadwork, embroideries, quilts, and coverlets.

Virginia

Colonial Williamsburg

http://www.colonialwilliamsburg.com/history/clothing/intro/index.cfm

Colonial Williamsburg has an extensive Web site that features essays providing an introduction to eighteenth-century clothing; detailed explanations and diagrams of men's, women's, and children's clothing; a description of millinery shops of the eighteenth century; and an introduction to costume design. Easily one of the best Web sites existing for research and information concerning eighteenth-century clothing.

Museum of the Confederacy

http://www.moc.org/excol.htm

The collection has "badges and ribbons from postwar veterans reunions . . . 550 flags including non-regulation oil-painted silk flags and government issue national colors" as well as "215 uniforms including prewar militia uniforms, plantation-made garments, late-war issues from the CSA's Richmond depot and the uniforms of well-known officers; 3,000 military accoutrements and 1,000 military buttons; and 5,000 domestic items featuring wartime 'ersatz' goods such as plantation wooden shoes and homemade soap, slave-woven coverlets and baskets, and articles associated with the employment of women in government bureau."

FILM AND THEATER

Thomas S. Hischak

Until Florida became the nation's number one tourist destination in the 1970s, many Americans were mostly familiar with the South only through movies, plays, and television shows. In many ways they still are, for the Florida that vacationers see is far from an accurate picture of the diversity of the South. And while the region has been depicted on stage and screen in an often cliché-ridden and over-simplified manner, some of that diversity has managed to rise to the surface. Perhaps no one play or movie has ever captured the complex variety of the South. In fact, the designations "southern play" and "southern film" are of little use. The stage pieces *Uncle Tom's Cabin* and *A Streetcar Named Desire*, and the movies *The Birth of a Nation* and *Li'l Abner*, could not be further apart from each other, yet all four would be labeled southern. But they do not share the same locality, language, social order, or regional point of view; four works from four different nations might have more in common with each other.

To non-southerners, the unifying element in conjuring up the South in one's mind has always been the region's distinctive sound: the much-parodied southern accent. Yet it doesn't take a very thorough examination to realize that even this feature is radically different as one travels from one part of the South to another. The rich Creole voice, the twangy Ozark tones, the European-like vocal gentility of certain cities, and the musical flavors of Appalachia are among the diverse sounds that make the region as difficult to pin down linguistically as to define stylistically. Broadway and Hollywood may have lumped them all into a "southern play" or a "Dixie film," but even in their vagueness the two media sometimes captured the unique qualities of one of the nation's most misunderstood regions.

EARLY THEATER IN THE SOUTH

American theater in the 1700s consisted of British theater in the upper colonies and French and Spanish theater in the South and Southwest. Theatrical troupes

The Oldest Playhouse in the South?

While there is some evidence that French- and Spanish-language theater troupes toured the South in the early 1700s, the oldest playhouse in the region was built in 1736 in Charles Town (later Charleston), South Carolina, as a venue for English-speaking productions. The New Theatre on Dock Street opened with a production of the London hit *The Recruiting Officer* and was an immediate hit at the playhouse, soon familiarly known as the Dock Street Theatre. It flourished for two years until the building was destroyed in the great Charleston fire of 1738. Two subsequent playhouses were constructed on the site, one in 1754 and a second in 1766, until it was replaced by a hotel in 1809. Historic preservationists had long sought to reconstruct the theater, and during the Depression their efforts were successful when, under the sponsorship of the Works Progress Administration (WPA), a replica of the original structure was built. It opened in 1937 with, appropriately enough, a production of *The Recruiting Officer*. Although it is now located on Church Street, the new Dock Street Theatre seats 563 patrons in pew-like seats that replicate the 1736 original. The playhouse was a busy venue during the Little Theater movement of the 1930s and early 1940s and continues to serve as a performance space as well as a landmark historic building. Though far from continuous in its operation, the Dock Street Theatre is in its own way the South's oldest playhouse.

from Europe gave limited tours in the New World, rarely in permanent playhouses, then returned home. Their motivation was financial, and the little bit of culture they brought to North America was more a by-product than a mission. The first troupe to arrive in America with plans to stay was that of the British actor-manager Lewis Hallam (1714–1956), who arrived in Williamsburg, Virginia, in 1752, having received permission from the colony to establish a permanent home there. But the small community could not sustain a professional theater company, so Hallam and his players toured to Philadelphia, New York, and Charleston, South Carolina, in their efforts to make a go of the venture. Charleston was the largest city in the South and was generally considered the region's most important cultural center. Theater productions were common there as early as 1736, when the first permanent playhouse in the South was constructed. The South Carolina seaport city rivaled Boston, New York, and Philadelphia (the other three major metropolises in the colonies) for its wealth and sophistication and would remain a jewel in the New World until after the Civil War.

Outside of the original thirteen colonies, New Orleans was the other major cultural center of the South. French actors had been performing there for some years before a revolution in Haiti forced a theater company from there to reestablish itself in New Orleans in 1791. By 1807 an English-speaking troupe made its debut in the Louisiana city, and for many years both French and English companies found success performing side by side. New Orleans enjoyed a theater boom starting in the 1830s when actor-manager James H. Caldwell (1793–1863) arrived and built the St. Charles Theatre, the city's premiere playhouse for many decades. Other structures followed, and New Orleans remained a flourishing theater center for the rest of the century, even continuing with success during the Civil War years.

Ambitious theater companies on the Atlantic coast realized that there was money to be made by following the homesteaders and performing out west. During the early decades of the 1800s, the "West" referred to the new territories in Kentucky and Tennessee. Lexington, Kentucky, had a permanent playhouse as early as 1808, and Nashville was a popular stop on the Appalachian tour circuits in the 1820s. As the young country expanded and the railroad network was developed, theatergoing was no longer only an urban pastime, and all small and mid-size cities throughout the South boasted playhouses that were frequently booked with local and touring productions. This activity suddenly came to a standstill during the Civil War and only returned haltingly during Reconstruction. In many ways, theater in the region disappeared along with the old southern way of life, and only in the twentieth century did touring theatrical productions become a significant enterprise.

THEATER IN THE TWENTIETH-CENTURY SOUTH

By the end of the 1800s, most theater in the South consisted of professional touring companies, many of whom were controlled by the powerful Theatrical Syndicate based in New York City. This monopolistic enterprise was ruthless in its business practices and knew how to turn playgoing into a nationwide money-making machine. While major cities such as Philadelphia, Chicago, Baltimore, San Francisco, and Boston boasted their own theater companies independent of New York–based tours, there were few such cases in the South. Even flourishing metropolises such as Atlanta and New Orleans depended on the Syndicate for its live theater. Not until the new century was half over did many southern cities provide professional homegrown theater as part of the growing regional (or resident) theater network. In the 1950s this movement started to replace the old community and little theaters across the land, and arts centers, built and promoted by the city, started to spring up. Atlanta was one of the first communities in the South to seize upon the new plan; by the end of the century it would boast dozens of professional, educational, and semiprofessional theaters. Richmond, Louisville, and cities in the Carolinas and Florida soon followed suit, and before long a major network of regional theaters across the South brought live

Tennessee Williams' South on Stage

William Faulkner, Eudora Welty, Flannery O'Connor, Carson McCullers, and others can comfortably be described as southern novelists and short story writers. But in the theater few playwrights have concentrated on the region, and often dramas and comedies set in the South were written by New Yorkers and other northern dramatists. But Tennessee Williams (1911–1983) is the genuine article: a true southern playwright. While his works may not give a balanced view of the region, they are nonetheless some of the most vivid depictions of characters and places in the South. He was born Thomas Lanier Williams in Columbus, Mississippi, but grew up and was educated in the Midwest. Yet Williams' writing rarely strayed far from his southern roots. His faded plantation belles, grasping Delta businessmen, small-town spinsters, oversexed itinerant studs, and conniving, predatory females encompass the decadent as well as the pathetic side of the region's inhabitants. He is also very astute in capturing the various southern locales, such as the sweltering suffocation of New Orleans in *A Streetcar Named Desire* (1947), the rigid small community with its strict proprieties in *Summer and Smoke* (1948), the wealthy but hollow Delta mansions as seen in *Cat on a Hot Tin Roof* (1955), an Italian American coastal town in Louisiana in *The Rose Tattoo* (1955), and the well-greased political machine in southern cities, as with *Sweet Bird of Youth* (1959). Williams is considered America's most poetic playwright. He did not write his dramas in verse but used a musical, highly lyrical form of dialogue that was as rhythmic as it was accurate. These rhythms can best be described as southern, each character speaking in a poetic dialect of one sort or the other. The blunt gruntings of Stanley Kowalski are contrasted with the fluttery tones of Blanche DuBois, both of *A Streetcar Named Desire*, just as in *Cat on a Hot Tin Roof* where Big Daddy's barking basso is set against Brick's quietly smoldering mumbles and Maggie's not-so-quiet sexual smoldering. No other playwright re-created the sounds of the South on stage with such theatrical and knowing aplomb. Since many of Williams' plays were filmed (although in most cases with abridged and censored screenplays), he remains one of Hollywood's most effective authors of southern films. Whether on stage or screen, Williams' South is feverishly alive in both media.

Jessica Tandy plays Blanche DuBois in a scene from the play *A Streetcar Named Desire* (1947). Photofest.

performance to many communities. While this movement rarely provided theater to rural areas as the Syndicate had done, it was nonetheless a renaissance of sorts. Among the many noteworthy regional theater companies in the South at the beginning of the twenty-first century were the Actors Theatre of Louisville; the Alabama Shakespeare Festival in Montgomery; the Alliance Theatre Company, the Georgia Shakespeare Festival, and the Academy Theatre, all in Atlanta; the Arkansas Repertory Theatre in Little Rock; the Asolo Theatre Company and the Florida Studio Theatre in Sarasota; the Barter Theatre in Abingdon, Virginia; the Charleston Stage Company in South Carolina; the Clarence Brown Theatre Company in Knoxville; the Playhouse on the Square in Memphis; the Playmakers Repertory Company in Chapel Hill, North Carolina; the Signature Theatre in Arlington, Virginia; and the Tennessee Repertory Theatre in Nashville. Curiously, New Orleans remained for many years the only major metropolis in the nation that could not nurture and support a first-class resident theater, an odd fact considering the city's wealth, history, education, culture, and civic pride.

FILM PRODUCTION IN THE SOUTH

The earliest American movies were filmed in and around New York City, where the acting, writing, directing, and producing talent was centered. Production moved into nearby New Jersey and Long Island for a time until the 1910s, when California was deemed the most suitable location for moviemaking because of its sunny climate and variety of topographical features. The same could be said for much of the South, but, for various reasons, filmmakers would not be drawn to the area for several decades. There was a period in the 1910s when the Jacksonville area of Florida was a popular location for filmmaking, but as Southern California rose in movie dominance, this "Southern Hollywood" soon faded away. When Hollywood wished to re-create the South on screen, it did so in the sound stages or on the back lots. *Gone with the Wind* (1939), considered the most southern of all movies, is a good example of moviemakers conjuring up a region without setting foot on the story's actual locale; Hollywood's Tara, Twelve Oaks, Atlanta, and other sites became the real thing in the studio system. It was not until the 1960s, and the waning of the old studio system, that producers looked outside of California to capture new vistas and often save money by filming in locations where goods and labor were cheaper. When it was learned that a movie set in Tennessee could be shot cheaper in Tennessee, moviemakers started to consider the South a practical production location. By the 1970s all the state governments and major cities set up film commissions to attract filmmakers to their area, knowing that movie production brought money into town and employed many people, even if for a short period of time. In remote districts where unions were not strong and prices were low, producers could save thousands of dollars even as they got the real thing. In some cases, movies not even set in the South were filmed there because of the budgetary perks. Although *Close Encounters of the Third Kind* (1977) took place in Indiana, it was shot in Alabama, while *Blue Velvet* (1986) had a midwestern setting but was filmed in North Carolina.

By the 1990s, Wilmington, North Carolina, had become the third most productive site for filmmaking in the nation, superseded only by Southern California and New York City. Not only movies but television series, such as *Dawson's Creek*, were filmed there. The state offered the production companies low-cost services, state-of-the-art communication and transportation, and even financial incentives. But the Wilmington environs were far from a

D. W. Griffith's South on Screen

The film medium's first great American artist, the director-writer D. W. Griffith (1875–1948), was a southerner, and often throughout his career his films returned not only to the region of his birth but to a southern temperament as well. Born David Wark Griffith in La Grange, Kentucky, and raised in Louisville, he was a product of the late Reconstruction era. His father had been a physician and served in the Mexican War, but the family was reduced to poverty. Griffith never forgot his family's plight, and a bitterness remained with him throughout his life. It also appeared in his movies, most memorably in the Reconstruction sections of his masterpiece, *The Birth of a Nation* (1915), which has been faulted for its blatant racism and glorification of the Ku Klux Klan. Griffith's southern films were also filled with sentimental affection for the old South and Victorian manners, high regard for the innocence of women, and a deep sense of patriotism. In his early one- and two-reelers made for the Biograph Studio, Griffith explored these themes, as well as the Civil War as the turning point in American history. A cowardly son finds inspiration from his patriotic father in *The Honor of His Family* (1910), a similarly weak soldier gets his courage from a sweetheart in *The Battle* (1911), while disgrace is brought on a family because of a soldier's desertion in *The House with Closed Shutters* (1910). In each case, a southern family is at the center of the story, just as *The Birth of a Nation* takes a southern point of view of the war and its aftermath. But even in Griffith's peacetime stories and movies, a lush romanticism and a sense of duty pervade the southern works. His later feature films such as *The White Rose* (1923) and *Topsy and Eva* (1927) retain the passion of his Civil War movies because Griffith was stubbornly old-fashioned in his outlook. The great pioneer developed and defined the language of the cinema, then quickly outdated himself by refusing to give up his Victorian and racist sensibility in a modern world. But as disturbing as his views of the South might seem to modern audiences, there is no question that Griffith captured the region on screen with fervor and a point of view shared by many southerners of his generation.

low-income, backward area. As the locality developed, costs rose, and soon North Carolina found itself in competition with foreign markets that could offer even lower wages and greater tax incentives. The most glaring example of Wilmington losing its predominance came in 2003 with the Civil War film *Cold Mountain*; although the story takes place in Virginia and North Carolina, the movie ended up being filmed in Rumania, where it cost much less to make.

But films continue to be made in North Carolina and throughout the South on a much more frequent basis than seen in the 1960s and 1970s. Also, independent filmmakers continue to thrive in the region. Victor Nunez (b. 1945), for example, has produced a number of feature "indies" in North Florida, such as *Gal Young 'Un* (1979), *A Flash of Green* (1984), *Ruby in Paradise* (1993), *Ulee's Gold* (1997), and *Coastlines* (2002). Younger artists, such as David Gordon Green (b. 1975), who set his movies *George Washington* (2000) and *All the Real Girls* (2003) in North Carolina, find the South ideal for making small-scale films with an alternative point of view. Today it is almost expected that a movie about the South should be filmed there. That is not always the case, but it happens more often than at any other time since the birth of American cinema.

DEAR OLD SOUTH

Regardless of where a "southern" film is shot or where a play about the South is presented, the final product usually holds a definite point of view about the region. Accurate or not, complimentary or not, each work depicts the South in some way. Whether this point of view comes from the source material, the screenplay, the playwright, the director, or the producers, the movie or play cannot help but say something about the world it inhabits. Since no one work can begin to encompass all of the opinions and viewpoints of the South, each film or theater piece tends to fall into a category that expresses the approach taken. These classifications are arbitrary and difficult to define, but we will try to cover some of the broad fields into which southern movies and plays may fall.

The nostalgic film or drama that presents an idealized view of the dear old South will be considered first. Because the way of life changed so drastically after the Civil War, there has always been a great deal of nostalgia for the past South. Sometimes this nostalgia takes the form of racism and bigotry, such as touting the Confederate flag or extolling the memory of slavery. But just as often the fondness for the long-gone southern ways is an emotional rather than a political one. Images of plantation life, with everyone living in harmony and the aristocratic gentility ruling the day, are considered more fantasy today than history, yet even non-southerners are drawn to this highly romantic view of a lifestyle that rarely existed. Viewers are also attracted to rose-tinted depictions of small-town life in the South: the quaint, close-knit community where honest and decent citizens in Tennessee, Arkansas, or elsewhere reaffirm one's faith in humanity. Sometimes these versions of the South can be unrealistically simpleminded, as in the film *Tammy and the Bachelor* (1957), in which a perky backwoods girl from the Louisiana bayou patches up all the problems that the rich sophisticates have, even winning the love of a handsome southern aristocrat along the way. Child stars Shirley Temple and Bobby Breen pulled off similar feats in some 1930s movies. In *The Littlest Rebel* (1935) and *The Little Colonel* (1935), the southern moppet Temple charms Union officers during the war and embittered colonels after the war, restoring warm affection where once hostility reigned. Breen, Temple's male counterpart during the Depression years, played a youth who inherits his father's plantation before the Civil War in *Way Down South* (1939). The chirping boy would much rather sing spirituals with his slaves than treat them harshly, and he even gets rid of some nasty overseers. But the movie still wallows in affection for the old ways, even suggesting that the slave system is fine if everyone sings together. Such highly escapist films as these border on the politically incorrect today (especially in their treatment of African Americans), yet one can understand their appeal; Hollywood sometimes presented a South that charmed audiences while it erased guilt.

Even plays and movies that were not so sunny in outlook managed to bask in the nostalgic glow of the old South. *Gone with the Wind* opens with a teary tribute to the lost land of cavaliers and ladies with the purple prose that fills the screen right after the opening credits. The text does not come from Margaret Mitchell's novel but from Hollywood, suggesting that one must love and lament the old ways in order to get into the spirit of the story that follows. Although *Gone with the Wind* exhibits great storytelling, it reflects the racism of the times and perpetuates the myth that a better world was lost when the South fell. Or consider the idealistic view of the Reconstruction era presented in the musical movie *Song of the South* (1946). Like Shirley Temple and Bobby Breen, it is the young Bobby Driscoll who breaks through the color barrier and befriends a former slave who tells him Uncle Remus stories. As charming as the film is, its use of stereotypes in depicting African Americans as lovable entertainers is disturbing. Even on its first release, NAACP leaders criticized the part-live action, part-animated feature, and years later the movie was pulled from television broadcast because networks did not wish to offend black audiences.

DEAR NEW SOUTH

It was easy to idealize the old South on stage and screen, but there was often nostalgia for the less glorious days as well. Generations of southerners growing up in the region without plantations and Negro folktales also held affection for the South. Thomas Wolfe, Carson McCullers, Pat Conroy, Truman Capote, Harper Lee, and others often wrote about the struggles of their past with a warmth of understanding, and these writings often made for superior theater and cinema. Lee's *To Kill a Mockingbird*, filmed in 1962, is perhaps the finest example. Dealing with racism in a small Depression-era town, the book (and Horton Foote's superb screenplay) cannot justly be called escapist. The issues are never buried, and even the children in the story are affected by the prejudices of some of the adults. But *To Kill a Mockingbird* is indeed nostalgic and offers, in the person of lawyer Atticus Finch, a figure that inspires hope and understanding of all races. Arguably the real heroine is Scout, who looks far ahead of where her father is able to go. Finch is an adult, more complex version of Temple and Breen, though bringing a dignity to his efforts that the youngsters never possessed. Finch even loses the case of an African American wrongly accused of rape, but it does not diminish his integrity. The film portrays a South struggling to throw off its racist past and presents a community that is sobered up by its own questionable actions.

McCullers' *The Member of the Wedding* was turned into a successful Broadway drama in 1950 and was filmed two years later with most of the stage cast. Also far from escapist, this portrayal of a lonely twelve-year-old girl, who finds emotional refuge in the arms of her family's black cook, is a poignant piece that never judges and always understands. Many critics now, including Grace Hale, might suggest that this drama perpetuates the Mammy stereotype. The situation of a white child developing a deep kinship with a Mammy-like figure runs through many southern

Gregory Peck as Atticus Finch in a scene from the movie *To Kill a Mockingbird* (1962). Photofest.

novels, plays, and movies (most recently seen again in the 2003 stage work *Caroline, or Change*), but *The Member of the Wedding* is perhaps the most subtle and fascinating. The cook Berenice (unforgettably played by Ethel Waters) in the movie version is not a saint; she is an oft-married, opinionated, and troubled black woman. Her charge Frankie (beautifully portrayed by Julie Harris) in the movie version is an awkward adolescent whose roller-coaster of emotion makes her as difficult as she is amusing. The relationship between the two is a classic southern paradox: unequal socially but emotionally unified. This is nostalgia of the highest order. McCullers' novel *The Heart Is a Lonely Hunter* was also filmed, and the 1968 movie offers a more sophisticated version of a Temple/Breen-like peacemaker. The deaf-mute, John Singer (given an understated performance by Alan Arkin), befriends a variety of misfits in a small southern town, helping each one put his or her life in perspective. But few of them consider Singer's own loneliness and needs, and only his death brings them to realize the impact he has had on their lives. In terms of plot it is not that far removed from *The Little Colonel*, but McCullers' characters are a fascinating cross section of a southern community: the bigoted black doctor and his estranged daughter, an alcoholic drifter, a yearning adolescent, and so on. This is the new South, and McCullers' affection for it is far from rose-tinted.

Pat Conroy's novels are mostly set in the Carolinas. One in particular, *The Water Is Wide*, is a good example of another southerner looking nostalgically back at efforts to better his homeland. Filmed in 1974 as *Conrack*, the movie tells of a teacher who attempts to educate the neglected African American children on a small island off the South Carolina coast. His backward students are at a disadvantage, but Conroy's unconventional methods eventually succeed with them and their suspicious parents. But just as Atticus Finch loses his case, Conroy is booted out by conservative school officials, and his efforts are only a warm memory. Based on the author's own experiences, the story still holds a romanticized view of the South. Conroy's failure to continue his teaching is a jolt of reality, but the movie can be categorized as idealistic all the same.

Many feel that two acclaimed films about poor, struggling African Americans— *Sounder* (1972) and *The Color Purple* (1985)—also tend to romanticize certain aspects of the South in order to illustrate the cruelty of other aspects. In the latter, the sexually, physically, and emotionally abused Celie withstands a series of troubles but survives to find herself eventually regenerated. Like the other black women in the film, Celie is selfless, uncomplaining, and as perfect as the black men are cruel, lecherous, and destructive. Alice Walker's novel was far more subtle, but director Steven Spielberg's lush and idyllic landscapes and simplistic characterizations were considered by many to turn an honest book into a romanticized movie. *Sounder*, based on William H. Armstrong's novel, portrays a family of black sharecroppers during the Depression who also override oppression to find self-worth. When the father is jailed for stealing meat to feed his family, his strong-willed wife and their adolescent son keep the family together until his return. Far more understated than *The Color Purple*, the well-acted *Sounder* nonetheless romanticized its vision, every member of the family being flawlessly understanding and nobly good. The film was a landmark of sorts, portraying African Americans as a closely knit unit of fellowship rather than the dysfunctional groups that usually were presented on screen. But for many, time has proven that the basic vision of the piece is idealistic and another case of romanticizing the South.

SOUTHERN GOTHIC

The flip side of these idealized visions of the South is the "Southern Gothic" play or movie. The term has been defined in various ways since it was first used in the 1930s as a negative connotation of decaying society and degenerate behavior. Erskine Caldwell's notorious novel *Tobacco Road* about Georgia "poor white trash" was turned into a record-breaking hit on Broadway in 1933 and filmed in 1941. The amoral Lester family of sharecroppers are not above selling off their daughters for marriage, throwing rocks at grandma when she irritates them, and even running mother over with an old car to make a point. Caldwell's depiction of such repulsive folks only draws laughs today, but the public's fascination with such low-lifes worried some in the Depression years, and the genre Southern Gothic was viewed as a sign of loosening morals. As the years passed, Southern Gothic took on a wider meaning that included eccentric and unique aspects of the South, from perverse recluses living in crumbling mansions to objectionable sexual activities such as incest. The richly unusual characters in Flannery O'Connor's short stories were colorful examples, but the works by William Faulkner and Tennessee Williams were also included. Today the designation Southern Gothic is less offensive and encompasses any person or activity that a non-southerner might look on as bizarre, such as the lovably dysfunctional sisters in the play *Crimes of the Heart* (1981; filmed in 1986) or the delightfully offbeat movie *Cookie's Fortune* (1999).

Eccentricity has long been viewed as a southern trait, suggesting that there are strange people in New England and California, but it takes a southerner to be a true eccentric. It is another regional cliché but not one without some basis of truth. While Southern Gothic is a literary style, it can also be a philosophy of life, and real-life eccentrics have always been noticed and often applauded. History, legend, and politics are filled with celebrities known for their quirky "southern ways," and the rest of the country often finds them amusing, even endearing. In her heyday, actress Tallulah Bankhead (1903–1968) was a glowing example. The Alabama stage and screen star rarely received noteworthy roles, but she managed to inject a highly mannered kind of eccentricity in most of her vehicles and carried that persona beyond the footlights. On the other hand, there are the film celebrities who exude a creepy, uncomfortable eccentricity in their performances. The actor-writer-director Billy Bob Thornton is a current example, his work in *Sling Blade* (1995) revealing the less pleasant side of the southern eccentric. Sometimes this kind of quirkiness sits in a gray area between comedy and horror, as in the movie *Crazy in Alabama* (1999), adapted from a novel by southern author Mark Childress, in which an abused wife chops off her husband's head and brings it with her in a hatbox when she sets off for California to become a movie star. When does eccentric behavior become psychopathic? It's a line often crossed in Southern Gothic. Many stage and screen comedies set in the South fall into this category of eccentricity. The off-Broadway hit *Steel Magnolias* (1987) and its 1989 screen version provide a mild example. The group of small-town women who gather at a local hair salon are far from dangerous, and few spectators would question their sanity. Yet there is a spirited quality in their talk and behavior that would not be possible in, say, Ohio. Southern playwright Beth Henley (b. 1952) moves closer to the edge of bizarre behavior in comedies such as *The Wake of Jamie Foster* (1982), *The Miss Firecracker Contest* (1984), which was filmed in 1989 as *Miss Firecracker*, and the already mentioned *Crimes of the Heart*. As with *Steel Magnolias*, Henley concentrates on spirited southern women who are as passionate about the details as they are about life and death. Some southern audiences groan at their wacky predictability, but outside the South they are welcomed as wholesome comic types. Such comedies of manners as *Crimes of the Heart* might be defined as satires elsewhere, but within the Southern Gothic they are considered real life.

Many critics called Robert Altman's film *Nashville* (1975) a satire, but one fails to find the target of its humor unless it is America itself. The complex comedy, which follows over a dozen characters during a few days in the Tennessee city, is a kaleidoscope of sorts, a mock documentary that finds humor in the music business, celebrity, politics, and whatnot. Had it been set in Boston, the movie might have been satiric; placed in the "Athens of the South," it comfortably fits into Southern Gothic. And while some of the characters are not even southerners, the tone of eccentricity is quite clear. The same can be said for *The Birdcage* (1996), the American adaptation of the popular French film *La Cage aux Folles* (1978). The gay lifestyle of South Beach in Miami is not so much satirized in the comedy as it is lovingly rendered as everyday life. The eccentricities of the characters are not exaggerations, they are a given. So too is the behavior of some of the Savannah characters in *Midnight in the Garden of Good and Evil* (1997), though that movie cannot comfortably be described as a comedy. The transvestite Lady Chablis might be right at home in South Beach, but his/her presence in the historic, conservative city is what makes the eccentricity so much fun. The fact that the role was not played by an actor but by the actual transvestite in the true story adds another level of eccentricity to the movie.

Sometimes Southern Gothic can be nostalgic, as in *The Grass Harp*, a Truman Capote tale that was dramatized on Broadway in 1952, musicalized off Broadway in 1971, and filmed (as a non-musical) in 1996. The eccentric behavior of Aunt Dolly is recalled fondly by those who loved her and saw nothing wrong with her retreating to a tree house when life's pressures were too great to bear. Nor does one question the shenanigans of con-man George C. Scott in the film farce *The*

Flim-Flam Man (1967), a man whose victims are more criminal than himself. Nostalgia creeps into *Fried Green Tomatoes* (1991), though the stories that the nursing home resident (Jessica Tandy) tells are rarely comic. These past events inspire the contemporary housewife Kathy Bates to rethink her life, just as Dolly and Scott have an inspiring influence on a youth in their vehicles. These nostalgic movies seem to say that eccentricity teaches one how to live.

GOTHIC HORROR AND GOTHIC DECADENCE

As charming as the eccentric comedies are, most of the Southern Gothic plays and films have been concerned with decadence, such as that found in *Tobacco Road*, or a particular branch of decay that can only be called Gothic horror. These nightmarish works see southern decay as the ideal backdrop for men's (and often women's) most sinister behavior. Unlike the traditional horror thriller that aims to scare the audience with surprises and supernatural creatures, Gothic horror need look no further than a deranged human mind to create uneasy chills. It is less a matter of whodunit than the shock of what has been done. Bette Davis hacking her lover to death in *Hush ... Hush, Sweet*

Scene from the movie *Midnight in the Garden of Good and Evil* (1997), filmed in Savannah, Georgia. Photofest.

203

Charlotte (1964) then retiring to her haunted plantation with her memories is a classic example. The unseen hero Sebastian in Tennessee Williams' drama *Suddenly Last Summer* (1958; filmed in 1959) uses his beautiful wife to attract men for his own sexual yearnings, which only leads, horrifyingly, to murder and cannibalism. In a Louisiana hospital Sebastian's mother hopes to have the wife lobotomized in order to keep the son's behavior secret. In Williams' *Orpheus Descending* (1957; filmed as *The Fugitive Kind* in 1959) and *Sweet Bird of Youth* (1959; filmed in 1962), castration is the fate for both heroes, while a woman cuts off her breasts after losing her child in the film *Reflections in a Golden Eye* (1967), adapted from a Carson McCullers novel. These lurid examples of the peculiar nature of Gothic horror show characters at the extreme edge of human behavior. Yet some films can be just as nightmarish and create similar uneasiness by staying within the realm of believability. A good example is *Deliverance* (1972), with a plot that would have been described as a "problem play" in past times. Four urban executives from Atlanta take a canoe trip down a remote Georgia river. When they leave civilization behind, they also leave the safety of the law as they know it. When two backwoodsmen rape one of the men at gunpoint, one of the foursome kills one culprit, and justice is now in the hands of the strongest. The four urbanites realize that city laws do not work here and decide to hunt down the surviving hillbilly and kill him. No haunted mansions or psychotics were needed to create the nightmare that was *Deliverance*; it was there close under the surface all the time. However, some have criticized the movie, calling it classist, anti-southern, and homophobic.

Less gruesome and more plentiful are the plays and movies about southern decadence. This theme recurs so often in the work of novelists, playwrights, and filmmakers that one starts to wonder if such a thing as a well-balanced southern family exists. Although such works are no more prevalent than those written about dysfunctional people in other regions, there is something about the Southern Gothic treatment of decadence that seems to fascinate audiences everywhere. Many of Tennessee Williams' plays (and their film versions) fall into this category, from the wealthy, hollow world of *Cat on a Hot Tin Roof* (filmed in 1958) to the repressed small-town sexuality of *Summer and Smoke* (filmed in 1961). But it was a lesser known Williams one-act play, *27 Wagons Full of Cotton* (1955), that was turned into his most decadent and infamous movie, *Baby Doll* (1956). An oversexed child-bride who sleeps in a crib and symbolically sucks her thumb, a husband who is a voyeur spying on his virgin wife, and a corrupt businessman who seeks to covet both his neighbor's wife and goods are the central characters in this notorious depiction of southern decadence. Condemned and berated at the time of its release, *Baby Doll* is indeed trashy, yet it is thematically in line with Williams' other works on the subject.

Sex and sexual promiscuity are often at the center of southern decadence. *The Story of Temple Drake* (1933), *The Sound and the Fury* (1958), *The Long, Hot Summer* (1958), *Sanctuary* (1961), *Walk on the Wild Side* (1962), *Body Heat* (1981), and many other movies can be added to those previously mentioned. But sometimes the decadence involves money, as seen in Lillian Hellman's dramas *The Little Foxes* (1939; filmed in 1941) and *Another Part of the Forest* (1946; filmed in 1948). Both plays deal with the money-hungry Hubbard family who are taking advantage of the corrupt politics during Reconstruction to amass a fortune. Not merely content to steal and cheat other businessmen, the family members turn on each other when necessary. The cold, sly Regina goes so far as to watch her husband die of a heart attack and not fetch his medicine, knowing it will be to her financial advantage. Money and power are not as sexy as sex, but in Hellman's hands the theatrics are both engrossing and decadently fascinating. Politics has also served as the subject for Southern Gothic works. Robert Penn Warren's novel *All the King's Men*, a thinly disguised portrait of Louisiana governor Huey Long, was filmed in 1949 to great effect. It is not clear why political corruption in the South should

Documenting the South

While documentary films rarely get the widespread distribution of the fictional Hollywood feature, the genre is perhaps the most potent when considering different regions of the United States. Documentaries about the South (particularly those made by southerners) are valuable tools in capturing the region's persona. Even a very biased or opinionated documentary sheds light on its subject (and filmmaker) and cannot be discarded in putting together the puzzle pieces that define the South. Two outstanding documentaries about the region were made in the 1930s: Pare Lorentz's 1939 film about the creation of the Tennessee Valley Authority, *The River*, and Elia Kazan's 1938 documentary about life in the Tennessee mountains, *People of the Cumberland*. Like the TVA project itself, *The River* was sponsored by the federal government. Kazan's film was made by Frontier Film Group, a leftist organization based in New York City. The Standard Oil Company produced Robert Flaherty's *Louisiana Story* (1948), a semi-documentary about oil drilling as seen through the eyes of a young boy in the bayou.

By the 1950s the new medium of television took over the documentary form, but the genre enjoyed a resurgence on celluloid in the 1960s. In the South this was a very appropriate moment because debates were raging over southern identity. Because of the infiltration of television and other mass media, many feared that the region's unique characteristics would be swallowed up by nationwide trends and be lost forever. The 1960s saw emphasis put on oral tradition and folklore in the southern states as music, legends, folk art, and craftsmanship were being recorded and preserved. Documentary film was an ideal method to secure the identity of the region, and many nonfiction movies were made about specific areas and particular groups of people. Most of these films were low-budget projects using 16 mm cameras, and distribution was limited; in fact, many were made for archival purposes only. But it was a fertile time for documentary filmmaking in the South.

Since then the region has continued to be documented on film, though infrequently with mainstream movies. In the 1970s Judy Peiser and Bill Ferris made a series of documentaries about the Mississippi Delta for the Center for Southern Folklore: *Mississippi Delta Blues* (1970), *Gravel Springs Fife and Drum* (1971), *Black Delta Religion* (1974), and others. Such projects were more typical than studio-backed documentaries. A laudable exception is *Mississippi Blues* (1983), a leisurely but potent look at southern customs, geography, and music that was made by French director Bertrand Tavernier and American author Robert Parrish. A selective list of recent film documentaries about the South includes *Tobacco Blues* (1998), about tobacco farmers in Kentucky; *The Bare Hick Project* (2000), concerning a journey through the south Alabama woodlands; *Behind Closed Doors: The Dark Legacy of the Johns Committee* (2000), an investigation into a communist witch hunt in Florida universities during the late 1950s; *The Murder of Emmett Till* (2003), about a teenager killed in Mississippi; and *Sheriff* (2004), which follows a North Carolina law officer on his job.

be more interesting than such practices elsewhere, but it seems no government potboiler is complete without a dishonest southern politico on the scene. *Louisiana* (1947) and *A Lion in the Streets* (1953) are older examples of the genre, while more recent films such as *Blaze* (1989) and *Bulworth* (1998) prove that interest in the political Southern Gothic has not disappeared.

Neither has audiences' fascination with law and order on the local level. Southern small-town sheriffs are still a popular staple, and they are usually bigoted as well as corrupt. When the subject is handled intelligently, the result is as thought-provoking as *In the Heat of the Night* (1967). But more often than not the sheriff is rascally, as in *Flamingo Road* (1949), or ridiculous, as in *Smokey and the Bandit* (1977) and its sequels, or downright vicious, as in the *Walking Tall* (1973) movies. When citizens take the law into their own hands, the outcome is a series of feuding movies usually set in the Appalachian Mountains. While some early plays, such as *In Old Kentucky* (1893), and silent films, such as *The Feud* (1919) and *Fighting Cressy* (1920), took the subject very seriously, most later works dealing with feuding were either bumbling comedies about hillbilly rivalry, such as *Kentucky Kernels* (1935) and *Feudin' Fools* (1952), or melodramas about star-crossed lovers who are separated by a feud, as in *Roseanna McCoy* (1949) and *The Trail of the Lonesome Pine* (1936).

THE BLACK SOUTH ON STAGE

There is no South without African Americans. Since African peoples were used as slave labor from the earliest days of settlement, there has never been a South without a significant black population. No novel, play, or movie set in the region can ignore their presence. The race is part of the landscape, the sounds, even the temperament of the South. So one cannot accurately categorize any southern play or film as a "Negro drama" or "black movie." The very nature of a southern work is that it includes African Americans. But one can consider plays and movies in which black characters were at the forefront of the story. This was not as common as one might suppose. Blacks were relegated to supporting or minor roles in the action because that was the position they were assigned in southern life for so many years. The slaves and former slaves in *Gone with the Wind* are secondary characters in the plot but are essential parts of the story and its milieu; the same could be said of the role whites assign African Americans in the South.

Black characters have appeared on the American stage since the mid-1700s, though they were usually played by white actors in blackface. This practice continued for over 200 years as both comic and serious roles were performed by whites without audiences questioning the odd juxtaposition. It is not difficult for theatergoers today to understand a white Othello, but the portrayal of southern Negroes by whites would strike modern audiences as unsatisfactory, not to mention in poor taste. Yet in the past, spectators preferred to see actors in blackface; they also preferred exaggerated portrayals of blacks. So white actors usually turned the characters into highly stylized caricatures and gave birth to many of the black stereotypes that would survive for so many decades. Even the minstrel show, a unique of African American invention, would usually be dominated by white performers. It seemed that Americans, in both the North and the South, liked their black entertainment filtered through a non-black sensibility. A parody of the real thing was valued more than the original.

But the portrayal of black characters by white actors did not seem to limit theater production. Dramas and comedies offered Negro characters in both minor and major roles, and all ages and types were presented on stage. One only has to look at the variety of black characters in stage versions of *Uncle Tom's Cabin* to see that the use of blackface actors did not narrow the field. Harriet Beecher Stowe's inflammatory novel was adapted for the theater soon after it was published and held the boards for an astonishing eighty years. Unauthorized dramatizations appeared everywhere, but it was an 1853 version by George L. Aiken that broke all records. *Uncle Tom's Cabin* was even more popular after the Civil War; in 1879 alone there were no fewer than forty-nine troupes of actors performing the piece across the country. Even as late as 1927, a dozen companies were still touring the melodrama with success. Many actors and acting families spent their entire stage careers performing *Uncle Tom's Cabin* (they were called "tommers" in the business and their trade was referred to as "tomming"), and audiences north and south never seemed to tire of the work. It was (and remains) the play seen by more Americans than any other.

Though rarely read or performed today, Stowe's infamous masterpiece has not aged well. Although it treats its black characters sympathetically, modern audiences (white and black) find them stereotypic and embarrassingly simpleminded. But the same can be said for the white characters in the piece, such as the snarling villain Simon Legree and the saintly Little Eva. Uncle Tom is so kindly and subservient that his very name later came to mean a spineless black man who bows unstintingly to all whites. The runaway slaves Eliza and George have much more backbone, but contemporary audiences cringe at Topsy, the half-wit "pickaninny" whose ignorance is meant to be amusing. Yet these were all bold and vital characterizations in their day, and audiences laughed and wept at the plight of both the white and black characters. *Uncle Tom's Cabin* was filmed over a dozen times between 1903 and 1958 (some of the adaptations were one-reelers dramatizing just one scene from the story), but it never was as popular on screen as the play was on stage. In fact, it was *The Birth of a Nation* that eclipsed it in movie houses. But Griffith's 1915 film offered a very different view of southern blacks that disturbed African Americans then as much as it does now. If the slaves and ex-slaves in *Uncle Tom's Cabin* were harmlessly simpleminded, they were downright dangerous in *The Birth of a Nation*. In the movie, the Ku Klux Klan is created to save the innocent white populace from the drunken, lascivious Negroes who were given too much power by Reconstruction. The film is a cinematic masterpiece in many ways, but as far as portraying African Americans on screen, it did more damage than any other movie ever made in America.

On stage, however, black characters were usually handled with sympathy, even if it was a condescending kind of sympathy. A popular theme running through so many plays from *The Octoroon* (1959) to *Show Boat* (1927) and beyond was the tragic fate of mulattos, usually female. These light-skinned characters of mixed blood found themselves ostracized by both white and black society, and the plays often concluded with the heroine's death, the only possible denouement for such unfortunates. Sometimes the characters are so light-skinned that they are not aware of their mixed ancestry and the drama revolves around their realization of the truth. *The Octoroon*, by Irish American Dion Boucicault (1820–1890), is set in the prewar South where the mulatto Zoe is to marry a prosperous plantation owner. Not only is her true identity revealed by a cruel Yankee overseer, but her freedom is threatened as the villain hopes to sell her. On her deathbed she praises her fiancé for his willingness to confess "without a blush" his love for an octoroon, an old expression for a mulatto. Unlike *Uncle Tom's Cabin*, *The Octoroon* is still produced on occasion and holds the stage very well. A male version of the same story can be found in *The Nigger* (1909), a powerful drama by Edward Sheldon (1886–1946) that was the talk of the town in its day. A southern governor finds out through a long-secreted letter that he is the son of a Negro slave. With the help of his faithful fiancée, he reveals the truth to the voters, passes legislation to help the African Americans in his state, and then steps down from office. Although the title offended some black and white audiences, the play was firmly ahead of its time in championing civil rights. The mulatto theme also is important in the landmark musical *Show Boat*, in the North Carolina play *In Abraham's Bosom* (1926), and in *The Mulatto* (1935), Langston Hughes' provocative drama that was a rare hit on Broadway for a black playwright. *The Nigger* was made into a silent film in 1915, and a mulatto woman was at the center of *Pinky* (1949), *Band of Angels* (1957), and many other movies.

Long before the civil rights movement of the 1960s, there were a handful of notable plays that dealt with African Americans in the South. Most, admittedly, were written by white playwrights, but they were cast with black actors and were bold attempts to approach the subject of race in a serious manner. Eugene O'Neill's *All God's Chillun Got Wings* (1924) depicted a tragic romance between an African American law student and a white woman who was his childhood friend. Despite threats from the Klan and some denunciations in the press, the play was applauded as an honest portrayal of an explosive issue. South Carolina playwrights Dorothy and Dubose Heyward's *Porgy* (1927) was a vibrant recreation of Charleston's Catfish Row tenement district and the rough and tumble life there, particularly for two unlikely lovers. Although the Heywards were white, they knew the neighborhood well and their characterizations were vivid and uncompromising. Because of the popularity of the folk opera version, *Porgy and Bess* (1935), the original play is rarely produced today. But it remains a potent piece of writing and an important step in the development of drama about southern African Americans. At the end of World War II, returning black G.I.s found America as segregated as when they had left. The subject was handled intelligently in the drama *Deep Are the Roots* (1945), about an African American man who returns to his southern homestead and finds that the new freedoms offered him in the army are denied at home. He has fallen in love with a local white woman who wishes to marry him, but the two come to realize that the community is not ready for such a thing. The play tended to be understated rather than melodramatic, and it ran on Broadway for over a year.

CIVIL RIGHTS AND WRONGS

Of the many "black" plays during the 1960s (and these *were* written by African American authors), most were set in cities up north where so many blacks had relocated. The issues were not only racial; drugs, gang warfare, alcoholism, poverty, and other elements figured into the dramas, and it seemed like the black experience in America was an urban one. But a handful of 1960s plays were focused on the South, most memorably Ossie Davis' *Purlie Victorious* (1961; filmed as *Gone Are the Days* in 1963) and James Baldwin's *Blues for Mister Charlie* (1964). The former work is unique in that it is a comedy, albeit still filled with social commentary. Davis himself played a preacher who returns to his Georgia community and tries to establish his own church by outfoxing the conservative old white Cap'n. (The comedy was later turned into the successful Broadway musical *Purlie*.) Baldwin's drama concerns the murder of an outspoken black youth in a southern town. The flashbacks that surround the trial illustrate both the white and black attitudes of the locals. While most African American playwrights in the 1970s and beyond concentrated on plays set outside of the South, the writer Charles Fuller has often returned to the region, writing a series of historical dramas about fighting for Negro rights in the years following the Civil War. Yet his most renowned work is *A Soldier's Play* (1981; filmed as *A Soldier's Story* in 1984), set on a Louisiana army base during World War II. Its plot revolves around the murder of a vicious black sergeant and the African American officers who must investigate it. At first the Ku Klux Klan is thought responsible for the crime, but the investigation reveals many levels of prejudice within the black unit, and the issue of racial strife is discovered to be much more complex than previously thought. It is an intelligent, thought-provoking play and film and one of the most accomplished of all southern dramas.

Hollywood had long recognized the potential of movies that appealed to African Americans across the country but did not think a "black movie" could be popular with mainstream audiences. So a series of "race" films were made, often on a cheap budget and with second-string production crews, and released in cities and rural communities with large African American populations. Yet once in a while a feature was made that was seen by a wider audience, and all of America had the chance to see southern blacks depicted honestly. Two of the earliest and finest examples were *Hearts in Dixie* and *Hallelujah* (both 1929), primitive talkies about rural life in the South. *Hearts in Dixie* is generally considered the first all-black feature, yet there is a polish to some of its scenes that is remarkable. The episodic tale follows the daily life of a Negro family who live on a plantation. Although some familiar character types are present, such as the wise, gray-haired grandfather and the lazy husband, the film mostly avoids stereotypes and aims for believable relationships among the family members. The plot of *Hallelujah* is more melodramatic but still effectively real. A cotton picker lusts after a gangland moll, then reforms himself, becoming a traveling preacher. But when she re-enters his life, he falls to temptation and even tracks down and murders the man who accidentally killed her. The atmospheric film was shot on location in the South, and its depictions of the cotton workers, revival meetings, and river baptisms have a documentary feel to them. The movie is also noteworthy for its use of music, with Negro spirituals and other songs filling the soundtrack.

But mainstream movies showing African Americans in the South were rare from the 1930s to the 1960s, and many of the films after that concentrated on other regions. It seemed politically weak to re-create black life in the southern states when the civil rights movement was advocating a progressive role for African Americans in all parts of American society. Films about the movement itself would surface in the 1970s and later, but only a handful of them dealt with the South. Yet some in-

Song of the South: Musicals

In view of the South's highly romantic nature and its heritage with blues, gospel, jazz, and other forms of American music, it is surprising that there are not more stage and screen musicals set in the region. But the majority of Broadway musicals were written about New York City and other sophisticated urban locations, and Hollywood often copied the theater in its subject matter, so rural (particularly rural South) settings were less frequent. For every *Oklahoma!* (1943) there were a dozen Manhattan or Paris musicals. Yet some distinctive stage and film musicals dealing with the South have always been featured in both media, and some of them are memorable. The American musical theater landmark *Show Boat* (1927) and its three movie versions (1929, 1936, and 1951) portray the region both romantically and with condemnation. The Mississippi River gives the show its thematic spine but, as expressed in the song classic "Ol' Man River," it is an uncaring, uncompromising force of nature. The characters find love on the river, yet, in its southern towns along the shore, they also find prejudice and the suffocating laws of segregation. This is most potently portrayed in the famous miscegenation scenes with the mulatto Julie Laverne. Another stage landmark is *Shuffle Along* (1921), one of the earliest and most successful of "Negro" musical shows that was actually written by African Americans. The musical is set in the fictional village of Jimtown and takes a more satirical view of southern small-town life than *Show Boat*. Deemed politically incorrect today, the stereotypic characters are nonetheless vibrant blacks whose political shenanigans echoed the kind of lighthearted corruption seen in mainstream musical comedies. Similar in its setting and tone is the richer *Cabin in the Sky* (1940), a folk tale musical that was beautifully filmed in 1943. African Americans were presented with whimsy in the Broadway fantasy *Finian's Rainbow* (1947; not filmed until 1968), which was waggishly set in "Missitucky"; in a handful of all-black Hollywood musicals such as *New Orleans* (1947); and in the prankish stage musical *Purlie* (1970) that lampooned stereotypes in the rural South. The folk opera *Porgy and Bess* (1935; filmed in 1959) took a much more serious look at southern neighborhoods such as Charleston's Catfish Row, as did the updated musicalization of the opera *Carmen* called *Carmen Jones* (1943; filmed in 1954), which retold the story of the sultry heroine with African American characters in the Deep South. On occasion a new musical would return to this more disturbing point of view, more recently in the Broadway musical drama *Marie Christine* (1999), which retold the Medea story within the French Creole society of Louisiana. On the other hand, Broadway has had more success in mocking aspects of southern life, such as Florida land boom speculation in the Marx Brothers' *The Cocoanuts* (1925; filmed in 1929), crooked business practices in *Louisiana Purchase* (1940; filmed in 1941), and Ozark hillbilly types in *Li'l Abner* (1956; filmed in 1959). Hollywood portrayed the region nostalgically, with musicals such as *Song of the South* (1946), with glamour, as in *Neptune's Daughter* (1949), and romantically, as with *Mississippi* (1935), *Moon over Miami* (1941), and others. Show business musicals, particularly biographical tuners, have also been popular. *Swanee River* (1940), *Dixie* (1943), *St. Louis Blues* (1958), *The Buddy Holly Story* (1978), *Coal Miner's Daughter* (1980), *Bird* (1988), and others celebrated the lives of southern-born songwriters and singers, though the facts about their lives were sometimes as inaccurate as the locales portrayed. Fictional show business musicals sometimes depicted the region more effectively, particularly later efforts such as *Honeysuckle Rose* (1980), *Honkytonk Man* (1982), and *Crossroads* (1986). Finally, of the handful of more recent Broadway musical dramas to take on serious issues, two southern works stand out: the pacifist Civil

War musical *Shenandoah* (1975) and the powerful *Parade* (1998), which looked at southern bigotry as directed toward Jews. As both stage and screen musicals get more adventurous, they will continue to return to the South for inspiration, as will light-hearted musical comedies.

dividual movies about blacks in the region stood out, either because of their popularity or their subject matter. In addition to the already-discussed *Sounder* and *The Color Purple*, audiences embraced *Driving Miss Daisy* (1989), which was based on a long-running 1987 off-Broadway play. Although the background of the intimate piece was southern discrimination against Jews as well as blacks, it was not a very disturbing movie and suggested that the kinship between the two main characters was strengthened by their understanding of each other's age as much as their races. More explosive was *Mississippi Burning* (1988), about three white civil rights workers murdered by the Klan. African Americans were more on the periphery than in the center of the action in the movie, but they were central in *Rosewood* (1997), about the destruction of a prospering black community in Florida in the 1920s. One member of the town is accused of raping a white woman, and the entire village is torched and innocent residents are killed. Both films were based on actual events, though in each case fictional additions were thought to weaken the final result. But such ambitious works were to be applauded when most Hollywood films were portraying African American males as cops, gangsters, and studs, and black women were observed only in terms of their relationships with such men.

THE CIVIL WAR IN FILM

If the Civil War is considered the pivotal point in creating present-day America, then one cannot underestimate the impact of that war in forming the personality of the South. The conflict between North and South defined the country by revealing what was best and worst about the nation its forefathers had forged. It is not difficult to understand the fascination the Civil War still holds for Americans, and much of that fascination has its roots in nineteenth-century war plays and twentieth-century films. During the actual struggle, patriotic and propaganda plays were produced both in the North and the South, but the scripts were not of lasting value. It was not until after the surrender that the theater successfully cashed in on the theatrics of the country's greatest turmoil. Oddly, of the many Civil War plays produced during the rest of the century, few dealt with slavery, battles, secession, or the beliefs that caused the war. Most were interested in the personal drama: lovers separated by the battle lines, brother turning against brother (or father against son) because of their beliefs, spies behind enemy lines, and families uprooted because of the conflict. It was the personal war that worked on stage, and audiences never seemed to tire of the endless variations on the same few themes.

The first important Civil War play was Dion Boucicault's *Belle Lamar* (1874), a melodrama about a southern wife who chooses her homeland over her Union officer husband. The drama was not a success, but it established the pattern for dozens of subsequent plays on the subject. While most of these works were written by northerners and first produced in New York City, their sympathies were often with the South—maybe not the political South, but the romantic one. The plays tended to agree that a northern victory was best for the country, but usually they admired the southern spirit, particularly the outspoken plantation belles and patriotic wives. Of course there were villainous rebels and lecherous Confederate officers, but just as often their counterparts were found on the Union side as well. Few of the plays concentrated on only one side of the conflict. A true Civil War play included both Northern and Southern characters because that was the whole point of a struggle that pitted Americans against Americans.

By the 1890s there were several dramas about the war that enjoyed long runs, critical acclaim, and even attention in decades to follow. Only a few are produced today, but when they are, they are surprisingly effective. Augustus Thomas' *Alabama* (1891) dealt with Reconstruction and a ruined southern family that is saved by a long-lost son who had joined the Union Army during the war. David Belasco's *The Heart of Maryland* (1895; filmed in 1915 and 1927) featured one of the most courageous of stage southern belles. Not only does she stab a treacherous Confederate officer so that her sweetheart can escape, she even climbs the bell tower and silences the clapper by swinging with it and keeping the alarm from warning the enemy. William Gillette (1853–1937) wrote and starred in *Secret Service* (1896) for many years, playing a northern spy posing as a Confederate captain. Clyde Fitch's *Barbara Frietchie* (1899) depicted another feisty southern belle, this one remaining faithful to the Union even when the rest of the town scorns her; she boldly displays the Stars and Stripes as Stonewall Jackson parades by. Finally, William C. de Mille's *The Warrens of Virginia* (1907) mixed spies and a North-South romance effectively into a taut melodrama. The fact that these plays held the boards for several years was a testament to their superior stagecraft and the continued interest in Civil War dramas.

Early movies concerning the war copied the stage works' reliance on romance and suspense. But it did not take filmmakers long to realize that the cinema could go beyond the confines of the theater and that the spectacle of battle could be portrayed on screen. D. W. Griffith's *The Birth of a Nation* was the first American film to effectively capture warfare on the screen, and the effect was overwhelming. Many feel it was the battle scenes and not the Ku Klux Klan storyline that made the movie so popular. Regardless, others followed in Griffith's footsteps, and a Civil War movie meant action scenes on a large scale. Yet the most popular Civil War sound movie, *Gone with the Wind*, offered no battle scenes at all and focused instead on how the war affected the South and its people. Most films about the era tried to have it both ways, mixing human interest and romance with spectacle and action. The fact that few were as successful (critically and financially) as *The Birth of a Nation* or *Gone with the Wind* has not been lost on Hollywood, which would go through periods when Civil War movies were strongly discouraged.

Since most of the war took place on southern soil, it stands to reason that most films about the Civil War were set in the South. Even when the central character is a Union soldier, as in *The Red Badge of Courage* (1951), the locale is usually southern. Yet there is a great deal of variety to be found in the many movies about the conflict, as witnessed by a selected few examples over the decades. *So Red the Rose* (1934) glorified the southern cause, showing strong, patriotic women managing the plantation even as the slaves cheered on the Confederate Army. *Virginia City* (1940) concerned a shipment of gold from Nevada to Richmond during the waning days of the war, complete with spies and counterspies trying to keep the gold from saving the South. In *Tap Roots* (1948), a group of Mississippi farmers who have abolished slavery try to secede from the Confederacy. *The Vanquished* (1953) dealt with a Confederate vet who, having spent time in a Union prison camp, returns to his southern home where he has to deal with some corrupt Reconstructionists. *The Horse Soldiers* (1959) was an action picture starring John Wayne about Union horsemen who must destroy a rail link deep in the Confederacy. *Shenandoah* (1965) was an antiwar film that focused on a Virginia farmer who hopes to keep his sons out of the war. By the late 1960s and the era of the Vietnam War protests, movies about the Civil War had little appeal, and few were made during the next two decades. But the success of *Glory* (1989), the first feature film to deal with African Americans who fought in the war, and *Gettysburg* (1993), one of the few Civil War movies not set in the South, spurred interest in the subject once again, and several films followed, including *Ride with the Devil* (1999), *Gods and Generals* (2003), and *Cold Mountain* (2003). Since interest in the War Between the States, as some southern factions prefer to call it, shows no sign of waning, other movies about various aspects of the war will undoubtedly follow.

Has the South been adequately portrayed on the stage and screen? Taken in small pieces, most of its elements have been touched upon by the two media, but the pieces make up a haphazard mosaic, and the total picture is far from balanced. While the major subject areas have been discussed here, there is so much more in the diverse region that has been neglected by Hollywood and the theater. For example, the world of the extensive Latino population in Florida has rarely been explored by the two media. The film *Popi* (1969) and the play *Anna in the Tropics* (2003) are among the few examples. The fundamentalist movement in the South, as seen in the play *Inherit the Wind* (1955; filmed in 1960), has been largely ignored. *Bayou* (1957) and *Scorchers* (1991) are among the too few movies to deal with life in the Cajun communities of Louisiana, while *Distant Drums* (1951) and *Joe Panther* (1976) are rare examples of films about Florida's Seminoles. In general, Native Americans in the South have been largely ignored by stage and screen; the subject was only touched upon in the epic play *The Kentucky Cycle* (1993). That ambitious drama was also one of very few works to look at the effect the closing of the coal mines in Appalachian had on its people. The list continues, for so much about the South does not have the visibility of a civil war or a civil rights movement. Yet Hollywood and Broadway have not failed to understand the intrinsic theatricality of the region, its ability to fascinate with its flamboyance, and the sparkling nature of its people. If the two media have sometimes reduced the South to a series of clichés, it has all been part of the talent the region has for flair. The South's diversity and complexity may have been overlooked on occasion, but the rest of the nation has never failed to notice its southern brother.

RESOURCE GUIDE

Printed Sources

Banham, Martin, ed. *The Cambridge Guide to Theatre*. New York: Cambridge University Press, 1992.

Bawden, Liz-Anne. *The Oxford Companion to Film*. New York: Oxford University Press, 1985.

The Best Plays. 82 editions. New York: Dodd, Mead and Co., 1894–1988; New York: Applause Theatre Book Publishers, 1988–1993; New York: Limelight Editions, 1994–2001.

Blum, Daniel. *A Pictorial History of the Silent Screen*. New York: G. P. Putnam's Sons, 1953.

Blum, Daniel, and John Willis. *A Pictorial History of the American Theatre, 1860–1980*. 5th ed. New York: Crown, 1981.

Bogle, Donald. *Toms, Coons, Mulattoes, Mammies and Bucks: An Interpretive History of Black in American Films*. Rev. ed. New York: Continuum, 1989.

Bordman, Gerald. *American Musical Theatre: A Chronicle*. 3rd ed. New York: Oxford University Press, 2001.

———. *American Theatre: A Chronicle of Comedy and Drama, 1869–1969*. 3 vols. New York: Oxford University Press, 1994–1996.

Bordman, Gerald, and Thomas S. Hischak. *The Oxford Companion to American Theatre*. 3rd ed. New York: Oxford University Press, 2004.

Campbell, Edward D.C., Jr. *The Celluloid South: Hollywood and the Southern Myth*. Knoxville: University of Tennessee Press, 1981.

Graham, Allison. *Framing the South: Hollywood, Television and Race During the Civil Rights Struggle*. Baltimore: Johns Hopkins University Press, 2001.

Halliwell, Leslie. *Halliwell's Film Guide*. 7th ed. New York: Harper and Row, 1989.

Henderson, Mary C. *Theater in America*. New York: Harry N. Abrams, 1986.

Hirschhorn, Clive. *The Hollywood Musical*. Rev. 2nd ed. New York: Crown, 1983.

Hischak, Thomas S. *American Theatre: A Chronicle of Comedy and Drama, 1969–2000*. New York: Oxford University Press, 2001.

———. *The Theatregoer's Almanac*. Westport, CT: Greenwood Press, 1997.

Katz, Ephraim. *The Film Encyclopedia*. 3rd ed. New York: Harper-Perennial, 1998.

Konigsberg, Ira. *The Complete Film Dictionary*. 2nd ed. New York: Penguin, 1997.

Langman, Larry, and David Ebner. *Hollywood's Image of the South: A Century of Southern Films*. Westport, CT: Greenwood Press, 2001.

Maltin, Leonard. *Movie and Video Guide*. 2003 ed. New York: Penguin Putnam, 2002.

Mast, Gerald. *A Short History of the Movies*. Indianapolis: Pegasus, 1971.

Theatre World. 56 editions. New York: Norman McDonald Associates, 1946–1949; New York: Greenberg, Publisher, 1949–1957; Philadelphia: Chilton, 1957–1964; New York: Crown, 1964–1991; New York: Applause Theatre Book Publishers, 1991–2000.

Wilmeth, Don. B., and Tice Miller, eds. *Cambridge Guide to American Theatre*. New York: Cambridge University Press, 1993.

Web Sites

All Movie Guide: www.allmovie.com (casts and production information)
Artslynx Theatre Resources: www.artslynx.org (theater support organizations and unions)
Box Office Magazine: www.boxoff.com (monthly trade publication online)
Broadway.Com: www.broadway.com (articles, news, reviews on contemporary theater)
Film Comment: www.filmlinc.com./fcm/online (bimonthly publication by Film Society of Lincoln Center online)
International Movie Data Base: www.imdb.com (American and international films and artists, thorough and clearly cross referenced)
Motion Picture Guide: www.tvguide.com/movies (production data and reviews)
Playbill on Line: www.playbill.com (articles and news regarding contemporary Broadway and regional theater)
Theatre History Online: www.theatrehistory.com (texts, archives, resources)
Variety: www.variety.com (weekly trade publication online)

Regional Film Festivals

Asheville Film Festival
PO Box 7148
Asheville, NC 28802
www.ashevillefilmfestival.com

Atlanta Film Festival
75 Bennett St. NW
Atlanta, GA 30309
www.imagefv.org

Carolina Film and Video Fest
University of North Carolina at Greensboro
Greensboro, NC 27402
www.uncg.edu/bcn/cfvf

Crossroads Film Festival
PO Box 22604
Jackson, MS 39225
www.crossroadsfilmfest.com

Cucalorus Film Festival
PO Box 2763
Wilmington, NC 28402
www.cucalorus.org

George Lindsey University of North Alabama Film Festival
UNA Box 5151
Florence, AL 35632
www.2.una.edu

IndieMemphis
1910 Madison Ave.
Memphis, TN 38104
www.indiememphis.com

Key West IndieFest
1107 Key Plaza #136
Key West, FL 33040
www.keywestindiefest.com

Magnolia Independent Film Festival
2269 Waverly Dr.
West Point, MS 39773
www.magfilmfest.org

Miami International Film Festival
300 NE 2nd Ave.
Miami, FL 33132
www.miamifilmfestival.com

Nashville Film Festival
PO Box 24330
Nashville, TN 37202
www.nashvillefilmfestival.org

New Orleans Film Festival
843 Cardondelet No. 1
New Orleans, LA 70130
www.neworleansfilmfest.com

North Carolina Gay and Lesbian Film Festival
Carolina Theatre
Durham, NC 27701
www.carolinatheatre.org

Ozark Foothills Filmfest
195 Peel Rd.
Locust Grove, AR 72550
www.ozarkfoothillsfilmfest.org

Pensacola Bay International Film and Video Festival
600 S. Barracks St.
Pensacola, FL 32502
www.pensacolafilmandtv.com

Sarasota Film Festival
635 S. Orange Ave.
Sarasota, FL 34236
www.sarasotafilmfest.com

Savannah Film Festival
216 E. Broughton St.
Savannah, GA 31401
www.scad.edu/filmfest

Sidewalk Moving Picture Festival
500 23rd St. S.
Birmingham, AL 35233
www.sidewalkfest.com

Tambay Film and Video Fest
16002 Saddle Creek Dr.
Tampa Bay, FL 33618
www.tambayfilmfest.com

VCU French Film Festival
Virginia Commonwealth University
Richmond, VA 23284
www.frenchfilm.vcu.edu

Virginia Film Festival
PO Box 400869
Charlottesville, VA 22904
www.vafilm.com

Regional Theaters and Theater Festivals

Actors' Playhouse National Children's Theatre Festival
280 Miracle Mile
Coral Gables, FL 33134
www.actorsplayhouse.org

Actors Theatre of Louisville
316 W. Main St.
Louisville, KY 40202
www.actorstheatre.org

Alabama Shakespeare Festival
1 Festival Dr.
Montgomery, AL 36117
www.asf.net

Alliance Theatre Company
1280 Peachtree St. NE
Atlanta, GA 30309
www.alliancetheatre.org

Appalachian Festival of Plays
Barter Theatre
Rox 867
Abingdon, VA 24212
www.bartertheatre.com

Arkansas Repertory Theatre
601 Main St.
Little Rock, AR 72201
www.therep.org

Art Within
1940 Minnewil Lane
Marietta, GA 30068
www.artwithin.org

BareBones Theatre Group 15-Minute Play Festival
Box 11111
Charlotte, NC 28220
www.barebones.org

Barter Theatre
Box 867
Abingdon, VA 24212
www.bartertheatre.com

The Blowing Rock Stage Company
Box 2170
Blowing Rock, NC 28605
www.blowingrockstage.com

Caldwell Theatre Company
7873 N. Federal Hwy
Boca Raton, FL 33487
www.caldwelltheatre.com

Centre Stage–South Carolina
PO Box 8451
Greenville, SC 29604
www.centrestage.org

Charlotte Repertory New Play Festival
129 W. Trade St.
Charlotte, NC 28202
www.charlotterep.org

Clarence Brown Theatre Company
1714 Andy Holt Blvd.
Knoxville, TN 37996
http:/theatre.utk.edu

Coconut Grove Playhouse
3500 Main Highway
Miami, FL 33133
www.cgplayhouse.com

Drama Rama
Box 70232
New Orleans, LA 70012
www.dramarama.org

Florida Repertory Theatre
PO Box 2483
Ft. Myers, FL 33902
www.floridarep.com

Florida Stage
262 S. Ocean Blvd.
Manalapan, FL 33462
www.floridastage.org

Florida Studio Theatre
1241 North Palm Ave.
Sarasota, FL 34236
www.fst2000.org

Gainesville Theatre Alliance
PO Box 1358
Gainesville, FL 30503
www.gainesvilletheatrealliance.org

The Hippodrome State Theatre
25 SE 2nd Pl.
Gainesville, FL 32601
http://thehipp.org

Horizon Theatre Company
Box 5376
Atlanta, GA 31107
www.horizontheatre.com

Horse Cave Theatre
PO Box 215
Horse Cave, KY 42749
www.horsecavetheatre.org

Humana Festival of New American Plays
Actors Theatre of Louisville
316 W. Main St.

Louisville, KY 40202
www.actorstheatre.org

Juneteenth Legacy Theatre
Box 3463
Louisville, KY 40201
www.juneteenthlegacytheatre.com

Kentucky Shakespeare Festival
1114 South Third St.
Louisville, KY 40203
www.kyshakes.org

Le Petit Théatre du Vieux Carré
616 St. Peter St.
New Orleans, LA 70116
www.lepetittheatre.com

MetroStage
1201 N. Royal St.
Alexandria, VA 22314
www.metrostage.org

Mill Mountain Theatre
1 Market Square
Roanoke, VA 24011
www.millmountain.org

National Black Theatre Festival
North Carolina Black Repertory Company
610 Coliseum Dr.
Winston-Salem, NC 27106
www.nbtf.org

New Theatre
4120 Laguna St.
Coral Gables, FL 33146
www.new-theatre.org

Playhouse on the Square
51 South Cooper
Memphis, TN 38104
www.playhouseonthesquare.org

Playmakers Repertory Company
CB #3235
Center for Dramatic Art
Chapel Hill, NC 27599
www.playmakersrep.org

Playwrights' Forum
Box 11265
Memphis, TN 38111
www.playwrights-forum.org

Poplar Pike Playhouse
7653 Old Poplar Pike

Germantown, TN 38138
www.ppp.org

Roadside Theatre
91 Madison Ave.
Whitesburg, KY 41858
www.appalshop.org/rst

Running with Scissors
2619 Royal St.
New Orleans, LA 70117
www.norunningwithscissors.com

The Shakespeare Tavern
The Atlanta Shakespeare Company at the New American Shakespeare Tavern
499 Peachtree St. NE
Atlanta, GA 30308
www.shakespearetavern.com

Southern Rep Theatre
333 Canal St.
New Orleans, LA 70130
www.southernrep.com

Spoleto Festival USA
PO Box 157
Charleston, SC 29402
www.spoletousa.org

Stage One: Louisville Children's Theatre
501 W. Main St.
Louisville, KY 40202
www.stageone.org

Summer Shorts
444 Brickell Ave.
Miami, FL 33131
www.citytheatre.com

Swine Palace Productions
Reilly Theatre
Tower Dr.—LSU
Baton Rouge, LA 70803
www.swinepalace.org

Tennessee Repertory Theatre
PO Box 198768
Nashville, TN 37219
www.tnrep.org

Theatre at Lime Kiln
14 S. Randolph St.
Lexington, VA 24450
www.theatreatlimekiln.com

Trustus Theatre
Box 11721

Columbia, SC 29211
www.trustus.org

Virginia Stage Company
Box 3770
Norfolk, VA 23514
www.vastage.com

YES New Play Festival
Northern Kentucky University
Highland Heights, KY 41099
www.nku.edu/-theatre

FOLKLORE

Jon Lohman

Mention of "the South" has generally conjured two related yet dichotomous images in the American imagination. On the one hand, the South is often portrayed as provincially backward—a region somehow living in the past. This perception is due in large part to negative stereotypes found in such popular television shows as *The Beverly Hillbillies* and *Hee-Haw*, and movies such as *Deliverance*, which portray the southerner as the "hillbilly," "redneck," "good ol' boy," or "cracker." Seen through these various conceptual lenses, southerners, and particularly southern whites, are often perceived as largely uneducated, unclean, and hostile. By the same token, southern blacks often fall prey to simplistic stereotypes such as "country," or as the "Uncle Tom," somehow overly complicit in some of the racist conditions that, while often understood primarily as a "southern problem," have existed in both rural and urban centers throughout the United States.

While these simplistic and negative stereotypes have colored the nation's understanding of the South, there seems to simultaneously exist an almost opposite, overly romanticized view of the South as somehow being more "authentic" than other regions of the country, inhabited by a more soulful people who possess a deeper connection to land and lore. It is in part this latter perception of the South that has traditionally drawn folklore collectors to the region.

The American Folklore Society (AFS) was founded in 1888 to help preserve and record the old songs, tales, ballads, and folk beliefs that many people feared would disappear as the region industrialized. The society's members immediately pointed their compasses southward, seeing as their primary mission preserving and documenting the "relics of old English folk lore," as well as the "lore of Negroes in the Southern states." The term *folklore* was coined by English scholar William Thoms, following the lead of folkloric studies in Germany. Thoms and his contemporaries defined "the folk" primarily as the "common people"—the "peasantry"—residing in rural areas. "Lore" referred to the primarily orally transmitted texts passed down from one generation to another—the tales, ballads, superstitions, and legends distinctive to a particular region or cultural group.

The field of folklore has evolved and changed substantially over time. Now, it is widely understood that folklore does not reside only in rural areas, among those that have remained somehow untouched by modernity. Rather, folklore can thrive in any setting, be it rural or urban, and among any group whatsoever that shares common traditions and expressive language. Also, the notion of "folklore" has been expanded to that of "folklife," which includes not only oral forms of expressive culture, but also forms of material culture such as crafts and clothing, as well as aesthetic forms as varied as vernacular architecture and foodways. Scholarly interest has moved beyond the mere collection of traditional stories and songs to focus on the cultural contexts in which they are enacted. These significant shifts in the ways in which folklore is understood, however, have done little to quell the interest among folklorists in the American South, an area that has always proved remarkably fertile ground for folk culture. And it is this vibrant folk culture that has contributed most significantly to the region's continued uniqueness and distinctive regional identity.

Though the American South has often been understood as a region somewhat "fixed in time," inhabited by folks who have remained in the same location for multiple generations, this perception is largely incorrect. The South has, in fact, experienced tremendous demographic shifts over time, perhaps to a greater extent than any other region of the country, and is far better understood as a region in constant diasporic flux.

History clearly shows that southerners have been moving into and out of the region for centuries. Early migrants included Spanish-, English-, or French-speaking settlers seeking new agricultural lands or escaping from religious persecution; Africans enslaved and brought to the region against their will; and French-speaking Acadians forced out of Canada who made a new life in southwest Louisiana. Southerners have seemingly been in constant movement within the region as well. Escaped slaves formed independent maroon communities or sought safe haven with groups of Native Americans. Later, rural-dwelling blacks and whites were often compelled to move to emerging urban centers such as Norfolk, Virginia, or Memphis, Tennessee, in search of work. And history has periodically witnessed dramatic movements of southerners out of the region, be it the forced expulsion of the Cherokee from western North Carolina to government reservations in Oklahoma, the large migration of southern blacks out of the region to escape the oppressive segregationist policies in the decades following the Civil War, or the movement of both rural whites and blacks in search of factory work in northern cities such as Detroit, Chicago, Cleveland, and Philadelphia. Recently, this trend seems to have somewhat reversed, as many residents of the Northeast and other regions of the country have increasingly moved south to work or retire. Cities such as Atlanta, Georgia, Charlotte, North Carolina, Tampa/St. Petersburg and Jacksonville, Florida, and Nashville, Tennessee, have experienced a steady growth in population, becoming major markets and important financial centers of the "New South."

How have these patterns of constant movement influenced the region's folklore? To begin with, the development of folklore in the South is a story of diverse cultural communities constantly coming into contact with one another. Native Americans, Spanish, French, English, and other European settlers, along with descendants of many African communities, as well as immigrant communities from lands as culturally and geographically varied as Southeast Asia and the Caribbean, have lived, worked, and played in remarkably close proximity in the South. These communities have, at various times, fought with one another, but they have also at various times cared for each other's children, eaten each other's food, and listened to each other's stories and music. The result, as cultural scholars have recently come to recognize, is not so much a blending or two or more cultures to create a hybrid of these original forms, but rather the creation of vibrant, completely new forms of folk expression unique to the region. While folklorists, sociologists, anthropologists, and other scholars used to refer to the processes of cultural contact as a form of syncretism, recent scholars have chosen instead a term borrowed from linguistic studies—*creolization*—which refers to the ways in which the mixing of two cultural forms can result in the creation of something completely new. In fact, though many folklorists flocked to the South to mine isolated and untouched folk traditions, it is likely that this process of creolization, more than anything else, has shaped the expressive culture of the region, as Charles Joyner eloquently states:

> Out of the convergence of African and European traditions, so different yet so alike, emerged a new southern folk culture, a folk culture with both an African and a European heritage yet as different from either as water is from hydrogen and oxygen. I believe that the sharing of cultural traditions in the South is more responsible than any other single factor for the extraordinary richness of Southern culture.[1]

This "extraordinary richness of Southern culture" is best revealed through an exploration of the region's folklore. The folklore and folklife of the South are incredibly diverse and decidedly local, deeply rooted in the social, cultural, and economic life of particular regions and communities. At the same time, these distinct folk expressions often transcend their local situations, responding to a universal impulse inside all of us to create the extraordinary from the ordinary, and to repeatedly express to each other "who we are."

LEGENDS AND TALES

Folktales are generally defined as the stories passed down orally from generation to generation within particular cultural communities. The great zeal for collecting folktales in the American South was largely in response to significant works published in Europe, particularly the seminal two-volume collection of folktales by the German brothers Jacob and Wilhelm Grimm. Their collection entitled *House Hold Tales* was published in Germany between 1812 and 1815 and subsequently translated into English in 1884. Known as Grimms' tales, this collection became immensely popular in the United States and largely spurred the creation of the American Folklore Society. This tremendous wave of folktale collecting eventually led to the publication of the *Motif-Index of Folk-Literature* by American scholar Stith Thompson (1885–1976) in the 1930s. Thompson and his colleagues produced what they believed was a comprehensive index for tracing a particular tale's diffusion and possible origin, and by which to identify the use of tales in literary works. This index, still used by many folklorists today, identified and meticulously classified common motifs evident in folktales (for example, motif N711.6, "Prince sees heroine at ball and is enamored"). Clearly evident from Thompson's work is his placement within the overriding methodological approaches to folklore studies of his time. The focus is on text rather than context, on the tale rather than its tellers, and the still dominant notion that the stories found in the Americas, particularly rich in the South, were largely survivals of European or African forms.

Folklorists casing the South soon encountered numerous folktales that appeared to be directly inherited from, or that possessed many motifs common to, those from the European *marchen* tradition, though clearly with their own distinctive versions. For instance, Europe's Cinderella story has been collected in a variety of forms in the southern tradition. The classic Brothers Grimm tale "Hansel and Gretel" exists in a version distinct to North Carolina called "Mutsmag." The story familiar to us as "Beauty and the Beast" appears in regional variations in Arkansas, North Carolina, and Virginia, and in Kentucky under the unique title "The Girl Who Married the Flop-Eared Hound Dog." Distinctive versions of *The Taming of the Shrew* have also been collected in Virginia, Kentucky, Arkansas, and Texas.

While early collections of folktales in the South focused first on those of European origin, and later of those of African origin, folktales clearly thrived in the South before the arrival of Europeans and Africans in the New World. Native American groups in the South including the Cherokees in the Great Smokies, the Choctaw of Tennessee and Mississippi, the Seminole of Florida, the Houma of Louisiana, and many others all had rich bodies of folklore.

NATIVE AMERICAN FOLKTALES

Early collections of Native American lore tended to be greatly colored by the pervading negative stereotypes of Native Americans as "savage," "primitive," and "uncivilized," or in the more positive, though perhaps equally misleading portrayal of the "noble savage," somehow representing a perfectly preserved culture of the distant past. In the South, in fact, early folklore collectors often ignored the presence of Native Americans altogether, in part because they often exoticized the cultures of southern blacks and poor rural southern whites in a similar fashion, and thus these groups remained the focus of their folkloric collections. There were, however, several significant early studies of Native American folklore, particularly among the Cherokee in North Carolina.

Having apparently migrated from the land that is now Ohio, the Cherokees became the mountaineers of the southeastern states until their displacement by white settlers, and the infamous Trail of Tears of 1838–1839, when most of the Cherokee Nation was forcibly moved to Oklahoma. A small group of fugitives was allowed to stay in western North Carolina, forming the Eastern Band of the Cherokees. James Mooney (1861–1921) and Horace Kephart (1862–1930) collected folktales, songs, customs, and other folklore from Cherokees in the late 1880s and at the turn of the century, respectively. Mooney, an ethnologist with the National Bureau of Ethnology, was assigned to conduct field research on the culture and beliefs of American Indians. He collected many sacred myths as well as sacred rituals and medical practices, and even studied Cherokee ball-play. While examination of

Mooney's notes reveals that he used trickery and deception to attain these sacred materials (the Cherokee were notoriously secretive about their rituals and sacred myths to outsiders), he appears to have been more respectful and empathetic than many of his scholarly contemporaries who never seemed to question the Darwinian framework of their own cultural superiority. Mooney's *Myth of the Cherokee* (1901) remains an important record of a culture on the cusp of dramatic transition.

Modernization, intermarriage and commerce with whites, Christianization, public schooling, and the general impact of contemporary American life have eroded many of the traditional folkways of the Cherokees. However, storytelling has remained an important aspect of Cherokee social and cultural life, and, many would argue, has likely played a large role in its very maintenance. Several contemporary Cherokee storytellers have gained national recognition on the storytelling and folklife festival circuit, such as Lloyd Arneach, who performed in front of large audiences on the National Mall in Washington, D.C., at the 2003 Smithsonian Folklife Festival. The following is Arneach's version of a Cherokee tale that dates back many generations, entitled "How the Mink Got His Dark Coat":

> Among the animals, the mink was known as a notorious thief. He stole all the time; he could never be trusted in any dealings in which he gave his word, because he always went back on his word—his word meant nothing. And they couldn't leave anything out that they possessed, because he would steal it. And if he couldn't use it, he'd destroy it.
>
> So the animals decided that they'd teach him a lesson. They caught the mink and built a large fire and threw him in the middle of it. And the fire was burning up very high and the mink was squirming around the fire, and every time he would jump out they'd throw him back in. They finally decided he'd been punished enough, so they let him out of the fire. But they discovered that his coat had been burned black and he smelled like roasted flesh. And to this day, the mink's coat is dark, and when he's excited or angry he gives off a smell very similar to roasted flesh.[2]

Arneach's story is representative of a thematic structure quite prevalent in Cherokee tales, as well as in other Native American tales throughout the region. Like the tale above, many Indian folktales of the South can be considered "origin tales." A survey of Native American tales throughout the region yields such titles as "How the Old Man Made People," "Why the Opposum's Tail Is Bare," "How Rabbit Brought Fire to the People," and the following tale, told by the Tuskegee Indians of Tennessee and Alabama, called "The Origin of the Earth":

> Before the beginning, water was everywhere. But no people, animals, or earth were visible.
>
> There were birds, however, who held a council to decide if it might be best to have all land or all water. "Let us have land, so we can have more food," said some of the birds. Others said, "Let's have all water, because we like it this way."
>
> Subsequently, they appointed Eagle as their Chief who was to decide one way or the other. Eagle decided upon land and asked, "Who will go and search for land?"

Dove volunteered first and flew away. In four days he completed his hunt and returned, reporting, "I could not find land anywhere."

Crawfish came swimming along and was asked by the council to help search for land. He disappeared under the water for four days. When he arose to the surface again, he held some dirt in his claws. He had found some land deep in the water.

Crawfish made a ball of the dirt and handed it to Chief Eagle, who then flew away with it. Four days later he returned and said to the council, "Now there is land, an island has been formed—follow me!"

The whole bird colony flew after Eagle to see the new land, though it was a very small island. Gradually, the land began to grow larger and larger as the water became lower and lower. More islands appeared and these grew together, creating larger islands into one earth.[3]

Clearly, many Native American communities throughout the South told these origin tales to help explain the many mysteries of life, such as how the earth began, or where fire came from. Early collectors describe these tales as being passed down from one generation to another, and report that some tribal members achieved a high level of prestige within their tribe as storytellers. Of course, Native Americans, like most cultural communities, told one another stories for enjoyment, recreation, and good humor. Tall tales, stories where the events, characters, and circumstances are greatly and often humorously exaggerated and larger than life, have their earliest roots in Native American societies. Such tales were told by Native Americans in what is now South Carolina to regale Spanish audiences as early as the 1520s. Tall tales were reportedly told throughout the rural and wooded South as early as the nineteenth century, particularly in Mississippi, Alabama, and Georgia. Distinct cycles of tall tales are also found among numerous cultural groups throughout the South.

TALL TALES IN CAJUN COUNTRY

Just as early folk collectors explored regions such as Appalachia for survivals of old English tales, the first scholars to explore the folklore of French Louisiana were primarily interested in tracing either the French or African origins of the traditional tales of the region. When Alcee Fortier collected his stories among black Creoles in New Orleans in the early twentieth century, he focused almost exclusively on animal tales in his efforts to draw direct cultural connections between the black Creole cultures of Louisiana and Africa. In the 1920s and 1930s, Calvin Claudel and

Juan Ponce de Léon. Courtesy Library of Congress.

Corinne Saucier searched for fairy tales among Cajun storytellers that would draw clear connections to French antecedents. It was not, however, until the collecting of Richard Dorson (1916–1981), and later the important work of Cajun-born scholar Barry Jean Ancelet that the lore of Cajuns and Creoles was viewed in terms of their own unique connections with the land, climate, and culture of southwest Louisiana. Ancelet freed himself from the relentless search for French or African "survivals" or "retentions" in his groundbreaking volume *Cajun and Creole Folktales*, focusing instead on the context of the tales as much as their texts—the tellers as much as the tales.

The Fountain of Youth

In the fifteenth century, a Caribbean legend described a miraculous spring, or fountain, in a land to the north. Stories in the region described this fountain as possessing curative powers that would restore one's youth. According to one tale, an Arawak chief named Sequene migrated from Cuba to Florida in search of this "fountain of youth" around the time of Christopher Columbus's first voyage to the New World in 1492.

One popular legend relates that Spanish explorer Juan Ponce de Léon was inspired by stories of the fountain of youth and sought its location during his explorations of the New World. Today, the Fountain of Youth Park in St. Augustine marks the place traditionally recognized as where de Léon first landed in Florida on April 2, 1513.

Ancelet collected numerous types of tales throughout French southwest Louisiana, including *contes merveilleux* (magic tales), *contes d'animaux* (animal tales), and *menteries et contes forts* (lies and tall tales). He also collected stories unique to specific regions within Cajun country. For example, *contes de Pascal*, or Pascal stories, are unique to the small town of Mamou, which is also known throughout the region for its Saturday morning Cajun dances and the unique customs associated with its celebration for Mardi Gras (see section on holidays and festivals). Pascal stories are so named after their protagonist, Pascal, and are characterized by a system of exaggerations, lies, and nonsense. Also, unlike many other forms of folktales which tend to follow a somewhat fixed text or storyline, the Pascal stories are always improvisational and often conversational in nature, as evidenced by the following interchange between Ancelet and Mamou storyteller Irving Reed:

> *Irving Reed*: Oh, old Pascal, they made him a state-trooper. And cars were speeding everywhere during the war. And they gave him a bicycle. He went after the cars. He couldn't catch them. So he took off the tires and he rode on the telephone lines on the rims. And when the car arrived, he would jump off in front of the car. His bicycle was well-trained! It could talk, "Mr. Pascal." The bicycle could talk.
> *Barry Jean Ancelet*: Oh?
> *Irving Reed*: Yeah! It called him Mr. Pascal. It spoke English.[4]

Ancelet collected numerous similar stories about Pascal, often featuring his exaggerated exploits on his bicycle. In one story, his bike was able to travel at speeds up to 700 miles an hour. Ancelet, being of the later generation of folklorists that viewed the storytelling context to be as integral to the tradition as the story texts, describes the ways in which these tales often are told to "top" the previous one. As the Pascal storytelling session went on, be it in a neighborhood bar or at a dinner party, each story would become increasingly fanciful, and Pascal's abilities would become increasingly outrageous. This almost competitive dynamic is often the case in other tall tale traditions, including the Jack tales of southern Appalachia.

THE JACK TALES OF APPALACHIA

Jack tales are long, humorous stories that tell of the adventures of the fictional hero named Jack, an Appalachian farm boy who possesses uncanny good luck and manages to continually stumble upon success. Jack is usually portrayed as somewhat unworldly or unsophisticated, yet possessing remarkable street smarts, being particularly imaginative, quick-thinking, and resourceful.

Folklorists became interested in Jack tales around the beginning of the twentieth century, but Richard Chase (1904–1988) collected the most comprehensive group of Jack tales in 1943. Numerous scholars have turned their attention to Jack tales since then, and many contributed to what is considered the seminal volume of work on the subject, the "Jack Tales" issue of the *North Carolina Folklore Journal* (September 1978). Jack tales have since been collected throughout the central Appalachian region, including eastern Kentucky, eastern Tennessee, and southwest Virginia, but they seem to thrive most strongly in the Beech Mountain region of northwestern North Carolina.

With the increasing popularity of folklife and storytelling festivals, tellers of Jack tales have emerged as some of the most beloved and sought-after participants. Ray Hicks (1922–2003), of Beech Mountain, who was somewhat of a celebrity on the storytelling festival circuit, became a memorable fixture at the signature festival in Jonesboro, Tennessee. Ray was one of eleven brothers and sisters in a family that boasted numerous generations of storytellers. He was the subject of a critically acclaimed documentary, *Fixin' to Tell about Jack*, and has been featured on numerous recordings. In 1983 Ray was awarded a National Heritage fellowship, the highest honor bestowed on traditional artists in the United States. The following is a transcript of Ray's version of "Jack and the Robbers":

Ray Hicks (1922–2003) of the Beech Mountain storytelling festival circuit, signature festival in Jonesboro, Tennessee. Photo by Donald Mussell.

Jack lived with his moma and daddy way back in the mountains. One day Jack wouldn't do his work. His moma' said Jack milk the cow, so Jack he just wouldn't do it. Mom said Jack get the water in from the springhouse, but Jack was lazy that evening and just wouldn't do nuttin'. So when Jack's daddy came home, he saw Jack hadnt done the work, he gave Jack a hard whippin'. Jack got mad and said I am running away from home and ain't never coming back. Jack slung what clothes he had over his back and down the road he went. He walked and walked till he came to a field, he looked out in that field and seen a big old steer, that old steer had its head hung down, going mooooooo, moooooo, mooooo, Jack walked up to that old steer he said you look pitiful, what's wrong with ya'? That old steer said I'm gettin' so old, I cant pull the plow no more, cant help the old master around the field, he gonna' get rid' of me tomorrow and get a new steer, Jack said you better come with me I'm gonna' run away from home, down the road Jack and the steer went.

They walked and walked on, till they come to another big field. Looked out in that field, there's an old donkey out there, heee haaa heeaaa, heee-haaaaaaaaa Jack walked up to that ol' donkey, said what's wrong with you, you sound plum awful? Ohhhhh said the donkey I'm getting so old my master cant ride on my back and I cant take him to town. He gonna' get rid' of me tomorrow and get a new donkey, well said Jack you better come with us, we gonna' run away from home, down the road Jack the steer and donkey went . . .

Characteristic of most Jack tales, Hicks draws this story out for quite some time as Jack experiences similar encounters with a long cast of animals, including a tomcat, a hound dog, and a rooster. The traditional story, in the temporary possession of the master teller Hicks, follows this parallel yet whimsical pattern, drawing the listeners in further:

. . . down the road, Jack, steer, donkey, cat, dog, rooster went, they walked on and on way into the night, they got in the woods and got lost. Jack said we better find a place to spend the night, untellin' what kinda' animals in these woods, well the old rooster flew up in the tree, and looked around, said Jack. I see a light shining off in the holler, Jack said who ever lives there might let us spend the night, well they all walked down into the holler till they came to the little house, Jack knocked on the door, wasn't nobody at home, Jack opened the door and went on into the house, all the animals came in behind him, they got in there and Jack looked around, in the corner was an old table, and on that table was some food, money, and old clothes, Jack said otto, the cat said what is it, Jack said we better get out of here this is the house of the highway robbers, the cat said no Jack we better hide, I here 'em comin' down the road now, well the cat jumped into the fire place, dog got behind a chair, Jack grabbed a stick and got behind the door, the donkey got out behind the steps, steer got up against the fence, and the ol' rooster flew up top the chimney, well here come seven highway robbers down the road, they got up to the fence and they all stopped, one of the robbers said, one of you boys go into the house and check around, see if anybody's been here while we were gone, if there ain't been nobody here, build a fire in the fire place and we'll come on in, that robber went in the house and didn't see nobody, he looked in the fire place, seen them two cat eyes a shinin', he thought they was fire coals, he got down on his knees, started blowing in the fireplace, blew ashes in the cat's eye, the cat got mad and went meawwwwwww, and scratched him in the eye, the robber jumped up, got to the chair, dog jumped out and with the two teeth he had left bit a chunk outta' his leg, well he got to the door, Jack hit him in the head with the back of that stick, knocked him outside, the donkey kicked him up to the fence, the steer grabbed him with that long horn threw him over the fence, and the rooster onto the chimney going cock-a-doodle-doo, cock-a-doodle-doo, the robbers took off down the road as hard as they could run, the other robber caught up with them about a mile down the road, keep a runnin' boys, don't go back to that house, its full of witches, devils and everything. I went to build a fire in the fireplace and a witch jumped out and scratched me in the face, got to the chair, a man jumped out with a butcher knife and cut a chunk outta' my leg, got to the door, a giant hit me in the head with his big ol' fist, and I don't know what it was that kicked me over to the devil, he grabbed me with a pitchfork and threw me over the fence, the worst part they was a man top the chimney, hollering, throw him up here boys when ya' get done with him, it scared them robbers to death, they left that country and was never seen again, but Jack, the steer, donkey, cat, dog, and the rooster moved into that little shack and lived happily ever after.[5]

This story is a typical Jack tale and classic Ray Hicks. Hicks was a master of tone and timbre in his telling. The pace of his telling gradually builds throughout the story, until the final chaotic events unfold in rapid-fire fashion. Ray Hicks died in 2003, but the surviving members of the storytelling Hicks family and other Jack tale tellers such as Ray Proffitt, Jr., continue to delight festival visitors across the country.

While folktales of similar structure and motifs are found in various cultures throughout the world, Jack tales appear to be most similar to European *marchen* and the various African American genres of trickster tales. It is likely that these tales, similar to many aspects of Appalachian folklore and folklife, emerged as a complex blending of the two cultural influences, resulting in the creation of a distinctly new, "Appalachian" folk expression. The origins of many of these tales are to be found in the stories and folk-speak of the Scots-Irish and English pioneers who settled in the region in the 1700s. It is also likely that Appalachian communities related well to the trickster tales of African Americans, particularly Brer Rabbit tales and Old John tales, which privilege a kind of folk intelligence of the protagonists over their perhaps more learned oppressors, and present an alternative narrative to the pervading negative stereotypes of rural folks.

THE AFRICAN AMERICAN TALES OF THE SOUTH

"John and Old Master"

Among the most common genres of southern African American folk narratives are stories of a slave named John and his dealings with the "Old Master" (often pronounced "Old Marster.") Part of a larger African-based tradition of trickster stories, John, the generic slave character, often uses his cunning to outwit his master, and many of these tales end with John winning certain special privileges, rewards, and even his own freedom. An interesting aspect of these tales is that John is usually portrayed as enjoying some measure of favoritism from his master. The interactions between John and the Old Master are often portrayed as being unusually genial and good-natured, though the ultimate power-dynamic remains painfully clear, and the explicit or implicit threat of the master's whip is never completely out of sight. Ultimately, the Old Master is most often depicted as being foolish and boastful. Many of the tales, in fact, focus on the Old Master's foolish bragging to his peers about the exaggerated skills and abilities of John himself. Often in these tales, John must find a way out of a troublesome situation, both to save face for his master and to avoid a variety of harsh consequences.

A good example is the story prolific collector B. A. Botkin (1901–1975) titles "The Coon in the Box." In this classic tale, the slave John leads Old Master into believing that he has telepathic powers. He does this by secretly listening in on the Master's conversations with his wife:

> One night when Old Master was eating supper he told his wife that he was going to plow the west forty acres the following day. After John heard that he goes home to bed; the next morning he gets up earlier than usual, and gets the tractor out and hooks up the plow. When Old Master came out John was all ready to go. So he said, "Well John, we're going to plow the west forty acres today." He said, "Yes, Master, I know, I got the rig all set up."

At first the Old Master doesn't think much of this "coincidence," but gradually he begins to take notice, and eventually becomes convinced that John can see into the future:

> So boss says, "what puzzles me is how a nigga' like you can figure out what I'm going to do every day before I tell you." He says, "Well that's all right Boss, I know everything." So Old Master shook his head and walks on up. So that night he was still puzzled at suppertime. John was still at the window. He listened to what his Boss was talking about. Old Master told his wife, "Well this slave we got around here, he's the smartest one I ever seen. Every morning I go out to tell him what to do he's already done it or he's telling me what we are going to do. And I don't know what to do about it."

Eventually, the Old Master sees a way to profit from his slave's supposed magical powers. He bets his friends that John can correctly guess what animal is hidden in a box. His friends take him up on the bet, and Old Master warns John that when the time comes, he better guess right. The problem for John, though, is that he never overhears Old Master revealing what's inside the box. One of Old Master's friends hides a raccoon in the box. When pressed to guess what's inside, John is forced to give up: "he didn't know in his mind what, so he just scratched his head and said, 'Well, it looks like you got the old coon at last!' "[6] In this humorous case, John unwittingly answers correctly, by referring to himself as "the old coon," a derogatory and racist expression.

These stories have been of particular interest to scholars because of the ways in which they often reveal some of the more complex and nuanced aspects of the slave-master relationship in southern plantation society. Often, slaves felt uneasy telling these John stories, in part for fear they might receive harsh punishment for referencing the "Old Marster" so directly. Thus, there was a parallel tradition, which experienced even greater distribution, of Brer Rabbit and other "magical animal" stories.

turn de handle w'iles you goes atter some water fer ter wet de grinestone,' sezee.

" Co'se, soon'z Brer Rabbit see Miss Fox go

atter de water, he jump down en put out, en dis time he git clean away."

" And was that the last of the Rabbit. too. Uncle

African American tales of the animal trickster Brer Rabbit were popularized by folklorist Joel Chandler Harris (1845–1908) in his folklore classic, *Uncle Remus Tales*. This illustration shows Miss Fox holding Brer Rabbit by the collar, from *Uncle Remus and His Friends* (1899). Courtesy Library of Congress.

Brer Rabbit

African American tales of the animal trickster Brer Rabbit were largely brought into the larger American consciousness by Joel Chandler Harris (1845–1908) in his folklore classic, *Uncle Remus Tales*. Harris, an Anglo-American scholar, published these tales primarily as a way to entertain other whites with what he termed the "quaint and homely humor of the negroes." Despite these questionable motivations, the impact of his work cannot be underestimated. Perhaps more than any other body of work, the *Uncle Remus Tales* sparked widespread interest in the collection of the "Negro folklore" of the South, particularly folktales.

Chandler published numerous Brer Rabbit tales in *Uncle Remus*, many of which have continued to be collected in various forms by folklorists to this day. For example, Daryl Cumber Dance, an African American folklorist, recently collected this version of the classic Brer Rabbit tale "The Tar Baby" in Richmond, Virginia:

> The animals were trying to catch Brer Rabbit; and Brer Rabbit would go down to the spring to get water. They thought that would be a good way to catch him. And so they made a Tar Baby and set it up at the spring 'cause Brer Rabbit was very inquisitive. And Brer Rabbit went down to drink, and he saw this Tar Baby; and he said, "Uh, who're you?" And he didn't say nothing, so then Brer Rabbit said, "You better tell me who you are!" And so the Tar Baby didn't say anything. So then Brer Rabbit went up there and say, "Well, I'll slap ya!" And the Tar Baby didn't say anything, so he slapped the Tar Baby, and his hand stuck, but the Tar Baby still didn't say anything. So he say, "I'll kick ya!" And he kicked 'im and his foot stuck.

Eventually, Brer Rabbit gets all of his limbs, and even his head, stuck on the tar baby. The animals soon find that they have successfully trapped Brer Rabbit:

> They say, "We gotcha! We gotcha!"
> He say, "Well, I tell you what to do. You throw me in the briar patch, be-

cause I don't like briar patches. You just throw me in the briar patch and you'll have me—then you can keep me forever."

So then they took him and threw him in the briar patch, and he say, "O-o-oh!" when he got in the briar patch. "O-O-OH! This is where I was born and raised—right in the briar patch!"

Then he ran down through the briars.[7]

In much the same way that "Old Master" seems unable to catch John in even the most poorly conceived lie, the other animals, particularly the often mentioned bumbling adversary Brer Bear, are unable to capture the trickster Brer Rabbit. It is not difficult to see how these tales achieved resonance within the African American community, both under the harsh institution of slavery and in the years of discrimination to follow.

OTHER ANIMAL TRICKSTER TALES: A VIEW FROM THE OZARKS

One of the most prolific folklore collectors of the South was Vance Randolph (1892–1980), who spent the majority of his time collecting in Arkansas and the greater Ozarks. Randolph published many important works on Ozark folktales, including *We Always Lie to Strangers: Tall Tales from the Ozarks* (1951), *Who Blowed Up the Church House? and Other Ozark Folk Tales* (1952), *The Talking Turtle and Other Ozark Folk Tales* (1957), and *Pissing in the Snow, and Other Ozark Folktales* (1976).

Randolph encountered many "magic animal tales," often featuring animals other than the standard Brer Rabbit and Brer Bear, among African Americans and whites in the region. The following is Randolph's version of "The Talking Turtle," a story he collected in Arkansas. While this version is unique to the Ozark region, it generally follows a common central motif, identified in Thompson's *Motif-Index* as "talking animal refuses to talk on demand."

One time there was a fellow named Lissenbee, and the trouble was that he couldn't keep nothing to himself. Whenever anybody done something that wasn't right, Lissenbee would run and blab it all over town. He didn't tell no lies, he just told the truth, and that's what made it so bad. Because all the people believed whatever Lissenbee said, and there wasn't no way a fellow could laugh it off.

If he seen one of the county officers going to a woman's house when her husband was not home, Lissenbee would tell it right in front of the courthouse, and so there would be hell to pay in two families. Or maybe some citizens liked to play a little poker in the livery barn, but there wasn't no way to keep it quiet, on account of that goddam' Lissenbee. And when the Baptist preacher brought some whiskey home, there was Lissenbee a-hollering before the preacher could get the keg out of his buggy. After while the boys was afraid to swipe a watermelon, for fear old blabbermouth Lissenbee would tell everybody who done it.

The last straw was the time Lissenbee found a turtle in the road. It was bigger than the common kind, so he stopped to look at it. The old turtle winked its red eyes, and it says, "Lissenbee, you talk too damn much." Lissenbee jumped four foot high, and then just stood there with his mouth a-hanging open. He looked all around, but there wasn't nobody in sight. "It must be my ears have went back on me!" says he. "Everybody knows terrapins is dumb." The old turtle winked its red eyes again. "Lissenbee, you talk too damn much," says the turtle. With that Lissenbee spun 'round like a top, and then he lit out for town.

When Lissenbee come to the tavern and told the people about the turtle that could talk, they just laughed in his face. "You come with me," says he, "and I'll show you!" So the whole crowd went along, but when they got there the old turtle didn't say a word. It looked just like any other turtle, only bigger than the common kind. The people was mad because they had walked away out there in the hot sun for nothing, so they kicked Lissenbee into the ditch and went back to town. Pretty soon Lissenbee set up, and the old turtle winked its red eyes. "Didn't I tell you?" says the turtle. "You talk too damn much."[8]

This tale, like many others discovered throughout the region, warns of the perils of talking too much. "Talking too much" can be interpreted in many ways, and its meanings are often closely associated with the particular storytelling context. Many tales associated with plantation society caution against talking too much, often in reference to the hazards associated with spreading rumors, particularly within earshot of the master or other oppressive forces. At other times, "talking too much" refers to excessive bragging or hubris. In still other stories, particularly in tales collected much later, cautions against "talking too much" may refer to concerns about revealing too much to "outsiders" or tourists, such as in the "Wormy Apple" tale collected in western North Carolina. In this tale a young boy tells a tourist woman that the cider at his family's fruit stand is made from wormy apples. When the boy's father learns what his son told the tourist, he gives the boy a whipping. The woman, having witnessed this display, gets upset and tells the man that it's not right to whip a child for telling the truth. The father responds that he'd punish his child for lying as well. The tourist, confused, wonders what the father is trying to teach the child, to which the father responds, "To keep his mouth shut." While speaking to the traditional "don't talk too much" motif of many folktales throughout the South, this tale clearly speaks to more contemporary tensions associated with the increasing encounters between locals and tourists within the region.

LEGENDS AND LEGENDARY FIGURES

In every region of the United States, certain historical figures have risen to the level of legend, and the South is no exception. In fact, the telling of legends by southerners has served to continually reassert their own heritage and the region's cultural and geographic uniqueness.

Many legends in the South speak to the region's vital role in the formation of early America. White southerners made it a point to continue to share legendary tales about "the lost colony of Roanoke," the first attempted colony in the New World, as well as legendary tales of Captain John Smith, who was supposedly saved from execution at Jamestown by the Powhatan princess Pocahontas. Southerners have largely been responsible for shaping the legends about Virginian George Washington, including the classic tale about him cutting down the cherry tree, as well for developing the legends around the life of the South's Renaissance man, Thomas Jefferson.

Though born in Pennsylvania, Daniel Boone became a legendary figure in the South for his various heroics throughout the Kentucky territory. Tennessee-born Davy Crockett became a legendary figure, and the subject of countless exaggerated tales for his heroics at the Alamo. The Civil War is responsible for many legendary figures in the South, and legends depicting the heroics of "Stonewall" Jackson, J.E.B. "Jeb" Stuart, and Robert E. Lee. Lee, in particular, has been the subject of countless tales, and accounts of his heroism seem to have only grown over time in many southern communities. The following tale, for example, appears in Botkin's classic collection of southern folklore:

In the legendary tale, Captain John Smith was supposedly saved from execution at Jamestown by the Powhatan princess Pocahontas. Courtesy Library of Congress.

> One day he met coming to the rear a gallant Georgian whose right arm was very badly shattered. "I grieve for you, my poor fellow," said the tenderhearted chief; "can I do any thing for you?" "Yes sir!" replied the brave boy with a proud smile; "you can shake hands with me, general, if you will consent to take my *left* hand." General Lee cordially grasped the hand of the ragged hero, spoke a few kind words which he could never forget, and sent him on his way rejoicing that he had the privilege of suffering under such a leader.
>
> One night some soldiers were overheard discussing the tenets of atheism around the campfire, when a rough, honest fellow cut short the discussion by saying: "Well boys, the rest of us may have developed from monkeys; *but I tell you none less than a God could have made sucha' man as 'Marse Robert!'* "[9]

As one can imagine, Lee has not attained the same legendary status in the South's African American communities. Instead, many southern black legends focus on the heroics of famous slave insurrectionists such as Denmark Vesey and Nat Turner, and on Maryland-born legendary figure of the Underground Railroad, Harriet Tubman. Other cultural groups have had their legendary figures as well. Native Americans have a long tradition of passing on legends about the mysterious power of nature. Creoles in Louisiana shared tales of the legendary voodoo queen Marie Laveau. Cajuns tell legends of the loup-garous, or werewolves. Local legends and legendary figures abound throughout the South as well, from charismatic politi-

The Civil War is responsible for many legends in the South depicting the heroics of Thomas "Stonewall" Jackson, J.E.B. "Jeb" Stuart, and Robert E. Lee. Courtesy Library of Congress.

cal figures like Louisiana governor Huey P. "The Kingfish" Long to sports legends like the late Alabama football coach Paul "Bear" Bryant.

Many of the best known legendary figures in the South, however, were blue-collar workers, such as the black railroad worker John Henry, the white railroad engineer Casey Jones, and the riverboatman Mike Fink. Many of these legendary figures have been immortalized not only through the telling of tales, but also through another important genre of southern folklore—the folk song.

FOLK SONGS

The early focus of U.S. folklore studies on old English folklore also had an impact on the study of songs and ballads. The search for old English ballads in the United States was largely inspired by the work in Europe of American-born academic Francis James Child (1825–1896), who gathered the lyrics of hundreds of old ballads and edited his work into a five-volume set entitled *The English and Scottish Popular Ballads* (1882–1894), the seminal collection of the genre. As noted earlier, both folk professionals and the general public believed that the South, and in particular the Appalachian region, was a storehouse of the more "authentic" forms of American folklore, and thus this region became the central locale for collecting folk songs.

One of the most prominent early collectors of old English folk songs in Appalachia was Cecil Sharp (1859–1924). Sharp, a well-known collector in England, was introduced to some of the collected folk songs of Appalachian residents during a visit to the United States to assist with the production of a Broadway play in New York. Sharp was amazed at the some of the surviving elements of the old English ballads in this region, and immediately recognized many variations of what had become known as the Child Ballads. In 1916 and 1918, Sharp traveled throughout the Appalachian region in search of traditional ballads with his former student, Maud Karpeles (1886–1976).

Sharp wrote the following letter during his time collecting in North Carolina on August 27, 1916:

> Last week I went to Hot Springs, where I got thirty beautiful songs from a single woman. The collecting goes on apace, and I have now noted 160 songs and ballads. Indeed, this field is a far more fertile one upon which to collect English folk songs than England itself. The cult of singing traditional songs is far more alive than it is in England or has been for fifty years or more. . . . This last week I took down three ballads given in Child which I have never before heard sung and to which there are no published tunes *Edward*, *Johnny Scott*, and *Fair Annie*. The first of these is one of the oldest ballads known, and is the prototype of *Lord Rendal*, a very rare and valuable find. I am simply amazed at what I have done in a month compared with what I have ever been able to do in England in that time.[10]

The woman who provided Sharp with thirty ballads was Mrs. Jane Gentry, one of countless informants Sharp encountered during his travels.

Compare Sharp's transcription of Gentry's version of "Edward" (which, as Sharp notes, was "one of the oldest ballads known") with the 1765 version that appears in Child's collection as Child Ballad #13:

Robert Johnson

Few artists have had such a profound impact on American music during so short a career as the enigmatic Mississippi blues legend Robert Johnson (1911–1938). He recorded only twenty-nine songs before his death, but this relatively small body of work includes numerous songs which have endured as blues standards, including "Sweet Home Chicago," "Love in Vain," "I Believe I'll Dust My Broom," and "Crossroads Blues." Johnson is remembered, however, not only for his masterful work but for the lore and rumors that surrounded him during his playing career and in the years following his death. Legend has it that Johnson "sold his soul" to the devil in exchange for his remarkable talent. This legendary exchange reportedly took place late one evening at the crossroads of highways 61 and 49 in Clarksdale, Mississippi, immortalized in his "Crossroads Blues": "I went down to the crossroads and fell down on my knees, asked the Lord up above for mercy, save poor Bob if you please."

The Crossroads Legend was only strengthened by the mysterious circumstances surrounding Johnson's untimely death—an alleged murder by poisoning by the jealous husband of a woman with whom he was having an affair. Johnson's Crossroads Legend also speaks to the convergence of numerous powerful motifs in African American folklore. The notion of the crossroads as a place of evil, for example, is quite common in the folklore of the African diaspora. And the blues, while mainstream today, was seen as a dangerous secular departure from church-based gospel music, and was often considered the "devil's music."

Edward

As sung to Cecil Sharp by Mrs. Jane Gentry at Hot Springs, North Carolina, August 24, 1916

Edward

As it appears in Francis Child's *The English and Scottish Popular Ballads*

How come that blood on your shirt sleeve?
Pray, son, now tell to me.
It is the blood of the old greyhound
That run young fox for me.

It is too pale for that old greyhound
Pray, son, now tell to me.
It is the blood of the old grey mare
That ploughed that corn for me.

It is too pale for that old grey mare.
Pray, son, now tell to me,
It is the blood of my youngest brother
That hoed that corn for me.

What did you fall out about?
Pray, son, now tell to me.
Because he cut yon holly bush
Which might have made a tree.

What will you tell to your father dear
When he comes home from town?
I'll set my foot in yonder ship
And sail the ocean round.

What will you do with your sweet little
      wife?
Pray, son, now tell to me.
I'll set her foot in yonder ship
To keep me company.

What will you do with your three little
      babes?
Pray, son, now tell to me.
I'll leave them here in the care of you
For to keep you company.

What will you do with your house and
      land?
Pray, son, now tell to me.
I'll leave it here in care of you
For to set my children free.[11]

What makes that blood on the point of
      your knife?
My son, now tell to me
It is the blood of my old grey mare
Who plowed the fields for me, me, me
Who plowed the fields for me.

It is too red for your old grey mare
My son, now tell to me
It is the blood of my old coon dog
Who chased the fox for me, me, me
Who chased the fox for me.

It is too red for your old coon dog
My son, now tell to me
It is the blood of my brother John
Who hoed the corn for me, me, me
Who hoed the corn for me.

What did you fall out about?
My son, now tell to me
Because he cut yon holly bush
Which might have been a tree, tree, tree
Which might have been a tree.

What will you say when your father comes
      back
When he comes home from town?
I'll set my foot in yonder boat
And sail the ocean round, round, round
I'll sail the ocean round.

When will you come back, my own dear
      son?
My son, now tell to me
When the sun it sets in yonder sycamore
      tree
And that will never be, be, be
And that will never be.

Sharp collected variants of "Edward" in other locations in North Carolina, as well as in parts of Virginia. As this comparison demonstrates, the singing of these traditional ballads, largely unchanged from their original forms, became one of the more compelling arguments that there were largely homogeneous populations of English descendants still living in the mountain regions of the South. The collection of these ballads, particularly those that closely resembled the Child Ballads, documented more than a century earlier, resulted in the publication of the two-volume *English Folk Songs from the Southern Appalachians*. This collection generated a tremendous amount of interest in the folklore of the Appalachian region and inspired the future work of a host of folklorists. For example, *Folksongs of West Virginia* was published by John Harrington Fox in 1929 and 1939. Arthur Kyle

Davis, Jr., published his *Traditional Ballads of Virginia* in 1929. Mississippi native Arthur Palmer Hudson (1892–1978) published his *Folksongs of Mississippi and Their Background* in 1936. Ozark ballads and other folk songs were collected by the prolific scholar Vance Randolph (1892–1980), resulting in the four-volume collection *Ozark Folksongs* in 1946–1950. Dorothy Scarborough (1878–1935), who collected mainly in the mountains of North Carolina and Virginia, produced *A Song Catcher in the Southern Mountains: American Folksongs of British Ancestry* in 1937. And perhaps the most prolific "song catchers" were Mississippian John Lomax (1867–1948) and his son Alan (1915–2002), who recorded folk songs throughout the Appalachian region and the South for the Folklife Archives at the Library of Congress.

The first published collection of southern black folk songs was *Slave Songs of the United States* (1867) by William Francis Allen (1830–1889), Charles P. Ware, and Lucy Garrison. This collection focuses primarily on black spirituals. Allen began his collecting work in 1863 on St. Helena Island off the coast of South Carolina. Allen and his coauthors amassed and transcribed "Negro spirituals" from throughout the southern states, including Virginia, the Carolinas, Georgia, Florida, Alabama, and Louisiana. Many of the folk songs he collected were to become the basis for popular standards in years to come, such as his collected version from South Carolina of "Michael, Row the Boat Ashore":

> Michael row de boat ashore, Hallelujah!
> Michael boat a gospel boat, Hallelujah!
> I wonder where my mudder deh (there).
> See my mudder on de rock gwine home.
> On de rock gwine home in Jesus' name.
> Michael boat a music boat.
> Gabriel blow de trumpet horn.
> O you mind your boastin' talk.
> Boastin' talk will sink your soul
> Brudder, lend a helpin' hand.
> Sister, help for trim dat boat.
> Jordan stream is wide and deep.
> Jesus stand on t' oder side.
> I wonder if my maussa deh.
> My fader gone to unknown land.
> O de Lord he plant his garden deh.
> He raise de fruit for you to eat
> He dat eat shall neber die.
> When de riber overflow.
> O poor sinner, how you land?
> Riber run and darkness comin'.
> Sinner roll to save your soul, Halleluja!

The authors of this volume came to understand that in these African American slave songs they were encountering a musical and lyrical sensibility startlingly different than in Western Anglo styles. Following the appearance of *Slave Songs of the United States*, numerous other African American folk songs and other forms of "Negro folklore" were published in such popular periodicals as *Century*, the

Atlantic, and *New England Magazine*. Often these articles were published by abolitionists and others interested in portraying a positive image of the cultural lives of African Americans.

The importance of African American folk song and folklore was broadly emphasized by Harris's publication of *Uncle Remus*. Unlike Allen, Ware, and Garrison, who focused almost exclusively on Negro spirituals, Harris published songs from other aspects of plantation life, including work songs and shouts. Included in his collection were slave work songs associated with the corn-shucking ceremony. According to folklorist Roger D. Abrahams, the corn-shucking harvest ceremony became an important seasonal event throughout the low-country areas of the Chesapeake, in the Tidewater regions of Virginia and North Carolina, in both lowland and upland settlements in the Carolinas and Georgia, and in Kentucky, Tennessee, Alabama, Mississippi, and eastern Texas. Harris provides the first written accounts of songs that accompanied such ritual enactments. A portion of the "Corn-Shucking Song" is presented below. Like many of his contemporaries, Harris chose to publish these songs using a phonetic spelling to elicit the spoken dialect:

Corn-Shucking Song

Oh, dofus news you know do day'l bo a breakin'—
(Hey O! Hi O! Up'n down do Bango!)
An' do fior be a burnin' en' do ash-cake a bakin',
(Hey O! Hi O! Up'n down do Bango!)
An' do hon'll be a hollorin' en do boss 'll be a wakin'—
(Hey O! Hi O! Up'n down do Bango!)
Better git up, nigger, en give yo'se'f a shakin'—
(Hi O, Miss Sindy Ann!)

Oh, work on, boys! give doze shucks a mighty wringin'—
(Hey O! Hi O! Up'n down do Bango!)
'fo' do boss come aroun' a dangin' en a dingin'—
(Hey O! Hi O! Up'n down do Bango!)

Git upen move aroun'! sot dom big han's ter swingin'—
(Hey O! Hi O! Up'n down do Bango!)
Git up'n shout loud! lot do w'ite folks year you singin'!
(Hi O, Miss Sindy Ann!)

For dolos' eli on yard is a huntin' for do mornin'
(Hi O! git long! go 'way!)
En shell ketch up widdus 'fo' we over git dis corn in.
(Oh, go 'way Sindy Ann!)[12]

The pervading belief among scholars well into the mid-twentieth century was that the early songs of African Americans were not the original creations of the slaves, but instead a product of the imitation of Euro-American songs. Early attempts were made to disprove this erroneous theory, however, most notably by Henry Edward Krehbiel (1854–1923) with his 1914 publication of *Afro-American Folk Songs*. Other important works followed, led by anthropologist Elsie Clews Parsons (1874–1971), who collected African American folklore both in the South and throughout the Caribbean. And one of the most prolific collectors of African American folklore in the South, though little known in her own time, was folklorist and novelist Zora Neale Hurston (1891–1960). Hurston was a student of the influential anthropologist Franz Boas (1858–1942). Boas provided Hurston with a fellowship that enabled her to conduct fieldwork in Georgia, New Orleans, and her hometown, Polk City, Florida. Hurston's work is distinguishable from earlier works by Chandler and others in that she was herself "of the culture," and her work depicts her subjects with an unprecedented level of admiration and dignity.

Hurston became one of the key participants in the Federal Writers' Project (FWP), which created an invaluable record of the voices of everyday folks in the South, including ex-slaves, Civil War veterans, and Native Americans, as well as other, often underrepresented voices in the South, including emerging immigrant communities. In Florida, for example, the WPA folklorists collected a number of important items from the Cuban American population, particularly in the southernmost region of the state. This ancient lullaby, sung to a WPA folklorist by Alva Rodriguez, is still very popular in the Cuban American community, particularly in Key West:

The Federal Writers' Project

The Works Progress Administration (WPA), an ambitious effort to create jobs and bolster American aesthetic and cultural life, was launched in 1935 as part of President Franklin Roosevelt's New Deal efforts to counter the Great Depression. An important component of the WPA was the Federal Writers' Project (FWP), which employed over 6,000 men and women throughout the country. FWP employees set out to interview everyday Americans to record their life stories, their personal struggles and successes, and their unique regional and local lore. This massive collecting effort ultimately resulted in the creation of a guidebook for each state. The FWP was particularly active in the South, which yielded some of its most valuable collections of oral materials, including extensive interviews with former slaves and Civil War veterans. The FWP's folklore division, headed by Benjamin A. Botkin (1901–1975), collected countless items of folklore including folk expressions, songs, tales, occupational lore, and folk customs. Many of the most fruitful studies of folklore came from the South, including Zora Neale Hurston's groundbreaking work in Florida, which eventually led to the publication of *Mules and Men* (1935) and *Their Eyes Were Watching God* (1937).

Duermate Mi Nina (Sleep My Child)	*Go to Sleep My Girl*
Key West, Florida, January 22, 1940	
Duermete mi nina,	*Go to sleep my girl,*
Que tenge que hacer	*For I have something to do*
Lavar los panales	*Wash out the napkins and sit down to sew.*
Y sentarme a ceser.	
Palomita blanca	*Little white dove, bill of coral*
Pico de coral	*When I am dead*
Cuando yo me muera	*Who will weep for me?*
Quien me va a llorar.	

The Federal Writers' Project collected tales and songs throughout the South, in communities defined by ethnicity, region, and occupation. The latter proved particularly fruitful, as folklorists discovered that particular types of work communities had their own vibrant forms of folklore. To this day, occupational lore has been a primary interest of folklorists.

WORK SONGS

As mentioned earlier, early folk collectors such as Joel Chandler Harris were particularly interested in recording the lore of work and play among the African Americans primarily for entertainment purposes. This motivation speaks to a long tradition of whites' somewhat voyeuristic interest in African American expressive forms, beginning with their earliest contact in the Americas. The earliest writings of southern plantation owners, for example, often refer to the social entertainments of their slaves, particularly in the area of music. Thomas Jefferson wrote of his slaves playing the "banjar" at Monticello, his Virginia home. The "banjar," scholars strongly believe, is a reference to an early version of the banjo, originally brought to American shores from Africa, an instrument that would eventually be the cornerstone of popular music throughout the region. Similar accounts of slave musical enactments were recorded on Sundays in "Place Congo" in New Orleans, which many music historians view as the birthplace of jazz.

The African American tradition of worksong, however, persisted well after its original plantation setting, and has survived in various forms well into the twentieth century, particularly in various black-dominated work contexts. Folklorists have collected forms of African American worksong among crab-pickers and fishermen along the South's coastal regions, sharecroppers and other farm workers throughout the rural South, and even "lining bar gangs" (also known in some portions of the South as gandy dancers), groups of African American men who worked to lay down railroad tracks and keep them in alignment. Lining track requires tremendous coordination, and is also very physically grueling and time-consuming work. The sophisticated use of worksong among trackliners responds to both of these conditions, serving both to ensure that each member of the gang is working in sync with the others, and to help make the time pass more quickly with friendly jests and laughter. The "shouts" or "calls" of the lining bar gang consisted of a call-and-response of "two-line ditties" between the lead caller and the crew. As this style of work often necessitated that the men spend weeks on end away from their wives, these songs often, not surprisingly, referred to women:

> I got a gal,
> In Baltimore,
> She make five dollars,
> And give me four!
>
> I got a gal,
> In Kansas City,
> The girl can't cook,
> But she sure is pretty!

Other lining bar songs would poke fun at "the Captain," a white man hired to supervise the gang:

> Look at the Captain,
> How he stands,
> More like a farmer,
> Than a railroad man!

Captain can't read,
Captain can't write,
How can he tell
When the track is right?[13]

   The worksong tradition is not exclusive to African Americans. Songs of and about work, particularly work that entails great physical labor and a measure of occupational hazard, are sung throughout the South. There is, in fact, a long-standing tradition of ballad singing throughout the South that speaks to the perils of not just railroad work but also other dangerous and often thankless occupations such as coal mining, logging, and commercial fishing. Often, these ballads focus on legendary tragic accidents that have occurred in these work settings, such as in this classic southern ballad about a train accident in Virginia, "The Wreck of the Old 97":

On one cloudless morning I stood on the mountain,
Just watching the smoke from below,
It was coming from a tall, slim smokestack
Way down on the Southern railroad.

It was 97,
The fastest train ever ran the Southern line,
All the freight trains and passengers take the side for 97,
For she's bound to be at stations on time. . . .

It's a mighty rough road from Lynchburg to Danville,
And the lie was a three-mile grade,
It was on that grade that he lost his air brakes,
And you see what a jump that she made.

He was going down the grade making 90 miles an hour,
When his whistle began to scream,
He was found in that wreck with his hand on the throttle,
He was scalded to death by the steam.

Did she ever pull in? No, she never pulled in,
And at 1:45 he was due,
For hours and hours has the switchman been waiting
For that fast mail that never pulled through.

Did she ever pull in? No, she never pulled in,
And that poor boy must be dead.
Oh, yonder he lays on the railroad track
With the cart wheels over his head.

97, she was the fastest train
That the South had ever seen,
But she run so fast on that Sunday morning
That the death score was numbered 14.

Now, ladies, you must take warning,
From this time now and on.
Never speak harsh words to your true loving husband.
He may leave you and never return.[14]

As these "tragedy" ballads and tales demonstrate, life has long proved difficult and even tragic for many southerners, particularly those living in poverty-stricken conditions in many rural and mountainous areas. Often, southerners turned to faith and religion to help get through the trials and tribulations of life, and to seek out answers to life's greatest questions. The region has often been referred to as the Bible Belt by outsiders, who marvel at the evangelical fervor so prevalent in the South (see chapter on **Religion**). Along with participation in various forms of established religion, however, the South has always been quite fertile ground for what some call superstitions, and folklorists prefer to call folk beliefs.

FOLK BELIEFS AND "SUPERSTITIONS"

Folklorist Jack Solomon views a folk belief as "an attempt to grapple with the mysteries of human life in our universe, to answer, interpret, understand, solve, control, or come to terms with the multitudinous questions, problems, obstacles, and dilemmas that confront our instinct to survive."[15] Folk beliefs in the South address countless numbers of life's mysteries, including death and dying, love and courtship, and good luck and misfortune. Folk beliefs are prominent in nearly every folk community in the South, and some are distinct to specific locations. For example, the following folk beliefs pertaining to childbirth were collected in 1920 by Daniel Thomas among the infamous horseback-riding midwives in Kentucky:

- A woman in travail should hold salt clenched in her two outstretched hands.
- In a case of child labor, place an axe edge up under the bed of the mother.
- If an expectant mother places her hand upon her body, the child will have a birthmark at the position on its body that she presses.
- An expectant mother should not have her teeth filled.
- In a case of child labor, cross hazel twigs, put them across an open Bible, and place them under the pillow.
- To hasten child-delivery, give a woman a drink of which another woman has partaken.
- The number of balls on the navel string of the first child shows the number of children that a woman will have.[16]

Some folk beliefs become associated with larger cultural groups, and are often found among these groups in a wide range of geographical contexts. The following beliefs concerning courtship, for example, have been collected by African American folklorists in various regions throughout the South:
You can make a man love you by . . .

- Putting his picture on a table and burning a candle on top of it for nine days.
- Writing his name nine times on a piece of paper and putting it under your pillow.
- Cutting some hair out of your man's head and putting it in a jar in a hole under your step (he won't be able to stay away from your house).
- Putting a lock of your hair in his shoe.

You can get rid of a man by . . .

- Sprinkling some pepper behind him when he leaves.
- Putting his picture face-up in the bottom of your shoe (he'll walk away from you).
- Buying him some new shoes (he'll walk away from you).[17]

In many rural communities throughout the South, the residents are by necessity particularly concerned with the weather. It is not surprising, then, that many folk beliefs offer their own kind of meteorological predictions. The following weather-related folk beliefs were collected among farmers in rural Alabama by students at Troy State University between 1958 and 1962:

- If soot falls down the chimney, it's a sign of rain.
- If bark grows heavy on trees in summer, look for a cold winter.
- Hollow moon turns west, the fish bite the best.
- If it lightens in the north after the sun goes down, and it does not rain in three days, it will not rain for three weeks.
- Thunder in February and it will frost on the same day in April.
- When grass is dry at morning's light, look for rain before the night.
- When the dew is on the grass, rain will never come to pass.
- For each time it thunders in February, it will frost on that day in May.
- If January is warm, this means that bad weather is in store for the rest of the year.[18]

GHOST STORIES

One of the more prominent folk beliefs, apparent not just in the South but throughout the country and the entire world, is the belief in ghosts. The researchers for the Federal Writers' Project Folklore Division collected many ghost-related folktales and beliefs throughout the country from the late 1930s to the mid-1940s. One location that proved particularly fruitful for ghost story collection was central and southeastern Alabama. This region was later revisited by folklore students at Troy State. The students collected the following ghost tale, "Scratch, Scratch, Scratch," from a man named T.M. Stroud in southeastern Alabama:

Back in 1888, each man in the country had to work on country roads for ten days out of every year. T.M. Stroud from Elba, Alabama, was working his ten days with two other men. They were camped for the night at Woodland Grove Church in Coffee County.

There was a man buried in the cemetery of Woodland Grove with an unusual story about him. It seems that before he died he ordered his casket and had it made where you could take off the top and slide back a panel and view him. He requested that he be put in a vault above the ground, and every ten years his family must slide back the panel and look at him. The family obeyed him four times and finally decided to bury him under the ground.

This particular night T.M. Stroud and the other two men had eaten their supper and prepared beds in the back of the church in front of the altar. As they turned out the light, they heard a scratching sound, similar to that of a dog. They lit their lanterns and went outside and searched under the church where the scratching sound had come from. There was no dog. They retired again but the scratching continued louder than ever. It sounded as if it came from the front door this time. They got up again and searched the church again but heard the scratching once more in the top of the church. They checked the church once more and checked the grounds outside the church to see if someone was trying to scare them. They found nothing at all. They retired again and were almost asleep with the scratching still going on, when they heard a window suddenly rise. They jumped up and no one was around. They don't know why it went up.

Finally they tried to ignore it and go to sleep. In the middle of the night they heard a tree fall right near the church. The next morning, they searched for the tree for two hours and never found one. The three men think it was this old man trying to rise out of his grave.[19]

Between 1937 and 1942, the Virginia Writers Project (VWP), a subsidiary of the Federal Writers' Project, collected stories throughout Virginia as part of a massive folklore-gathering effort that altogether amassed over 3,850 items of oral, customary, and material folklore from sixty-two counties around the state. A surprising number of ghost stories were collected in Virginia, including this tale, told by Leonard E. Carter to the folk collector James Taylor Adams in the southwestern mountains of Virginia in 1941:

The Headless Ghost of Griffith's Wife

Over here in Russell County, about Sword's Creek, a man named Henry Griffith killed his wife and a feller named Lawson and his wife one time. I don't know exactly when it happened but sometime after the railroad was built through the country. I heard some railroad men talkin' 'bout seein' things up thar down at Norton about fifteen years ago. This feller Griffith was jealous of his wife, they said, an' she was afraid of him an' had done gone to stay with a family named Lawson. I believe Lawson had married her sister, or maybe it was that she was Lawson's sister. Maybe no kin at all. Anyway, she had left her man an' went to stay at Lawson's. An' late one evenin' the three of 'em was down by the Clinch River, fishin' maybe, I don't know. Griffith foun' out about them bein' down thar an' he slipped up on them an' killed all three of 'em an' cut off their heads an' throwed 'em in the Clinch River. It was a month or two before they was found. A railroad man found 'em, I think. They say Griffith's wife head was not foun'.

Well, Griffith was tried and sent to prison for a long time. An' not long after that a train was comin' down Clinch River one night, an' when it was passing the place where the people was killed the engineer looked on ahead an' there on the bank of the river he seed a woman without any head, but carryin' some sort of light in her hand. An' she acted jes like she was searchin' for sumpin' along the edge of the water, an' her no head now. What do you know about that?

Well sir, about the same time the engineer seed her the fireman seed her too. He looked at the engineer an' the engineer looked back at him. Neither one spoke until they had got a way past the place. Then they axed one another if the other seed anything. An' they both said they had seed a woman without any head an' carrying a light as if she was lookin' for somethin'.

They say that ever since then you can go by thar at night an' you will see her, always with a light, walkin' along the edge of the don't know what about it. It might be that way.[20]

JOKES

Though much folklore in the South focuses on such morbid topics as death and tragedy, and often deals with deep-seated fears or anxieties, it would be misleading to suggest that the region's folklore is devoid of good humor. In fact, it could be said that one of the most familiar sounds of the South, along with the ringing of the banjo in the hills of Appalachia, or the sound of the Cajun-style accordion and fiddle in the bayous, is that of laughter. As our brief exploration of the Brer Rabbit and Jack tales shows, good humor has always been a central, overriding feature of southern folk traditions. The telling of jokes, in particular, has long been a vibrant activity in the region. From the earliest period of folkloric research, collectors have reported of epic joke-telling sessions throughout the region, and of individuals who have gained a measure of notoriety within their own villages and hamlets for their comedic prowess.

In recent times, the television has often replaced traditional family and community story- and joke-telling gatherings. New suburban subdivisions have often forgone the traditional front-porch architectural style. Many traditional community joke-telling venues such as the barbershop, the five-and-dime, or the soda fountain have been replaced by less hospitable and often impersonal shopping malls. Yet even with these developments, joke-telling still manages to thrive in the South. One area where joke-telling has remained strong is, perhaps not surprisingly, in close connection with another remarkably resilient form of southern folklife—traditional country music.

Bluegrass and country musicians throughout the South have traditionally made joke-telling a central aspect of their performance. Often, the group's banjo player is either the primary teller or the primary butt of these jokes. One likely reason is that the banjo requires an excessive amount of tuning in comparison to the other instruments. There are countless ways to tune a banjo, and the banjo player often has to dramatically switch tunings between numbers. Likewise, the banjo often slips out of tune in response to the humid conditions common in the South during the summer, the busiest time for bluegrass festivals. The "dead air" between songs while the banjo is tuned is often filled with banjo-related jokes. It has often been said that banjo players spend half their time tuning and the other half playing out of tune. The following is a sampling of "banjo jokes" collected at bluegrass gatherings throughout the South:

Q: What is the range of a banjo?
A: About 10 meters if you throw it hard enough.
Q: What's difference between a banjo and a fish?
A: You can tuna fish . . .
Q: What is the definition of perfect pitch?
A: Throwing a banjo into a toilet without hitting the seat.
Q: Do you know how to tell when a banjo player is playing out of tune?
A: His fingers are moving.

Q: How long does it take to tune a banjo?
A: Nobody knows.[21]

While most forms of popular music tend to privilege youth over experience, traditional music tends to embrace older players. This is particularly the case in southern mountain bluegrass and traditional country music, as well as in the folk music of the Deep South such as Cajun, zydeco, and the blues. In fact, it could be argued that the acceptance of and reverence for older musicians and the intergenerational exchange within these musical forms is one of the most important reasons for their continued resilience and vibrancy in the twenty-first century.

While older musicians are revered and celebrated, however, they are certainly not free from friendly mockery. Rare it is to attend a bluegrass concert without at least one joke about old age. Often jokes poking fun at elder musicians even come from those musicians themselves, such as this one, told by eighty-four-year-old bluegrass musician "Papa Joe" Smiddy, collected by the author in southwest Virginia:

Papa Joe: "I went to the doctor recently and he told me I had to take these pills the rest of my life."
Bandmember: "Well, heck, that's no so bad, is it?"
Papa Joe: "Yeah, but he only gave me five of them!"

This same zest for life evidenced by the rich tradition of joke-telling throughout the South can also be seen in the ways in which southerners celebrate.

HOLIDAYS AND FESTIVALS OF THE REGION

It can be argued that no region in the United States celebrates more often, and likewise that no other region can claim such an integral role of festivity in the formation and maintenance of community folk culture, than the South. Along with uniquely southern takes on nationally celebrated holidays such as Independence Day, Thanksgiving, and Labor Day, as well as religious holidays such as Christmas, Easter, and Hanukkah, there are more regionally specific holidays and celebrations observed throughout the South. Robert E. Lee has his own state holiday in Virginia. The legendary pirate Gasparilla is the focus of a major licentious celebration in Tampa, Florida. Southerners, some have argued, will throw a festival to celebrate anything. New Orleans, historically known for its propensity to party, is noted not only as the primary location in North America for the transatlantic pre-Lenten celebration of Carnival, but for its year-round cycle of festivals, parades, and revelry. In many New Orleans communities, particularly among African Americans, even one's funeral becomes an occasion to parade, sing, dance, and revel. New Orleans rhythm and blues diva Irma Thomas perhaps puts it best: "As you know, in New Orleans we celebrate anything and everything. We celebrate frogs, roaches, mosquitoes, red beans and rice, gumbo, okra, headaches, divorce, separation, and when our pregnancy tests come back negative!"[22]

A similar compulsion to celebrate can be seen throughout the southern region. A sampling of some of the festive offerings on any given Saturday during the spring and summer reveals communities celebrating everything from shrimp and petroleum (Morgan City, Louisiana), crawfish (Breaux Bridge, Louisiana), moonshine whiskey (Climax, Virginia), and rhodo-dendrons (Mentone, Alabama), to "slugburgers" (Corinth, Mississippi), fish stock (Punta Gorda, Florida), rat-tlesnakes (Claxton, Georgia), water-melon (Pageland, South Carolina), and even ramps, a rather pungent-smelling wild garlic (southwest Virginia, and throughout the Appalachian region). Festivals often commemorate local he-roes or significant local historical events. For example, there are festivals honoring Davy Crockett, Doc Watson, Elvis Presley, and Daniel Boone. Often the featured subjects of these festivals prove incidental to the nature of the events. Most often, these community festivals center on music, dancing, eat-ing, drinking, and good old community camaraderie.

Numerous festivals unique to the South have become major tourist at-tractions, and have come to influence (for better or worse) how the region is perceived and understood by outsiders. For example, Mardi Gras in New Or-leans (and to a lesser extent in southwest Louisiana and Mobile, Alabama) has risen above the status of local folk cele-bration and now draws over 3 million revelers to the city each year. While many tourists tend to view Mardi Gras as the weekend and days leading up to "Fat Tuesday," many folk groups in New Orleans view Carnival as a year-round enterprise, as float preparations, costume-making, marching band prac-tice, and other activities become an organizing force in participants' lives. A unique embodiments of this level of commitment are the "Mardi Gras Indians"—black residents of New Or-leans who spend the better part of the year hand-sewing elaborate beaded and feathered "Indian suits" to wear each Mardi Gras, in honor of the Native American tribes that once gave shelter to maroon slaves.

The legendary pirate Gasparilla is the focus of a major celebration in Tampa, Florida. Photo c. 1940. Photo by Burgert Bros. Florida Photographic Collection.

Mardi Gras in New Orleans draws over 3 million revelers to the city each year. Pictured are Mardi Gras court costumes at the Mardi Gras of Imperial Calcasieu Museum, New Orleans, Louisiana. Louisiana Office of Tourism.

251

Along with these large- and small-scale community celebrations, there are countless festivals throughout the South that specifically highlight folklife and community-based aesthetic traditions. Annual events such as the Blue Ridge Festival in Ferrum, Virginia, the Storytelling Festival in Jonesboro, Tennessee, the Festival Acadiens in Lafayette, Louisiana, and many, many more serve to highlight, celebrate, and reinforce the myriad cultural folkways that make the South one of the most culturally vibrant regions of the country. A partial listing of these festivals, along with other sources for further exploration of southern folklore, is found in the Resource Guide.

RESOURCE GUIDE

Printed Sources

Ancelet, Barry Jean. *Cajun and Creole Folktales: The French Oral Tradition in South Lousiana*. New York: Garland Publishing, 1994.

Botkin, B. A. *A Treasury of Southern Folklore*. New York: Crown Publishers, 1949.

Dance, Daryl Cumber, ed. *From My People: 400 Years of African American Folklore*. New York: W. W. Norton, 2000.

Joyner, Charles. *Shared Traditions: Southern History and Folk Culture*. Urbana: University of Illinois Press, 1999.

Kinser, Sam. *Carnival, American Style: Mardi Gras at New Orleans and Mobile*. Chicago: University of Chicago Press, 1990.

Lindahl, Carl, ed. *Perspectives on the Jack Tales and Other North American Marchen*. Bloomington: Indiana University Press, 2001.

Solomon, Jack, ed. *Ghosts and Goosebumps: Ghost Stories, Tall Tales, and Superstitions from Alabama*. Athens: University of Georgia Press, 1994.

Toelken, Barre. *The Dynamics of Folklore*. Boston: Houghton Mifflin, 1979.

Videos/Films

Always for Pleasure. Les Blanc Productions, 1978. Color, 58 min. An intense insider's portrait of New Orleans street celebrations and unique cultural gumbo: Second-line parades, Mardi Gras, Jazz Fest. Features live music from Professor Longhair, the Wild Tchoupitoulas, the Neville Brothers, and more.

Being a Joines: A Life in the Brushy Mountains. Delaplane, VA: Davenport Films, 1976. 28 min. UNC/Tom Davenport film on social change and cultural traditions in the stories of Blanch and "Frail" Joines from western North Carolina.

Fixing to Tell about Jack. Whitesburg, KY: Appalshop Films, 1975. Color, 25 min. Elizabeth Barret made this wonderful film about legendary Jack tale teller Ray Hicks.

Gandy Dancers. 1994. 30 min. Maggie Holtzberg-Call and Barry Dornfeld film, with demonstrations and documentary footage of track lining and interviews with former railroad track crew men about the work songs and their social context.

The High Lonesome Sound. Berkeley, CA: Center for Media and Independent Living, 1963. B&W, 28 min. John Cohen film on Roscoe Holcomb, banjo picker and singer from Kentucky mining region, with Old Regular and Holiness church services, Bill Monroe concert, dances, etc.

Festivals

Festivals USA
http://www.festivalusa.com

Includes a comprehensive listing of many folk and music festivals throughout the South.

Traditional Arts Program Network
http://afsnet.org/tapnet

Official Web site of the Traditional Arts Programs Network. Includes links to state folk-life programs throughout the South, as well as regional and national programs.

Organizations, Museums, Special Collections

The American Folklife Center at the Library of Congress
101 Independence Ave. SE
Room LJ G-49
Thomas Jefferson Building
Washington, DC 20540-4610
http://www.loc.gov/folklife/afc.html

The collections in the center's Archive of Folk Culture include folk cultural material from all fifty states, as well as United States trusts, territories, and the District of Columbia. Most of these areas have been served by the American Folklife Center's cultural surveys, equipment loan program, publications, and other projects. There are numerous collections of WPA fieldwork, primarily conducted in the South.

American Routes
Public Radio International
Amroutes@aol.com
http://www.americanroutes.com/

Hosted by Nick Spitzer from New Orleans, American Routes is a radio program from Public Radio International that covers the vast American musical landscape, spanning genres and eras from Aretha Franklin to George Jones, Los Lobos to Howlin' Wolf, Count Basie to Beck, Gershwin to Dylan, Armstrong to Marsalis, a cappella to zydeco. It often focuses on southern music.

The Southern Council for Folk Culture
512 S. Ellison Lane
Waynesboro, VA 22980
voicemail: (540) 941-1168

Founded in 1997, this is a private, nonprofit educational organization dedicated to the documentation and presentation of traditional, folk, and ethnic expressive culture (music, dance, narrative, worship, folklife), especially those vernacular artists and art forms found in the contemporary American South.

Alabama

The Alabama Center for Traditional Culture
410 North Hull Street
Montgomery, AL 36104
(334) 242-3601
fax: (334) 269-9098
http://www.arts.state.al.us/actc/index-folkarts-actc.html

Alabama Folklife Association
Alabama Center for Traditional Culture
410 North Hull Street
Montgomery, AL 36104
http://alabamafolklife.org

Alabama Folklife Program
Alabama State Council on the Arts
201 Monroe Street
Montgomery, AL 36104
(334) 242-4076, ext. 225
fax: (334) 240-3269
http://www.arts.state.al.us/folklife/folklife.htm

The Alabama Folklife Recording Series produced on the Alabama Traditions label includes documentary recordings that have been produced with public support from the Alabama State Council on the Arts.

Arkansas

Annual World Championship Duck Calling Contest and Wings over the Prairie Festival
Downtown Stuttgart
(800) 810-2241
http://www.stuttgartarkansas.com.

Celebrate the last weekend in November with one of the oldest festivals in the state. Duck calling contest and duck gumbo cook-off with arts and crafts, carnival and midway, 10K race, sportsmen's dinner/dance.

Arkansas Arts Council
232 Center Street, Suite 1500-Tower Building
Little Rock, AR 72201
(501) 324-9148
fax: (501) 324-9154
http://www.arkansasarts.com/

The Department of Arkansas Heritage
1500 Tower Building
323 Center Street
Little Rock, AR 72201
(501) 324-9150
http://www.arkansasheritage.com/

Since 1975, the Department of Arkansas Heritage has been promoting and coordinating the discovery, preservation, and presentation of Arkansas's natural and cultural resources.

Ozark Folk Center
Mountain View, AR 72569
(501) 269-8102
http://www.ozarkfolkcenter.com/

Arkansas' Ozark Folk Center State Park is America's only facility that works at preserving the Ozark heritage and presenting it in such an entertaining way. Tap your toes to mountain music. See blacksmithing, pottery making, and over eighteen other pioneer skills and crafts. Learn to play the dulcimer or autoharp, to jig dance, or to grow an organic herb garden. Design your own workshop for the study of the traditional crafts demonstrated here.

Florida

Florida Folklife Program/Bureau of Historic Preservation
500 South Bronough Street
Tallahassee, FL 32399-0250
(850) 245-6333
(800) 847-7278
fax: (850) 245-6437
http://dhr.dos.state.fl.us/folklife/index.html

The Florida Folklife Program, a component of the Florida Department of State's Division of Historical Resources, documents and presents the folklife, folklore, and folk arts of the state. Its full-time staff of professional folklorists and administrative support personnel form a base in the Bureau of Historic Preservation. The Florida Folklife Program coordinates a wide range of activities and projects designed to increase the awareness of Floridians and visitors alike about the state's traditional culture.

Folklife Days
500 S. Bronough Street
Tallahassee, FL 32399-0250
http://dhr.dos.state.fl.us/folklife/rfd.html

Folklife Days brings local folklife demonstrations to thousands of schoolchildren through two host organizations each year. During this three-day event in Tallahassee in late November, folk artists demonstrate traditional crafts, occupations, and leisure activities. Teachers are provided with educational materials to incorporate the information into classroom learning.

Historical Museum of Southern Florida
101 West Flagler Street
Miami, FL 33130
(305) 375-1492
fax: (305) 274-5390
http://www.historical-museum.org/folklife/folkllife.htm

Stephen Foster State Folk Culture Center
Florida Park Service
White Springs, FL 32096
(386) 397-2733
http://www.floridastateparks.org/stephenfoster

This unique state park is named in honor of Stephen Foster, the nineteenth-century composer whose tunes for the family parlor and traveling minstrel show remain American favorites. His composition "Old Folks at Home" immortalized the Suwannee River. Since 1935 it has also been Florida's state song.

Georgia

Chattahoochee Folklife Project
P.O. Box 553
Bueno Vista, GA 31803-0553
(229) 649-6957
http://www.hcc-al-ga.org

The Chattahoochee Folklife Project is an extended effort to build an ongoing and viable program of folklife activities and research in the region. The project is sponsored by the Historic Chattahoochee Commission, a bistate agency serving valley counties in both

8。。。

Alabama and Georgia. A major component of the commission's work is the development of programs and publications that focus on the distinctive nature of the region and its traditional culture and history.

Georgia Folklife Program, Georgia Council for the Arts
260 14th Street, N.W., Suite 401
Atlanta, GA 30318-5360
(404) 685-2786
fax: (404) 685-2788
http://www.gaarts.org/grants_programs/folklife/

The Georgia Folklife Program actively documents, supports, preserves, and educates the public about Georgia's traditional folk culture.

South Georgia Folklife Project
315 Continuing Education Bldg.
Valdosta State University
Valdosta, GA 31698
(229) 293-6310
fax: (229) 293-6387
http://www.valdosta.edu/music/SGFP

The South Georgia Folklife Project is a collaboration between the College of the Arts at Valdosta State University and the Georgia Council for the Arts Folklife Program to identify, document, encourage, and present through public programs the traditional arts and folklife of South Georgia.

Kentucky

Appalshop
91 Madison Avenue
Whitesburg, Kentucky 41858
(606) 633-0108
fax: (606) 633-1009
http://www.appalshop.org

Appalshop is a nonprofit, multidisciplinary cultural center located in the Appalachian coalfields of eastern Kentucky. Appalshop's mission is to document, disseminate, and revitalize the lasting traditions and contemporary creativity of Appalachia; to tell stories the commercial cultural industries won't tell, challenging stereotypes with Appalachian voices and visions; to support communities' efforts to achieve justice and equity and solve their own problems in their own ways; to celebrate cultural diversity as a positive social value; and to participate in regional, national, and global dialogue toward these ends. Appalshop recently produced a documentary film about Appalachian storyteller Ray Hicks entitled *Fixing to Tell about Jack*.

Kentucky Folklife Festival
Frankfort, Kentucky
(same contact as below)
http://history.ky.gov/Programs/Folklife/Kentucky_Folklife_Festival_03.htm

The Kentucky Folklife Festival takes place in September and showcases music, dance, crafts, games, food, storytelling, and other forms of cultural expression.

Kentucky Folklife Program
100 West Broadway

Frankfort, KY 40601
(502) 564-1792
toll free: (877) 444-7867
fax: (502) 564-0475
http://history.ky.gov/Programs/Folklife/index.htm

The mission of the Kentucky Folklife Program is to identify, document, and conserve the state's diverse cultural traditions, generally referred to as folklife. An interagency program of the Kentucky Historical Society and the Kentucky Arts Council, the Kentucky Folklife Program strives to increase awareness of the state's folklife through diverse cultural programming.

Louisiana

Folklife in Louisiana/Louisiana Division of the Arts Folklife Program
P.O. Box 44247
Baton Rouge, LA 70804
(225) 342-8180
fax: (225) 342-8173
http://www.louisianafolklife.org/

The Louisiana Folklife Program, within the Division of the Arts, is designed to identify, document, conserve, and present the folk cultural resources of Louisiana. Folklife includes living traditions learned informally over time within ethnic, regional, occupational, and family groups.

Louisiana Folklife Center
Northwestern State University
Box 3663, NSU
Natchitoches, LA 71497
(318) 357-4332

Louisiana Folklife Festival
1800 Riverside Drive
Monroe, LA 71201
(318) 324-1665
fax: (318) 324-1665
Luster@aol.com
http://www.louisianafolklifefest.org

The Louisiana Folklife Festival highlights the continuing work of the Louisiana Folklife Program within the Louisiana Division of the Arts, Department of Culture, Recreation, and Tourism in order to document, preserve, and promote Louisiana's folk culture resources. Taking place each year during the second weekend of September in Monroe, Louisiana, the festival celebrates Louisiana heritage derived from many countries, cultures, and ethnic groups.

Louisiana Voices, Folklife in Education Project
715 South Eugene Street
Baton Rouge, LA 70806
(225) 387-6535
http://www.louisianavoices.org

Louisiana Voices is a pioneering online education guide that provides rich teaching resources on Louisiana folk and traditional arts and culture, offering an academically sound basis for both multicultural and technology education.

New Orleans Jazz & Heritage Festival
1205 North Rampart
New Orleans, LA 70116
(504) 522-4786
folklife@nojazzfest.com
http://www.nojazzfest.com

The New Orleans Jazz & Heritage Festival, aka Jazz Fest, is an eleven-day cultural feast in which thousands of musicians, storytellers, cooks, and craftspeople welcome 500,000 visitors each year during the last weekend in April and the first weekend in May.

Mississippi

Center for the Study of Southern Culture
University of Mississippi
University, MS 38677
http://www.olemiss.edu/depts/south/

Over the past twenty years the Center for the Study of Southern Culture at the University of Mississippi has become a focal point for innovative education and research on the American South. The center was founded in 1977 after two years of planning by a campus-wide committee of faculty and administrators who saw its potential for strengthening the university's instructional program in the humanities, promoting scholarship on every aspect of southern culture, and encouraging public understanding of the South through publications, media productions, lectures, performances, and exhibitions. By almost any standard the center has far surpassed the goals of its founders.

Mississippi Arts Commission Heritage Program
239 N. Lamar St., Suite 207
Jackson, Mississippi 39201
(601) 359-6030
fax: (601) 359-6008
http://www.arts.state.ms.us/crossroads

The Mississippi Arts Commission Heritage Program Crossroads of the Heart is an online exhibit of Mississippi traditional culture including Teacher's Guide and Resource Guide. From the sands of the Mississippi Gulf coast to the flat, fertile land of the Delta, from the forests of the Piney Woods to the foothills of the Appalachians, Mississippians express their heritage and soul through creativity and tradition.

North Carolina

Center for Documentary Studies
1317 West Pettigrew Street
Lyndhurst House
Duke University
Durham, NC 27705
(919) 660-3610
fax: (919) 681-7600
http://cds.aas.duke.edu/

The Center for Documentary Studies (CDS), an interdisciplinary educational organization affiliated with Duke University, is dedicated to advancing documentary work that combines experience and creativity with education and community life. Founded in 1989, CDS connects the arts and humanities to fieldwork, drawing upon photography, filmmaking, oral history, folklore, and writing as catalysts for education and change.

258

North Carolina Arts Council, Folklife Program
Department of Cultural Resources
Raleigh, NC 27601-2807
fax: (919) 715-5406
http://www.ncarts.org/arts_folklife.cfm

The Folklife Program of the N.C. Arts Council documents, promotes, and celebrates the rich traditional culture of North Carolina in a number of ways, including commercial recordings, books, videos, cassettes, slides, and photographs, as well as programs like the N.C. Folk Heritage Awards. Folklife also collects scholarly journals and newsletters from around the region concerning folk culture.

North Carolina Folklore Society
c/o Box 726
Fountain, NC 27829
http://www.ecu.edu/ncfolk/

Founded in 1913, the North Carolina Folklore Society promotes the appreciation and study of North Carolina's folklife. In its early years, members guided by Frank C. Brown of Duke University collected songs, stories, customs, and superstitions for the Frank C. Brown Collection of North Carolina Folklore, the most extensive collection of a state's folklore. Each spring the society holds its annual meeting/conference, which includes panels, discussions, lectures and slide talks, video screenings, traditional music performances, and the presentation of society awards.

South Carolina

McKissick Museum
University of South Carolina
Columbia, SC 29208
(803) 777-2515
fax: (803) 777-2829
http://www.cla.sc.edu/mcks/folklife/index.htm

McKissick's Folklife Resource Center was created in 1985 as a repository for fieldnotes, photographs, slides, audio tapes, video tapes, albums, publications, and other information of value to southern folklife scholars and interested members of the general public. The center is also a repository for materials generated by independent researchers, and maintains vertical files on South Carolina folk artists, as well as on folk arts related organizations in and outside the state. The Folklife Resource Center also produces the Fall Folklife Festival annually.

South Carolina Arts Commission, Folklife and Traditional Arts
1800 Gervais Street
Columbia, SC 29201
(803) 734-8697
fax: (803) 734-8526
cstinson@arts.state.sc.us
http://www.state.sc.us/arts/grants/organizations/folklife.htm

Tennessee

Arts Center of Cannon County
P.O. Box 111
Woodbury, TN 37190
(615) 563-2787 or (800) 235-9073

fax: (615) 563-2788
http://www.cannonartsctr.org

The Arts Center of Cannon County serves over 100 craft artists, 400 performing artists, and more than 19,000 students annually in its facility located in Woodbury, Tennessee.

Center for Popular Music, Middle Tennessee State University
Murfreesboro, TN 37132
(615) 898-2449
http://popmusic.mtsu.edu/

The Center for Popular Music is an archive and research center devoted to the study of American popular music from the pre-Revolutionary era to the present. It was established in 1985 as one of the sixteen Centers of Excellence at universities in the Tennessee Board of Regents system.

Center for Southern Folklore
130 Beale Street, P.O. Box 226
Memphis, TN 38101-0226
(901) 525-3655
http://www.southernfolklore.com/

Through its research and interpretive programs, the Center for Southern Folklore has enriched the understanding of the people and traditions of the South for over thirty years. The center uses public events, performances, exhibits, and media to creatively present folk culture to audiences of all ages. The Center for Southern Folklore produces the Memphis Music and Heritage Festival each Labor Day weekend.

Tennessee Arts Commission, Folklife Program
401 Charlotte Avenue
Nashville, TN 37243-0780
(615) 532-9795
fax: (615) 714-8559
robert.cogswell@state.tn.us
http://www.arts.state.tn.us

Virginia

Blue Ridge Institute and Museum
Ferrum College
Ferrum, VA 24088
(540) 365-4416
http://www.blueridgeinstitute.org

For more than two decades Ferrum College's Blue Ridge Institute and Museum has documented, interpreted, and presented the traditional culture of the Blue Ridge and its people. Designated the State Center for Blue Ridge Folklore by the Virginia General Assembly in 1986, the institute promotes an understanding of regional folklore past and present for all ages.

The Virginia Folklife Program
Virginia Foundation for the Humanities
145 Ednam Drive
Charlottesville, VA 22901-3207
(434) 243-5523
fax: (434) 296-4714
http://www.virginiafolklife.org

From the bluegrass gatherings of Galax to the ceremonial Hmong dances of Arlington, from the intricately carved snake sticks of the Shenandoah to the duck decoys of the Eastern Shore, the forms of folklife in Virginia are as varied as the communities that create them. Whether sung or told, hand-crafted or performed, a group's folklife refers to those "arts of everyday life" that signify a tangible sense of traditional knowledge, communal belonging, and shared identity. Folklife is in the songs we sing, the stories we tell, the stews we cook, and the crafts we create. Folkways are not simply surviving relics of past ways, but are constantly evolving, given new life and cultural relevance as they engage new tradition bearers.

The Virginia Folklore Society
University of Virginia
Department of English
219 Bryan Hall
P.O. Box 400121
Charlottesville, VA 22904-4121
http://www.virginia.edu/~vafolk/

Founded on April 17, 1913, the Virginia Folklore Society is one of the oldest state folklore societies in the country. The Virginia Folklore Society serves a broadly based public interest in folklore and tradition and includes among its members academic and public sector folklorists, teachers, students, and interested lay and professional people having a wide range of backgrounds and experience. It is the host of the Kevin Barry Perdue Archive of Traditional Culture, one of the finest archives of Virginia and southern folklore.

FOOD

*Susan Tucker and
Sharon Stallworth Nossiter*

If Southerners from vastly different backgrounds meet, it is quite safe to assume that food will be a topic that gives them common ground. The overwhelmingly agricultural and rural past of the region; the feeling of a citizenry set apart by the legacies of slavery and the Civil War; the long years of isolation from modernity as a result of poverty and other problems; and the dishes held in common by their reliance on cornmeal, greens, and pork—all tie the South together.

Food, to southerners, tells of a past that draws from the Americas, Africa, and Europe; the complication of hunger amid plenty; distinct geographic areas covering what are generally called the Upper South (Virginia, North Carolina, Kentucky, and parts of Tennessee) and the Deep South (South Carolina, Georgia, Florida, Mississippi, Alabama, Louisiana, Arkansas, and parts of Tennessee); and ethnic groups who have shaped the region's culinary pride. In short, the southern table serves a rich meal of social and economic history, distinctive and delicious foods, and connections among people.

NATIVE AMERICAN FOOD IN THE SOUTH

The first settlers in the area, the Native Americans, ate a richly diverse diet. For example, the Seminoles in Florida made extensive use of over 120 plants as food. The Creeks, Chickasaws, Choctaws, and Cherokees of Tennessee and Alabama grew crops of corn, beans, pumpkins, squash, sweet potatoes, and melons.[1]

Daily fare, for many, was a pudding of ground roots, fish, and wild game. All southeastern Native Americans gathered sunflowers, hickory nuts, acorns, pecans, and other nuts for food, drinks, and oils. From sassafras leaves they made medicine, tea, and beer. Among the fruits they gathered, persimmon was the most important, but they also picked and cooked with grapes, cherries, papaws, tart crab apples, plums, prickly pears, maypops, and berries. These fruits were eaten raw, cooked, or dried; they became drinks, sauces, and condiments as well.

Deer, squirrels, rabbits, opossum, bears, wild turkey, grouse, quail, ducks, geese, and turtle (boiled or smoked) provided the meat in Native American diets. Bear was even more important for its fat, which provided an essential cooking oil. Bison and buffalo were also important meats, though they became rather rare by the 1700s in the Southeast. Coastal Native Americans added other protein sources such as crab, clams, oysters, and crawfish.

Most important, as in all the Americas, the southeastern Native Americans grew and used corn. One of the principal dishes of the Natchez of Mississippi and Louisiana, for example, was scorched corn—ground, then burned in ashes until it was red, then pounded with dried beans. The Natchez also ate *boota copassa*, a finely ground, parched green corn, what the French explorers called "cold meal" (later, *coush-coush*, a term they borrowed from the Africans). Similarly, all southeastern Indians made a ceremonial hominy corn drink. The Choctaws served this drink, called *tan fula*, in a horn-shaped spoon, which awaited guests on a small wooden platform.[2]

The centrality of corn is apparent when one looks at Native American names of the calendar and feast days. For the Natchez, the third moon (May and the time of planting) was Little Corn; the seventh moon (August, the time of harvest) was Great Corn; and the eleventh moon (January, when corn would be reaching short supply) was Cold Meal, the same name the French carried with them in their accounts, and probably the same food they carried in their traveling satchels. For the Choctaws, the Great Green Corn Dance in early summer was the biggest celebration of the year.

THE COLONIAL SOUTH

Studies of food in the colonial South begin in Florida and Alabama in the early 1500s with the explorations of Ponce de Léon, Panfilo de Narvaez, Hernando de Soto, and Tristan de Luna, and in Virginia in the late 1500s with Sir Walter Raleigh's first expedition. The dual forces of plenty and hunger, so symbolic of the South until the present day, began in these early European glimpses. The Spanish left pigs, oranges, lemons, other tropical fruit, and peaches across the landscape.

The English left habits of the table and telling descriptions of foodstuffs. From the early 1600s onward, British accounts described the land in Virginia and North Carolina as temperate and rich, capable of offering meals of wild boar, venison, and other meats as excellent as any that could be had in England. The soil of Virginia was praised as the most fruitful in the world. Yet, for these settlers, having enough food here would be a very difficult undertaking, and many would starve.

Though not without its own period of great hunger, the 1607 Jamestown settlement was a lasting one because it could feed its inhabitants. Here colonists learned from earlier failures about the necessity of relying on the expertise of the Native Americans. They also began with adequate food from England, bringing and importing pigs, ale, ciders, cattle, and other foodstuffs.

In 1619 the first group of some twenty slaves arrived on a Dutch ship. With them and the millions more Africans who followed came foodstuffs, knowledge, and skills with okra, plantains, sweet potatoes and yams, rice, and other fruits, vegetables, and legumes that would form the bedrock of African American cooking traditions. Discussed more fully below in terms of signature dishes, African American cooking especially made use of those parts of the pig spurned by well-to-do whites.

Other English and French colonial settlements on the Gulf coast and in South Carolina show the same basic history as that of the Virginia colonists—the initial reliance on European food imports, the necessity of adopting Native American foods and skills, and the introduction of new foods and cooking styles from Africa. Most valued among imports would have been flour, since the wet climate precluded raising much wheat. Folk legends along the Gulf coast recount stories of women who staged "petticoat" rebellions to protest their longing for wheat flour. To the rescue, during a 1722 protest in New Orleans, a Madame Langlois organized a cooking school to teach young French women how to make cornmeal, hominy grits, and succotash—dishes she learned from the Native Americans. Others like her found help from the Africans, who greatly expanded the food the Southeast could eat and export. Rice, for example, allowed the colonies to feed themselves and made South Carolina one of the richest areas.

The great mix of colonial culinary traditions included others as well: the Scotch-Irish in the Upper South and Georgia, French Huguenots in South Carolina, the French fur traders and French settlers working in Kentucky, and the Acadians who came to Louisiana from Canada. As will be shown in various sections below, all brought lasting culinary traditions.

CULINARY RICHNESS

The era of the plantation South reached its peak in the 1850s, and its culinary history has been romantically told in cookbooks, travel accounts, and other sources. But this period also tells another story, that of the culinary history of the non-elite—the small farmers and slaves—and the trade in foodstuffs between these various groups and between distant points within and outside the South.

The often mythic plantation South offered the best of all native and imported foods. For example, a dinner served at Monticello might have begun with consommé julienne and continued with a Virginia ham, corn pudding, celery with almonds, scalloped tomatoes, puréed cymlings, boeuf à la daube, damson plum preserves, Jerusalem artichoke pickles, and a wild turkey. Almost all of the ingredients would have been grown or raised on the plantation. The wines, however, would have been French.

The planters visited in the cities and mingled their culinary ways with the leisurely lifestyles of people in New Orleans, Savannah, Charleston, Mobile, and other old cities. Here, the families of merchants and traders ate plentifully from such dishes as shrimp soup and shrimp croquettes, shrimp-stuffed peppers, creamed oysters, redfish, court bouillon, turtle stew, sautéed artichokes, and Huguenot torte.

The port cities had great access to food, but in all cities and many towns food soon began to be sold at established markets. Travelers wrote of the generosity with which they were seated at southern tables and campfires, and of the colorful calls of fruit and vegetable vendors. This was the picture presented to the world, but this South was made possible only by an ever-growing population of slaves. Their labor produced tobacco, cotton, rice, and sugar which, in turn, enabled the planters and merchants to purchase food for their well-provided tables.

Thomas Jefferson

Well known to all Americans, Thomas Jefferson (1743–1826) holds a special place in the history of southern food. The reach of his interests extends to this day. Even his failures offer southerners the chance to look at large issues of abundance and want in our democracy, and lesser issues such as how to grow grapes in a wet climate.

Called America's first gourmet, Jefferson began a lifelong interest in agriculture in his boyhood home, Shadwell. In his early twenties, he began to keep notes in a *Garden Book* that would extend over half a century. This and his *Farm Book* (1774–1822) are still used today by readers wishing to learn more about food in Virginia. As a young student at William and Mary, he explored further a love of science but chose to study law and philosophy. Despite this decision, his practical inventions concerned with growing and serving food were many. These included the dumbwaiter, the lazy Susan, and new designs for a pump within an icehouse and for the moldboard plow.

In the beloved home of his adulthood, Monticello, Jefferson directed the labor of slaves in growing a bounty of fruits and vegetables. He was among the first white Americans to cultivate peanuts, pecans, eggplants, broccoli, endives, and tomatoes. Although he himself was primarily a vegetarian, he introduced the first broad-tailed Merino sheep and Calcutta hogs to America. He built vineyards of grapes, and orchards of orange, apple, cherry, peach, plum, chestnut, and mulberry trees.

As ambassador to France from 1785 to 1789, he delved further into culinary matters. For both its architecture and its symbolic centrality to French bread, he loved especially the municipal grain market in Paris. From his travels within the French countryside, he wrote enthusiastically of the olives of Provence, the gooseberries at Beaujolais, the almonds of Lyons, and other delights. He returned from France with much wine, a French cook, and an even greater interest in agriculture and food.

In Monticello and in the White House, he entertained lavishly, continued to write of his farming experiments, and charted the course of blending the best native ingredients with the methods of French cooking. He served as wine advisor to Washington, Adams, Madison, and Monroe, and during his own presidency brought a French chef to the White House. He popularized the drinking of Champagne, and himself brought some 20,000 bottles of wine to the White House. Here, he also served the first french fries and offered for dessert something that today is called Baked Alaska.

Of course, too, he secured for the United States the Mississippi River and the large territory that would become fourteen states, many of them our most important wheat-producing areas. As he wrote about this purchase, "Let the land rejoice for you have bought Louisiana for a song."

The rest of the South, the enslaved themselves and the poor, did not eat so well. On one plantation, for example, slaves were allotted meal, rice, vegetables, salt, molasses, some sort of pork, and occasionally fish and coffee. On some plantations, such rations were adequate. Or, where law or custom allowed, slaves were allowed time to hunt, fish, or grow their own vegetables to supplement the allocations of staples. On other plantations, however, the slaves' rations would not have met the needs of people engaged in heavy labor, and they very infrequently had time to grow or hunt for supplementary food. For poor whites, especially those who lived in mountainous areas with poor soil, cornmeal formed the core of the diet, with wild game, vegetables, and beans adding the only variety.

Scholars agree, however, that for some the supply of food was probably greater than what they had known in Africa or Europe. An often told account revolves around a newly arrived Irishman of the 1850s who was chided for lying when he wrote home that he ate meat two times a day. He responded that his lie was intentional: no one in Ireland would believe him if he told the truth—that he ate meat three times a day.[3]

In addition, the food at hand was often shared. Hospitality, often written about in terms of the plantation owners, was even more common among the less fortunate. Church picnics and other communal feasts gave the chance to share the first return of fishermen and hunters. The first days of cold weather became the occasion for large families to hold hog killings, and for each family to take home meat for the winter.

The Upper South and increasingly all the area east of the Mississippi River benefited also from the expansion of trade. More and more food would become known and tasted during the period 1776–1860. Early in the days of the new republic, the nation acquired the port of New Orleans and the Mississippi River. After this, vegetables and flour from the North could be brought up river in autumn and winter. Steamboats transported barrels of oysters for holidays to places like Memphis and Louisville, as well as more commonplace food to all points. The South's production of virtually all the nation's rice, much of its sugar, and almost half its supply of corn and pork meant that interior roads had to be built and maintained as well.

Ideas about food also passed between communities on such routes. Slaves from plantations and poor whites repeated recipes as they peddled extra produce in towns and cities. And in new hotels, taverns, and inns, travelers tasted and talked of coffee, tea, chocolate, and alcoholic beverages.

CULINARY ISOLATION

Much of the opulence of plantation tables vanished after the Civil War, but also changed were the eating habits of all southerners. After the war, only sugar remained a viable food crop, and the shipping trade itself diminished as the railroads began to ship more products east and west. Subsistence farmers often were not ready for, or able to shift to, the market economy that had descended upon the South. Sharecroppers working with tobacco and cotton had little time for their own gardens, even less time for putting foods away for winter, usually no money before crops were harvested, and often no place to buy food but plantation stores. The South in the years between the Civil War and World War II lagged far behind the rest of the United States: it had fewer roads, railroads, automobiles, and chances for improvements such as running water and electricity. Public education was also inadequate.

It was within this environment that hunger became part of the daily lives of many southerners. The steady diet of the poor remained one of salt meat, cornbread, syrup or sorghum, and some sweet potatoes. Tooth decay, growth retardation in children, and even rickets were ever-present problems. Clay eaters, answering both the call of hunger and the craving for iron, were well known; even today one can find people who remember eating clay. A tendency to indolence or, less gravely, slowness—both hallmarks of the region's reputation—rested on malnutrition.

Thus, on a national level, the South became the launching ground for many federal food programs. The establishment of land grant colleges in the late nineteenth and early twentieth centuries to teach agriculture brought some of the first positive changes to the poorly fed South. The Smith-Laver Act of 1914 (named for two southern congressmen, Hoke Smith of Georgia and A. F. Lever of South Carolina) furthered the work of county extension agents and Farm Bureau agents. As community-based teachers, these agents brought to countless homes the chance for education in agriculture, home economics, and other practical subjects. Although southerners often claimed that the Depression was hardly noticed in their already poverty-stricken states, events in Mississippi provided the impetus for government aid to the hungry. To keep prices from falling, 6 million young pigs slaughtered in the state in 1933 were carried to a dump instead of being sold as food. The resulting outrage propelled the Roosevelt administration to establish a federal relief program.[4]

In this period, too, the great incidence of pellagra in the South became the impetus for adding nutrients to food. Caused by a deficiency in tryptophan and niacin, neither of which is found in cornmeal, pellagra—"the plague of the polenta eaters"—was always a disease of the poor. Characterized by scabs on the skin, with progressively worsening conditions leading to death, pellagra is cured by the seemingly simple addition of milk or meat to the diet—but not all southerners had money to buy such products. An essential part of the story of food in the South, then, is the work of Joseph Goldberger (1874–1929) and others who waged a campaign to have niacin added to flour, cornmeal, and other foods, something achieved uniformly by the mid-1940s.

Other problems of poverty and diet were more pronounced in the South than in other regions, and remain so. Writers who eloquently noted the malnutrition of southern children and politicians who launched the War on Poverty in the 1960s often began their work in Mississippi, Alabama, and Appalachia. Even today, food stamp use in all southern states except Virginia exceeds the average usage figures for other states. High blood pressure, heart disease, and other health problems related to diet continue to plague southerners, more so than other Americans.

Within this environment, the southern table found itself the testing ground for communal resourcefulness, for the ability to do much with little and the willingness to offer what was at hand to others. To be sure, this was common in other parts in the United States, but in the South the communal gathering around food became a source of pride, a powerful reiteration of southern hospitality. Within this tradition, the families of sharecroppers waited eagerly for trips to town and for the coming of the rolling stores—wagons and vans sent by local, and sometimes national, stores—where they might buy or trade eggs for flour to make biscuits for a special meal. Within this tradition, country-bred southerners moved to nearby cities or the industrial North, and from newly found jobs and lives, provided money to feed those remaining at home. Within this tradition, southern food—its memory and its recipes—moved away from and back to the South. In countless reminiscences, the special summer meals of fried chicken, green beans, creamed corn, and peach pie are remembered in terms of how mothers, fathers, aunts, and uncles—some at "home" only for a few days—planned for a day of feasting. The isolation the South felt from other more prosperous areas of the country and the isolation many of its migrating people felt from their families made the celebration of foods from home all the more important.

DAYS OF REST, HOLIDAYS, AND SPECIAL OCCASIONS

Until the mid-twentieth century, the rural South's working, resting, and eating schedules were governed directly and indirectly by habits somewhat unique to the region. Sunup to sundown schedules for nine months of the year were the norm for farmers and sharecroppers. Their needs spilled over into towns, where stores closed on Wednesday or Thursday afternoon for a half-day of rest. Saturday, when stores were open all day, was the day to shop for groceries.

Most people ate an early breakfast, their biggest meal in the middle of the day, and a light supper. The workforce population and segregation laws affected who ate where and when. For example, since 88 percent of all African American women who worked outside the home during the early 1900s were domestic workers, their schedules (and cooking) influenced the eating habits of their own families and those of their employers. The typical schedule for a domestic worker was daily, with Thursdays and every other Sunday off. Thus, on Thursday night, dinner in many homes was different than on other nights.

Segregation laws governed who could eat in what restaurants until the 1960s. Custom, for a long while afterwards, also dictated who served at tables. Restaurant signs noting ownership by a private club were, for the most part, reactions to segregation or to its demise.

In the summer, at the end of harvests, African Americans and whites alike had picnics and church suppers featuring beloved tomatoes, salads of Vidalia onions, peaches baked every sort of way, and other delicacies not seen at other times of the year. In the late fall most families held some sort of shared hog-killing.

Christmas and New Year's Day called for special dishes and beverages. In addition to oranges, traditional Christmas fare, past and present, has included egg nog (not uniquely southern but often given prominence), the spiced round beef most well known in Tennessee (made from a beef roast that has been shot through with pork fat), syllabub (described in the sweets section), and charlotte russe. The latter is made with a Bavarian cream or a blancmange poured into a mold lined with ladyfingers. Homemade lemon curd is a popular gift item.

New Year's Day is always celebrated with

Oranges at Christmas

The most southern of Christmas foods are oranges and orange-based candies and desserts. Harvested on the Gulf coast and in Florida in late autumn, oranges were remembered as Christmas gifts by former slaves interviewed in the 1930s. Candied orange peel (first popularized in 1847 in Sarah Rutledge's cookbook) was, and continues to be, a holiday treat. Southern children also continue to find an orange in their stockings on Christmas morning. Finally, there is ambrosia on the Christmas Eve table. Concocted of layers of sliced oranges, shredded coconut, sugar, and sometimes wine, ambrosia has been popular since colonial times.

Holiday dining at Brennan's (1946), a grand New Orleans restaurant. Courtesy Louisiana Office of Tourism.

black-eyed peas, said to bring good luck for the year and to symbolize copper coins. According to some writers, the turnip greens served alongside the peas symbolize folded green money.

January 6, the day of the Three Kings or Epiphany, is celebrated in Louisiana and some places along the Gulf coast with a king cake. These are brioche-like breads, baked in a ring mold and decorated with purple, gold, and green sugar. A small ring, bean, or baby (now made of plastic) is hidden in the cake, and the person who wins the charm must buy the next cake.

Other holidays celebrated in the South—Easter, July the Fourth, Juneteenth, Labor Day, and Thanksgiving—follow national customs. Easter is one of the few times that southerners eat lamb or mutton, for example. July the Fourth is celebrated with traditional barbecue and potato salad dishes common to the rest of the country, though buttermilk ice cream is special to the South on this day. Juneteenth, with its strawberry sodas and its barbecue, though more recently taken up in the South than in Texas, nevertheless follows customs established there. Labor Day has the last plenty of summer, and Thanksgiving, turkey and pumpkin pie. One difference at Thanksgiving is that many southerners do not serve mashed Irish potatoes, but, as in the past, rely upon sweet potato and rice dishes.

A holiday unique to Kentucky is Derby Day. Foods suggested for serving then are tea sandwiches with Benedictine spread (a seasoned cream cheese), ham and biscuits, mint juleps, Derby pie (pecans with bourbon and chocolate), and bourbon balls.

Funeral foods, taken by friends and neighbors to the house of the bereaved, are said to be the best southern food, though no standard dishes seem to exist.

For many southerners, Sunday dinner in the middle of the day meant and still means a time for family and friends. Chicken is a traditional Sunday entrée, biscuits are almost always served, and dinnertime is usually between one and three o'clock.

CLIMATE, GEOGRAPHY, AND ETHNIC GROUPS

The climate of the South has been generally advantageous for growing food. The growing season is hot and long—as long as nine months along the Gulf coast—and winters are neither long nor very cold. Fertile soils have given rise to successful crops of rice, sugar cane, citrus fruits, soybeans, peanuts, sweet potatoes, and other foodstuffs. Seafood from both the Atlantic Ocean and the Gulf of Mexico has always played an important role. In recent years, livestock, catfish, and crawfish have been added to the list of southern products.

Distinctive geographic areas have produced distinctive foods, including a number of regional specialties, discussed in detail below. To cooking traditions based on topography and climate were added the other great shapers of recipes—the people and the foods brought to the South from other places. None has been more important than the African influence. The four most important foods brought by the slaves were peanuts, okra, cowpeas, and sesame seeds—all palatable long after harvesting and also easily grown in the South.

In addition, the gifts of other ethnic groups can be found throughout the region. As noted above, Georgia and South Carolina grow the priceless peaches brought first by the Spanish. Florida remains famous for the other gift of the Spanish—oranges. In Louisiana, the mix of French, Spanish, African, and Native American traditions produced an entire cuisine. Later, Italians in Louisiana would bring a talent for making muffuletta sandwiches, stuffing artichokes, and cultivating strawberries.

CREOLE AND CAJUN FOODS

Mark Twain called the food of New Orleans "as delicious as the less criminal forms of sin." From its founding in 1718, New Orleans has been seen as a culinary island of sophistication and epicurean delight. Its port; founder Jean Baptiste Le Moyne, Sieur de Bienville's decision to bring German farmers to a nearby rural area to supply town dwellers with food; the willingness of the city's first French women to learn Native Americans dishes; the mixing of the French love of fine food, the Spanish affinity for spices, and the Africans' skill as cooks and bakers—all provided the basis for the early beginnings of this reputation.

The result was Creole cuisine—a style of cooking that relies on the use of rice, onions, celery, tomatoes, bell peppers (green peppers), green onions (instead of shallots), thyme, and bay leaf. Also key to any description of Creole food are okra; roux, a mixture of flour and fat carefully browned as a basis for many dishes; and delicate blends of seafood, sausages, spices, and other foods.

New Orleans specialties—all dating from the nineteenth century or earlier—include gumbo, which can be made some forty different ways, and jambalayas, probably based on the Spanish paella and made of rice cooked with ham, seafood, chicken, sausage, and tomatoes. Oysters are eaten raw or cooked in many ways. Café au lait is made with rich, dark coffee and often served with chicory to make it even stronger. Leftover bread becomes pain perdu or bread pudding with whiskey sauce. Leftover rice is incorporated into a breakfast fritter called calas.

Red beans and rice are a traditional Monday dish. Pralines—French-derived candies made from local pecans and brown sugar—are another specialty, though they can be found along the Gulf coast from Pensacola to Texas as well. Turtle soup and bouillabaisse are also early dishes that have remained somewhat important to Creole cuisine.

The country cousin to Creole food, Cajun food, is based around traditions brought to Louisiana by the Acadians who had been ousted by the British from Canada in the mid-1700s. Settling in the southern part of the state, the Cajuns developed a cuisine with a great reliance on game and seafood found in forests, swamps, and bayous. The Creoles often purchased their sausage from

New Orleans Restaurants

New Orleans is best known for its restaurants—the grand ones with international reputations, and the small ones where one can eat quite cheaply. Among the former are Antoine's (in existence since 1840), Galatoire's (1905), Arnaud's (1918), and Brennan's (1946). Some signature dishes of these restaurants are oysters Rockefeller, pompano en papillote, turtle soup, soufléed potatoes, bread puddings made in various ways, and bananas Foster. New additions to the list of internationally known restaurants are Susan Spicer's Bayona and Paul Prudhomme's K-Paul's Louisiana Kitchen.

Neighborhood restaurants in the city serve Creole tomatoes, shrimp remoulade, okra and tomatoes, mirlitons stuffed with crab, and red beans and rice, as well as the popular po'boy sandwiches and muffulettas. It is often said that one cannot eat badly in New Orleans.

Neighborhood restaurants in New Orleans are well known for Acadian-style food such as mirlitons stuffed with crab. Courtesy Louisiana Office of Tourism.

the Cajuns, who once a year had their boucheries. The two principal sausages are boudin and andouille. Creole sausage is made too, but it is not as spicy or smoky.

Both types of southern Louisiana home cooking rely heavily on local ingredients, and are cooked by rich and poor residents alike. Dishes not generally found in restaurants are daube glacée and Creole cream cheese, to name just two.

As in other parts of the United States, many other immigrants also influenced the cooking of the South. The Greeks, the Chinese, the Cubans, the Mexicans, the Vietnamese, the Poles and Slavs, and the Haitians have all added significant traditions in food preparation, restaurants, and the fishing industry. Atlanta today has the fastest growing Hispanic population in the country, and their cuisine can be found in many restaurants and all grocery stores. Too, almost every southern state has a few long-standing Greek restaurants, which specialize in steaks or seafood, and gave southerners their first taste of feta cheese. Chinese Americans have lived in Mississippi for over 100 years, and Chinese food is probably the best known of all Asian food. Jews arrived early along the eastern seaboard, in the port of New Orleans, and up through the rural areas of the Deep South; their traditions of noodle puddings, chicken soups, blinis, and pound cakes also seeped into southern cooking. To this mix, the Cubans have added a rich tradition of meat sandwiches and other dishes. Mexican foods are sold throughout the South, even in some very small towns. The Vietnamese of New Orleans, living on the west bank of the Mississippi River and in New Orleans East, have a colorful Saturday market, grocery stores that sell produce grown on the levees, and a number of highly rated restaurants. Other Asian populations also settled along the Mississippi and Alabama Gulf coasts where they have pursed traditional fishing interests. Poles, Austrians, Acadians, Croats, Serbs, and Slavs have also added to the seafood industry.

CULINARY PRIDE

Perhaps because of the combination of peoples, painfully lived periods of want, and rich traditions continually asserting themselves, southerners have always had a profound interest in their food. Even in the face of national food chains, changing demographics, poverty, and plenty, southern food is characterized by the retention of past habits. The region's food remains rooted in cornbread once a week for many people, even as it is recalled in the Krispy Kreme sign in New York City. Southern food remains on the table of the family reunion, even if one eats lean salads for most other meals. Finally, the fact that southerners of different races sit down together to eat is perhaps one of the most important markers of a changed society.

With all its diversity, southern food is a subject worthy of conversation, high and low. In the South, southern cookbooks remain the best sellers among all books, but cookbooks on southern cuisine also sell well outside the South. African American and poor white eating habits are studied by scholars in order to understand such topics as resistance, adaptation, and the market economy. Food festivals and agricultural fairs draw tens of thousands each year. These studies and events underlie the well-practiced southern folk art of food.

Meats

Pork

Southerners were hardly the first to make thorough use of the pig. Pork is the leading meat worldwide, the most economical, and the most widely used. But the South has earned its name as the Republic of Pork—the home of the first thirteen pigs, brought by Hernando de Soto in 1542 to an area near what is today Tampa; the site of many innovative uses of every part of the pig; and a place where the choice parts of the pig graced the tables of the wealthy, while the poor made do with the scraps. In the South, then, the pig becomes our country hams, ham hocks and salt pork for flavoring, pickled pigs' feet, pig ears and pig tails simmered together, brains

National Shrimp Festival scene in Gulf Shores, Alabama. Courtesy of the Alabama Bureau of Tourism & Travel. Photo by Grey Brennan.

scrambled with eggs, spareribs for barbecuing, chitterlings (the very well cleaned intestines), hog maw (the belly), hogshead cheese (souse), pork chops, sausages, and cracklings.

In the nineteenth century, the best hogs were fed with corn at least six weeks before they were killed. But according to Mississippian Kathy Starr, three to four weeks is enough. Starr gives fairly explicit instructions on butchering a hog in her 1989 book, *The Soul of Southern Cooking*: "shoot him, knock him in the head, or cut his throat," she writes, going on to describe blood-letting, boiling, and butchering.[5] Most people today buy their pork at the grocery store, although some are still fortunate enough to know countrymen who raise their own hogs and butcher them for hams and homemade sausage.

The most distinguished end for a pig is bound to be the country ham, as traditionally prepared in Virginia, Kentucky, and Tennessee. Its classic companions are, for formal occasions, the beaten biscuit, and, at more informal affairs such as breakfast, red-eye gravy.

Smithfield, Virginia, is the best-known source of southern-style country hams, and has been shipping them worldwide for more than 200 years. A Smithfield ham has been peanut-fed, salt-cured, smoked, and aged for at least six months. Country hams, a more generic term, have generally also been salt-cured and aged. Their creation is a lengthy process, for they are cured in dry salt for about five weeks, often smoked with smoldering hardwoods from two weeks to two months, and then hung up to age. The completion of this process yields a rich reddish-brown ham with a smoky aroma. Connoisseurs note that anything shorter than eight months has not been sufficient time to produce a country ham. The ham is then scrubbed clean of any salt and mold, soaked overnight, boiled slowly, and then, oftentimes, baked or glazed in the oven with anything from pineapples and cloves to peanut butter and brown sugar.

There is a certain etiquette in eating such a ham, and writers such as Marjorie Kinnan Rawlings have noted the delicacy of small bites. Historians tell of hams used for centerpieces, and advertisements for country hams often have pigs themselves singing about their desire to be such an ornament.

Less refined than the ham, but wildly popular, are chitterlings, also spelled chitlins or chit'lins, but always pronounced with two syllables, not three. Some people eat them boiled, with plenty of hot sauce, while others find that frying them makes them more palatable. Mississippian Craig Claiborne reminisced about the annual chitlin suppers at his mother's boardinghouse in Indianola, where they were served. "The chitlins (or chitterlings, if you prefer) were always served with vinegar and hot pepper flakes plus turnip greens and corn bread. Prior to that annual feast, she would give the boarders ample notice that it was about to happen, and if they didn't like it they could simply dine elsewhere," said Claiborne, who went on to become a food critic and writer for the *New York Times*.

South Carolina native Vertamae Smart-Grosvenor also remembered chitlins: "People think chitterlings is something only the southern nigras eats but let me tell you about the time I was in this fancy restaurant in Paris and the people said, 'Let us order, we know this place.' . . . So these people order for me . . . this enjoyable rare dish. Well thank you Jesus the food arrives and it ain't nothing but CHITTERLINGS in the form of sausage. They call it andouillette."[6]

One last delicacy to mention is hogshead cheese, traditionally, made of the hog's head, boiled with all the bones removed. Cooks today often do not use the head, but pork shoulder or other meaty parts instead. The meat is mashed and seasoned with hot peppers, vinegar, nutmeg or sage, and bell pepper. The mixture is allowed to gel overnight, then sliced for eating. Some people eat it on crackers or melt it over their grits for breakfast.

One of the best ways to eat pork, and one that has spawned imitations well outside the South, is barbecued—whole hogs, spareribs, country-style ribs, Boston butts or shoulder slow-cooked and chopped for sandwiches. Whole books have been written about barbecue, and controversies have ensued over cooking methods, fuels, and sauce ingredients. Mutton (in Kentucky), goat, and beef all have their fans, but in the South as a whole, barbecue means pork.

Barbecue cultures are found in Tennessee, Kentucky, Georgia, and the Carolinas, although good barbecue can be found in isolated pockets of other southern states. (Texas is outside the purview of this chapter, and Texans prefer beef.) Each barbecue center has its preferences as to what is barbecued, what fuels the fire, how long to cook the meat, how to cut it, and what to put on it afterwards.

The two schools of barbecue cooking are direct and indirect. As the names imply, one favors cooking the meat directly over the wood, coals, or charcoal, with the juices from the meat dripping down and then adding flavor to the meat. The other school cooks with hardwood (oak, hickory, pecan), with the meat juices rarely touching the flame.

In the South as a whole, barbecue means pork. This North Carolina farmer barbecues pork over an open pit. Courtesy of the North Carolina State Archives.

Sauces are generally vinegar-based, tomato-based, or mustard-based. The last is the least common, most of its fans being in South Carolina.

Barbecues, both the food and the occasion for a party, have been popular in the South since the late eighteenth century. Some food writers have linked barbecues exclusively to the settlement of the mountain areas and to the frontier campfires; others have linked them to gatherings of indentured servants and slaves.

As in the past, barbecues today almost always are celebratory affairs. Barbecue contests have developed in recent times, where cooks gather for competitions. Local winners often work their way up through larger contests to the big leagues of Memphis in May, or the Big Pig Jig in Vienna, Georgia.

Beef and Game

There are few typically southern dishes made from beef. One is grillades and grits, a New Orleans dish typically made with beef round steak or veal. Daube, or pot roast, is also popular in New Orleans, served hot with spaghetti or chilled to a gelatinous firmness and served in thin slices. Spiced round is a popular Christmas dish in Tennessee, where it was introduced by Swiss and German immigrants.

Another beef dish, found, curiously enough, in the little towns along the Mississippi River, is hot tamales. Probably introduced by Mexican migrant workers in the early 1900s, tamales are usually made of beef, although pork or chicken tamales are also popular.

Wild game is an important part of the southern meat-eating tradition, although far less essential to the table than it once was. One of the feast dishes of the Choctaw and the Chickasaw involved skewering chunks of turkey meat, venison, and bear meat. The bear meat was prized for its fat, which then flavored the other meat. For just this reason, bear continued to be important well into the twentieth century. As late as the 1950s, food writer Mary Land was giving recipes for bear ribs, steaks, and ragout.[7] The bear is a protected species now.

Other game is still eaten, however. The opening of various hunting seasons is occasion for gatherings at remote cabins, called camps, where men and women seek deer, doves, duck, or quail. Farm-raised quail is also popular, and easier to come by for those who don't hunt.

Small game animals—opossums, raccoons, muskrat, and rabbit—are still hunted as well, although vanishing habitat makes it difficult to rely on their presence. Two traditional southern stews of small game are Brunswick stew and burgoo. Both called originally for squirrel or rabbit, but now are also made with chicken and vegetables, especially butterbeans and okra.

Brunswick stew, called the most famous dish of pioneer America, is said to have been created around 1828 in Brunswick County, Virginia, by a slave, Uncle Jimmy Matthews, who made it from squirrels, butter, onions, stale bread, and seasoning. Brunswick stew later became popular for church suppers and fundraisers—with many variations. Mrs. S. R. Dull, a longtime Atlanta food editor, listed several recipes for Brunswick stew in her 1928 compendium, *Southern Cooking*. Most of these were modified by various meat parts, chili sauce, ketchup, and Worcestershire sauce.

A Kentucky favorite, burgoo, was a similarly slow-cooked stew of small game, or more recently, beef, chicken, or lamb, with vegetables, including okra and butterbeans. Food writer Marion Flexner advised that it be served a day or two old, reheated, alongside corn pones.

Salt and Pepper

In the past, salt production took place in Kentucky, Louisiana, Virginia, Florida, and Tennessee. Salt played an important role in the Civil War, when salt shortages made the preservation of foods a constant problem for both civilians and the military. Several key battles were waged unsuccessfully to defend those places where salt could be made. Today, Louisiana still maintains important evaporated salt production facilities and salt mines.

Avery Island is one of five salt islands along the Gulf coast and home to Louisiana's most famous manufactured product, Tabasco brand hot sauce. First compounded in 1868 by the McIlhenny family, Tabasco sauce takes as its base Tabasco peppers—a special variety of red capsicum peppers from Mexico. The peppers are crushed, aged with vinegar and salt, strained, bottled, and sold around the world.

Poultry

For special occasions, southerners have always preferred chicken to a pork roast, and chickens themselves have played an important part in southern history. In many parts of the nineteenth-century South, chickens were sold by African Americans, often their one source of cash in times of slavery and sharecropping. Louisiana's Huey Long, like many other politicians, used the chicken as a symbol of prosperity, promising "a chicken in every pot" for Sunday dinner. Long knew that too many people depended on their hens to lay eggs to cook one for dinner very often. Farm women and even women in small towns traded eggs for groceries when money was scarce.[8]

The quintessential southern chicken dish is, of course, fried chicken. Fried chicken, thanks to Colonel Sanders and his ilk, has become internationally famous, although the version one buys as fast food—heavily breaded, deep-fried, and greasy—is a slur on the dish that for many southerners evokes Sunday dinner, picnic lunches, and family reunions.

Southern cooks have been frying chicken the same way for at least 180 years, generally following the 1824 advice of Mary Randolph, who wrote about dredging the pieces in flour, sprinkling them with salt, and frying them a light brown in hot lard. Vegetable oil is a more popular frying medium today. Some cooks add bacon drippings for flavor.

The quintessential southern chicken dish is fried chicken. Courtesy Georgia Department of Economic Development.

Some people soak their chicken in buttermilk or sweet milk before dredging it in flour, or in cornmeal, breadcrumbs, or crushed cornflakes, or a mixture of such; or they dip the chicken in an egg-and-water mix before dredging it. Others add herbs or spices to the mix, or hot sauce to the milk. Some people deep-fry, but most home cooks pan-fry the chicken in a skillet, turning it until it is golden brown and crisp.

Gravy, made from the leavings in the skillet and water or milk, is a requirement for many, and some even smother their chicken in the gravy. But most people want a crispy, tender piece of chicken.

The South raises more chickens than any other area in the country. Georgia, Arkansas, Alabama, North Carolina, and Mississippi together raised over half of the 8.5 million broilers produced in the United States in 2002.[9] While fried chicken has received nearly universal acclaim, other southern chicken dishes, though less well known, are equally delicious. Chicken and dumplings is one favorite, the chicken stewed to rags, and the flour dumplings boiled in the chicken broth. South Carolina's chicken pilau (or perloo) is a classic chicken cooked with rice and seasoning vegetables, water, or broth, until the liquid has been absorbed by the rice.

Chicken pie is another popular Sunday dinner dish. The chicken is stewed and usually deboned, then put into a pie with its gravy, often enriched with cream. The pie can be made of a flour crust, or it might be simply biscuits on top. One unique recipe from South Carolina calls for cooked, buttered rice to be pressed into a pie plate. The chicken is added, along with corn and broth, and more rice is layered on top. Cooked vegetables such as asparagus, peas, carrots, or potatoes can be added to the pie, and some recipes use hard-boiled eggs.

"Country captain" is less often seen, but it is a true southern specialty, claimed by Savannah, Georgia, but found in South Carolina as well. It is a sort of mild curry, accented with currants, almonds, and sometimes crisp bacon bits, and served with rice and chutney. The *Oxford English Dictionary* defines a country captain as "(a) a captain stationed in the country; (b) Anglo-Ind. a captain of a native ship; also a peculiar dry kind of curry," but Savannahians say the recipe was brought to them by a sea captain in the spice trade.

Seafood

The southeastern United States has many natural advantages when it comes to the eating of seafood and other fish. Only Arkansas, Kentucky, and Tennessee lack some outlet to the ocean, and even these states are honeycombed with rivers and lakes.

The first Virginia and Gulf coast settlers found the Native Americans fishing for saltwater catfish that weighed more than 100 pounds, and other large fish such as the sturgeon, paddlefish, and gar pikes. The Native Americans also ate smaller fish such as shad, croaker, mullet, bass, sunfish, and perch.

Early cookbooks give instructions for curing herrings and pickling oysters or sturgeon, common methods of preservation in the days before refrigeration. In *The Virginia Housewife*, Mary Randolph records English- and French-derived recipes for fish, including how to cook eels, perch, oysters, carp, and cod. She also provides interesting instructions on "how to curry a catfish" and how to "caveach" fish, an ancient recipe in which the fish is fried, then marinated, cold, in vinegar.

Today, the Gulf of Mexico, which borders Texas, Louisiana, Mississippi, Alabama, and western Florida, is the United States' national fishing hole, providing 82 percent of the annual shrimp catch, 57 percent of the oysters, and 17 percent of the crabs. Mississippians in the Delta farm catfish where cotton used to grow. Tennesseeans farm trout. Florida fishermen reap a bounty from the Gulf as well as the Atlantic Ocean. Frogs' legs are a commercial industry located in the Gulf coast states from Florida to Louisiana. Breaux Bridge, Louisiana, claims the title of crawfish capital of the world. In 1999 Louisiana produced more than 13 million pounds of crawfish, and in the decade 1990–2000 accounted for 90 percent of the global crawfish production. Seventy percent of this yield was consumed within the state of Louisiana. (A surprise even for many in Louisiana is the fact that this treasured food was avoided by Creoles and Cajuns alike until the twentieth century.)[10]

Around the coastal perimeter of the South and in the backwoods near its rivers and bayous, restaurants specializing in seafood abound. These serve roasted oysters, whole fried catfish or smoked mullet, fried shrimp, hushpuppies, crab claws, and cole slaw.

Seafood restaurants vary a great deal, from barebones oyster bars and fish camps, to family-style establishments, to elegant city spots where trout amandine or pompano en papillote are the local favorites.

What the crawfish is to Louisiana, the stone crab is to South Florida. Stone crabs are harvested from October to May. They are boiled and the claw meat is most often dunked in a mustardy mayonnaise. Conch fritters are another popular shellfish dish of Florida, especially in the Keys. West Indies salad, the creation of a steakhouse in Mobile, Alabama, is a simple dish of chilled white lump crabmeat layered with finely chopped onion and marinated with cider vinegar and oil.

Reciting the list of seafood dishes for which the South is famous is indeed a

Shrimp boats in Alabama. The Gulf of Mexico is the United States' national fishing hole, providing 82 percent of the annual shrimp catch. Courtesy of the Alabama Bureau of Tourism & Travel. Photo by Ami Simpson.

mouthwatering exercise. A few are seafood gumbo, shrimp remoulade, crawfish etouffée, deviled crabs, oysters Bienville, broiled pompano, soft-shell crabs, fried frog legs, stuffed red snapper, planked shad, boiled crabs, boiled crawfish, and boiled shrimp. Another specialty, Charleston she-crab soup, is made in midwinter when the crabs are full of eggs (although out of season it can be made with the crumbled yolks of hard-boiled eggs substituting for the roe). South Carolina also has muddle, a fish stew comprising a "mess of fish," grouper or snapper, shrimp, and scallops.

Seafood boils are popular wherever an assortment of seafood is available, and South Carolina's celebration of Frogmore stew, which contains boiled shrimp, crab, spicy sausage, corn, and vegetables, is a welcome feast. The name Frogmore derives from an old settlement on St. Helena Island, a remnant of African American Gullah culture.

Seafood gumbo ingredients. Courtesy Louisiana Office of Tourism.

Historic Southern Cookbooks

The first printing of a cookbook in America took place in Williamsburg, Virginia, in 1742. Entitled *The Compleat Houswife; or, Accomplish'd Gentlewoman's Companion*, this English reprint established a link between many future southern recipes, particularly those for sweets, and British traditions.

One of the most important cookbooks of the nineteenth century, and the first American regional cookbook, was Mary Randolph's *The Virginia Housewife* (1824). Subtitled "Method Is the Soul of Management," this book ran through some twenty editions even before the close of the Civil War. Many scholars believe it to be the most influential of all nineteenth-century American cookbooks. Its popularity assured that Americans outside the South were well aware of many regional dishes. Here beaten biscuits, okra gumbo, and a number of recipes for greens and pork made their way into the mainstream. Perhaps building upon Thomas Jefferson's early interest in combining the bounty of his state with French cuisine, the book lent a certain status to southern food and placed Virginia in the minds of many Americans as a site of hospitality.

Mrs. Randolph herself was a relative of Jefferson and other Virginia notables. Like a number of later cookbook writers, she was known as a gracious hostess in her own home and, in hard times, in her Richmond boarding house. Her recipes lent both a practical and an aristocratic air, and she herself was nicknamed "The Queen."

A number of nineteenth-century cookbooks added to the regional reputation established by Mrs. Randolph. These included Lettice Bryan's *The Kentucky Housewife* (Cincinnati, 1839); P. Thornton's *The Southern Gardener and Receipt Book* (Camden, South Carolina, 1840); Sarah Rutledge's *The Carolina Housewife, or House and Home* (Charleston, 1847); *Confederate Receipt Book* (Richmond, 1863); Annabella Hill's *Mrs. Hill's New Cook Book* (New York, 1867); May Joseph Waring's *The Centennial Receipt Book* (Charleston, 1876); Marion Cabell Tyree's *Housekeeping in Old Virginia* (Louisville, 1879); Abby Fisher's *What Mrs. Fisher Knows about Old Southern Cooking* (San Francisco, 1881), today considered the first book filled with recipes by an African American; the Christian Woman's Exchange's *The Creole Cookery Book* (New Orleans, 1885); Lafcadio Hearn's *La Cuisine Creole, a Collection of Culinary Recipes from Leading Chefs and Noted Creole Housewives, Who Have Made New Orleans Famous for Its Cuisine* (New Orleans, 1885); Mrs. Henry Lumpkin Wilson's *Tested Recipe Cook Book* (Atlanta, 1895); and Emma Rylander Lane's *Some Good Things to Eat* (Clayton, Alabama, 1898).

Handwritten journals of recipes from the seventeenth through the nineteenth centuries, intended to pass family recipes between generations, are today found in such books as Harriet Pinckney Horry's *A Colonial Plantation Cookbook* (edited by

Richard J. Hooker, 1984), *Martha Washington's Book of Cookery* (edited by Karen Hess, 1981); and *Nelly Custis Lewis's Housekeeping Book* (edited by Patricia Brady Schmit, 1982).

In the early twentieth century, the southern cooking repertoire was expanded by such books as the Picayune's *The Creole Cook Book* (New Orleans, 1900); Louisa Smithye Stoney's *Carolina Rice Cook Book* (Charleston, 1901); Celestine Eustis's *Cooking in Old Creole Days* (New York, 1904); and Martha McCulloch Williams's *Dishes and Beverages of the Old South* (New York, 1913).

Later important milestones in southern cookbook history were Lena Richard's *The New Orleans Cook Book* (1940), Harriet Ross Colquitt's *The Savannah Cook Book* (Charleston, 1933); Helen Bullock's *The Williamsburg Art of Cookery* (Williamsburg, 1938); Marian Flexner's *Out of Kentucky Kitchens* (1949); and Marion Brown's *The Southern Cook Book* (Chapel Hill, 1951).

During these years, Kentuckian Duncan Hines started his guides to America's eating places, thus also extending the reach of how one could learn of southern food. The popular Junior League cookbooks (began in 1950s Montgomery, Alabama) also spread during these years.

In the last quarter of the twentieth century, many southern writers who achieved national prominence taught readers about the region's food, foremost among them being such notables as Craig Claiborne, Eugene Walter, and Lillian Hellman. Contemporary writers such as Peter Feibleman, John Egerton, John T. Edge, Jessica Harris, Edna Lewis, Scott Peacock, Bill Neal, Vertamae Smart-Grosvenor, and Damon Fowler have followed in this tradition of combining historic recipes, social history, and fresh ingredients.

Vegetables and Legumes

Southerners are fond of vegetables. A dinner in the middle of the summer might, even today, hold a feast of eggplant patties, sliced tomatoes, fried okra, corn pudding, black-eyed peas, and summer squash served with cornbread and iced tea. Such a meal also reflects the mixture of heritages that characterizes southern food, combining African, European, and Native American.

The settlers of the South found riches in the variety of vegetables. Native Americans were already growing squash or pumpkins, maize, and different sorts of beans, and also gathering onion, garlic, leeks, and various roots and tubers. A list of food foraged by southeastern Indians would include red coontie and white coontie, the roots of smilax and zamia, respectively; Indian potatoes or groundnuts; the wild sweet potato or wild morning glory, which has a root that can weigh up to thirty pounds, and swamp potatoes collected from the root of arrowhead.[11]

In her 1954 *Louisiana Cookery*, Mary Land listed thirty-five different wild pot and salad herbs and tubers—from American lotus to yucca. These sorts of gleanings were tremendously important to the diets of Native Americans. Tastes differ, and not many of the wild plants the Native Americans collected made the transition to the tables of white settlers or their black slaves. But some did, including Jerusalem artichokes, hearts of palm (swamp cabbage), dried sassafras leaves, and ramps. Wild leeks, or ramps, remain a favorite in springtime North Carolina, West Virginia, and Tennessee.

Corn was the staple grain, but it was also, when young and tender, an important vegetable. Succotash, a mixture of young corn and butterbeans, is one Native American dish that is still commonly eaten today. Sagamite, which is corn and green beans, survives as well, although it's not called that anymore. The Indians also ate their corn roasted, and of course, ground into meals and paps.

Sweet potatoes are probably not native to the southern United States, but they were grown here as early as 1610. Simply roasted or fried, or made into fritters, pies, biscuits, and elaborate casseroles with brown sugar, pecans, and marshmallows, they help define the southern table.

Black and white colonists soon added to the variety of foodstuffs with seeds and slips of plants they imported. Human nature being what it is, people generally prefer the familiar to the exotic. And so to the Native American plants were added okra, asparagus, lettuces, white (always called Irish) potatoes, cabbage, tomatoes, sorrel, and turnips.

That last, turnips, is most important, the most southern of all vegetables. At least, its tops—its greens—are. Several other kinds of greens are also eaten in the South—collards, mustard greens, and beet greens. Even dandelions and radish tops can be stewed. The water in which greens are cooked becomes something delicious in its own right. It's called pot liquor, and some people prefer it to the greens, especially when it is poured over hot cornbread.

Okra is another popular vegetable not often found in American cooking outside the South, although it is part of African, Indian, and Middle Eastern cuisines. Most often, it is sliced and fried, or added to south Louisiana's gumbo for its unique flavor and thickening qualities. In Charleston, a dish called Limpin' Susan is made with okra and rice. Okra is also good left whole and cooked with tomatoes, or browned with onions, or served cold with a vinaigrette. The Angolan name for okra is gombo, or rather, kingombo.

Vegetables themselves are highly desired, as witnessed by the huge popularity of farmers' markets in places like Montgomery, Asheville, and Atlanta. The list of other southern vegetable dishes is long, ranging from asparagus soup to down-home recipes like candied sweet potatoes, pickled beets, corn oysters, stuffed bell peppers, and fried green tomatoes.

Frying isn't limited to green tomatoes, of course, although those are possibly the most famous fried vegetables. Okra, zucchini, yellow summer squash, eggplant, and even dill pickles (which used to be a vegetable, back when they were cucumbers) are all potential candidates.

Stuffing is another popular method of cooking vegetables such as tomatoes, eggplant, squashes, and bell peppers. New Orleans chef Paul Prudhomme often takes it a step further and combines the two methods, first hollowing out his vegetable, then frying it, then stuffing it.

Various vegetable pickles are traditional, okra and green beans as well as the more common cucumber. Spicy relishes such as chili sauce and chow-chow also enliven the table.

For long years, most vegetables in the South were cooked with pork, or at least seasoned with a little salt pork; this is true even today. Slaves were said to salvage bits of meat (called meat tits), especially salt pork, in bags, and then put them to simmer in one pot. This has also meant a long tradition of one-pot cooking. Peas, beans, and greens are rarely eaten without such seasoning. South Carolina's Hoppin' John, which is rice and black-eyed peas cooked with bacon, and New Orleans-style red beans and rice, cooked with ham hocks, are good examples, along with green beans slow-cooked with ham and all those collard, mustard, and turnip greens.

The origin of the name "Hoppin' John" is not clear. Raymond Sokolov says it dates to at least 1841 when, according to the story still told in Charleston, it was sold in the streets by a crippled black man called Hopping John. Food historian Karen Hess, however, proposes a more scholarly explanation, relating the name to a Hindu word for cooked rice, *bhat*, which in another form, *Bahatta*, could have evolved to 'hoppin,' and the Malaysian word *kachang*, which applies to various legumes, or pulses (peas), for 'John.' Both words could have arrived in South Carolina, where the dish first became known to whites, with their African slaves, she says.[12]

Salads

When it comes to salads, southerners are not generally identified with crisp green salads. However, mache or corn salad—newly popular in upscale salad bars and groceries—has been eaten for 100 years or more in the South, along with artichokes vinaigrette, asparagus, and watercress.

"Poke salat," made from the tender green shoots of poke weed (the roots and lower shoots of which are poisonous), along with other salads made of the first greens of spring, such as dandelion, were relished by early settlers. The "salat" can be simply dressed with salt, pepper, and vinegar, or boiled with salt pork.

"We would relish a dish of mixed greens—poke leaves before they unfurled, lamb's quarters, and wild mustard," wrote Edna Lewis, who grew up in a small farming community in Virginia that was settled by freed slaves. "We also had salad for a short period made of either Black-Seeded Simpson, or Grand Rapids, loose-leaf lettuce that bolted as soon as the weather became warm. It was served with thin slices of onion before they begin to shape into a bulb—the tops used as well—in a dressing of vinegar, sugar, and black pepper."[13]

The descendants of Florida's Spanish settlers were eating another soupy salad, gazpacho or gazpachee, a hundred years before the rest of the country became aware of it. For authenticity, say the authors of *The Florida Cookbook*, this mixture of tomatoes, cucumbers, onions, and bell pepper should be thickened with hardtack, which is the type of cracker carried by sailors for long voyages.

Salads made with gelatin have a certain popularity as well. Gelatin salads range from the delicate tomato aspic, a toothsome delight on summer tables, to the weightier salads of more recent vintage which include anything from pineapple, marshmallows, and whipped cream to shredded cabbage and carrots.

Dried Beans and Peanuts

Finally, the cowpea is one of the most important of the foods brought from Africa, reaching Florida in the 1700s. Since English peas are hard to grow in hot climates, the cowpea quickly became popular. In 1797 Washington bought forty bushels of cowpea seeds for sowing on his plantation. A number of different types remain important, particularly the black-eyed pea and the crowder pea (Purple Hull, Lady, and others). In the South, these peas are dried and then cooked slowly with bacon or

George Washington Carver

Born a slave in Missouri, George Washington Carver (1861–1943) contributed more than any other one person to the food of the South. Living most of his life in Tuskegee, Alabama, he influenced the planting of crops that brought the South into the modern era.

From boyhood, he held a focused interest in plants. The story of his education itself shows an unparalleled dedication to scientific pursuit, especially since he was often hindered by segregation, prejudice, and lack of money. His skills included growing plants, painting, cooking, knitting, and crocheting. Truly a Renaissance man, he homesteaded in Kansas, and then returned to various academic pursuits, finally earning an advanced degree from Iowa State College of Agriculture at Ames in 1896.

Arriving in Tuskegee in 1898, he directed an agricultural experiment station for forty-seven years, educating students and others. Revered by many for his never-ending and generous commitment to human welfare, he invented hundreds of products, mostly related to food, patenting only one of his least important. He could not be bothered to take the time to seek reward for his other products, devoting himself instead, to influencing the planting of cowpeas, soybeans, plums, and other neglected crops in place of cotton. He thus helped southern farmers recover some of the richness of their soil lost to the sole planting of cotton.

He also made sure that African American agricultural extension agents were used effectively, creating an unprecedented "movable school of agriculture and home economics" whereby equipment could be carried to remote rural areas. From these wagons, agents under his direction taught about soil conservation, plant protection, and new farm products. Long before others, he also worked on food dehydration.

Most important, his work made possible the development of peanuts and sweet potatoes from noncommercial crops to leading ones in the South. By 1938 peanuts were the chief crop of Alabama. For the nation, the development of peanut butter was his biggest accomplishment, adding to the American diet this now commonplace and quick source of protein.

Honored nationally and internationally, Carver worked away from the mainstream of scientific research and lived during the worst years of segregation. He directed much of his work toward the people he believed most needful of his help—African American farm families.

ham hocks. Often called beans in national grocery stores, cowpeas are highly nutritious.

Another great food brought by way of Africa is the peanut, or as early Americans called it, the groundnut. Although some were grown for export from the Carolinas in the early 1800s, most were produced by slaves for their own use. Peanut soup was an early Virginian favorite dish among slaves. Boiled peanuts covered with molasses were a treat. Easily transported, roasted peanuts became popular during the Civil War. Peanuts were especially popular at cotton picking and ginning times, and later, of course, became the basis for one of the most important of all twentieth-century American foods, peanut butter.

Rice and Grits

Rice was first grown in America on the orders of Virginia governor Sir William Berkeley, who in 1647 had a half bushel planted. It did so well that, on the advice of some of Virginia's slaves, more rice was grown; it was even exported to the West Indies and New England for at least fifty years.

South Carolina was the first state to make rice its primary cash crop. South Carolina became known for its rice from the mid-1680s, when a Captain John Thurber gave Charles Town resident Dr. Henry Woodward a small amount of rice from Madagascar. By 1690 South Carolinians were growing so much rice that they asked that it be added to the list of commodities with which they might pay their quitrents. By 1700 planters had grown more rice than there were ships to export it.

But the end of slavery foretold the end of the rice era in South Carolina. Without a supply of unpaid labor, and with increasing competition from states further south, cultivation in South Carolina declined. Over about twenty years, four hurricanes devastated the rice fields, and the last commercial crop was planted there in 1927. Today, rice is grown commercially in Louisiana, Texas, Arkansas, Mississippi, and, surprisingly enough, California, which has taken the lead in recent years due to the demand for specialty rice.

Still, the original cultivation of rice in South Carolina left behind a body of dishes that Karen Hess defines as a "rice kitchen," comparable to that of other, older rice-eating cultures in China, India, and Africa.[14] And although some rice breads, waffles, fritters, dumplings, croquettes, custards, and puddings of South Carolina are little used today, other regional favorites remain. Hoppin' John and Limpin' Susan, discussed above, are the best known. In New Orleans, a rice kitchen also developed with such dishes as red beans and rice, red rice (cooked with tomatoes), jambalaya (cooked with ham and seafood), and calas, the hot breakfast cakes made of cooked rice sweetened and fried. Late eighteenth- and early nineteenth-century refugees from Haiti also added parched rice, rolled in a ball and eaten with sugar or salt.

Both South Carolina and Louisiana produced stern instructions on how best to cook rice—by boiling and then steaming it. That said, sales of rice cookers, which purport to do the same thing automatically, are strong in South Carolina and south Louisiana, where rice is still served very often—some say as much as twice a day. Old cookbooks also have a number of recipes for rice breads, waffles, fritters, dumplings, croquettes, custards, and puddings, few of which are seen today. Louisiana settlers of the late eighteenth century and the nineteenth century gave rice-parching parties, a method of cooking rice that came to New Orleans from the West Indies with the refugees from the slave uprisings in what is now Haiti.

A rice dish specific to south Louisiana is dirty rice, so called because of the color given it by the finely chopped chicken livers and gizzards which flavor it along with sausage or some other ground meat.

The other great grain of the South is dried corn, which, hulled, becomes hominy, the Indians' saccamite. "It was the Indians around Louisiana who first taught the use of hominy," according to the Picayune cooks. "They used to take the dried Indian corn and thresh it till all the yellow, hardened outer germ or hull came off, the grain being left white." The dried corn was sometimes bleached and hulled in lye, procured from the ashes of hardwood fires, then washed and cooked. C. C. Robin wrote of corn—of its infinite renditions into cornmeal mush, sagamite or hominy, and even coush-coush served in gumbo.

Grits are dried hominy or whole dried corn ground into coarse meal. They are much loved by southerners but disparaged by others. Grits are generally served at breakfast, with butter or gravy, never sugar. Texture is a very im-

Southeastern Native Americans grew and used corn. This shows Timucua men cultivating a field and Timucua women planting corn or beans. Courtesy The Art Archive/New York Public Library/HarperCollins Publishers.

portant element of grits, which can be runny if carelessly made. Grits are not the same as polenta, which is finer and smoother-textured, though both are made from ground hominy.

A popular variation is cheese grits, generally made with cheddar, served at breakfast or as a side dish for lunch or dinner. Leftover grits get very firm. Chilled and cut into shapes, they make fried grits, which can serve as a base for sauces or can be eaten alone. Charleston has a breakfast specialty of shrimp and grits, while in New Orleans, grillades and grits are a popular brunch item, the grits serving as a sop for the tomato gravy of the grillades. A sauce of sautéed wild mushrooms makes a delicious topping for grits cakes.

Breads

The South is a region rich in the history of bread, and is particularly known for its cornbreads and biscuits. Cornbread came as a gift from the Native Americans. As that inveterate travel writer Harriet Martineau noted, corn was more valuable than gold to the early colonies. Indian women taught white settlers how "to bruse or pound [corn kernels] in a mortar, and thereof make loaves or lumps of dowishe bread." The meal was flattened into cakes, and baked on heated stones, within the hot coals themselves, or on paddles of wood or hoes. The former two methods yielded ash cakes, and the latter, hoecakes. Both remained a part of the diet of some southerners well into the twentieth century.[15]

This was so because heavy rainfalls and high temperatures prohibit wheat production, and corn itself requires little skill in cultivation and milling. Cornmeal is served up in spoonbread, cracklin' bread, shortenin' bread, mush cakes, coush-coush, hush puppies, corn pone (from the Native American word *appone*, meaning corn cake), griddle cakes, scratch back, and any number of other recipes.

A number of these breads have their origin in Africa (most assuredly, coush-coush) or in the adaptations of the Africans and poor whites to the ingredients readily available. Cracklin' bread, for example, uses pork cracklings to provide fat to the bread. (Crackling is the solid substance remaining in the pot after lard has been rendered.) Seasoned with onions, fried cornmeal bits are called hush puppies, named because black cooks, in charge of both food and animals around the campfires of fishing camps, told the dogs to be quiet.

Cornbread itself has many incarnations, though its humble beginnings of only cornmeal, salt, and water remain in recipes that now call for cream, butter, and eggs. Today sugar is frequently added to the mix, but many southerners insist that this is a clear indication of the influence of some culture outside the South.

Cornbread was and is served with all meals, with sweet or savory touches added, and its history has been written in the memory of all southerners. George Washington had his "small mush cakes" for breakfast; early-twentieth-century children carried pails of cornbread and molasses for their school lunches. Today restaurants, plain and fancy, serve up cornbread as a delicacy with various dishes. All the while cornbread is still eaten in homes across the South, and corn muffin mixes are among the best selling of all such offerings in grocery stores.

The commonplace, however, stands in contrast to biscuits, which southerners often reserve for special meals and company. At least one writer has called hot biscuits the successor to hot hoecakes. And for another writer, the South could be distinguished from other areas by "the dividing line between cold bread and hot biscuits."[16] Baskets of biscuits set within an ironed cloth mark the table of prosperity.

Beaten biscuits (apoquiniminc cakes), famed in Virginia and often served with ham, carry the basic biscuit recipe of flour, shortening, and milk and are therefore rather hard. Their dough is beaten with a mallet or a rolling pin, traditionally with an axe handle, for twenty to thirty minutes to create an airy texture. Each bun is then pricked with a fork and baked.

Other types of biscuits became more popular after the invention and marketing of baking powder and baking soda in the late nineteenth century, and after soft midwestern wheat came to be sold by White Lily of Knoxville and Martha White of Nashville in the early twentieth century. Some recipes add ham or cheese, or cooked puréed sweet potato, to the basic mix.

Early favorites among other hot breads were rolls, buttermilk bread, Sally Lunn, batterbread, flannel cakes, waffles, French rolls, and muffins. Most of these and many others relied upon yeast, made then from hops or potatoes or gathered from the air. Early cookbooks and family recipe books give much attention to the making of yeast. In addition, yeast breads themselves were much treasured. Planters took loaves of white bread home with them, for example, when they returned from cities to their plantations. Gifts of bread were common at Christmas, and store-bought sliced white bread prized enough, as late as the 1950s, to be given as a present to a teacher.

Local breads once popular were the South Carolina Awendaw (made from cornmeal, milk, rice, eggs, and butter), rice scones, and rice cakes; Carolina egg bread (a spoon bread enriched with extra eggs), calas, (rice beignets sold on the streets of New Orleans, often by women of color); and the sweet potato buns of Virginia. Today, the fried beignet, a sort of souffléed square of a doughnut, remains popular in New Orleans, and sweet potato buns are served in fine restaurants in the Upper South.

However, until the mid-twentieth century, the biggest difference among breads eaten in the South would have been between rural and urban areas. In rural areas, cornbread and home-baked bread predominated. In nineteenth-century cities, bread-baking at home for the wealthy involved a furnace (measuring one foot in diameter) in the yard or, for others, a brick beehive oven built in next to the chimney in the days when cooking took place over an open fireplace.

For the most part, after the 1870s, cities lured bakers who sold their products wholesale to groceries, and the public responded by giving up most home baking except for special occasions. For example, in New Orleans by 1871, there were some 149 bakers, with Alsatian and German names predominating.

Technology, changing consumer habits, and governmental regulations brought the opening of many more retail bakeries in the early twentieth century and made store-bought bread more frequent on the southern table. In addition, bakers in southern seaports were also known for their production of tack, hard crackers supplied to sailors for long journeys.

By the end of the twentieth century, however, commercially produced bread became standardized across the South. This has meant the closure of almost all local bakeries and a decline in the variety of bread available. Only in a few large cities are artisanal breads making a slow comeback. Refrigerated dough, shipped from cities across the United States, now enables fresh bread to be sold in grocery stores, but among the majority of the population, sliced white bread, generally made far away, predominates.

On the other hand, southern sweet rolls—notably Krispy Kreme doughnuts, first sold in North Carolina with a recipe created in Arkansas—now have a national market. And many a southern Sunday dinner table holds more biscuits, cornbreads, or rolls than do similar tables in other regions. The line between the North and South is still evident on a table set with cold versus hot bread.

Sandwiches, Southern Style

Sandwiches of regional fame include the po'boy (sometimes spelled poor boy, but never pronounced that way) of New Orleans and the Gulf coast, and the muffuletta, unique to New Orleans. Different stories are told about the origin of the po'boy. Some say it was the sandwich of choice for nineteenth-century Gascony-born butchers of the French Quarter and the Poydras Markets. These men went to work before dawn and ate a very big breakfast upon leaving their stands at 11 A.M. Others date the sandwich more specifically to the New Orleans streetcar workers' strike of 1929. During this time, Martin's Grocery began selling the long loafs with meat for a nickel, to help the "poor boys" who were on strike. Martin's ordered its bread from John Gendusa, whose bakery opened in 1927.

To this day, the Gendusa family, along with Leidenheimer and Binder Bakeries, make bread for po'boy sandwiches—two inches wide and thirty-six inches long. New Orleans po'boy bread is crispy and light, while in other places along the Gulf coast it is a softer bread, lacking the crisp crust. On the Mississippi coast, this bread is often made by Desporte's Fine Breads in Biloxi, which still uses the brick ovens its founder constructed in 1939.

A local favorite is the oyster po'boy, in which the whole of the bread is hollowed out and filled with fried oysters, tartar sauce, tomatoes, and lettuce. This would be an oyster po'boy dressed; an undressed po'boy lacks the trimmings. Traditionally made with broiled or creamed oysters, it was called the Peacemaker, or La Médiatrice, because a husband detained downtown too long would bring it home to his wife to soften her heart.

Some food writers liken the po'boy to the hero sandwich. A po'boy can contain any variety of ingredients, but traditional ones are roast beef and gravy, ham and cheese, sausage, fried trout, shrimp, soft-shell crabs, or tunafish salad. Except in the case of the oyster po'boy, mayonnaise (and only very rarely butter) is used on these sandwiches.

The muffuletta, that other New Orleans sandwich, made its debut through the efforts of one Salvatore Lupo in 1906 at his French Quarter shop, Central

The "Peanut Butter and Jelly" of the South: Pimento Sandwiches

The pimento cheese sandwich, called the peanut butter and jelly of southern childhoods, is best made with thin white bread spread with a mixture of homemade mayonnaise, grated cheddar cheese, jarred pimentos, and other seasoning ingredients such as jalapeño peppers or perhaps a little grated onion. A fixture at southern wakes and weddings, pimento cheese sandwiches are a constant on lists of "How to Know If You Are a Southerner," but rarely appear in cookbooks.

Grocery, which can still be visited today. Based on a Sicilian sandwich (the Roma) and named after the sesame seed crusted bread that looks like the top of a mushroom, muffulettas contain an olive salad, cheeses (mozzarella and provolone), ham, and salami.

In Louisville, two sandwiches claim a birthplace. One is the Louisville Hot Brown, created at the Brown Hotel in the 1920s, and made with turkey and bacon (with optional tomato), held together on toast by a white or cheese sauce. The other famous Louisville sandwich is a Benedictine, noted earlier as a Derby Day dish. Jenny Benedict, who created it, now has a Kentucky highway marker noting her fame.

In Tampa (especially its Ybor City) and in Miami, the Cuban sandwich is popular. First made for those working in late-nineteenth-century cigar factories, the Cuban sandwich is comprised of cheese, pork, ham, pickles, tomatoes, and sometimes sausage (thought to be the influence of the Italians who worked alongside the Cubans). Butter and mustard are used on Cuban bread (long loaves with a crisp crust on the outside and lightly textured inside), which is then pressed flat in a sandwich iron.

Other sandwiches regularly eaten by southerners, not unique to this region but certainly more abundant here than in many other places, are barbecued pork or beef sandwiches.

Beverages

In the South, thirst occupies a consistent place in the long, hot summers. More so than the mythology of other regions, that of the South has often been linked to beverages. Drink is written large in the jazz of New Orleans and the blues of Mississippi, and in the usually religious-based prohibitions against alcohol that have made some southern counties dry and others wet.

Many southern beverages have a long history. The Native Americans created a sort of milk from hickory nuts; drank ceremonial drinks made from yaupon holly, hominy, or persimmons; and settled near rivers with adequate water supplies.

Alcoholic Drinks

As in their homelands, the European settlers arrived expecting that fermented drinks would be much safer than pathogen-packed waters. Thus they carried with them imported spirits, but also instructions on how to make fermented drinks. By 1609 alcohol production was a daily, necessary part of work that fell to both men and women.

Most alcoholic beverages were made at home and were meant for the consumption of the family—young and old alike—until the late nineteenth century. Daily fare would have included ciders of various sorts. However, one of the most commercially viable of all U.S. wines was made in North Carolina by Paul Garrett: the Virginia Dare scuppernong wine.

Alcohol contributed to many deaths among the Native American, European, and African population, but the popularity and economic importance of southern spirituous drinks grew steadily. For special occasions, Madeira was an imported favorite, as was homemade brandy. Rum particularly occupied a crucial place in the early politics of the South. When the French established high tariffs on sugar cane and molasses to save their own homeland sugar industry, the West Indian plantation owners began an earnest trade with the British colonies. The Molasses Act of 1733 halted some of this trade, but not before rum had become an established part of American, including southern, life. George Washington himself gave some seventy-five gallons of rum to potential supporters in his bid for the Virginia House of Burgesses, and rum runners came into being along the Atlantic and Gulf coasts during the colonial period.

Whiskey, though, became and remains the alcoholic beverage most associated with the South. Its central place in the lore of Virginia, Tennessee, and Kentucky, as well as other mountainous areas, is undisputed. As early as 1622, corn whiskey was made in Virginia, and by the early eighteenth century the Scotch-Irish settlers in various states had achieved some fame for their Scottish-based recipes, their stills, and, most important, their experiments with both corn and rye whiskey.

The first bourbon is sometimes attributed to a Baptist minister, one Elijah Craig, said to have distilled it in 1787. However, most accounts date the transformation of corn whiskey into bourbon sometime after the 1794 Whiskey Rebellion, when Scotch-Irish Pennsylvania settlers moved to escape taxes. In their new home in what would become Kentucky, they began experimenting with water that had passed through limestone.

This innovation was one factor in creating what has been called Dixie nectar, or bourbon, named for the county in which it was first produced. Bourbon is made of at least 51 percent fermented corn grain, almost always sour mash (corn, barley, wheat, or rye mixed with pure water, and folded into an older mash and fresh yeast), distilled to a maximum of 160 proof, and then aged for at least two years, and usually four, in charred oak barrels. Bourbon's best-known use is as the key ingredient in mint juleps (although rye, brandy, and rum also are choices).

From the eighteenth century onward, whiskey making—commercially and as a home-based effort—was economically important to residents in the Appalachian and Ozark mountains. Corn transformed into whiskey could be more easily transported than could corn itself, and the rugged terrain of these areas lent itself to the hiding of illegal stills.

Tenders of stills, makers of moonshine, have appeared in endless books and films about the South. Called by some "scared whiskey," southern moonshine became known across America in the escapades of Li'l Abner by Al Capp, and Barney Google and Snuffy Smith by William De Beck.

City dwellers popularized yet other drinks. Savannah made famous the Chatham Artillery punch—first served in the 1850s and still valued today for its mix of tea, lemon, sugar, brandy, whiskey, and Champagne. The cocktail claims a very nearly undisputed heritage in New Orleans, from the bitters and brandy served in egg cups (coquetiers) by Antoine Peychaud in the late 1700s. Other New Orleans–created drinks include the Sazerac, the Ramos gin fizz, and the hurricane. New Orleans itself stands out as the U.S. home of absinthe and, later, herbsaint production.

New Orleans was also the site of the nation's first commercial ice plant (1865). Ice before this time was universally found only in the homes of those wealthy enough to have a stone springhouse with spring waters channeled through it. Imported ice, shipped from the Northeast as ballast for empty ships that would return with agricultural products, was stored in the cool springhouse. Ice in drinks, however, was first seen as a health threat.

Tea, Coffee, Milk, Juice, and Soft Drinks

Yet, iced tea—or, as some southerners say, sweet tea—was destined to become one of the staples of the table. Southern colonialists were tea drinkers from the seventeenth century onward, and early cookbooks such as that of Lettice Bryan attest to its use as a cold beverage early in our history.

Tea itself is grown in a number of private southern gardens. Since the 1840s, South Carolinians have commercially harvested and merchandised some tea. Until 2002 Wadmalaw Island, South Carolina, had the only working tea plantation in the United States. (It was acquired in 2003 by Bigelow Tea, which had plans for reopening production.)

Though not ever-present on the dinner table, coffee also holds a key role in southern foodways. In the late nineteenth century, Nashville entered coffee's history when Atlantic and Pacific Company salesman Joel Cheek marketed a blend he named after the city's Maxwell House Hotel. Today New Orleans coffee merchants still package a coffee and chicory mixture, something not as readily available in other parts of the United States. The city's serving of café brulot (a mixture of orange peels, cinnamon, coffee, and brandy) also gained notoriety well before the twentieth century.

Accompanying coffee might be what southerners call sweet milk, to distinguish it from sour buttermilk. Buttermilk was the drink of choice until recent times. The early colonists drank goat's milk, the poor and enslaved drank skim milk (if any dairy products at all), and only the very rich received fresh milk. In the nineteenth century, however, some families began to keep one cow, and so buttermilk and clabber (curdled milk) figure heavily in southern memory and printed recipes. In the early twentieth century, cornbread soaked in buttermilk was a supper for many, and buttermilk remains a drink of older southerners.

The raising of citrus fruits in Florida and along the Gulf coast meant that lemonade and orange juice attained early status as regional treats. By the mid-1700s, one Jessie Fish saw the commercial possibilities of orange juice and shipped two caskets of the drink to a northern port. However, it wasn't until after World War I that Florida oranges themselves began to be shipped widely, and not until World War II that orange juice followed suit. Today, the making of Florida orange juice is a multibillion dollar business, and orange juice is the state drink of Florida.

By mid-nineteenth century, the temperance movement had helped along the popularity of fruit drinks and their near cousins, what southerners call soft drinks (southerners very, very rarely call these drinks sodas or pop). The South was home to the founding of Coca-Cola (in 1886 in Atlanta, Georgia, by John S. Pemberton); to Pepsi Cola (in 1898 in New Bern, North Carolina, by Caleb Bradburn); to Barq's Root Beer (in 1901 in Biloxi, Mississippi, by Edward A. Barq); to Buffalo Rock Ginger Ale (in 1908 in Birmingham, Alabama, by Sidney Lee); and to Blenheim Ginger Ale (in 1904 in Blenheim, South Carolina, by John May). The tremendous and sometimes global success of those carbonated drinks would follow the post–World War I decline in sugar prices, with other southern drinks including RC Cola, founded in 1933 by a group who worked for Claude Hatcher in Columbus, Georgia. Mostly local soft drinks were Pop Rouge in Louisiana, Dr. Enuf in Tennessee, and Ale 8 in Kentucky. Coca-Cola became the most success-

Several soft drink companies originated in the South, including Coca-Cola and RC Cola. Natchez, Mississippi, 1940. Courtesy Library of Congress.

ful of these drinks when the U.S. Army made Cokes part of the ration given each soldier during World War II.

Sweets

Pecan pie, sweet potato pie, and praline candy are now served all over the world, with the descriptive adjective "southern" attached to them. Other sweets also associated with the region—candies and cakes made from peanuts and sesame seeds, bread puddings, fruit pies of many sorts, berries, melons, and molasses cookies, not to mention various breads and drinks—appear again and again in any culinary history of the region.

To the first inhabitants of the American South, the Native Americans, the inclination to end a meal with a sweet or to save it for later consumption would not have appeared odd in the least. Sir Walter Raleigh wrote enthusiastically of the Virginia strawberry, and Le Page du Pratz equally so about small sweet oranges (satsumas) in Alabama. Dried cherries, blueberries, huckleberries, blackberries, and red and white grapes were similarly noted by early observers of the Native Americans.

To these early traditions, the African, the French, the Spanish, and especially the British (whom scholars say always have consumed more sweets than other groups) added variations that have been passed down in written form since the 1600s. Early manuscript books often began with, or devoted whole sections to, puddings, custards, creams, and sweet breads. Baking was highly prized, and recipes abound for pies, pastries, large loaf cakes, breads, cookies, gingerbreads, fruit preserves and jellies, and jumbles—all, for the most part, copying English traditions.

The treasured place of sweets is evident in Martha Washington's *A Booke of Sweetmeats*, which she began with instructions for clarifying sugar and the successive stages of syrup making, followed by over 100 recipes for preserving fruit. Similarly, her granddaughter's cooking notebook began by telling how best "to keep butter" and proceeded to recipes for some 100 desserts.

Ice cream too was often noted in accounts of the time, as were Indian pudding (sweetened cornmeal) and syllabub (a frothy concoction of sherry, white wine, ale, or cider mixed with cream). The poor of English or French descent or the enslaved Africans, as well as the descendants of both these groups, would not have known such desserts, but instead soaked their cornbreads (from hoecakes to spoon breads) in honey or molasses for part or all of their meal itself. Later sweet treats for those on a small budget might have been stage planks (rather hard gingerbread rectangles) or Moon pies (round marshmallow sandwich cookies sold first to coal miners by the Chattanooga Bakery in the early 1900s).

Southerners also ate humble fruits like the watermelon. By the mid-seventeenth century, this fruit was grown in both Florida and Virginia, and was beginning to spread throughout the South. Requiring a 120-day growing season, the watermelon and other gourds (many used for serving dishes) became the most common fruits of summer.

Despite its sweetness and its beauty as a large red fruit, the watermelon has a complex place in southern thought. Since a number of white illustrators placed African Americans and watermelons in scenes involving theft or laziness, the watermelon has a conflicted place within race politics. Even today, watermelons have remained both popular and maligned. A traditional southern folk tune, *Watermelon on the Vine*, was one of the earliest recordings of southern country music; and the blues song *Watermelon Man* identified the melon as a symbol of sexual power. In 2003 a *New York Times* food critic wrote of how she became ashamed of her love of this summertime fruit. Nevertheless, African American scholar Jessica Harris featured watermelon rind pickles as a product of the African diaspora; summer festivals centered around the watermelon abound; and the roadside sale of watermelons is a beloved summer tradition.

African Americans influenced the overall development of southern sweets made from peanuts, pecans, rice, and sweet potatoes. The word *goober*, from the Congo name *nguba*, remains well known in the South today. Goo Goo Clusters, a commercial concoction of caramel, marshmallows, peanuts, and chocolate, even today hails itself as "the South's Favorite Candy."

Found in at least nine southern states from the Carolinas to Texas, pecans too came to be sweetened with molasses or honey. Pecan pie, a fairly recent dish, dating only from the beginning of the twentieth century, utilizes syrup usually made from sugar cane. Rice too could be made into a sweet, although this was rarely done in the coastal areas. Rice blancmange and other rice puddings with a custard base were the norm in the inland South.

Sweet potatoes and pumpkins, both among the foods eaten by the Native Americans, became favorites throughout the South, probably because they could be grown in small gardens by slaves while other work was being accomplished for the plantations. The sweet potato ripened late in the growing season and thus could be used all winter. It could be baked into pies or sweetened as a whole and then eaten like a banana. Well into the twentieth century, a potato in the South meant a sweet potato.

Southerners reveled too in other recipes such as those for Emma Lane's Prize Cake (published first in 1898 in *Some Good Things to Eat*), chocolate bourbon balls, white divinity fudge, and various fruit and nut cakes. Banana pudding, too, was a southern favorite, made especially in port cities where shipments of bananas were frequent.

For everyday sweets, most southern households up until the late twentieth century canned and preserved fruits. Using crockery jars until the early twentieth century and glass thereafter, canning and preserving meant a yearly gathering of female friends and family.

In addition to these foods that had overarching appeal to all southerners, various regional sweets also came into play. Hernando de Soto planted bitter oranges in 1539, and descendants of these bigarades remain today in the wild orange trees growing yet in underdeveloped areas of Florida. The key lime pie of southern Florida and the peach dishes of Georgia and South Carolina remain favorites. Charleston African Americans gave us benne brittle and benne wafers (from benne, or sesame seeds, first brought from Africa). Another South Carolina favorite is Lady Baltimore cake, a white layer cake with white icing filled with nuts and raisins. Fried pies and boiled custards are popular in Tennessee and Georgia. Mississippi mud cake, pinto bean cake (which had precedents in both African American and American Indian tradition), and testament cake, beloved among the teaching methods of many a Sunday school teacher—found their way onto the table of many a church supper, especially in the rural South. Finally, pralines became a favorite along the Gulf coast. Created from a French recipe for sugared almonds or almond paste, pralines were sold on the streets of Mobile and New Orleans by African American women in the nineteenth century. Today, devotees are usually divided between the creamy praline and the sticky praline.

Southern Sugar

Today, Florida provides the largest crop of sugar cane in the United States—with Palm Beach, Hendry, Martin, and Glades counties producing half the nation's sugar. Louisiana follows as the second biggest producer. An important player in the production of sugar is Savannah Foods (in Georgia, but now owned by a Texas company), which markets Dixie Crystals. Dixie Crystals were first made by generations of Cajuns, transplanted to Georgia in the 1910s.

In Louisiana, the early cultivation of sugar cane proved pivotal to the national consumption of sweets. Although the crop was grown in the mid-eighteenth century, it was not until 1796 that Etienne de Boré perfected his method for crystallizing brown sugar from cane. Soon molasses from sugar cane began to replace sorghum molasses and maple syrup from the Upper South. As cookbook writer Mary Parloa noted in 1887, "The finest molasses came from Porto Rico, and the next best from New Orleans."

Both Louisiana and Florida have social and economic histories long tied to sugar. Prior to the Civil War, some 1,300 Louisiana plantations, with a slave population numbering 125,000, grew and ground cane. After the war, the number of plantations decreased and cooperative agriculture and union organizing were attempted but failed. Some technological changes were made, however. The Reserve refinery, which in 1917 became the largest in the United States, was owned and run by French-born Jewish merchant Leon Godchaux, himself known as the Sugar King.

The growth of Florida as a sugar-producing area occurred continually from colonial times to the present. Since the 1960s, with the importation of Cuban sugar banned and with the skills and knowledge of Cuban refugees, Florida has increased its output, such that the sale of raw sugar and molasses in the 1990s meant millions of dollars in profit and several thousand full-time equivalent jobs in Florida.

RESOURCE GUIDE

Printed Sources

Egerton, John. *Southern Food: At Home, on the Road, in History*. New York: Alfred A. Knopf, 1987.

Harris, Jessica. *The Welcome Table: African American Heritage Cooking*. New York: Simon and Schuster, 1995.

Hilliard, Sam Bowers. *Hog Meat and Hoecake: Food Supply in the Old South, 1840–1860*. Carbondale: Southern Illinois University Press, 1972.

Hudson, Charles. *The Southeastern Indians*. Knoxville: University of Tennessee Press, 1976.

Neal, Bill. *Biscuits, Spoonbread, and Sweet Potato Pie*. Chapel Hill: University of North Carolina Press, 1996.

Rogers, Mara Reid, et al. *The South Beautiful Cookbook*. San Francisco: Collins Publishers, 1996.

Taylor, Joe Gray. *Eating, Drinking, and Visiting in the South: An Informal History*. Baton Rouge: Louisiana State University Press, 1982.

Walter, Eugene. *American Cooking, Southern Style*. New York: Time-Life Books, 1975.

Web Sites

AnythingSouthern.Com. AnythingSouthern Foodways Page. 2002. Accessed October 10, 2003.
http://www.anythingsouthern.com/listing.asp?CategoryID=1142
This page gives links to recipes, as well as sites that explore southern culinary history.

James, Portia, and Psyche A. Williams-Forson. Still Cooking by the Fireside: African Americans in Food Service. 2000. Smithsonian Institution Women's Committee. Accessed October 10, 2003.
http://anacostia.si.edu/food/index.htm
This online exhibit and bibliography explore African Americans as food vendors, waiters, and cooks in various periods of American history.

Johnson, Pableaux, and John T. Edge. The Southern Foodways Alliance Home Page. September 17, 2003. Center for the Study of Southern Culture. Accessed October 10, 2003.
http://www.southernfoodways.com/index.shtml

The mission of the SFA is to celebrate, preserve, promote, and nurture the traditional and developing diverse food culture of the American South. Take here a tour of barbecue country, learn about various documentary projects, and read about books on southern cooking.

Louisiana State Museum. Freshly Brewed: The Coffee Trade and Port of New Orleans. 2002. Accessed October 10, 2003.
http://lsm.crt.state.la.us/site/coffee/coffee1.htm

This exhibit explores the port of New Orleans, the role of coffee importers, and the banana trade in the nineteenth and twentieth centuries.

Mitchel, Jennifer. Culinary Oral History and Survey of Regional Resources on Food in the South. April 11, 2003. Deep South Regional Humanities Center at Tulane University. Accessed October 10, 2003.
http://deepsouth.tulane.edu/programs/southern_cooking.html

The Oral History Project and Survey investigate foodways in Louisiana, and provide listings of printed materials and films on food in the South, and a description of the culinary-related holdings of libraries and archives in Alabama, Arkansas, Louisiana, Mississippi, and Tennessee.

The Mount Vernon Ladies Association. Eighteenth-Century Foodways: A Research Guide. 2000. Mount Vernon Library and Curatorial Collections. Accessed October 10, 2003.
http://www.mountvernon.org/library/books/food.html

An extensive annotated bibliography with links giving recipes from Martha Washington's kitchen.

Olvar, Lynne. Culinary History Timeline: Social History, Manners, Menus. October 4, 2003. Morris County Library, New Jersey. Accessed October 10, 2003.
http://www.gti.net/mocolib1/kid/food1.html

This site lists links to important Web sites on U.S. culinary history and has an extensive timeline, running from prehistory to the present, also with links. Many southern foods are explored here.

Prewitt, Terry, and others. The Culture of Southern Food. Fall 1996. University of West Florida. Accessed October 10, 2003.
http://www.anythingsouthern.com/frameset.asp?Address=http://www.uwf.edu/tprewitt/sofood/welcome.htm

This Web site explores culinary history in Virginia, Appalachia, and the Gulf coast, using the methods of practicing anthropologists.

Videos/Films

Beyond Measure: Appalachian Culture and Economy. Dir. Herb E. Smith. Appalshop, Inc., 2002.
Brunswick Stew. Dir. Stan Woodward. Agee/Ross Spears, 1998.
Fried Green Tomatoes. Dir. Jon Avenet; written by Fannie Flagg and Carol Sobieski. Filmax International, 1991.
It's Grits. Dir. Stan Woodward. Agee/Ross Spears, 1997.

Lost Restaurants of New Orleans. Dir. Peggy Scott Laborde. WYES TV, 2002.
Smokestack Lightning: A Day in the Life of Barbecue. Dir. Scott Stohler and Lolis Eric Elie. Bay Package Productions, 2001.
Soul Food. Dir. George Tillman. Starring Vanessa Williams. Twentieth Century Fox, 1997.
Southern Stews. Dir. Stan Woodward. Stan Woodward, 2001.

Organizations, Museums, Special Collections

Mariners' Museum
100 Museum Drive
Newport News, VA 23606
http://www.mariner.org/

The Mariners' Museum contains artifacts, paintings, and photographs that illuminate life on the sea. Recent exhibits included an exploration of African Americans as oystermen, crab pickers, cooks and waiters on steamboats, oyster shuckers, and fishmongers.

Maritime and Seafood Industry Museum
Point Cadet Plaza
P.O. Box 1907
Biloxi, MS 39533
http://www.maritimemuseum.org/aboutus.html

This museum preserves and interprets the maritime history and heritage of Biloxi and the Mississippi Gulf coast, as well as shrimping, oystering, recreational fishing, and other subjects.

Monticello
Thomas Jefferson Foundation
P.O. Box 316
Charlottesville, VA 22902
http://www.monticello.org/about/index.html

The historic home of Thomas Jefferson offers the chance to explore a plantation and the grounds where many foods were raised.

Southern Foodways Alliance
Center for the Study of Southern Culture
Barnard Observatory
University, MS 38677
http://www.southernfoodways.com/index.shtml

The mission of the SFA is to celebrate, preserve, promote, and nurture the traditional and developing diverse food culture of the American South, through an annual symposium, held in October, and various documentary projects.

Vorhoff Library and New Orleans Culinary History Group
Newcomb College Center for Research on Women
Tulane University
New Orleans, LA 70118
http://www.tulane.edu/~wclib/culinary.html

The Library has over 2,000 cookbooks and culinary history books. The Culinary History Group works on special projects, such as an oral history of New Orleans cuisine, a bibliography of New Orleans cookbooks, and the survey of regional resources on culinary history housed online at the Deep South Regional Humanities Center (see http://deepsouth.tulane.edu/programs/southern_cooking.html).

Events

Alabama

Bayou la Batre Blessing of the Fleet
St. Margaret Catholic Church
P.O. Box 365
Bayou La Batre, AL 36509
(251) 824-2415
http://www.arts.state.al.us/actc/articles/blessing.htm

Held annually in May. Part religious ceremony, part local heritage celebration and part tourist attraction, this parade of boats opens the shrimping season.

Franklin County Watermelon Festival
P.O. Box 44
Russellville, AL 35653
(256) 332-1760
franklincounty@charter.net
http://www.franklincountychamber.org

Held annually in August. Activities and foods centered around watermelons and other melons.

Arkansas

Annual Bradley County Pink Tomato Festival
Chamber of Commerce
206 N. Myrtle
Warren, AR 71671
(870) 226-5225
http://www.bradleycountychamberofcommerce.com

Held annually in June. All-tomato luncheon, tomato eating contest, chili cook-off, and other activities.

Annual Hope Watermelon Festival
Chamber of Commerce
P.O. Box 250
Hope, AR 71801
(870) 777-3640
http://www.hopemelonfest.com

Held annually in August. Watermelon eating and seed spitting contests, watermelon judging and auction, and Watermelon Olympics.

Annual Purplehull Pea Festival & World's Championship Rotary Tiller Race
City of Emerson
P.O. Box 1
Emerson, AR 71740
(870) 547-2707 or (501) 315-7373
http://www.purplehull.com

Held annually in June. World's Championship Tiller race, the World Cup Purplehull Pea Shelling Competition, purple hull pea booth, the Great Purplehull Peas & Cornbread Cook Off.

Florida

La Belle Swamp Cabbage Festival
La Belle, FL
http://members.aol.com/browne/scf.html

Held annually in February. Celebrates Florida's most unusual vegetable.

Central Florida Peanut Festival
Williston, FL
(352) 528-5552
http://www.floridasecrets.com/AnnualEvents/WCevents/WCSpotlight/CentralFlorida
PeanutFestival.htm

Held annually in October. Contests, dishes made with peanuts and more.

Isle of Eight Flags Shrimp Festival
P.O. Box 6146
Fernandina Beach, FL 32035
(866) 4-Amelia or (904) 261-3248
http://www.shrimpfestival.com

Held annually in May. Contests and activities around seafood from Florida waters.

Georgia

Big Pig Jig Festival
Dooly County Chamber of Commerce
Vienna, GA 31092
(229) 268-8275
http://www.bigpigjig.com

Held annually in October. Georgia's Barbecue Cooking Championship with specialty food vendors, a hog calling contest, and the popular People's Choice Tasting contest.

Brunswick Seafood Festival
30 Nimitz Dr.
Brunswick, GA 31520
(912) 265-4032
http://www.brunswickgeorgia.com

Held annually in May. A weekend-long event filled with delicious seafood, the Scrap-yard Navy Race, and a Blessing of the Fleet.

Vidalia Onion Festival
P.O. Box 504
Vidalia, GA 30474
(912) 538-8687
http://www.searchvidalia.com

Held annually in April. Celebrating the harvest of the world's most delicious Vidalia.

Kentucky

Headquarters for International Bar-B-Q Festival
St. Ann Street
Owensboro, KY 42304
(800) 489-1131
http://www.bbqfest.com

Held annually in May. Cooking teams and ten tons of mutton, 5,000 chickens, and 1,500 gallons of burgoo.

Marion County Country Ham Days
Lebanon-Marion County Chamber of Commerce
21 Court Square
Lebanon, KY 40033
(270) 692-9594
http://www.hamdays.com

Held annually in September. Festival featuring country ham breakfast, Country Ham Jam street dance, Pokey Pig 5K Run, and other events.

World Chicken Festival
London-Laurel County Tourist Commission
140 West Daniel Boone Parkway
London, KY 40741
(606) 878-6900
http://www.chickenfestival.com

Held annually in September. World's largest known stainless steel skillet serving delicious fried chicken.

Louisiana

Breaux Bridge Crawfish Festival
P.O. Box 25
Breaux Bridge, LA 70517
(337) 332-6655
http://www.bbcrawfest.com/generalinfo.html

Held annually in April/May. The Breaux Bridge Crawfish Festival has been named a top festival in the country.

French Food Festival
Larose Regional Park & Civic Center
P.O. Box 1105
Larose, LA 70373
(985) 693-7355
Fax: (985) 693-7380
http://www.BayouCivicClub

Held annually in October. Celebrates Creole and Cajun Cuisine and music.

Jambalaya Festival
P.O. Box 1243
Gonzales, LA 70707-1243
(800) 680-3208
(225) 647-9237
http://www.ascensionparish.com/festival/jambalaya/contact.html

Held annually in May. Gonzales, the "Jambalaya Capital of the World," opens its doors so that others may taste over forty kinds of gumbo.

Louisiana Shrimp and Petroleum Festival
Morgan City
P.O. Box 103
Morgan City, LA 70381

(985) 385-0703

http://www.shrimp-petofest.org/

Held annually in August/September. The event is free and has grown to become one of the country's premiere festivals.

New Orleans Jazz and Heritage Festival
1205 North Rampart St.
New Orleans, LA 70116
(504) 522-4786
http://www.nojazzfest.com

Held annually in April and May. The festival celebrates the indigenous music and culture of New Orleans and Louisiana, and has food from selected vendors, food demonstrations, and panel discussions concerning the folklore, recipes, and history of food.

Strawberry Festival
Ponchatoula Strawberry Festival, Inc.
P.O. Box 446
Ponchatoula, LA 70454
(985) 542-7520
(800) 917-7045

Held annually in April. Prides itself as being one of the few festivals in which nonprofit organizations are the only vendors on the official festival grounds.

Mississippi

Pioneer and Indian Festival
P.O. Box 69
Ridgeland, MS 39158
(601) 856-7546
http://members.aol.com/frankt29/thomfilm/pioneer.htm

Held annually in October. Celebrates Native American food in Mississippi.

World Catfish Festival
P.O. Box 385
Belzoni, MS 39038
(800) 408-4838
http://www.catfishcapitalonline.com

Held annually in April. Celebrates the cooking of catfish in many different ways.

North Carolina

The Barbecue Festival
P.O. Box 1642
Lexington, NC 27293
(336) 956-1880
http://www.barbecuefestival.com

Held annually in October. Celebrates Lexington barbecue.

North Carolina Apple Festival
NC Apple Festival Headquarters
P.O. Box 886
Hendersonville, NC 28793

(828) 697-4557
apple1@ncapplefestival.org
http://www.ncapplefestival.org

Held annually in August. Celebrates apples grown in North Carolina.

North Carolina Peach Festival
Downtown Candor and
Fitzgerald Park on Railroad Street
Candor, NC 27229
(910) 576-6011
http://www.southfest.com/festivals/ncpeach.shtml

Held annually in July. Peach dishes, games, and other entertainment.

South Carolina

Okra Strut Festival
P.O. Box 406
Irmo, SC 29063
(803) 781-7850
http://www.irmookrastrut.com

Held annually September. The festival is now a two-day event featuring a street dance, parade, arts and crafts, rides and amusements, petting zoo, and lots of festival food.

Squealin' on the Square (Barbecue Cook-off)
Main Street Laurens USA, Inc.
P.O. Box 1736
Laurens, SC 29360
(864) 984-2119
mail@mainstreetlaurens.org
http://www.mainstreetlaurens.org/calendar.html

Held annually in October. This festival has barbeque samples from BBQ cook teams and other contests.

Tennessee

Allardt Pumpkin Festival and Weigh-off
City of Allardt
P.O. Box 448
Allardt, TN 38504
(931) 879-7607
http://www.picktnproducts.org/tourism/festivals.html

Held annually in October. This festival showcases the weighing of giant pumpkins, watermelons, and other oversized vegetables.

Memphis in May
Memphis in May International Festival Inc.
245 Wagner Place, Memphis, TN 38103
(901) 525-4611
http://www.memphisinmay.org/

Held annually in May. A series of festivals throughout the month, including the Barbeque World Championships and the Great Southern Food Festival.

Scott County Sorghum Festival
P.O. Box 4442
Oneida, TN 37841
(423) 569-6900 or (800) 645-6905
http://www.scottcounty.com/Events/annual.cfm

Held annually in September. Sorghum, table-grade syrup, is here celebrated through many games, tastings, and other activities.

Virginia

Urbanna Oyster Festival
Drawer C
Urbanna, VA 23175
(804) 758-0368
Fax: (804) 758-9052
oysterfestival@oasisonline.com
http://www.urbannaoysterfestival.com/

Held annually in November. At this festival food is provided by over fifty vendors.

Virginia Food Festival
RIR on Strawberry Hill
Richmond, VA
(804) 643-3555
FoodFestival@att.net
http://www.vdacs.state.va.us/news/releases-b/091203foodfest.html

Held annually in August. This festival celebrates the many foods that are produced in Virginia. Scrumptious edibles such as ham, crabs, peanuts, and eggs complete the menu available to the thousands who come to the fairgrounds.

Virginia Pork Festival
P.O. Box 1001
Emporia, VA 23847
(804) 634-3485
http://www.vaporkfestival.com

Held annually in June. This festival is one of the East Coast's largest food festivals, with outstanding pork dishes. Dishes range from barbecued loin chops and spare ribs to chitterlings and sausage burgers.

LANGUAGE

Michael Montgomery

The linguistic landscape of the American South is as diverse and complex as that of any region in the country, with five centuries of contact between Old World and New World languages that originated on three continents. European languages arrived in permanent settlements in the early sixteenth century with Spanish in Florida and South Carolina; in the seventeenth century with English in Virginia and French in South Carolina and Louisiana (the latter much more prominent); and in the eighteenth century with German (in Virginia, by way of Pennsylvania). Many others came having fewer speakers and less permanence. Many native and European languages have disappeared (or are rapidly doing so), having left their mark in place names, local vocabulary, or otherwise. The South remains a very heterogeneous place and has become even more so since 1990, with speakers of many types of Spanish, Haitian Creole, and other tongues, especially diverse Asian languages, forming sizable immigrant communities that appear to be maintaining their languages more than other recent waves of newcomers. A comprehensive linguistic history has yet to be written, but a good place to begin reading about language in the region is the "Language" section of the *Encyclopedia of Southern Culture* (see especially the section's overview essay).[1]

NATIVE LANGUAGES

At least thirty (and possibly more than twice that number) native languages were once spoken in the South. They include members of five families (Algonquian, Muskogean, Iroquoian, Siouan, and Caddoan) and at least six other unaffiliated languages (Timucua in Florida and Georgia, and Yuchi in South Carolina and Georgia, among others). Most had been in the region for millennia, but some arrived in comparatively recent times (for example, the Cherokee to Mississippi from what is now the Midwest). As early as the sixteenth century, contact with the Spanish in Florida and South Carolina put the existence of many small groups under

305

pressure from disease, forced labor, and competition for land. The identity, even the existence, of some of them and the language they spoke are known only from a highly fragmentary record and from considerable detective work (for example, Apalachee in Florida). Recording equipment and professionally trained linguists arrived barely in time in the 1930s to make a record of several (e.g., Tunica in Mississippi). By the end of the twentieth century the future of all remaining native languages was in danger, with few people under the age of twenty having a native command. The extinction of these languages seemed inevitable, aided by deliberate policy in the nineteenth century to remove their speakers forcibly to Indian Territory (modern-day Oklahoma), prohibition against the use of native languages in tribal schools until recent years, and the dominance of English speakers numerically, economically, and politically. However, many revival movements have sprouted, even where the ancestral language is known only from decades-old recordings (e.g., among the Catawba in South Carolina.[2] More courses in tribal languages are offered in schools and community centers today than ever before, and Cherokee has for the first time become a required course in one local high school in western North Carolina. Thus, the future of native languages is by no means as dire as it looked a few short years ago. For the best general surveys of the subject, see James Crawford's *Southeastern Indian Languages* (1976), which has an extensive survey of the literature of twenty-nine languages, and Hardy and Scancarelli's *Native Languages of the Southeastern United States* (2004). That literature dates to the late eighteenth century, when British, Spanish, and French traders and missionaries began collecting word-lists. Though handicapped by trying to analyze languages very different in almost every way from familiar European ones, and lacking tools such as a phonetic alphabet, early workers left a rich record for scholars and tribal officials (including revivalists) to mine later.

Sequoyah, inventor of the Cherokee alphabet. Courtesy Library of Congress.

The historic contribution of Native American and other languages to English can be judged best from the *Dictionary of American Regional English* (see below), whose editors have produced indexes to the first three volumes, which cover A–O; these borrowings are mainly names for plants. Therein one finds three terms in American English from Cherokee (e.g., *conohany*), seven from Choctow (e.g., *appaloosa*, *bayou*), two from Creek (e.g., *catalpa*), and one from Seminole (*coontie*). No in-depth study has superseded Mathews' *Some Sources of Southernisms* (1948), which treats words and geographical nomenclature that entered southern English from Muskogean languages (Creek, Chickasaw, Choctaw, Seminole, etc.) and Nahuatl (e.g., *chicle, mesquite*). What English has borrowed from native languages of the South is surprisingly little and obscure, the exception being Algonquian languages (especially Powhatan) in Virginia, which gave John Smith and his followers *raccoon, possum*, and other common terms for things completely new to Europeans. In western North Carolina, eastern Tennessee, and north Georgia, the Cherokee intermarried with whites and introduced a substantial part of their traditional culture (e.g., herbal cures) to them, but their linguistic influence was tiny.

EUROPEAN LANGUAGES OTHER THAN ENGLISH

Spanish, the first European language to establish itself in the region, left an imprint on the place names of Florida and to a much lesser extent in South Carolina, Louisiana, and other colonies/states. Among the oldest Spanish-language communities in the region are those in Florida deriving from Cuba (greatly enlarged in the 1960s) and the Isleños of southeastern Louisiana, who came from the Canary Islands in the 1770s.[3] Today the number of Spanish speakers is growing rapidly, by several-fold in only a decade in the Carolinas, Georgia, and elsewhere. According to the 2000 Census, 4.24 million (6 percent) of the 67.5 million people in the eleven-state region spoke Spanish, a figure that will almost certainly continues to increase. Florida led with 15 percent, followed by North Carolina (4.7 percent) and Virginia (4.4 percent). With its many varieties of Spanish from the Caribbean, Central America, and South America, and the influx of other groups recently, South Florida has become the most linguistically diverse and the most polyglot part of the South.

French, once spoken in much of the Lower Mississippi Valley, first came to Louisiana more than three centuries ago. The three general varieties of Louisiana French include one directly from France that was close to the Parisian standard; Cajun French, which arrived from Acadia (Nova Scotia and New Brunswick) in the mid-eighteenth century; and Creole French (sometimes called Gumbo or Gombo), produced by contact between Europeans and Africans and perhaps also Native Americans.[4]

The heartland of German language use and influence in the United States is Pennsylvania, and most of the German found in the South was or is a product of secondary migration from that state. Two centuries ago, German dialects were commonly heard in the Shenandoah Valley of Virginia, where their speakers migrated as early as 1726. By the time of the Revolution, German speakers comprised 5 percent of Virginia's population. Today use of the language depends on the survival of two conservative religious denominations, the Old Order Amish and Old Order Mennonites.[5] Beginning in the seventeenth century, German speakers settled in South Carolina in four stages, contributing such terms as *saddle horse, sawbuck, spooks,* and *I want off* to the state's English.

Underappreciated is the cultural and linguistic diversity of arrivals from the British Isles. To be sure, those who came from Scotland and Ireland (less so for Wales) usually spoke English rather than a Celtic language, but they did not consider themselves to be "English." Very rarely did these groups come early, form their own communities, or use a Celtic language outside the home. The major ex-

307

ception was the Highland Scots, who first came to North Carolina's Cape Fear Valley in the 1730s. They usually had Scots Gaelic for their first language and used it there for well over a century. Even in that part of North Carolina, however, Gaelic left no mark.[6]

OVERVIEW OF ENGLISH IN THE SOUTH

Few traits identify southerners so readily as the way they speak English. It's what non-southerners often notice first, sometimes with ridicule but sometimes also with admiration; southerners are known for their ability to tell stories, for example. For many southerners, the way they speak English marks their loyalties and their identity, but they often face stereotypes and prejudice when they travel away from home, and not infrequently in southern schoolrooms as well. Over the past forty years more than 100 popular glossaries—often tourist-shop caricatures—have expressed the range of attitudes southerners have toward their own speech. When Jimmy Carter ran for president in 1976, a spate of these appeared, including the best-known member of the genre, Steve Mitchell's *How to Speak Southern* (1976), which went through dozens of printings and had at least two spin-offs.

The South is the most recognized speech region in the United States and is often perceived to be homogeneous. Some features are used by most southerners of all social classes (for example, pronouncing *pen* and *pin* alike), but the region is hardly more uniform than the country as a whole and is distinctive most for its mix of varieties. The Mason-Dixon Line has never set the region apart in speech, and the "isolation" of the South (or parts of it) has been greatly exaggerated. Linguistic research can identify no common denominator that can safely identify a "southern accent" or a "southern dialect."

Rather than the hot climate or slower pace of life, factors to which many features of southern life are often attributed, the region's speech habits can be explained by history, demography, social factors, and psychology (that is, the consciousness of the region's people). The most unusual types of speech are found on the periphery of the South, in areas such as the mountains of southern Appalachia and Arkansas and such coastal areas as the Outer Banks of North Carolina, the Chesapeake Bay Islands of Virginia, and the Sea Islands of South Carolina and Georgia.[7] Many speech patterns differentiate people within the region socially as much as geographically, such as the lack of pronunciation of *r* in *car* and *bird*, which among whites in the Deep South is less common in the working class and among younger speakers. Although no unique linguistic features distinguish the South by its speech, two factors differentiate it from other regions: a unique combination of linguistic features, and the use of these features more often by a wider range of people than elsewhere.

Southern Grammar

General features of grammar that are southern, some of which do not have exact equivalents in other types of American English, include the following: (1) *y'all* and *you all* (the second being the somewhat more formal variant) as second-person plural pronouns; (2) *liked to*, "almost," as in *I liked to died*; (3) adding *all* after pronouns to indicate inclusion, as in *what all, who all* (*Who all did you see?*); (4) verbs with the same form in all tenses, as *come, run*; (5) the helping verb *done* to emphasize, as in *he done broke the television*; (6) double helping verb constructions such as *might could* and *might can*; (7) verbs whose principal parts are made regular (*blowed, heared*); (8) use of a "personal dative" pronoun, as in *I bought me a dog*; and (9) *fixin' to*, meaning "be about to, getting prepared to."

Southern Pronunciation

Among general features of southern pronunciation are the following: (1) prolonging and splitting of vowels into two syllables (*bed* as *bay-uhd*, *hit* as *hee-uht*, sometimes known as the "southern drawl"); (2) modifying "long i" to *ah*, so that *my right side* sounds like *mah raht sahd* and *mile* rhymes with *mall*; (3) shifting of accent to the first syllable (*EN-tire, PO-lice*); (4) the "breaking" of some vowels, especially common in the Upper South, so that *steel* is pronounced like *stale*, and *stale* like *stile* (sometimes called the "southern vowell shift"); (5) similar pronunciation of front vowels before nasal consonants, so that pairs of words like *pen* and *pin* and *hem* and *him* are pronounced alike; (6) nasalization of vowels in words like *pumpkin*; and (7) final *l* reduced or lost in words like *ball, boil*.

Dialect Divisions and Affinities

As shown by research of the Linguistic Atlas project (see below), the South is divided into two broad subregions in speech: the Lower South (also known as South or Deep South, covering the Atlantic coastal plain from eastern Virginia to Texas, and the South Midland (sometimes known as Upland Southern or Upper South, encompassing the Piedmont and the southern Appalachians from Virginia through South Carolina, the hill areas above the Piedmont in Georgia and Alabama, and the northwest half of Arkansas).

The speech of the Lower South has some affinities (as in the pronunciation of vowels) to that of London and the southern counties of England, and the speech of the Upper South is akin (especially in grammar) to the speech of the north of England, Scotland, and Ulster (the northernmost province of Ireland). The contribution by Scotch-Irish immigrants from Ulster (who were the dominant group in many parts of the Carolina and Virginia backcountry in pre-Revolutionary days) has been significantly underestimated. To southern English they contributed *cracker* (originally "a boaster," then "a person from the backwoods," and now "a rural white person from Georgia or Florida"), *galluses* for "suspenders," *gumption* for "common sense, good judgment, shrewdness," *wait on* for "wait for," and many other terms and grammatical patterns, perhaps even *y'all*.[8]

We can speak of three broad streams in the formation of southern English, contributed by settlers from England, Ulster, and Africa. Broad connections with British speech patterns are discernible because fewer non-English speakers from continental Europe settled in the South than in the North. But the influx of large numbers of Africans over a period of two and a half centuries, speaking dozens of languages, has made the situation far more complex. No type of English came to American shores without immediate changes. Everywhere competing dialects and languages were the norm, even in more remote places. Popular beliefs that seemingly isolated areas like the Outer Banks or the southern Appalachian Mountains preserve "pure Elizabethan English" or "pure Scotch-Irish English" from centuries ago are powerful and attractive and are held ardently by local people as well as outsiders, but they are great exaggerations and usually based on only a small handful of usages.

South Midland speech derives primarily from the colonial settlements in the Delaware Valley of Pennsylvania. It was carried southwestward into eastern Virginia and the Carolinas and then in the nineteenth century across the northern parts of Georgia, Alabama, and Mississippi and also across Tennessee, Kentucky, and Arkansas. Typical South Midland vocabulary includes *blinds* for "window shades," *little piece* for "short distance," *skillet* for "frying pan," *red worm* for "earthworm," and *quarter till* for "quarter to." Coastal southern speech was also carried southwestward from the colonial settlements in Virginia and the Carolinas into southern Georgia, Alabama, Mississippi, and Louisiana and then northward into eastern Arkansas and western Tennessee and Kentucky, and also into Florida. Typical Coastal southern vocabulary items include *lightwood* for "kindling" and *piazza* for "porch." Crossing migration patterns have blended these two general varieties of speech in the interior South, so that the more clear-cut distinctions found in the Atlantic states diminish as one moves west. The two regions differ from one another most in vocabulary: for example, the South Midland has *chigger* and *redworm*, while the Coastal South has *redbug* and *earthworm*.

The Planting of English

When it arrived in Virginia, English had yet to develop a standard written form, much less a spoken one. Spelling was quite inconsistent. For a century or more the English of the South Atlantic colonies was largely an Atlantic variety with similarities to the English spoken in New England as well as Britain. It was in constant and rapid flux from the arrival of more and more speakers, and it grew constantly by borrowing from other tongues, both native and European. Little is known with certainly about the diverse English of early settlers, however, because few records survive with direct evidence until well into the eighteenth century. All indications are that they brought quite different types of English to North America, and no doubt the competition of languages and dialects in the early days of settlement involved a leveling of differences and an amalgamation, producing a middle ground between dialects in many places.

In the late eighteenth century writers like Noah Webster and the Reverend John Witherspoon noted (and condemned) characteristic southern usages as contrary to a national ideal, so the South was developing (or was perceived to have) its own speech by that time. In the first half of the nineteenth century, southern speech became more and more distinctive from that of the rest of the country, probably because this was the period when the region achieved a strong regional consciousness. During that period commentators in the South first began compiling glossaries and observations; several of these, from Virginia, Georgia, and Tennessee, are gathered in *The Beginnings of American English*.[9]

In some respects English in the South (not just in more isolated areas) has been more conservative than other regional types of American English, preserving eighteenth- and nineteenth-century usages that are rarely found today in Great Britain or elsewhere in the United States. Most of these older forms are vocabulary (e.g., *poke*, "paper bag"; *tote*, "carry"; *carry*, "take, escort"), but some southern pronunciations are also preservations from centuries ago. *Git* for *get*, the pronunciation of the suffix-*ing* as *-in* in words like *talking* and *sleeping*, and the absence of *r* after vowels were all fashionable in Great Britain in the 1700s, though today they and other usages are often labeled "nonstandard" and discouraged in the twenty-first-century schoolroom.

Change and Innovation

Many grammatical forms that were brought by immigrants from Britain or Ireland have developed new patterns or meanings in the South. For example, especially among African Americans the verb *be* came to refer to a habitual or frequent activity (*he be talking*, "he talks all the time"). Speakers of English everywhere use *whatever* and *whoever*, but in the South these developed the inverted forms *everwhat* and *everwho* (*Everwho it was didn't call back*). *Might could* is known in Ulster and Scotland (its place of origin), but many other similar southern combinations of helping verbs, such as *might would*, are not.

Change and innovation have been constant in all categories of southern speech. The social and political alienation that affected the former Confederate states for decades after the Civil War apparently intensified the region's dialect identity, so much so that some scholars argue that southern English as we now know it was mainly a post–Civil War development, produced by isolation and demographic changes not affecting other parts of the country.[10]

Thus, some of the most radical changes in southern speech began, or at least spread rapidly in the late nineteenth century, continuing into the twentieth century as the South became more and more urbanized and industrialized. Some of these were and have been divergent, but others converged with other types of American English. Changes in vocabulary were dramatic and were primarily in the direction of homogeneity with the rest of the country (for example, southerners increasingly use *green beans* rather than *string beans* and *bag* rather than *sack*). A recent study of local students at a small western North Carolina college found a striking loss of regional vocabulary, with *living room*, *gutters*, *mantel*, and *attic* completely replacing *big house*, *eaves trough*, *fireboard*, and *loft*. Ellen Johnson has done a comprehensive study of the subject.[11]

But pronunciation is another matter. The "southern vowel shift" appears to be spreading rapidly. Pronouncing "long i" as *ah* is holding its own, as the speech of the two main candidates for president in 2000 attested. One recent study in a small Alabama city showed that young men use the southern drawl more than older women, which indicates the desire of southerners to preserve their speech. Thus, in some regards the pronunciation of southern speech is becoming less like that of the rest of the country, and television can hardly be the culprit for this.

The forces bringing about more uniformity in contemporary American English are upward mobility, mass education, and the shift of population to urban areas since World War II. In the South these have blurred traditional distinctions in speech lingering from the days of greater social stratification. The speech of natives in Charlotte or Memphis today often differs greatly from that of a generation ago, but that of small towns not nearly so much. Young, middle-class speakers of the urban and suburban South today are often much closer to their peers in the urban North and West.

These social and demographic forces have meant that the regional dialects in the South are increasingly being replaced by social dialects (often based on age) and that regional dialect boundaries are shifting in the South. Coastal cities such as Savannah and Richmond exercised influence from the eighteenth well into the twentieth century, but the exploding metropolises of the Upper South, such as Atlanta and Nashville, are now the centers for linguistic change and new regional standards of speech. Whereas older speakers in Columbia, South Carolina (halfway between Charleston and Charlotte), often pronounce *Mary*, *merry*, and *marry* with three different Lower southern vowel sounds, their grandchildren more often than not pronounce all three words with the same vowel of *merry*, the South Midland pattern.

Black/White Dimensions of Speech

The question of how speech differs between blacks and whites in the South has produced much research, commentary, and controversy. Scholarly views differ widely.[12] The question is first a historical one. One extreme view is that the speech of blacks (except for Gullah, spoken on the Sea Islands of South Carolina and Georgia; see below) retains only a very small handful of nouns (e.g., *goober*, *gumbo*, *juke*) and names from African languages and that all other features of black speech derive from an older type of southern speech shared with whites. An intermediate view is that African and Caribbean languages strongly influenced the speech of the Sea Islands, but influenced that of African Americans much less so elsewhere (this view links the absence of the verb *be*, as in *you kiddin'*, to such an influence). This view also argues that the African contribution to American English is generally underappreciated; one exponent of this view, David Dalby, discusses Africanisms and probable Africanisms in American English and presents eighty forms in a glossary with etymological notes.[13] At the other extreme is the view that present-day African American English as spoken everywhere is only superficially English and is ultimately derived from a creole language like Gullah, spoken on southern plantations throughout the South in the nineteenth century. J. L. Dillard in *Black English: Its History and Usage in the United States* (1972) argues for this position and holds that many usages in southern white speech are due to the influence of African Americans.

It is this last view that was espoused by the Oakland, California, School Board and that sparked the highly publicized and emotional "Ebonics" controversy beginning in December 1996. It produced a large body of literature and public discussion.[14] The case for a distinct "Black English" or "African American English," however, is easier to make in the urban North than in the South, where far fewer linguistic forms are used exclusively by either blacks or whites. African American English in Detroit and Chicago is to a large extent, especially in pronunciation, southern English transported and quite different from local white varieties there.

Early commentators on the speech of southern blacks emphasized its conservativeness, some even calling it "Shakespearean." But there is much evidence that for the past century it has been one of the most innovative varieties (or collection of varieties) in the country, both in the South and in the urban North, where most research has been concentrated in recent decades. This is true not just for vocabulary. African American English has developed many new grammatical features in the past two or three generations (e.g., *steady* in *he steady working*, "he works constantly").[15] However, northern teachers and linguists have routinely labeled as "Black English" many other features, such as the helping verb *done* (*I done told you to stop that*), that are quite common in southern white speech.

Gullah

About forty years ago linguists began noting profound structural similarities between many English-based creole languages of the West Indies, from the Bahamas to Belize to Trinidad and Guyana. It became clear that Gullah (also called Geechee), a creole spoken by African Americans from the northern coast of South Carolina to the Florida border, shared many of these similarities. Historical research revealed that in the eighteenth century many slaves were brought from the Caribbean (Jamaica and especially Barbados, the parent colony of South Carolina in 1670) and only later from Africa. Today there are perhaps 200,000 Gullah speakers, perhaps half of them using it daily, but such an estimate is quite tentative, for many reasons. Gullah is not a language distinct from English in the way that French and Spanish are; some degrees of Gullah are close to the local English, others much less so. Nearly all Gullah vocabulary is shared with English (only 5 percent comes from African or Caribbean sources), but Caribbean-based grammatical rules, rhythms, and sometimes the meanings of words make Gullah not easily comprehensible to English speakers elsewhere, including African Americans from the rural South two or three hours away by car. Speakers of Gullah usually have the ability to shift quite dramatically between superficial and deep levels, depending on their purposes and who they are talking to.

The first significant and still most important study of Gullah is Lorenzo Dow Turner's *Africanisms in the Gullah Dialect*.[16] It is the foundation upon which all later work rests, though its focus is primarily on items that can probably or possibly be traced to West African languages. This study has sample Gullah texts and sections on Gullah grammar, pronunciation, and intonation, as well as an exhaustive list of Gullah names and vocabulary (e.g., *nini*, "female breast," from Mende; *moco*, "witchcraft, magic," from Fula) compared to words of similar form and meaning in thirty African languages. In all, Turner identified approximately 4,000 Africanisms, but 90 percent of these were personal names rather than usages in the everyday language of the Gullah community. His book is often technical, but a recent reprinting (2002) features a lengthy new introduction for the general reader and includes a biography of the author, the first professionally trained African American linguist.

Today the Sea Islands are experiencing a cultural renaissance, and interest in Gullah food, music, storytelling, literature, and traditions has extended to language. The most dramatic evidence of this is a Bible translation undertaken by the Sea Island

Dictionary of American Regional English

At its inception in 1889 the American Dialect Society saw as a primary mission the collection of material for a full-scale, historically based dictionary of the country's regional English on a scale comparable to Joseph Wright's *English Dialect Dictionary* (1898–1905). It began publishing word-lists and glossaries submitted by its members from around the country in its journals *Dialect Notes* (1890–1939) and *American Speech* (1925–). Not until 1985, however, did volumes of the *Dictionary of American Regional English* (*DARE*) begin to appear. This extraordinary work on the country's regional English contains tens of thousands of entries and hundreds of thousands of quotations, and is based on the widest possible range of oral and written sources the editors could find, including all the material in the two American Dialect Society periodicals identified above. *DARE* is particularly useful because it employs a wide-ranging system of regional and social labels for words, meanings, and pronunciations. When a usage is found to be prevalent more or less in an area or among a group, this is specified. For example, 215 terms from letters A to O are labeled "Appalachian" (*beal*, "of a sore: to fester"; *discomfit*, "to inconvenience") and 411 "Black" (e.g., *buddygee*, "a friend, buddy"; *crab-apple switch*, "large pocket-knife"). The labels are not only numerous, but also more valid than those found in any other dictionary; because *DARE* has nationwide coverage, its editors could tell with assurance when a term was confined to a certain area or group, that is, both where it was used and where it was not. The range of labels is wide: "affectionate," "African," "Alabama," "Alaska," "Allegheny Mountains," "Amish," "aphetic," and so on.

Translation Team of the Wycliffe Bible Translators, at work since 1979.[17] Two Gospels have appeared—*De Good Nyews Bout Jedus Christ Wa Luke Write* (1995) and *De Good Nyews Bout Jedus Christ Wa John Write* (2003)—with the entire New Testament scheduled to appear in late 2004. Other than Native American languages like Cherokee, Creek, and Choctaw, Gullah is the only language in the South to have its own translation of Scripture.

While popular attention has, following Turner's footsteps, focused on its African roots, Gullah's more immediate historical connections to Caribbean creoles have drawn more scholarly analysis. The language and the culture associated with it preserve both, but it is the Caribbean flavor that visitors more often notice when they hear the lilt of Gullah for the first time, imagining they are on Jamaica.

The Study of Southern English

There is more commentary on the speech of the American South than on that of any other region of the country. The South is the only region to have a book-length bibliography devoted to its speech. The *Annotated Bibliography of Southern American English* lists nearly 4,000 items and is a point of departure for exploring countless topics on language in the region.[18]

The largest effort to survey the South's English has involved three regional linguistic atlases, projects that stemmed from a vision in the late 1920s of the Linguistic Society of America and the American Council of Learned Societies. The object was to survey the traditional vocabulary, pronunciation, and grammar of English-speaking North America by interviewing older, mainly rural speakers using a standard questionnaire. Following fieldwork interviews for the *Linguistic Atlas of New England* (1931–1933), work commenced on the *Linguistic Atlas of the Middle and South Atlantic States* (*LAMSAS*) and was finished in the early 1950s after being interrupted by World War II. *LAMSAS* interviewed 1,162 people from New York to northeastern Florida, including 154 people in Virginia, 157 in North Carolina, 156 in South Carolina, 110 in Georgia, and 9 in Florida. Linguistic information collected was to be correlated with geography and such cultural and historical phenomena as settlement and migration.

Three volumes from the first two surveys have been produced. *Word Geography of the Eastern United States* shows the geographical distribution of traditional vocabulary in the Atlantic states on 163 maps.[19] Whereas popular belief is usually that the eastern states have a simple North versus South division in speech, Kurath's book demonstrated conclusively the existence of a third, intermediate region, the Midland, having a North Midland and a South Midland subdivision. He found that the territory from Virginia southward fell into seven dialect areas, four in the South proper (or Lower South) and three in the South Midland region. The latter share much vocabulary with West Virginia and especially Pennsylvania, the colony from which the interior of Virginia and the Carolinas was largely settled in the eighteenth century. Kurath's introduction provides the best account of settlement history from a linguistic perspective and identifies more than 200 words that are more or less confined to one dialect area or another.

A Survey of Verb Forms in the Eastern United States uses the same records to detail eighty-eight verb features, including principal parts, subject-verb agreement, negative constructions, infinitives, and modal verbs. *The Pronunciation of English in the Atlantic States* uses pronunciation to demarcate dialect areas and describes how individual words are pronounced throughout the region.[20] Its 180 maps show the distribution of pronunciations of key words. In general, the three-way North/Midland/South division is not as evident for verbs and pronunciation as it is for vocabulary. Much of the most important information in these volumes is summarized by Raven McDavid, Jr., in his introduction to regional dialects of the Atlantic states.[21] He links the development of dialect differences to settlement history and social factors, presents characteristic pronunciation, vocabulary, morphology, and syntax of the three main dialect areas and eighteen sub-areas identified by the *Linguistic Atlas*, and discusses social class dialects and the influence of foreign-language communities, including French, German, and African, on southern English.

The *Linguistic Atlas of the Gulf States* (*LAGS*) carried the same survey into the interior South, interviewing 1,121 people in Alabama, Arkansas, Florida, Georgia, Louisiana, Mississippi, Tennessee, and East Texas, a territory of nearly a half-million square miles.[22] In contrast to previous atlases, however, *LAGS* interviewed many younger and more urban speakers, as well as more minorities. As a result, it has drawn a more complex picture of southern speech, countering the simple Coastal South versus South Midland dichotomy previously outlined. It identified at least eleven major subregional dialects in the eight states and as many as fourteen urban dialects. Some usages correlate with geography (for example, map 3 in *LAGS* shows the distribution of *chigger* in the South Midland vs. *redbug* in the South for the mite that crawls under the skin and causes an itch). But other terms show a pattern that is more social (for example, *wishbone* was found to cluster in urban areas, *pully bone* in rural ones; see map 4 in *LAGS*). Kentucky remains the only state not mapped for its dialect areas. Fieldwork was conducted there in the 1950s as part of the *Linguistic Atlas of the North-Central States* (also including Michigan, Ohio, Indiana, Illinois, and Wisconsin), but has never been analyzed.[23]

CONCLUSION

It is commonplace today to believe that a national form of American English is rapidly diluting and eroding the country's regional varieties as well as driving out other varieties both in the South and worldwide. Though there is undoubtedly some truth in this, the continued vitality of language variety in the South shows that it is only part of the story.

RESOURCE GUIDE

Printed Sources

General Works

Bernstein, Cynthia, Thomas Nunnally, and Robin Sabino, eds. *Language Variety in the South Revisited*. Tuscaloosa: University of Alabama Press, 1997. Scholarly collection indicating topics of interest to researchers.

Brooks, Cleanth. *The Language of the American South*. Mercer University Lamar Memorial Lectures No. 28. Athens: University of Georgia Press, 1985.

Campbell, Lyle. *American Indian Languages: The Historical Linguistics of Native America*. New York: Oxford University Press, 1997.

Carver, Craig M. *American Regional Dialects: A Word Geography*. Ann Arbor: University of Michigan Press, 1987. Comprehensive description of character of American geographical dialects, based on lexical and morphological data from Linguistic Atlases and *Dictionary of Regional English*.

Eliason, Norman E. *Tarheel Talk: An Historical Study of the English Language in North Carolina to 1860*. Chapel Hill: University of North Carolina Press, 1956. A compendium of linguistic, historical, and cultural material from unpublished letters, diaries, plantation books, church records, legal papers, and other manuscripts, including a survey of the vocabulary, grammar, pronunciation, language attitudes, and language variation revealed in these documents.

Goddard, Ives, ed. *Handbook of North American Indians*. Vol. 17, *Languages*. Washington, DC: Smithsonian Institution, 1996.

Kretzschmar, William, Jr., Virginia G. McDavid, Theodore K. Lerud, and Ellen Johnson, eds. *Handbook of the Linguistic Atlas of the Middle and South Atlantic States*. Chicago: University of Chicago Press, 1994. Chapter 8, "The Dialects of the LAMSAS Region," gives a short overview, pp. 147–153.

Montgomery, Michael, ed. *The Crucible of Carolina: Essays in the Development of Gullah Language and Culture*. Athens: University of Georgia Press, 1994.

Nagle, Stephen J., and Sara L. Sanders, eds. *English in the Southern United States*. Cambridge: Cambridge University Press, 2003. Essays written for an advanced undergraduate audience.

Randolph, Vance, and George P. Wilson. *Down in the Holler: A Gallery of Ozark Folk Speech*. 1953. Reprint, Norman: University of Oklahoma Press, 1979. Comprehensive description from thirty years of study and observation by first author, a noted folklorist; covers grammar, pronunciation, archaisms, taboos and euphemisms, wisecracks, and the dialect in fiction; has an extensive glossary.

Read, William A. *Indian Place Names in Alabama*. Louisiana State University Studies no. 29. Baton Rouge: Louisiana State University Press. Reprint, Tuscaloosa: University of Alabama Press, 1984.

Rickford, John Russell, and Russell John Rickford. *Spoken Soul: The Story of Black English*. New York: Wiley, 2000. General treatment of contemporary African American English analyzing its social, stylistic, and linguistic dimensions and its treatment in the media; discusses the Ebonics controversy and implications for employment and education.

Schneider, Edgar W. *American Early Black English*. Tuscaloosa: University of Alabama Press,

1989. Historical work analyzing grammatical patterns in ex-slave narratives collected by the Federal Writers' Project in the 1930s.

Wood, Gordon R. *Vocabulary Change: A Study of Variation in Regional Words in Eight of the Southern States.* Carbondale: Southern Illinois University Press, 1971. A study of generational and subregional patterns of 1,200 words and expressions in Alabama, Arkansas, Florida, Georgia, Louisiana, Mississippi, Oklahoma, and Tennessee, using figures and maps to relate these patterns to agricultural regions and nineteenth-century migration across the South.

Bibliographies

Brasch, Ila Wales, and Walter Milton Brasch, eds. *A Comprehensive Annotated Bibliography of American Black English*. Baton Rouge: Louisiana State University Press, 1974.

Christian, Donna. *American English Speech Recordings: A Guide to Collections*. Washington, DC: Center for Applied Linguistics, 1986. Organized by state; lists collections of recordings and where they are held in public or private hands; for each collection gives number of recordings, whether transcripts have been made, number and social profiles of speakers, and the topics covered.

Linn, Michael D. "Appendix: Resources for Research." In *American Dialect Research*, ed. Dennis R. Preston, 433–450. Amsterdam: Benjamins, 1993. Annotated list of resources, collections, and archives of recordings.

Linn, Michael D., and Maarit-Hannele Zuber. *The Sound of English: A Bibliography of Language Recordings*. Urbana: National Council of Teachers of English, 1984. An annotated list of mostly commercial recordings of historical varieties of English, American English, and other materials.

McMillan, James B., and Michael Montgomery. *Annotated Bibliography of Southern American English*. Tuscaloosa: University of Alabama Press, 1989. Annotated and cross-referenced compilation of 3,800 items from Maryland to Texas; includes work by historians, folklorists, and linguists, divided into twelve chapters by subject matter: Historical Studies, Phonetics and Phonology, Lexical Studies, Morphology and Syntax, Place Name Studies, Literary Dialect, etc.

Randolph, Vance. *The Ozarks: A Bibliography*. 2nd ed. Columbia: University of Missouri Press, 1987. The standard bibliography, by a lifelong student of Ozark lore.

Reinecke, John, et al., eds. *A Bibliography of Pidgin and Creole Languages*. Honolulu: University Press of Hawaii, 1975. Reprinted as Eric Document 121 121. Annotated; includes chapter on Gullah texts and descriptions, pp. 468–480.

Woodbridge, Hensley C. "A Tentative Bibliography of Kentucky Speech." *Publication of the American Dialect Society* 30 (1958): 17–37.

Dictionaries and Glossaries

Bradley, Francis W. "A Word List from South Carolina." *Publication of the American Dialect Society* 14 (1950): 3–73.

Farwell, Harold F., Jr., and J. Karl Nicholas. *Smoky Mountain Voices: A Lexicon of Southern Appalachian Speech*. Lexington: University Press of Kentucky, 1993. Compilation of published and unpublished material from Horace Kephart.

Geraty, Virginia. *Gulluh fuh Oonah Gullah for You: A Guide to the Gullah Language*. Orangeburg, SC: Sandlapper, 1997.

Gonzales, Ambrose E. *The Black Border*. Columbia, SC: State Company, 1922. Includes glossary of Gullah, pp. 277–340, which is condensed at www.gullahtours.com/gullah_dictionary.html.

Green, Bennett Wood. *Word-Book of Virginia Folk-Speech*. Richmond: Jones' Sons, 1912. Reprint, New York: Blom, 1971.

Major, Clarence. *Juba to Jive: Dictionary of Afro-American Slang*. New York: Penguin, 1994.

Montgomery, Michael. *From Ulster to America: The Scotch-Irish Heritage of American English*. Belfast: Ulster Historical Foundation, forthcoming.

Montgomery, Michael B., and Joseph S. Hall, eds. *Dictionary of Smoky Mountain English*. Knoxville: University of Tennessee Press, 2004. Comprehensive historical dictionary of southern Appalachian speech; also contains survey of grammar.

Smitherman, Geneva. *Black Talk: Words and Phrases from the Hood to the Amen Corner*. Boston: Houghton Mifflin, 1984.

Valdman, Albert. *Dictionary of Louisiana Creole*. Bloomington: Indiana University Press, 1998.

Wilson, George P. "Folk Speech." In *The Frank C. Brown Collection of North Carolina Folklore*, 505–618. Durham: Duke University Press, 1952. Glossary of 1,500 North Carolina items, including pronunciations, unusual meanings, names, and grammatical usages, figurative expressions, humorous rhymes, salutations and replies, etc.

Encyclopedias

Flora, Joseph, and Lucinda H. Mackethan, eds. *The Companion to Southern Literature*. Baton Rouge: Louisiana State University, 2002.

Haskell, Jean, and Rudy Abramson, eds. *Encyclopedia of Appalachia*. Knoxville: University of Tennessee Press, forthcoming. The section on language has twenty-nine entries on such topics as "Cherokee," "Medical Terminology," and "Spanish."

Wilson, Charles R., and William Ferris, eds. *Encyclopedia of Southern Culture*. Chapel Hill: University of North Carolina Press, 1989. The section on language has twenty-six entries on such topics as "Folk Speech" and "Place Names."

Special Topics

Atwood, E. Bagby. *A Survey of Verb Forms in the Eastern United States*. Ann Arbor: University of Michigan Press, 1953.

Bailey, Guy. "Digging Up the Roots of Southern American English." In *Studies in the English Language II: Conversations Between Past and Present*, ed. Anne Curzan and Kim Emmons, 450–460. Berlin: Mouton de Gruyter, 2004.

———. "When Did Southern American English Begin?" In *Englishes Around the World I*, ed. Edgar W. Schneider, 255–275. Amsterdam: Benjamins, 1997.

Bayley, Robert, and Ruth King. "Languages Other than English in Canada and the United States." In *Needed Research in American English*, ed. Dennis Preston, 163–230. Durham: Duke University Press, 2004.

Berlin, Ira, Joseph P. Reidy, and Leslie S. Rowland, eds. *Freedom: A Documentary History of Emancipation, 1861–1867*. Series 2, *The Black Military Experience*. Cambridge: Cambridge University Press, 1982.

Christian, Donna, Walt Wolfram, and Nanjo Dube. *Variation and Change in Geographically Isolated Communities: Appalachian English and Ozark English*. Tuscaloosa: University of Alabama Press, 1984.

Crawford, James, ed. *Southeastern Indian Languages*. Athens: University of Georgia, 1976.

Dalby, David. "The African Element in American English." In *Rappin' and Stylin' Out: Communication in Urban Black America*, ed. Thomas Kochman, 170–186. Urbana: University of Illinois Press, 1972.

Dillard, J. L. *Black English: Its History and Usage in the United States*. New York: Random House, 1972.

Fischer, David H. *Albion's Seed: Four British Folkways in America*. New York: Oxford University Press, 1989.

Fyfe, Christopher, ed. *"Our Children Free and Happy": Letters from Black Settlers in Africa in the 1790s*. Edinburgh: Edinburgh University Press, 1991.

Green, Lisa. *African American English: A Linguistic Introduction*. Cambridge: Cambridge University Press, 2002.

Hardy, Heather K., and Janine Scancarelli, eds. *Native Languages of the Southeastern United States*. Lincoln: University of Nebraska Press, 2004.

Huffines, Lois. "German Language." In *Encyclopedia of Southern Culture*, ed. Charles R. Wilson and William Ferris, 771–773. Chapel Hill: University of North Carolina Press, 1989.

Hull, Alexander. "French Language." In *Encyclopedia of Southern Culture*, ed. Charles R. Wilson and William Ferris, 770–771. Chapel Hill: University of North Carolina Press, 1989.

Index by Region, Usage, and Etymology to the Dictionary of American Regional English, Volumes 1 and 2. Publication of the American Dialect Society 77, 1993.

Index by Region, Usage, and Etymology to the Dictionary of American Regional English, Volume 3. Publication of the American Dialect Society 82, 1999.

Johnson, Ellen. *Lexical Change and Variation in the Southeastern United States, 1930–1990*. Tuscaloosa: University of Alabama Press, 1993.

Jones-Jackson, Patricia. *When Roots Die: Endangered Traditions on the Sea Islands*. Athens: University of Georgia Press, 1987.

Klingler, Tom. *If I Could Turn My Tongue Like That: The Creole of Point Coupee Parish, Louisiana*. Baton Rouge: Louisiana State University Press, 2003.

Kretzschmar, William. "Linguistic Atlases of the United States and Canada." In *Needed Research in American English*, ed. Dennis Preston, 25–48. Durham: Duke University Press, 2004.

Kurath, Hans. *Word Geography of the Eastern United States*. Ann Arbor: University of Michigan Press, 1949.

Kurath, Hans, and Raven I. McDavid, Jr. *The Pronunciation of English in the Atlantic States*. Ann Arbor: University of Michigan Press, 1961.

Labov, William, Sharon Ash, and Charles Boberg. *Atlas of North American English: Phonetics, Phonology and Sound Change*. Berlin: Mouton de Gruyter, forthcoming.

Lanehart, Sonja, ed. *Sociocultural and Historical Contexts of African American English*. Amsterdam: Benjamins, 2001.

Mathews, Mitford McLeod, ed. *The Beginnings of American English: Essays and Comments*. Chicago: University of Chicago Press, 1931.

———. *Some Sources of Southernisms*. University: University of Alabama Press, 1948.

McDavid, Raven I., Jr. "The Dialects of American English." In *The Structure of American English*, ed. W. Nelson Francis, 480–543. New York: Ronald, 1958.

Meinig, D. W. *The Shaping of America: A Geographical Perspective on 500 Years of History*. Vol. 1, *Atlantic America, 1492–1800*. New Haven: Yale University Press, 1986.

Meyer, Duane. *The Highland Scots of North Carolina, 1732–1776*. Chapel Hill: University of North Carolina Press, 1961.

Mitchell, Steve. *How to Speak Southern*. New York: Bantam, 1976.

Montgomery, Michael. "British and Irish Antecedents." In *Cambridge History of the English Language*, Vol. 6, *English in North America*, ed. John Algeo, 86–153. Cambridge: Cambridge University Press, 2001.

———. "The Celtic Element in American English." In *Celtic Englishes II*, ed. Hildegard Tristram, 231–264. Heidelberg: Benjamins, 2000.

———. "Review Essay of Basic and Descriptive Materials of the Linguistic Atlas of the Gulf States." *American Speech* 68 (1993): 263–318.

————. "The Scotch-Irish Influence on Appalachian English: How Broad? How Deep?" In *Ulster and North America: Transatlantic Perspectives on the Scotch-Irish*, ed. Curtis Wood and Tyler Blethen, 189–212. Tuscaloosa: University of Alabama Press, 1997.

Montgomery, Michael, and Guy Bailey. Introduction to *Language Variety in the South: Perspectives in Black and White*, 1–29. University: University of Alabama Press, 1986.

Pederson, Lee, Charles E. Billiard, Susan E. Leas, Guy Bailey, and Marvin Bassett, eds. *Linguistic Atlas of the Gulf States: The Basic Materials*. Microform Collection. Ann Arbor: University Microfilms, 1981. Two formats: 1,199 microfiche cards or 54 microfilm reels.

Pederson, Lee, Susan Leas McDaniel, and Marvin H. Bassett, eds. *The Linguistic Atlas of the Gulf States: A Concordance of the Basic Materials*. Ann Arbor: University Microfilms, 1986. 154 microfiche.

Pederson, Lee, Susan Leas McDaniel, et al., eds. *The Linguistic Atlas of the Gulf States*. 7 vols. Athens: University of Georgia Press, 1986–1992.

Shores, David L. *Tangier Island: Place, People, and Talk*. Newark: University of Delaware Press.

Teschner, Richard. "Spanish Language." In *Encyclopedia of Southern Culture*, ed. Charles R. Wilson and William Ferris, 782–784. Chapel Hill: University of North Carolina Press, 1989.

Thernstrom, Stephen, ed. *Harvard Encyclopedia of American Ethnic Groups*. Cambridge, MA: Harvard University Press, 1982.

Turner, Lorenzo Dow. *Africanisms in the Gullah Dialect*. Chicago: University of Chicago Press, 1949. Reprinted in 2002 by the University of South Carolina Press with a new introduction by Katherine W. Mille and Michael Montgomery.

Williams, Cratis D. *Southern Mountain Speech*. Ed. Loyal Jones and Jim Wayne Miller. Berea: Berea College Press, 1992.

Wilson, Charles R., and William Ferris, eds. *Encyclopedia of Southern Culture*. Chapel Hill: University of North Carolina, 1989.

Wolfram, Walt, and Natalie Schilling-Estes. *Hoi Toide on the Outer Banks: The Story of the Ocracoke Brogue*. Chapel Hill: University of North Carolina Press, 1997.

Wright, Joseph, ed. *English Dialect Dictionary*. 6 vols. London: Henry Frowde, 1898–1905.

Videos/Films

American Tongues. Prod./Dir. Louis Alvarez and Andrew Kolker. New American Media, 1989? This hour-long video profiles the accents and dialects of linguistic communties throughout the country, and discusses dialect stereotypes, linguistic prejudice, and the role of the media in shaping language. Also available in a forty-minute high school version; see www.cnam.com/more_info/ameri3.html.

Family Across the Sea. South Carolina Educational Television, 1990. Focuses on the slave trade and documents and explores similarities in language, folkways, music, and culture between the Sea Islands and West Africa, particularly Sierra Leone; has an accompanying teacher's guide booklet.

Indian by Birth. North Carolina Language and Life Project, Humanities Extension/Publications, North Carolina State University, 2000. Presents the language and heritage of the Lumbees, a community of mixed African American, white, and Native American ancestry.

The Language You Cry In. California Newsreel, 1998. Tells how a funeral chant in Mende recorded by Lorenzo Dow Turner seventy years ago in the Georgia Sea Islands was traced to a small village in the Sierra Leone interior, where it was also remembered by only one woman. www.newsreel.org/films/langyou.htm.

Mountain Talk: Language and Life in Southern Appalachia. Prod. Neal Hutcheson. North Carolina Language and Life Project, Humanities Extension/Publications, North Carolina State University, 2003. The language of small communities in the North Carolina mountains.

The Ocracoke Brogue: A Portrait of Hoi Toider Speech. North Carolina Language and Life Project, Humanities Extension/Publications, North Carolina State University, 1997. Examines the dialect of the Outer Banks Island and its role in creating and sustaining local identity.

The Story of English. British Broadcasting Corporation, 1986. A seven-part series with two episodes relating to the American South: "The Guid Scots Tongue," which links Scotland and Ulster with Appalachia, and "Black on White," which links Africa to the United States. The program has a companion book: Robert McCrum, William Cran, and Robert MacNeil, *The Story of English* (New York: Viking, 1986).

Yeah You Right. Prod./Dir. Louis Alvarez and Andrew Kolker. New American Media. Presents the diverse speechways of New Orleans.

Web Sites

American Dialect Links
www.evolpub.com/Americandialects/AmDialLnx.html

Comprehensive list of Web sites, of widely varying quality, organized by region and state.

American Dialect Society Home Page
www.americandialects.org

Features news of ongoing research on American dialects from the society and other sources.

American English Speech Sample Index
www.uta.fi/FAST/REF/samples.html

Atlas of North American English (formerly Phonological Atlas of the U.S.) at the University of Pennsylvania
www.ling.upenn.edu/phono_atlas/home..html

A survey of pronunciation changes in progress, based on a nationwide survey using randomly selected telephone interviews; analysis of material in preparation for publication by Labov et al.

Deep South Humanities Center at Tulane University
deepsouth.tulane.edu/resources.html

Searchable database on the archives and collections in the mid-South.

The Dialect Survey
www.hcs.harvard.edu/~golder/dialect

Ongoing project on regional vocabulary.

Documenting the American South at the University of North Carolina at Chapel Hill
docsouth.unc.edu/dasmain.html

Contains numerous autobiographies, memoirs, diaries, slave narratives, and Civil War letters that document nineteenth-century southern English.

HistoricalVoices.org
www.HistoricalVoices.org

An archive of early recordings.

International Dialects of English Archive at Kansas University
www.ukans.edu/~idea.northamerica.html

Has sound samples from all states in the region (e.g., ten from Alabama), with speakers identified by race, sex, year of birth, and place of birth; provides model accents for dialect training and coaching.

Klingler, Thomas A., Home Page.
www.tulane.edu/~klingler

Contains audio samples of Louisiana French Creole (accessed April 10, 2004).

Linguistic Atlas Projects, University of Georgia
www.hyde.part,uga.edu/index.html

This site, from the headquarters of the Altas project, has information and material from *LAMSAS* and *LAGS*. For *LAMSAS* this site has data for 153 questionnaire items. At hyde.park.uga.edu/lamsas/lingmaps.html one can use this material to draw electronic maps of hundreds of words and pronunciations. For example, there are forty-four terms with the meaning "thunderstorm"; one of them (*squall*) occurs fifty times and shows a coastal distribution from Maryland to Florida (see map 5 in *LAGS*). Informant profiles for the entire project are on line, as well as transcriptions of approximately sixty interviews conducted with African American speakers, including the twenty-one by Lorenzo Dow Turner in the early 1930s (www.hyde.part,uga.edu/afam/information.html).

For *LAGS* it has a description of the project. *LAGS* is the only completed atlas project to have been tape-recorded in full. All recordings (5,300+ hours) are archived at both Emory University and the University of Georgia. Components of the project also include (1) microfiche collections of the complete transcriptions and concordance; (2) seven volumes of analysis, including a Handbook, General Index, Technical Index, Regional Matrix, Regional Pattern, Social Matrix, and Social Pattern (the last four have one or more overlay map transparencies); and (3) electronic files of all responses, available at the project Web site, along with a step-by-step protocol for analyzing the data in these files (hyde.park.uga.edu/protocol.txt).

National Archives and Records Administration Digital Classroom
www.archives.gov/digital_classroom/lessons/civil_war_documents/civil_war_documents.html

Has audio file of interview with John Salling, last surviving Confederate veteran, one of earliest-born speakers of southern English who has been recorded.

New South Voices
www.newsouthvoices.uncc.edu/trial.jsp

An archive of oral and video interviews and narratives; a resource for studying the history and language of the South.

Schiffman, Harold, Bibliographies on the Subject of African-American Vernacular English (AAVE) and/or Black English.
ccat.sas.upenn.edu/~haroldfs/540/handouts/aave/aave.html (accessed April 10, 2004).

Libraries

Numerous libraries in the region hold manuscripts of linguistic interest (usually nineteenth-century letters from less-educated individuals whose speech intrudes into their writing). Among those that have the largest and richest collections and the best online catalogues are the following:

Alderman Library of the University of Virginia
www.uva.edu/manuscripts.html

Louisiana and Lower Mississippi Valley Collection at Louisiana State University
www.lib.lsu.edu/special/llmvc.html

Perkins Library at Duke University
www.lib.duke.edu

South Caroliniana Library at the University of South Carolina at Columbia
www.lib.sc.edu/socar

Southern Historical Collection at the University of North Carolina at Chapel Hill
www.lib.unc.edu/mss

By far the largest and most varied collection of recordings from the South is held by the Archive of Folk Culture (now incorporated into the American Folklife Center) at the Library of Congress (www.loc.gov/folklife). It contains thousands of recorded interviews, stories, sermons, and other verbal lore collected from the late 1920s to the present from every part of the South and from the entire range of ethnic and social groups. At the Archive librarians have compiled a Spoken Word Catalog, a master listing of this material. The collection, includes recordings of ex-slaves (listed at www.loc.gov/folklife/guides/slave.html), which were transcribed by linguists and published in Guy Bailey, Natalie Maynor, and Patricia Cukor-Avila, *The Emergence of Black English: Text and Commentary* (Amsterdam: Benjamins, 1991; some of these are available in audio versions at "Remembering Slavery" (http://rememberingslavery.soundprint.org/index.html), a project of the Smithsonian Institution.

Published Transcripts
African American Interest

The type of document most frequently published is the ex-slave narrative and these interviews. The Federal Writers' Project interviewed about 2,000 ex-slaves in the 1930s; these interviews were loosely transcribed in George P. Rawick, *The American Slave: A Composite Autobiography*, 41 vols. (Westport, CT: Greenwood Press, 1972–1979).

Numerous other projects have drawn on written documents from African Americans of the late eighteenth or nineteenth century. The Freedman and Southern Society project at the University of Maryland has published several volumes of documents from National Archives collections from Civil War and early Reconstruction times, including many letters from African American soldiers in Ira Berlin et al., ed., *The Black Military Experience* (Cambridge: Cambridge University Press, 1982), each with a detailed historical context provided by editors. A summary of the project and sample documents that vividly speak for themselves can be found at www.history.umd.edu/Freedmen. Christopher Fyfe, ed., *"Our Children Free and Happy"* (Edinburgh: Edinburgh University Press, 1991), is an account of African Americans who were allied with the British in the Revolutionary War, mainly in South Carolina, and retreated with them to Nova Scotia. A decade later, 2,000 of them relocated to Sierra Leone in search of a warmer climate and better circumstances. The volume includes transcripts of forty-one letters and petitions between 1792 and 1800.

Civil War Letters and Other Documents

These are held by numerous archives, historical societies, and libraries, public and private, throughout the region. In addition, many documents have been published. For a comprehensive bibliography of published sources, see the Web site of the United States Civil War Center at Louisiana State University: www.cwc.lsu.edu.

Representative publications include Gustavus W. Dyer et al., eds., *Tennessee Civil War Veterans Questionnaire*, 5 vols. (1922; Reprint, Easley, SC: Southern Historical Press, 1985), which has verbatim questionnaires, often in halting English, returned by elderly Confederate and Union veterans; and J. Roderick Heller III and Carolyn Ayres, eds., *The Confederacy Is on Her Way up the Spout: Letters to South Carolina, 1861–1864* (Athens: University of Georgia Press, 1992).

LITERATURE

Susan V. Donaldson

For me there is seldom a "the South," for simple characterizations eliminate the reality of sharp conflicts over just about everything in southern culture, slavery most of all.

Nell Irvin Painter

This country is so complicated that when I start to think about it I begin talking in a Southern accent.

Norman Mailer

Probably no other regional literature produced in the United States is as burdened with static, radically simplified stereotypes as is "southern literature." The mere utterance of the phrase conjures up white columns, gallant white cavaliers, radiant white belles, and muted black retainers—in short, a novel like Margaret Mitchell's *Gone with the Wind*. But even an iconic narrative like Mitchell's 1936 best seller reveals, upon close perusal, fractures in the columns and unsettling ambiguities and contradictions in the portraits of seemingly one-note characters like Ashley Wilkes and Scarlett O'Hara, who are not quite the effortless bearers of white nostalgia for the world of Tara that they initially seem. In those fractures can be detected a host of alternative, contesting stories revealing a far more complicated and multivoiced South than generally acknowledged by popular—and even scholarly—assessments of the region. Two generations of writers since the publication of *Gone with the Wind*, in fact, have made it their business to interrogate, complicate, and explode those emblematic images of a timeless plantation South, among them Margaret Walker in *Jubilee* (1966), Dorothy Allison in *Bastard out of Carolina* (1992), and Alice Randall in *The Wind Done Gone* (2001).

In doing so, they remind us of the multiple and contending narratives that have mapped and remapped the American Southeast since the earliest days of European exploration and invasion, when a host of radically different cultures—Spanish,

French, English, Irish, Scottish, Ashanti, Fulani, Ibo, Malagasy, Mandingo, and Yoruba—came in contact with indigenous cultures—from the Mississippian societies of mound builders, sun worshippers, and corn cultivators to the confederations of the Catawba, Cherokee, Creek, Chickasaw, and Choctaw arising from the wreckage of two centuries of violent encounters. From these exchanges emerged a cacophony of stories of multiple, miscegenated antecedents—from captivity narratives by Spanish, English, and African American wanderers to contemporary, self-reflexive historical novels that seek to excavate stories forgotten or submerged in the never-ending project of inventing and reinventing southern identity, literature, and community.

To pay heed to these multiple voices and antecedents—and to move beyond those all-too-ready stereotypes of plantations, nostalgia, and lost traditions—we need to approach southern literature as plural, contested, and dialogic—stories, poems, songs, histories, plays, and life writings engaged in never-ending exchanges, quarrels, and responses echoing with earlier voices and narratives whose own configurations are shaped by preceding and succeeding efforts to tell about the region that became the South. We need, in short, to read southern literature from the perspective of its earliest beginnings, that is, as a "contact zone," in Mary Louise Pratt's words, where different cultures confront, intersect, and interpret one another's otherness. What this kind of "contact perspective" reveals are the multicultural origins of a region stereotyped and classified for far too long in homogeneous terms, from the Slave South to the Solid South. We discover instead a region that has long functioned as the nation's imaginative borderlands, an arena of conflicting and merging cultures, something like a witches' brew of otherness conjured up by four centuries of literary representations both creating and repressing multiplying possibilities of difference and hybridity.

ENCOUNTERING OTHERNESS

Literature of the Indigenous and the Settlers

The earliest literary efforts to issue from the southeastern part of what is now the United States reflected in form and content the shock of encounter between the region's richly diverse indigenous societies—constituting roughly 1,294,000 inhabitants by the estimates of anthropologist Charles Hudson—and Spanish, French, and English explorers and adventurers. Spanish forays into the mainland north of the Caribbean, where conquistadors quickly established their domain two decades after Columbus' 1492 voyage, were driven by the imperative of conquest—for slaves to work the mines and plantations established throughout the Caribbean basin and for riches comparable to those offered by the Aztecs in Mexico. What Hudson calls "the first ethnographic description" of native cultures in North America, *De Orbe Novo*, or *The New World* (1511–1530), by Pietro Martiere d'Angiera (or Peter Martyr, as he was known in English), emerged from a slaving expedition to the coast of present-day South Carolina.

The stories of gems, pearls, and wealthy native societies that circulated from that early expedition fueled the Spanish exploratory ventures that followed and the narrative accounts they inspired, chief among them the firsthand account offered by what is arguably the American South's first captivity narrative—the chronicle by the Panfilo de Narvaez expedition's treasurer, Alvar Nunez Cabeza de Vaca, of the ill-fated attempt in 1528 to establish a Florida colony. First published in 1542 and then reissued in 1555, Cabeza de Vaca's extraordinary account of living "lost and naked" among the Indian cultures of Florida, Texas, New Mexico, Arizona, and Mexico was circulated as *La Relacion*. Written and published to persuade Charles V of Spain to colonize Florida and the Southwest, Cabeza de Vaca's account narrates his eight years among native societies, first as a shipwreck survivor, then as a captive, and finally as an acculturated native who became a tradesman and then shaman for the indigenous peoples with whom he had come to identify. The result is a story of the remaking and hybridization of identity as Cabeza de Vaca ends his narrative with a strong sense of identification with the Indians with whom he lived and whom he felt charged to protect against "the Christians" to whom he eventually returned.

His report, historian Alan Taylor declares, would inspire the next two expeditions of Spanish conquistadors—of Francisco Vásquez de Coronado through the Southwest to the Great Plains, and of Hernando de Soto to Florida through the Southeast to the Mississippi. De Soto's 4,000-mile expedition in 1539–1543 produced four chronicles, three firsthand by Rodrigo Rangel, de Soto's secretary, Luys Hernández de Biedma, the royal factor, and an unnamed Portuguese gentleman of Elvas. A secondary account, titled *La Florida del Inca* (1605) and likely based on the stories of one of the expedition's survivors, was authored by Garcilaso de la Vega, a mestizo born in Peru who pronounced himself "El Inca."

The de Soto expedition wreaked considerable havoc on the heavily populated Mississippian cultures of mound builders, corn cultivators, and sun worshippers in territory extending from Florida to present-day East Texas. Something of that impact was captured in the eloquent speech, recorded in Garcilosa de la Vega's account, of a chieftain who opposed the Spaniards' advance in northern Florida—and stoutly resisted their self-representation as superior beings requiring submission:

These Spaniards are the same people who committed cruelties against us in the past [i.e., Pánfilo de Narváez's army]. They are demons, not sons of the Sun and Moon, for they go about killing and robbing. They do not bring their own women, but prefer to possess the wives and daughters of others. They are not content to colonize a particular piece of land because they take such pleasure in being vagabonds, living upon the labor of others. They are thieves and murderers. Warn them not to enter my land, for no matter how brave they are, they shall never leave it, for I shall destroy them all.

Despite his defiant words, the chieftain and his people suffered heavy losses at the hands of the Spaniards in a battle known by the name of the chieftain's principality—Napituca—and in battles to follow, like Mabila, where a force of 5,000 indigenous people suffered a loss of 3,000 at the hands of de Soto's men—thereby foreshadowing the wreckage to come.

Competing with the Spanish were tentative French explorations along the coasts of South Carolina, Georgia, and Florida. Under the leadership of René Goulaine de Laudonnière, a French Huguenot colony established a brief foothold in Florida—Fort Caroline—near the mouth of St. John's River in 1564, but the settlement was extinguished a year later by Spanish forces. Narrative accounts of those early French ventures and of the Fort Caroline settlement, though, were left first by Laudonnière himself in his *A Notable Historie Containing Foure Voyages Made by Certaine French Captaines unto Florida*, translated and published by Richard Hakluyt in 1587, and then by Jacques Le Moyne de Morgues, the official artist and cartographer for the French colony. Le Moyne managed to escape the Spanish attack on Fort Caroline and subsequently wrote and illustrated a short history of Laudonnière's doomed colony that was published in Frankfurt in 1591 under the title *Brevis narratio* and then issued again by Theodore de Bry, with engravings of the Le Moyne illustrations. Le Moyne also produced what is very probably the first painting of Native Americans and European settlers in the New World, a representation in watercolor and gouache on vellum portraying—tellingly enough—French explorers as conquerors welcomed by Indians who had begun worshipping a column left by an earlier explorer, Jean Ribaut.

Le Moyne's lovely painting hauntingly evokes something of the vast cultural upheaval that was already devastating indigenous communities. At the time of contact with the Spaniards, by many estimates, the Southeast as a whole boasted a population of some 1.29 million divided up into multiple tiny chiefdoms, some with as many as 5,000 inhabitants, and villages ranging from 300 to 500. At least several different language groups—Muskogean, Iroquoian, Catawban, Caddoan, Alongkian, Tunican, and Timucan—divided up the region, and those groups in turn could each be broken down into several different languages. Dominating the area between northern Florida and eastern Texas was a loose grouping of societies, marked by mound-building, corn cultivation, and sizable towns, that anthropologists now call Mississippian, existing roughly between 800 and 1600 C.E. This was a world, though, that went into rapid decline in the wake of de Soto's pillaging for food and slaves. Worse yet was the expedition's lingering legacy of smallpox, measles, and typhus epidemics that depopulated whole villages and towns. By 1685, according to historian Peter Wood's estimates, the total Indian population of the Southeast had declined precipitously, to around 199,400, and by 1790 to around 55,900.

Early English Literature from America

Contributing to that decline—and recording it in a series of exploration/ethnography narratives and promotional tracts—were the English explorers and then colonizers who began appearing on the eastern seaboard just a few decades after the 300 survivors of the de Soto expedition straggled back to Mexico in 1543. English accounts of exploration along the Atlantic coast of the region began with Thomas Harriot's *A Briefe and True Report of the New Found Land of Virginia* (1588), relating Harriot's experiences on the second Roanoke expedition in 1585 under Sir Richard Grenville, brother-in-law to Sir Walter Raleigh, and that account in turn was reissued in 1590 by Theodor de Bry with engravings based on watercolor drawings of Native Americans by John White. William Strachey in turn produced the first detailed account of the founding of Jamestown in 1607 and English relations with Powhatan's kingdom in his 1612 manuscript *The Historie of Travaile into Virginia Britannia*.

The most famous of those English narratives of exploring the Southeast, though, were the multiple volumes issued by adventurer, entrepreneur, and soldier of fortune Captain John Smith, who helped establish the first permanent English colony of Jamestown, Virginia, in 1607, and who played no small role in defining Virginia's myths of origins—and creating identities of "Indian" and "settler." Following the lead of travel narratives established by Richard Hakluyt's *The Principall Navigations, Voiages and Discoveries of the English Nation* (1589), the prolific and self-promoting Smith issued first *A True Relation of such occurrences and accidents of noate as hath hapened in Virginia* (1608), the first publication to emerge from British North America, and then *A Map of Virginia, with a Description of its Commodities, People, Government, and Religion* (1612), *A Description of New England* (1616), and most famously *A Generall Historie of Virginia, New England, and the Summer Isles* (1624).

All told, Smith authored some eight books celebrating his own adventures and promoting Virginia as a land of plenty awaiting the pleasure of English settlers, and together they helped portray him as a larger-than-life frontier hero foreshadowing the likes of Davy Crockett and Daniel Boone. Above all, though, his volumes, particularly the 1624 *Generall Historie of Virginia*, etched in the initial outlines of triumphant white Virginian settler and submissive Indian bowing to the "progress" of civilization. It was in the 1624 volume that he offered his signature tale of nearly suffering execution at the hands of the Powhatan Indian chief Wahunsunacock, only to be delivered by the chief's "dearest daughter" Matoaka, nicknamed Pocahontas; that story in turn would be closely associated with the region's burgeoning mythology of sectional identity, as critics like Gordon Sayre have pointed out. Whether or not the story was true would be the subject of heated debate—often along sectional lines. No less a figure than Henry Adams would later accuse Smith in an 1867 *North American Review* essay of inventing the story, a calculated attempt, Sayre says, "to discredit the South and aid the Union war effort." Later commentators would speculate that the impending execution feared by Smith was really a ceremony overseen by Powhatan to initiate Smith into his society, with Pocahontas as a sponsor of sorts.

That this most famous of Virginian myths has been subject to such debates suggests what is at stake in these first exploration/ethnography narratives to emerge from British North America—the authority to name, define, map, and control a polyglot, emerging New World. At a time when the success of the Jamestown colony was very much in the balance, as settlers struggled with disease and their dependence upon Indian communities for food and sustenance, Powhatan's kingdom, according to historian James Axtell, was "one of the most powerful Indian polities in eastern America," a chiefdom made up of some thirty tribes totaling between 13,000 and 14,000 people and over 3,000 warriors. But within forty years, Axtell adds, Powhatan's kingdom had largely disappeared from Tidewater Virginia. "By 1700," he notes, "the native population of eastern Virginia had fallen 87 percent to only 1,900; by no coincidence, whites and blacks together marked 60,000." Disease, wars, and the advance of white settlements were primarily responsible, but so too in a manner of speaking were the histories and travel accounts, offspring of the earliest exploration narratives, which played no small role in producing and defining racial difference and racial categories as they were emerging in the New World. As Indian populations receded, representations of Native Americans took on a curiously fixed character—one of defeat, submission, and decline—in the histories and travel accounts that began to emerge from European settlers by the early years of the eighteenth century, and culminated with Thomas Jefferson's *Notes on the State of Virginia* (completed in 1784 and published in 1785). Robert Beverley's *The History and Present State of Virginia* (1705) singled out that decline as an occasion for lamentation and speculated that intermarriage between settlers and Indians might well have prevented both the preceding century's wars and the rapid decrease in the colony's native population. Indeed, he appropriated for himself the identity of "Indian" as "a native and inhabitant of the place," but still felt compelled to write the volume to answer "misrepresented" accounts of his country and in particular the popular assumption in England "that the country turns all people black who go to live there." "Indian" though he saw himself, Beverley nevertheless contributed to a growing discursive tradition of racial categorization delineating the boundaries between white selves and dark others.

The drive to catalogue, categorize, and contain was impelled in part by the emergence of an unruly frontier world of multiple, shifting cultures decidedly disreputable by English standards of respectability. So disinclined were the earliest settlers at Jamestown to abide by those standards—and the imperative to labor—that the president of the Virginia Company denounced them as a "damned crew" given to drunken binges and vomiting. A whole subgenre of rogue literature, of ballads, poems, and satires of raucous colonial life, sprang up, the most famous of which was Ebenezer Cooke's long poem *The Sot-Weed Factor* (1708) of colonial Maryland. Travel accounts of the early eighteenth century with more sober aims of describing and cataloguing were just as likely to bring attention to the region's more disreputable inhabitants. John Lawson in his 1709 exploration account *A New Voyage to Carolina*, summarizing eight years of travel through the back country and the Indian nations of the Carolinas, pointedly noted in his preface that "most of our Travellers . . . are Persons of the meaner Sort, and generally a very slender education." William Byrd II of Westover was if anything even franker in descriptions of backwoods life along the Virginia–North Carolina border in the account he wrote about traveling for a 1727–1728 commission to settle boundary disputes between the two colonies. Unpublished in his lifetime and circulated among his friends in Virginia and England, *The History of the Dividing Line Betwixt Virginia and North Carolina* and the satirical *The Secret History of the Line* lambasted the "slothfulness" of North Carolinians living along the line and thereby initiated a long narrative tradition about poor whites and white trash that would include nineteenth-century Southwest humorists, Erskine Caldwell's inhabitants of *Tobacco Road*, and the twentieth-century blue-collar Kentuckians of Bobbie Ann Mason's short stories.

Slavery as a Topic in Early American Southern Literature

Byrd reinforced as well the drive to establish boundaries—on maps, in class and racial categories, and in narrative—that early on became characteristic of British America's imaginings of each colony, in the words of Gordon Sayre, "as a fort, with high walls blocking out the dangers and temptations of the wilderness." Providing some of the impetus for that drive a century earlier was the introduction of twenty Africans by a Dutch slave trader into the colony at Jamestown in 1619, thereby laying the foundation of both slavery and the codification of race in Virginia law.

By the eighteenth century African slaves by far formed the largest population group brought into British America—some 1.5 million, triple the number of European immigrants. Accompanying that influx was the move among colonial governments to codify slavery—Virginia, for one, tightened and expanded its slave code in 1705—and the drive among European descendants to map the boundaries between blackness and whiteness, most notably in *Notes on the State of Virginia*, by Thomas Jefferson, the revolutionary leader who had arguably done the most to define the emerging new vocabulary of liberty and equality for white Americans in the Declaration of Independence.

Even in the Declaration, though, that vocabulary emerged as racially coded. A crucial clause Jefferson had included in a draft of the document had condemned King George for fostering the "execrable commerce" of the African slave trade but was ultimately deleted by his colleagues in the Continental Congress. Later proposals made by Jefferson to stop the slave trade and to implement a gradual emancipatory scheme in Virginia were struck down as well. *Notes on the State of Virginia*, written for a small French audience and published anonymously in France, would reveal Jefferson's own hesitations in addressing the abolition of slavery and his implication in a burgeoning discourse defining the lines dividing white, red, and black—and ultimately between the South as a region and the rest of the country.

Among the most cited passages in *Notes* are those in which Jefferson expounded, with considerable anguish, upon the corrupting influence of slavery on both white and black and his fears for the new republic's future if slavery as an institution continued. The best hope for the future, he argued toward the end, lay in an agrarian republic, protected from the urban ills of Europe. Life on the land, though, which Jefferson pronounced the most virtuous of economies, had already become defined in Virginia by slavery, an institution that Jefferson warned was inherently corrupting: "The whole commerce between master and slave is a perpetual exercise of the most boisterous passions, the most unremitting despotism on the one part, and degrading submissions on the other." Worse yet, the very presence of slavery contradicted the rationale of the republic: "[C]an the liberties of a nation be thought secure when we have removed their only firm basis, a conviction in the minds of the people that these liberties are of the gift of God?"

The answer, he maintained, lay in gradual emancipation—but only if accompanied by deportation and colonization elsewhere of freed slaves. Racial distinctions, he declared, were too strong not to result ultimately in "the extermination of the one or the other race." In passages that would haunt his legacy—and fuel for centuries to come the controversy over his relationship with his slave Sally Hemings—Jefferson speculated, "as a suspicion only, that the blacks, whether originally a distinct race, or made distinct by time and circumstances, are inferior to the whites in the endowments both of body and mind," and concluded that any freed blacks "must be removed beyond the reach of mixture." As one of his points of evidence, he cited the contrast offered, he declared, between the native eloquence of American Indian speakers and what he perceived as the limitations of black articulation, never "above the level," he declared, "of plain narration." What black writing there was, he concluded, whether that of Phillis Wheatley or Ignatius Sancho, could not be categorized as genuine literature.

Jefferson's dismissal—in particular, his refusal to afford recognition to black writing—anticipated the narrative assumptions of generations of white southern writers to come, that African Americans had no voice in the making of the community imagined by southern writing, that slaves by definition, as historian Philip Morgan has argued in his study of eighteenth-century Virginia and South Carolina, were not part of the polity, local or otherwise. Jefferson himself, David B. Davis observes in *The Problem of Slavery in the Age of Revolution*, retreated into studied silence on slavery after his return from his extended stay in France. Slavery, though, would generate considerable polemic and literature from white southerners in the antebellum period to follow, but like Jefferson, they would respond to African American voices—in abolitionist tracts and slave narratives—with dismissal, with charges of fraud, with censorship, and with silent refusals to acknowledge those voices.

That silence, ironically enough, was shaped and impelled by a growing clamor of African American voices finding their first articulation in autobiographical narratives of crime, slavery, and captivity in the latter part of the seventeenth century. The earliest accounts of individual African Americans, Frances Smith Foster reports in *Witnessing Slavery*, were criminal narratives that appeared in New England as well as Virginia, but by the eighteenth century African Americans were beginning to produce both Indian captivity tales and narratives of escaping from slavery. Roughly at the same time that Jefferson's *Notes on the State of Virginia* was issued anonymously in Paris, John Marrant published one of the first books written by an African American, an account of his captivity under the Cherokee on the South Carolina frontier so popular that its last edition was issued in 1835. Shaped by the structure of spiritual narratives and his own experience of conversion under traveling evangelist George Whitefield, Marrant's book crossed many of the boundaries being drawn in white texts by tracing his shifting identities in free black, white, and Cherokee cultures. Equally transgressive were the texts of those who experienced the Middle Passage and enslavement and drew from both from Indian captivity tales and from spiritual narratives for both form and content. One of the earliest was the story of a Muslim merchant named Ayuba Suleiman Diallo, whose travail of kidnapping and enslavement was captured by white Marylander Thomas Bluett, who published the account in London in 1734 under the title *Some Memoirs of the Life of Job*.

By 1789, when *The Interesting Narrative of the Life of Olaudah Equiano, or Gustavus Vassa, the African* was published in London, slave narratives had emerged as powerful indictments of slavery—and of Western definitions of whiteness and blackness. Equiano wrote his narrative as the African-born son of an Ibo tribal elder who experienced the abuses of the Middle Passage and of slavery in Virginia, Philadelphia, Georgia, and the West Indies, supervised cargoes of slaves in the Atlantic, and finally

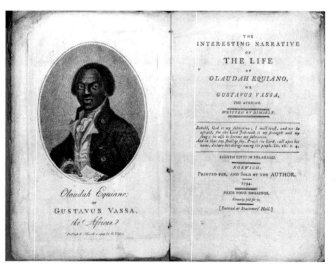

Olaudah Equiano, b. 1745. Courtesy Library of Congress.

redefined himself as a Christian and an Englishman. As such, his was a powerful voice emerging from the huge amorphous underworld of seamen, slaves, pirates, indentured servants, and Irish migrants that historian Peter Linebaugh sees defining the seventeenth- and eighteenth-century Atlantic and serving as "a vector of revolution that travelled from North America out to sea and southward to the Caribbean." This was the wide-ranging community, Linebaugh adds, that would play no small role in spreading the antinomian democracy of evangelist George Whitefield, one of the leaders of the First Great Awakening in the New World, and in fueling the rebellions that unfolded in the slave societies of the Americas beginning in the 1720s, 1730s, and 1740s in Jamaica, South Carolina, New York, Georgia, Virginia, and Bermuda.

Native Americans and Early Literature

Part of that huge amorphous Atlantic community were the new Indian confederations emerging in the eighteenth century out of the wreckage of the Mississippian cultures, of which only the Natchez in southern Mississippi and small Gulf coast communities remained in 1700. Those new confederations, chief among them the Catawba, Choctaw, Chickasaw, Creek, and Cherokee, "exemplified," according to Alan Taylor, "the widespread process of colonial 'ethnogenesis'—the emergence of new ethnic groups and identities from the consolidation of many people disrupted by the invasion of European peoples, animals, and microbes." Indian territory was, in fact, highly heterogeneous, attracting, historian Thea Perdue declares, colonial officials, traders, fugitives, and runaway slaves as well as captives taken from settlements and pioneer caravans. By 1825, 25 percent of the Cherokee were of mixed heritage, and the children of Europeans in particular became increasingly important in Cherokee governance as the Cherokee themselves shifted from hunting and gathering to agriculture.

Emerging from this world in flux were voices that reflected that heterogeneous world, like the speeches of Nancy Ward, or Nan-ye-hi in Cherokee, often hailed as a Cherokee Pocahontas for her role in saving white settlers on the Tennessee frontier, and a prominent leader in Cherokee councils as a War Woman and Beloved Woman. Serving as intermediary between the Cherokee and the new U.S. government in the 1780s, Nan-ye-hi by her presence and through her speeches resisted the exclusion of women mandated by U.S. negotiators and left behind an eloquent record of pleas for peace and for her right to be heard as a mother and a Cherokee leader. Nan-ye-hi was followed first by George Gist, known as Sequoyah, who completed a writing system for the Cherokee—an eighty-six-symbol syllabary—that was adopted in the 1820s, and then by Elias Boudinot, or Gallegina, whose journalistic negotiations between Cherokee and white American worlds led him to be pronounced both the "Father of American Indian Journalism" and "traitor" to the Cherokee. Claiming Cherokee-Scotch ancestry as well as descent from one of the members of the de Soto expedition, Boudinot published two major defenses of Cherokee culture and arguably the first piece of Indian fiction, a short story, "Poor Sarah." In 1827 he began editing the bilingual Cherokee national newspaper *The Cherokee Phoenix* and for the next four years called for assimilation into white culture, promoted Cherokee nationalism, and vigorously fought the movement for removal of all Indians to territory west of the Mississippi. His editorials on removal in particular were reprinted throughout the United States, but Boudinot himself came to support removal and signed the 1836 Treaty of New Echota stipulating the cession of Cherokee lands in Georgia and setting in motion the departure in late 1838 of 13,000 Cherokee on the Trail of Tears for present-day Oklahoma.

The Cherokee were joined in Indian Territory by the other so-called civilized tribes, but left behind were a good many communities of Indians who had intermarried with African Americans—the Lumbee in North Carolina, the Mattaponi in Virginia, and the Nanticoke in Maryland, as well as the Seminole in Florida, who harbored runaway slaves for generations and fought three fierce wars with the U.S. government in the first half of the nineteenth century. Left behind as well was a rich oral tradition of rabbit/trickster tales reflecting long-term African and Native American interaction, "a cycle of stories," David Elton Gary reports, "unique to the southeastern United States." As folklorists like George Lankford have argued, the trickster folktales emerging from these communities revealed multiple cultural exchanges—Ashanti-Creek, Fan-Creek, Bakongo-Biloxi, and Ibo-Creek. By the time Joel Chandler Harris began collecting stories of Brer Rabbit from ex-slaves in late nineteenth-century Georgia, ethnologists were already bringing attention to the parallels between Brer Rabbit and the Rabbit stories of the Creek and the Cherokee, especially the stories of the Tar Baby and the Rabbit's race with the turtle.

Edgar Allan Poe

Southwestern humor won the praise of no less a figure than Edgar Allan Poe, often hailed as the preeminent white writer of the antebellum South, who pronounced Longstreet's *Georgia Scenes* "a sure omen of better days for the literature of the South." As a gypsy journalist/editor and aspiring man of letters, Poe himself experimented with a range of narrative voices, from the highly rational to the demented, in stories like "The Black Cat" (1843) and "The Fall of the House of Usher" (1839) and tried his hand as well with black dialect in stories like "The Gold-Bug" (1843). His work as a whole reverberated with voices and narratives drawing from the region's multiple voices and encounters, in part because he was so deeply immersed in the periodical culture of the Anglo-American Atlantic. British and German gothicism shaped many of his most famous poems and stories, like "Ligeia" (1838), "The Masque of the Red Death" (1842), and "The Raven" (1845), but so too did African American folklore and slave narratives, as Joan Dayan and Teresa Goddu have both persuasively argued.

Significantly, Poe began his career in letters in earnest at the *Southern Literary Messenger* in Richmond, Virginia, during the 1830s, a decade of mounting crisis over slavery, beginning with the Nat Turner Revolt in 1831, and a good deal of his work in the 1830s and 1840s suggests an engagement with and appropriation of conventions characterizing both proslavery and antislavery literature. Short stories slyly evoking insurrection and conflagration, like "Hop-Frog" (1849), "The Man that Was Used Up" (1839), "The Murders in the Rue Morgue" (1841), and "A Tale of the Ragged Mountains" (1844), hinted at, as Richard Gray has suggested, the white South's "secret fears and guilts," and one of Poe's few long works, the adventure novel *The Narrative of Arthur Gordon Pym* (1838), resonated with scenarios of apocalyptic racial wars predicted by proslavery apologists warning of the consequences of emancipation. But *Pym*'s elaborate plotting of flight, entrapment, masquerade, deceit, and escape by sea also suggests Poe's familiarity with slave narratives dating back to Olaudah Equiano's accounts of seafaring adventures and stints aboard slave-trading ships. Those intertextual borrowings in turn underscore both the muting of multiple southern voices as the slavery debate came to dominate literary production in the region and, in Goddu's words, "the crossfertilization of pro- and antislavery pamphlets in the South in the 1830s."

Hybrid Cultures of the South in Its Early Literature

Farther west, miscegenated and multilingual cultures were emerging in the evolving mestizo culture of what would later become the Texan-Mexican border country and in the multiracial world of French Louisiana. By the late eighteenth century the equestrian drama *Los Comanches*, probably written by a rancher named Pedro Bautista Pino, was being performed regularly to celebrate the 1779 defeat of the Comanche chief Cuemo Verde in the costly Comanche wars waged by the Spanish. Notable as well were the popular ballads circulating throughout the border country down through the nineteenth century and beyond, among them indita ballads ("little Indian songs") relating historical and personal tragedies; trovos, musical contests waged by two troucadores, and especially corridos, ballads tracing their descent from Spanish songs brought to Mexico and usually focusing on Anglo-Mexican conflicts. Arguably the most famous of the corridos was "The Ballad of Gregorio Cortez," relating the war waged by a heroic Texan-Mexican rancher against Anglo lawmen. In the twentieth century novelist and folklorist Américo Pardes would capture the most comprehensive version of the corrido in his dissertation and in his 1958 book *With His Pistol in His Hand: A Border Ballad and Its Hero*. French New Orleans for its part produced the two earliest Spanish-language newspapers in the United States—*El Misisipi*, founded in 1808, and *El Mensagero Lusianés*, founded in 1809. Far more extensive, though, was the Francophone literature that emerged from the city acquired through the Louisiana Purchase. Despite the prohibition against publication leveled against New Orleans's *gens de couleur libres*, the Crescent City produced the first anthology of poetry by writers of color ever published, *Les Cenelles* (1845), edited by a free man of color named Armand Lanusse. Included in the anthology were eighty-five poems by seventeen black Louisiana poets, among them Victor Séjour, Camille Thierry, Pierre Delcour, Mirtil Ferdinand Liotau, and Joanni Questi. Significantly, three of those contributors eventually felt compelled to move to France—Sejour, Delcour, and Thierry.

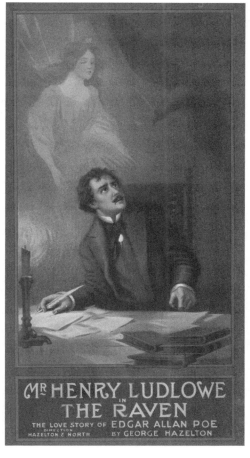

Edgar Allan Poe is often hailed as the preeminent white writer of the antebellum South. Courtesy Library of Congress.

Something of early North American hybridity also lingered in the short stories and sketches of horse swaps, revival meetings, con games, and sporting contests that emerged from the areas in the Old Southwest opened up to European American settlement by Indian Removal and that appeared in the 1830s, 1840s, and 1850s in regional and national newspapers, but most particularly in the New York *Spirit of the Times*, edited by William T. Porter. Now categorized generally as southwestern humor, these sketches of southern backwoods life—"the nether side of Southern life," as one late nineteenth-century commentator put it—were written for the most part by lawyers and journalists who generally cast distant and amused eyes upon the shenanigans and vernacular of frontier denizens, as did Joseph Glover Baldwin, who declared in his 1853 *Flush Times of Alabama and Mis-*

sissippi: "The condition of the country may be imagined:—vulgarity—ignorance—fussy and arrogant pretension—unmitigated rowdyism—bullying insolence, if they did not rule the hour, *seemed* to wield unchecked dominion." Among the earliest publications to appear in this vein were a series of volumes published under Davy Crockett's name relating his adventures and highlighting his distinctive "rip-roaring" backwoods voice and Augustus Baldwin Longstreet's 1835 volume *Georgia Scenes*, a collection of sketches that appeared originally in the Milledgeville *Southern Recorder* and later in the Augusta *States Rights Sentinel*.

Longstreet's sketches in turn paved the way for a subgenre of sketches and short stories that would enjoy popularity for the next two decades, among them Johnson Jones Hooper's 1845 volume *Some Adventures of Captain Simon Suggs*, whose title character utters the memorable line, "It's good to be shifty in a new country," and two volumes compiled by William T. Porter, *The Big Bear of Arkansas* (1845), featuring the title story by Thomas Bangs Thorpe that became emblematic of southwestern humor, and *A Quarter Race in Kentucky* (1846). Other celebratory volumes of country and small-town life were William Tappan Thompson's *Major Jones's Courtship* (1843), Henry Clay Lewis' *Odd Leaves from the Life of a Louisiana Swamp Doctor* (1850), published under the pseudonym Madison Tensa, William Gilmore Simms' *As Good as a Comedy* (1852), *Paddy McGann* (serialized in 1863), and "How Sharp Snaffles Got His Capital and Wife" (published posthumously in 1870), and most notably George Washington Harris' *Sut Lovingood: Yarns Spun by a Nat'ral Born Durn'd Fool* (1867), perhaps the prime exemplar of the genre and its highlighting of voices drawn from the southern backcountry.

SLAVERY VERSUS ANTISLAVERY

In the first half of the nineteenth century, the debate over slavery came to dominate literary productions of and about the South as the region's slaveholding elite retreated to a siege mentality—in politics and in narrative—as challenges mounted to the region's "peculiar institution." The year 1800 saw the aborted slave conspiracy in Richmond, Virginia, known as Gabriel's Rebellion, inspired in no small part by the successful ten-year slave revolt that transformed Saint-Domingue, the Caribbean jewel of the French empire, into the Western Hemisphere's second republic—Haiti. One southern state after another had responded as early as the 1790s with legal barricades, first against the slave trade, then against the entry of West Indian blacks into southern seaports, and finally against the distribution of literature about the newly established black republic. To a great extent, as historian Alfred Hunt argues, the white South's intellectual blockade against the free discussion of ideas began not with the widespread circulation of northern abolitionist pamphlets in the 1830s but with those early attempts to stave off the contagion of rebellion emanating from the Caribbean at the turn into the nineteenth century.

Slave Narratives

What followed, though, were three decades of proliferating slave rebellions and conspiracies in the U.S. South—the Easter Plot of 1801–1802, the Louisiana insurrections of 1811–1812, the Denmark Vesey conspiracy of 1822, the 1829–1830 publication and distribution of David Walker's *Appeal* for slave resistance, and the 1831 Nat Turner Revolt in Southampton County, Virginia—the most active period of slave uprisings in American history. Accompanying armed resistance to slavery was a mounting tide of autobiographical narratives by fugitive slaves attacking slavery as an institution and calling for its abolition—eventually totaling some 6,000 extant works, by Frances Smith Foster's estimate, from one-page interviews to book-length volumes, many of them best sellers spawning multiple editions and translation into foreign languages.

In the eighteenth century the earliest versions of slave narratives had emerged in both the Northeast and the South in the form of crime confessions, spiritual narratives, and Indian captivity narratives, and a few had even offered autobiographical accounts by Africans, like *A Narrative of the Life and Adventures of Venture, a Native of Africa* (1798). By the 1820s and 1830s, though, slave narratives began to emerge as a peculiarly southern genre, one defined by its opposition to slavery as an institution and to the white South that fostered it. A forecast of what was to come was the 1825 volume *Life of William Grimes, the Runaway Slave*, a first-person account of a man who spent thirty years as a slave in the South and was finally forced to purchase himself from his master. "He was the first black autobiographer in America," William Andrews declares, "to picture the South in what would become a standardized image in abolitionist propaganda: the plantation as rural chamber of horrors, a nightmare world presided over by near-demonic whites as capricious as they were sadistic."

Grimes' account was followed first by David Walker's electrifying *Appeal to the Coloured Citizens of the World* (1829), rewriting the Declaration of Independence as a call for organized resistance to slavery, and then by *The Confessions of Nat Turner* (1831), a remarkable account of the Southampton revolt pitting Turner's voice and rationale for the rebellion as divinely inspired against that of his court-appointed attorney, Thomas Gray, who served as Turner's amanuensis and saw the narrative as a cautionary tale about religious fanaticism and the looming dangers of slave rebellion. The distribution of Walker's *Appeal* in 1830–1831 in southern seaports up and down the Atlantic coast—by black sailors, preachers, and maroon communities in outlying areas—led to seizures of available copies, mass arrests, quarantines of black sailors, and new legislative sanctions on the distribution of seditious literature and slave education. *The Confessions of Nat Turner*, 50,000 copies of which were printed, as well as the revolt it recorded, helped ignite the Virginia legislative debates on the future of slavery in 1831–1832 and helped instigate heightened restrictions on black assembly and an outright ban on black preachers—legislative acts that foreshadowed, like the seizures and arrests greeting David Walker's *Appeal*, the silence, denial, and withholding of recognition with which white southerners would receive black narratives to come.

These two texts, accompanied by a host of slave narratives to come, also arguably helped prompt the formulation of the proslavery argument as it began to emerge in pamphlets and speeches, but particularly in novels mapping yet another new southern genre—the plantation tradition—implicitly responding to, countering, and rewriting slave narratives. Just months after the Nat Turner Revolt in Virginia, a Baltimore writer named John Pendleton Kennedy produced *Swallow Barn* (1832), a congenial epistolary novel about life on a shabbily genteel Tidewater Virginia plantation that charms its northern narrator and by implication pleads with its readers to consider the benefits of a rural, hierarchical way of life based on slavery. Kennedy's views on the virtues of an organic, fixed, hierarchical society would be echoed by the historical romances that would continue to be produced during the 1830s, in particular by Boston-born Caroline Howard Gilman, who made a career for herself as an editor and writer in Charleston and whose 1837 novel *Recollections of a Southern Matron* made a considerable contribution to the region's plantation tradition by insisting upon the devotion of slaves to their white masters and mistresses—and her title character's own sense of reciprocity to her "servants."

Antislavery Literature

Despite qualms articulated by Kennedy in particular regarding the morality of slavery as an institution, Kennedy's and Gilman's novels in many respects paralleled the argument for slavery as a positive good expounded by South Carolinian John C. Calhoun on the floor of the U.S. Senate, but the benevolent picture of slavery painted in those novels—and in proslavery arguments—would be countermanded by two South Carolina–born white aristocrats, Angelina and Sarah Grimké, who moved to the North in the 1820s and allied themselves with the forces of immediate abolitionism led by William Lloyd Garrison, who began editing *The Liberator* in 1831. Both converts to Quakerism at early ages, the Grimké sisters began speaking to women on abolitionism in New York City, first in parlors and then in churches. In doing so—and in writing public appeals on antislavery—they helped to articulate an alliance between abolitionism and feminism and to define new roles for white women in the public sphere. That same year Angelina Grimké published her *Appeal to the Christian Women of the South* through the American Anti-Slavery Society, arguing that slavery violated the spirit of the Bible and the Declaration of Independence and urging wives, mothers, sisters, and daughters of southern lawmakers to speak and act on slavery. Concurrently, Sarah Grimké published *An Epistle to the Clergy of the Southern States*, also through the American Anti-Slavery Society, followed two years later by *Letters on the Equality of the Sexes and the Condition of Woman, Addressed to Mary S. Parker, President of the Boston Female Anti-Slavery Society*. Angelina took yet another step into the public sphere in 1838 when she became the first woman to speak before a legislative body—yet again on slavery. "I stand before you as a southerner," she told a legislative committee of the Massachusetts House of Representatives, "exiled from the land of my birth, by the sound of the lash, and the piteous cry of the slave. I stand before you as a repentant slaveholder."

At the same time the Grimké sisters were making their presence felt in antislavery publications, the number of slave narratives steadily rose as antislavery organizations began to make use of fugitive slaves and their narratives as political weapons against slavery. In 1836 *Slavery in the United States: A Narrative of the Life and Adventures of Charles Ball* was issued under the editorship of Isaac Fisher; in 1837 the *Narrative of the Adventures and Escape of Moses Roper* appeared, "the first fugitive slave narrative since Grimes's," Andrews reports, "to be composed and written by the slave himself"; and in 1838 the *Narrative of James Williams* was published under the auspices of the American Anti-Slavery Society, the first slave narrative to receive the society's sponsorship. By the early 1840s a charismatic escaped slave from Maryland who had taken the name Frederick Douglass was giving public speeches as a lecturing agent for the Massachusetts and American antislavery

Angelina and Sarah Grimké allied themselves with the forces of immediate abolitionism. The Grimké sisters began speaking to women on abolitionism in New York City and writing public appeals on antislavery. They helped to articulate an alliance between abolitionism and feminism and define new roles for white women in the public sphere. Courtesy Library of Congress.

societies and making a considerable impact on his spellbound listeners, some of whom doubted that so well-spoken a man could have actually been a slave. In response Douglass produced his pivotal *Narrative of the Life of Frederick Douglass, an American Slave* (1845), the first of three autobiographies, including *My Bondage and My Freedom* (1855) and *The Life and Times of Frederick Douglass* (1881). Within just five years, Douglass' 1845 volume had sold 30,000 copies, and by 1848 it had gone through nine editions in England.

Douglass' first account became in many respects the most famous slave narrative of them all, one that highlighted the crucial link between literacy and freedom and insisted upon the project of self-definition in opposition to everything that slavery represented. But nearly as popular were slave narratives that followed—William Wells Brown's narrative went through four editions in 1847, the year it was published, and *The Life of Josiah Henson, Formerly a Slave, Now an Inhabitant of Canada*, issued in 1849, sold 6,000 copies its first three years of publication. So prominent had slave narratives become by mid-century that Ephraim Peabody, a Unitarian minister in Boston, pronounced them a "new department" in "the literature of civilization."

Early African American forays into belles lettres, in turn, revealed their antecedents in slave narratives and antislavery sentiment. In 1829 *The Hope of Liberty*, by George Moses Horton, a North Carolinian slave, appeared—the first book of poetry by a southern black poet as well as the first book by an African American issued by an American publisher. Horton had written the book to earn enough money to buy his freedom, and though he failed in that aim, he published two other volumes of poetry, *The Poetical Works of George M. Horton* (1845) and *Naked Genius* (1865), and included in those volumes were poems that resonated with the yearnings for freedom shaping so many slave narratives. William Wells Brown in turn produced the 1853 novel *Clotel*, a daring account of Thomas Jefferson's mixed-race daughter that Brown published in England and revised several times over fourteen years, and then followed five years later with the first play by an African American—*The Escape: or, A Leap for Freedom: A Drama in Five Acts* (1858). Most militant of all was Martin Delany's *Blake; or, The Huts of America* (1859), a proto–black nationalist novel that traces the trajectory of a slave from fugitive to armed insurrectionist taking refuge in Cuba.

Harriet Jacobs' extraordinary slave narrative *Incidents in the Life of a Slave Girl* (1861) reaped the benefits of those early literary experiments. Jacobs' story of fending off the sexual advances of her mistress' father, hiding in her grandmother's house for seven years, and finally escaping to the North revealed the author's thorough familiarity not just with the masculine tradition of slave narratives epitomized in Douglass' writing but also with sentimental and gothic novels of the period, which helped shape her own narrative. *Incidents* was replete with dramatic confrontations, chase scenes, and a sexual frankness startling in a nineteenth-century text. Jacobs' text also suggested a thorough familiarity with the proslavery argument as it had emerged in plantation novels, and her narrative took careful aim at some of the most cherished features of the plantation myth, including the benevolent patriarch-steward, the nurturing southern lady, and the familial underpinnings of slavery itself.

These were books, though, that were received with studied silence in the white southern press—except for references here and there to antislavery agitators as frauds and imposters. One after another defenders of slavery concentrated their energy instead on repudiating egalitarianism and insisting upon slavery as the foundation of civilization: Thomas R. Dew's *Review of the Debate in the Virginia Legislature* (1832); William Harper in *Memoir on Slavery* (1838); James Henry Hammond in *Two Letters on Slavery in the United States Addressed to Thomas Clarkson, Esq.* (1845); Henry Hughes in *Treatise on Sociology: Theoretical and Practical* (1854); and George Fitzhugh's two books rejecting Jeffersonianism and capitalism altogether, *Sociology for the South: or the Failure of Free Society* (1854) and *Cannibals All! or Slaves Without Masters* (1857). To this argument Thornton Stringfellow added a plea for the biblical grounding of slavery in *A Brief Examination of Scripture Testimony on the Institution of Slavery* (1850). John C. Calhoun offered indirect support for the proslavery position in two treatises, published posthumously, arguing for inequality as the basic human condition and against the dangers of governing by numerical majority: *A Disquisition on Government* and *Discourse on the Constitution of the United States*, both included in his *Works* (1851–1855).

The Legacy of *Uncle Tom's Cabin*

The antislavery book that attracted the most furious white southern response, though, was not a best-selling slave narrative but a novel drawing a good deal of its material from slave narratives and in particular from *The Life of Josiah Henson*—Harriet Beecher Stowe's *Uncle Tom's Cabin*, serialized in the antislavery newspaper *The National Era* in 1851–1852 and issued as a separate volume in 1852. So great was the popularity of Stowe's antislavery novel that it sold more copies, Elizabeth Ammons reports, "than any book in the world except the Bible." Ten thousand copies were sold almost immediately, and 300,000 within the year in the United States alone. Stowe's novel also created a firestorm in the slaveholding South, where it was seen as a call for massive resistance to the recently passed Fugitive Slave Act, which required northern legal authorities to return runaway slaves. Notable as well, though, was the foregrounding of dissenting and marginal voices in *Uncle Tom's Cabin*—runaway slaves like Eliza and George Harris, aiders and abettors of runaways like plantation mistress Louisa Shelby, saboteurs like Cassie, and covert abolitionists like Augustine St. Clare and his daughter Eva. These were voices that white southerners had sought to block at southern seaports and in post offices and to repress or silence altogether in white plantation novels. It was little wonder, then, that generations later Louisiana writer Grace King would describe the best-selling novel as that "hideous, black, dragon-like book that hovered on the horizon of every Southern child."

Still, as George Frederick Holmes, one of the southern reviewers of *Uncle Tom's Cabin*, acknowledged, "We shall be indebted to the continuance and asperity of this controversy for the creation of a genuine Southern literature—in itself an inestimable gain to our people." Besides inspiring slashing reviews—by South Carolinian Louisa McCord, for one, the only woman, historian Marli Weiner notes, to publish regularly in the region's major periodicals—Stowe's novel also instigated a new wave of plantation novels so expressly configured in opposition to *Uncle Tom's Cabin* that they became known as "anti-Tom" novels. Over twenty books responding to the best seller were published before the Civil War, among them John W. Page's *Uncle Robin in His Cabin in Virginia, and Tom Without One in Boston* (1852); William Gilmore Simms' *Woodcraft* (1854), featuring two of his more memorable characters, Captain Porgy and his body servant, Tom, who refuses to accept proffered freedom; and a revised edition of *Swallow Barn* (1852), expanded, as John Pendleton Kennedy declared, to refute "abolitionist mischief." Eight of those anti-Tom novels were by white southern women, among them Caroline Lee Hentz's *Marcus Warland* (1842) and in particular *The Planter's Northern Bride* (1854), which featured the unmasking of a slave abolitionist as a fraud; Mary H. Eastman's *Aunt Phillis's Cabin; or Southern Life as It Is* (1852); Maria McIntosh's *The Lofty and the Lowly; or, Good in All and None All-Good* (1853); Martha Haines Butt's *Anti-Fanaticism: A Tale of the South* (1853); Mary E. Herndon's *Louise Elton; or Things Seen and Heard* (1853); Mrs. Henry R. Schoolcraft's *The Black Gauntlet, a Tale of Plantation Life in South Carolina* (1860); and Virginia Terhune's *Moss-Side* (1857).

Women Writers in the Nineteenth-Century South

Many of these novels were best sellers and to a great extent heralded the beginning of white women's writing in the South at a time when women novelists in the Northeast were becoming so prevalent that they would attract Nathaniel Hawthorne's now-famous denunciation dismissing "that damn'd mob of scribbling women." In the 1840s and early 1850s, a few white women, among them Caroline Lee Hentz and E.D.E.N. Southworth, had resorted to literature to support their families, and those efforts had turned out to be so successful that other writers, including Augusta Evans and authors of anti-Tom novels, were encouraged to follow in their footsteps. By 1857 Southworth's best-selling novels, often about women thrown upon their own resources, were earning roughly $6,000 a year, and Augusta J. Evans' third novel, *Beulah* (1859), about a young woman struggling with religious doubt, made something of a sensation among southern women readers.

By and large opposed to the women's movement emerging in the North, as well as to the antislavery movement, the South's first white women writers nonetheless found themselves being drawn into the public sphere as the Civil War engulfed North and South. "The Civil War," Drew Gilpin Faust argues in *Mothers of Invention*, "made thousands of white women of all classes into authors—writers of letters and composers of journals recording the momentous and historic events as well as creators of published songs, poetry, and novels." Indeed, with so many men at the front, women, Faust adds, became for all intents and purposes the custodians of white southern culture, and their literary contributions to the war effort—in the form of songs, poems, stories, and essays—filled the pages of southern periodicals. Augusta Evans herself wrote the most famous novel of the Confederacy, *Macaria; or Altars of Sacrifice* (1863), the story of two ambitious young single women who eventually submerge their intellectual and artistic impulses in service to the Confederacy. Evans' novel proved so popular in both armies that one Union general felt compelled to ban it as detrimental to troop morale.

In terms of popular impact, Evans' novel would overshadow to a striking degree the poetry by South Carolinian Henry Timrod, often posthumously pronounced the "Poet Laureate of the Confederacy" on the strength of his 1861 poem "Ethnogenesis," celebrating the birth of the Confederacy. But so too would perhaps the greatest literary accomplishments to emerge out of the wartime South—Civil War diaries produced by white women in striking numbers, many of them published at the turn of the twentieth century, among them Mary Ann Harris Gay's *Life in Dixie During the War* (1897), Sarah Rice Pryor's *Reminiscences of Peace and War* (1904), Eliza Andrews' *The War-Time Journal of a Georgia Girl, 1864–1865* (1908), Sarah Morgan Dawson's *A Confederate Girl's Diary* (1913), and perhaps most famously Mary Chesnut's *A Diary from Dixie* (1905). A far more extensive version of Chesnut's diary, which has become in many respects one of the seminal literary documents of the nineteenth-century South, would be published in 1981 and edited by C. Vann Woodward as *Mary Chesnut's Civil War*. As a whole, her Civil War diary suggests the double-edged nature of journal-writing that Drew Gilpin Faust sees for women like Chesnut, who found in those journals opportunities not just to record the course of Confederate lives during the war but also to explore the possibilities of alternative selves that might well prove antithetical to the worlds they inhabited. "We shall never any of us be the same as we have been," wrote one of those women diarists in a prescient moment in 1862. It was a remark that suggested something of the new literary directions—many of which would be pioneered by late nineteenth- and early twentieth-century women writers, white and black, that Civil War diaries by women anticipated.

MEMORY AND COUNTER-MEMORIES

Literature from the Civil War

In the immediate wake of the war, John Esten Cooke, who had served with both Stonewall Jackson and J.E.B. Stuart, issued a flurry of Civil War novels, *Surry of Eagle's Nest* (1866), *Mohun* (1869), and *Hilt to Hilt* (1869), but they would be overshadowed by the continuing success of domestic novels by southern white women following the national trend. Augusta Evans, for one, managed to surpass the success of *Macaria* with her 1866 novel *St. Elmo*, the story of a plucky young woman writer who, through sheer dint of moral will, transforms a rake into a sober minister and husband. *St. Elmo* became one of the biggest best sellers of the nineteenth century, a book so widely read for the next half-century and more that Allen Tate would despairingly refer to it as an example of the South's feeble literary tradition, and Eudora Welty would remember in *One Writer's Beginnings* (1984) the "classic advice given to rose growers on how to water their bushes long enough: 'Take a chair and *St. Elmo*.'"

Years later Evans' success, and that of other women writers, would still rankle for writers like Paul Hamilton Hayne, who had been chief—and unpaid—editor of Charleston's *Russell's Magazine*, the center of an active literary circle just before the war attracting the talents of William Gilmore Simms and Henry Timrod, among others. In an 1874 article for the *Southern Magazine* titled "Literature at the South: The Fungous School," he lamented the accolades awarded to "Mrs. Duck-a-Love's 'pathetic and passionate romance, that marvellous revelation of a woman's famishing heart'" and "Mrs. General Aristottle Brown's 'profound philosophic novel,'" which, he declared, could be summed up as "an exponent of effervescing commonplace, with much fizz, fussiness and froth." From Hayne's perspective that success contrasted sharply with his own difficulties making a living through letters and his poetry and with the plight of his friend Henry Timrod, whose poetry he took the responsibility for collecting and publishing after Timrod's untimely death in 1867. Perhaps more to the point, such writing for Hayne, who was often referred to as the "Poet Laureate of the South" in the last twenty years of his life, also appeared to distract white southern writers from the task of holding high the banner of southern distinctiveness in the literary realm—a point that he made startlingly clear in an 1866 article for *Scott's Monthly*: "Overthrown in our efforts to establish a political nationality by *force of arms*, we may yet establish an intellectual dynasty more glorious and permanent by *force of thought*."

In the 1870s, in fact, beginning with a series on "The Great South" by Edward King for *Scribner's Monthly*, northern publishers and magazine editors began to show a heightened interest in the defeated Confederacy as a region offering an exotic contrast with the strains of urbanism, industrial capitalism, labor troubles, and mounting immigration characterizing the Northeast. Readers of *Lippincott's* and *Scribner's Monthly* applauded the musical lyrics of Sidney Lanier's poems celebrating southern landscapes and small farms, especially "Corn" (1875), "The Symphony" (1875), and "The Marshes of Glynn" (1878). In the next two decades, local color fiction, celebrating the nooks, crannies, country dialects, and odd traditions, seized control of the national imagination and fostered the careers of a host of writers, particularly white women like Mary Noailles Murfree, who, writing under the pseudonym Charles Egbert Craddock, found a large audience for her novels and stories about the Tennessee mountains; Mollie Moore Davis, who wrote historical novels about Texas and French Louisiana; northern-born Constance Fenimore Woolson, who wrote about life in Florida; and Grace King, who produced a series of volumes on the history of New Orleans, Louisiana, and Florida, as well as fiction about French Creoles.

The Black Character in Post–Civil War Literature

Stories and poems with black dialect became particularly popular, starting with Irwin Russell's poems, most notably "Christmas-Night in the Quarters" (1878), which caught the eye of a white Georgian journalist named Joel Chandler Harris who had been experimenting himself with black dialect sketches in the *Atlanta Constitution*. In quick succession volumes examining the byways of southern life, explicated partly through dialect, appeared on the national scene—*Like unto Like* (1878), by Sherwood Bonner, the pen name of journalist Kate Bonner McDowell; *Old Creole Days* (1879) and *The Grandissimes* (1880), by a New Orleans accountant named George Washington Cable; and *Uncle Remus: His Songs and Sayings* (1880), by Harris himself, who would later praise Irwin Russell for discovering "the literary possibilities of the negro character."

Harris' volume turned out to be a best seller, averaging $4,000 in sales a year, inspiring a whole series of Uncle Remus volumes, and pointing the way for a reconfiguration of the plantation romance as the white South's postbellum narrative of legitimation, one that could reestablish white authority and black subordination in the aftermath of emancipation. Harris based the stories in the Uncle Remus volumes on folktales he had collected from former slaves, but the tales themselves were always framed by Harris' central conceit—that of a former slave telling stories to a white boy. In many respects the stories were as much about the act of storytelling as they were about the adventures of a trickster rabbit and his woodland fellows, and that narrative shift signaled the formation of a new arena for literary productions of and about the region—stories themselves. The seemingly innocuous scenario of Uncle Remus, a kindly former slave, telling what seemed like children's stories, helped inaugurate one of the region's central images of self-definition, that of a community of storytellers who felt compelled to "tell about the South" and its past, and the audiences summoned into being by that telling were always envisioned as white.

No one wielded that scenario of self-conscious storytelling about the region more persuasively or powerfully than did Thomas Nelson Page, whose 1884 story "Marse Chan" borrowed Harris' narrative framing by a former slave looking back fondly at plantation days before the war and emancipation and taking it upon himself to tell the story of the white family that once owned him. "Marse Chan" would serve as the linchpin of Page's 1887 collection of short stories *In Ole Virginia*, which, together with the Confederate monuments that began appearing all over the turn-of-the-century South, laid the foundation for the defining narrative of the postbellum white South—the "myth of the Lost Cause." Page's narrative and those that followed for all intents and purposes seized control of regional memory and transformed the antebellum southern past into a realm of charming cavaliers and belles and pastoral plantations, where slavery was viewed as stewardship and not as a central cause of the Civil War. So popular did *In Ole Virginia* and its imitators prove to be both in the South and in the North that by the lights of former Union officer and Reconstruction judge Albion Tourgée the South finally won in literary wars what it had lost at Appomattox.

The White View: Post-Reconstruction Literature

It was precisely that kind of triumph that worried southern dissenters, white and black, like George Washington Cable, Mark Twain, and Charles W. Chesnutt, all of them attracted to local color fiction but resolutely opposed to the emerging cult of the Lost Cause and its rewriting of postbellum southern history to suit the needs of white nostalgia. To a startling degree, Cable offered a highly prescient critique of the kind of storytelling undertaken by Page in "Marse Chan" in his 1880 novel *The Grandissimes*, set in 1803 Louisiana but aimed unmistakably at the growing racism of the post-Reconstruction South. Cable's novel follows the adventures of an immigrant to Louisiana who learns to make sense of "the newly found book, the community of New Orleans" by listening to the stories told by white and black members of the French Creole family called the Grandissimes, and chief among those stories is the tale of a runaway slave whose eventual reconciliation to the family and death is told again and again by the Grandissimes in a white communal rite of affirmation. It is, one white Grandissime tells the newcomer, the story that "turns the edge of our tools," and for Cable, concerned about the rise of legalized segregation in New Orleans, the consequences of those stories were racial oppression, injustice, and silence for anyone who resisted their narrative momentum.

From Mark Twain's perspective, Cable was a southerner who, in his own words, "did not write in the southern style," a characterization Twain himself—pronounced by William Dean Howells "the most desouthernized Southerner I ever knew"—found much to his liking. Twain's own antecedents in antebellum Missouri had drawn him to southwestern humor in his own experiments with tall tale-telling, like "The Jumping Frog of Calaveras County" (1865), a story he may have heard from black laborers on the Mississippi, but the imaginative trips he took back to his native region—in *Life on the Mississippi* (1883), *The Adventures of Tom Sawyer* (1876), *Adventures of Huckleberry Finn* (1885), and *Pudd'nhead Wilson* (1894)—revealed a growing distaste for revered white regional traditions, from the honorific posturing of gentlemen to the institution of slavery itself. Nowhere was he franker than in *Adventures of Huckleberry Finn* about the dangers and violent consequences of romantic pretensions and obsessions with honor, all exemplified by the Grangerford-Shepherdson feud. Perpetuated by obsessions with honor and concluding in a horrifying massacre, the feud drives runaways Huck and Jim back to the safety of the river.

If anything, black writer Charles W. Chesnutt, who had been mentored early on in his career by George W. Cable, was even more adamant about the connections to be made between stories of honor and tradition and consequent violence, and nowhere more so than in his 1901 novel *The Marrow of Tradition*, a roman à clef of the 1898 race riot in Wilmington, North Carolina, and a work that anticipates to an uncanny degree the violent impact of Thomas Dixon's rabidly racist retellings of recent southern history, *The Leopard's Spots* (1902) and *The Clansman* (1905). With unflinching clarity Chesnutt's novel exposed the connections to be made between the racial violence engulfing a thinly disguised Wilmington and the newspaper stories of rape and murder concocted by a trio of white political leaders determined to reinstate the political and economic hegemony of whites. It was a novel ahead of its time. Even ordinarily sympathetic white reviewers like William Dean Howells pronounced it "bitter," and Chesnutt's literary career for all intents and purposes came to an end with its publication.

The only contemporary black fiction that would match the anger of *The Marrow of Tradition* was found in the self-published volumes by Texas-born minister Sutton E. Griggs, who kept up for several years a steady drumbeat of daring and incendiary novels: *Imperium in Imperio* (1899), *Overshadowed* (1901), *Unfettered* (1902), and *The Hindered Hand; or, The Reign of the Repressionist* (1905?). W.E.B. DuBois, in contrast, resorted to the coded language and double meanings of southern black culture "behind the veil" in his deeply personal excavation of the African American past in *The Souls of Black Folk* (1903), written during his years on the faculty at Atlanta Clark University. Booker T. Washington also retreated to a certain extent in his use of the language and form of slave narratives in his autobiography *Up from Slavery* (1900), which also included a kind of masking that earlier slave narrative writers would have readily recognized. A few years later James Weldon Johnson would highlight the vexed relationship between black narrators and white readers in his *Autobiography of an Ex-Coloured Man* (1912), published anonymously largely as a ploy to unsettle white audiences confronted with the permeability of the color line that plantation literature had helped construct.

Those brief, daring forays against the cult of white southern memory were in many respects surpassed by the work of African American women writers, who began to publish in sizable numbers well before the turn into the twentieth century. The year 1892, as Frances Smith Foster argues, marked "the beginning of a new era in African American women's literary tradition." That year Frances Ellen Watkins Harper, antislavery activist, essayist, and poet, brought out *Iola Leroy; or Shadows Uplifted*, tracing the travails of a woman raised as white whose mixed-race heritage is eventually revealed to her and who chooses ultimately to define herself as black. *Iola Leroy* set itself the task of retelling the story of the Civil War and Reconstruction from a specifically black perspective, and as such, emerges as a novel, in John Ernest's words, "about writing (authoring) the self—and, beyond that, about writing the race." She was joined in that project with the publication that same year of *A Voice from the South*, by Anna Julia Cooper, later to become famous as teacher and principal of the M Street High School (later Dunbar High School) in Washington, D.C. Cooper saw her collection of essays on women and writing as a bid to give voice to the "other side" of southern life and literature, and declared that the status of the African American woman in the coming century would determine what kind of society America would make. Also marking 1892 was the publication of *Southern Horrors: Lynching in All Its Phases* by journalist Ida B. Wells-Barnett, who directly attacked white rationales for the accelerating outbreaks of lynchings throughout the region. She followed that initial pamphlet with her 1895 volume *Red Record*. All of those initial volumes were contemporary with Alice Dunbar-Nelson's *Violets and Other Tales* (1895) and *The Goodness of St. Rocque and*

Other Tales (1899) and Eloise Bibb Thompson's poems and short stories about passing and the color line in the world of Creoles of color.

The Birth of Modern Southern Literature

Such works resolutely brought attention to the voices, political issues, and counter-memories repressed or appropriated by regional memories constructed in white plantation literature and the burgeoning Cult of the Lost Cause. Hence critics like Carol S. Manning have argued that the celebrated southern literary renaissance, usually designated as occupying the two decades between World War I and World War II, should be extended to incorporate these writers, along with Kate Chopin, Grace King, and Ellen Glasgow, as the earliest pioneers of the critical temper usually associated with the regional flowering of letters in the first half of the twentieth century. Traditionally, historians of the southern renaissance have taken their cue from Allen Tate's famous 1945 characterization of modern southern literature's origins: "With the war of 1914–1918, the South reentered the world—but gave a backward glance as it stepped over the border: that backward glance gave us the Southern renascence, a literature conscious of the past in the present." Tate's reference to World War I, though, presupposes that the writers who most concern him are young men who distanced themselves from their native region through military experience abroad—an assumption that Tate doubtless inherited from Malcolm Cowley's exclusive focus on white male writers catapulted into modernism by World War I in his pioneering history of modernism, *Exile's Return*. Not surprisingly, this paradigm of the southern renascence takes for granted the dismissal and categorization of white women writers like Kate Chopin, Ellen Glasgow, and Mary Johnston as local color practitioners, writers in a minor vein, and ignores altogether women writers of color.

Ironically, novelists like Chopin, Glasgow, and Johnston anticipated by a generation and more the self-styled rebels in the 1920s who won so much praise from critics like H. L. Mencken for their hard-nosed critiques of the region. Chopin's short stories in the 1890s brought a sharp eye to bear on the gap between gender conventions and personal desires, and her 1899 novel *The Awakening*, with its forthright, nonjudgmental portrait of one woman's discovery of her sexuality, was scandalous enough to make Chopin retreat from the public eye on the remainder of her life. Johnston in turn moved from Lost Cause novels like *The Long Roll* (1911) to open support of women's suffrage in the her 1913 novel *Hagar*. Most iconoclastic of all was Richmond-born and bred Ellen Glasgow, who early on declared, "What the South needs is blood and irony," and proceeded to produce an impressive multinovel social history of Virginia exploring interdicted topics like class, interracial sex, and economic exploitation. Chief among her concerns was the dehumanization imposed upon women by the ideal of white southern womanhood, a theme she explored to devastating effect particularly in *Virginia* (1913) and in her best-known work, *Barren Ground* (1925).

These were writers who paved the way for Elizabeth Madox Roberts, who in 1925 published *The Time of Man*, a story of a rural Kentucky woman, as well as two of the most innovative and daring white writers of the 1920s, Tennessee-born Evelyn Scott and Atlantan Frances Newman, both of whom experimented with modernist narrative techniques and produced taboo-breaking portraits of female sexuality. Scott proved herself a rebel early on by eloping to Brazil at the age of twenty with a man two decades her senior, and then went on to produce ten novels, a collection of novellas, two books of poetry, a play, an autobiography, and a wide array of essays, reviews, and short stories, among them a vivid Civil War novel, *The Wave* (1929). Frances Newman was not nearly as productive as Scott, but her first novel, *The Hard-Boiled Virgin* (1926), a satirical portrait of a southern new woman weighed down with the legacy of southern belledom, earned rapturous praise from H. L. Mencken and Richmond novelist James Branch Cabell, then at the height of his fame for his racy novels of fantasy and male quest. Her second novel, *Dead Lovers Are Faithful Lovers* (1928), skewered the ideal of marriage and played havoc with traditional notions of devoted wife and predatory mistress.

Newman died suddenly in 1928, too soon to enjoy the fruits of her second novel's fame, but she did attract the critical eye of a Vanderbilt University professor and poet named Donald Davidson, who denounced *The Hard-Boiled Virgin* in a 1928 review for its "malignant intent of puncturing some convention, especially the conventions of the Old South as represented in the St. Cecilia Society of Charleston and the aristocracy of Peachtree Street, Atlanta." Years later he would accuse Newman and other feminist women writers of not being southern at all, and significantly, the essays and books that he and his fellow-poet southern activists—chief among them John Crowe Ransom, Allen Tate, and Robert Penn Warren—wrote in the decades to come would rule out Newman, most white women, writers of color, and leftist activists in a careful remaking of modern southern letters in the self-image of the group known first as the Fugitive poets, then as the Southern Agrarians, and finally as the southern New Critics and virtual inventors of modern "southern literature."

Davidson's criticism of Newman, though, also hinted at the Fugitives' own troubled engagement with southern tradition through most of the 1920s and the 1930s. By the mid-1920s Davidson was celebrating in his poetry fabled Tennessee's frontier heritage and the legacy of "The Tall Men," as well as frankly condemning the present in poems like "Fire on Belmont Street." Tate and Ransom, in contrast, were far more equivocal about the southern past and their ability as moderns to penetrate the barriers of time and change—an ambivalence that Tate in particular captures in his most famous poem, "Ode to the Confederate Dead," begun in 1925 and revised over the next decade. The poem's effort to conjure up the phantasms of the past results in the speaker's withdrawal from his contemplation of the past and its ruins: "Leave now, / The shut gate and the decomposing wall."

The Agrarian Tradition and Its Response in Literature

It was a conclusion, strangely enough, that Tate reached in his own contribution, "Religion and the Old South," to the celebrated 1930 Agrarian manifesto, *I'll Take My Stand: The South and the Agrarian Tradition*, put together by Davidson, Tate, Ransom, and Warren, along with eight other contributors. The essays as a whole differed widely, united in only the loosest sense by John Crowe Ransom's opening statement of aims, contrasting the preference of the contributors for an agrarian, traditional South over the lures of northern industrialism, urbanism, and progressivism. Dividing the contributors were their markedly different ideals of the region—Davidson evoked the benefits of a folk culture, while Ransom extolled the rewards of an organic, hierarchical society with antecedents in European aristocratic societies. Tate, as always, was the most ambivalent, arguing that the South lacked the traditions of a genuinely conservative-minded society and hinting that the very project of retrieving and reviving tradition was doomed by its modern self-consciousness and thus required—much to the scandal of many a reviewer—the taking hold of tradition "by violence." Lewis P. Simpson's shrewd assessment of the Agrarian engagement with regional history could not be more apt: "No American writers ever worked harder at inheriting their inheritance than the Agrarians."

Still, the image of the past evoked by the Agrarians was one that was studiously white and, in the words of one angry black reviewer, "neo-Confederate"—as though to offer a counter-representation to the images of southern blackness that had already been excavated and popularized by the writers of the Harlem Renaissance. The southern past written into being by the writers and painters of the Harlem Renaissance, in fact, had already made a deep public impression in the 1920s, and the South their works summoned—that of the rural black farmers and laborers and a rich culture of spirituals, blues, jazz, signifying, and veiled defiance being transplanted into northern cities—was far different from the oddly ethereal world of eighteenth-century white aristocrats envisioned by John Crowe Ransom. The Georgia that Jean Toomer captured in the landmark 1923 volume *Cane* evoked the piney woods of backbreaking labor and sudden racial violence as well as the vibrant night life of Seventh Street in Washington, D.C. The private worlds of African American women were given voice in the poetry of Washington writer Georgia Douglas Johnson, famous for her "Saturday night" literary salons, and of Anne Spencer of Lynchburg, Virginia. James Weldon Johnson captured the lyrical accents of black preaching in *God's Trombones* (1927), while Missouri-born Langston Hughes explored the possibilities of jazz and blues in *The Weary Blues* (1926) and *Fine Clothes to the Jew* (1927) and experimented with drama in *Mulatto: A Tragedy of the Deep South*, produced in 1935. Sterling Brown and Zora Neale Hurston for their part set themselves the task of collecting black folklore, a project earlier dominated by white folklorists who more often than not had made use of it to bolster white memories of a lost plantation South. The result of their folklore forays into the rural black South was a slew of publications popular among black and white readers alike: Brown's 1932 poetry volume *Southern Road* and Hurston's premier folk collection *Mules and Men* (1935) as well as two novels, *Jonah's Gourd Vine* (1934) and *Their Eyes Were Watching God* (1937). Louisiana-born Arna Bontemps in turn began excavating African American history, particularly slave rebellions ranging from Virginia to Saint-Domingue, and produced three novels in the 1930s, *God Sends Sunday* (1931), *Black Thunder* (1936), and *Drums at Dusk* (1939). Richard Wright too would turn southward, inspired by the proletarian fiction of the 1930s, and produced first *Uncle Tom's Children* (1938), a short story collection focusing largely on black tenant farmers in the region, and then two volumes offering literary responses to the Great Migration of African Americans out of the South—*Native Son* (1940) and *Twelve Million Black Voices* (1941).

No historical project was more ambitious or more radically opposed to everything the Southern Agrarians represented, though, than W.E.B. DuBois' magisterial *Black Reconstruction* (1935), which rebutted the white southern version of post–Civil War history as one of black failure and white redemption. For DuBois southern history, and southern stories, for that matter, quite simply offered an arena of contesting narratives. "Shall we accept the conventional story of the old slave plantation and its owner's fine, aristocratic life of cultured leisure?" he asked at the end of the volume. "Or shall we note slave biographies, like those of Charles Ball, Sojourner Truth, Harriet Tubman and Frederick Douglass; the careful observations of Olmsted and the indictment of Hinton Helper?"

A few white writers had already anticipated those questions by mining the artistic potential of black folk culture in sympathetic volumes that won the praise of no less a figure than DuBois himself, then editor of the NAACP's journal *The Crisis*. Included in this group were T. S. Stribling, who examined the consequences of the Great Migration in *Birthright* (1922); DuBose Heyward, who produced *Porgy* (1924), a story of Charleston black life that later metamorphosed, with the help of George Gershwin's music, into the opera/musical *Porgy and Bess* (1929); Julia Peterkin, who raised white South Carolinian hackles by publishing a series of books with wholly black perspectives—*Green Thursday* (1924), *Black April* (1927), *Scarlet Sister Mary* (1928), and *Bright Skin* (1932); and playwright Paul Green, whose 1926 play *In Abraham's Bosom* won the Pulitzer Prize.

Concurrently, a growing number of writers explored the plight of those who rarely figured in the white plantation myth except in the most marginal of ways—poor whites, black and white sharecroppers, yeoman farmers, mountaineers, mill workers, and the lower middle class. Edith Kelley proved to be an early pioneer in this vein with her 1923 novel *Weeds*, followed by Thomas Wolfe, who drew from his own background growing up in an Asheville boardinghouse and then seeking a life of letters in the Northeast for his highly autobiographical novels *Look Homeward, Angel* (1929) and *Of Time and the River* (1935). Anticipating William Faulkner's Snopes saga, T. S. Stribling traced the rise of a poor white family in *The Forge* (1931), *The Store* (1932), and *The Unfinished Cathedral* (1934). The onset of the Great Depression inspired a slew of proletarian novels, including a number responding to labor struggles in North Carolina and Tennessee, among them Olive Tilford Dargan's *Call Home the Heart* (1932), Grace Lumpkin's *To Make My Bread* (1932), and Myra Page's *Gathering Storm* (1932). Wisconsin-born Marjorie Rawlings expressed similar sympathies with backwoods Florida life in *South Moon Under* (1933), *Golden Apples* (1935), and *The Yearling* (1938), which won the Pultizer Prize. Playwright Lillian Hellman also drew considerable inspiration from the social activism of the 1930s and produced a series of plays examining the wielding of sexual, economic, and political power—*The Children's Hour* (1934), *The Little Foxes* (1939), *Watch on the Rhine* (1944), and *Another Part of the Forest* (1946). Considerably more comic in his orientation to the world of the southern poor would be Erskine Caldwell in *Tobacco Road* (1932) and *God's Little Acre* (1935), but his collaboration with photographer Margaret Bourke-White in *You Have Seen Their Faces*—like a very similar volume, James Agee's *Let Us Now Praise Famous Men* (1941), including photographs by Walker Evans—made an earnest effort to speak out for those who had been left voiceless by the Great Depression.

William Faulkner

These were writers, though, that tended to be given short shrift by the Southern Agrarians, who by the mid-1930s had begun to write extensively on modern southern letters—what they were and who could be designated a genuinely southern writer. Tate and Ransom in particular were given to dismissing everyone from Ellen Glasgow and James Branch Cabell to DuBose Heyward and other white Charleston writers, but two novels published in 1929 by a white Mississippian named William Faulkner would eventually catch their attention—*Sartoris* and in particular *The Sound and the Fury*. In the latter novel they would recognize a voice akin to their own—that of Quentin Compson, agonizing over the steady decline of his aristocratic family and the moral fall of his sister Caddy. In the literary histories and criticism that New Critics like John Crowe Ransom, Allen Tate, Robert Penn Warren, and Cleanth Brooks produced over the next several decades, Faulkner took center stage in the fabled southern literary renaissance as the master storyteller of the fall of the Old South and the rise of a new, commercial South increasingly overrun by money-minded entrepreneurs like the ever-multiplying Snopes family.

With the publication of *Light in August* (1932), *Absalom, Absalom!* (1936), *The Unvanquished* (1938), *The Hamlet* (1940), and *Go Down, Moses* (1942), among other texts, Faulkner would also emerge as the central critic of that characterization. As he experimented with one genre after another, he revealed himself as a storyteller whose increasingly self-reflexive meditations on the politics of southern storytelling—which voices were heard and which were not and what identities would emerge from those exchanges—took issue with those who set themselves to interpret and categorize his work. He was frankly skeptical of the master narrative that critic Malcolm Cowley used to shape his editing of *The Portable Faulkner* (1946), that of "a parable or legend of all the Deep South's project." Faulkner's response to that overview was very nearly dismissive: "I don't see too much Southern legend in it."

Faulkner's burgeoning reputation as the region's master storyteller—and his own proto-postmodern critique of that master narrative—would shape southern letters for decades to come, in terms of rebellion and revision as well as imitation. In *Absalom, Absalom!* the plight of writers working in his shadow was eerily foreshadowed by Quentin Compson, trying to come to terms with what it means to understand the South and its history and finding himself trapped in a labyrinth of ever-recurring stories and memories. Those sentiments—the pull of past stories and memories and their paradoxical

William Faulkner. Courtesy Library of Congress, Prints & Photographs Division, Carl Van Vechten Collection.

claustrophobia and elusiveness—would be anticipated to a startling degree in Caroline Gordon's first novel, *Penhally* (1931), which posits women's custodianship of the past against male mismanagement of land and history and slyly rewrites *I'll Take My Stand* from a woman's point of view, a perspective that she continued to explore in the eight novels to follow, as well as in a host of short stories. Similarly, Katherine Anne Porter's character Miranda in "the Old Order" stories published in *Pale Horse, Pale Rider* (1939) and *The Leaning Tower and Other Stories* (1944) receives family stories about the past and ideal white womanhood with equivocation and even resistance. Something of that same ambivalence would mark the most famous female character in southern letters, Margaret Mitchell's Scarlett O'Hara, who made her appearance in *Gone with the Wind* the same year that *Absalom, Absalom!* was published. Scarlett would find herself hesitating between past ideals, exemplified by her mother and Ashley Wilkes, and the freedom, sexual fulfillment, and material comfort offered by Rhett Butler, who would himself return to Charleston and the corridors of the past and memory at the very end of the novel. W.J. Cash's *The Mind of the South* (1941) offered a startling nonfiction examination of that ambivalence as well and argued that the fanciful vision of the past fostered in so many southern novels was simply the product of myth-making. No one text, though, would capture the claustrophobic consequences of southern white memory more vividly—and with greater consequences—than *Killers of the Dream* (1949), Lillian Smith's monumental assault on the culture of segregation that sought in a mixture of memoir and polemic to probe the forces of white Protestantism, racism, and sexual repression girding the white South's cult of memory—and by implication trapping Quentin Compson himself into an endless retelling of old stories.

Even Robert Penn Warren, who had a large hand in forging William Faulkner's reputation as the greatest southern writer of them all, took the measure of the difficult and sometimes dangerous task of probing the past and memory in *All the King's Men* (1946), his magisterial roman à clef of Louisiana politician Huey Long that itself echoes with the voices and stories Warren had inherited from Faulkner and Thomas Wolfe. These are voices that very nearly threaten to overpower Warren's narrator, Jack Burden, who in Compsonian fashion carries with him everywhere the burdens of weighing and judging the past. Tellingly, the novel concludes with an anticipated farewell to the past so that the narrator may depart "into the convulsions of the world, out of history into history and the awful responsibility of time."

REWRITING THE SOUTH IN A POSTMODERN WORLD

The memorable last words of Warren's novel have led at least one literary critic to pronounce it the final volume of a rapidly dying Southern Renascence as the South itself entered a new post–World War II world rendered unfamiliar and unsettling by accelerating new forces of industrialization, urbanization, and huge demographic shifts of African Americans into the urban North. By that time Faulkner himself had completed his most fruitful period of literary production and had turned to an increasingly self-reflexive mode pondering the nature of his creative output. As early as the 1940s, in fact, a number of writers, among them Eudora

Welty, Tennessee Williams, and Carson McCullers, were experimenting with a new self-reflexivity, pioneered by Faulkner himself in *Absalom, Absalom!* and *Go Down, Moses*, that questioned inherited narratives of order and tradition, brought attention to their economies of representation, and foregrounded their provisionality. In doing so, they helped dislodge Quentin Compson's voice from its dominating position in southern letters and unearthed a multiplicity of voices and stories interrogating accepted conventions of community, gender, race, and sexuality in a manner that anticipated postmodernism.

For Welty, Williams, and McCullers in particular, that project meant resorting in part to a mode of representation that Faulkner had wielded to good effect in stories like "A Rose for Emily" (1930), "Dry September" (1931), *Sanctuary* (1931), and *Absalom, Absalom!*—southern gothicism and the grotesque, a genre that revealed its roots in British romanticism and Edgar Allan Poe's ghost stories through its imagery of dark houses, spectacles of suffering, figures of alienation, and haunted histories. Welty herself would object to her work being termed as such, but her first two short story collections, *A Curtain of Green* (1941) and *The Wide Net* (1943), as well as her second novel, *Delta Wedding* (1946), would resort to the gothic and the grotesque in covert ways to give voices to characters usually relegated to the sidelines of southern communities, from sideshow performers to women driven half-mad with misfortune and grief. To do so also meant to examine the limits of inherited southern stories—those in which many of her characters found themselves trapped—as did, for that matter, the characters figuring in the plays of Tennessee Williams and the novels of Carson McCullers. Like Welty, both Williams and McCullers underscored the entrapment of figures by old memories and older stories and the desperate efforts of their protagonists to wrench themselves free—McCullers in her best-known novels, *The Heart Is a Lonely Hunter* (1940), *The Member of the Wedding* (1943), and *The Ballad of the Sad Café* (1951), and Williams in his earliest and greatest plays, *The Glass Menagerie* (1945), *A Streetcar Named Desire* (1947), *Summer and Smoke* (1948), *Cat on a Hot Tin Roof* (1955), and *Suddenly Last Summer* (1958). For Welty, as critics like Barbara Ladd, Rebecca Mark, and Patricia Yaeger have ably argued, emancipation would come, in a manner of speaking, in rewriting her own inherited stories—those of Faulkner and of Western male heroic narratives in her pivotal volume *The Golden Apples* (1949)— and in exploring the consolations of memory and its confluences in *Losing Battles* (1970) and *The Optimist's Daughter* (1972).

Emancipation could also come from parody, "perhaps the only type of power available (or desirable) to a writer or critic," Michael Kreyling speculates, "living in the post-conscious sequel to a successful age of inimitable originals, as Mannerism followed Michelangelo." Flannery O'Connor's primary preoccupation was with "the action of grace in territory held largely by the devil" in her short stories and novels of "the Christ-Haunted South"—*Wise Blood* (1952), *A Good Man Is Hard to Find and Other Stories* (1955), and *The Violent Bear It Away* (1960)—but her attentive ear to regional rhythms and her sharp eye for the ridiculous also prompted parodies of southern manners, taboos, and in particular reverence for the past and history. Parody also figures in the work of a good many southern writers to follow, like Peter Taylor, whose carefully crafted short stories of Tennessee life skewer the preoccupation of upper-class white southerners, and whose last nov-

Ralph Ellison and *Invisible Man*

No one would make more brilliant use of parody and satire—and thereby unlock possibilities for a multiplicity of voices and narratives—than Ralph Ellison, whose brilliant 1952 novel *Invisible Man* anticipated desegregation two years before *Brown v. Board of Education* signaled the beginning of the end of Jim Crow in the U.S. South—and by implication a long tradition of white southern narratives and representations premised on the marginalization, invisibility, and silencing of African Americans. Signifying on the anonymity of slave narratives and their time-honored motifs of flight and escape, *Invisible Man* took aim at myths of the American Dream, Booker T. Washington's work ethic, Emersonian idealism, white anxieties of miscegenation, communist political activism, and above all the meaning and representation of blackness and whiteness in American culture. In doing so, the novel offers a bursting archive of black cultures and memories and, in Eric J. Sundquist's words, "an archaeology of African American identity" that cannot, in the end, be cordoned off from white American culture. "Who knows but that, on the lower frequencies," the narrator concludes, summoning into being new readers and new stories, "I speak for you?"

els, *A Summons to Memphis* (1986) and *In the Tennessee Country* (1994), interrogate the value of the past and tradition. Even more antagonistic were Walker Percy's battles with tradition, which Percy often associated with his cousin and adopted father, William Alexander Percy, a writer himself whose 1941 memoir *Lanterns on the Levee* counseled a reverent stoicism for white southern aristocrats in the face of defeat and decline. In contrast, Percy's protagonists, from Binx Bolling in *The Moviegoer* (1961) to Will Barrett in *The Last Gentleman* (1966) and *The Second Coming* (1980), are solitary male pilgrims estranged from the past and their forebears and cast adrift amid the weightless simulacra of American mass culture. John Barth as well experimented, like Percy, with European existentialism in his first two novels, *The Floating Opera* (1956) and *The End of the Road* (1958), but resorted to rollicking parody in *The Sot-Weed Factor* (1960), which found its antecedents in one of Maryland's earliest literary productions. Similarly, Reynolds Price, Michael Kreyling has argued, saw his task early on in his career—in novels like *A Long and Happy Life* (1962) and *A Generous Man* (1966)—as parodying and exorcizing the revered motifs he had inherited from Faulkner and a long line of southern writers—that of young men achieving manhood through male rituals of community and hunting. Price's primary concern in more than a dozen novels, among them *The Surface of the Earth* (1975), *The Source of Light* (1981), *Kate Vaiden* (1986), *Good Hearts* (1988), *A Whole New Life* (1994), and *The Promise of Rest* (1996), is the drama of the family, the origin, Price declares, of "[a] lot of the madness and violence in Southern fiction."

In his truly seminal novel, *Invisible Man*, Ralph Ellison anticipated to a striking degree a growing self-consciousness and experimentation among both poets and novelists whose preoccupation with region turned increasingly inward in the second half of the twentieth century. Lewis P. Simpson among others has interpreted that move as constituting something like a second phase of the Southern Renascence, one more inclined to undertake existential searches than to explore past obsessions with regional memories. Certainly the long career of Robert Penn Warren reveals such a shift as his work progressed from the 1950s to the early 1980s, moving from the epic perspectives of *Brother to Dragons* (1953), *Band of Angels* (1955), *Wilderness* (1961), and *The Legacy of the Civil War* (1961) to increasingly interior and self-reflexive poetry in *Incarnations* (1968), *Audubon: A Vision* (1969), *Now and Then* (1978), and *Being Here* (1980).

Poetry and Experiments in Genre and Narrative

A good deal of poetry in Warren's wake has followed suit with increasingly private visions stressing memory, family, and rural landscapes, most notably work by Randall Jarrell, A. R. Ammons, James Dickey, Donald Justice, Jonathan Williams, James Seay, Fred Chappell, Robert Morgan, Wendell Berry, Dabney Stuart, George Garrett, James Applewhite, George Scarbrough, Dave Smith, and Andrew Hudgins. At the same time their poetry resonates with an ever-widening range of voices, from those rendered in Appalachian dialect to the musical phrasing of Charlie Parker. Contemporary southern poets, David Kirby has suggested, "use brief, trenchant references to the South to energize larger worldviews." Among these writers are Earl S. Braggs, Betty Adcock, Elizabeth Seydel Morgan, John Wood, Charlie Smith, Susan Ludrigson, Richard Katrovas, Katherine Soniat, Alane Rollings, Brenda Marie Osbey, and Susan Montez. Ellen Bryant Voigt, a distinguished poet in her own right, sees southern writers as playing a crucial role in "the wholesale reemergence of narrative in contemporary poetry," and credits in particular David Bottoms, Henry Taylor, David Huddle, Rodney Jones, Leon Stokesbury, T. R. Hummer, and Andrew Hudgins. Particularly notable in this vein is the poetry of Natasha Trethewey, whose latest volume, *Bellocq's Ophelia* (2002), imaginatively constructs the life of one of the prostitutes in early twentieth-century New Orleans photographed by E. J. Bellocq.

Experiments with multiple voices and narratives have also drawn a growing number of writers, black and white, whose works cross multiple genres and fairly vibrate with self-reflexive turns, assemblages of mass culture, and shifting, splintering narrators. In *Mumbo Jumbo* (1972) Ishmael Reed counters the "monoculture" of contemporary America with the hybridity and multiculture of "Voodoo aesthetic," rooted in the multiple West African antecedents of the southern past. In *Flight to Canada* (1976), he merges the time-honored plot of escape from slavery narratives with jet planes, fragments of contemporary pop culture, and a narrator who is as slippery as his name—Raven Quicksill. Raymond Andrews's characters take on a comparable liminal quality in *Appalachee Red* (1978), which critic Keith Clark sees as a rewriting of Faulkner's stoically enduring African Americans. A celebration of flux and instability also marks the work of Barry Hannah, who has pointedly voiced his resistance to telling "some cranked up southern story again" and whose fiction, beginning with *Airships* (1978) and *Ray* (1980), luxuriates in multiple perspectives and jumbled collages of pop culture fragments and yet hearkens back, as Fred Hobson argues, to the broad humor of the Southwest. Albert Murray as well celebrates the "composite" and "multicolored" heart of American culture in his genre-crossing nonfiction, like *The Omni-Americans: Black Experience and American Culture* (1970), and follows the lead of his old friend Ralph Ellison by resorting to the rhythms of jazz and blues in his memoir/travel book *South to a Very Old Place* (1971). Lewis Nordan acknowledges a similar hybrid heritage in his fiction, particularly *The Music in the Swamp* (1993) and *Wolf Whistle* (1995), both of which resort to the blues as an idiom crossing racial boundaries.

The Civil Rights Revolution and the Women's Movement

Nothing, though, would inspire the proliferation of new voices and stories more than the great social movements of the 1960s—the civil rights revolution and the women's movement. The decade, Fred Hobson suggests, functioned as "a watershed in southern thought," the backdrop, from the perspective of Jean François Lyotard, for a postmodern splintering of grand metanarratives into "micronarratives" and "local" voices/histories. Martin Luther King, Jr., Alice Walker argued in a 1972 essay, reversed the forces of "dispossession" that had driven so many African Americans out of the South. "He gave us back our heritage," she declared. "He gave us back our homeland, the bones and dust of our ancestors, who may now sleep within our caring *and* our hearing. . . . He gave us continuity of place, without which community is ephemeral. He gave us home." Repossessing the region emerged in many respects as a central motif for a generation of African American writers, like poet Margaret Walker and novelist Ernest Gaines, who both rewrote *Gone with the Wind* from slave perspectives, Margaret Walker in *Jubilee* (1966) and Gaines in *The Autobiography of Miss Jane Pittman* (1971). Repossession as well was a major concern for Walker herself, who sought her own literary voice in an excavation of her Georgia childhood and of rural black culture in *The Third Life of Grange Copeland, In Love and Trouble* (1974), *Meridian* (1976), *The Color Purple* (1982), and *In Search of Our Mothers' Gardens* (1983), a search she expanded to West African antecedents in *Possessing the Secret of Joy* (1992).

Joining her in the project of repossession were writers participating in the black arts movement of the 1960s, among them Henry Dumas, Julia Fields, Ted Shine, Nikki Giovanni, Etheridge Knight, and Sonia Sanchez, who invited the readers of her poetry to "Come into Black geography" and to hear how she "became / this woman with razor blades between / her teeth." The civil rights movement would inspire as well Pauli Murray's 1956 memoir *Proud Shoes* and Maya Angelou's series of autobiographies, beginning with *I Know Why the Caged Bird Sings* (1970), along with James Alan McPherson's fiction and Rita Dove's most famous volume, *Thomas and Beulah* (1986), as well as *On the Bus with Rosa Parks* (1999). Similarly, Alice Childress and Ernest Gaines returned to their own southern antecedents by unearthing half-forgotten rural worlds, Childress to the Gullah culture of the Georgia Sea Islands in her plays *Sea Island Song* (1977) and *Gullah* (1984), and Gaines to the Louisiana back country of Cajuns, African Americans, and Creoles in novels culminating with *A Gathering of Old Men* (1983) and *A Lesson Before Dying* (1994). More recently, Anthony Grooms has turned his sights on Birmingham in the civil rights era in *Bombingham* (2001). Paule Marshall and Gayle Jones have been inspired to look even farther afield, past the conventional geographic boundaries of the U.S. South to the rest of the Americas, in their own projects of retrieval—Marshall to the West Indies in *Praise Song for the Widow* and *The Chosen Place, the Timeless People* (1969) and Jones to Brazil in *Corregidora* (1976). Yusef Koumenyakaa's Pulitzer Prize-winning poetry attempts similar boundary-crossing ventures in forays bridging his Louisiana childhood and his military experiences in Vietnam.

Women Writers

The example of the civil rights movement contributed as well to the most impressive flowering of southern letters in the second half of the twentieth century—that of women writers from all walks of life and ethnic/racial backgrounds. West Virginian Mary Lee Settle led the way early on with her now-famous *Beulah Quintet* (1956–1982), historical novels of Appalachia extending from the English Civil War to Vietnam. As the system of Jim Crow was slowly dismantled under the pressure of boycotts, Freedom Rides, demonstrations, and voter registration, the region's defining preoccupation, race, came under increasing scrutiny—in Elizabeth Spencer's *The Voice at the Back Door* (1956) and much later *Marilee: Three Stories* (1991); Harper Lee's *To Kill a Mockingbird* (1961); Alice Childress' play *Wedding Band* (1966); Ellen Douglas' *Black Cloud, White Cloud* (1963) and *The Rock Cried Out* (1979); Shirley Ann Grau's *Keepers of the House* (1964); and Doris Betts' *Beasts of the Southern Wild* (1973) and *The River to Pickle Beach* (1972). Rewriting age-old racial scripts—and the difficulties therein—engaged the energies of Anne Moody in *Coming of Age in Mississippi* (1968), arguably the most famous autobiography to emerge from the civil rights era, and of Toni Cade Bambara in *The Salt Eaters* (1980), as well as Rosellen Brown in *Civil Wars* (1984), Linda Beatrice Brown in *Rainbow Roun Mah Shoulder* (1984), Shirley Anne Williams in *Dessa Rose* (1986), Kaye Gibbons in *Ellen Foster* (1987), Shay Youngblood in *The Big Mama Stories* (1989), Dori Sanders in *Clover* (1990) and *In Her Own Place* (1993), Nancy Kincaid in *Crossing Blood* (1992), Bebe Moore Campbell in *Your Blues Ain't Like Mine* (1992), Thulani Davis in *1959* (1992), and Gloria Naylor in *Mama Day* (1993).

The age-old ideal of white southern womanhood fell under scrutiny as well in fiction revising and transforming the novel of manners—by Gail Godwin in *A Mother and Two Daughters* (1982) and *A Southern Family* (1987); Josephine Humphreys in *Dreams of Sleep* (1984), *Rich in Love* (1987), and *The Fireman's Fair* (1991); Jill McCorkle in *The Cheerleader* (1984), *Tending to Virginia* (1987), *Ferris Beach* (1990), and *Carolina Moon* (1996); and Kaye Gibbons in *A Virtuous* Woman (1989), *A Cure for Dreams* (1991), *Charms for the Easy Life* (1993), and *Sights Unseen* (1995). Diane McWhorter for her part has examined the legacy of whiteness in Alabama in her 2001 memoir *Carry Me Home: Birmingham, Alabama: The Climactic Battle of the Civil Rights Movement*. A similar kind of interrogation of gender roles also informs plays produced by Marsha Norman and Beth Henley, among them *'night, Mother* (1983), *Crimes of the Heart* (1983), and *The Miss Firecracker Contest* (1985). Both gender and race are scrutinzed by Suzan Lori-Parks in plays that reconfigure African American history and memory, among them *Imperceptible Mutabilities of the Third Kingdom* (1986–1989), *The Death of the Last Black Man in the Whole Entire World* (1989–1992), *The American Play* (1992–1994), and *Venus* (1996), and her Pulitzer Prize–winning *Topdog/Underdog* (2001).

Also deriving inspiration from the civil rights movement has been the surge of transnational Hispanic literatures over the past thirty years that have played no small role in expanding representations of the American South beyond its traditional North American (and Confederate) boundaries and excavating some of the region's own forgotten histories of multilingualism and multiculturalism. Leading the way were Chicano activists and pioneers allied with César Chávez's United Farm Workers, like Rodolfo "Corky" Gonzales, whose 1967 poem "I Am Joaquín" gained wide attention, as well as Abelardo Delgado, Raymundo "Tigre" Perez, Ricardo Sánchez, Alturista (Alberto Urista), and especially Luis Valdez, who established El Teatro Campesino (The Farmworker's Theater) in 1965. These writers in turn claimed as precursors José Antonio Villareal, whose novel *Pocho* was issued in 1959, and Américo Paredes, a native of Brownsville, Texas, who wrote bilingual poetry and published poems in Spanish-language newspapers like San Antonio's *La Prensa* and whose novels *George Washington Gomez* and *The Shadow* were not published until the 1990s. These pioneers were quickly joined by a generation of Chicano writers published by mainstream English-language houses, among them Rudolfo Anaya, Ana Castillo, Lorna Dee Cervantes, Denise Chávez, Sandra Cisneros, Leroy V. Quintana, Tomás Rivera, Jimmy Santiago Baca, Helen María Viramontes, and Evangelina Vigil. A good many writers whose work began to appear in the 1970s and 1980s consciously associated themselves with the borderlands cultures of South Texas and with hybridity and bilingualism, including Rolando Hinojosa, Pat Mora, and Gloria Anzaldúa. Indeed, one of the distinguishing traits of contemporary Hispanic letters, according to anthologist Nicholás Kanellos, has been its strong transnational character, defined by "the crossing of political, geographic, cultural, and racial boundaries." Crossing boundaries has given voice to a new generation of Puerto Rican writers, including Miguel Algarín, Judith Ortiz Cofer, Victor Hernández Cruz, Sandra María Estevez, Miguel Piñero, Piri Thomas, and Ed Vega, along with a rising group of Cuban American writers, among them Roberto Fernández, Cristina García, Oscar Hijuelos, Carolina Hospital, Elías Miguel Muñoz, Gustavo Pérez-Firmat, and Virgil Suárez. Dominican, Colombian, and Guatemalan writers have also made their presence known, most prominently Julia Alvarez, Jaime Manrique, Francisco Goldman, and Junot Diaz.

Gay Writers

The flowering of Hispanic and African American letters in the wake of the civil rights revolution has been paralleled by a new visibility in queer letters inspired in part by earlier but far more sexually reticent writings by Tennessee Williams, Truman Capote, Carson McCullers, William Alexander Percy, William Goyen, and Lillian Smith, all of which nonetheless lend, in Gary Richards's words, "a distinctly lavender tint" to southern literature of the mid-twentieth century. Pioneering the way were first Patricia Highsmith in *The Price of Salt* (1952) and then two second-wave feminists, Rita Mae Brown and Lisa Alther in their best-selling lesbian coming-of-age novels, *Ruby Fruit Jungle* (1973) and *Kinflicks* (1975), followed by Harlan Greene in his 1984 novel *Why We Never Danced the Charleston* and Blanche McCrary Boyd in *The Revolution of Little Girls* (1991), and especially Tony Kushner in his landmark epic *Angels in America* (1992), followed by his most recent play, a musical called *Caroline, or Change* (2003), which explores the painful bonds binding a black maid and the son of the Jewish family that employs her in Louisiana. In a similar pioneering spirit, Randall Kenan has unearthed stories of black homosexuality in the rural South in *A Visitation of Spirits* (1989) and *Let the Dead Bury Their Dead* (1992), and Dorothy Allison has explored her own sense of being a "cross-eyed and working-class lesbian" in poems, short stories, essays, and most notably her 1992 novel *Bastard Out of Carolina*.

The South Confronts Diversity, Mass Culture, and Social Change

Dorothy Allison's work overlaps with yet another group of local narrative/histories emerging in the second half of the twentieth century with the decentering of Quentin Compson's voice and story—that of marginalized backcountry and blue-collar worlds confronting the bewildering economic and social changes represented by the civil rights movement, the Vietnam War, and the proliferation of mass culture and consumerism in the form of strip malls, Walmarts, and television culture. Often focusing on class but also drawing attention to marginalized pockets of regional life from Appalachia to Cajun country to remnants of Native American cultures, this loose grouping includes the work of writers who often voice their reluctance to be identified as "southern" writers, among them Lee Smith, who argues that the Appalachian settings and communities of her novels, like *Black Mountain Breakdown* (1980), *Oral History* (1983), *Family Linen* (1985), *Fair and Tender Ladies* (1988), *The Devil's Dream* (1992), and *Saving Grace* (1995), exempt her from being grouped with writers more directly concerned with the burdens of slavery, race, and regional history. Harry Crews has also resisted the label "southern" for his novels of regional underworlds and marginal cultures, from *The Gospel Singer* (1968) to *Celebration* (1998), and sees even the south Georgia backwoods of his memoir *A Childhood* (1978) as a place apart from representations of region defined by literary tradition. For writers of this group, like Anne Tyler and Bobbie Ann Mason, place is largely defined by the trappings of mass culture—from shopping malls to fast food—and hence the difficulties of maneuvering through that world and its ever-accelerating currents of change dominate their fiction, as in Tyler's *Dinner at the Homesick Restaurant* (1982), *The Accidental Tourist* (1985), *Breathing Lessons* (1988), and most recently *The Amateur Marriage* (2004), to name just a few among her sixteen novels, and Mason's short stories and novels, most notably *Shiloh* (1983) and *In Country* (1985). Other writers, like Larry Brown, Tim Gautreaux, Mary Hood, Donald Harrington, Nancy Kincaid, Mark Childress, R. T. Smith, Linda Hogan, Marilou Awiakta, Joy Harjo, Janisse Ray, Peter Mathiessen, and Jack Butler, have resorted to a range of settings, from Lousiana Cajun country to Florida pockets of Native Americans to Appalachia, to explore voices of those usually relegated to the corners of regional life, from Larry Brown's blue-collar fathers and sons to R. T. Smith's lost tribes of Tuscarora, Choctaw, and Cherokee who learn, as suggested in his poetry, that "the trail of tears never ends." A growing number of contemporary writers, as Robert Brinkmeyer has argued, have even changed their fictional locales from the South to the West in an effort to step free of "the web of culture" and address dramas of individual identity and action, among them Richard Ford, Barry Hannah, Clyde Edgerton, Rick Bass, Doris Betts, Cormac McCarthy, Barbara Kingsolver, Madison Smartt Bell, Frederick Barthelme, Chris Offutt, and Carl Hiassen. Others have shifted attention to the emergence of new enclaves of Indochinese immigrants and refugees on the Gulf Coast and in global-oriented cities like Atlanta, from Tom Wolfe in his much-heralded *A Man in Full* (1998) to Robert Olen Butler's *A Good Scent from a Strange Mountain* (1993), Mary Gardner in *Boat People* (1995), and Lan Cao in *Monkey Bridge* (1997), described by Maureen Ryan as the first novel by a Vietnamese American refugee.

All of these micronarratives and "local" histories—from Tim Gautreux's fiction of Cajun Louisiana to Linda Hogan's excavation of lost Native American Floridi-

Ralph Ellison, novelist and author of the widely acclaimed *Invisible Man*, was elected a member of the National Institute of Arts and Letters in 1964. Courtesy AP/Wide World Photos.

ans in *Power* (1998)—suggest the kind of challenging of consensus and acknowledgment of difference usually associated with postmodernism as defined by critics like Linda Hutcheon, who argues that "one of the lessons of post-modernism is the need to respect the particular and the local." Providing an equally powerful challenge to consensus and the master narrative associated with the voice of Quentin Compson is the postmodern historical fiction that has emerged from the region since the 1960s with the publication of William Styron's *The Confessions of Nat Turner* (1967) and *Sophie's Choice* (1979), novels that Hutcheon would describe as "historiographic fiction," interrogating official histories with alternative stories of the past and commenting on their own operations of representation in the spirit of self-reflexive fiction. Joining Styron in this endeavor have been writers as wide-ranging as Barbara Chase-Riboud in *Sally Hemings* (1979), Octavia Butler in *Kindred* (1979), Toni Morrison in *Beloved* (1987), Ellen Douglas in *Can't Quit You, Baby* (1988), Connie May Fwloer in *River of Hidden Dreams* (1994), Madison Smartt Bell in his Haitian trilogy, *All Souls' Rising* (1995), *Master of the Crossroads* (2000), and *The Stone that the Builders Refused* (2004), Barbara Kingsolver in *The Poisonwood Bible* (1998), Donald McCaig in *Jacob's Ladder* (1998), James Kilgo in *Daughter of My People* (1998), Josephine Humphreys in *Nowhere Else on Earth* (2000), Alice Randall in *The Wind Done Gone*, and Edward P. Jones in *The Known World* (2003). These are all books that offer alternative histories—from Morrison's "remember-

Eudora Welty won the 1973 Pulitzer Prize for fiction for her novella *The Optimist's Daughter* (1972). Courtesy AP/Wide World Photos.

ing" of repressed memories and stories of slavery to Jones's account of black slaveholders in antebellum Virginia—and in doing so they bring into question not just "official" versions of southern history but also the very definitions, categories, and boundaries with which southern literary productions have been associated since the earliest days of European exploration and settlement. Above all, these are historical novels that question the way southern narratives have traditionally been constructed—their implication in the construction of race and region, their definitions of southern selves and otherness, and their negotiations in the borderlands of community and identity determining which voices have been heard and which have been repressed.

This is the project, ultimately, of Barry Unsworth's 1992 Booker Prize–winning novel *Sacred Hunger*, which questions the very categorization of southern literature not just by virtue of the author's nationality—British—but also by the story it tells—of a slave ship mutiny and an interracial maroon community in eighteenth-century Spanish Florida. The novel exposes, in a sense, the untold, repressed, forgotten stories that have long haunted southern literature and southern history, in this case the story of an ancient mulatto beggar in early nineteenth-century New Orleans who talks "of a Liverpool ship, of a white father who had been doctor aboard her and had never died, a childhood of wonders in a place of eternal sunshine, jungle hummocks, great flocks of white birds rising from flooded savannahs, a settlement where white and black lived together in perfect accord." Concluding the novel is an account of the dying beggar mourning the loss of his childhood paradise, of a South that might have been but never was, and of his own lost story, the only place now where that forgotten little paradise exists. In presenting this tale as one that is lost—but haunts the opening narrator and us as readers, for that matter—Unsworth suggests something like the unfinished task contemporary southern writers now face: the necessity of interrogating, remapping, and re-envisioning the southern stories handed down to the present generation, of transgressing the boundaries they attempt to pose, and exploring their silences and margins to reinstate the dialogues and multiple possibilities that have been lost.

RESOURCE GUIDE

Printed Sources

Anthologies and Readers

Andrews, William L., and Henry Louis Gates, Jr., eds. *The Civitas Anthology of African American Slave Narratives*. Washington, DC: Civitas/Counterpoint, 1999.

Andrews, William L., et al., eds. *The Concise Oxford Companion to African American Literature*. New York: Oxford University Press, 2001.

———, et al., eds. *The Literature of the American South*. New York: Norton, 1998.

Ayers, Edward L., and Bradley C. Mittendorf, eds. *The Oxford Book of the American South: Testimony, Memory, and Fiction*. New York: Oxford University Press, 1997.

Cortina, Rodolfo, ed. *Hispanic American Literature: An Anthology*. Lincolnwood, IL: NTC Publishing Group, 1998.

Forkner, Ben, and Patrick Samway, eds. *A Modern Southern Reader: Major Stories, Drama, Poetry, Essays, Interviews, and Reminiscences from the Twentieth-Century South*. Atlanta: Peachtree Publishers, 1989.

———, eds. *A New Reader of the Old South: Major Stories, Tales, Poetry, Essays, Slave Narratives, Diaries, and Travelogues, 1820–1920*. Atlanta: Peachtree Publishers, 1991.

Gates, Henry Louis, Jr., ed. *Norton Anthology of African American Literature*. New York: Norton, 1997.

Higgs, Robert J., ed. *Appalachia Inside Out*. Knoxville: University of Tennessee Press, 1995.

———, et al., eds. *Voices from the Hills: Selected Readings of Appalachia*. New York: Frederick Ungar, 1975.

Howorth, Lisa, ed. *The South: A Treasury of Art and Literature*. New York: Hugh Lauter Levin Associates/Macmillan, 1993.

Kanellos, Nicolás, ed. *Herencia: The Anthology of Hispanic Literature of the United States*. New York: Oxford University Press, 2002.

Kilcup, Karen L., ed. *Native American Women's Writing, 1800–1924: An Anthology*. Oxford: Blackwell, 2000.

Littlefield, Daniel F., Jr., and James W. Parins, eds. *Native American Writing in the Southeast: An Anthology, 1875–1935*. Jackson: University Press of Mississippi, 1995.

Mann, Barbara Alice, ed. *Native American Speakers of the Eastern Woodlands: Selected Speeches and Critical Analyses*. Westport, CT: Greenwood Press, 2001.

General Guides

Aberjhani and Sandri L. West. *Encyclopedia of the Harlem Renaissance*. New York: Facts on File, Inc., 2003.

Bain, Robert, and Joseph M. Flora, eds. *Contemporary Poets, Dramatists, Essayists, and Novelists of the South: A Bio-Bibliographical Sourcebook*. Westport, CT: Greenwood Press, 1995.

———, eds. *Fifty Southern Writers Before 1900: A Bio-Bibliographical Sourcebook*. Westport, CT: Greenwood Press, 1987.

Bassett, John E., ed. *Defining Southern Literature: Perspectives and Assessments, 1831–1952.* Madison, NJ: Farleigh Dickinson University Press, 1997.

Flora, Joseph M., and Robert Bain, eds. *Contemporary Fiction Writers of the South: A Bio-Bibliographical Sourcebook.* Westport, CT: Greenwood Press, 1993.

———, eds. *Southern Writers after 1900: A Bio-Bibliographical Sourcebook.* Westport, CT: Greenwood Press, 1987.

Flora, Joseph M., and Lucinda H. MacKethan, eds. *The Companion to Southern Literature: Themes, Genres, Places, People, Movements, and Motifs.* Baton Rouge: Louisiana State University Press, 2002.

Foster, Mamie Marie Booth, comp. *Southern Black Creative Writers, 1829–1953: Bio-Bibliographies.* Westport, CT: Greenwood Press, 1988.

Gray, Richard, and Owen Robinson, eds. *The Blackwell Companion to Literature and Culture of the American South.* Oxford, U.K.: Blackwell, 2004.

Hubbell, Jay B. *The South in American Literature, 1607–1900.* Durham, NC: Duke University Press, 1954.

Jordan, Casper LeRoy. *A Bio-Bibliographical Guide to African-American Women Writers.* Westport, CT: Greenwood Press, 1994.

Matuz, Roger, ed. *Contemporary Southern Writers.* Detroit: St. James Press, 1999.

Perry, Carolyn, and Mary Louise Weaks, eds. *The History of Southern Women's Literature.* Baton Rouge: Louisiana State University Press, 2002.

Reisman, Rosemary M. Canfield. *Contemporary Southern Men Fiction Writers: An Annotated Bibliography.* Lanham, MD: Scarecrow Press, 1998.

———. *Contemporary Southern Women Fiction Writers: An Annotated Bibliography.* Metuchen, NJ: Scarecrow Press, 1994.

Rubin, Louis D., Jr., ed. *A Bibliographical Guide to the Study of Southern Literature.* Baton Rouge: Louisiana State University Press, 1969.

———, et al., eds. *The History of Southern Literature.* Baton Rouge: Louisiana State University Press, 1985.

Snodgrass, Mary Ellen. *Encyclopedia of Southern Literature.* Santa Barbara: ABC-CLIO, 1997.

Wages, Jack D. *Seventy-Four Writers of the Colonial South.* Boston: G. K. Hall, 1979.

Weaks, Mary Louise, and Carolyn Perry, eds. *Southern Women's Writing: Colonial to Contemporary.* Gainesville: University Press of Florida, 1995.

Williams, Jerry T., ed. *Southern Literature, 1968–1975: A Checklist of Scholarship.* Boston: G. K. Hall, 1978.

Wilson, Charles Reagan, and William Ferris, eds. *Enclopedia of Southern Culture.* Chapel Hill: University of North Carolina Press, 1989.

Histories, Critical Studies, and Collections

Abernathy, Jeff. *To Hell and Back: Race and Betrayal in the Southern Novel.* Athens: University of Georgia Press, 2003.

Andrews, William L. *To Tell a Free Story: The First Century of Afro-American Autobiography, 1760–1865.* Urbana: University of Illinois Press, 1986.

Anzaldúa, Gloria. *Borderlands/La Frontera: The New Mestiza.* 2nd ed. San Francisco: Aunt Lute Books, 1999.

Awkward, Michael. *Inspiriting Influences: Tradition, Revision, and Afro-American Women's Novels.* New York: Columbia University Press, 1989.

Axtell, James. *The Indians' New South: Cultural Change in the Colonial Southeast.* Baton Rouge: Louisiana State University Press, 1997.

Baker, Barbara A. *The Blues Aesthetic and the Making of American Identity in the Literature of the South.* New York: Peter Lang, 2003.

Bakker, Jan. *Pastoral in Antebellum Southern Romance*. Baton Rouge: Louisiana State University Press, 1989.

Beaulieu, Elizabeth Ann. *Black Women Writers and the American Neo-Slave Narrative: Femininity Unfettered*. Westport, CT: Greenwood Press, 1999.

Beck, Charlotte H. *The Fugitive Legacy: A Critical History*. Baton Rouge: Louisiana State University Press, 2001.

Bellin, Joshua David. *The Demon of the Continent: Indians and the Shaping of American Culture*. Philadelphia: University of Pennsylvania Press, 1991.

Bennett, Barbara. *Comic Visions, Female Voices: Contemporary Women Novelists and Southern Humor*. Baton Rouge: Louisiana State University Press, 1998.

Berry, J. Bill, ed. *Located Lives: Place and Idea in Southern Autobiography*. Athens: University of Georgia Press, 1990.

Blight, David W. *Race and Reunion: The Civil War in American Memory*. Cambridge, MA: Harvard University Press/Belknap Press, 2001.

Bradbury, John M. *Renaissance in the South: A Critical History of the Literature, 1920–1960*. Chapel Hill: University of North Carolina Press, 1963.

Brantley, Will. *The Feminine Sense of Southern Memoir: Smith, Glasgow, Welty, Hellman, Porter, and Hurston*. Jackson: University Press of Mississippi, 1993.

Brennan, Jonathan. *When Brer Rabbit Meets Coyote: African-Native American Literature*. Urbana: University of Illinois Press, 2003.

Brinkmeyer, Robert. *Remapping Southern Literature: Contemporary Southern Writers and the West*. Mercer University Lamar Memorial Lectures No. 42. Athens: University of Georgia Press, 2000.

———. *Three Catholic Novelists of the South*. Jackson: University Press of Mississippi, 1985.

Brundage, W. Fitzhugh, ed. *Where These Memories Grow: History, Memory, and Southern Identity*. Chapel Hill: University of North Carolina Press, 2000.

Bryant, J. A., Jr. *Twentieth-Century Southern Literature*. Lexington: University Press of Kentucky, 1997.

Bryant, Jerry H. *Victims and Heroes: Racial Violence in the African American Novel*. Amherst: University of Massachusetts Press, 1997.

Carby, Hazel. *Reconstructing Womanhood: The Emergence of the Afro-American Woman Novelist*. New York: Oxford University Press, 1986.

Carr, Duane. *A Question of Class: The Redneck Stereotype in Southern Fiction*. Bowling Green, OH: Bowling Green State University Press, 1996.

Cartwright, Keith. *Reading Africa into American Literature: Epics, Fables, and Gothic Tales*. Lexington: University Press of Kentucky, 2002.

Cash, W. J. *The Mind of the South*. 1941. New York: Vintage, 1969.

Castille, Philip, and William Osborne, eds. *Southern Literature in Transition: Heritage and Promise*. Memphis: Memphis State University Press, 1983.

Chametzky, Jules. *Our Decentralized Literature: Cultural Mediations in Selected Jewish and Southern Writers*. Amherst: University of Massachusetts Press, 1986.

Clark, Keith. *Contemporary Black Men's Fiction and Drama*. Urbana: University of Illinois Press, 2001.

Cohn, Deborah N. *History and Memory in the Two Souths: Recent Southern and Spanish American Fiction*. Nashville: Vanderbilt University Press, 1999.

Conkin, Paul. *The Southern Agrarians*. Knoxville: University of Tennessee Press, 1988.

Cook, Sylvia Jenkins. *From Tobacco Road to Route 66: The Southern Poor White in Fiction*. Chapel Hill: University of North Carolina Press, 1976.

Core, George, ed. *Southern Fiction Today: Renascence and Beyond*. Athens: University of Georgia Press, 1969.

Couch, William T., ed. *Culture in the South*. Chapel Hill: University of North Carolina Press, 1934.

Cowan, Louise. *The Fugitive Group: A Literary History*. Baton Rouge: Louisiana State University Press, 1959.

Cutrer, Thomas W. *Parnassus on the Mississippi: "The Southern Review" and the Baton Rouge Literary Community, 1935–1942*. Baton Rouge: Louisiana State University Press, 1984.

Daniell, Rosemary. *Fatal Flowers: On Sin, Sex, and Suicide in the Deep South*. New York: Holt, 1980.

Davenport, F. Garvin. *The Myth of Southern History: Historical Consciousness in Twentieth-Century Southern Literature*. Nashville: Vanderbilt University Press, 1970.

Davis, David Brion. *The Problem of Slavery in the Age of Revolution, 1770–1823*. Ithaca, NY: Cornell University Press, 1975.

Dayan, Joan. "Poe, Persons, and Property." In *Romancing the Shadow: Poe and Race*, ed. J. Gerald Kennedy and Liliane Weissberg, 106–126. New York: Oxford University Press, 2001.

Dryer, Joyce, ed. *Bloodroot: Reflections on Place by Appalachian Women Writers*. Lexington: University Press of Kentucky, 1998.

Ehle, John. *Trail of Tears: The Rise and Fall of the Cherokee Nation*. New York: Anchor/Doubleday, 1988.

Entzminger, Betina. *The Belle Gone Bad: White Southern Women Writers and the Dark Seductress*. Baton Rouge: Louisiana State University Press, 2002.

Evans, Sara. *Personal Politics: The Roots of Women's Liberation in the Civil Rights Movement and the New Left*. New York: Vintage Books, 1980.

Fabi, M. Giulia. *Passing and the Rise of the African American Novel*. Urbana: University of Illinois Press, 2001.

Fabre, Geneviève, and Michel Feith, eds. *Temples for Tomorrow: Looking Back at the Harlem Renaissance*. Bloomington: Indiana University Press, 2001.

Fabre, Geneviève, and Robert O'Meally, eds. *History and Memory in African-American Culture*. New York: Oxford University Press, 1994.

Faery, Rebecca Blevins. *Cartographies of Desire: Captivity, Race, and Sex in the Shaping of an American Nation*. Norman: University of Oklahoma Press, 1999.

Fahs, Alice. *The Imagined Civil War: Popular Literature of the North and South, 1861–1865*. Chapel Hill: University of North Carolina Press, 2001.

Faust, Drew Gilpin. "Altars of Sacrifice: Confederate Women and the Narratives of War." In *Southern Stories: Slaveholders in Peace and War*, 113–140. Columbia: University of Missouri Press, 1992.

———. *Mothers of Invention: Women of the Slaveholding South in the American Civil War*. Chapel Hill: University of North Carolina Press, 1996.

Folks, Jeffrey J. *In a Time of Disorder: Form and Meaning in Southern Fiction from Poe to O'Connor*. New York: Peter Lang, 2003.

———. *Southern Writers and the Machine: Faulkner to Percy*. New York: Peter Lang, 1993.

———. *Southern Writers at Century's End*. Lexington: University Press of Kentucky, 1997.

Foster, Frances Smith. *Witnessing Slavery: The Development of Ante-Bellum Slave Narratives*. 2nd ed. Madison: University of Wisconsin Press, 1994.

———. *Written by Herself: Literary Production by African American Women, 1746–1892*. Bloomington: Indiana University Press, 1993.

Gardner, Sarah E. *Blood and Irony: Southern White Women's Narratives of the Civil War, 1861–1937*. Chapel Hill: University of North Carolina Press, 2004.

Garrett, George. *Southern Excursions: Views on Southern Letters in My Time*. Baton Rouge: Louisiana State University Press, 2003.

Gilman, Owen W. *Vietnam and the Southern Imagination*. Jackson: University Press of Mississippi, 1992.

Goddu, Teresa A. *Gothic America: Narrative, History, and Nation*. New York: Columbia University Press, 1997.

Goldfield, David. *Still Fighting the Civil War: The American South and Southern History*. Baton Rouge: Louisiana State University Press, 2002.

Gossett, Louise Y. *Violence in Recent Southern Fiction*. Durham, NC: Duke University Press, 1965.

Grammar, John. *Pastoral and Politics in the Old South*. Baton Rouge: Louisana State University Press, 1996.

Gray, Richard. *The Literature of Memory: Modern Writers of the American South*. Baltimore: Johns Hopkins University Press, 1979.

———. *Southern Aberrations: Writers of the American South and the Problems of Regionalism*. Baton Rouge: Louisiana State University Press, 2000.

———. *Writing the South: Ideas of an American Region*. New York: Cambridge University Press, 1986.

Greene, J. Lee. *Blacks in Eden: The African American Novel's First Century*. Charlottesville: University of Virginia Press, 1996.

Gretlund, Jan Nordby, ed. *The Southern State of Mind*. Columbia: University of South Carolina Press, 1999.

Griffin, Farah Jasmine. *"Who Set You Flowin'?" The African-American Migration Narrative*. New York: Oxford University Press, 1995.

Gwin, Minrose. *Black and White Women of the Old South: The Peculiar Sisterhood in American Literature*. Knoxville: University of Tennessee Press, 1985.

Gwinn, Matthew. *After Southern Modernism: Fiction of the Contemporary South*. Jackson: University Press of Mississippi, 2000.

Hale, Grace Elizabeth. *Making Whiteness: The Culture of Segregation in the South, 1890–1940*. New York: Pantheon, 1998.

Hall, Jacquelyn Dowd. " 'The Mind that Burns in Each Body': Women, Rape, and Racial Violence." In *Powers of Desire: The Politics of Sexuality*, ed. Ann Snitow, Christine Stansell, and Sharon Thompson, 328–349. New York: Monthly Review Press, 1983.

Harris, Trudier. *Exorcising Blackness: Historical and Literary Lynchings and Burning Rituals*. Bloomington: Indiana University Press, 1984.

———. *The Power of the Porch: The Storyteller's Craft in Zora Neale Hurston, Gloria Naylor, and Randall Kenan*. Mercer University Lamar Memorial Lectures No. 39. Athens: University of Georgia Press, 1996.

Harris-Lopez, Trudier. *South of Tradition: Essays on African American Literature*. Athens: University of Georgia Press, 2002.

Harrison, Elizabeth Jane. *Female Pastoral: Women Writers Re-envisioning the American South*. Knoxville: University of Tennessee Press, 1991.

Hinks, Peter P. *To Awaken My Afflicted Brethren: David Walker and the Problem of Antebellum Slave Resistance*. University Park: Pennsylvania State University Press, 1997.

Hobson, Fred. *But Now I See: The White Southern Racial Conversion Narrative*. Baton Rouge: Louisiana State University Press, 1999.

———. *Serpent in Eden: H. L. Mencken and the South*. Baton Rouge: Louisiana State University Press, 1978.

———. *The Southern Writer in the Postmodern World*. Mercer University Lamar Memorial Lectures No. 33. Athens: University of Georgia Press, 1991.

———. *Tell about the South: The Southern Rage to Explain*. Baton Rouge: Louisiana State University Press, 1983.

Hoennighausen, Lothar, and Valeria Gennaro Lerda, eds. *Rewriting the South: History and Fiction*. Tuebingen: Franke Verlag, 1993.

Holman, David Marion. *A Certain Slant of Life: Regionalism and the Form of Southern and Midwestern Fiction*. Baton Rouge: Louisiana State University Press, 1995.

Howard, John, ed. *Carryin' On in the Lesbian and Gay South*. New York: New York University Press, 1997.

Hudson, Charles. *Knights of Spain, Warriors of the Sun: Hernando de Soto and the South's Ancient Chiefdoms*. Athens: University of Georgia Press, 1997.

Humphries, Jefferson, ed. *Metamorphoses of the Raven: Literary Determinedness in France and the South since Poe*. Baton Rouge: Louisiana State University Press, 1985.

———. *Southern Literature and Literary Theory*. Athens: University of Georgia Press, 1990.

Humphries, Jefferson, and John Lowe, eds. *The Future of Southern Letters*. New York: Oxford University Press, 1996.

Hunt, Alfred N. *Haiti's Influence on Antebellum America: Slumbering Volcano in the Caribbean*. Baton Rouge: Louisiana State University Press, 1988.

Inge, M. Thomas, and Edward J. Piacentino, eds. *The Humor of the Old South*. Lexington: University Press of Kentucky, 2001.

Inge, Tonette Bond, ed. *Southern Women Writers: The New Generation*. Tusacaloosa: University of Alabama Press, 1990.

Jablon, Madelyn. *Black Metafiction: Self-Consciousness in African American Literature*. Iowa City: University of Iowa Press, 1997.

Jenkins, McKay. *The South in Black and White: Race, Sex, and Literature in the 1940s*. Chapel Hill: University of North Carolina Press, 1991.

Jones, Anne Goodwyn. *Tomorrow Is Another Day: The Woman Writer in the South, 1859–1936*. Baton Rouge: Louisiana State University Press, 1981.

Jones, Anne Goodwyn, and Susan V. Donaldson, eds. *Haunted Bodies: Gender and Southern Texts*. Charlottesville: University of Virginia Press, 1987.

Jones, Suzanne W. *Race Mixing: Southern Fiction since the Sixties*. Baltimore: Johns Hopkins University Press, 2004.

Jones, Suzanne W., and Sharon Monteith, eds. *South to a New Place: Region, Literature, Culture*. Baton Rouge: Louisiana State University Press, 2002.

Jordan, Winthrop D. *White over Black: American Attitudes Toward the Negro, 1550–1812*. Baltimore: Penguin Books, 1968.

King, Richard. *A Southern Renaissance: The Cultural Wakening of the American South, 1930–1955*. New York: Oxford University Press, 1980.

King, Richard, and Helen Taylor, eds. *Dixie Debates: Perspectives on Southern Cultures*. New York: New York University Press, 1996.

Kirby, David. "Is There a Southern Poetry?" *Southern Review* n.s. 30 (1994): 869–880.

Kissel, Susan S. *Moving On: The Heroines of Shirley Ann Grau, Anne Tyler, and Gail Godwin*. Bowling Green, OH: Bowling Green State University Press, 1996.

Kreyling, Michael. *The Figure of the Hero in Southern Narrative*. Baton Rouge: Louisiana State University Press, 1987.

———. *Inventing Southern Literature*. Jackson: University Press of Mississippi, 1998.

Kubitschek, Missy Dehn. *Claiming the Heritage: African American Women Novelists and History*. Jackson: University Press of Mississippi, 1991.

Ladd, Barbara. *Nationalism and the Color Line in George W. Cable, Mark Twain, and William Faulkner*. Baton Rouge: Louisiana State University Press, 1996.

Lawson, Lewis A. *Another Generation: Southern Fiction since World War II*. Jackson: University Press of Mississippi, 1984.

Lewis, Jan Ellen, and Peter S. Onuf, eds. *Sally Hemings and Thomas Jefferson: History, Memory, and Civic Culture*. Charlottesville: University of Virginia Press, 1999.

MacKethan, Lucinda Hardwick. *Daughters of Time: Creating Woman's Voice in Southern Story*. Mercer University Lamar Memorial Lectures No. 32. Athens: University of Georgia Press, 1990.

———. *The Dream of Arcady: Place and Time in Southern Fiction*. Baton Rouge: Louisiana State University Press, 1980.

Magee, Rosemary M., ed. *Friendship and Sympathy: Communities of Southern Women Writers*. Jackson: University Press of Mississippi, 1992.

Maguire, Merrill. *The Folk of Southern Fiction*. Athens: University of Georgia Press, 1972.

Malvasi, Mark G. *The Unregenerate South: The Agrarian Thought of John Crowe Ransom, Allen Tate, and Donald Davidson*. Baton Rouge: Louisiana State University Press, 1997.

Manning, Carol, ed. *The Female Tradition in Southern Literature*. Urbana: University of Illinois Press, 1993.

McDonald, Robert L., and Linda Rohrer Paige, eds. *Southern Women Playwrights: New Essays in Literary History and Criticism*. Tuscaloosa: University of Alabama Press, 2002.

McDowell, Deborah E. *"The Changing Same": Black Women's Literature, Criticism, and Theory*. Bloomington: Indiana University Press, 1995.

McDowell, Deborah E., and Arnold Rampersad, eds. *Slavery and the Literary Imagination*. Baltimore: Johns Hopkins University Press, 1989.

McIlwaine, Shields. *The Southern Poor White from Lubberland to Tobacco Road*. Norman: University of Oklahoma Press, 1939.

McPherson, Tara. *Reconstructing Dixie: Race, Gender, and Nostalgia in the Imagined South*. Durham, NC: Duke University Press, 2003.

Miller, Danny. *Wingless Flights: Appalachian Women in Fiction*. Bowling Green, OH: Bowling Green State University Press, 1996.

Millichap, Joseph R. *Dixie Limited: Railroads, Culture, and the Southern Renaissance*. Lexington: University Press of Kentucky, 2002.

Mixon, Wayne. *Southern Writers and the New South Movement, 1865–1913*. Chapel Hill: University of North Carolina Press, 1980.

Monteith, Sharon. *Advancing Sisterhood? Interracial Friendships in Contemporary Southern Fiction*. Athens: University of Georgia Press, 2000.

Morgan, Philip D. *Slave Counterpoint: Black Culture in the Eighteenth-Century Chesapeake and Lowcountry*. Chapel Hill: University of North Carolina Press for the Omohundro Institute of Early American History and Culture, 1998.

Morris, Christopher, and Steven G. Reinhardt, eds. *Southern Writers and Their Worlds*. Walter Prescott Webb Memorial Lectures No. 29. College Station: Texas A&M University Press for the University of Texas at Arlington, 1996.

Morrison, Toni. *Playing in the Dark: Whiteness and the Literary Imagination*. Cambridge, MA: Harvard University Press, 1992.

———. "Unspeakable Things Unspoken: The Afro-American Presence in American Literature." In *Within the Circle: An Anthology of African American Literary Criticism from the Harlem Renaissance to the Present*, ed. Angelyn Mitchell, 368–398. Durham, NC: Duke University Press, 1994.

Moss, Elizabeth. *Domestic Novelists of the Old South: Defenders of Southern Culture*. Baton Rouge: Louisiana State University Press, 1992.

Nelson, Dana D. *The Word in Black and White: Reading "Race" in American Literature, 1638–1867*. New York: Oxford University Press, 1993.

Nelson, Richard. *Aesthetic Frontiers: The Machiavellian Tradition in the Southern Imagination*. Jackson: University Press of Mississippi, 1990.

Nicholls, David G. *Conjuring the Folk: Forms of Modernity in African America*. Ann Arbor: University of Michigan Press, 2000.

O'Brien, Michael. *Conjectures of Order: Intellectual South and the American South, 1810–1860*. 2 vols. Chapel Hill: University of North Carolina Press, 2004.

———. *The Idea of the American South, 1920–1941*. Baltimore: Johns Hopkins University Press, 1979.

———. *Rethinking the South: Essays in Intellectual History*. Baltimore: Johns Hopkins University Press, 1988.

O'Dell, Darlene. *Sites of Southern Memory: The Autobiographies of Katherine Du Pre Lumpkin, Lillian Smith, and Pauli Murray*. Charlottesville: University of Virginia Press, 2001.

Painter, Nell Irvin. "Of *Lily*, Linda Brent, and Freud: A Non-Exceptionalist Approach to Race, Class, and Gender in the Slave South." In *Half Sisters of History: Southern Women and the American Past*, ed. Catherine Clinton, 93–109. Durham, NC: Duke University Press, 1994.

Parrish, Nancy C. *Lee Smith, Annie Dillard, and the Hollins Group: A Genesis of Writers*. Baton Rouge: Louisiana State University Press, 1998.

Payne, Ladell. *Black Novelists and the Southern Literary Tradition*. Athens: University of Georgia Press, 1981.

Perdue, Thea. *"Mixed Blood" Indians: Racial Construction in the Early South*. Mercer University Lamar Memorial Lectures No. 45. Athens: University of Georgia Press, 2003.

Petesch, Donald A. *A Spy in the Enemy's Country: The Emergence of Modern Black Literature*. Iowa City: University of Iowa Press, 1989.

Powell, Dannye Romine, ed. *Parting the Curtains: Voices of the Great Southern Writers*. New York: Anchor Books, 1995.

Pratt, Mary Louise. "Criticism in the Contact Zone: Decentering Community and Nation." In *Critical Theory, Cultural Politics, and Latin American Narrative*, ed. Steven M. Beel, Albert H. Le May, and Leonard Orr, 83–102. Notre Dame, IN: University of Notre Dame Press, 1993.

———. *Imperial Eyes: Travel Writing and Transculturation*. London: Routledge, 1992.

Prenshaw, Peggy Whitman, ed. *Women Writers of the Contemporary South*. Jackson: University Press of Mississippi, 1984.

Pyron, Darden A., ed. *Re-Casting: "Gone with the Wind" in American Culture*. Miami: University Press of Florida, 1983.

Richards, Gary. "'With a Special Emphasis': The Dynamics of (Re)Claiming a Queer Southern Renaissance." *Mississippi Quarterly* 55 (2002): 209–230.

Ridgely, J. V. *Nineteenth-Century Southern Literature*. Lexington: University Press of Kentucky, 1980.

Roberts, Diane. *The Myth of Aunt Jemima: Representations of Race and Region*. New York: Routledge, 1994.

Rodgers, Lawrence P. *Canaan Bound: The African American Great Migration Novel*. Urbana: University of Illinois Press, 1997.

Romine, Scott. *The Narrative Forms of Southern Community*. Baton Rouge: Louisiana State University Press, 1999.

Rowe, Anne E. *The Enchanted Land: Northern Writers in the South, 1865–1910*. Baton Rouge: Louisiana State University Press, 1978.

Rubin, Louis D., Jr., ed. *The American South: Portrait of a Culture*. Baton Rouge: Louisiana State University Press, 1978.

———. *The Edge of the Swamp: A Study in the Literature and Society of the Old South*. Baton Rouge: Louisiana State University Press, 1989.

———. *The Faraway Country: Writers of the Modern South*. Seattle: University of Washington Press, 1963.

———. *A Gallery of Southerners*. Baton Rouge: Louisiana State University Press, 1982.

———. *The Literary South*. Baton Rouge: Louisiana State University Press, 1986.

———. *The Wary Fugitives: Four Poets and the South*. Baton Rouge: Louisiana State University Press, 1978.

Rubin, Louis D., Jr., and Robert D. Jacobs, eds. *South: Modern Southern Literature in Its Cultural Setting*. Garden City, NY: Doubleday, 1961.

Rubin, Louis D., Jr., and James Jackson Kilpatrick, eds. *The Lasting South*. New York: Regnery, 1957.

Rushdy, Ashraf. *Neo-Slave Narratives: Studies in the Social Logic of a Literary Form*. New York: Oxford University Press, 1999.

Sayre, Gordon M. *Les Sauvages Américains: Representations of Native Americans in French and English Colonial Literature*. Chapel Hill: University of North Carolina Press, 1997.

Segrest, Mab. *My Mama's Dead Squirrel: Lesbian Essays on Southern Culture*. Ithaca, NY: Firebrand Books, 1985.

Seidel, Kathryn Lee. *The Southern Belle in the American Novel*. Tampa: University of South Florida Press, 1985.

Silber, Nina. *The Romance of Reunion: Northerners and the South, 1865–1900*. Chapel Hill: University of North Carolina Press, 1993.

Simpson, Lewis P. *The Brazen Face of History: Studies in the Literary Consciousness of America*. Baton Rouge: Louisiana State University Press, 1990.

———. *The Dispossessed Garden: Pastoral and History in Southern Literature*. Athens: University of Georgia Press, 1975.

———. *The Fable of the Southern Writer*. Baton Rouge: Louisiana State University Press, 1994.

———. *The Man of Letters in New England and the South: Essays on the History of the Literary Vocation in America*. Baton Rouge: Louisiana State University Press, 1973.

Singal, Daniel Joseph. *The War Within: From Victorian to Modernist Thought in the South, 1919–1945*. Chapel Hill: University of North Carolina Press, 1982.

Spivey, Ted R. *Revival: Southern Writers in the Modern City*. Gainesville: University Press of Florida, 1986.

Stephens, Robert O. *The Family Saga in the South: Generations and Destinies*. Baton Rouge: Louisiana State University Press, 1995.

Sundquist, Eric J. *To Wake the Nations: Race in the Making of American Literature*. Cambridge, MA: Harvard University Press, 1993.

Tate, Linda. *A Southern Weave of Women: Fiction of the Contemporary South*. Athens: University of Georgia Press, 1994.

Taylor, Alan. *American Colonies: The Settling of North America*. New York: Penguin, 2001.

Taylor, Helen. *Scarlett's Women: "Gone with the Wind" and Its Female Fans*. London: Virago Press, 1989.

Tracey, Susan J. *In the Master's Eye: Representations of Women, Blacks, and Poor Whites in Antebellum Southern Fiction*. Amherst: University of Massachusetts Press, 1995.

Twelve Southerners. *I'll Take My Stand: The South and the Agrarian Tradition*. 1930. New York: Harper Torchbooks, 1962.

Walker, Alice. *In Search of Our Mothers' Gardens*. New York: Harcourt Brace Jovanovich, 1983.

Walker, Melissa. *Down from the Mountaintop: Novels in the Wake of the Civil Rights Movement*. New Haven, CT: Yale University Press, 1991.

Warren, Nagueyalti, and Sally Wolff, eds. *Southern Mothers: Fact and Fictions in Southern Women's Writings*. Baton Rouge: Louisiana State University Press, 1999.

Watson, Charles L. *The History of Southern Drama*. Lexington: University Press of Kentucky, 1997.

Watson, Ritchie Devon. *Yeoman Versus Cavalier: The Old Southwest's Fictional Road to Rebellion*. Baton Rouge: Louisiana State University Press, 1993.

Westling, Louise. *Sacred Groves and Ravaged Gardens: The Fiction of Eudora Welty, Carson McCullers, and Flannery O'Connor*. Athens: University of Georgia Press, 1985.

Whitt, Jan. *Allegory and the Modern Southern Novel*. Macon, GA: Mercer University Press, 1994.

Wintz, Cary D. *Black Culture and the Harlem Renaissance*. Houston: Rice University Press, 1988.

Wray, Matt, and Annalee Nevitz. *White Trash: Race and Class in America*. New York: Routledge, 1997.

Wright, J. Leitch. *The Only Land They Knew: The Tragic Story of the American Indians in the Old South*. New York: The Free Press, 1981.

Wyatt-Brown, Bertram. *Hearts of Darkness: Wellsprings of a Southern Literary Tradition*. Baton Rouge: Louisiana State University Press, 2003.

———. *The House of Percy: Honor, Melancholy, and Imagination in a Southern Family*. New York: Oxford University Press, 1994.

Voigt, Ellen Bryant. "Narrative and Lyric: Structural Corruption." *Southern Review* n.s. 30 (1994): 725–740.

Yaeger, Patricia. *Dirt and Desire: Reconstructing Southern Women's Writing, 1930–1990*. Chicago: University of Chicago Press, 2000.

Young, Thomas Daniel. *The Past in the Present: A Thematic Study of Modern Southern Fiction*. Baton Rouge: Louisiana State University Press, 1981.

Web Sites

African American Webliography (LSU Lilbraries)
http://www.lib.lsu.edu/hum/african.html

American Life Histories: Manuscripts from the Federal Writers' Project, 1936–1940
http://rs6.loc.gov/ammem/wpaintro/wpahome.html

American Slave Narratives: An Online Anthology
http://xroads.virginia.edu/~hyper/wpa/wpahome.html

The American South/Internet Resource Center
http://www.ibiblio.org/south/#pubs

American Studies at the University of Virginia
http://xroads.virginia.edu

Archives of Appalachia
http://www.cass.etsu.edu/archives/index.htm

Center for Documentary Studies at Duke University
http://cds.aas.duke.edu

Center for Southern Literature/Margaret Mitchell House and Museum
http://www.gwtw.org/csl.html

Database of African-American poetry, 1760–1900
http://etext.lib.virginia.edu/aapd.html

First-Person Narratives of the American South
http://docsouth.unc.edu/fpn/fpn.html

Language of the Land/Journeys into Literary America—The South
http://lcweb.loc.gov/exhibits/land/landsout.html

Library of Southern Literature (University of North Carolina at Chapel Hill Libraries/Documenting the American South)
http://docsouth.unc.edu/southlit/southlit.html

The Mississippi Writers Page
http://www.olemiss.edu/mwp

Rare Books, Manuscripts, and Special Collections Library—Duke University
http://scriptorium.lib.duke.edu/#collecctions

Society for the Study of Southern Literature: Bibliography
http://www.missq.msstate.edu/sssl

Southern Literature and Culture on the Internet
http://academics.vmi.edu/english/southern.htm#Bibliography

Southern Literature: Women Writers
http://falcon.jmu.edu/~ramseyil/southwomen.htm

Southern Studies Jumpgate
http://www.ibiblio.org/sostudies/jump.htm

Story South: The Best from New South Writers
http://www.storysouth.com

University of Mississippi Libraries (Department of Archives and Special Collections)
http://www.olemiss.edu/depts/general_library/files/archives/index.html

Welcome to Yoknapatawpha: The Ole Miss Faulkner Home page
http://www.mcsr.olemiss.edu/~egjbp/faulkner/faulkner-and-material_culture.html

State Centers for the Book

Alabama

Alabama Center for the Book
Center for the Arts & Humanities
Auburn University
Pebble Hill
Auburn, AL 36849-5637
phone: (334) 844-4947 / fax: (334) 844-4949
e-mail: alabamabookcenter@auburn.edu
http://www.alabamabookcenter.org

Arkansas

Arkansas Center for the Book
Arkansas State Library
1 Capitol Mall
Little Rock, AR 72201
phone: (501) 682-5288 / fax: (501) 682-1693

Florida

Florida Center for the Book
Broward County Library
100 S. Andrews Ave.
Ft. Lauderdale, FL 33301
phone: (954) 357-7404 / fax: (954) 357-7399
e-mail: trebbi@browardlibrary.org
http://www.floridacenterforthebook.org/

Georgia

Georgia Center for the Book
DeKalb County Public Library
215 Sycamore St.
Decatur, GA 30030
phone: (404) 370-8450 / fax: (404) 370-8469
e-mail: gcb@mail.dekalb.public.lib.ga.us
http://www.dekalblibrary.org/gcb

Kentucky

Kentucky Center for the Book
Dept. for Libraries and Archives
300 Coffee Tree Rd., Box 537
Frankfort, KY 40602-0537
phone: (502) 564-8300, ext. 315 / fax: (502) 564-5773

Louisiana

Louisiana Center for the Book
P.O. Box 131
Baton Rouge, LA 70821
phone: (225) 342-4923 or (888) 487-2700 (toll free) / fax: (225) 219-9840
http://www.state.lib.la.us/Dept/cftb/index.htm

Mississippi

Mississippi Center for the Book
Mississippi Library Commission
P.O. Box 10700
1221 Ellis Ave.
Jackson, MS 39209
phone: (800) 647-7542 / fax: (601) 354-6713
e-mail: info@book.lib.ms.us

North Carolina

North Carolina Center for the Book
4640 Mail Service Center
Raleigh, NC 27699-4640
phone: (919) 807-7416 / fax: (919) 733-8748
http://statelibrary.dcr.state.nc.us/ld/nccftb/cftb.htm

South Carolina

Palmetto Book Alliance
South Carolina State Library
1500 Senate St., P.O. Box 11469
Columbia, SC 29211
phone: (803) 734-8666 / fax: (803) 734-8676
http://www.state.sc.us/scsl/lib/pba/

Tennessee

Tennessee Center for the Book
Humanities Tennessee
1003 18th Ave. South
Nashville, TN 37212
phone: (615) 320-7001 / fax: (615) 321-4586

Virginia

Virginia Center for the Book
Virginia Foundation for the Humanities
145 Ednam Dr.
Charlottesville, VA 22903-4629
Virginia Foundation for the Humanities phone: (434) 982-2983 / fax: (434) 296-4714
e-mail: mfr@virginia.edu

Conferences and Literary Festivals

Anything Southern: Books and Literature
http://www.anythingsouthern.com/listing.asp?CategoryID=61

Anything Southern: Literary Festivals and Events
http://www.anythingsouthern.com/listing.asp?CategoryID=1085

Arts and Education Council on Southern Literature
http://artsedcouncil.org/1/lit/fellows.htm

Celebrating Literature in Virginia
http://www.library.vcu.edu/guides/va_authors.html

Southern Arts Federation
http://www.southarts.org

Southern Literature Council of Charleston
http://www.southernlit.org

Virginia Festival of the Book
http://www.vabook.org

MUSIC

David Sanjek

While it may seem to be hyperbole to assert that the South is the cradle of American music, much evidence exists to support this view. The creators of a number of the essential vernacular genres of American music—including blues, jazz, gospel, country, rhythm and blues, rock and roll, funk, soul, and rap as well as such wholly regional variants as zydeco and swamp pop—were residents of the South, as were some of the most influential proponents of these musical styles. It is hard, in fact, to think of a single form of American music that does not bear some degree of southern influence. The principal exception to the geographical primacy of the South in American music could be said to be the body of expression associated with New York City, specifically, the wealth of material bred in the musical theater associated with Broadway and the heritage of popular song collectively ascribed to the inhabitants of Tin Pan Alley. Yet, even here the influence of the South can be detected, for example, in the groundbreaking evocation of the region in Jerome Kern (1885–1945) and Oscar Hammerstein's (1895–1960) *Show Boat* (1927) or the repertoire composed by such successful tunesmiths as Harold Arlen (1905–1986), Hoagy Carmichael (1899–1961), or Johnny Mercer (1909–1976).

In *Southern Music/American Music*, Bill C. Malone and David Stricklin note that the South has exerted its sway over American musical culture in two ways: "as a source of images and symbols, both positive and negative, which have fueled the imaginations of musicians and songwriters, and as an incubator of entertainers and styles that have shaped the entire realm of American popular music."[1] In effect, the South has acted as a catalyst, both literally and figuratively, upon national musical culture. The southern influence, felt through the actions and imaginative conceptions of a wide range of individuals, has waxed and waned, but nevertheless has been an undeniable component of the music produced in the United States.

Several themes run through the history of music in the South: the racial dynamic of southern musical culture; the romanticizing of the region's output; the commercial context in which the material has been created; and the technological means by which we continue to enjoy and study the music. The subject is vast, and only a few representative examples can be discussed here.

First, the South's music opens a particularly informative window on the inescapable, and often agonizing, presence of race in American society. African American, European, and other sources, sometimes existing in isolation but more often in combination, have contributed to the region's music. One illuminating aspect of American musical culture is that the parameters between races when they create music have a porous quality rarely found in other contexts of daily life. That is not to say that all musicians, or their audiences, adopt a color-blind mentality, but they have often been more willing to accommodate the kind of assimilation that rarely occurs on the social plane in the cultural arena. One reason for this open-mindedness is that musicians often have a uniquely ecumenical attitude toward repertoire. They acquire their material through what Tony Russell calls "omni-racial media."[2] He adds, "The great quality of the common stock was adaptability; its great power, assimilation; it was neither black nor white, but a hundred shades of gray."[3] In some rare circumstances, such assimilation was acknowledged from both sides of the equation. Furthermore, race often played a crucial role in who profited from the promotion of musical culture. Often, whites "covered" the works of blacks and treated the material as if it were created in a vacuum devoid of race or other impediments. The transmission of musical forms both breached and broke upon the impediments of race, and sometimes class as well, in complex ways.

Second, the musical by-products of southern culture have met with both adulation and abjection from the public. As often as those raised outside the South have acquired an admiration for the region through its musical expression, they just as frequently have treated that material dismissively. That narrowing of a complex body of culture can range from the ridiculing of mountain residents in the form of the caricatured hillbilly or redneck to the romanticizing of traditional rural ways of life. Examples of either attitude abound, from the assumption that a television show like *Hee-Haw* reflected reality to the belief that those raised in rural isolation adopted a more coherent way of life than those caught up by the copious attractions of urban life. Ascribing authenticity to the pastoral is the by-product of a body of cultural and ideological assumptions often unexamined by those who esteem the "simple life."

Third, some southern music has been produced and marketed to reach a very broad public. In the minds of some listeners, this commodification of indigenous culture demeans or damages the very substance of the music itself. It must be acknowledged, however, that much of this work would be lost or reach only a very narrow audience were it not for the recording industry, and listeners are not forced to hear or appreciate music only in the form through which it has been marketed.

NINETEENTH-CENTURY SOUTHERN MUSIC

Four nineteenth-century phenomena contributed crucial elements that are found, in a variety of forms, in the subsequent development of southern musical forms: blackface minstrelsy, the music of Stephen Foster, spirituals, and the study of traditional southern music.

Blackface Minstrelsy

The antebellum practice of white performers embodying the romantic myth of the southern plantation through deliberate impersonation of the stereotypic phenomenon of the "happy" slave began to take hold on the stage in the 1830s. Oddly, few of its progenitors came from the South. Non-southern individuals like New Yorker Thomas D. "Daddy" Rice (1808–1860), who originated the "Jim Crow" persona, and Ohioan Daniel Emmett (1815–1904), to whom the composition "Dixie" is attributed despite the likelihood of its black origins, established the parameters of the form. They created a popular fantasy of black masculinity that attracted many followers, black and white alike. Many blackface performers thereafter took up instruments like the banjo and tambourine, engaged in dance forms like "patting juba," took on the role of recurrent figures like "Tambo" and "Bones," and found a wildly enthusiastic audience, particularly in the urban working class. For many years, blackface minstrelsy has been viewed pejoratively as a wholly manipulative and inextricably racist form of cultural appropriation. Recently, however, scholars have seen a more complex dynamic at work, one in which affection as much as abjection governed the investment by audiences and practitioners alike in the form. As Eric Lott observes, "the very form of blackface acts—an investure in black bodies—seems a manifestation of the particular desire to try on the accents of 'blackness' and demonstrates the permeability of the color line."[4] Fascination as much as derision was at work in blackface minstrelsy and amounted, Lott argues, to "less a sign of absolute white power and control than of panic, anxiety, terror and pleasure."[5] The manner in which certain members of the audience, particularly disenfranchised working-class youths, found in the adoption of the superficial characteristics of another race a means both of defining themselves and setting themselves apart from mainstream norms has a long history.

Stephen Foster

The songs of Pittsburgh-born Stephen Foster (1826–1864) have had a longstanding influence on American music. A number of his works were written for the minstrel stage, such as "Oh! Susanna" (1847), and they embody the form's depiction of blacks as simple, illiterate laborers who occupy their limited free time with carefree singing and dancing. It is, however, his nonethnic and exceedingly romanticized celebrations of a bygone era of southern domesticity that have held the greatest sway over audiences. "Old Folks at Home" (1851), "Massa's in de Cold Ground" (1852), and "My Old Kentucky Home, Good Night" (1853) encapsulated his contemporaries' yearning for a simpler, pre-industrial epoch. The appeal of these songs lay as much in their denial of the ascendance of urbanization as in the teary-eyed evocation of a stress-free past. Unlike his minstrel pieces, these songs broke free from racial stereotypes and brought to mind instead timeless and universal yearnings for family, home, and childhood. Moreover, Foster's achievement is equally if not more consequential for its commercial dimension, as he is credited as being the first American songwriter to make a living from his compositions. That does not mean that he made a lavish income, as near his life's end, he sold off all future rights to thirty-six of his compositions for less than $2,000.

Still, both his ambitions and his limitations laid claim to the fact that the South could be mined for musical ore and that one could profit from that enterprise.

Spirituals

As influential as Foster's songs was the vernacular repertoire drawn from the spiritual. Long a part of African American private lives as a portion of their religious consciousness, the "sorrow songs," as W.E.B. DuBois called them, first entered the larger American consciousness as formal musical literature with the publication in 1867 of *Slave Songs in the United States*, edited by William Francis Allen, Charles Pickard, and Lucy McKlim Garrison. Groundbreaking as this volume was, the nation was more indelibly marked by the performance of the material as part of an academic enterprise. This was the celebrated, and still practicing, Fisk Jubilee Singers, founded at the historically black Fisk University in Nashville, Tennessee, in 1867. The catalyst was the school's financial uncertainty, a circumstance well known to George White, Fisk's white treasurer. He brought the ensemble north in 1871 and met with a wildly enthusiastic reception. The group's repertoire was admittedly representative of the black vernacular tradition, but White saw to it that the songs were delivered without excess enthusiasm. The group's polite and restrained vocal style matched the interest on the part of white, middle-class Americans in "cultural uplift." It demonstrated the docility of former slaves while, at the same time, validating the importance and substance of their musical talents. Other black institutions took up Fisk's example, including Hampton and Tuskegee, and sought the sympathies of northern philanthropists. The Fisk ensemble toured Europe for the first time in 1872, and their cultivated delivery captivated foreign audiences. A number of concert composers, including Antonin Dvorak (1841–1904), approved of the "sorrow songs" and even integrated them in their own work, thereby giving what had begun as a vernacular enterprise the imprimatur of the concert hall.

Traditional Southern Music Study and Preservation

Academics, as much as commercial songwriters, recognized in the nineteenth century that southern music could be examined for its intellectual and ideological wealth. Equally, the material these individuals focused on gave credence to a specific and narrow slice of southern life. If these scholars' motives were more elevated than the commercial ambitions of writers like Emmett, Rice, or Foster, they similarly corroborated a narrow-minded yet influential depiction of the region. Key to this process, which would be continued by crucial figures like Cecil Sharp (1859–1924) and Alan (1915–2002) and John Lomax (1875–1948), was the collection by Harvard Shakespearean scholar Francis James Child (1825–1896) of what he considered the most distinctive British ballads. Very much a literary analyst, Child examined his songs as altogether verbal texts divorced from melodies as well as the social or cultural context in which they were created and performed. In addition, his choice of material was governed by a considerable class bias, for he disdained the unschooled masses that had written the material. He also bowdlerized his material to remove the rude or what he considered obscene. Over the course of ten volumes released between 1882 and 1898, Child amassed in *The English and*

Scottish Popular Ballads a canon of some 305 texts that came to be regarded by future researchers as a sine que non of Anglo-Saxon musical expression.

Child's work is important in this context in that when Cecil Sharp traveled to America in 1916 and visited the South in search of exemplary forms of mountain music, he chose and appreciated his material using the criteria established by Child. While Sharp might have valued the work he uncovered as music to be sung, and wished to encourage its integration into people's everyday lives, he similarly believed that the material supported the supremacy of Anglo-Saxon culture. He saw the repertoire as a means of renovating and reinforcing habits of mind lost to the influence of modernization, and wished that its proponents would resist any possible benefits from that process to their circumscribed lives. Furthermore, he esteemed their musical expressions less for their inherent value than for how they might act as raw materials with which more sophisticated individuals could construct complex compositions. For Sharp and others, as Benjamin Filene observes, the call to "use folk song education to pass on WASPs' 'racial inheritance' sounds like a bid to preserve the centrality of Anglo-Saxon culture against outside influence."[6] His ambition will come to mind later on when the business interests in Music City construct the "Nashville sound" to combat the ascendance of rock and roll or when the producers of *O Brother, Where Art Thou?* attempt to reinvigorate the vernacular repertoire as an antidote to the supremacy of what they regarded as mindless pop drivel.

EARLY SOUTHERN MUSIC RECORDING

In the early twentieth century the commercial recording industry began to promote southern music. Did the industry preserve or simply plunder the copious musical culture it encountered? On more than one occasion, business interests found the performers foreign to their own experience and the music they produced not to their taste. With the record business in its infancy, the market for different types of music had yet to be systemically ascertained. Recordings were often pressed in small numbers at first until a genuine market was established. Yet the public flocked to purchase the work of southern performers almost immediately. In time their material received generic designations, but it is important to underscore that the performers themselves did not necessarily define their work so much as allow the marketplace to give it a name.

This was particularly the case with country music, for which advertisers also used the names "hillbilly" and "old-timey." It should also be stressed that the recording industry defined the parameters of southern musical genres by virtue of how they chose the repertoire of the artists they released. Some variants of southern music had less of a presence on wax than in public performance, as was the case, for example, with black string bands during the 1920s. Finally, the long-term value of southern music was something only the most perspicacious of record executives recognized. Most notably, Ralph Peer (1892–1960) made sure to copyright the work of his artists and retain the rights to its publication.

The First Jazz Recordings

Jazz had been evolving in New Orleans and elsewhere since before the turn of the twentieth century, yet not until 1917 did the major labels make an effort to preserve it. The first known group was not African American, but white. The Original Dixieland Jass Band took root in New Orleans but moved to Chicago in 1916 and then to New York City. They changed the name of what they played to "jazz" and cut a side for Columbia, yet it was shelved. In 1917 the Victor Talking Machine Company (later RCA Victor and more recently BMG-Bertlesman) released "Livery Stable Blues" backed by "Dixieland Jazz Band One-Step." It captured the public imagination, and the group had a fervent if brief following even though their efforts sparked a fascination with the genre as a whole. It was not until six years later, however, in 1923, that the preeminent black musicians from New Orleans, where the genre can be said to have incubated, entered the recording studio. The cornet player and bandleader Joseph "King" Oliver (1995–1938), along with his protégé, the magisterial Louis Armstrong (1901–1971), cut sides for the Paramount and Gennett labels. Whether the delay was caused by the potentially apocryphal assertion that Oliver in particular feared his horn licks being stolen by competitors should he document them, or by the overt racism if not the simple obliviousness of the record industry, is a matter of conjecture. Whatever the case, one mourns the loss of much music to history.

The First Blues Recordings

Blues recordings were made, albeit by white theatrical artists, during the second decade of the twentieth century. The first publication by a black writer of a blues song has been assigned to W. C. Handy (1873–1958), known as the "Father of the Blues." He released "Memphis Blues (Mr. Crump)" in 1912 and followed it with his most memorable composition, "St. Louis Blues," in 1914. Custom, however, has it that the first blues record for the general public was made in 1920, specifically by an African American singer and musicians. The principal agent in this process was the Alabama-born Perry Bradford (1893–1970), a theatrical producer and songwriter. He believed that black music could become culturally desegregated only by convincing a record company to release a composition by him performed by members of his own race. The two principal companies of the day, Victor and Columbia, turned him down, but the General Phonograph Company, owner of the Okeh label, took the risk. The singer Bradford employed was Mamie Smith (1883–1946), and their first effort was in the popular mode favored by Tin Pan Alley. It failed, but Smith performed their second effort in 1920, "Crazy Blues," in the refined (and to present-day ears, theatrical) mode of the emerging genre and found a substantial audience. Ralph Peer, associated with Okeh at the time, deemed the material Bradford had created "race records," and other labels took up the gauntlet. For several years, the bulk of the artists they hired were women, like Smith, with sophisticated performing styles. Their ranks were joined in 1923 by Bessie Smith (1894–1937), the "Empress of the Blues." She brought to the material a ferocity and depth of emotion that made her peers seem delicate by comparison and established her as the preeminent female performer in the genre until her untimely death in an automobile accident in 1937.

Not until two or three years after the release of "Crazy Blues" did record companies discern a similar market for blues recorded by male performers, and from 1926 to 1930, some 2,000 pieces were released. The type of material featured in this impressive wealth of music varied considerably in terms of instrumentation, lyrical content, and vocal style. While many bluesmen were solo artists, some were part of jug bands (Gus Cannon's [1883–1979] Jug Stompers); some played as part of piano/guitar duos (Leroy Carr [1905–1935] and Scrapper Blackwell [1903–1962]), and some were even skillful enough to accompany jazz ensembles (Lonnie Johnson [1899–1970]). Lyrics were drawn from diverse sources, including gospel (Blind Willie Johnson [1902–1947]) and the range of public styles from the prior century whose proponents were known as songsters (Henry "Ragtime Texas" Thomas [1874–?] and Mississippi John Hurt [1893–1966]). Some of the most haunting and influential players emerged from the Mississippi Delta. Accompanying themselves with a guitar style that at times mimicked and at others augmented their mesmerizing vocals, men like Charley Patton (1887–1934), Son House (1902–1988), Tommy Johnson (1895–1956), and Skip James (1902–1969) were raised within the plantation system. Their material responded to the plight of their peers with a haunting form of expression that offers, in the view of southern scholar James C. Cobb, "an insider's perspective on the communal search for self-determination and stability that dominated the postemancipation emancipation of black southerners as a group."[7] In their capacity to both mirror the rigors of segregation and embody an alternative to that turmoil, the blues epitomize, in Albert Murray's memorable phrase, "rituals of resilience and perseverance through improvisation in the face of capricious disjuncture."[8]

Many of the blues artists that historians and fans now credit as being the best in the genre were not so viewed at the time their recordings were made. Their material sold few copies, and their reputations were local in nature. The posthumous veneration of Robert Johnson (1911–1938) is a case in point. Early record buyers did not venerate the dark and brooding inhabitants of the Delta and were drawn instead to material that was, by contrast, lighthearted or overtly comic. By way of illustration, two of the most successful and influential early pieces were released in 1928: Leroy Carr's "How Long—How Long Blues" and "It's Tight Like That," played by Tampa Red (1904–1981) and Georgia Tom Dorsey (1899–1993). Carr was a tasteful pianist with a conversational vocal style that has led some to call him the first blues crooner. The material played by Red and Dorsey epitomized a form known as "hokum" that was upbeat and deliberately employed double entendres.

The First "Country" Music Recordings

While the research of Sharp and others indicated a wealth of musical culture among the White residents of the South, recording studios did not seek out the material so much as have its proponents find them. In 1922 two fiddlers, Arthur Campbell "Eck" Robertson (1887–1925) and Henry Gilliland, traveled to New York City. Dressed, respectively, in Confederate garb and a cowboy suit, the two men buttonholed the Victor label to record them. Some of their works were subsequently released without much impact on the market, although Robertson's solo version of "Sallie Gooden" remains a country standard. Their fanciful exploits failed to benefit others until 1923, when an Atlanta-based record dealer, Polk Brockman (1902–1985), convinced Ralph Peer to record the contest-winning Fiddlin' John Carson (1868–1949) for the Okeh label. While Peer did so, he found the two selections—"The Little Old Log Cabin in the Lane" and "The Old Hen Cackled and the Rooster's Going to Crow"—"plu-perfect awful." He therefore issued the record without any advertising or a label to indicate the track names and artists. He even excerpted it from the company's catalogue and then shipped the disc exclusively to the Atlanta market. Within a month, it sold 500 copies, Brockman's faith in the appeal of Carson was validated, and a new market and genre were born.

The record industry, eager to pigeonhole country music, saddled its performers with the pejorative appellation "hillbillies." The term first appeared in advertising in 1925, applied to Al Hopkins' string band, and for many urbanites it echoed an unexamined impression of the South as benighted by backwardness, superstition, and racism. This viewpoint was influenced by the resurrection of the Klu Klux Klan, the rising incidence of lynching, and the fundamentalist ideology dramatized by the Scopes trial. The reality was that the early performers of country music came from a wide range of backgrounds and classes, and a number of them saw a recording career as a way out of poverty. The range of material they played also illustrated how stereotypes about the region failed to illuminate its diversity. Much of the music was drawn from traditions that urban audiences had forgotten about or turned aside from: variants of British ballads of the sort Sharp studied, frontier fiddle melodies, camp meeting songs, hymns draw from shape-note manuals, and the popular commercial repertoire from the nineteenth century. This diverse repertoire mirrored the complexity of the region and its sense of itself. In Malone and Stricklin's words, "It was a melding of rural and urban influences; it was simultaneously southern and American; and its performers and audience were torn by opposing desires, clinging to a self-image of rustic simplicity while at the same time striving to be accepted in an urban, middle-class milieu."[9]

Some of the most evocative and influential material of the early country era embodied the interracial dimension of American musical culture, despite the perception that segregation dominated every aspect of southern life. Country artists of the era drew from a diverse array of traditional material, for, as Tony Russell asserts, "the bearers of tradition are not purists, but eclectics."[10] "The traditional music of the countryman," he continues, "was a repertoire shared by black and white; a common stock. Some tunes or songs might be associated by some of their users with one race rather than the other, but most would have no racial connotations."[11] Banjo player Dock Boggs (1898–1971) counted among his most celebrated sides "Down South Blues" and "Mistreated Mama Blues," both recorded by the black blues queens of the 1920s—Sara Martin (1894–1935) in the case of the former, and Clara Smith (1884–1955) in the latter. Uncle Dave Macon (1870–1952), a professional banjo player and prolific recording artist from the 1920s to his death in 1952, had a repertoire whose diversity reflected the ecumenical style of the black songster. The playing style of many early country guitarists mirrored the work of black players, particularly in their evocative use of the bottleneck to stretch and draw out notes. This practice can be heard in the music of such celebrated performers as Frank Hutchison (1891–1945); Tom Darby (1884–1971), who performed in tandem with Jimmie Tarlton (1892–1979); and

Riley Puckett (1894–1946), the blind guitarist with Gid Tanner's (1895–1960) Skillet-Lickers. Furthermore, in some more limited instances, interracial bands recorded together, as when Jimmie Davis (1899–2000), best known as the writer-performer of "You Are My Sunshine," cut sides with black Mississippi guitarist Clifford Gibson (1901–1963) and the all-black Louisville Jug Band.

COUNTRY MUSIC

The Grand Ole Opry

Country music expanded its audience quite notably in 1925 with the emergence of one of the nation's longest-lasting public musical broadcasts, the Grand Ole Opry. The inspiration of George D. Hay (1895–1968), an experienced broadcaster, the Opry was heard (as it still is) on WSM in Nashville, Tennessee, owned by the National Life and Accident Insurance Company. The program began in November of that year as the WSM Barn Dance and received its current name in 1927. Broadcast live before a studio audience and carried over a signal that assured the performers a geographically broad audience, the Opry was regulated by Hay so as to ensure that it remained an informal, listener-friendly, down-home avenue for country music. Hay rigorously reinforced a questionably circumscribed image of country music through the Opry. He gave the featured ensembles such rural designations as the Fruit Jar Drinkers or Possum Hunters; required that they wear floppy hats and overalls rather than suits and ties; and posed them in publicity photographs in cornfields and pigpens. By contrast, a number of the featured musicians were professionals—watchmakers, auto repairmen, and even police—rather than rural landowners. Nonetheless, the image they projected on the air was pastoral in the extreme, even when, as the Opry became a runaway success, the broadcast and the booking service it established took on a particularly regimented and professionalized dimension.

Like George D. Hay, Ralph Peer recognized and profited from the emerging audience for country music. No longer associated with Okeh, he had been hired by Victor in 1925 when they wished to augment their presence in the country field. A savvy businessman, Peer signed a unique contract with the label: he worked without salary but retained control of the copyrights for whatever he produced. He established as well a going rate for each individual session: $50 a tune and a miniscule royalty for each record sold, yet no rights in the song itself. Peer recognized the profits to be made in the field in 1926 when material cut by Ernest "Pop" Stoneman (1893–1968) sold 60,000 copies with no promotion, earning the artist $3,600 in royalties while Peer pocketed $250,000. Eager to find other equally marketable performers, Peer set up an open recording session in Bristol, Tennessee, in July 1927. Among the individuals and ensembles who answered the call, two stood out from the crowd. Together they constitute what many consider the core of the country canon: the Carter Family—songwriter and occasional vocalist A.P. (1881–1960), his guitarist-vocalist wife Sara (1899–1979), and her guitarist-vocalist cousin Maybelle (1909–78)—and Jimmie Rodgers, the Blue Yodeler (1897–1933).

The Carters came from the mountains of Virginia and had only the barest of professional careers prior to meeting Peer. Even after they became audience favorites, they retained in both their repertoire and the presentation a domestic approach. Hearing them on the radio, on records, or in person brought one, as it were, into their living room, for they treated audiences as if they were guests, not passive consumers of a repertoire that validated the consecrated values of hearth and home. Allen Lowe considers them the "aural equivalent" of *American Gothic*, Grant Wood's celebrated evocation of Middle America.[12] Their several hundred recordings embodied the worldview of the Protestant South and its yearning for stability in a fluctuating environment. Their genius was, in the words of biographers Mark Zwonitzer and Charles Hirshberg, "giving a modern sustain to decades- and centuries-old song."[13] That wealth of song was largely the work of A.P., though to call him a songwriter stretches the term, in that he adopted a significant portion of the Carter Family's material from nineteenth-century popular songs that he found in published collections or heard during trips to hunt up songs. He was sometimes accompanied on those excursions by a black guitarist, Leslie Riddle (1905–1980), who acted as his musical amanuensis and had a significant influence too on Maybelle's celebrated Carter style of finger picking. A.P. infrequently sang, but the balanced harmonies of Maybelle and Sara possessed a gorgeous sympathy. Some of their songs have become perennials of American music, like "Keep on the Sunny Side," "Wildwood Flower," and "Will the Circle Be Unbroken?" The last was a testament to the security of faith, yet took on an even more telling tone when the trio performed after A.P. and Sara divorced. Some of the Carter Family continued to perform, when Maybelle and her daughters Helen, June, and Anita performed together as Mother Maybelle and the Carter Sisters. June Carter later married Johnny Cash (1932–2003), whom she met at a Grand Ole Opry performance.

If the Carters embodied tradition and stability, Jimmie Rodgers projected the image of an itinerant rounder who sought release from convention in the freedom of the open road. Born in Mississippi, he was a railroad worker starting in his teens until the tuberculosis that eventually killed him took hold and he supported himself as an entertainer. At age thirty, when he met Peer, he was a professional musician who had, through his travels, sampled a wealth of vernacular styles. Among them was the evocative yodel he added to one of the songs he played for Peer at Bristol, an old lullaby also recorded by Riley Puckett, "Sleep Baby Sleep." The incorporation of the technique exemplified the adaptability seen again and again in Rodgers' 111 recordings. If he seems at times a kind of musical magpie, it is the ecumenical dimension of American vernacular music coming through. Jazz players as well as Hawai'ian musicians accompanied Rodgers on some of those sides in addition to the increasingly customary instrumentation of the country singer. He incorporated as well the syncopation and delivery of rural blues in his sequence of Blue Yodels, the best known of which is played as "T for Texas." That eclecticism would make Rodgers a model for musicians in all genres, and even lead to his induction into the Rock and Roll Hall of Fame.

Many historians of country music have drawn upon the opposition of the Carters and Rodgers as constituting the two strains of the genre, and southern music as a whole, one might add: the one associated with tradition and stability, and the other drawn by evolution and the transitory. Even those who ramble, however, yearn for security, while the resolution connected to a sense of permanence can become a yoke to the spirit. Few country artists, or musicians in general, are single-minded about their material or the life that it illustrates. As Malone and Stricklin note, "Hillbilly music, like the people who produced and nourished it, was typically ambivalent about home, the country, and the South, idealizing them while exhibiting a fascination with rambling. Home was often extolled after it was abandoned, and the wandering life was sometimes gloried after it was unattainable."[14] Should it be a surprise that Rodgers' favorite of all his songs was "Daddy and Home"?

Documenting Traditional Music of the South

Southern music, as did all commercial productions, suffered a significant loss of audience during the Great Depression. In the process, the efforts made in the 1920s to seek out performers in the field dissipated, and an emerging group of professional folklorists with the aid of portable recording equipment took up the cause of uncovering talent wherever it could be found. They meant the results to serve the interests of preservation, not professionalism, yet some of the performers uncovered influenced commercial music or went on to have careers of their own. Primary among those researchers was the father and son team of John and Alan Lomax; the former assembled the first published collection of cowboy songs, and the latter became one of the most influential documentarians of vernacular music at home and abroad. Supported by the American Council of Learned Societies and the Library of Congress' Archive of American Folk Song, the duo took to the road in 1933 and most notably "discovered" Huddie Ledbetter or Leadbelly (1888–1945), a forty-four-year-old convict serving a sentence for murder in Louisiana's Angola Prison. The Lomaxes had come to the institution in search of performers untouched by commercial influence, a noble but misguided quest.

Leadbelly brought them a wealth of material, yet despite his incarceration, he was a man of the world. The Lomaxes hoped as well to uncover a native vernacular repertoire equal to that espoused by Francis Child and Cecil Sharp, and Leadbelly embodied for them that goal. To him, we owe such perennial songs as "Midnight Special" and "Goodnight Irene," yet he also illustrates the shortcomings of the ambitions inherent in what Benjamin Filene calls the Lomaxes' "outsider populism": the urge "to locate America's strength and vibrancy in the margins of society."[15] In doing so, the Lomaxes, and others then and since, exoticized the individuals they encountered by assuming that they epitomized all manner of innocence and irrationality rather than meeting them on their own terms. Understandably, therefore, despite all he owed them for helping to arrange his release, Leadbelly disliked the Lomaxes' insistence that he wear prison garb when he performed. This demand led to their eventual separation and the guitarist's efforts to make a living as a professional singer on his own, always appearing in a neat coat and tie.

Bluegrass Music

New forms of musical expression from the South moved into the commercial marketplace in the 1930s, most notably the phenomenon of bluegrass. Its progenitor, Bill Monroe (1911–1996), a mandolin player born in the mountains of Kentucky, had an undeniably affecting high tenor voice. Monroe assembled the instrumentation of the string bands and added an unrelenting velocity. The genre's compelling vigor led Alan Lomax to describe it in a 1959 *Esquire* article as "folk music with overdrive." Speed and instrumental virtuosity were, however, not the sole salient characteristics of the form, for the keening sound of Monroe's vocals and the evocative delineation of rural ways in the lyrics gave rise to the feel of the material known as "the high lonesome sound." It possessed a mournfulness, an acknowledgment of life's vicissitudes, that attracted rural and urban audiences alike. Monroe's ensembles also acted for decades as a workshop not only for the development of the genre but also for training generation after generation of musicians. Primary among them were the guitar-banjo duo of Lester Flatt (1914–1979) and Earl Scruggs (1924–   ), who on their own attracted vast audiences and became an indelible element in the national consciousness when they played the theme to the 1960s situation comedy *The Beverly Hillbillies*. To this day, bluegrass has preserved its commitment to acoustic instrumentation and a traditional repertoire and has acted for many as a means of withstanding the encroachment of modernization.

Gospel Music

Another genre that took hold in the 1930s is gospel. Church music has long been a mainstay of southern life, and the commercial reproduction of material written and performed by professional entertainers for a sacred audience became common at this time. Many choirs recorded music in the 1920s, and many bluesmen incorporated sacred material in their repertoire. The first songwriter to create a unique and enormously successful body of gospel song was Thomas Dorsey, paradoxically the Georgia Tom of "It's Tight Like That." He began his career in the blues world as the pianist for Ma Rainey (1886–1939), one of the earthiest of the blues queens. The son of a Baptist minister, he left the secular world behind in 1929, and in 1932 published his most famous song, "Precious Lord, Take My Hand," inspired by the loss of his wife and son. Countless individuals have treated "Precious Lord" as their own statement of faith. Dorsey also encouraged the growth of the field by the incorporation in Chicago of the Gospel Singers Convention, at which he displayed his material for use in churches across the land. Over the course of time gospel has welcomed the talents of countless superlative performers, from solo artists to quartets to choir leaders, among them the Golden Gate Quartet, Mahalia Jackson (1911–1972), Five Blind Boys of Alabama, Swan Silvertones, and many, many more. In the years to come, as rhythm and blues established itself as a new musical format, many of its performers obtained their training in the church, and the habits of call and response or melismatic elaboration of lyrics endemic to gospel were transposed to a secular context.

Cajun-Zydeco and Swamp Pop

Regional expression in Louisiana also took root in the interior bayous inhabited by the French-speaking communities of both Whites and African Americans. The former had migrated from Canada in the mid-seventeenth century after having been expelled by the British. The process, known within the community as Le Grand Derangement, led them to Louisiana. Central to their culture was the music they played on guitars, accordions, and fiddles and featured at the dances that gave pleasure and relief from a hardscrabble life. Sung in their native French, the lyrics of their songs focused on the quotidian pleasures of love and labor, and incorporated specific references to the places and habits of their bayous. In turn, the African Americans constructed a body of music that has come to be known as zydeco, whose instrumentation and lyrics resemble that of the Cajun culture. The first commercial interest in the region's repertoire dates from 1928, when a white French-speaking singer and accordion player from Rayne, Louisiana, Joseph Falcon (1900–1965), accompanied by his guitar-playing wife, Ceoma Breaux Falcon, recorded "Allons à Lafayette" (Let's Go to Lafayette). Industrial interest in the form was intermittent, although certain zydeco artists, particuarly Clifton Chenier (1925–1987) and Boozoo Chavis (1930–2001), released popular songs. The field eventually took off in the mid-1960s when independent companies that specialized in vernacular musical forms, most notably the California-based Arhoolie label, brought Chenier's work to prominence in communities outside the Deep South. It was not, however, until the 1980s that this musical culture achieved success on the national record charts, when "My Toot Toot" (1982) by Rockin' Sidney (1939–1998) not only sold in the millions but also was covered by other artists, including those not native to Louisiana. That same year, Che-

A musician plays the washboard at the Zydeco Music Festival, Louisiana. Courtesy Louisiana Office of Tourism.

nier won a Grammy Award, and another noted artist in the genre, Buckwheat Zydeco (1947–   ), was signed to a contract with a major company, Island Records.

The region, like much of the rest of the South, was an incubator for generic crossover, as musical practices intermingled and, in the process, led to new forms of composition and performance. One such was swamp pop, so named by British journalists enamored of the material. It was a conglomeration of blues, rhythm and blues, rock criss-crossed with zydeco, and Cajun. Played by young musicians from both the white and black communities, it achieved success regionally and, on occasion, even on a national basis when companies purchased master recordings produced by small, independent local labels. The repertoire included slow, emotive ballads like Cookie and the Cupcakes' "Matilda" (1961) and upbeat rockers like "This Road Should Go On Forever" (1959) by Rod Bernard (1930–   ). Another regional phenomenon of the period was an evocative subgenre of the music dubbed swamp blues, principally released by the local Excello label. Artists like Slim Harpo (1924–1970), Lonesome Sundown (1928–1995), and Lazy Lester (1933–   ) concocted a stripped-down, hypnotically evocative sound which, like swamp pop, found many aficionados, including the Rolling Stones, who covered Harpo's "I'm a King Bee" early in their career.

Recording

Memphis

The success of regional music scenes in the South was widespread. Small labels took advantage of the concentration of songwriters, musicians, and performers that formed scenes and capitalized upon their collective talents. One of the most important and prolific music centers of this kind was Memphis, Tennessee. It had been a focal point of blues in the 1920s with the work of Gus Cannon or the Memphis Sheiks and would become a seedbed for the formation of rock and roll and the proliferation of rhythm and blues. Beale Street was the focal point of black culture in the city and offered ample opportunities for musical entertainment. Alabama-born Sam Phillips (1923–2003) saw the city and the black neighborhood as a kind of promised land and spent a fabled career mining the unique talents he discovered there on his legendary Sun label. Well versed in the manipulation of sound, Phillips was particularly interested how his artists' unique marks could be captured in the recording studio. To achieve that end, Phillips employed tape echo, distortion, and whatever else would work in order to bring out the core of whoever stood before his microphones. Phillips sought uniqueness and worked to transfer the one-of-a-kind temperaments he uncovered to the aural arena. In his own words: "I tried my best to let people be individuals. If it took a week or a month to get out of a person what they really, truly had to say, this is what we did. A lot of times you've just got to *unlock* that person. I think freeing up a man's thoughts can be the catalyst for his creativity in any field, especially music."[16] The catalogue of artists on the label is astonishing. In addition to pioneers of rock and roll like Elvis Presley (1935–1977), Jerry Lee Lewis (1935–), Carl Perkins (1932–1998), Johnny Cash, and Roy Orbison (1936–1988), he mined the black world through the talents of B. B. King (1925–), Howlin' Wolf (1920–1976), Junior Parker (1932–1971), Little Milton (1934–), Roscoe Gordon (1934–2002), and Rufus Thomas (1917–2001).

Stax Records

Memphis once again made its mark on the national scene in the 1960s with the efforts produced by the Stax label. Started in 1961 by Jim Stewart (1930–) and Estelle Axton (1919–2004), over time it became a competitor to the Detroit-based Motown and was viewed by some as more down-home and rooted in black musical conventions than its northern competitor. In addition, the company stood out for its interracial staff, both in the back room and the recording studio. Peter Guralnick has written of the rhythm and blues or soul music movement of the 1960s as embodying the energies of the civil rights movement reconstituted in musical form, and few companies symbolized those efforts as vividly as Stax. He states, "Southern soul music represented a temporary victory, a momentary cessation of hostilities in which the combatants hesitantly set aside their differences and for an instant, however brief, joined arms in a sea of troubles against a common foe."[17] The principal backup group for the company, which also had a notable solo career, was the biracial Booker T. and the MGs. Both as writers and musicians, the ensemble assisted in the careers of Carla Thomas (1942–), Eddie Floyd (1935–), and Isaac Hayes (1942–), among many others, and laid down a spare, yet uniquely effective groove that has continued to influence others, both in and out of black music. Stax was not alone, however, in the musical renaissance in Memphis during the height of the soul era. The Gold Wax and Hi labels participated as well, the latter led by producer-writer-arranger Willie Mitchell (1928–), whose collaborations with Al Green (1946–) in the 1970s kept soul music alive.

New Orleans

New Orleans is another city to take on cultural precedence in American music during the 1920s. Long associated with jazz, it became one of the focal points for the development of the new musical genre known as rhythm and blues, the name given by *Billboard* magazine to upbeat black popular music in 1949. Part of the reason the city flowered a music center was the plethora of capable players and singers, but equally consequential was the role played by writer-producer-arrangers like Dave Bartholomew (1920–) and engineers like Cosimo Matassa (1926–). Bartholomew led the band and wrote many of the singles for pianist Fats Domino (1928–), one of the best-selling performers of the 1950s and a persistent crossover from the black to the pop charts. Bartholomew also aided in the work of Smiley Lewis (1913–1966) and Lloyd Price (1933–) and set the standard for other writer-producer-arrangers like Paul Gayten (1926–1991). New Orleans was also a focal point for gifted piano players who concocted new ways of employing the keyboard, like Professor Longhair (1918–1980), Archibald (1912–1979), and James Booker (1939–1983). They, and others, embodied the city's unique syncopation, referred to as the "third line," that gave a novel rhythmic accent to American popular music. Bartholomew set standards that his successor as the focal producer-arranger in New Orleans in the 1960s and 1970s, Allen Toussaint (1938–), would match with his work alongside Lee Dorsey (1924–1986), Irma Thomas (1941–), Aaron Neville (1941–), and others.

Allen Toussaint (1938–) was inducted into the Rock and Roll Hall of Fame in 1998 for the wealth of material he wrote, and in some cases recorded, in the 1960s and 1970s when he was arguably New Orleans' leading songwriter/producer. He entered the business when his legendary predecessor, Dave Bartholomew, hired Toussaint in 1955 at age seventeen to stand in on keyboards for Fats Domino on recordings. He capitalized on that break in 1958 when he arranged the instrumental hit for Lee Allen, "Walkin' with Mr. Lee." Subsequently, Joe Banashak, A&R man for the new Minit label, selected him as producer-writer for a string of hits, including Jessie Hill's "Oooh Poo Pah Do" and Ernie K-Doe's "Mother-in-Law." After a spell in the military, Toussaint collaborated with Marshall Sehorn in forming Sansu Enterprises, which accounted for some of the most infectious and successful New Orleans releases, most notably the long-term partnership with vocalist Lee Dorsey, who belted out such Toussaint classics as "Working in a Coal Mine" and "Yes We Can." Many of the Sansu sides utilized a house band that went on to major status on their own as the Meters. Toussaint released several solo albums in the 1970s and had a number one single with LaBelle's cover of his "Lady Marmalade."

The Neville Brothers are one of the familial units that have transformed New Orleans music. As both soloists and an ensemble, they have participated in the music industry of the region for some fifty years, starting with oldest brother, Art

(1937–), in 1954, when he cut "Mardi Gras Mambo" with his high school band, the Hawketts. Vocalist Aaron (1941–) struck out on his own and climbed the charts in 1966 with the smooth ballad "Tell It Like It Is." Simultaneously, Art was at work as one of the Meters, and when that ensemble broke up in 1977, the Neville Brothers collaboration took hold. Brothers Cyril (1948–) and Charles (1939–) took part, and the group recorded for several labels, most successfully for A&M with 1989's "Yellow Moon" and 1990's "Brother's Keeper."

Nashville

In the late 1940s, Nashville, a radio center since the start of the Grand Ole Opry, also became a recording center for country music. Focal in that process was Hank Williams (1923–1953), whom many consider the best country songwriter of all time and the most charismatic performer since Jimmie Rodgers. Georgia-born, the lanky, self-destructive, and poetically gifted performer found the equivalent of Ralph Peer in the person of publisher Fred Rose (1897–1956), who assisted in writing and merchandising his material. Williams made his initial mark in 1949 through a cover of a 1920s Tin Pan Alley tune, "Lovesick Blues." The song was recorded in 1929 by the blackface white vocalist Emmett Miller (1906–1962), who

Hank Williams. Photofest.

significantly influenced Williams' delivery. Yet it was his own material that created his reputation and helped make a mark for country music as a whole when it was covered by pop artists like Tony Bennett (1926–). As Bill Malone observes, "Williams' style and repertory were curious blends of country gospel and honky-tonk, a mixture that was rare in Hank's own day and is almost unknown now."[18] His vocal delivery was as diverse as his material, for he could put across blues, gospel, fast novelty pieces, and mournful love songs. At the same time, it was as much the suddenness of his demise at twenty-nine, brought about by drugs and alcohol abuse, that created the myth about Williams. He set a standard both of songwriting and hell-raising for country performers then and now.

The success of Williams' songs helped obliterate the perception of country music as a genre performed solely by and for hicks from the sticks. During the 1950s, it made a beachhead in the national consciousness, only to be overshadowed by the rise of rock and roll in the middle of the decade. Convinced that country must not sound like country in order to gain a mainstream audience, producers in Nashville—key among them Owen Bradley (1915–1998) and Chet Atkins (1924–2001)—promoted what has come to be known as the Nashville sound. It smoothed out if not removed altogether the instrumental markers that codified the genre and added layers of strings and backup singers that appealed to a middle-of-the-road, urban consciousness. Condemned by some as a sell-out and categorized by others as "soft-shell" in contrast to mainstream "hard-core" country, the Nashville sound won many adherents. It sped up the careers of artists like Eddie Arnold (1918–), Jim Reeves (1923–1963), and Patsy Cline (1932–1963), the last of whom, paradoxically, has come to be viewed over time not as middle-of-the-road but country to the core.

Icons of Southern Popular Music

Robert Johnson

While the Depression hurt the music business, the search for new artists resumed when circumstances became less dire. Contemporary audiences view one discovery from this period as a key figure in American music, yet he sold few records at the time and had only the barest of followings. This was Robert Johnson, about whom myth and mystification have accumulated over time. Few nowadays believe the account that he gained his technical proficiency by encountering the devil at the crossroads. Others, however, agree with Peter Guralnick's effusive description of him as "the personification of the existential blues singer, unencumbered by corporeality or history, a fiercely incandescent spirit who had escaped the bonds of tradition by the sheer thrust of genius."[19] The small repertoire Johnson recorded does include a number of pieces that have come to be regarded as masterworks: "Love in Vain," "Cross Road Blues," and "Ramblin' on My Mind." The 1991 reissue of his complete output set sales records for the blues, and he is regarded as perhaps the most influential bluesman of all time. This should not sway us from reintegrating Johnson into the world of his time, acknowledging his own influences and adaptations from other performers, or recognizing that the construction of both his personality—the facts about which remain largely unknown—and technical skills remain a posthumous matter. Other musicians of comparable skill and consequence performed at the time, and while their lack of fame should not diminish Johnson's achievement, it reminds us that musical history, like all forms of narrative, is a selective affair.

Elvis Presley

Of all the musicians that emerged from the South, it is Elvis Presley who has had the most epochal influence on the national culture and beyond. Stating that, one feels compelled to treat his legendary emergence from poverty and obscurity into wealth and prominence as some kind of sui generis occurrence. Quite the contrary—one can map out the factors that influenced his style, his stance, and even his presumably unintended demise. None of that matters, however, when one considers that what Elvis made of his forebears and fanaticisms exceeded the sum of their parts. His influence on the culture at the time of his first recording in 1954 is something we can only partly measure, for, hyperbole though it might appear, he liberated a tense and repressed society when he shook his hips and twitched his lip. His sense of fun and sexual ferocity made a mockery of the starched-collar appearance of his peers, and he, in turn, liberated them to gain access to the energies, musical and otherwise, that lay, hibernating it would seem, in the mass culture all around them. The arc of the career that followed that initial release possessed a quality both of tragedy and its companion, comedy. The latter can be illustrated by the avidity with which Elvis acquired all the external markers of status and success, an eagerness that could not help but come across as gauche. Yet, what did one expect? He wanted to become a success and a name to contend with, and he succeeded, most likely, beyond his most cherished fantasies. The tragedy occurs with what he can be said to have sacrificed in the process. He acquiesced to the

Elvis Presley. Photofest.

whims and plots of his manager, Colonel Parker, in return for filthy lucre, and insipid Hollywood vehicles and second-rate singles were the price for the prize. The dramatic arc does, at the same time, contain a kind of resurrection in the 1968 television special, on which he comes across as recovering not only his love of the music but also the energy that led him to pursue it in the first place. After that, Vegas, isolation behind the gates of Graceland, physical deterioration, and drug abuse: the full litany of decline.

And yet, much as we might mourn a substantial talent given over to excess and exploitation, the weight of what Elvis embodied, its reflection of southern, and national, culture, and the continuing influence it has on our lives have not diminished. This is aptly summarized by one of the singer's best analysts, Greil Marcus:

> At his best Elvis not only embodies but personalizes so much of what is good about this place [the South]: a delight in sex that is sometimes simple, sometimes complex, but always open; a love of roots and a respect for the past; a rejection of the past and a demand for novelty; the kind of racial harmony that for Elvis, a white man, means a profound affinity with the most subtle nuances of black culture combined with an equally profound understanding of his own whiteness; a burning desire to get rich, and to have fun; a natural affection for big cars, flashy clothes, for the symbols of status that give pleasure both as symbols, and on their own terms. Elvis has long since become one of those symbols himself.[20]

In his own way, as Walt Whitman said of the American consciousness, Elvis contained multitudes, and in that variousness assimilated the complexities and contradictions of his region, his race, and his nation.

Muddy Waters

If a portion of the country community tailored their material to consolidate their position in the marketplace, the principal proponents of blues achieved wider success by remaining true to its roots and not diluting its energy. The career of Muddy Waters (1915–1983) epitomizes this phenomenon. One of the many African Americans who participated in the groundswell of migration from the rural South to the industrial North, he began his career in the delta of Mississippi. His talents were first documented in 1941 as part of the field recording excursions of Alan Lomax, who had traveled to the region in part in search of Robert Johnson, whom he did not know had died. At this point, Waters was an acoustic performer, influenced by local masters like Son House but equally aware of and responding to currently successful commercial recording artists like Leroy Carr, whose discs he bought. Once north, Waters transformed his approach to fit the sonic demands of loud, jam-packed local clubs by plugging in his guitar and adding a jolt of amplified energy to the genre. He exemplified for his peers in the black community the self-possessed and sexually aggressive male in songs like "Hoochie Coochie Man" and "Got My Mojo Working." Recording on the Chicago-based Chess label, Waters experienced an ironic reception when he first traveled to Europe in the 1950s. The audience recoiled from the audacity of his electrified repertoire, as the accepted mode of performance at the time for blues fans was the more low-key

Muddy Waters. Photofest.

acoustic format with which he began his career. However, when he returned to the continent the following decade, a number of foreign artists like the Rolling Stones having become captivated by his commercial material, his reversion to acoustic backup was rejected as lacking the ferocious fire of the Chess catalogue. Waters also had a notable influence on blues as a field in that his backup bands acted as an incubator for individuals who achieved substantial careers in their own right, among them harmonica player Little Walter (1930–1968), pianist Otis Spann (1930–1970), and guitarist Jimmy Rogers (1924–1997).

Otis Redding

Of the numerous exemplary rhythm and blues performers associated with Memphis, few, perhaps, possessed more potential to cross over to a mass audience than Otis Redding (1941–1967), and few left in the wake of their untimely death so many ardent and mournful fans. The Georgia-born Redding came up the hardscrabble path of journeymen performers, playing, while still a teenager, in an ensemble called Johnny Jenkins and the Pinetoppers and acting as the leader's chauffeur. In 1962, when Jenkins had forty minutes left over during a recording session, Redding seized the opportunity. He had a self-penned song, "These Arms of Mine," ready, and knew how to put his material across. Throughout his career,

Redding employed a deliberately stripped down and utilitarian instrumental style, epitomized by Booker T. and the MGs. The band sought to become a cohesive voice that supported Redding's unabashedly emotional delivery without calling undue attention to themselves. Redding quickly caught the public's ear, and he earned the sobriquet "Mr. Pitiful" for his sequence of heartfelt ballads: "Pain in My Heart" and "That's How Strong My Love Is." He was, at the same time, capable of a driving, vigorous attack, as in "Respect" and his cover version of the Rolling Stones' "Satisfaction." His hell-bent version of the British group's hit illustrated Redding's canny ability to transform others' material into his own voice, which he did masterfully with an old Tin Pan Alley standard, "Try a Little Tenderness." The manner in which the recording took the listener from a slow rendition of the chorus only to end with a ferociously vigorous recasting of the material was masterful and routinely brought audiences to their feet. In 1967 Redding was on the verge of claiming the mass audience as he had the black public when he appeared at the Monterey Pop Festival and captured the crowd of laid-back hippies with his calculated energy and the professional sheen of his stage act. Sadly, he died in December of that year in a plane crash. His biggest hit, the posthumous "(Sittin' on) The Dock of the Bay," tantalized listeners with the trajectory his career might have taken had fate not intervened.

James Brown

The height of the soul era in the 1960s saw the efflorescence of the career of James Brown (1933–), even though he had been having hits and making a mark in the black community since the early 1950s. Singles of his like "(Say It Loud) I'm Black and I'm Proud" (1968) gave musical expression to the unfulfilled yearnings in the urban ghetto for social as well as economic parity. So persuasive was his presence that when the inner cities lit up, community leaders called on Brown to allay the turmoil. However, even more influential was his dance material, which crossed over to the pop charts with regularity. Brown treated his troops of backup performers as if the whole band were a rhythm section, and, in the process, concocted a unique kind of percussive voice. Punctuating horn riffs, high-energy exhortations from the backup singers and chicken-scratch riffs from his guitars washed over a firm and undeniably effective set of bass figures and drum accents. Brown even used his very voice like a drum, weaving together words, screeches, and idiosyncratic expostulations that held a crowd hypnotized. He was known colloquially as the "hardest working man in show business," and his performances were tribal evocations of the fury of funk that few others could match. When DJs in the hip-hop community years later would ransack the recorded past for riffs and rhythms to form backup tracks, Brown's catalogue would be one of the most sampled in all of American music.

Concurrent in the 1960s with the electrification of southern music and the energetic solicitation of wider and wider audiences not drawn by the qualification of region alone, other forms of musical expression took a less aggressive path and found a small but exceedingly loyal public. One of the most fascinating in this regard was the reemergence of elderly blues musicians—most notably Son House, Mississippi John Hurt, and Skip James—whom young, white blues record collectors "found" in their home territories and brought back to the present-day public. Although the effort was not meant to be a kind of cultural exhumation, listeners drawn to these men wished to fix them, and their art, in time. Consequently, when these performers indicated an awareness of and fascination with mainstream pop material, their interests were deemed inauthentic, and they instead were flooded with requests to play material from their youth. Some were no longer able to marshal the drive or interest to do so, yet others illustrated that time cannot extinguish the fire of creativity. Son House, for example, is said to have had to be retaught songs he had not played in years, whereas Mississippi John Hurt seemed to possess a bottomless repository of tunes and limitless desire to share them with a new generation.

RECENT SOUTHERN POPULAR MUSIC

The impact of rock and roll on southern musicians again took a notable turn in the late 1960s and early 1970s with the ascendance of a group of bands collectively labeled "southern rock." They were diverse in format, however, despite the coincidence of their geographical origin. Lynyrd Skynyrd from Florida became arena-based favorites with long jam tunes like "Freebird," but also indicated a lyrical sensitivity with songs such as "Sweet Home Alabama," a caustic response to Neil Young's (1945–) accusatory "Southern Man." The Charlie Daniels Band of Tennessee played mainstream rock, but veered as well into polemical territory with "Still in Saigon." The most successful and influential group of this array was the Allman Brothers Band, founded by brothers Greg (1947–) and Duane (1946–1971), the latter a guitarist who gained a reputation playing numerous rhythm and blues sessions. Their instrumentally sophisticated long jams incorporated elements of blues, rock, jazz, and free-form improvisation into a satisfying brew that was, sadly, cut short by Duane's untimely death in a motorcycle accident in 1971.

Nashville in the 1970s and 1980s reflected the impact of other musical genres, in part through the incorporation of rock-style instrumentation, but even more so in its continuing efforts to accumulate the diverse audience institutionalized by the Nashville sound. This led, in part, to having numerous non-country artists releasing material with the genre's name affixed, like the pop stars John Denver (1943–1997) and Olivia Newton-John (1948–), as well as courting the mainstream through Hollywood affiliations with the success of the John Travolta vehicle *Urban Cowboy* (1980). Elements in the country community attempted to counter what they regarded as a dilution of the genre through a resurrection of the strong personal voice associated with Jimmie Rodgers and Hank Williams, most notably in the persons of Willie Nelson (1937–) and Waylon Jennings (1937–2002). Even RCA's attempt to capitalize on their efforts by labeling the endeavor the "outlaw" movement did not diminish the sequence of superior recordings these individuals released. Nor did it obliterate the influence of the kind of personalized and idiosyncratic songwriting from the likes of Kris Kristofferson (1936–) or Billy Joe Shavers (1939–) that found its way to Nashville.

The Miami Sound

In the 1970s, another regional music center, Miami, Florida, ascended in the public consciousness, particularly through the popularity of dance music, soon to become part of the disco explosion. One label in particular, T.K. Records, started by Henry Stone (1921–) in 1972, formed the seedbed of some of the most successful recordings from the region. Stone was a New Yorker bred in the fast-hustle environment of the independent musical entrepreneur. He worked for the West Coast–based Bihari brothers after World War II, then moved to Miami in 1947. While he occasionally dabbled in releasing his own product, such as some of the first sides by Ray Charles cut in 1951, he more often created material that he sold to more established concerns. These include the 1971 tribute to feminine self-assertion by Betty Wright (1953–), "Clean-Up Woman," put out by Atlantic's subdivision, Alston Records. While the company had hits on the R & B charts, it conquered the mainstream with the release in 1975 of "Get Down Tonight" by K.C. and the Sunshine Band, led by Harry Wayne Casey (1951–) and Rick Finch (1954–), who had both been contract employees at the company. Their simple but rock-steady groove took off with the phenomenon of disco, and Stone catered to the fever by offering all his dance material on twelve-inch vinyl, whose superior dynamics and rich bass tones captivated DJs. While T.K. rode the crest of the disco wave, it crashed and expired when the vogue extinguished, closing its doors in 1981.

Other artists triumphed in Miami. The vibrant Cuban community saw one of its own, Gloria Estefan (1957–), merge the island's syncopations with the commercial rhythms of salsa music. She joined a local wedding band led by her husband-to-be, Emilio Estefan, and they eventually released their first Spanish-language LP in 1979. The couple caught the ear of non-Latin audiences with "Dr. Beat" in 1984, then increased their fan base exponentially with their first English-language release, *Primitive Love*, the following year. It included three Top Ten hits, which was exceeded by the four contained on 1988's *Let It Loose*, including "The Rhythm Is Gonna Get You." Estefan has gone on to become the most successful crossover artist in Latin music, with an international sales mark of over 50 million units. Another Miami-based group that achieved acclaim as rap became the most successful genre in the commercial sphere was the notorious 2 Live Crew. Led by Luther Campbell (196?–), the quartet assembled in 1987 and clinched a short-lived but fervent hold on the public by combining simple, even at times infantile, beats with equally simple-to-follow lyrics that routinely incorporated a strong strain of misogyny and a heavy dose of blue language. Public officials took them on in high-stakes pornography trials more than once, yet the group made their most long-standing artistic and legal mark by winning a case against the estate of Roy Orbison in 1994. Their satire of the singer's "Oh, Pretty Woman" certified that the literary mode could stand up in court as a justifiable form of expression in popular music, even when civil libertarians felt that the material was more valuable as a test case of principles than as the embodiment of poetic skill.

Progressive Rock, Blues, and Country

The special character of music that emerges from and speaks about the South as a region often was lost in the ascendance of mainstream music industry in the 1980s and 1990s with its emphasis on superstars, million-sellers, and mass market expectations. At the same time, pockets of the South continued to encourage out-of-the-ordinary efforts by venturesome musicians or the continuation of earlier formats that had lost their hold on the record charts. In the former case, the college town of Athens, Georgia, became a hotbed for alternative rock in the 1980s. Bands like R.E.M. and the B-52s first made their mark on college radio and the club circuit, and eventually secured major record deals and mainstream success without, for the most part, losing touch with their roots. In the latter case, both old-school rhythm and blues and hard-core blues retained a position in the marketplace through the efforts of, respectively, independent labels like Mississippi's Malaco and Fat Possum. Their owners recognized that a small but loyal audience retained an affection for artists that the national public ignored. Malaco, for instance, had a million-seller in Z. Z. Hill's (1935–1984) *Down Home Blues* (1984), and Fat Possum caught the ear of younger audiences eager to encounter what they considered authentic expression with the stripped-down but evocative hill country drone of blues played by Junior Kimborough (1930–1998) and R. L. Burnside (1926–   ). Some may have disapproved of the phenomenon of illiterate black men in their seventies and older playing rock clubs to the cheers of college crowds who encouraged them to remain as down and dirty as possible, while others believed such efforts kept the genre healthy if not vigorous.

Nashville in the 1990s by and large took an opposite approach, continuing to appeal to the mainstream crossover audience by once again downplaying much of what some listeners felt was endemic to country. In the process, the million-selling Garth Brooks (1962–   ) and Shania Twain (1965–   ), for example, became international stars, both of whom incorporated plentiful elements of rock in their presentation. Many frowned even more vigorously when a song like Billy Ray Cyrus' "Achy Breaky Heart" (1961–   ) seemed a calculated attempt to bring the genre onto the dance floor with its infectious and audience-friendly chorus. Still others continued to espouse the values of hard-core country sentiments, even if the charts and the corporate offices seemed to pay them little attention. The Americana movement, in particular, sought to combine personally styled songwriting with country instrumentation and feel, and, in the process, groups like Wilco retained a fervent, if limited, audience.

CONCLUSION

In the early twenty-first century, interest in and commercial acceptance of the full range of southern music continue apace. Earlier antagonisms bred of regional pride as well as a recalcitrance to accept local custom and practice have fallen away. If nothing else, it is undeniable that over the last twenty-five years, population and financial power have shifted southward to the Sun Belt. In the process, the South has become not simply the source of American musical culture, but its financial and political bedrock. That rabid growth and rise to prominence have changed the constitution of the local population. Many current residents of the region are not natives, yet acclimate themselves to the customs driven by time and tradition. A sufficient body of musical culture has accumulated over the course of this transition that it comes as no surprise that organizations and institutions have engaged in the celebration—some might argue calcification—of the historical record of the region's musical history. The country music community was one of the first to do so, when, concurrent with the formation of the Country Music Association, they instituted the Country Music Foundation. Since 1960 it has documented, preserved, and disseminated information about and material germane to the wealth of country music. More recently, the city of Memphis, in conjunction with the Smithsonian, opened the Memphis Rock and Soul Museum illustrating the history of the city's musical wealth in the context of national patterns of growth and development. And, even more recently, forces connected to the now-defunct Stax label opened a museum and foundation on the site of the original studios and offices. Memphis also has paid tribute to the blues for twenty-five years through the auspices of the Blues Foundation and the annual ceremony of the Handy Awards for the best in blues music. Additional awards

Jazz performers in Preservation Hall, New Orleans, Louisiana. Courtesy Louisiana Office of Tourism.

and honors are given to regional artists by the federal government as well as the Rock and Roll Hall of Fame, the Country Music Hall of Fame, and the Rhythm and Blues Foundation, among others.

Southern music is not a thing of the past. It flourishes all around us, and new recordings indicate its health as well as its ongoing diversity. One case in point is the unexpected success of the soundtrack for the Coen Brothers' *O Brother, Where Art Thou?* (2001), spearheaded by T. Bone Burnett (1945–). The story is set in the 1930s, and the material assembled by Burnett evokes the period by mixing gospel choruses, string band songs, Delta blues, and a capella mountain classics. The acoustically performed and technologically unadulterated sound that resulted captivated more than 6 million buyers and won the collection several Grammy Awards. It also brought back to public visibility one of the venerated proponents of the high lonesome sound, Ralph Stanley (1928–), whose unaccompanied rendition of the classic "O, Death" remains a standout. If Burnett's efforts did not lead to a wholesale conversion by the recording industry to the kind of back-to-basics sound he espoused, it reminded one nonetheless that audiences can make unexpected consumer choices in eager pursuit of what they conceive of as novelty.

A second example is the ambitious release by the Drive-By Truckers of *Southern Rock Opera* in 2002, illustrating how both instrumental ferocity and lyrical thoughtfulness can combine in a genre not always known for its ambitiousness or calculated self-consciousness. The material is dedicated to Lynyrd Skynyrd, whose near-wholesale demise in a plane crash is hauntingly evoked in the final track, "Angels and Fuselage." It incorporates as well a song that castigates the late George Wallace (1919–1998) for his appeals to racist sentiments, but nowhere else on this expansive two-CD effort does the group simplify the complexity of the region's beliefs or prejudices. The material remains focused on what they call the "duality of the southern thing": its capacity for both the best and worst of human nature. As the final, repeating chords of the last track evoke the tragedy and beauty in the loss of several of the South's most gifted musical sons, the Drive-By Truckers remind one that southern music can demand the whole of our understanding as effectively as anything produced since Thomas Edison first enabled notes and voices to be preserved for the course of time.

RESOURCE GUIDE

Printed Sources

Blackface

Cockerell, Dale. *Demons of Disorder: Early Blackface Minstrels and Their World*. Cambridge: Cambridge University Press, 1996.

Emerson, Ken. *Doo-dah! Stephen Foster and the Rise of American Popular Culture*. New York: Simon and Schuster, 1997.

Lhamon W. T., Jr. *Raising Cain: Blackface Performance from Jim Crow to Hip Hop*. Cambridge, MA: Harvard University Press, 1998.

Lott, Eric. *Love and Theft: Blackface Minstrelsy and the American Working Class*. New York: Oxford Universy Press, 1995.

Russell, Tony. *Blacks, Whites and Blues*. New York: Stein and Day, 1970.

Sacks, Howard L., and Judith Rose Sacks. *Way Up North in Dixie: A Black Family's Claim to a Confederate Anthem*. Washington, DC: Smithsonian Institution Press, 1993.

Toll, Robert. *Blacking Up: The Minstrel Show in Nineteenth Century America*. New York: Oxford University Press, 1974.

Bluegrass

Cantwell, Robert. *Bluegrass Breakdown: The Making of the Old Southern Sound*. New York: Da Capo Press, 1992.

Rosenberg, Neil. *Bluegrass: A History*. Urbana: University of Illinois Press, 1993.

Blues

Barlow, William. *Looking Up at Down: The Emergence of Blues Culture*. Philadelphia: Temple University Press, 1989.

Charters, Sam. *The Blues Makers*. New York: Da Capo Press, 1991.

———. *The Country Blues*. New York: Rinehart, 1959.

Cohn, Lawrence, ed. *Nothing but the Blues: The Music and the Musicians*. New York: Abbeville, 1993.

Davis, Francis. *The History of the Blues: The Roots, the Music, the People from Charley Patton to Robert Cray*. New York: Hyperion, 1995.

Dixon, Robert M.W., and John Godrich. *Recording the Blues*. New York: Stein and Day, 1970.

Evans, David. *Big Road Blues: Tradition and Creativity in the Folk Blues*. New York: Da Capo Press, 1982.

Guralnick, Robert. *Searching for Robert Johnson*. New York: Dutton, 1989.

Handy, W. C. *Father of the Blues*. New York: Da Capo Press, 1991.

Jones, LeRoi. *Blues People*. New York: Morrow, 1963.

Lomax, Alan. *The Land Where Blues Was Born*. New York: Pantheon, 1993.

Murray, Albert. *Stomping the Blues*. Twenty-fifth anniversary ed. New York: Da Capo Press, 2000.

Oliver, Paul. *Blues off the Record: Thirty Years of Blues Commentary*. New York: Da Capo Press, 1988.

———. *Songsters and Saints: Vocal Traditions on Race Records*. Cambridge: Cambridge University Press, 1984.

———. *The Story of the Blues*. New York: Chilton, 1969.

Palmer, Robert. *Deep Blues*. New York: Viking, 1981.

Titon, Jeffrey Todd. *Early Downhome Blues*. Urbana: University of Illinois Press, 1977.

Wald, Elijah. *Escaping the Delta: Robert Johnson and the Invention of the Blues*. New York: Amistad, 2004.

Wolfe, Charles, and Kip Lornell. *The Life and Legend of Leadbelly*. New York: Harper, 1994.

Cajun-Zydeco and Swamp Pop

Bernard, Shane K. *Swamp Pop: Cajun and Creole Rhythm and Blues*. Jackson: University Press of Mississippi, 1996.

Broven, John. *South to Louisiana: The Music of the Cajun Bayous*. London: Pelican, 1983.

Stivale, Charles. *Disenchanting les Bon Temps: Identity and Authenticity in Cajun Music and Dance*. Durham, NC: Duke University Press, 2003.

Tisserand, Michael. *The Kingdom of Zydeco*. New York: Arcade, 1998.

Country

Country Music Foundation. *Country: The Music and the Musicians. Pickers, Slickers, Cheatin' Hearts and Superstars*. New York: Abbeville, 1988.

Malone, Bill C. *Country Music U.S.A.* Rev. ed. Austin: University of Texas Press, 1985.

Peterson, Richard. *Creating Country Music: Fabricating Authenticity*. Chicago: University of Chicago Press, 1997.

Tichi, Cecilia. *High Lonesome: The American Culture of Country Music*. Chapel Hill: University of North Carolina Press, 1994.

Tosches, Nick. *Country: The Twisted Roots of Rock 'n' Roll*. New York: Da Capo Press, 1996.

Wolfe, Charles. *A Good-Natured Riot: The Birth of the Grand Ole Opry*. Nashville: Country Music Foundation Press and Vanderbilt University Press, 1999.

Zwonitzer, Mark, and Charles Hirshberg. *Will You Miss Me When I'm Gone? The Carter Family and Their Legacy in American Music*. New York: Simon and Schuster, 2002.

Folk

Bluestein, Gene. *Poplore: Folk and Pop and American Culture*. Amherst: University of Massachusetts Press, 1994.

Cantwell, Robert. *When We Were Good: The Folk Revival*. Cambridge, MA: Harvard University Press, 1996.

Filene, Benjamin. *Romancing the Folk: Public Memory and American Roots Music*. Chapel Hill: University of North Carolina Press, 2000.

Whisnant, David. *All That Is Native and Fine: The Politics of Culture in an American Region*. Chapel Hill: University of North Carolina Press, 1983.

General

Applebome, Peter. *Dixie Rising: How the South Is Shaping American Values, Politics and Culture*. New York: Harcourt, Brace, 1997.

Cobb, James C. *Redefining Southern Culture: Mind and Identity in the Modern South*. Athens: University of Georgia Press, 1999.

Hamm, Charles. *Yesterdays: Popular Music in America*. New York: W. W. Norton, 1979.

Levine, Lawrence W. *Black Culture and Black Consciousness: Afro-American Folk Thought from Slavery to Freedom*. New York: Oxford University Press, 1977.

Lowe, Allen. *American Pop from Minstrel to Mojo: On Record 1893–1956*. Redwood, NY: Cadence Jazz Books, 1997.

Malone, Bill C. *Singing Cowboys and Musical Mountaineers: Southern Culture and Country Music*. Athens: University of Georgia Press, 1993.

———, and David Stricklin. *Southern Music/American Music*. Rev. and expanded ed. Lexington: University Press of Kentucky, 2003.

Gospel

Goff, James. *Woke Me Up This Morning: Black Gospel Singers and the Gospel Life*. Jackson: University Press of Mississippi, 1997.

Harris, Michael W. *Rise of Gospel Blues: The Music of Thomas Andrew Dorsey in the Urban Church*. New York: Oxford University Press, 1992.

Heilbut, Anthony. *The Gospel Sound: Good News and Bad Times*. New York: Simon and Schuster, 1971.

Reagon, Bernice Johnson, ed. *We'll Understand It Better By and By*. Washington, DC: Smithsonian Institution Press, 1992.

Jazz

Armstrong, Louis. *Satchmo: My Life in New Orleans*. New York: Prentice-Hall, 1954.

Charters, Sam. *Jazz New Orleans 1885–1963*. New York: Oak Publications, 1963.

Foster, Pops, as told to Tom Stoddard. *Pops Foster: The Autobiography of a New Orleans Jazzman*. Berkeley: University of California Press, 1971.

Hadlock, Richard. *Jazz Masters of the Twenties*. New York: Da Capo Press, 1988.

Marquis, Don. *In Search of Buddy Bolden: First Man of Jazz*. Baton Rouge: Louisiana State University Press, 1978.

Schuller, Gunther. *Early Jazz: Its Roots and Musical Development*. New York: Oxford University Press, 1989.

Turner, Frederick. *Remembering Song: Encounters with the New Orleans Jazz Tradition*. New York: Da Capo Press, 1994.

Memphis

Bowman, Rob. *Soulsville U.S.A.: The Story of Stax Records*. New York: Schirmer Books, 1997.

Escott, Colin, and Martin Hawkins. *Good Rockin' Tonight: Sun Records and the Birth of Rock 'n' Roll*. New York: St. Martin's Press, 1991.

Gordon, Robert. *It Came from Memphis*. Boston: Faber and Faber, 1995.

New Orleans

Berry, Jason, Jonathan Foose, and Tad Jones. *Up From the Cradle of Jazz: New Orleans Music since World War II*. New York: Da Capo Press, 1992.

Broven, John. *Walking to New Orleans: The Story of New Orleans Rhythm and Blues*. Gretna, LA: Pelican Press, 1974.

Rock

DeCurtis, Anthony, and James Henke, with Holly George-Warren, eds. *The Rolling Stone Illustrated History of Rock and Roll*. New York: Random House, 1992.

Gillett, Charlie. *The Sound of the City: The Rise of Rock and Roll*. New York: Pantheon, 1983.

Palmer, Robert. *Rock and Roll: An Unruly History*. New York: Harmony Books, 1995.

Rhythm and Blues

George, Nelson. *The Death of Rhythm and Blues.* New York: Pantheon, 1988.

Guralnick, Peter. *Sweet Soul Music: Rhythm and Blues and the Southern Dream of Freedom.* New York: Harper and Row, 1986.

Hirshey, Gerri. *Nowhere to Run: The Story of Soul Music.* New York: Times Books, 1984.

Hoskyns, Barney. *Say It One Time for the Broken-Hearted: Country Soul in the American South.* London: Bloomsbury, 1998.

Shaw, Arnold. *Honkers and Shouters: The Golden Years of Rhythm and Blues.* New York: Macmillan, 1978.

Ward, Brian. *Just My Soul Responding: Rhythm and Blues, Black Consciousness, and Race Relations.* Berkeley: University of California Press, 1998.

Recordings

Allman Brothers Band. *Filmore East Concerts.* Deluxe Edition. Polydor, 1997.

Arnold, Eddy. *Ultimate Eddy Arnold.* BMG Heritage, 2003.

B-52s. *Nude on the Moon.* Rhino, 2002.

Bernard, Rod. *Swamp Pop Rock & Roller.* Ace, 1986.

Boggs, Dock. *Complete Early Recordings 1927–29.* Revenant, 1997.

Booker, James. *New Orleans Piano Wizard Live.* Rounder, 1977.

Booker T & the MGs. *The Essential.* Rhino, 2002.

Brooks, Garth. *The Hits.* Liberty, 1994.

Brown, James. *Showtime.* Polydor, 1991.

Buckwheat Zydeco. *Ultimate Collection.* Hip-O, 2000.

Burnside, R. L. *Too Bad Jim.* Fat Possum, 1991.

Carr, Leroy. *Whisky Is My Habit, Women Is All I Crave.* Sony Legacy, 2004.

Carter Family. *In the Shadow of Clinch Mountain.* Bear Family, 2000.

Cash, Johnny. *American Recordings.* Sony, 1994.

———. *The Essential Johnny Cash 1955–83.* Sony Legacy, 1992.

Chavis, Boozoo. *The Lake Charles Atom Bomb.* Rounder, 1990.

Chenier, Clifton. *Zydeco Dynamite.* Rhino, 1993.

Cline, Patsy. *Ultimate Collection.* MCA International, 1998.

Cookie & the Cupcakes. *Kings of Swamp Pop.* Ace, 1997.

Daniels, Charlie. *A Decade of Hits.* Epic Legacy, 1983.

Dorsey, Lee. *Wheelin' and Dealin': The Ultimate Collection.* Arista, 1997.

Drive-By-Truckers. *Southern Rock Opera.* SDR, 2001.

Estefan, Gloria. *Let It Loose.* Epic, 1988.

Flatt & Scruggs. *The Complete Mercury Sessions.* Mercury, 1992.

———. *'Tis Too Sweet to Be Remembered: The Essential Flatt & Scruggs.* Sony Legacy, 1997.

Floyd, Eddie. *Knock on Wood. The Best of Eddie Floyd.* Atlantic, 1997.

Golden Gate Quartet. *Travelin' Shoes.* Bluebird/RCA, 1992.

Gordon, Rosco. *Just a Little Bit: Very Best of Rosco Gordon.* Collectibles, 2001.

Green, Al. *Absolute Best.* Right Stuff, 2004.

Harpo, Slim. *Excello Singles Anthology.* Hip-O, 2003.

Hayes, Isaac. *Man! The Ultimate Isaac Hayes 1969–77.* Stax, 2001.

Hill, Z. Z. *Down Home Blues.* Malaco, 1982.

House, Son. *Father of Delta Blues: The Complete 1965 Sessions.* Sony Legacy, 1992.

Howlin' Wolf. *His Best, Volumes 1 & 2.* Chess-MCA, 1997, 1999.

Hurt, Mississippi John. *Avalon Blues. The Complete 1928 Okeh Sessions.* Sony Legacy, 1996.

———. *Complete Studio Recordings.* Vanguard, 2000.

Jackson, Mahalia. *Gospel, Spirituals and Hymns.* Sony Legacy, 1991.

Jennings, Waylon. *Only Daddy That'll Walk the Line RCA Years*. RCA, 1993.

Johnson, Blind Willie. *Dark Was the Night*. Sony Legacy, 1998.

Johnson, Lonnie. *Steppin' on the Blues*. Sony Legacy, 1990.

Johnson, Robert. *King of the Delta Blues*. Sony Legacy, 1997.

Kimbrough, Junior. *All Night Long*. Fat Possum, 1992.

King, B. B. *Anthology*. MCA, 2000.

Kristofferson, Kris. *Essential Kris Kristofferson*. Sony Legacy, 2004.

Lazy Lester. *I Hear You Knockin'*. Excello, 1994.

Leadbelly. *King of the 12-String Guitar*. Sony Legacy, 1991.

———. *Where Did You Go Last Night?* Smithsonian Folkways, 1996.

Lewis, Jerry Lee. *All Killer No Filler*. Rhino, 1993.

Lewis, Smiley. *I Hear You Knockin': The Best of Smiley Lewis*. Capitol, 1992.

Little Milton. *Greatest Hits*. Chess-MCA, 1997.

Lomax, Alan. *Alan Lomax Sampler*. Rounder, 1997.

Lonesome Sundown. *I'm a Mojo Man*. Excello, 1995.

Lynyrd Skynyrd. *30th Anniversary Collection*. MTV, 2003.

Macon, Uncle Dave. *Classic Sides 1924–38*. JSP, 2004.

Miller, Emmett. *Minstrel Man from Georgia*. Sony Legacy, 1996.

Monroe, Bill. *The Essential Bill Monroe 1945–49*. Sony legacy, 1996.

———. *Very Best*. MCA, 2002.

Nelson, Willie. *Nite Life. Greatest Hits & Rare Tracks 1959–71*. Rhino, 1989.

———. *Revolution in Time: The Journey 1973–93*. Sony Legacy, 1995.

Neville Brothers. *Treacherous: A History of the Neville Brothers*. Rhino, 1986.

Orbison, Roy. *All Time Greatest Hits*. DCC, 1997.

Original Dixieland Jazz Band. *75th Anniversary*. RCA/Bluebird, 1992.

Parker, Junior. *Backtracking. Duke Recordings, Vol. 2*. MCA, 1998.

———. *Junior's Blues. Duke Recordings, Vol. 1*. MCA, 1992.

Patton, Charlie. *Screamin' and Hollerin' the Blues*. Revenant, 2000.

Perkins, Carl. *Original Sun Greatest Hits*. Rhino, 1986.

Presley, Elvis. *Complete Sun Sessions*. RCA, 1987.

———. *Essential Collection*. RCA, 1988.

Price, Lloyd. *Greatest Hits: Original ABC Recordings*. MCA, 1994.

Professor Longhair. *Fess: The Professor Longhair Anthology*. Rhino, 1993.

Redding, Otis. *The Otis Redding Story*. Rhino, 1993.

Reeves, Jim. *Anthology*. BMG, 2003.

R.E.M. *Best of R.E.M.* EMI, 1998.

———. *In Time 1988–2003*. Warner Brothers, 2003.

Rockin' Sidney. *My Toot Toot*. Ace, 1986.

Rodgers, Jimmie. *The Singing Brakeman*. Bear Family, 1992.

Shaver, Billy Joe. *Restless Wind: Legendary Billie Joe Shaver, 1973–97*. Razor & Tie, 1995.

Smith, Bessie. *The Essential Bessie Smith*. Sony Legacy, 1997.

Stanley, Ralph. *Saturday Night and Sunday Morning*. Freeland, 1998.

Tampa Red. *Complete Bluebird Recordings 1934–38*. BMG-Bluebird, 1997.

Thomas, Carla. *Gee Whiz! Greatest Hits*. Rhino, 1997.

Thomas, Henry. *Texas Worried Blues: Complete Recordings 1927–29*. Yazoo, 1989.

Thomas, Irma. *Sweet Soul Queen of New Orleans*. Razor & Tie, 1996.

Thomas, Rufus. *Do the Funky Somethin': Best of Rufus Thomas*. Rhino, 1996.

Twain, Shania. *Gone on Over*. Mercury, 1997.

2 Live Crew. *As Nasty as They Wanna Be*. Atlantic, 1989.

Waters, Muddy. *His Best 1947–55, 1956–64*. Chess/MCA, 1997.

Various Artists

Another Saturday Night. Ace, 1990.
Anthology of American Folk Music. Smithsonian Folkways, 2000.
Bristol Sessions. Country Music Foundation, 1991.
Get Down Tonight: Best of TK Records. Rhino, 1990.
O Brother, Where Art Thou? Mercury, 2000.
White Country Blues 1926–38. Sony Legacy, 1993.

RELIGION

Paul Harvey

In Thomasville, Georgia, in the mid-1990s, a young white woman named Jaime L. Wireman gave birth to a child she named Whitney, after the contemporary black singer Whitney Houston. Wireman's husband, an African American man named Jeffrey Johnson, worked odd jobs locally, and the two lived together in a trailer just outside the southwest Georgia town. The child, born with a skull not fully formed, died after just nineteen hours. Jaime Wireman wanted the baby to be buried with her maternal grandfather in the cemetery of the Barnetts Creek Baptist Church. After her burial, however, deacons of the church, who had not known previously that the father was black, asked the family to remove the child from the historically all-white cemetery. When the embarrassing incident came to light, church members criticized the deacons' action and permitted the child to remain buried in the cemetery. With some prodding from Whitney's maternal grandmother, the deacons and the pastor of the church met the family, apologized for their actions, and asked for forgiveness. "Our church family humbly asks you to accept our apology," the chairman of the board of deacons told the family. "I believe people are sorry," the child's grandmother concluded. "She was just a baby."

This story set in the contemporary South allegorically retells familiar themes of southern history: racial intermingling and separation, exclusion and segregation, sin, forgiveness, and an ambiguous healing. Racial division runs headlong into biracial sex and an innocent childhood disrupted by the intrusion of an unjust social world. The culmination, on the face of it, brings healing. Just as importantly, the story puts into relief a paradox of southern, and American, religious history: namely, the deep contradiction between human spiritual equality in the eyes of God and divinely ordained social inequality in the everyday world. Nowhere has this painful paradox been so evident as in the American South, where American Christianity may be seen simultaneously at its most tragic and its most triumphant. Speaking of her own experience, Lillian Smith said of this paradox, "I, myself, being a Deep South white, reared in a religious home and the Methodist church realize the deep ties of common songs, common prayer, common symbols that bind our two races together on a religio-mystical level, even as another brutally mythic idea, the concept of White Supremacy, tears our two people apart."

The South still commonly appears as the land of the Bible Belt, of evangelical Protestant hegemony. Despite the rapidly increasing immigration from all parts of the world to the region, there is still justification for such a view. Stereotypes are sometimes true. Scholarship in southern religious history, including titles such as *At Ease in Zion* and *Churches in Cultural Captivity*, furthers this seemingly timeless image of the "God-haunted" South, here referred to as the evangelical belt. The prevalence of southern accents on the airwaves of televangelism cements this image in the public mind. To study religion in the South, then, is to examine the influence of a dominant evangelical culture that has shaped the region's social mores, cultural forms, charged racial interactions, and political practices. In no other widely dispersed region, save for the Mormon regions of the Rocky Mountain West, does one family of religious belief and expression hold such sway over so many people and throughout such a large area. The biracial nature of evangelicalism in the South, as well, lends it a distinctive history and culture that alternately puzzles, repulses, and fascinates outsiders.

Cultural modernists since the twentieth century have attributed many of the problems of the South to what they have seen as the region's behaviorally repressive, socially racist, and intellectually restrictive Protestant culture. In the 1920s H. L. Mencken slammed the South as "a cesspool of Baptists, a miasma of Methodism, snake-charmers, phony real-estate operators, and syphilitic evangelists." In the 1930s John Dollard's *Caste and Class in a Southern Town* (1937) underscored how southern churches reinforced the caste system of the region. In his 1941 classic, *The Mind of the South*, Wilbur J. Cash said that there was no mind of the South but only a temperament torn between a "hell-of-a-fellow" sociability and a primitive religious fundamentalism, a tension that built up and periodically exploded like an August thunderstorm.

In recent years, however, the South has undergone a renaissance. With it has come a revitalized scholarship, largely freed of older defensiveness and denominational hagiography on the one hand, and academic iconoclasm on the other. In the 1960s and 1970s, an initial burst of interest in southern religious history, spurred on by both the civil rights movement and the resistance to it, established the field. Works by scholars such as Samuel S. Hill, Jr., John B. Boles, and Donald G. Mathews ushered in an era of serious historical inquiry that continues today. Meanwhile, the burgeoning field of slavery studies produced classics in the study of antebellum southern religion, most notably Eugene D. Genovese's provocative and brilliant *Roll, Jordan, Roll* and Albert J. Raboteau's synthetic *Slave Religion: The "Invisible Institution" in the Antebellum South*. Most recently, Christine Leigh Heyrman's suggestive and artfully written *Southern Cross: The Beginnings of the Bible Belt*, focusing on the early days of southern evangelicals and their accommodation to the moral reality of a patriarchal slave society, shows how much can still be gleaned from rereading the sources with a fresh set of questions.

If religion in the Old South has become a mature field of study, scholarship on the era since the Civil War is still, relatively speaking, in its adolescence. Numerous questions remain open. For example, women's historians seeking to understand social reform in the South repeatedly have discovered religion at the center of it.

In the process, they have added significantly to the body of literature on southern religion, even though many of the studies are not focused on religion per se. Some important areas, such as the history of southern Pentecostalism, cry out for more research. There is hardly any substantial scholarship on some key figures, such as Charles Harrison Mason, founder of the Memphis-based black Pentecostal Church of God in Christ. Some topics (such as Appalachian Mountain religious expression) have drawn the attention of anthropologists but not often of historians. We also lack a general study that serves as the equivalent of Donald Mathews' *Religion in the Old South*; however, the impact of a new generation of scholarship and the recent establishment of the *Journal of Southern Religion* (one of the first of a growing number of wholly online journals, with the permanent Web address http://purl.org/jsr) should provide a secure scholarly future.

HISTORICAL BACKGROUND

Any discussion of southern religion must begin with the landmark works of Samuel S. Hill, Jr., whose 1967 *Southern Churches in Crisis* and subsequent books, including *Religion in the Solid South* (1972) and *The South and the North in American Religion* (1980), have defined the field. If historians, as the cliché goes, are divided into lumpers and splitters, Hill is a classic "lumper." That is, Hill's original work concerned itself not with variety and diversity within a tradition so much as with what unites the tradition, what made southern religion *southern*. Focusing almost exclusively on whites, *Southern Churches in Crisis* defined the archetypal "culture-religion" of southern Christianity, one more experiential and emotional, less doctrinal and intellectual than religion outside the region. Southern orthodoxy, according to Hill, sees individual conversion (rather than social reform or any larger purpose) as the central role of religious institutions—an argument later dubbed the "conversionist paradigm." Southern believers historically have seen their own region as a Zion, set apart from the secularizing currents of the rest of the country, and thus more pure, more godly. Thus, southern believers have been "otherworldly" even while theologically defending the southern status quo. *Southern Churches in Crisis* evinced considerable skepticism about whether there were any forces that could break the stranglehold of the insular nature of southern belief patterns.

The irony, of course, is that it was New England, not the South, that was the Bible Belt of early America. The South, by contrast, was known for Deism among intellectuals such as Thomas Jefferson, high-church Anglicanism among white planters, rabble-rousing in the backcountry among Scots-Irish folk famously indifferent or hostile to organized religion of any kind, enslaved people whose religious views appeared to whites to be largely inscrutable and unknowable, and Native American in dozens of religious groupings varying by geography and tribal groupings.

Native American religious history in the South is relatively "invisible." Without a major proselytizing and recording group such as the Jesuits were among the Iroquois in upstate New York and Canada, or as the Franciscans were in the region that became the American Southwest, southern Native Americans have not often received the same scholarly or popular attention. And the sheer bewildering variety of Native American religions in the South and elsewhere makes it difficult

Native American dancers, Grand Village of the Natchez Indians. Courtesy Mississippi Development Authority/Division of Tourism.

to issue generalizations beyond the most banal. Thus, in studies of southern religion (including this one) that emphasize the interaction of white and black Christian belief and practice, Native American religion is not often considered; it just seems to be a subject filed under a different category.

What is perhaps most important to note here is the crucial role of Native Americans in a number of the key episodes of southern history. Scholars now see the mythology of Virginia white men, the chief Powahatan, and the young Indian girl Pocohantas as part of Native American ceremonial traditions in which others were adopted into tribes—in this case, Pocohantas' famous action being a sort of prescribed role among Native Americans in the region. Later, African American runaways teamed with the Seminoles in Florida to constitute formidable guerilla forces which frightened whites and led to a beefed-up military presence in the Southeast (and led to significant syncretic faiths which married African and native practices and beliefs). In the nineteenth century, the wars over lands in Alabama and Georgia often pitted native against native, as Christianized Indians who had economic relationships with whites tended to ally with or marry white traders, while other tribal factions sought a renewal of Native American religious life precisely through war against the white invaders. Christian missionaries worked extensively with southeastern Native Americans, especially the Cherokees, and left their mark in converts who married Native American religious custom to Protestant belief structures. Some missionaries took up the cause of the Native Americans against the Jacksonian policy of ethnic cleansing, taking their case to the Supreme Court (leading Andrew Jackson to challenge the Chief Justice to enforce the law that he had just ostensibly made). Later, after the massive forced migrations of southeastern Native Americans to the nether regions of Oklahoma, missionaries continued their work, leaving large and now thriving Christian communities among Native Americans in those areas.

If in the eighteenth century one were to predict where the term "Bible Belt" would be applied in the twentieth and twenty-first, the historic South would have been a guess laughed out of the conversation. Just how the South gained its distinctive religious character has been a historical puzzle that the last generation of historians has tried to piece together.

The Southern Evangelicals' Accomplishments

It was the great accomplishment of nineteenth- and twentieth-century southern evangelicals to have so radically transformed the South's religiosity from indifference to intensity, a feat of proselytization analyzed by historians such as John Boles (*The Great Revival*), Donald Mathews (*Religion in the Old South*), Randy Sparks (*Religion in Mississippi*), Lynn Lyerly (*Methodism and the Southern Mind*), Rhys Isaac (*The Transformation of Virginia, 1740–1790*), Mechal Sobel (*Trabelin' On: The Slave Journey to an Afro-Baptist Faith*), Albert Raboteau (*Slave Religion: The "Invisible Institution" in the Antebellum South*), and Christine Heyrman (*Southern Cross: The Beginnings of the Bible Belt*). The story these scholars tell is complex and, in some measure, contested. It is intimately bound up with the rise of a slaveholding republic, the national Second Great Awakening, the coming of "civilization" to the rustic southern backcountry and newly opening states of the Deep South, the innovative methods (such as circuit-riding preachers and mass-produced pamphlet literature) employed by the newly rising evangelical denominations, and the concerted (and partially successful) effort to evangelize among enslaved people.

Counterbalancing this rise of southern evangelicalism was a masculine culture of honor that prized self-assertion and devalued shame in inverse proportion to the way evangelicals valorized shame of one's sin and distrusted the self (a theme discussed with illuminating insight in Ted Ownby's *Subduing Satan: Religion, Recreation, and Manhood in the Rural South, 1865–1920*). That was a major obstacle for the evangelicals. Christine Heyrman's prize-winning study *Southern Cross* is especially innovative in its emphasis on how evangelical preachers aligned themselves with women in the household and gradually insinuated themselves into southern life, despite the suspicion and hostility they often encountered from male patriarchs. Gradually, enough men came to accept the message and to support missionaries (such as the wealthy planter in Liberty County, Georgia, Charles Colcock Jones) who evangelized among the slaves. Antebellum white evangelicals considered themselves faithful purveyors of the gospel message to a people bound down by heathenism and barbarism.

Southern Christianity and Enslaved Americans

The uses enslaved people made of Christianity, of course, differed radically from the plans of the planters and missionaries. In the late eighteenth century, a brief moment of opportunity for a biracial religious order seemed to present itself. Whites and blacks in backcountry congregations worshipped together. They called each other by the respectful evangelical titles "brother" and "sister" and wept to each other's exhortations. Some ministers declared slavery to be a sin, freed their own slaves, and advocated lifting restrictions on black men who wished to preach the gospel in public.

But this moment was illusory. It quickly became evident that whites valued the blossoming of their evangelical institutions and would make the necessary moral accommodations to achieve that. As Virginians and Marylanders had established as early as the 1660s, freedom from the bondage of sin did not equal freedom from human bondage. Despite the presence of the occasional odd antislavery southern divine, white southern Christians erected a wall of separation between the realms of spiritual and temporal equality. By the 1830s, especially after Nat Turner's uprising in 1831, white evangelicals who previously had questioned slavery were defending it as a divinely sanctioned social order. In South Carolina, where few whites challenged the peculiar institution even during the revolutionary era, Baptists in the early nineteenth century worked feverishly on a Christian proslavery apologetic, even making trips to the North to debate abolitionists. Southern evangelical intellectuals argued that God sanctioned American slavery to bring the Christian message to heathen Africans and teach superior peoples to care for the inferiors entrusted to them. God watched over humanity; husbands provided for and protected wives and children and received obedience and respect in return; masters provided for and protected slaves and demanded obedience. By the 1850s such a view reigned as a virtually unchallenged orthodoxy among white southern evangelicals, be they elite divines or folk exhorters.

Enslaved Christians found in African American evangelicalism a faith that provided many with the sustenance to fight off the worst psychological abuses perpetrated by whites. But black Christianity in the antebellum era empowered few slaves in any overt political way. It rarely intended to do so. When Nat Turner, the well-known slave rebel and Baptist messianist, was asked by his lawyer how he interpreted his impending execution for leading a bloody slave uprising, he answered simply, "Was not Christ Crucified?" For most enslaved Christians, however, the evangelical faith provided not so much the fuel for violent revolt as spiritual protection from the heinous system of racial subjugation supported by their white brethren as God's plan to Christianize the heathen.

From the 1820s forward, black congregations sometimes were allowed a separate existence from their white parent churches. Over 150 separate black churches were formed, many with separate buildings, pastors, and deacons. Despite the increasingly hostile attitudes of whites to black religious independence, institutions such as the First African Baptist Church of Savannah managed to maintain a separate if not autonomous existence. The very presence of these congregations testified to the faith of enslaved Baptists in the power of the Christian message to overcome the most unpromising of conditions. The churches were not independent, but they nurtured independent spirits.

Most southern congregations in the antebellum era often claimed a substantial membership of enslaved African Americans. With the enslaved members sitting in segregated parts of the building, presiding ministers solemnly recounted biblical injunctions to obey the masters. This lesson on the cultural captivity of southern ministers was not lost on the slaves. Frederick Douglass, the escaped slave and prominent black abolitionist, delighted northern audiences with his renditions of the hypocritical solemnities of southern ministers, messages he remembered well from Maryland churches. In these white-run antebellum churches, blacks participated to a larger degree than historians once understood. White ministers tutored black protégés for missionary work, on occasion even setting these ministers free. Black members were considered part of churches, even if only their first names might be recorded on the roll book.

Enslaved Christians in the antebellum South fashioned a religious culture which synthesized Euro-American Christian beliefs and African expressive styles into a unique, sustaining form of Christianity. This faith took shape partly under the suspicious eyes of watchful but devout whites, but more importantly developed in the sacred spaces the slaves created for themselves in private worship. Sometimes noticed (and often ridiculed) by whites, slave religion found its fullest expression in the brush arbors and secret places where enslaved Christians could express religious faith in the way they chose. In these private gatherings, the deepest desires for freedom found expression among people otherwise compelled to dissemble before old master. One Texas minister, illiterate during slavery and told by the master to preach obedience, countered his restrictions in private: "I knew there was something better for them but I darsn't tell them so lest I done it on the sly. That I did lots. I told the Niggers, but not so Master could hear it, if they keep praying that the Lord would hear their prayers and set them free." From these settings came some of the most profoundly beautiful creations of American culture—the spirituals, the ring shouts, and the African American chanted sermon.

Black believers saw in the Civil War the fulfillment of prayers for emancipation, education, and the right to worship freely in churches of their own directing. After the war, independent churches and denominational organizations sprung up quickly in black communities, including thousands of small local congregations and major national organizations such as the African Methodist Episcopal Church and the National Baptist Convention. Only a decade after the war, hardly any black parishioners still worshipped in the historically white southern churches. Through the last part of the nineteenth century black church membership grew rapidly. By the 1906 religious census, the National Baptist Convention claimed more than 2 million communicants, or over 61 percent of black churchgoers. The African Methodist Episcopal Church (AME) numbered some 500,000, the African Methodist Episcopal Zion (AMEZ) denomination about 185,000, the Colored Methodist Episcopal (CME) sect approximately 173,000, and the Methodist Episcopal Church (MEC) about 60,000 black adherents. Catholics claimed around 38,000 African American worshippers, while the Presbyterians and Congregationalists together counted some 30,000. Altogether, church membership among African Americans rose from 2.6 million to 3.6 million from 1890 to 1906. The church was widely acknowledged to be at the center of African American social and cultural life, and remained so through the era of segregation and, much later, the civil rights movement.

During and after the Civil War, white evangelicals entered the public arena as never before. Gradually, they came to dominate their culture in a way that simply was impossible in the antebellum era. The Confederate cause increasingly was defined as a righteous and godly one, and the South's military heroes—Robert E. Lee, Stonewall Jackson, and others—demigods praised for their piety as much as for their military prowess. Evangelicals took the lead in furthering the Lost Cause, too, another way in which the Civil War was "Christianized." The title of Charles Reagan Wilson's classic work on this subject—*Baptized in Blood*—perfectly captures the sanctification of the South through the Lost Cause.

The Meaning of "Redemption" for Southern Christians

The term "Redemption," used by historians to describe the end of Reconstruction in the mid-1870s, assumed an especially powerful meaning for white southern believers. Redemption signified individual salvation as well as deliverance from "cursed rulers." Submission to the North in politics, many white southern Christians feared, would mandate what some called "Yankee faith"—theological liberalism and racial egalitarianism. As would be the case a century later during the civil rights movement, white Democratic politicians during Reconstruction employed an evangelical language of sin and redemption combined with measures of political organization and extralegal violence. When some African American men exercised rights of political citizenship, it appeared to white conservatives as an overturning of a divinely ordered hierarchy. Their polemic against "the gospel according to Radicalism" proceeded from many of the same assumptions regarding natural hierarchy that had guided the proslavery argument. White southern Christians viewed their Redemptionist activity as essentially religious, an extension of the cosmic struggle between order and disorder, civilization and barbarism, white and black.

Despite a period of sharp postwar decline due to southern defeat and even more so to the mass withdrawal of African Americans from the major religious institutions of the region, white evangelical churches reestablished themselves after the war. They still faced some of their old competitors and enemies, such as the honor culture of the Old South that prized masculine assertiveness, as well as the poverty and isolation that gripped so much of the region. Nevertheless, evangelicals largely captured the culture of the region. They overcame some of their earlier suspicion of the use of state power and governmental authority and seized on progressive initiatives to improve public life through education, sanitation, and prohibition. Indeed, despite their reputation for stalwart conservatism, southern evangelicals in fact led the progressive movement in the early twentieth century. Good roads, better schools, improved sanitation, elimination of alcohol, and the proper ordering of the races through "modern" mechanisms such as urban segregation, they realized, only aided their cause.

The dominant understanding of evangelicalism in the South since the Civil War, the so-called cultural captivity thesis, explains how southern Christians were "captive" to southern culture. In its simplest formulation, the thesis runs like this: Compelled to choose between Christ and culture, southerners chose culture. For example, white religious institutions and practices in the nineteenth- and twentieth-century South reflected and reinforced racism. Slumbering in a reactionary form of evangelicalism, southern whites faltered before the moral challenges posed to them, from abolitionism through Reconstruction and later the civil rights movement. Black religious institutions, dormant until their revitalization in the 1950s and 1960s, primarily served to console parishioners worn out by the travail of surviving life under segregation.

The Civil Rights Revolution and Religion

There are obvious and important truths here. Writing in the midst of the civil rights revolution, scholars such as Samuel Hill and John Lee Eighmy could not help but see cultural captivity when stiff-necked deacons and ushers stood cross-armed at church house doors, defending "segregation now, segregation forever." More recently, scholars of the civil rights era have pointed out the fact that prominent black ministers avoided association with the movement, with some clearly complicit in the oppressive system. In this sense, the cultural captivity thesis damns both white and black churches.

Yet the dominant classes rarely have espoused theologies of equality. More commonly, they adopt theologies that sanctify inequality. "We do not believe that 'all men are created equal' . . . nor that they will ever become equal in this world," a prominent Southern Baptist cleric said in the 1880s. The white southern theology of class, blood, and sex was premised on God-ordained inequality. It was an unstable foundation in the context of American liberal democracy, but one common in human history. White southern religious ideas of the social order of the races, moreover, could be intellectually grounded in a conservative vision of the role of hierarchy in preserving order and staving off anarchy. These notions were not merely hypocritical cant intended to void the clear biblical message, for particular biblical passages clearly explained why spiritual equality does not (and must not) imply temporal equality. The reasoning went like this: God created the world. If inequality exists, then God must have a reason for it. Without inequality—without rulers and ruled, without hewers of wood and drawers of water—there could be only anarchy. Men cannot govern themselves on a plane of equality. Realizing this, God sanctions Himself to head the church, men to lead women and children, slaveowners to direct the lives of slaves, and white people to guide the destiny of black people. Godly societies were orderly societies, conservative southern divines said, and orderly societies required such hierarchies as God clearly had ordained—of class, blood, and gender. Presbyterian elders, Episcopalian divines, and even Baptist and Methodist preachers aspiring to the status of "gentleman theologians" understood that formulating a distinctive theological tradition for their section constituted part of their calling as apostles of respectability.

Post–Civil War southern theologians responded to defeat in the war by emphasizing human weakness, fallibility, and dependence on God. For many white southern theologians, defeat in the Civil War also shored up orthodoxies of race and place. The Negro—as a beast, a burden, or a brother—was there to be dealt with by whites, who were the actors in the racial drama. After the Civil War, by using the term Redemption, white southerners expressed a deeply religious understanding of the tumultuous political events of the 1870s. The divinely ordained social/racial hierarchy had been restored by southern martyrs, and the South atoned, renewed. As the *New Orleans Advocate* (the Louisiana white Methodist newspaper) crowed in 1879, "Not a Negro at the polls. This is just as it should be. . . . Let the Negroes and Chinamen and Indians suffer the superior race of white men to whom Providence has given this country, to control it."

In the twentieth-century South, however, constructing a theological defense of segregation was more complicated. After World War II, the American creed required white southern theologians to mouth the words "all men are created equal." To justify the state-mandated inequality of segregation, they resorted to constitutional arguments ("interposition"), appeals to tradition, and outright demagoguery. They dug up references to "render unto Caesar" and formulated obscurantist renderings of Old Testament passages such as the Son of Ham mythologies.

During the mid-twentieth century, religious segregationists peopled the white churches of the region, but they were difficult to organize into concerted action. More so than ministers, many of whom were relatively silent during the civil rights crises, or who attempted to use the language of "moderation" to paper over differences, white laymen in the South articulated, defended, and enforced what amounted to a folk theology of segregation. It was more pervasive among southern laymen and laywomen and among ministers outside the denominational hierarchy than in the circles of denominational leadership. This sanctification of segregation was important in making the white South so obsessed with purity, and concerned with defending (in the words of scholar Jane Dailey) the sacred triad of sex, segregation, and the sacred. Only a proper ordering of the races would maintain white southern purity against defilement—the sexual metaphors behind the race politics were obvious and restated endlessly. The frequent phobia of impurity, seen in the frequent references to "filth" and "social disease" that pervaded segregationist literature, clarifies that segregationism was something deeper than custom, that it had been sanctified. It was about not being "forced to go into those *intimate* things that I don't wish to go," as Dallas Baptist superstar minister W. A. Criswell put it, perfectly capturing the obsession with purity that haunted white southern conservatives. A theology of segregation may be found recycled through the ephemeral literature of the era—in letters to editors, in newspaper columns, and frequently in private correspondence. White supporters of civil rights quoted Acts 17:26: "Of one blood has God made all nations." Segregationists, in response, explicated the second half of the verse, which referred to God assigning to his creatures the "bounds of their habitation." For biblical literalists such as most southerners were, passages such as Acts 17:26 correlated to the specific social customs of God's Zion, the American South.

Progressive Christianity in the South

Like religious expression elsewhere, religion in the post–Civil War American South has been both priestly and prophetic. It often has undergirded, and less frequently challenged, the social order. If white southern theology generally sanctified southern hierarchies, evangelical belief and practice also at times subtly undermined the dominant order. Churches as institutions were conservative, but progressive Christians drew different lessons from the Bible than regional religious leaders often understood. The actions of individual churchmen and women outstripped the cautious defensiveness that often marked the public stance of the religious institutions. While religious institutions were resistant to change, many religious folk devoted themselves to social change precisely because they perceived God as the author of it.

At no time was this more apparent than during the great social revolution of twentieth-century American history: the civil rights movement. Although drawing on multiple influences both secular and religious, the freedom struggle was sustained through the religious vision of the ordinary black (and a few white) southerners who made up its rank and file, braved harassment and intimidation, and transformed the consciousness and conscience of the country.

Progressive and radical social activism in the South quite often came from people imbued with the same evangelical upbringings as those who adamantly defended the social order. Writing about the rise of southern liberalism, the historian John Egerton explains that churches and universities were wellsprings "for the intellectual and philosophical stimulation out of which some reform movements came— but when the institutions themselves shrank from joining the fray, it was often their sons and daughters, acting in new alliances or as individuals, who moved the dialogue and the action to a higher plane." Petty daily harassment, economic coercion, beatings, death threats, and even assassination have hounded religious prophets for social change in a region historically hostile to radical seers—most especially those committed to racial justice. But the very pervasiveness of evangelicalism in the region also provided the religious language from which these social prophets drew their inspiration. They knew that, as a severe and righteous judge, God would condemn the historic patterns of brutality and injustice endemic to an impoverished and racially segregated region.

Scholars have rightly seen evangelicalism as a legitimator of the southern status quo, one that gave divine sanction to the peculiar social mores of the region. But religious belief was also a prophetic voice warning against God's judgment on a people willing to tolerate unrighteousness. Some of the most self-consciously religious social activists served in the Student Non-Violent Coordinating Committee in the 1960s. SNCC's "distinctively idealistic belief that fortitude, determined action, and fearlessness would result in momentous social change," Southern Methodist daughter and civil rights activist Mary King has explained, "stemmed to a great degree from the Protestant upbringings of most of its workers." She connected her vision specifically to Wesleyan theology, that "through grace and redemption each person can be saved," a view that "reinforced" SNCC's belief that the "good in every human being could be appealed to, fundamental change could correct the immorality of racial segregation, and new political structures could be created."

African-American Protestantism empowered the most important social struggle in twentieth-century American history, one that fundamentally redefined citizenship for disfranchised peoples. Civil rights leaders employed multiple arguments, many of them involving constitutional protections. But beneath that ran the powerful stream of black Protestant ideas (translated sometimes through Gandhian and Catholic Worker notions of civil disobedience and active resistance) that moved southern folk and pushed forward a leadership that otherwise remained cautious and circumspect. Evangelical Protestantism among black southerners historically appeared to be apolitical. Critics called it "otherworldy" or "compensatory." But the implicit potential of southern folk faith—what contemporary scholars might call the "hidden transcript" of religious belief and behavior—bears close attention, for it defeated an enemy superior in number and resources. Scholar Robin D.G. Kelley has argued that "we need to recognize that the sacred and the spirit world were also often understood and invoked by African Americans as weapons to protect themselves or to attack others. . . . Can a sign from above, a conversation with a ghost, a spell cast by an enemy, or talking in tongues unveil the hidden transcript?" One might add, can one's private and communal prayer when facing down racist sheriffs and voting registrars, shotguns blasted through a window, or snakes thrown on one's front porch serve as the antidote to the poison of apartheid? The freedom struggle brought the hidden transcript to the surface. The assassins who bombed the 16th Street Baptist Church in Birmingham and numerous other ecclesiastical buildings recognized this as clearly as anyone.

When one looks beyond the church itself, the empowerment provided by the tradition of intense personal evangelicalism appears more clearly. As Charles Payne has written, "faith in the Lord made it easier to have faith in the possibility of social change," even if in the Delta towns he studied, such as Greenwood, Mississippi, the movement grew despite ministerial recalcitrance. Those on the movement's front line, in the words of one participant, had that "something on the inside." For many ordinary southerners, nothing else besides this "something on the inside," this religious vision of redeeming the South, sufficed for the sacrifices required by the struggle. The civil rights movement represented the culmination of a religious vision, the realization (however temporary) of the beloved community. Even if this utopian language ultimately was bound to disappoint, such a vision energized ordinary black southerners stifled by a repressive social system.

In the 1980s and 1990s, the longer-range effect of the civil rights movement appeared paradoxical. On the one hand, African Americans entered southern social institutions in numbers and in an unselfconscious way that stunned many older southern people, white and black, who remembered the drama of the freedom struggle of the 1950s and 1960s firsthand. Southern churches mostly remained separated by race, but in other areas of social life pluralism came to the once solid South. Indeed, by the late 1990s it was becoming apparent that immigration from Mexico, Central and South America, and Asia was dramatically changing particular biracial southern patterns. On the other hand, in much of the South, especially the rural areas where the biracial pattern still remained evident, white and black people remained quite separate, and the extent of black poverty rivaled that of the worst areas of the country. Many problems formerly seen as "northern," such as gangs and drugs, infiltrated southern communities in places such as the Mississippi Delta, where the civil rights movement never made a serious dent on the disheartening statistics of black poverty. In short, "national" patterns of race relations, including increasing racial segregation of housing (a distinct change from the historic southern pattern of closely mingling and sometimes intersecting white and black residential areas, in part due to the economy of domestic service on which white households depended), became part of the "southern way of life." In politics, gerrymandered districts ensured the continued tension between a white Republican and a black Democratic South in many areas. In business, a rising and substantial black middle class increasingly had more in common with their white middle-class suburban compatriots than with the black poor in cities and in declining rural areas.

The "southern" trend in religion, too, mirrored the national scene, as black and white evangelicals were "divided by faith." The common thread of evangelicalism running through the southern tradition could not mask the very different social interpretations given to faith by black and white church communities. In particular, the evangelical individualism that was such a deep part of southern white religious history prevented many good-hearted white southerners from seeing what their black brethren knew very well, that the deep racial and structural divide in American life would not be broken down by "changing hearts" or other nostrums dear to the hearts of evangelicals. Like the first Reconstruction, then, the civil rights movement, sometimes called the second Reconstruction, is an unfinished revolution—nowhere more so than in southern religion.

Southern Evangelicals and the Move to the Political Right

Southern evangelicalism has never been as removed from engagement in this world's affairs as its adherents (and many historians since) typically have claimed. Such remains the case today, when the activist impulse has migrated rightward and lodged itself firmly in the hands of a (mostly) white evangelical leadership. Since the 1960s, social activism in southern religion largely has passed from the civil rights coalition, whose primary focus was racial justice in the South, to the religious right, seen in the rise of figures such as Jerry Falwell, Pat Robertson, and Ralph Reed. Learning from the techniques of the civil rights movement, the contemporary religious-political right has deployed the language of social righteousness. In this case, though, social activism has been used not so much to pull a backward region forward as to reclaim a lost heritage of a once supposedly "Christian America."

By the 1970s, many white southern believers accommodated themselves with remarkable ease to the demise of white supremacy as fundamentally constitutive of their society. Thus, in the recent controversies within southern church organizations, race has been one of the very few items on the agenda *not* in dispute. Today's conservatives, for the most part, have repudiated the white supremacist views of their predecessors, as seen in the 1995 resolution of the Southern Baptist Convention (SBC) officially apologizing for the role historically played by white southerners in defending slavery and segregation. Since the 1960s the standard biblical arguments against racial equality have become relics, embarrassments from a bygone age. But their philosophical premises have not. Indeed, they have found their way rather easily into the contemporary religious conservative stance on gender. For religious conservatives generally, patriarchy has supplanted race as the defining first principle of God-ordained inequality. Nowhere is this more evident than in the self-described "conservative resurgence" inside the nation's largest Protestant denomination, the Southern Baptist Convention.

In 1979 a group of conservative Southern Baptist men led by Paige Patterson and Paul Pressler, one a theologian and the other a lawyer and conservative district judge, set out to win control of the largest Protestant organization in the United States, the Southern Baptist Convention. Earlier attempts by less well connected fundamentalists in the early 1970s had failed. But this effort did succeed in formulating a strategy for ultimate victory: place the right men in the presidency of the SBC, and then use the appointive power of the executive office to slot political and ideological allies in key positions. Patterson and Pressler, the two Texans who served, respectively, as the theologian and strategist of the movement, estimated (with remarkable prescience) that in ten years conservatives would own a controlling majority on seminary trustee boards and denominational agencies. A politically charged battle through the 1980s for control of the SBC as an organization thus ensued. By 1991 the conservatives had won a complete victory, in what they referred to as a "conservative resurgence" and the defeated moderates called a "fundamentalist takeover."

Theological modernism and political liberalism, the conservatives argued, were weaning Southern Baptists away from their historic defense of Reformed Christianity. The moderates responded that the fundamentalists were conducting a political purge. The moderates, however, lacked any clear political leadership. By the very nature of being moderates, they lacked the capacity to fight with a single-minded will. By contrast, conservative leaders pronounced that they were "going for the jugular," and it was the moderates' blood supply that would be stanched. In the end, Southern Baptist moderates and progressives, who were often accused of being too preoccupied with things of the world, turned out to be too spiritually and irenically inclined to organize themselves as a "movement culture" or engage in effective power politicking in the convention. The conservatives, who proclaimed themselves defenders of the spirituality of the church, in fact were savvy political operators.

Behind the recent battle for control of the Southern Baptist Convention has been a deep divide between those for whom human equality and autonomy reign as fundamental principles, and those for whom communal norms and strictures and a divinely ordained hierarchy remain determinative of social life. In some ways, the struggle has taken the form of a classic division between philosophical liberalism and communalist conservatism. For the latter group, gendered patterns of hierarchy are fundamental to godly structures of religious, social, and political life. Of course, southern conservatism always intertwined race and gender hierarchies. The foundational conservative principles of order and hierarchy, and the literalist biblical exegesis undergirding the philosophy, underlay each. Just as was the case with the antislavery biblical argument, liberals have been compelled to rely on broader readings of the biblical texts, which by definition leave them suspect and intellectually vulnerable within an evangelical culture that prizes strict constructionist readings of sacred passages—whether of the Bible or of the U.S. Constitution.

The relationship among race, gender, and contemporary white southern evangelical identity was forged in the wake of civil rights era controversies. That is not to say that race was the real issue behind the southern culture wars (such as the controversy over control of the SBC) of the 1980s and 1990s. It was not. It is to say, however, that moderates and conservatives, as well as a few liberals, formed distinct groupings during the civil rights years. Those factions played out their battle (over a very different terrain of issues) from 1979 to the early 1990s, when conservatives coalesced in part against the moderate and gradualist leadership of many Southern Baptist agencies. It was no accident that religious conservatives came to national prominence following the demise of race as the central issue of southern life. Their political movements updated venerable philosophical defenses of social hierarchy as necessary for a properly ordered liberty. No longer defenders of a discredited racial hierarchy, the conservatives advanced their positions in favor of an unapologetic patriarchy.

The restructuring of American religion outlined by the sociologist Robert Wuthnow followed a pattern similar to the changes in American politics through the New Deal and civil rights years. Late in the Depression, southern conservatives led by figures such as Josiah Bailey, a Southern Baptist newspaper editor and senator from North Carolina, effectively had formed a conservative coalition that stymied FDR's social agenda. In particular, opposition to a federal antilynching law was an effective organizing tool for the proto-Dixiecrats. They argued that the Democratic Party had become something very different than the party of their fathers. It had become a vehicle for the schemes of the New Deal, not the stalwart defender of decentralized and limited government as was the southern Democratic conservative philosophy. Moreover, the southern conservatives looked on with dismay as their party became a multiethnic patchwork. They were especially uneasy as blacks deserted the party of Lincoln for the party of Roosevelt. A decade later, their efforts would take shape in the Dixiecrat revolt of 1948.

The descendants of this restructuring of southern politics and religion led the later conservative movements, this time with more success. For them, race was not the primary issue, even if it lay just barely beneath the surface at times. In fact, some tentative cross-racial conservative coalitions—organized particularly around the issues of abortion, public education, and women's rights—have markedly distinguished contemporary southern religious conservatives from their avowedly white supremacist predecessors. More to the point, the civil rights struggle reformed southern denominations, splitting them along the lines of conservatives, moderates, and liberals that typically form cross-denominational alliances. It took the coalescing of divisions over race to fracture and create new religious alliances. The new groupings on the right quickly left behind the dishonorable racist past of their predecessors, but inherited their well-honed theological defenses of hierarchy, submission, and order.

RELIGIONS OF THE REGION

Protestant evangelicalism has obviously been the dominant religion of the region since the rise of the Bible Belt in the nineteenth century and the expanding southern religious empires (especially that of the Southern Baptist Convention) in the twentieth century. At the same time, the dominance of evangelicalism is not quite as simple as portrayed in the term "Bible Belt." Southern evangelicals are in effect at ease in Zion and uneasy in Babylon at the same time. Southern evangelicals have dominated their region religiously, and still do to a large extent; they have heavily influenced their region politically, and still do in some areas; and yet they have never felt completely secure in their cultural reign in the region, and have less reason now than ever before to feel such confidence.

The South's own self-image of being *at ease in Zion* has been shaken in recent years. Indeed, the very term "southern identity" itself has been called into question. What does it mean to call a region an evangelical belt when, according to the 2000 Census data, 40 percent of those surveyed were either uncounted or unaffiliated with any church? The closest competitor to the category of "unaffiliated or uncounted" for the South was "Baptist," with 19 percent of the total regional population identified as adherents (a category more expansive than that of "members"). The category "Historically Black Protestant" registered at 12 percent. The only other group coming in at a figure of over 10 percent were the Catholics. In looking at current growth trends, moreover, evangelical hegemony appears on the wane. For example, while 27 percent of Tennesseans claim affiliation with the Baptists, the growth rate of the denomination has not kept pace with the rapid percentage growth of population in the Volunteer State.

Statistics can tell many stories, of course. If the numbers crunched above show an evangelical belt that is, at best, holding its own, other tales from the tables suggest a different conclusion. In a poll conducted in 1998, 20 percent of southerners indicated that they attended church services more than once a week, a rate more than double that for non-southerners. More southerners (almost 42 percent, in comparison to 33 percent for those outside the region) agreed with the statement that religion was "extremely important" in their lives. Six of ten southerners said they accepted the account of creation in Genesis over Darwin. A large proportion of the "unchurched" in the region still believes in God and afterlife. The predominance of southern preachers on the airwaves provides the kind of oral soundtrack many Americans associate with conservative Protestant Christianity more generally. In other words, even if 40 percent of southerners are uncounted or unaffiliated, many register as believers if counted by other measures.

Catholicism, Judaism, and Asian Religions in the South

Historically, the South has been distinctive for its overwhelming predominance of a biracial culture, with relatively few "white ethnics" or other groups to complicate the mix. It has also been distinctive for the remarkable strength, resilience, and durability of evangelical Protestantism in the region, far exceeding that of any other region in the country. Until recently, Catholics have been concentrated primarily in particular sub-regions (Louisiana and Texas, in particular), Jews have never made it even to 1 percent of the population base, Latinos were scarce outside of Texas, and Asians represented the tiniest minority at all. As a result, scholars have been able to speak of a "solid South" in religion, one that has room for high-church Christianity for the elite and for Catholics in particular regions, but one that is fundamentally defined by Southern Baptists, Methodists, Presbyterians, and (more recently) Pentecostals. This is a far remove from the United States as a whole, where (for example) Catholics form the single largest religious grouping, while in the South, Catholics (at least outside of Louisiana) have always struggled for legitimacy and recognition.

Thus, in looking at "minority" religions in the South (which include Catholicism, Judaism, Asian religions, and Islam), one faces first their near invisibility in the region, at least until quite recently. This does not mean they were nonexistent. In a few particular cases, such as New Orleans and surrounding regions of Louisiana, Catholics were actually predominant, and evangelical Protestants were the relative upstarts. But even in Louisiana, once traveling far enough northward Baptists and Methodists displaced Catholics. The same holds true for Florida, where the relative anomaly of southern Florida gives way to a more familiar white and black evangelical Protestant scene in the northern half of the state and particularly in the Panhandle.

Like the rest of the country, the South has undergone radical demographic changes over the last generation, and this too has been reflected in religion. Thus, a scholar assigned to write a chapter for a cultural regions volume 100 years from now would produce a very different chapter indeed, and likely one in which the stress on biracial evangelical Protestantism has become one of many topics to be discussed rather than the major topic. One may start the discussion of minority religions in the South, and the diversification of southern religion itself, with the Catholics. Over 15 percent of southerners polled in 1999 claimed a Catholic identity. As one may expect, the majority are still comprised of historic Louisiana Catholics, Mexican Americans in Texas, and Cuban Americans in Florida. But Catholicism has found its way into the Deep South as well, and increasingly mixes in unobtrusively with the familiar landscape of evangelical Protestant churches. Immigration accounts for part of this; more significant, however, is migration, as national firms draw in increasing numbers of workers from other parts of the country. In particular urban regions—Atlanta, Charlotte, the Research Triangle, and even in the evangelical Vatican of Nashville—Catholics have assumed a regular-

Outdoor tile mural at Ursulines Convent, French Quarter, New Orleans. Courtesy Louisiana Office of Tourism.

ized presence in the southern landscape, such that to be southern and Catholic no longer seems the anomaly that it was in the past.

Black Catholics, too, have grown out of their Louisiana base and have found homes elsewhere. Historically, the Catholic Church in the South tried to promote itself among black southerners as one church that did not discriminate, one that welcomed all. As black Catholics well knew, this was partly a sham. Parochial schools in the South, including New Orleans, were segregated through the late nineteenth century, and many Catholic churches increasingly took to segregating pews during services or even to requiring blacks to stand at the back and receive communion last when whites filled up all the pew spaces. "You couldn't help but feel a certain degree of hatred," one black Louisiana Catholic recently reminisced, reflecting back on his experience of second-class citizenship in the Catholic Church. In this way, despite the heroic efforts of some priests and the attempts by Catholics to avoid the segregated church model of the Protestants, Catholics increasingly fit into a southern mold as well.

Jews have an intriguing relationship as well with the history of religions in the South. Jews established a significant presence early in southern history—significant not in terms of numbers, but in terms of occupying important and respected spots in the region's economic and cultural elite (including in Jefferson Davis' Confederate Cabinet). Jews held a respected spot, too, in the cultural imagery of southern evangelical Protestants, since Jews were, after all, descended from Abraham and Moses and David. Thus, biblical literalists had to give them respect, even if they knew nothing in particular of what Judaism was actually about. Thus, in the eighteenth and nineteenth century, the South was relatively free of overt anti-Semitism. This changed dramatically in the early twentieth century with the brutally tragic lynching of Leo Frank, the pencil factory owner falsely accused of murdering a young teenage girl, Mary Phagan, who worked in Frank's establishment. When Frank's sentence of death was commuted to life imprisonment, Georgia demagogues and politicos such as Tom Watson urged all red-blooded white men to do their duty—and they did, by dragging Frank out of his jail, and later carrying home souvenirs from his body.

Later in the twentieth century, Jewish southerners, including many well-known department store owners and merchants in cities such as Birmingham, Memphis, and Atlanta, had a complicated relationship with the civil rights struggle. Many were supportive of the black freedom struggle, both privately and publicly. A few were well-known segregationists. Others were privately supportive but joined southern moderates in urging caution and gradualism—earning one rabbi a spot of infamy on the list of religious "moderates" famously skewered by Martin Luther King Jr.'s "Letter from a Birmingham Jail." Some Jewish leaders—notably Rabbi Perry Nussbaum in Mississippi—saw their synagogues and houses bombed for their presumed identification with elements sympathetic to black civil rights. The most careful study of the subject, Clive Webb's *Fight Against Fear: Southern Jews and Black Civil Rights* (2001), has abundantly documented case studies of dozens of southern Jews who actively participated in, or at least gave aid and comfort to, southern blacks in the civil rights movement. Most of these received little publicity (particularly compared to the much better known efforts of northern Jews, many of whom volunteered for groups such as the Student Non-Violent Coordinating Committee), and many lived under a cloud of suspicion and resentment coming from both white and black communities. While some blacks expressed disappointment that more Jews were not at the forefront of publicly supporting the movement, white segregationists such as the notorious Louisiana Leander Perez

Temple Ohev Sholem school, Orlando, Florida, 1932. Courtesy Florida Photographic Collection, MOSAIC Collection.

identified "Zionist Jews" as "leaders in forcing communistic integration." Since the civil rights era, Jews have joined Catholics as increasingly "blended in" to the southern religious landscape, especially in the largest urban areas and in university communities. Thus, despite the hideous legacy of the Frank episode, cities such as Atlanta boast thriving Jewish communities that rival those of many other American cities, and rabbis have taken their place alongside Protestant ministers and Catholic priests in the category of regional "religious leaders" that receive attention in religious columns in the newspapers and are given ritual obeisance by politicians seeking to identify themselves with something other than the dirty world of the legislative hall.

Finally, some mention should be made of the recent demographic explosion of Asian religions in the South. In the 2000 Census, immigrants to the South numbered just over 8 million people. Comparing Census data from

Interior of the Shrine at Our Lady of the Angels Monastery in Hanceville, Alabama. Courtesy of the Cullman Area Chamber of Commerce.

1960 and 2000, one sees a quadrupling of the South's foreign-born population. The largest percentage of these consist of Latino immigrants, especially to Texas and Florida; but they have increasingly been joined by Asian immigrants to southern cities (the most visible evidence of which, of course, was the expansion of restaurant dining options for southerners beyond the dreary sameness of the older Chinese places serving up kung pao chicken, so much so that in larger urban areas one may now choose which regional variety of Thai food one most desires on a particular evening). By 2000, for example, the city of Atlanta included some 10,000 Buddhists, 12,000 Hindus, and 30,000 Muslims. Nearly 25,000 Vietnamese had taken up residence in Louisiana, and close to 50,000 Asian Indians (mostly of Hindu or Sikh faiths) in Georgia. In North Carolina, nearly 115,000 Asians had taken up residence in the state by the 2000 Census, and evidence of their impact could be seen in Hindu statues, Thai temples, Cambodian wats, and Vietnamese Catholic shrines that were popping up even in the most unexpected parts of the southern landscape (including a Theravada Buddhist temple in Fort Smith, Arkansas, a proliferation of Korean Baptist churches, and a Hindu temple in Morrissville, North Carolina. Perhaps because they are still a *relatively* small percentage of the population yet (in spite of their explosive growth in real numbers), or perhaps because they have filled vital niches in the southern economy (including everything from hotel maids to software engineers), Asian immigrants to the South have experienced surprisingly little of the harassment that traditionally greets newer foreign-born groups. It is too soon to say, however, how Asian religions will change the southern religious landscape. Most probably, they will become part of the landscape, noticed by those looking for evidence of their presence and likely unnoticed by the millions of Baptists and Methodists driving to their church parking lots.

Demographics of Religions in the South

Tilt the prism another way, and yet another perspective emerges. Since the 1970s, religious diversity in the South has intensified. The increasing pluralism of the region's population has brought in substantial Catholic, Hindu, Buddhist, and Jewish populations to the urban South. In 1999 more than one in five affiliated with some faith outside of Protestantism. Latinos and Asians now make up almost 14 percent of Southerners. Fourteen percent of Texas residents and 17 percent of Floridians were born outside the United States. In North Carolina, Latinos and Asians constituted less than 2 percent of the population in 1990, but that rose dramatically in the subsequent decade. In North Carolina alone, the 77,000 Latinos counted in 1990 grew to 377,000 ten years later. Durham County's Hispanic population rose by over 700 percent in 1990s, and Durham is now a "majority-minority" city: 48 percent white, 39 percent African American, 8 percent Hispanic, and 3 percent Asian. While the "distinctive South" still survives, the demographic distinctiveness of the South is in decline, in large part because of the influx of Latinos and Asians.

Even that story must be complicated and studied in specific subregions, for immigration patterns are intense in very particular areas and nonexistent in others. Hispanics gravitate toward specific locales where work awaits them—in the carpet factories in and around Dalton, Georgia, for example, the gigantic hog farms of North Carolina, and the migrant labor crop-picking camps in the Southeast. Asians may be found largely in growing metropolitan urban areas—Atlanta, Charlotte, the Research Triangle, Richmond and northern Virginia, and Nashville. Thus, the South may be colored with a dominant background of white and black Baptists, Methodists, Presbyterians, and Pentecostals along with a sprinkling of other groups in particular areas. There is still a decided Bible Belt where white and black evangelicals predominate in numbers akin to Mormons in Utah, and that belt stretches across several states and millions of religious adherents. Evangelicals still represent "religion" in terms of interaction with public culture, as in the nationally known case of Roy Moore, the Alabama judge famous for the gigantic Ten Commandments stone he smuggled into his federal courthouse (before later being ordered to remove it), or the Protestant evangelical–style prayers before commencement ceremonies or football games, or the insistence of state legislators on preserving other traditional symbols of southern evangelical dominance. Even this interaction of religion and public life appears likely to change, however, as (for example) Hispanic Catholics and Pentecostals make their voices heard, and highly educated Asians in the university and medical communities grow more assertive in public expression of their Hindu, Buddhist, Catholic, Sikh, or other faiths.

According to the American Religious Identification Survey (ARIS), the South stands as having the highest percentage of churchgoers within the region who affiliate themselves with Baptist (23.5 percent), Presbyterian (3 percent), and black Protestant (14 percent, well over half of whom are Baptists) denominations. Combining the data for white Baptists and black Protestants, and disaggregating blacks who are Baptist from the more general figure of black Protestant, one may see the considerable credence of the older notion of a "Baptist South." No other region comes close in terms of Baptist affiliation statistics. One may compare the presence of Baptists in the region to the figure of 5.7 percent of Baptists within the region of New England and a national low of 3.8 percent in the coastal Northwest. The South also counts the highest percentage by region of white non-Hispanic Methodists (6.9 percent) and a relatively high percentage of white non-Hispanic

Baptism at Dunham Springs, Louisiana, 1925. Southern Baptist Historical Library and Archives, Nashville, Tennessee.

Pentecostal/Charismatic adherents (3 percent). Moreover, in the ARIS data, the South has the lowest count of those who responded "no religion" when asked generally about their religious beliefs and affiliations (10 percent within the region), and nearly the lowest count for white Catholics (9.7 percent of churchgoers within the region).

State-level data provide equally informative numbers. According to data provided online in the North American Religion Atlas, evangelical Protestant members as a percentage of the total population peak in Alabama (32 percent, the highest in the region) and Mississippi (31 percent), followed closely by Tennessee (29.4 percent) and Kentucky (26.7 percent). Mainline Protestant members—a figure that would include the substantial membership of United Methodists, for example—result in another 7 percent of the population of Alabama, 7.5 percent in Mississippi, 7.3 percent in Tennessee, and 6.7 percent in Kentucky. In terms of the entire South region, when measuring adherents as a percentage of total population, 19 percent are counted as Baptist adherents, and 12.4 percent as historically African American Protestant. One may compare all these figures to the national average of 6.6 percent of Baptist members as a percentage of population, or 8.5 percent if measured in terms of adherents, and 7.4 percent of the national population listed in the historically African American Protestant category.

Measured nationally and aggregating together all evangelical Protestant adherents as a percentage of total population, the South measures some 25.5 percent; another 10.2 percent are listed as mainline Protestant adherents. Measured by members rather than adherents, a more stringent category, the South has almost 20 percent counted as actively participating attendants of evangelical Protestant congregations, a figure that stands in stark contrast to 1.7 percent of New Englanders and 2.9 percent of the population of the Middle Atlantic states.

This is not to suggest that evangelical Protestantism has a uniform dominance across the region. On the contrary, evangelical Protestant adherents as a percentage of population are heavily concentrated in particular regions and counties, especially in a broad swath that cuts directly through the historic cotton country and some up-country regions of the Old South. This is why the term "evangelical belt" is apt, for evangelical Protestant dominance measured by county does look very much like a belt when mapped on a county-by-county basis (albeit with a considerable belly overhang in regions of the Upper South).

A contrast of two states in the region makes this point clearly. In Mississippi, Baptist adherents (excluding historically African American Protestants) number 34 percent of the total population, and historically African American Protestant adherents account for another 29 percent of residents of the Magnolia State. Just over 16 percent of Mississippians are "unaffiliated or uncounted." Jews exist in too small numbers to form even a 1 percent slice on the pie chart. Some counties of Mississippi actually have zero percent reporting "unaffiliated or uncounted." In Amite County, Mississippi, for example, 44 percent of the population counts itself as Baptist, and 42 percent are adherents of historically black churches. With Methodists at 5 percent and Mormons racking up a surprisingly high 4 percent of the county's population, Amite County stands as one of the most religious in the entire country. Virtually every individual is affiliated and counted as being an adherent of some religious tradition.

In Virginia, by distinct contrast, almost half the population goes into the unaffiliated or uncounted category—a larger percentage than for the country as a whole. Baptist adherents, excluding historically African American churches, count for 12 percent of the state, a figure approximating the national average (in contrast to much of the rest of the South). The religiosity of Amite County, Mississippi, stands off against the relative indifference of Albermarle County, Virginia. The county that includes Charlottesville and the University of Virginia as its centerpiece ranks unusually high, by either regional or national standards, in the category of "unaffiliated or uncounted," almost 64 percent of its population. Baptist adherents account for only 8 percent of the population, and black Protestants just 3 percent. On the whole, Albermarle County looks more like the Pacific Northwest or other regions of high levels of indifference than it does most counties in the South region.

Even Rockingham County, in the Shenandoah Valley of Virginia, stands out for its 43.5 percent of the population being unaffiliated or uncounted, even as its historic role as home to Pietists and Anabaptists (such as the Mennonites) means that these groups stand at 20 percent of total population. Rockingham County bears considerable resemblance to up-country and historically white counties of the Deep South, including Cobb County, Georgia. Historically outside of the cotton and plantation belts and home mostly to poorer whites, such counties included many highly religious folk who were not necessarily church members, in part because of a lack of religious institutions in the regions. In 2000, Cobb County, just north and west of Atlanta, stood at 48.5 percent unaffiliated or uncounted. Even there, the importance of the Baptist faith is clear, as Baptist groupings claim about

19 percent of the northern Georgia area's population. Carroll County, historically home to a high proportion of white subsistence farmers who were suspicious of Georgia's elite, stands at nearly 40 percent unaffiliated or uncounted, again a relatively high percentage for what one would consider the evangelical belt.

In short, the South's religiosity is relatively high, but varies considerably by region. There is a clear "historically black Protestant belt," and one equally clear for an evangelical belt. Mapping the two together, one finds an almost exact parallel in the Deep South states to the historic region of southern staples, cotton and tobacco. The evangelical and black Protestant belts cut a wide swath through the Deep South and, nearing the coastlines and reaching into the northern half of Virginia or the lower half of Florida, fade from view almost entirely.

The particular demographic of the evangelical belt significantly influences the character of public life in those regions. The influence of religion on politics in the evangelical belt is significant, and will become more so as the conservative wing of the Republican Party strengthens its hold on believers in the region. In exit polling data from the 2000 election, 27 percent of voters surveyed in the South region indicated affiliation with evangelical Protestantism, the highest of any region (the next closest was the Midwest, at 25 percent; both contrasted starkly with New England, where just 1.8 percent claimed evangelical affiliation and 5.8 percent mainline Protestantism). Nationally, evangelicals voted in landslide proportions for George W. Bush over Albert Gore in the 2000 presidential race, by a combined margin of 78.7 to 19.4 percent. One immediately notes the contrast with historically black Protestant adherents, 91 percent of whom cast a ballot for Gore according to the exit polling data. These figures are similar across regions, with the Pacific Northwest and other Coastal regions having somewhat less discrepancy between Gore and Bush supporters among the evangelicals, but even then with a wide three-to-one margin remaining. As the most statistically evangelical Protestant of all the regions, the distinctive South clearly plays a key role in national elections. White southern evangelicals still live in the "Solid South," but one that is solidly conservative Republican; the other Solid South is that of historically black Protestants, who are even more highly partisan in the other direction. The racial alignments of southern voting patterns in national elections are remarkably monolithic.

Regional religious traditions appear even more significantly in data compiled by John Green of the University of Akron. He finds that the South has the highest percentage of those who self-identified (in his survey) as "evangelical" or "historically black Protestant" (41 percent and 16 percent, respectively), alongside the lowest percentage of Catholic adherents (12 percent), and the lowest number claiming to be non-Christian or secular (12 percent). When applied to the abortion issue, the evangelical belt remains solidly pro-life, by a margin of 67 percent pro-life to 33 percent pro-choice. In the Pacific Northwest, by contrast, evangelicals are also pro-life, but by a narrow margin of 52 to 48 percent. The South as a whole tops the poll in terms of "high views" of the Bible (that is, those who gave their endorsement to some variant of the statement that the Bible is the inspired word of God). In this survey, 68 percent of southerners profess belief in the Bible as the inspired word of God, in comparison to 47 percent of Pacific region respondents surveyed. All religious groups in the South—evangelical, mainline, black, Catholic, "Other Christian," Jewish, and (most interestingly of all) those self-identified as "secular"—are more likely (usually considerably so) to claim a "high view" of biblical authority. Eighty-five percent of southern evangelicals claim a high view, as do 62 percent of mainline Protestants and 30 percent of secularists. The corresponding figures for each group in the Pacific region are 78, 50, and 9 percent.

The South, then, is the most solidly evangelical region of the country, and the South's evangelicals are the most conservative in terms of voting patterns, views of biblical authority, and attitudes toward significant social issues. Ironically, it is those evangelicals who feel, as a recent book title puts it, "uneasy in Babylon," as they see a formerly almost monolithically evangelical culture gradually slipping from them. Perhaps more significantly, white and black southern evangelicals remain "divided by faith," as the historical differences between the two groups in terms of applying faith to social life remain apparent in the contemporary setting.

Sermon, Song, and Supernaturalism

The South may be the Bible Belt, but like Joseph's coat, it is a belt of many colors, embroidered with a rich stitching together of words, sounds, and images from the inexhaustible resource of the scriptures. More than any other region of the country, the South has been defined by its close identification with evangelical styles of religious expressions and its intense relationship with scriptural texts, one simultaneously literalist (hence the association of southern religion with fundamentalism), visionary, and musically creative. The rigid Bible Belt conservatism associated with the common understanding of religion in the South contrasts dramatically with the sheer creative explosiveness of southern religious cultural expression. Indeed, it is southern religion that was at the heart of much of twentieth-century American culture.

If the image of southern evangelicalism seems dominated by spare and plain meeting houses, fundamentalist fire-and-brimstone sermons, and repressive behavioral restrictions, the southern artistic imagination nevertheless has been infused with rich biblical imagery that has exploded in word, sound, and the visual arts. This is evidenced in the rich literary tradition of figures such as Flannery O'Connor, William Faulkner, Alice Walker, and Walker Percy; in the musical sounds of shape-note singing, the black spirituals, and white and black gospel; in the oratorical artistry of countless chanted sermons and well-known evangelists such as Billy Graham; and it is also wonderfully expressed by the visionary artworks of figures such as Howard Finster.

Religion in the South has deeply influenced American life less through theology, ritual, or formal structures than through cultural forms. Southern sermonic and oratorical forms reverberated through the majestic cadences of Martin Luther King, Jr., and American revivalism took a distinctively modern form through southern barnstorming preachers such as Billy Sunday and, later in the century, through Billy Graham. More recently, this has been reinforced by the prevalence of southern preachers on the airwaves, including Jerry Falwell's "Old Time Gospel Hour," Pat Robertson's "700 Club," the comical figures of Jim and Tammy Faye Bakker and their Christian theme park in South Carolina, and Jimmy Swaggart, nationally known Louisiana Pentecostal and first cousin to Jerry Lee Lewis, who carried the energy and fire of Pentecostalism into his music. The migration of black Americans from the South to the rest of the country through much of the twentieth century, moreover, ensured that African American sermonic forms developed over two centuries in the South would spread and become known in national politics through the likes of Jesse Jackson, a native of South Carolina.

More than anyplace else, in music the religious South deeply imprinted and shaped American life. In black spirituals, Americans learned of the deep theology and culture of the nation's most despised and oppressed people. Through black and white variants of gospel music and in the rhythmic intensity that black and white Pentecostals carried forward through the twentieth century, Americans recaptured a deep soulfulness and spiritual dance and listened avidly to thinly-veiled secularized versions of those forms in the popular music of the post–World War II era. In many ways, southern religious expressive forms, with their deep intermixing of white and black forms and styles, became America's cultural sensibility.

Racial segregation in post–Civil War southern religion was normal. But in liminal spaces—in novelty acts, revivals, and the creation of new religious and musical traditions—the bars of race came down, if only temporarily. When they did come down, however, they opened up possibilities for cultural interchange that fed into the "shared traditions" outlined by historian and anthropologist Charles Joyner. Like Huck and Jim on the raft, black and white southerners, Joyner argues, "continued to swap recipes and cultural styles, songs and stories, accents and attitudes. Folk culture simply refused to abide any color line, however rigidly it may have been drawn." White and black southern religious folk cultures drew from common evangelical beliefs and attitudes and swapped musical and oratorical styles and forms. On occasion, they shared liminal moments of religious transcendence, before moving back into a Jim Crow world where color defined and limited everything.

In the post–Civil War era, missionaries, travelers, reporters, and early anthropologists presented believers in the region as culturally other. For these observers, southern religion was emotion—overwrought, anti-intellectual, too given to personal experience over formalized understandings of faith. In short, it was too "Negro." There were obvious differences—including class distinctions—in white and black traditions, yet a regional style persisted. Southern evangelical enthusiasm provided ample opportunity for ridiculing primitive whites so backward as to practice customs tinged with folk Negritude.

Racial interchange figured importantly in early southern Holiness/Pentecostalism, the most innovative and important twentieth-century religious movement. A faith not born in the South, but attracting white and black southern folk disaffected by the embourgeoisement of dominant urban religious institutions, early Pentecostalism functioned much like early national camp meetings. In both cases, mobile common folk created a democratic religious impulse that impelled close bonds, a strict moral code forbidding worldly pleasure, and hypnotic worship practices that induced receptivity of bodies to the Spirit. Whites and blacks drank in the Spirit together, and blacks delivered a message that, for a time, whites eagerly embraced. Once these initial enthusiasms settled into institutional routines, white and black believers moved into separate and (usually) distinct religious organizations.

The vivid encounters with the Spirit evident in Pentecostal experience strongly influenced southern evangelical music. From the early intermingling of Protestant hymns and African styles in spirituals, to the mixing of white and black country and gospel sounds on radio dials, two streams of musical religious culture flowed beside each other, never merging but often intersecting. As rural southerners made their treks from countryside to town in the early twentieth century, and as many of them found their way to northern cities later in the century, they carried their churches with them, marking them for the derision of their urban neighbors. Later in the twentieth century, however, Pentecostalism became one of the fastest growing religious groupings in America, confounding a generation of interpreters who condemned it as the opiate of the dispossessed. These primitives instead provided much of the soundtrack and many of the expressive forms that reshaped American cultural styles later in the twentieth century. Like the black Pentecostals in the Church of God in Christ (COGIC), white Pentecostal churches served as training grounds for a remarkable number of figures (such as Presley, Johnny Cash, and Oral Roberts) who deeply imprinted American popular culture.

Twentieth-century southern gospel music illustrates these shared traditions. The gospel music business, according to the historian Bill Malone, evolved from shape-note singing schools and evangelical revivals, "but drew much of its dynamism and much of its personnel from the Holiness-Pentecostal movement of the late nineteenth century and early twentieth century. By 1900 a great stream of religious songs, fed by the big-city revivals of the era, flowed into American popular culture." Publishing houses, both within and outside denominations, cranked out paperback hymnals for church meetings and singing schools. White gospel singing groups learned from hearing the shape-note hymnals and instruction in singing schools, and from barbershop and black gospel quartets who toured the region and received wide regional radio airplay. And beyond church walls, white and black secular and religious performers traded licks, vocal styles, and lyrics.

Holiness/Pentecostalism provided fertile ground for musical interchange among white and black southerners, just as the great camp meetings of the early nineteenth century provided a similar forum for cultural interchange. Guitars, tambourines, and other rhythmical instruments, once seen as musical accompaniments for the devil, found their way into black Pentecostal churches in the early twentieth century. C. H. Mason's Church of God in Christ congregations immediately adopted them. White Pentecostalists soon picked them up, and the two shared hymns and holy dancing. Not bound by respectable conventions, white Pentecostals borrowed freely from all traditions. The derisive term "holy roller music" referred to gospel hymns, refrains, and chants belted out in an enthusiastic and syncopated style. White and black Pentecostal musical styles remained distinct, but they intersected at many points. Both employed rhythmical accompaniments, enthusiastic hollers, and holy dancing. Holiness and Pentecostal preachers and singers were among the most culturally innovative and entrepreneurial of twentieth-century plain folk southerners. As Bill Malone explains, "whether black or white, Pentecostal evangelists . . . armed with guitar and Bible, accompanied perhaps by a mandolin-strumming or tambourine-shaking wife, and preaching on street corners, under brush arbors, in tents, or in storefront churches, took their places alongside the shape-note teachers and gospel quartets as major agents in the fashioning of the southern gospel music repertory."

Black and white Pentecostals seized on the opportunities provided by mass media to spread their message. Gospel music publishing companies, led by the

Tennessee-based Vaughan empire and its numerous offshoots, profited from marketing their own tunes by sending out gospel quartet groups that sang their copyrighted songs in appealingly innovative styles. In this way, plain folk southerners learned new songs (typified by the 1930s hit "I'll Fly Away") that addressed their millennial hopes and daily struggles during the Depression. Among whites, the Vaughan family in Tennessee, and their rivals the Stampps-Baxter Company, introduced a whole new catalogue of southern religious songs that could be adapted by white gospel groups, or by bluegrass musicians such as Bill Monroe, or by black gospel soloists, quartets, and choirs. Black publishers and composers were just as aggressive. Many of the black gospel pioneers came out of the Baptist and Methodist churches, but the influence of Holiness/Pentecostal performance styles broke the stranglehold of "respectable" music that had defined urban bourgeois black services. Black gospel during these years developed its own tradition, its favorite touring quartets and choirs and first star soloists (such as Mahalia Jackson), its own fierce internal competitions among publishing outfits, composers, and traveling singing groups. In gospel, then, the streams of southern religious music, white and black, flowed alongside one another, sometimes exchanging tunes and lyrics and styles, while remaining distinct. Radio became their most effective medium, for it reached out-of-the-way places where many parishioners lived.

Later in the twentieth century, those raised as products of this racial interchange in religious expression entered the public world of broadcasting and performing. Radio orators, barnstorming evangelists, gospel singers, bluegrass pioneers, and pop stars—nearly all with roots in the low-church southern religious traditions—permanently changed American popular culture. Any number of country and soul singers and black gospel stars, from Hank Williams and Bill Monroe to Ray Charles and Sam Cooke, come to mind. Hank Williams' "Honky-Tonk Angels" bore a marked resemblance to the white gospel classic "Great Speckled Bird" made famous by Roy Acuff; Bill Monroe's innovative jamming on mandolin often backed gospel crooning that was obviously influenced by black quartet singing; Ray Charles' "Baby What I Say" was little more than a gospel vamp backing Charles' eroticized refrain; and Sam Cooke set a model for later singers such as Al Green in his move from gospel to soul and back again. Perhaps more than anyone else, however, Elvis Presley illustrates this point.

The young Elvis borrowed freely from sacred performers in creating his own musical persona. Elvis committed to memory an entire catalogue of church music, from both the white and black traditions, and could produce on command church songs of all sorts. Along with his friends in Memphis, Presley enthusiastically sampled African American religious culture both in person and on the radio. Unlike the rowdies (both white and black) who made sport of southern religious solemnities, Presley was affected by his encounter particularly with African American Pentecostalism, recognizing its kinship to his own Assemblies of God tradition. He listened to black religious orator Herbert Brewster on the radio and visited local meetings of the Church of God in Christ.

Presley's cultural pastiche emerged from a larger cultural transmission from black to white and back again, seen most clearly in the early history of Holiness/Pentecostalism and its relationship to the evolution of southern religious music. In both cases, whites and blacks borrowed theologies, performance styles, and cultural practices freely (if often unwittingly) from one another. Presley, for example, absorbed the sounds, the rhythms, and the stage manner (including the leg shake) that shaped his own electric performances. By Presley's time, white and black teenagers were eager to break down the rope lines that segregated them at rhythm and blues events, and white teenagers found black styles alluringly imitatable. White secular and religious performers learned from—some might suggest they stole—the doo-wop singing (with its own roots in black gospel quartets), religious "holy-roller" dancing, and the melismatic singing that coursed through African American church music. In the process they created sacred entertainments that shaped American popular culture. Sacred passion, expressed most obviously in white and black southern Pentecostalism, was at the heart of R & B, as well as rock-and-roll.

Southern evangelical culture also varied greatly by subregion—between city and country, Southeast and Southwest, Virginia and Texas, Florida and Kentucky, the Appalachian Mountains and the low country, the piney woods and the Black Belt, the Dust Bowl and the Florida swamplands. Where historians have (until recently) generalized about the regional religion, scholars from other disciplines, especially folklore, musicology, and religious studies, have brought their expertise into the study of practices that exist on the margins of dominant evangelicalism. Pioneered by Lawrence Levine's *Black Culture and Black Consciousness: Afro-American Folk Thought from Slavery to Freedom* (1978), scholars have addressed subjects such as ring shouts, conjure rituals, chanted sermonizing, and blues hollers. In such activities, students of religious culture have discovered a rich tradition of black expressive culture underneath the smothering rhetoric of "uplift" pervading black church organizations.

The blues were one medium for older African-derived spiritualities driven underground by the assimilationist tendencies of late nineteenth-century black religious leaders. Bluesmen spun tales of selling their souls to the devil—most famously, Robert Johnson's story of selling his soul to the devil at the crossroads—but they may have done so, theomusicologist Jon Spencer speculates, precisely because they were not that frightened of the evil presence. Closer to the trickster gods of Africa than to the darkly powerful Satan of Western Christianity, the devil in African American folklore was a force at once attractive, amusing, and frightening, just as were the bluesmen themselves. As Spencer summarizes, the country blues "tended to be more ritualistic than performance oriented . . . tended to be more priestly than artistic . . . tended to be more committed than merely appreciative." The preachers and the bluesmen pitted themselves as ferocious competitors in a zero-sum game. They offered two seemingly contradictory but ultimately complementary versions of black folk spirituality. Providing neither the collective solace of spirituals nor the optimistic swing of gospel, the blues instead commented on the inability of humans to sustain relationships, improve their condition, or encounter the Sacred as something other than a trickster. The country blues sketched a collective folk theodicy that spoke truth to power but also reinforced social enmities.

The power of folk traditions as both internally cohesive and destructive forces in southern black communities also is evident in the practice of conjure, or "black magic," as sensitively explored in Yvonne Chireau's study of four centuries of the practice in *Black Magic: Religion and the African American Conjuring Tradition* (2003) and Deborah Vansau McCauley's *Appalachian Mountain Religion* (1995). Chireau's work provides a most fascinating contribution to the long ongoing discussion of "magic" and "religion," of how informally envisioned and formally/theologically wrought worlds of the supernatural interact, collide, complement, and supplement one another. The practice of conjure, a form of healing and counter-harming that drew from both Christian and African-based religious elements, was primarily the province of poor southern blacks who were its primary practitioners (although whites formed a substantial clientele base). Fears of unseen powers—signified by specially concocted mixtures of roots, plants, and bags—compelled frequent recourse to conjure men. Belief in conjure—or at least a willingness to suspend disbelief—pervaded much of the Deep South. Many southern believers, black and white, engaged in a Pascalian wager, trusting in their Christianity but also keeping one foot in the world of spirits invoked by conjurers and narrated in popular tales. It was self-evident wisdom to place some stock in both. Bernice White of Leflore County, Mississippi, recalled how the people she grew up with in the first part of the twentieth century were "still scared. Oh, they would talk about they see things at night, the people come back and talk to them. Every once in a while I hear that now. I don't believe it. I never believed it, but I didn't take a chance on it not being true." Deeply held notions that imparted spiritual meanings to objects in the natural world thus remained a resilient part of southern folk understandings. For white and black religious reformers, Christianity and conjure were inherently contradictory. For many black southerners, they were complementary, able to address spiritual needs at different life moments.

The parallel among whites may be found most strongly in the Appalachian Mountains, where a variety of distinctive subregional religious traditions, with considerable folk and supernatural roots of their own, lived on in the face of the rise to respectability of the southern denominations. Appalachian Mountain religious worship and theology derive from a mixture of Scots-Irish "sacramental revivalism," German Pietism, colonial Baptist revival culture, and the anti-missions impulse in the southern backcountry. All of these came together after the camp meetings of the early nineteenth century (centered in the Upland South, particularly in Cane Ridge in Kentucky) to form what later became "mountain religion." In the antebellum era, as the benevolent empire began its march through America's religious heartland, religious folk in the Upland South took a determined stand against the increasingly Arminian theology of standard American evangelicalism. They remained true to their doctrines of waiting with a "sweet hope" for the action of the Spirit. Later in the nineteenth century, Protestant denominations began extensive home missions work in the mountains, disparaging the vital religiosity of the people while ignoring the tradition of native preaching. This continued in the twentieth century with the retranslation of "Social Gospel" ideas into current-day "liberation theology" in the mountains, again assuming the paternalist's prerogative of shining the light of true religion to deprived folk.

CONCLUSION

Studies of southern religion now make up a vital part of American religious history. The distorting influence of racial segregation is being dissolved as scholars attempt culturally complex histories of southern religious cultures. The overemphasis on the homogeneity of evangelical Protestantism in the region is giving way to an appreciation of diversity and complexity within the regional religious traditions. Simplistic interpretations of sectarian movements, especially Holiness/Pentecostalism, while still prevalent in American religious history generally, will not survive the coming generation of scholarship on this topic, much of it now unpublished but soon to have a major impact on the field.

Important questions and avenues of scholarship remain. The discovery of southern Jewish history goes on apace. Meanwhile, the diversification of the contemporary South brings religious pluralism to the region. Thomas Tweed's study of a Cuban Catholic shrine in Miami is one of the first of what will be many more works on non-Protestant religious expressions in the recent South. Since much of this concerns contemporary groups, anthropologists and sociologists have been the pioneers of this work. Important questions remain in understanding religion in the present-day South. The new South, symbolized by rising mega-regions such as Atlanta, Dallas, and Houston, stems in part from the successes of local leaders in attracting corporate enterprises to their region. Can southern religion remain "distinctive" in such settings? Is "Sun Belt religion" a different species than "southern religion," given that the religion of the Sun Belt is attracting business enterprise while the religion of the South historically has provided spiritual comfort to those in relative poverty?

Most importantly, the field awaits a successful integration of scholarship on white and black religious traditions. A number of scholars have attempted studies that present southern religion as the product of mutual interactions, hostilities, and influence between whites and blacks. No one, really, has succeeded fully in that venture yet. Southern religious history since the Civil War awaits the synthetic work that captures southern religious expressive cultures in all their complexity, tragic pain, and reconciling possibilities.

RESOURCE GUIDE

Printed Sources

Primary Sources

Allen, William Frances. *Slave Songs of the United States*. Orig. ed. 1867. Bedford, MA: Applewood Books, 1996.

Raines, Howell, ed. *My Soul Is Rested: Movement Days in the Deep South Remembered*. Reprint, New York: Viking Press, 1983.

Shurden, Walter B., and Richard Shepley, eds. *Going for the Jugular: A Documentary History of the SBC Holy War*. Macon: Mercer University Press, 1996.

Washington, James, ed. *Testament of Hope: The Essential Writings and Speeches of Martin Luther King, Jr.* Reprint ed. San Francisco: Harper, 2003.

Waters, Donald, ed. *Strange Ways and Sweet Dreams: Afro-American Folklore from the Hampton Institute*. Boston: G. K. Hall, 1983.

Zuckerman, Phil, ed. *DuBois on Religion*. Walnut Creek, CA: Altamira Press, 2000.

Secondary Sources

Boles, John B. *The Great Revival, 1787–1905: The Origins of the Southern Evangelical Mind*. Lexington: University Press of Kentucky, 1972.

Campbell, James T. *Songs of Zion: The African Methodist Episcopal Church in the United States and South Africa*. New York: Oxford University Press, 1995.

Cash, Wilbur J. *The Mind of the South*. New York: Knopf, 1941.

Chireau, Yvonne. *Black Magic: Religion and the African American Conjuring Tradition*. Berkeley: University of California Press, 2003.

Egerton, John. *Speak Now Against the Day: The Generation Before the Civil Rights Movement in the South*. Chapel Hill: University of North Carolina Press, 1994.

Eighmy, John Lee. *Churches in Cultural Captivity: A History of the Social Attitudes of Southern Baptists*. Ed. Samuel S. Hill, Jr. Knoxville: University of Tennessee Press, 1972.

Evans, Eli N. *The Provincials: A Personal History of Jews in the South*. New York: Atheneum, 1973.

Garrow, David J. *Bearing the Cross: Martin Luther King, Jr., and the Southern Christian Leadership Conference*. New York: Vintage, 1986.

Genovese, Eugene D. *Roll, Jordan, Roll: The World the Slaves Made*. New York: Pantheon Books, 1974.

Goff, James. *Close Harmony: A History of Southern Gospel*. Chapel Hill: University of North Carolina Press, 2001.

Hall, Randal Lee. *William Louis Poteat: A Leader of the Progressive-Era South*. Lexington: University Press of Kentucky, 2000.

Harrell, David Edwin. *Oral Roberts: An American Life*. Bloomington: University Press of Indiana, 1985.

Harvey, Paul. *Freedom's Coming: Religion, Race, and Culture in the South, Civil War Through Civil Rights*. Chapel Hill: University of North Carolina Press, forthcoming.

Heyrman, Christine Leigh. *Southern Cross: The Beginnings of the Bible Belt*. New York: Knopf, 1997.

Higginbotham, Evelyn Brooks. *Righteous Discontent: The Women's Movement in the Black Baptist Church, 1880–1920*. Cambridge, MA: Harvard University Press, 1993.

Hill, Samuel S., Jr. *Encylopedia of Religion in the South*. Reprint, Macon: Mercer University Press, 1998.

———. *Southern Churches in Crisis*. New York: Holt, Rinehart, and Winston, 1967.

———, ed. *Religion and the Solid South*. Nashville: Abingdon Press, 1972.

Isaac, Rhys. *The Transformation of Virginia, 1740–1790*. Chapel Hill: University of North Carolina Press, 1982.

K'Meyer, Tracy Elaine. *Interracialism and Christian Community in the Postwar South: The Story of Koinonia Farm*. Charlottesville: University Press of Virginia, 1997.

Larson, Edward J. *Summer for the Gods: The Scopes Trial and America's Continuing Debate over Science and Religion*. New York: Basic Books, 1997.

Levine, Lawrence H. *Black Culture and Black Consciousness: Afro-American Folk Thought from Slavery to Freedom*. New York: Oxford University Press, 1978.

Luker, Ralph. *The Social Gospel in Black and White: American Racial Reform, 1885–1912*. Chapel Hill: University of North Carolina Press, 1991.

Lyerly, Lynn. *Methodism and the Southern Mind, 1780–1810*. New York: Oxford University Press, 1998.

Manis, Andrew. *A Fire You Can't Put Out: The Civil Rights Life of Birmingham's Reverend Fred Shuttlesworth*. Tuscaloosa: University of Alabama Press, 1999.

Marsh, Charles. *The Last Days: A Son's Story of Sin and Segregation at the Dawn of a New South*. New York: Basic Books, 2001.

Martin, Joel. *Sacred Revolt: The Muskogees' Struggle for a New World*. Boston: Beacon Press, 1991.

Mathews, Donald G. *Religion in the Old South*. Chicago: University of Chicago Press, 1977.

McCauley, Deborah Vansau. *Appalachian Mountain Religion: A History*. Urbana: University of Illinois Press, 1995.

Montgomery, William E. *Under Their Own Vine and Fig Tree: The African-American Church in the South, 1865–1900*. Baton Rouge: Louisiana State University Press, 1993.

Morris, Aldon D. *The Origins of the Civil Rights Movement: Black Communities Organizing for Change*. New York: The Free Press, 1984.

Nelson, John K. *Blessed Company: Parishes, Parsons, and Parishioners in Anglican Virginia, 1690–1776*. Chapel Hill: University of North Carolina Press, 2002.

Norman, Corrie, et al., eds. *Religion in the South: Yesterday, Today, and Tomorrow*. Knoxville: University of Tennessee Press, 2004.

Owen, Christopher H. *The Sacred Flame of Love: Methodism and Society in Nineteenth-Century Georgia*. Athens: University of Georgia Press, 1998.

Ownby, Ted. *Subduing Satan: Religion, Recreation, and Manhood in the Rural South, 1865–1920*. Chapel Hill: University of North Carolina Press, 1990.

Raboteau, Albert J. *Slave Religion: The "Invisible Institution" in the Antebellum South*. New York: Oxford University Press, 1978.

Schweiger, Beth Barton. *The Gospel Working Up: Progress and the Pulpit in Nineteenth-Century Virginia*. New York: Oxford University Press, 2000.

Sobel, Mechal. *Trabelin' On: The Slave Journey to an Afro-Baptist Faith*. New ed. Princeton: Princeton University Press, 1988.

Spencer, Jon Michael. *Blues and Evil*. Knoxville: University of Tennessee Press, 1993.

Stowell, Daniel W. *Rebuilding Zion: The Religious Reconstruction of the South, 1863–1877*. New York: Oxford University Press, 1998.

Tweed, Thomas A. *Our Lady of the Exile: Diasporic Religion at an Cuban Catholic Shrine in Miami*. New York: Oxford University Press, 1997.

Wilson, Charles Reagan. *Baptized in Blood: The Religion of the Lost Cause, 1865–1920*. Athens: University of Georgia Press, 1980.

———. *Judgment and Grace in Dixie: Southern Faiths from Faulkner to Elvis*. Athens: University of Georgia Press, 1995.

Web Site

Journal of Southern Religion
http://purl.org/jsr
Scholarly journal devoted to the study of religion in the South.

Videos/Films

The Apostle. 1997. Directed by Robert Duvall.

This Far by Faith. 2003. PBS video series based on Juan Williams and Quinton Dixie, *This Far by Faith: Stories from the African-American Religious Experience* (New York: William Morrow, 2003).

Recordings

Roots n' Blues: The Retrospective, 1925–1950. 4 CDs. Sony, 1992.

Southern Journey. Compiled by Alan Lomax. 13 CDs. Rounder Record Select Series, 1997.

Wade in the Water. 4 CDs. Smithsonian Folkway Series, 1997.

Museums, Special Collections

"Coming Home! Self-Taught Artists, the Bible and the American South." Curated by Carol Crown. Art Museum of the University of Memphis (and traveling exhibition), 2004– . At http://www.people.memphis.edu/~artmuseum/ComingHome.html.

SPORTS AND RECREATION

Bruce Adelson

Recreational pursuits in the South, with its geographic breadth and abundance of natural resources, have long centered on outdoor activities. From the earliest recorded Native American sports in the Age of Discovery to today's wildly popular stock car racing, the South has a rich, full sporting tradition. The region's recreational tradition, however, has been heavily influenced by its experience with slavery and racial discrimination. Until the late twentieth century, sports and recreation were largely segregated by race. Indeed, in some parts of the South, such as Birmingham, Alabama, and the state of Louisiana, participating in integrated athletic and recreational activities was at one time a criminal offense, punishable by a jail term. Ironically, however, the region's, and the country's, first prominent athletes were slaves who, beginning in the eighteenth century, were paid to be jockeys. Many of these early sports heroes became stars in America's first national pastime, competitive horse racing.

NATIVE AMERICAN AND COLONIAL ERA SPORTING ACTIVITIES

One of the earliest recorded accounts of sports in the South was penned by Réné Laudonnière (1529–1582), a French explorer who witnessed Native Americans in Muskogee, Georgia, playing "at ball" in 1563. He observed that "they set up a tree in the midst of a place which is 8 or 9 fathoms high, in the top whereof there is set a square mat made of weeds and bulrushes, which whosoever hitteth in playing therat, winneth the game."

Native Americans in the South had an active recreational tradition. Through the colonial period, they were widely engaged in hunting, archery, fishing, swimming, and ball sports, including a variation of lacrosse. As early as 1609, Henry Spelman, a colonist captured by Powhatan Indians in Virginia, saw several Indians playing soccer during his captivity. Most historians date soccer's beginnings to eleventh-century England. Soccer did not become popular among European Americans until the late nineteenth century.

As colonial society evolved, so did American sport and recreation. Early European American sport was largely informed by the environment and the settlers' Old World roots. The colonists took many cues from the Indians, as they imitated the methods Native Americans used in hunting, fishing, and musketry competitions. From the early seventeenth century through the American Revolution, colonists' primary individual recreation was hunting. Shortly after arriving in the New World and acquainting themselves with their new surroundings, European Americans became avid hunters of the various kinds of game and fish that abounded throughout the South. Readily available wildlife, which was unfenced and belonged largely to no one, and the almost universal possession of firearms helped make hunting a sport open to all. In addition, this activity had a strong subsistence component since participants found various utilitarian uses for their kills.

While men were this sport's primary participants, women occasionally joined their ranks. For example, in 1710 British Army Colonel Philip Ludwell (1672–1726) wrote of his amazement at seeing a "very civil" Mrs. Francis Jones, a planter's wife, who "shews nothing of ruggedness" successfully hunting deer, turkey and other animals in the wilds of the Virginia–North Carolina border.

The settlers also brought with them to the South many European games, such as bowling, ninepins, and cards. However, their game playing was often hampered by the paucity of equipment for these pursuits, although local taverns usually had the necessities for interested game players. Faced regularly with such shortages, colonists invariably turned to what the natural world had to offer.

Social Differences and Blood Sports

By the late seventeenth century, social stratification began to influence southern colonial sport. The wealthy landed gentry became the primary organizers of and participants in organized sport, such as horse racing, and individual competitions, including running and walking races, skating, fishing, and an embryonic form of cricket. Many such competitions were held on plantations, making it easy for organizers to limit access to select audiences. One exception to this exclusionary practice was wrestling, which was popular in the South throughout the colonial and post–Revolutionary periods. While many matches took place on plantations, with landowners as participants and referees, poor southerners often were part of the audience.

So-called proper society became concerned about controlling access to sport and reining in the "unbridled" passions and dissipations of the lower classes, as they increasingly saw taverns, where all sorts of gaming and gambling had flourished for years, as places of ill repute. By approximately 1670, some colonial governments, Virginia's for example, sought to limit the number of taverns in their jurisdictions. The participants in taverns' activities tended to be non-landowners and other members of the working classes.

Wealthy individuals scorned some of the more violent sports engaged in by their less well-off brethren in the southern colonies. These included fisticuffs, cudgeling (a brutal activity where two men beat each other with large sticks until one could no longer stand), and gouging, where two men grappled with each other, using their thumbs to gouge out their opponent's eyeballs.

Fire-hunting was another popular recreation engaged in by non-landed colonists but shunned by the wealthy. In fire-hunting, several men would encircle deer and set fire to the surrounding brush. The resulting flames were intended to trap the deer, which, panic-stricken with no place to run, eventually became easy prey for the hunters. Fire-hunters were often wounded by other hunters who shot blindly through the conflagration and hit compatriots on the opposite side of the flames.

Cockfighting was another fiercely popular blood sport in the South. Its appearance there dates to the late sixteenth century. Matches were arranged by newly arriving Spanish and English explorers, and extended to others, who bet prodigious sums on the deadly outcomes. Cockfights continued to be popular in the southern states, and were significant sources of gambling revenue well into the nineteenth century.

Beyond the blood sports and outdoor recreations, badminton, fives, and tennis attracted some interest through the colonial and Revolutionary periods. Badminton was mainly considered a children's game, however. Fives was similar to modern handball and was played against a wall or in a confined area with designated "alleys" serving as the court. The paucity of records concerning these sports makes it difficult to determine how popular they were.

Youth Sports

Southern children enjoyed a wide array of games during the colonial period, including some, such as leapfrog and hopscotch, which have survived until today. Children also played a game called "badger the bear" or "bait the bull." These games, perhaps children's variants of adult blood sports, involved one boy kneeling on the ground, with a guardian to shield him from the blows of twisted handkerchiefs wielded by other boys standing over him.

HORSE RACING—AMERICA'S FIRST SPECTATOR SPORT

In terms of popularity, all other sports paled in comparison to horse racing, which dates in America to the early seventeenth century. This sport was a great social leveler, since it attracted people of all classes and races. With its universal appeal, horse racing was America's first true national pastime. Not surprisingly, horse racing also attracted much gambling. Bets were actively made before and during the races.

Eventually, Americans invented quarter racing, a truly New World variant of European horse racing. Faced with seemingly endless acres of woodlands in the New World and no prospect for laying out racecourses of a mile or more like those in England, the colonists created paths through the woods ten to twenty-four feet wide and one-quarter mile long, hence the name quarter racing. Courses were kept as uniform as possible so that the results of different races could be compared. The North Carolina-Virginia border, which became known as "the race horse region," was a hotbed of quarter racing during the colonial era.

Horse Racing's African American Tradition

Through the Civil War, most quarter race jockeys were slaves who were paid in cash, perquisites, or goods. However, slave jockeys, while enjoying their brief freedom and the opportunity to compete and excel in sport, were often cruelly reminded of who they were, being physically beaten by their masters, for example, for cheering too demonstratively against a rival owner's horse. There were white jockeys as well. Many so-called gentleman jockeys rode the horses they owned.

Austin Curtis, born in approximately 1759, was perhaps America's first sports star. A slave in Roanoke, Virginia, Curtis helped his owner, Willie Jones (1741–1801), develop a powerful stable of race horses that few comers were willing to take on. Curtis and Jones also developed a unique relationship, with Jones entrusting his prize jockey with responsibilities unusual for a slave in the eighteenth century. Curtis often crossed state lines, for instance, without Jones, to prepare for various races. In 1778 and 1779, Curtis also safeguarded Jones's horses from invading British troops. Curtis became his master's partner and gained his freedom in 1791 when he was at the top of his form as the South's premier jockey. After Curtis died on January 5, 1809, his obituary appeared in a Raleigh, North Carolina newspaper. It was almost unheard of at that time for a black person's death to be recognized in a newspaper, but Austin Curtis was no average man. As his obituary noted, he was "well known for many years past, as keeper of race horses. . . . His character was unblemished; his disposition mild and obliging . . . he possessed the esteem of *many*—the respect and confidence of all who knew him."

Horse Racing Expands

It did not take long for horse racing to become popular throughout the South. It expanded into all the southern colonies and moved on to the frontier areas. Kentucky's first quarter race course was built in 1780. Horse races were also held in the streets of Louisville beginning in 1783. Within four decades, Kentucky had established itself as the unchallenged leader in thoroughbred horse breeding, which was also popular in Florida.

By the 1820s, Tennessee rivaled Virginia as the horse racing capital of the South. Andrew Jackson (1767–1845), future president and an inveterate horse breeder and racing fancier, developed a prominent horse racing center in Nashville that was also famous for its horse breeding.

South Carolina was another haven for America's national sport. In the late eighteenth century, Washington Course opened in Charleston. By all accounts, this was America's first major sports facility, and women reportedly frequented the course in large numbers. In the early 1800s, it was still highly unusual for women to be seen at sporting events, spectacles considered unseemly for women's gentle dispositions.

The end of the Civil War led to an upsurge in the popularity of horse racing, which was largely suspended during the conflict, when horses could not be spared for the frivolity of sport. Between 1867 and 1875, the three events that today comprise thoroughbred horse racing's Triple Crown were created: the Belmont Stakes in New York (1867), the Preakness Stakes in Baltimore (1873), and the Kentucky

Derby (1875) in Louisville. The Kentucky Derby has evolved into the most famous horse race in the United States, and perhaps the entire world.

The Kentucky Derby

The Kentucky Derby was originally conceived by its founder, Colonel M. Lewis Clark (1856–1899), as a match between the best thoroughbreds of Kentucky and Tennessee. However, after returning in 1873 from a two-year trip to Europe where he viewed several racecourses, Lewis changed his plan, expanding the Derby to encompass all comers. He also lengthened his original mile and a quarter track to a mile and a half, after England's renowned Epsom Derby. The first Kentucky Derby was run on May 17, 1875. Aristides, a three-year-old chestnut colt, was the first winner. He was ridden by Oliver Lewis, an African American. The nearly century-old tradition of star black jockeys continued well beyond the Civil War. Indeed, Isaac Murphy (1871–1896) was arguably the greatest African American jockey in Derby history, winning three races in Louisville in the late nineteenth century. The Derby endures as one of the world's preeminent racing events.

SPORTS AND SLAVERY

Slaves engaged in many other sport and recreational pursuits in addition to horse racing. Southern plantations during the antebellum period were the focal point for organized sporting activities. In coastal areas of the South, plantation owners organized boat races, similarly between rival slave teams.

Many plantation owners also arranged boxing matches, pitting their slaves against those of neighboring plantations. Boxing matches were so popular among slaves and many plantation owners that they often generated more gambling revenue than horse racing. A widely told story, apocryphal or not, relates that the best "boxer slaves" earned enough money through fighting to buy their freedom and move north, where they became relatively wealthy as boxers.

Tom Molineaux (1784–1818) was one slave who did buy his freedom with $500 he earned in a boxing match against a slave from another plantation. He was perhaps America's first boxing star. In 1810 Molineaux fought for the boxing title against British heavyweight champ Tom Crib. After thirty-nine exhausting, brutal rounds, Molineaux collapsed and Crib was declared the winner.

Sundays were typically treated as days off for slaves. Many plantation owners also gave their slaves time off for either all or part of Saturday. Frederick Douglass (1818–1895) postulated that slaves were afforded leisure time on weekends and holidays as a control mechanism, to keep down "the spirit of insurrection among the slaves." Slaves engaged in many sports and recreations on these off days. Hunting and fishing were common pastimes that afforded slaves the opportunity to supplement their diets. Some planters also allowed their slaves to sell their bounty. However, many whites complained that slaves were such successful hunters and fishermen that they were monopolizing fishing and hunting opportunities in their communities. In 1831 fifty-six white residents of New Bern, North Carolina, asked the state legislature to ban slaves from hunting and fishing unless accompanied by a white person.

On weekends and holidays, slaves often visited nearby towns, where many different sports were enjoyed. Enslaved African Americans played ball sports, pitched quoits (horseshoes), ran footraces, wrestled, and played marbles among themselves on plantations or when they ventured into town. Slaves in the New Orleans area played a game called raquette, a Native American sport similar to lacrosse. Some male slaves also placed wagers, alongside white men, on cockfights and horse races. This interaction led some states, such as North Carolina (1830) to ban slaves from playing games of chance, with a penalty of thirty-nine lashes for violators.

CIVIL WAR ERA SPORTS

During the Civil War, Confederate soldiers carried their sports with them into battle. Cockfighting was so popular that it even delayed the march of General Stonewall Jackson's (1824–1863) army during the Shenandoah Valley campaign of 1862. Officers were unable to order their men, lured by the prospect of cockfighting and its attendant gambling, back into ranks. One Virginia regiment's troops took cockfighting so seriously that they even had their own trainer-coach to help give them an edge in competition against other regiments.

Footraces, jumping and swimming competitions, horse races, and snowball fights were popular pastimes in Confederate Army camps. While Confederate sports and recreations were basically the same as those played by southern civilians, returning troops after the war introduced a relatively new sport, and the concept of team play, to the South.

Baseball in the Nineteenth Century

During the war, Confederate prisoners watched their Union captors play baseball, a game they were largely unfamiliar with. Union troops, imprisoned in Confederate prison camps, also showed off the new game to their southern counterparts. A lithograph depicting Union prisoners playing a game at a prison camp in Salisbury, North Carolina, demonstrates baseball's spread below the Mason-Dixon Line. Northerners, carpetbaggers, and Union troops helped spread the game throughout the South in the years after the war. Although largely new to the South, baseball was nevertheless played in New Orleans before 1860.

The end of slavery dovetailed with baseball's introduction to bring a new kind of recreational democracy to the South. Baseball was open to all and was not subject to the caprices of wealthy landowners, who no longer controlled access to sporting competitions as they did during the antebellum period. Indeed, baseball was embraced by all classes of southerners, black and white. Men formed clubs and played against their rivals. Schools and colleges also adopted baseball, and began establishing teams and rules. Boys organized pick-up games in rural and urban areas. Soon semi-professional and professional teams began to appear as the sport's appeal continued to spread.

During industrialization, baseball continued to surge in popularity. By the 1880s, several entrepreneurs sought to establish a professional baseball league in the South with teams in major cities. In 1885 the Southern League of Professional Baseball Clubs was founded, with teams in Georgia (Atlanta, Augusta, Macon, and Columbus), Tennessee (Nashville, Memphis, and Chattanooga), and Alabama

(Birmingham). Atlanta won the first Southern League Championship, edging Augusta for the title.

Among the new league's stalwart players was Bill Hart (1865–1936). A right-handed pitcher, Hart was one of only two hurlers on Chattanooga's 1885 staff. However, because the other pitcher often mysteriously disappeared on game days, Hart frequently had to do double duty, sometimes pitching three or four days in a row. During one four-game series, he started and won all four games. In addition, Hart also played right field. In 1886 he began an eight-year major league baseball career when he debuted with Chicago. After his big league playing days were over, Hart returned to the Southern League in 1907, where he spent four more seasons, finally retiring from baseball in 1910 at the age of forty-five.

Separate and Unequal: Jim Crow, Baseball, and Southern Spectator Sports

Overlaying the rise to prominence of spectator sports in the last half of the nineteenth century was de jure segregation, the invidious reality that permeated every sector of southern life. By the early twentieth century, the South's golf courses, public parks, stadiums, sandlots, and basketball courts were all segregated by race.

Jim Crow also resulted in the segregation of two of the South's newly created sporting extravaganzas—the Orange Bowl (1935, based in Miami) and the Sugar Bowl (1934, based in New Orleans). Both bowls, together with California's Rose Bowl and El Paso's Sun Bowl, featured New Year's Day college football matchups between some of the nation's best teams. Local businessmen created the bowls, hoping that the games' national media attention would garner extra revenue for their businesses and communities. However, the games were segregated, since northern universities with black players on their teams were conspicuously not invited to attend. These schools quietly acquiesced in this discrimination until the late 1940s, when the integration of major league baseball changed America forever.

In 1947 the Brooklyn Dodgers' Jackie Robinson broke baseball's color line as he became the first African American in the twentieth century to play major league baseball. Robinson's debut had a stunning impact on the nation, by showing irrefutably that a black man could successfully compete with and excel against his white counterparts. Such a notion was quite subversive to unreconstructed segregationists in the South and elsewhere.

Dodgers president Branch Rickey decided to take advantage of Robinson's prominence by organizing a spring 1948 barnstorming tour for the Dodgers to several southern cities, including Asheville, North Carolina, and Fort Worth, Texas. Record-setting integrated crowds greeted the Dodgers at virtually every stop on their tour. Never before had blacks and whites in the South attended professional team sporting events in such great numbers. These cities, as with nearly all in the South of the 1940s, had also never seen a professional team sporting event with white and black players. This truly was a revolutionary concept at that time. Until at least the 1970s, baseball was overwhelmingly the most popular American spectator sport, especially in the South, where more than 150 professional baseball teams competed through the early 1960s. Given its popularity and widespread appeal, the impact of baseball desegregation would shake the very foundation of Jim Crow southern society.

While most southern ballparks had separate facilities for the races, blacks and whites had some occasions to mingle with each other, as they did in Asheville on April 8 and 9, 1948. On these dates, the Brooklyn Dodgers opposed the local minor league baseball team, the Asheville Tourists, before more than 9,000 spectators at McCormick Field. This old ballpark had a capacity of approximately 3,500, but the Tourists did their best to accommodate the record number of people wanting to see the Dodgers and their black star. Before each game, Robinson was greeted warmly by his newfound fans. When the Dodgers returned to Asheville in 1951 with a second black player, Roy Campanella, joining Robinson, another attendance record was set when 6,579 fans turned out to see Campanella drive in the winning run in Brooklyn's 9–8 victory over Asheville.

Buoyed by his 1948 success, Rickey arranged a larger, more ambitious tour in 1949. The Dodgers barnstormed in Florida and Georgia, touching down in Macon, Atlanta, West Palm Beach, and Miami. As in 1948, the team drew appreciative, record-setting crowds almost everywhere they played. Fans clamored for a chance to see Robinson. A crowd of 6,400 filled 4,000-seat Luther Williams Field in Macon to see Robinson and the Dodgers.

Unlike 1948, the 1949 tour encountered resistance from the Ku Klux Klan, which threatened boycotts and other acts of protest when the Dodgers crossed into Georgia. The Klan stepped up its declamations on the eve of Brooklyn's arrival in Atlanta, where they planned to play the Crackers, the city's minor league baseball team. In a seminal rebuff to segregation, Crackers owner Earl Mann ignored the Klan and welcomed the Dodgers to his ballpark. Over a three-game span at Ponce de Leon Park, more than 50,000 black and white fans watched the two teams play. No such numbers had ever attended an Atlanta team sporting event before. For the first time, Mann even opened a section of the grandstand to accommodate the record-setting number of black fans who paid their way into his park.

The 1948 and 1949 tours paved the way for integrated professional and collegiate sports in the South, although not before segregationists fought a last stand to protect their way of life. Massive southern resistance to the U.S. Supreme Court's *Brown v. Board of Education* decision in 1954, which declared segregated public schools to be unconstitutional, resulted in the erection of as many road-blocks as possible to prevent social integration. The anticipation of the *Brown* decision and the ruling itself led cities such as Memphis and Birmingham to criminalize interracial athletics and recreations. Violators in Birmingham, for example, faced a jail term of up to six months and/or a $100 fine for playing any integrated game in public.

In the late 1950s, Louisiana and Mississippi acted similarly on a statewide basis, while Georgia tried unsuccessfully to do so in 1955. These efforts largely ended in 1958 when a landmark decision declared segregated sports unconstitutional. Three federal judges in Louisiana upheld the claim of a black boxer, Joseph Dorsey, that he had the constitutional right to fight professionally against white and black men. Dorsey had fought in New Orleans and was prevented from fighting white boxers by the state's interracial sports ban.

It was not until 1964 that all of the South's more than 150 minor league baseball teams had integrated. In the 1950s and early 1960s, with minor league baseball teams in virtually every corner of the South, this sport had by far the greatest reach of all spectator recreations. Also, as the national pastime, omnipresent southern baseball had a tremendous impact on southern leisure time and attitudes. Its desegregation influenced people and southern society far beyond the ballpark. Baseball integration helped lay the foundation for the eventual integration of the South.

Although some southern colleges began breaking down color barriers starting in late 1947 when the University of Virginia hosted an integrated football squad from Harvard, collegiate sports and recreation in the South were not fully integrated until the early 1970s.

The Negro Leagues

Formed in response to professional baseball's segregation in the 1880s, the Negro leagues were loosely organized until 1920, when the Negro National League was founded. The formation of the Negro American League in 1937 led to spirited competition between the two circuits. Many historians consider the period from the mid-1930s through World War II the golden age of black baseball.

F. W. Purdue of Birmingham, Alabama, founded the Negro Southern League (NSL) in 1920. The league, which stayed in business until the mid-1950s, at one time featured some of the South's greatest Negro league teams, among them the Birmingham Black Barons, Nashville Elite Giants, Memphis Red Sox, and Monroe (Louisiana) Monarchs. This league was considered a Negro "minor league," feeding the major league Negro National and Negro American leagues. However, the NSL had its own brief moment in the big time, serving as one of the Negro major leagues in the 1930s.

The South featured legendary Negro league stars and teams in Atlanta, Chattanooga, Little Rock, Louisville, and many other cities. The Birmingham Black Barons were probably the best of the South's Negro league teams and featured such stars as Lorenzo "Piper" Davis (1917–1997), considered one of the best infielders in black baseball during the 1940s; Hall of Famer Willie Mays (1931–); and Sam Hairston (1920–1997), who became the first black player for major league baseball's Chicago White Sox in 1951.

The Memphis Red Sox, another prominent southern team, had its own history of stalwart players, including Bob ("The Rope") Boyd, who batted more than .370 three times in his Memphis career, and leading pitcher Verdell Mathis. Many of the Negro leagues' greatest players—among them Mississippi's James "Cool Papa" Bell (1903–1991), Virginia's Ray Dandridge (1913–1994), Georgia's Josh Gibson (1911–1947), Alabama's Monte Irvin (1919–) and Satchel Paige (1906–1982), North Carolina's Walter "Buck" Leonard (1907–1997), and Florida's John Henry "Pop" Lloyd (1884–1965)—were southern natives who are today members of baseball's Hall of Fame.

The integration of sports also led to the demise of the Negro leagues in the South and throughout the United States. Once Jackie Robinson broke big league baseball's color line, Negro league players became interested in trying to jump to the majors. By the mid-1950s, virtually all of the Negro leagues' most talented players had left to try so-called organized (heretofore white) baseball, leaving this proud institution, once a fixture of life among southern blacks, a shell of what it had been.

The South has given birth to many other great baseball players too numerous to mention. Perhaps the most famous is Alabama's Hank Aaron (1934–), whose 755 lifetime home runs remain an all-time baseball record. Aaron spent part of his Hall of Fame career with the Atlanta Braves, who debuted in 1966 as the Old South's first major league sports team.

Leo "Muscle" Shoals

Industrial baseball leagues from the mid-twentieth century fielded numerous competitive teams with star players, many of whom went on to enjoy professional careers. One of the most heralded and colorful of these industrial league stars was Leo "Muscle" Shoals (1916–2000). Like his industrial league compatriots, Shoals, who worked for a shovel manufacturer, earned extra money during the Great Depression as a slugger for his company's team.

Shoals, a barrel-shaped man with enormous arms, starred on the industrial sandlots of West Virginia, bashing balls over the fences until he signed a professional baseball contract with the St. Louis Cardinals in 1937. St. Louis sent Shoals to its farm team in Monessen, Pennsylvania, where he began a fifteen-year pro career, playing largely for teams in such southern states as Louisiana, North Carolina, South Carolina, and Tennessee.

Shoals quickly developed a reputation as a hell-raiser. He was shot after a barroom brawl and nearly came to blows with one of his managers. These incidents undoubtedly contributed to his never reaching the major leagues. But he did develop quite a following in the region formed by the confluence of Virginia, Tennessee, and North Carolina. Here Shoals spent his most productive seasons playing in Reidsville, North Carolina, and Kingsport, Tennessee, where he was the most feared slugger of his era from 1946 to 1955. In 1949 he slammed fifty-five homers for the Carolina League's Reidsville club. This mark remains a Carolina League record today. His home run hitting caught the attention of several big league teams, which offered him contracts. However, Shoals turned them down, finding that he made more money as a southern minor league star than he would as a major league rookie. Shoals regularly supplemented his meager baseball salary with the free meals, cars, and other gifts he received from fans and businesses. He also benefited from the tradition of passing the hat. In the small towns of the South during the 1940s and 1950s, when a home run was hit by a hometown player, fans passed the hat among themselves, collecting money to be given in tribute to their hero. Shoals often received several hundred dollars per week from these hats.

Shoals batted .427 for Kingsport in 1953 and led his league in home runs seven times, including 1955, when he topped the Appalachian League with thirty-three homers. Shoals ended his career with 363 home runs, ranking him among the most prolific sluggers in minor league history. In 1989, despite two hip replacement surgeries, Shoals began a new baseball career as a volunteer coach for the Patrick Henry High School Rebels of Abingdon, Virginia. He remains one of the greatest players and characters in southern baseball and industrial league history.

STATE FAIRS AND SPORTING TRADITION

Boxing

State fairs became popular sporting venues in the last quarter of the nineteenth century. Invariably, horse racing was the best attended sporting event at state fairs. Grandstands and racecourses were built to accommodate the large crowds. At North Carolina's fair, horses raced daily, with winning purses typically ranging from $50 to $350.

Atlanta, New Orleans, Memphis, and Charleston, with their large populations and comparative wealth, were major sporting and recreation centers. New Orleans developed into a premier boxing mecca, and was the showplace of the golden age of southern boxing, from approximately 1880 to 1892. During this time, most of the country's greatest fights were held in the South. The high-water mark came in 1892 when New Orleans hosted three world championship fights over consecutive days, with the finale featuring James Corbett defeating boxing legend John L. Sullivan.

Although the South's reign as boxing capital of the United States effectively ended in 1892, the region later gave birth to two of the greatest boxers of all time.

The Grapefruit League

Beginning in the 1930s, major league baseball teams headed south for spring training. Over the next two decades, more teams opted for Florida's sun and warm temperatures to prepare for the long baseball season. By the end of the 1950s, Florida was the established spring home of virtually all major league teams.

Today, spring training is big business, generating billions of dollars for Florida and its host communities. New ballparks dot Florida, such as Legends Field in Tampa and Roger Dean Stadium in Jupiter. Many exhibition games are sold out long before the teams hit Florida's diamonds in February. With billions of dollars at stake, spring training will likely remain a vital component of Florida's economy.

The John L. Sullivan–Jake Kilrain boxing match at Richburg, Mississippi, c. 1889. Courtesy Library of Congress.

Joe Louis (1914–1981) was born in Lafayette, Alabama. Known as the Brown Bomber, he was heavyweight champion of the world from 1937 to 1949. Muhammad Ali was born in 1942 in Louisville as Cassius Clay. He was the world's premier boxer during the 1960s and 1970s and remains a worldwide personality to this day.

Shooting

Shooting competitions were also popular state fair sports. They often featured matches with gun and drill clubs, newly created following the Civil War, as well as individual competition. The drill clubs or teams were a direct outgrowth of the war. These fraternal organizations were created to recapture the glory of the South's Lost Cause by embodying a military ethos and featuring displays of marching and parading.

Amusement Parks

Amusement parks have played a prominent role in southern recreation into the twenty-first century. Since Disney World opened in Orlando, Florida, in 1971, theme amusement parks have spread throughout the South. The first large theme park with a distinctive southern flavor was Nashville's Opryland, which opened in 1972 seeking to capitalize on the growing appeal of country music.

Opryland is like a mini version of the popular image of the (white) South. The food is quintessentially southern, with biscuits and gravy, fried chicken, and iced tea among the featured items. Souvenirs with a southern flair, including some with the Confederate flag, are also widely available. The *General Jackson*, a replica of the old-fashioned paddle wheeler that first plied Tennessee's Cumberland River in 1817, is another popular attraction. The music is largely country, although other genres are also honored here. But with the Grand Ole Opry, country music's historic home on the premises, this is country's theme park. The success of Opryland led to the creation of Dollywood in Pigeon Forge, Tennessee. This park honors country music singing star Dolly Parton, who grew up in the nearby Smoky Mountains.

Colonial Williamsburg is another kind of theme park. It is a privately run historic recreation of the colonial town of Williamsburg, which at one time was the capital of Virginia. The public buildings have all been designed to resemble their counterparts from the mid-1750s. Staff dressed in period costumes are omnipresent and help add a touch of historic realism to this setting.

Colonial Williamsburg's historic theme is also captured at several southern sites that memorialize the Civil War. Many of that conflict's most significant battlefields have been preserved as national monuments. Vicksburg, Mississippi; Fredericksburg, Virginia; and Chattanooga and Chickamauga, Tennessee, are three of the most popular battlefields for visitors seeking to understand more about the Civil War.

Gambling

Early southern fairs and amusement parks were also well known for gambling opportunities, another powerful regional tradition that lives on. Since the early 1990s, riverboat gambling has made a dramatic return to the South. Legalized gambling provides an important source of revenue, in the form of tourism and gambling dollars, to the communities featuring riverboat gaming.

In the antebellum period, riverboats plied southern waters and offered several types of gaming. However, more than 100 years after the Civil War, riverboat gambling was legalized. In 1989 Iowa became the first state to allow gaming on the water, followed by Missouri, Illinois, Indiana, Louisiana, and Mississippi.

Legalized riverboat gambling provides an important source of revenue to the communities along the Mississippi River. The *Mississippi Queen* is shown as it travels past Baton Rouge, Louisiana. Courtesy Louisiana Office of Tourism.

Today, Baton Rouge, Louisiana, has two old-fashioned riverboats offering various types of gaming. In Mississippi, riverboat gambling is typically offered on permanently docked barges, the most popular of which are docked along the Gulf coast. Both states allow twenty-four-hour gambling aboard their riverboats.

Wrestling

Wrestling, a sport that uniquely captures the southern imagination, dates back to the beginning of the colonial era, when grappling, boxing, and hand-to-hand combat blood sports were highly popular. Professional and amateur wrestling both are true institutions, perhaps because of the region's physical athletic culture. This sport grew in popularity in the mid-twentieth century.

Like all southern recreations, wrestling was at one time segregated by race. In some places, black wrestlers battled each other before African American audiences. Black wrestlers sometimes fought in sanctioned associations, such as in Georgia, which recognized the Negro Men's Heavyweight Championship Title in 1959.

Sputnik Monroe

One of the most entertaining and influential of a bevy of southern grapplers is Rock Brumbaugh, better known by his professional name, Sputnik Monroe. He was the king of professional wrestling in Memphis during the 1950s. Born in Mobile, Alabama, Monroe was a flamboyant bull of a man, weighing over 220 pounds and sporting a white streak in his hair. Unlike most white wrestlers of his time, Monroe did not shy away from crossing the color line. During his matches, he played to black fans and cultivated many friendships with African Americans. When Monroe was being booed by white patrons before a match, as he was routinely, black fans invariably came to his defense, drowning out the jeers with their own thunderous ovations. Monroe championed an end to segregated seating at wrestling matches in Memphis and Louisville, while also successfully breaking down other racial barriers throughout Memphis. Later in his career, Monroe teamed with an African American wrestler, in what many consider the first interracial pairing in southern wrestling.

BASKETBALL

In the South, college basketball is king. Teams such as Kentucky, North Carolina, and Duke have forged storied dynasties throughout the history of men's collegiate hoops. Adolph Rupp (1901–1977) coached the Kentucky Wildcats from 1930 to 1972 and won four NCAA titles, along with one NIT championship. Kentucky also won NCAA titles in 1978, 1996, and 1998. Kentucky, a member of the Southeastern Conference, has maintained a strong rivalry with the cross-state Louisville Cardinals, who won the NCAA tournament in 1980 and 1986. Kentucky also played in what many consider the best college basketball game ever—the 1992 Eastern Regional Final versus the Duke Blue Devils, which Duke won 104–103 on an improbable last-second shot.

Beginning in the 1930s, North Carolina became the center of southern basketball. Duke, North Carolina, and North Carolina State universities led the way on the college level. Factory leagues were created in such cities as Winston-Salem and Kannapolis, at the center of the state's textile industry, to foster corporate pride and teamwork among employees. These so-called Textile Leagues featured a high caliber of play by women and men and attracted much local interest.

The ACC and Tobacco Road

The Atlantic Coast Conference (ACC) has emerged as one of the best (if not the best) basketball conferences in the nation, year in and year out. Over the years, Clemson, Duke, Georgia Tech, Maryland, North Carolina, North Carolina State, Virginia, and Wake Forest have provided intense rivalries on the college hardwood. North Carolina's Research Triangle (encompassing Raleigh-Durham and Chapel Hill) is also home to the famed "Tobacco Road" basketball tradition, especially that of the backyard rivalry between the Carolina Tarheels and Duke Blue Devils, recognized as one of the greatest in all of sports. Students regularly camp outside to get in line for tickets to Duke-Carolina games. The tradition of both schools features Hall of Fame coaches—Carolina's Dean Smith (1931–) and Duke's Mike Krzyzewski (1947–)—as well as numerous All-Americans.

Basquette

In 1891 James Naismith (1861–1939), a high school teacher in Springfield, Massachusetts, invented basketball, with rules initially only for men. His game quickly spread throughout the country and made significant inroads in the South. Notably, Clara Baer of Sophie Newcomb College in New Orleans invented a version of the women's game in 1895, six years before standard rules for women's basketball were adopted in 1901. Baer sought Naismith's permission to publish the rules of her game. However, Naismith declined, prompting Baer to call her new sport "basquette."

Basquette was quite different from basketball and was conceived to emphasize "grace and skill of movement" rather than merely scoring a basket. In keeping with the 1890s concern about health, vitality, and exercise, Baer intended basquette to give women an opportunity to be physically active without being "unladylike." The emphasis on deportment was consistent with the times, when social norms dictated that women were delicate and not suited to physical strain. Instead, bicycling, calisthenics, and walking were thought to be more appropriate for women.

Baer's version of Naismith's game included frequent rest periods and no guarding or other interference with the player holding the ball. Baer also divided the court into seven zones, with players assigned to each zone. This pattern was designed to spread the players across the court and thus eliminate the pell-mell running about in the men's game. Many of her innovations for the women's game were eventually adopted nationally.

In women's basketball, the University of Tennessee forged winning traditions. Tennessee's Lady Volunteers won six national championships between 1987 and 1998 under coach Pat Summitt (1952–   ), a member of the Basketball Hall of Fame and the most successful coach in women's collegiate sports history.

Today professional and collegiate male and female teams flourish. The National Basketball Association has teams in Atlanta, New Orleans, Charlotte, Miami, and Memphis. The Women's National Basketball Association has a southern beachhead in Charlotte.

FOOTBALL

By the end of the nineteenth century, yet another new team sport, football, had geographically and psychically established itself in the South. Football spread to the South after 1869, when the first intercollegiate game was played between two northern universities, Princeton and Rutgers. In 1877 Washington & Lee College and Virginia Military Institute, both in Lexington, Virginia, played the first football game between southern colleges. However, football's introduction to the South did not go smoothly at first. Football encountered more opposition than baseball among southern religious stalwarts, who primarily objected to the violence of the game. In the late nineteenth century, football players, in a woefully mistaken display of perceived manliness, did not wear helmets. Indeed, some college coaches encouraged their players to grow their hair long to better protect their heads. Unfortunately, this plan did not succeed. Some players died from head injuries, while many others were seriously injured on the gridiron. Despite the objection of many southern churches and their followers to this northern intrusion into their perceived polite society, football quickly entrenched itself as perhaps the premier team sport in the South.

By the late nineteenth century, southern colleges and universities had become significant players in sports and recreation. By 1890 the universities of Virginia and North Carolina, Vanderbilt University, and Trinity College, which later became Duke University, had all established football programs. The game then moved to the Deep South, with the University of Georgia, Georgia Tech, the University of Alabama, Tulane, and Louisiana State University quickly following suit and forming their own teams.

While southern colleges and universities led the way with their football programs, high schools and fraternal clubs also picked up the new sport. Communities identified with their local high school football teams, making the weekly match into more than a mere game. Intense rivalries between schools developed, and continue to this day. Indeed, throughout today's Deep South, across Arkansas, Louisiana, Alabama, Mississippi, Florida, and Georgia, the weekly high school football game has few rivals for passionate sporting interest. The South's largely rural character initially fostered the intensity of the early football tilts. The games were outward manifestations of community pride among disparate rural towns and united their communities behind their local teams.

Perhaps the deep affinity southerners have for football explains why one of the game's most prominent early innovators was a southerner. John Heisman (1869–1936), for whom the Heisman Trophy (given annually to college's best football player) is named, developed the idea of using offensive linemen to block for running backs. He also advocated dividing a football game into four quarters, rather than two halves. Heisman's Georgia Tech football teams were undefeated from 1915 to 1917, a string of thirty-two games. Heisman and other southern coaches also pioneered the use of the forward pass. By early in the twentieth century, several southern universities—Clemson, Alabama, Vanderbilt, and the University of the South—had become national football powers.

Heisman set the standard for future generations of southern football coaches. The list of nationally renowned southern football coaches is lengthy. Some of the more noteworthy were Daniel McGugin, whose University of the South teams won thirteen titles in his thirty seasons as coach; Bob Neyland (1892–1962), who won 173 games over a lengthy career at the University of Tennessee that began in 1925; and Frank Broyles (1924–   ), who won seven conference championships at the University of Arkansas and is regarded as the greatest coach in that school's history.

Paul "Bear" Bryant (1913–1983) was the legendary coach of the universities of Maryland, Kentucky, and Alabama as well as Texas A&M University, whose record for most wins was eclipsed by Eddie Robinson. Bryant primarily made his mark at Alabama, where he earned a reputation for innovative play calling while wearing his trademark fedora. Bryant's legacy, however, is marred by his resistance to desegregation of college football and athletics generally. As the premier coach of his day, his resistance carried weight and slowed the inevitable integration of the sport.

SEPARATE TRADITIONS AND HISTORICALLY BLACK COLLEGES

By the twentieth century's dawn, the South had developed rigid lines of racial segregation. This was partly due to the end of Reconstruction in 1876 and the conservative, racist backlash against carpetbaggers, freed blacks, and their political power. Blacks and whites went to separate colleges and engaged in separate recreations. All aspects of everyday life grew increasingly segregated. Although integrated baseball, for example, had prospered in the New Orleans of the 1880s, by the late 1890s it was a relic of the past. From the 1890s until the early 1970s, the South's sports and recreations were overwhelmingly influenced by race; blacks and whites virtually never met in organized competitions or activities until the 1950s.

African Americans who attended black colleges energetically embraced the country's newest team sports on their campuses. In 1892 Biddle University and Livingstone College became the first black colleges to play an intercollegiate football game. Biddle bested Livingstone, with a 4–0 victory. Baseball was the first intercollegiate sport played at Atlanta Bible College, having made its debut in 1890. That year, Atlanta formed the South's first collegiate city baseball league, composed of five black colleges, including Atlanta Bible College.

Today, many southern historically black colleges retain their historic athletic traditions and continue to attract legions of fans. In the days of segregation, these and other institutions competed exclusively against each other. Tuskegee Institute and Tennessee State University have accumulated many national women's track championships. Tennessee State also won three consecutive men's basketball titles from 1956 to 1958, with John McClendon (1915–1999) as the coach. The 1957 title was historic, marking the first time that a historically black college had defeated a white university for a championship. McLendon, a member of the National Basketball Hall of Fame, won 523 games as a college coach and also coached professionally. In 1961, as coach of the American Basketball Association's Cleveland Pipers, he became the first black man to lead an integrated professional major league team.

Clarence "Big House" Gaines (1923–   ), another Basketball Hall of Famer, won 823 games in forty-seven years as a coach of the Winston-Salem State College men's basketball team. Gaines is the third winningest college basketball coach of all time. Only Adolph Rupp and Dean Smith have more victories.

In football, Grambling University in Louisiana has a storied past. Grambling's Eddie Robinson (1913–   ) is the winningest coach in college football history, with 408 victories. Enshrined in the College Football Hall of Fame, this native of Jackson, Louisiana, coached Grambling's men's football team for fifty-five years and had a streak of twenty-seven consecutive winning seasons, 1960–1986. Robinson's teams also won seventeen Southwestern Athletic Conference Championships and nine Black College National Championships. More than 200 of his players have enjoyed National Football League careers. Many of these Grambling alumni are members of the Pro Football Hall of Fame.

Even tiny Morris Brown College in Atlanta has made a large impact on the athletic field. This school has won two national collegiate championships (1940 and 1951) and has sent several players to the National Football League.

GOLF AND TENNIS

Golf and tennis, introduced in the South in the late 1800s, remained sports almost exclusively of the middle and upper classes until after World War I. The lower classes also largely shunned these sports as creations of the North. However, their popularity began spreading in the 1920s. Through the 1920s, tennis was primarily recreation for the wealthy since almost all tennis courts were at country clubs. It was not until the 1930s that public courts were built in significant numbers, although the sport's country club image persisted well into the 1960s. Neither golf nor tennis has gripped the interest of southerners as have football, basketball, horse racing, car racing, and baseball. This lag continued until many years after World War II.

Although tennis was never a wildly popular recreation in the South, the emergence of several star southern players helped broaden the game's appeal. Althea Gibson (1927–2003), born in Silver, South Carolina, quickly became a prominent player on the black tennis circuit. From there, Gibson went on to break two of tennis's racial barriers. In 1950 she became the first African American to play at the U.S. Open in Forest Hills, New York. The following year she broke another barrier, as the first black woman to play at Wimbledon, England.

In the 1960s, Arthur Ashe (1943–1993) took Gibson's achievements one step further. A native of Richmond, Virginia, Ashe was the first black man to star in professional tennis. During his career, he won thirty-five amateur and thirty-three professional titles. In 1973 Ashe became the first black player to reach the South African Open final, at a time when the government's apartheid policy was still very much alive.

Chris Evert, born in 1954 in Ft. Lauderdale, Florida, was one of the world's top tennis players in the 1970s and 1980s. In her eighteen-year career, she won 157 tournaments and more than $8.5 million in prize money. A three-time winner of the Wimbledon women's singles title, she also captured thirteen U.S. and French Open titles. Her prodigious success inspired many girls to follow in her footsteps.

In 1934 the first Masters Golf Tournament was held in Augusta, Georgia. The inauguration of what has become one of the most renowned golf tournaments and courses in the United States helped raise public interest in the sport throughout the South. As popular as this tournament became, southern interest in golf in the early twentieth century owed more to one of the region's first golf stars. Bobby Jones (1902–1971) was born in Atlanta and quickly rose to golfing prominence. Jones played in the 1916 U.S. Amateur golf tournament when he was fourteen. In his career, he won thirteen major golf championships, including the sport's Grand Slam in 1930, when he captured titles at the British Open, British Amateurs, U.S. Open, and U.S. Amateurs.

Jones also was instrumental in creating the Masters course at Augusta. He championed his sport throughout the South and almost single-handedly helped increase its popularity. With the construction of several golf courses during the Great Depression of the 1930s through federal financial assistance, Jones's ambition of spreading golf throughout the South became a reality.

The interwar period also featured the birth and growth of fraternal organizations in the South. Boy Scout and Girl Scout troops were popular. The annual Boy Scout Jamboree is still held in Virginia. After Congress passed the Smith-Lever Act, which created the Cooperative Extension System, county agents and community leaders began creating more local 4-H Clubs throughout rural areas. This was also true in the South.

The popularity of YMCAs also grew after World War I. Going back to 1856, when the first student YMCA opened at Tennessee's Cumberland University, this organization always had a place in southern life. The YMCA's connection to education continued in 1919 when Vanderbilt University helped create the southern YMCA College and Graduate School in Nashville.

CAR RACING AND THE BIRTH OF NASCAR

Between the two world wars, automobiles became more prevalent in the South than ever before. In the 1930s, cars also made inroads into the South's rural areas. During the Great Depression, some southerners used their cars to transport homemade liquor, more commonly known as moonshine, and also tobacco in hopes of evading law enforcement and the taxing authorities. Soon these liquor and tobacco drivers began racing each other informally. These races, as well as those held by others not necessarily engaged in illegal pursuits, led to the evolution of stock car racing, an original southern sporting institution.

After World War II, car ownership in the United States increased dramatically. Southerners enthusiastically embraced the car craze that was sweeping the country. Races began springing up throughout the region. Most of the fans and participants in car racing tended to be members of the lower classes, so-called rednecks, virtually all of whom were white. Reflecting the background and viewpoints of drivers and fans, Confederate flags were prominently displayed at races.

Early southern car races attracted true hell-bent-for-leather characters. Alcohol and fistfights were common features of these early tilts.

This outlaw atmosphere was abetted by the race organizers, often shady characters in their own right who thought nothing of escaping with the night's purse without splitting it with the drivers. There also was no national sanctioning body to bring order to the chaotic new sport.

In the late 1940s, Daytona Beach, Florida, became a hotbed for cars and informal car racing. Drivers, most of whom were men, proudly displayed their cars on Daytona's famed beach road, where autos are still driven today on the sand within feet of the ocean. Big Bill France (1909–1972), who came to Daytona in 1935 to open a service station and eventually organized some car races on the side, envisioned calming car racing. His dream of doing so was realized on December 14, 1947, when the National Association of Stock Car Racing (NASCAR) was formed in a Daytona Beach hotel. France was installed as its first president. NASCAR's founders intended this new organization to bring order and consistency to the madcap world of stock car racing.

The true birthplace of stock car racing remains a mystery, with many southern locales vying for the honor. Champion stock car racer Tim Flock (1924–1998), from Fort Payne, Alabama, once claimed that modern stock car racing was born in a cow pasture outside Atlanta. Here, according to Flock, drivers regularly wagered against each other. Sometimes as much as $20,000 was bet in a single night of racing.

Stock car racing remains an intensely popular recreational activity in the South today. NASCAR racing at Atlanta Motor Speedway. Courtesy Georgia Department of Economic Development.

Stock car racing's gender barrier was broken by several women, especially Ethel Flock and Sara Christian, who won NASCAR's 1949 Woman Driver of the Year award. Louise Smith of Greenville, South Carolina, was another pioneering woman driver. Driving since she was seven years old, Smith had a reputation for being able to go toe to toe with the men, in driving, drinking, and fighting.

Danville, Virginia's Wendell Scott (1921–1990) became NASCAR's first African American driver in 1947. He faced taunts from fans and fellow drivers and also was prohibited from competing at several southern racetracks because of laws and customs concerning segregation. He raced professionally for many years and won the Grand National race at Jacksonville Speedway in December 1963.

With the advent of NASCAR, sponsors became more involved in stock car racing and began manufacturing products specifically designed for high-speed automobiles. For example, in 1952 Pure Oil Company developed the first true stock car racing tire. Before this, street tires were used exclusively since no alternatives were available.

Stock car racing remains an intensely popular recreational activity in the South today, although its reach now extends much further. NASCAR has fans nationwide, with sanctioned stock car races from New England to California. This sport has also broadened its appeal. Many women and minorities are avid stock fans, and many middle- and upper-class citizens follow the sport, a far cry from its bootlegging roots in the 1930s.

The soul of stock car racing, however, remains in the South. This region retains the most storied tracks in stock car history, dating back to its formal beginnings in the late 1940s. South Carolina businessman and racing enthusiast Harold Brasington traveled to Indianapolis in 1948 to visit that city's famed Indy 500 Speedway. With ideas for his own version, Brasington returned home to Darlington where he got to work. Although his track was shorter, it retained the Indianapolis Speedway's asymmetrical design. On September 4, 1950, Darlington hosted its first race, a 500-mile event won by Johnny Mantz (1918–1972) before 20,000 fans. Darlington was the South's first paved racecourse and its first true speedway. When this track opened, it featured one toilet, one spigot with running water, and one working telephone, a far cry from the accoutrements of the modern stock car track.

Charlotte, North Carolina, Richmond, Virginia, and Talladega, Alabama, are also home to famous stock car tracks and host annual races of international renown. The Daytona Beach International Speedway, with its annual Daytona 500 race, is perhaps the most famous stock car racing track, located in the birthplace of NASCAR.

Among NASCAR's many racing personalities, the Earnhardts from Kannapolis, North Carolina, stand out as among the most prominent. Dale Earnhardt (1951–2001) was a six-time championship driver who had an enormous following among racing fans. He died from injuries suffered during a race. In 2000 Dale Earnhardt, Jr., joined the NASCAR circuit and continues to carry on his father's legacy.

Today NASCAR boasts a national television audience of more than 150 million, approximately 300 corporate sponsors of racing teams, and more than 15 million paying fans who attend its various races. Two television networks have paid $2.4 billion over six years for the right to telecast NASCAR races. The larger racetracks easily draw more than 100,000 fans for high-profile races, and space on the tracks' infields is snapped up quickly by fans. In an effort to broaden stock car racing's appeal, race days now are billed as family events, and are not just for white men anymore. As at football games, tailgate parties are common sights at NASCAR tracks. Order has been brought to stock car racing, from its wild beginnings to its more modern, buttoned-down image in the early twenty-first century. Executive suites and amenities abound at today's NASCAR tracks, which cannot completely escape their turbulent, redneck roots. For example, Confederate flags can still be seen flying among spectators in many of its venues, albeit in smaller numbers than in the past.

HOCKEY

Given its more temperate climate compared to the North and Midwest, the South has not had an extensive winter sports tradition. Indeed, the South's first National Hockey League (NHL) team, the Atlanta Flames, fled the South for Calgary in 1980 after several seasons of disappointing attendance in Georgia.

Since then, hockey's southern fortunes have changed dramatically. Intent on capturing some of the recreation interest and dollars in the South, the NHL decided to move south of the Mason-Line in the 1990s, with several franchises from Canada and Minnesota shifting out of the cold belt. There are now four NHL teams: the Florida Panthers (Sunrise, Florida), Nashville Predators, Carolina Hurricanes (Raleigh), and Atlanta Thrashers. Hockey returned to Georgia's biggest city in 1998.

Perhaps a more significant development than the presence of four National Hockey League teams in this region is the arrival of pro hockey's minor league version. The East Coast Hockey League, one of the feeder circuits for the NHL, boasted sixteen teams scattered across the South for the 2002–2004 season.

These teams, and the sports they play, have made heretofore unknown inroads in communities with virtually no winter recreation tradition and precious little experience with outdoor snow and ice. The East Coast Hockey League has teams in Arkansas, Louisiana, Mississippi, and Florida. Squads with colorful names such as the Augusta (Georgia) Lynx, Greenville (South Carolina) Grrrowl, Lexington (Kentucky) Men O'War, and Florida Everblades have become surprising sporting fixtures in their cities. The teams play in small, regional facilities where perhaps 5,000 fans per game are regular attendees. These teams' success has also sparked the creation of recreational hockey leagues and prep teams.

TRACK AND FIELD

Track and field has flourished in the South warm temperatures. Perhaps the culmination of this sport's southern popularity was the 1996 Olympic Games, which were held in Atlanta. Although the memory of these games may be permanently marred by the terrorist bombing that killed one person and injured many others, many Olympic athletes and teams established significant milestones here.

Carl Lewis (born in Birmingham, Alabama, in 1961) starred in the 1996 Olympic Games. He won a gold medal in the long jump competition and became one of four athletes ever to win nine gold medals over his Olympic career and one of three to win the same individual event four times. At the 1984 Olympics, he matched the record of Jesse Owens (1913–1980) by winning four gold medals in track events.

Owens, a native of Danville, Alabama, was a grandson of slaves. He not only became a great track star, but his victories at the 1936 Olympics in Berlin before Adolf Hitler are emblematic of one of the great acts of athletic heroism in modern sports history.

Running track at the 1936 Games was no small feat for a black man. The Germany of that time was ruled by Hitler and the Nazis. Believing themselves to be racially superior, the Nazis had begun imprisoning Jews and other minorities from Germany and other countries in concentration camps. Hitler planned to use the 1936 Olympics to showcase alleged Germanic ascendancy and scorned the presence of ten blacks on the U.S. team, decrying their ostensible inferiority. Owens' response was to win four gold medals, a feat unequaled until Lewis matched his total in 1984. The sight of Owens standing on the victory platform, saluting the American flag while German athletes gave the raised-arm Nazi salute, was a poignant reminder of all that Owens accomplished at these Olympic Games.

SOCCER

In 1996 women's soccer debuted as an Olympic sport. While the U.S. men's team disappointed its fans in Atlanta, the opposite was true for the women, who captivated the hometown crowd in Atlanta, playing before increasingly bigger crowds as the tournament progressed. The gold medal game was the culmination point. In one of the most anticipated soccer games in U.S. history, the American team won the first Olympic gold medal in women's soccer. More than 76,000 fans and a national television audience watched history being made.

Several unsuccessful attempts were made to capitalize on the women's team's success. Professional soccer leagues did not generate a consistent level of interest and revenue and ultimately proved untenable. However, sandlot, high school, and college soccer remain highly popular in the United States, including the South. Indeed, the South boasts some of the nation's top collegiate soccer programs, such as those at Central Florida University and George Mason University (Virginia). In addition, the University of North Carolina at Chapel Hill Fields the best women's soccer team in the country almost every year. Indeed, the women's team is the embodiment of success since the advent of Title IX in the 1970s opened up collegiate sports to women. The UNC squad has compiled a phenomenal run of dominance. Since the team was formed in 1979, the school has won sixteen national championships, a record of success virtually unparalleled in American collegiate and professional sports history. North Carolina women also made significant contributions to the 1996 Olympic gold medal team. Of the sixteen players on that squad, seven were either North Carolina alumnae or active players for the Tar Heels. Mia Hamm (1972–   ), the most famous women's soccer player in the United States, is a North Carolina native and UNC alumna. She was also a starring member of the 1996 gold medal team.

Soccer had remained mostly static in popularity until the 1980s. Then, helped by Title IX's requirement of parity between women's and men's sports, participation in this sport boomed. Indeed, women's collegiate soccer is one of Title IX's greatest success stories. By the late 1990s, there were more women's collegiate soccer teams than men's. In 1980, 900,000 women and girls participated in organized soccer. By 1990, this number more than doubled, to 2 million. At the end of the twentieth century, it was estimated that more than 2.5 million girls and women participated in soccer programs.

OUTDOOR RECREATIONS

Outdoor recreation has always been very popular in the South. Fishing in particular, as a pastime and as a livelihood, is enjoyed by many southerners who benefit from the fact that one-half of the U.S. coastline is below the Mason-Dixon Line. In addition to providing many recreational opportunities, fishing is the lifeblood of many southern communities. For example, Gulf of Mexico fishing for shrimp, grouper, and other marine creatures continues to be important economically for the states lining the Gulf basin. Louisiana, Virginia, and North Carolina rank among the national leaders in annual fish catches.

Millions of recreational fishing licenses are sold each year throughout the South. Salt and fresh water fishing are both available. Since more than 60 percent of

Deep-sea fishing is a pastime enjoyed by many southerners who benefit from the fact that one-half of this country's coastline is below the Mason-Dixon Line. Courtesy Palm Beach County Convention and Visitors Bureau.

southerners live less than two hours from a saltwater coast, fishing in these waters is very popular. The Outer Banks of North Carolina are a haven for saltwater fishing aficionados.

Hiking, camping, mountaineering, mountain biking, and similar outdoor pursuits are also popular southern pastimes. This region has two of the country's most frequently visited national parks, Great Smoky Mountain National Park in North Carolina and Tennessee, and Shenandoah National Park in Virginia. Indeed, Great Smoky Mountain attracts more visitors annually than any other national park in the United States. Other popular nationally protected attractions in the South include Cape Hatteras National Seashore in North Carolina and Everglades National Park in Florida. Hot Springs National Park in Hot Springs, Arkansas, is the country's only national park featuring bathhouses. Hot Springs' houses date from the early twentieth century and use this city's still active historic hot springs.

HIGH SCHOOL AND COLLEGE SPORTS

Today, although pro sports in the South are in the ascendancy, amateur athletics remain the lifeblood of the region. Sandlot, high school, and collegiate sports are often the center of attention in cities and towns throughout the South, especially in rural areas. Indeed, on Friday night, southern skies are invariably brightened by the lights from countless high school football stadiums, where fervent crowds pack the grandstands to cheer on their local heroes. These games unite and divide communities at the same time, pitting neighbor against neighbor. They also can serve as metaphors for competing societal priorities—sports versus academics, a competition that plays out each week from Louisiana to Virginia.

Alabama-Auburn game. Throughout the twentieth century, football emerged as an immensely popular southern institution, at the professional, collegiate, high school, and schoolyard levels. Courtesy of the *Tuscaloosa News*.

While scholastic and collegiate sports are closely followed in every region of the country, the South has long exhibited a particular passion for these recreations. This may partly be explained by the comparatively late arrival of major league sports (with the Atlanta Braves in 1966) in the South—later than in any other part of the United States except the Mountain West. Without big league sports, fans naturally turned to the next best alternative—amateur athletics. The South's historically rural character may also explain this phenomenon. With rural communities far from big city attractions and diversions, sporting events at the local high school and college were often the only weekend entertainment available, and these institutions developed a ready-made, intensely loyal following that persists to this day.

The Alabama-Mississippi All-Star Classic is emblematic of the South's fascination with scholastic athletics. The Classic began in 1988 and features the best high school football players from each state battling for the honor of state and school pride. These games receive much media attention and are always well attended by highly spirited fans. They have also been the jumping-off point for many players headed to collegiate and professional football careers.

College sports have their own spirit and dedicated following. The South is home to many of the nation's preeminent athletic universities, with long records of success in basketball or football, the South's most watched collegiate sports. Such schools as the University of Miami, Florida State University, and the University of Georgia have excelled on the gridiron, while Duke University, the University of North Carolina, and the University of Kentucky have long been associated with top basketball teams. Not to be overlooked, Louisiana State University is frequently at the top of the nation's collegiate baseball rankings.

In college football, the annual New Year's extravaganza, the Orange Bowl, often decides the national collegiate championship. The Orange Bowl is the South's most prominent college football event. The University of Miami Hurricanes were a perennial powerhouse through the 1990s and often vied for the national title. Intense college football rivalries abound in the South, such as those between Auburn University and the University of Alabama; Florida and Florida State universities; and the University of Mississippi and Mississippi State University. These schools' stadiums are routinely packed on fall Saturday afternoons, when the sport's archrivals face each other in historic competition.

School Spirit

Together with athletic excellence, southern universities also have strong traditions of school spirit. Examples abound. At Florida State University, the Sod Cemetery stands as a monument to school pride. This tradition began in 1962, when, after beating archrival Georgia, FSU team captains returned to campus with pieces of sod from their opponent's field. The sod was presented to Florida State's dean, then planted in the corner of the football team's practice field and memorialized with a "tombstone." Since then, so-called sod games, which are always played on the road, have also included victories in bowl games and upset victories when the school was regarded as a significant underdog. Just as in 1962, each piece of sod is buried in the cemetery and given its own tombstone.

The Clemson University men's football team has a tradition known as "running down the hill," which dates from 1942. After completing warm-ups before home games at Clemson Memorial Stadium in Clemson, South Carolina, the team returns to its locker room, boards buses, and drives to the stadium's east entrance. The team positions itself at the top of the stadium and waits for a signal. Before starting down the hill, each football player rubs Howard's Rock, a rock from Death Valley that is mounted on a pedestal. The rock was given to the university by former coach Frank Howard and was first rubbed by the football team on September 23, 1967, before a 23–6 victory over Wake Forest University. Since then, before each Clemson home game, every uniformed football player has sought the luck of Howard's Rock.

At the sound of a cannon blast, the band strikes up and the team charges down some 100 feet onto the playing field. Fans cheer wildly as the football players dash downhill through the crowd. The Clemson Tigers have carried this tradition through nearly 300 football games. Running down the hill began rather prosaically. In 1942 the locker rooms were at the top of the stadium, so going down (the players walked at first) through the grandstand was the quickest route to the field. Even after new locker rooms were built at field level, the tradition remained.

Georgia Tech University's football teams have long been known as the Rambling Wreck of Georgia Tech, symbolized by an old car, which leads the football team onto the field before each game. Rambling Wreck dates to 1927 and refers to a 1914 Ford owned by the university's dean of men. In the 1950s, university officials decided that the school needed an official "wreck" that would be a permanent mascot for its team. On September 30, 1961, the wreck, a 1930 Ford coupe, was unveiled for the first time at the school's home opener against Rice University and led Georgia Tech onto the field. The car was restored in 1982 and remains a fixture at Tech football games.

Since the 1920s, University of Arkansas Razorbacks fans have had a stirringly unique cry to support their athletic teams. The famous Hog Call resounds through the stadium and arena to rally the Razorbacks. *WOOOOOOOOOOOOOOO, pig! SOOIE!* has become a legendary cry heard throughout Arkansas.

Cheerleading and Twirling

Together with college and high school athletics and the spirit they invoke, cheerleading is very popular in the South. The University of Kentucky is perhaps the leading university in the United States in cheerleading. Its squads are regularly ranked among the best in the country. Indeed, Kentucky's cheerleaders have won the collegiate national championship an unprecedented twelve times—in 1985, 1987, 1988, 1992, and 1995–2002. They are the only cheerleaders to have won back-to-back titles and to have won eight successive championships. Kentucky's eight-year streak was broken in 2003 by representatives of another southern institute of higher learning, Central Florida University.

Cheerleading as a sport in the United States likely began at eastern and midwestern universities, and then spread throughout the rest of the country. In the South, this new activity became a hit almost instantly. At its inception in the late nineteenth century, cheerleading squads consisted of up to five members, invariably men. Unlike today's cheerleaders, their "uniforms" were indistinguishable from their classmates' garb. They wore sweaters with their school's colors and pants.

Early cheerleading was linked to athletics and was intended to inspire loyalty and school pride among students. After World War I, as more women attended college, they also participated in unprecedented numbers in extracurricular activities. After World War II, women replaced men as cheerleaders. Cheerleading squads also expanded to include as many as twenty women.

In 1948 the first cheerleading camp was held in Huntsville, Texas. Fifty-two women were schooled in the art of leading a crowd and speaking correct English by Lawrence "Herkie" Herkimer, the father of modern cheerleading, and his faculty of English and speech teachers. Herkimer, a former cheerleader himself at Southern Methodist University, is famous for many cheerleading innovations that can still be seen today. For example, in 1956 he invented the pom-pom by tying colored streamers to batons. He also pioneered the use of gymnastics and dance to lead cheers.

Today cheerleading is at the height of its appeal and popularity. Since the late 1980s, men in the United States have again become involved in the sport. In 2003 college cheerleading squads were split roughly 50–50 between men and women. Cheerleading has also spread to countries in Asia and Europe, becoming a truly worldwide phenomenon.

Cheerleading has also grown far beyond its roots as merely something to inspire other students. It has become a business and entertainment property. Cheerleading competitions are held nationwide and many are televised on ESPN. The participants' routines have also grown increasingly complex and athletically daring. Many cheerleaders have been seriously injured while attempting to perform these ever more difficult maneuvers.

Twirling is ineluctably linked to cheerleading and, like its close relative, is also quite prominent on southern high school and college campuses. The earliest twirlers were men when this activity began in the early twentieth century. Women supplanted men by the 1930s and led twirling into its golden age after World War II, when women flooded college campuses in record numbers and school spirit rallying cries were legion throughout the South. Then, as today, twirlers used batons, flags, and other objects to lead bands and spark crowds. Interestingly, although twirling was apparently not invented in the South, it nonetheless may have strong southern roots. Historian Robert Farris Thompson postulates that the familiar baton-twirling pose of the twirler's hand on her hip comes from southern black dance influences. Today, the National Baton Twirling Institute, one of the world's largest twirling schools, is held annually at the University of Mississippi.

THE RISE OF PROFESSIONAL SPORTS IN THE SOUTH

Professional team sports have been in the ascendant in the South since the end of the twentieth century. Major league baseball and football teams now span the entire South, from Charlotte, North Carolina, to New Orleans, Louisiana. The reputation of these cities has benefited from the enhanced attention the presence of major league sports invariably attracts. Indeed, some argue that Charlotte and Atlanta have grown economically as a result of new business opportunities surrounding their professional football and baseball teams. Even if the economic benefits derived from hosting major league teams are small, these and other southern cities are now more readily accorded the recognition and respect given the nation's largest cities, such as New York and Boston, who have sported major league baseball and football teams for as long as a century. In any case, major league southern teams provide increased recreational opportunities for those living in and visiting the host communities.

CONCLUSION

High schools and colleges remain at the core of southern sports and recreation. Many of the nation's top athletic programs can be found in the South, a region that has produced numerous prominent and innovative athletes and coaches in American sports history.

Chipper Jones of the Atlanta Braves. Courtesy Georgia Department of Economic Development.

In the early twenty-first century, sports in the South are arguably in their heyday. Major league sports, because of their prestige, omnipresence, and size, are at the forefront of southern sports and recreation. Professional sport franchises are found in virtually all of the South's large cities, and through radio, the Internet, and television touch more southern households than ever before.

In addition, southern major league teams are also in the midst of their greatest on-field successes, with the Florida Marlins (baseball) and Tampa Bay Buccaneers (football) winning championships in the early twenty-first century. There are more southern major league sports teams than ever before, and the record popularity of NASCAR makes this region a true mecca for professional sports.

RESOURCE GUIDE

Printed Sources

Adelson, Bruce. *Brushing Back Jim Crow: The Integration of Minor League Baseball in the American South*. Charlottesville: University Press of Virginia, 1999.

———. "Shoals' Strong Will Matched Powerful Arms." *USA Today Baseball Weekly*, April 14–20, 1993.

Altherr, Thomas L., ed. *Sports in North America*. Multivolume set. Gulf Breeze, FL: Academic International Press, 1992– .

Ayers, Edward L. *The Promise of the New South: Life after Reconstruction*. New York: Oxford University Press, 1993.

Billard, Mary. "Nascar Nirvana: R.V.'s, Rock Bands and Jell-O Shots." *New York Times*, October 17, 2003.

Bisher, Furman. "The Sports Revolution in the South." *Sport* (September 1964).

———. "What about the Negro Athlete in the South?" *Sport* (May 1956).

Bissinger, H. G. *Friday Night Lights*. New York: Da Capo Press, 2000.

Bowman, Larry. "Breaking Barriers: David Hoskins and Integration of the Texas League." *Legacies* 3, no. 1 (Spring 1991).

Byrd, William. *The Secret Diary of William Byrd of Westover, 1709–1712*. New York: Ayers Co., 1972.

Cash, W. J. *The Mind of the South*. New York: Vintage Books, 1991.

Chalk, Ocania. *Black College Sport*. New York: Dodd, Mead, 1976.

Clark, Dick, and Larry Letser, eds. *The Negro Leagues Book*. Cleveland: Society for American Baseball Research, 1994.

Culin, Robert Stewart. *Games of the American Indians*. New York: AMS Press, 1907.

Dean, Pamela. "Dear Sisters and Hated Rivals: Athletics and Gender at Two New South Women's Colleges, 1893–1920." *Journal of Sport History* (Fall 1997).

Doyle, Andrew. "Foolish and Useless Sport: The Southern Evangelical Crusade Against Intercollegiate Football." *Journal of Sport History* (Fall 1997).

Fitzpatrick, Frank. *And the Walls Came Tumbling Down: The Basketball Game that Changed American Sports*. New York: Simon and Schuster, 1999.

Hotaling, Edward. *The Great Black Jockeys*. Rocklin, CA: Prima Publishing, 1999.

Jefferson, Thomas. *The Papers of Thomas Jefferson*. Ed. Julian P. Boyd. Princeton, NJ: Princeton University Press, 1953.

"Journal of the Meetings of the President and Masters of the William & Mary College." *William & Mary College Quarterly*, 1st Series, 2, no. 2 (October 1893).

Keena, Sheila. *Encyclopedia of Women in the United States*. New York: Scholastic Press, 1996.

Martin, Charles H. "Integrating New Year's Day: The Racial Politics of College Bowl Games in the American South." *Journal of Sport History* (Fall 1997).

Sports and Recreation

Miller, Patrick. "The Manly, the Moral, and the Proficient: College Sport in the New South." *Journal of Sport History* (Fall 1997).

O'Neal, Bill. *The Southern League.* Austin, TX: Eakin Press, 1994.

Osborn, Kevin. *Encyclopedia of Sports in the United States.* New York: Scholastic Press, 1997.

Rollen, David C., and Robert W. Twyman, eds. *Encyclopedia of Southern History.* Baton Rouge: Louisiana State University Press, 1979.

Struna, Nancy L. "The Formalizing of Sport and the Formation of an Elite: The Chesapeake Gentry, 1650–1720s." *Journal of Sport History* (Winter 1986).

Sumner, Jim. "The State Fair and the Development of Modern Sports in Late Nineteenth Century North Carolina." *Journal of Sport History* (Summer 1988).

Voigt, Quentin David. *American Baseball.* Vol. 1. University Park, PA: Pennsylvania State University Press, 1983.

Wiggins, D. "Good Times on the Old Plantation: Popular Recreations of the Black Slave in the Antebellum South, 1810–1860." *Journal of Sport History* (Spring 1982).

Wilson, Charles Reagan, and William Ferris, eds. *Encyclopedia of Southern Culture.* Chapel Hill: University of North Carolina Press, 1989.

Wright, Louis, ed. *A Journey to the Land of Eden: The Prose Works of William Byrd of Westover. Narratives of a Colonial Virginian.* Cambridge, MA: Harvard University Press, 1966.

Web Sites

Amateur Athletic Association
www.aafla.com

Offers free access to a large library of articles about sports and recreation from several sources, including the *Journal of Sports History*, the *Journal of Olympic History*, and *Sporting Traditions* (accessed August 8, 2003).

Kentucky Derby 130
www.kentuckyderby.com

Maintained by Churchill Downs, Inc. (accessed October 22, 2004).

NASCAR.com
www.nascar.com

Sponsored by Turner Sports Interactive, this site provides information on NASCAR sponsored stock races and events as well as a brief history of the sport (accessed October 12, 2003).

Negro League Baseball Dot Com
www.negroleaguebaseball.com

Published by P. Mills, 2003 (accessed October 22, 2004).

Events

FedEx Orange Bowl
703 Waterford Way
Suite 590
Miami, FL 33126
(305) 341-4700
www.orangebowl.org

This college football game is played annually on January 1 and often features teams playing for the national championship.

The Kentucky Derby
Churchill Downs
Louisville, KY

The nation's premier horse race is held annually at Churchill Downs Racetrack. For information, access www.kentuckyderby.com.

The Masters
P.O. Box 2047
Augusta, GA 30903
www.masters.com

The Masters Golf Tournament, held each April in Augusta, Georgia, is the premier golfing event in the United States. Tickets for practice rounds have been sold for tournaments years in advance. Tournament ticket sales have been closed for many years. The above address provides information on how to add names to the practice round ticket lottery for future Masters.

Organizations

Alabama Sports Hall of Fame
2150 Civic Center Boulevard
Birmingham, Alabama 35203
(205) 332-6665
Email: alashof@bellatlantic.net

This is one of the finest sports museums in the United States, and features exhibits on Alabama's greatest athletes, including Hank Aaron, Willie Mays, and Paul "Bear" Bryant.

International Association of Sports Museums and Halls of Fame
180 N. LaSalle St. Suite 1822
Chicago, IL 60601
(312) 551-0810
Fax: (312) 551-0815
Email: info@sportshalls.com
www.sportshalls.com

Gives information about sports Halls of Fame and related museums throughout the South and the world.

TIMELINE

18,000–8000 B.C.E.	Paleo-Indian America: descendants of Asian peoples settle in the South.
1493	Spanish explorers sailing with Columbus first make landfall on Puerto Rico and St. Croix, the latter one of what would come to be called the Virgin Islands.
1497–1498	John Cabot sails to New England and southward along the coast to South Carolina; this exploration becomes the basis for English claims to North America.
1508	Settlement of Caparra founded by Spanish explorer and conqueror Ponce de León, on a bay he named Puerto Rico; in 1521 this settlement is moved to the present location of San Juan.
1524	Giovanni da Verrazano crosses the Atlantic and navigates the coast from North Carolina to Newfoundland for Francis I of France, laying the basis for France's North America claims.
1565	Pedro Menéndez de Avilés founds St. Augustine, Florida, for the Spanish Crown.
1570	Spaniards establish settlement and Jesuit mission of Ajacan, on what would come to be called the York River, in Virginia; the settlement is destroyed the next year by the Powhatan.
1584	Walter Raleigh sends expedition to America. Roanoke Island colony founded; Queen Elizabeth names new land Virginia.

1585	John White's *American Indians at Play*, first drawing of Indians, showing participation in lacrosse, archery, and other sports.
1587	Virginia Dare born, first white child of English parents born in North America.
	Manteo, the first Indian convert to Protestant Christianity, baptized into the Church of England; he is named Lord of Roanoke by Sir Walter Raleigh.
1600	Indian population in what would become the United States approximately 1 million.
1607	Founding of Jamestown Colony.
1609	Raising of corn (maize) learned from Indians.
1612	Captain John Smith's *A Map of Virginia* published in London.
	Cultivation of tobacco begun by John Rolfe in Virginia.
1619	Earliest arrival of Africans for permanent settlement in Virginia; this date is generally taken to mark the beginning of the African diaspora and of slavery in what would become the United States.
1670	Founding of Charleston, South Carolina.
1682	Sieur de la Salle explores the Mississippi basin and claims the region drained by the Mississippi and its tributaries for France; the region is called Louisiana.
1733	Founding of Savannah, Georgia.
1788	George Washington of Virginia elected the first president of the United States; after his successor, John Adams of Massachusetts, three Virginians serve consecutively: Thomas Jefferson, James Madison, and James Monroe. All four of these early Virginia presidents served two terms.
1789	North Carolina ratifies the Constitution, making it the fourth southern state among the original thirteen (the others being Georgia, Virginia, and South Carolina).
1792	Kentucky admitted to the Union.
1793	Eli Whitney invents the cotton gin in Georgia, revolutionizing southern agriculture.
1796	Tennessee admitted to the Union.
1808–1810	Cherokee chiefs and headmen tell Jefferson some of their tribe want to migrate westward, thus beginning the move into what is now known as Oklahoma.
1812	Louisiana admitted to the Union.
1813–1814	Creek War. Andrew Jackson defeats the Creek at the Battle of Horseshoe Bend. The Creek confederacy cedes two-thirds of its lands in the peace treaty.

1817	Mississippi admitted to the Union.
1819	Alabama admitted to the Union.
1820–1821	Missouri Compromise enacted by Congress under the leadership of Henry Clay of Kentucky; prohibits the westward extension of slavery above 36°30' north latitude.
1828	Andrew Jackson of Tennessee elected to the presidency; he serves two terms. Though a native of the border area straddling North and South Carolina, Jackson moved with his family westward and is considered the first "western" or "frontier" U.S. president.
1829	Jackson announces his policy of removal of Indians from the South.
1832	In *Worcester v. Georgia*, the U.S. Supreme Court acknowledges the sovereignty of the Cherokee people within the state of Georgia. President Jackson says of Chief Justice John Marshall, "He has made his decision, now let him enforce it."
	Virginia planter and scientific agriculturist Edmund Ruffin publishes results of fifteen-year study on restoring fertility to soil; he then launches the influential *Farmer's Register.*
1834	Cyrus McCormick of Virginia patents the reaping machine he had first successfully demonstrated three years earlier.
1835	By the dubious New Echota treaty, a minority segment of the Cherokee people cedes its lands in Georgia, North Carolina, and other states.
	The Seminole War begins, pitting the U.S. Army against that Native American people of Florida; the protracted conflict, extraordinarily costly in lives and money, ends only in 1842 with the expulsion of most of the Seminole to the West.
1836	Texas secedes from Mexico and wins its independence.
	Arkansas admitted to the Union.
1838–1839	The removal of the Cherokee in a forced march that comes to be known as the "Trail of Tears." Thousands are moved west of the Mississippi to Indian Territory (later known as Oklahoma); deaths from hunger, exposure, and illness are numerous.
1845	Florida (March) and Texas (December) admitted to the Union.
1846–1848	The Mexican War, seen by many in the United States as a war to extend the slave system. The United States conquers half of Mexico, in a result sealed by the Treaty of Guadalupe-Hidalgo.
1850	Fugitive Slave Law enacted by Congress as part of the Compromise of 1850, strengthening similar, earlier law of

	1793; required the return of fugitive slaves to their masters.
	Textile industry firmly established as South's most important; more than 200 mills operate.
1851–1852	Publication of *Uncle Tom's Cabin* by Harriet Beecher Stowe, Connecticut-born daughter of Congregationalist minister Lyman Beecher. The book, along with its dramatization by G. L. Aiken, becomes a major cultural factor in the United States' cultural polarization over slavery.
1854	Kansas-Nebraska Act repeals the Missouri Compromise of 1820, establishing two separate states, with the issue of slavery to be left to the settlers of each.
1857	Supreme Court rules in *Scott v. Sandford* against the plaintiff, Dred Scott, who sought recognition of his freedom in the West; in this infamous ruling, the Court held, among other things, that "Negroes had no rights which the white man was bound to respect."
1860	Following Lincoln's election, South Carolina secedes from the Union in December. It is joined by Mississippi, Florida, Alabama, Georgia, Louisiana, and Texas in early 1861, then by Arkansas, North Carolina, Virginia, and Tennessee—giving the Confederacy eleven states.
1861	Civil War begins.
1863	President Lincoln's Emancipation Proclamation frees slaves in nearly all the Confederacy.
	State of West Virginia admitted to the Union; its political destiny had diverged from that of the rest of Virginia since most in the western part of the state opposed secession.
1864	Union Gen. W. T. Sherman's Atlanta campaign, begun in the spring, culminates in the occupation and burning of that city in September.
1865	Assassination of Lincoln. Confederate States surrender at Appomattox Courthouse, Virginia, ending the Civil War.
1866	During the period of Reconstruction, the first African Americans serve in state governments and the U.S. Congress.
1876	Disputed election between Tilden and Hayes settled by deal between parties; Hayes wins presidency, Union to withdraw troops, ending Reconstruction.
1879–1890	African American former slaves move into the Plains region.
1880–1889	Disfranchisement of black voters in the South through poll taxes, literacy tests, and other means; African American voting declines by up to 60 percent in some states.

	Early peak of convict labor system in the South; prisoners are leased out to private employers, agricultural and industrial, and perform road and other government work.
1886	Newspaperman Henry Grady of Georgia gives his famous "New South" address in Boston.
1890–1899	Some 1,100 African Americans are lynched, nearly all in the South—the peak decade for the phenomenon.
1891–1893	Populist Tom Watson of Georgia first serves in the U.S. Congress as a Farmers' Alliance Democrat. He is eventually elected to the U.S. Senate in 1920. His populism includes virulent attacks on African Americans, Roman Catholics, Jews, and socialists.
1892	Supreme Court decision in *Plessy v. Ferguson* confirms segregation.
1898	Spanish-American War. United States conquers Cuba, Puerto Rico, and the Philippines from Spain.
1901	President Theodore Roosevelt dines with Booker T. Washington, causing a racist uproar.
1901–1910	Peak decade of reimposition of "Black Codes" by southern state governments. Measures to limit black mobility include vagrancy laws, restrictions on labor recruiting.
1913	Woodrow Wilson becomes president, the first southerner to occupy the White House since the Civil War. Remembered as idealist in his foreign policy, Wilson was retrograde in his racial politics; he held a White House screening of *The Birth of a Nation*.
1914–1918	U.S. participation in World War I. War-driven expansion of factory production leads to demand for labor; significant white and black migration from the South occurs.
1915	*The Birth of a Nation*, directed by Kentuckian D. W. Griffith, and based on the 1905 novel *The Clansman* by Thomas Dixon of North Carolina, depicts African American men as a sexual menace to white womanhood and sympathetically portrays the KKK.
	Carter G. Woodson of Virginia, son of ex-slaves, founds the *Journal of Negro History*.
1920–1930	Nearly a quarter-million black South Carolinians (some 30 percent of the total) leave the state; throughout the South, this decade is a first peak of the Great Migration, a long process begun in the last quarter of the nineteenth century.
1925	Launching of the Grand Ole Opry over Nashville radio station WSM; the Opry goes on to become the longest-running radio program in U.S. history.

1926	Educator Carter G. Woodson initiates the first Negro History Week in February; later the observance evolves into Black History Month.
1927	Virginia's Carter Family makes famous recordings in Bristol, Tennessee; Mississippi-born Jimmie Rodgers participates in the same epoch-making recording session.
1928	Huey P. Long is elected governor of Louisiana, initiating a long, famous political career.
1932	Georgia's Richard B. Russell is elected to the U.S. Senate, where he serves until his death in 1971.
1934	*Li'l Abner*, a comic strip drawn by Al Capp, first appears in U.S. newspapers in distribution by United Features Syndicate. It rapidly becomes a hit, and its portrayal of poor whites in Appalachia becomes one of the most enduring images of the South in the national consciousness.
1936	*Gone with the Wind*, by Atlanta-born writer Margaret Mitchell, wins a Pulitzer Prize; the novel is brought to the movie screen in 1939.
1937	*Their Eyes Were Watching God*, a portrait of southern black community life by Alabama-born, Florida-raised writer and folklorist Zora Neale Hurston, is published. Its influence, and its author's renown, are largely delayed.
1940	Publication of North Carolinian Wilbur J. Cash's *The Mind of the South*, an exploration of the (white) southern outlook that exerts wide influence in succeeding decades.
1941–1945	World War II.
1941	Gunnar Myrdal's *An American Dilemma* an influential look at racism.
1946	Populist "Big Jim" Folsom wins Alabama governorship; he would be reelected in 1952.
1947	Georgia-born Jackie Robinson of the Brooklyn Dodgers, enduring racist anger and incidents, becomes the first African American to play major league baseball in the twentieth century.
	A Streetcar Named Desire, by Mississippi-born dramatist Tennessee Williams, is awarded the Pulitzer Prize. His *Cat on a Hot Tin Roof* would be similarly honored in 1955.
1948	Bill France founds stock car racing association NASCAR in Daytona Beach, Florida.
	President Truman orders the desegregation of the U.S. Armed Forces.
	Strom Thurmond leads the segregationist "Dixiecrats" as presidential candidate.

1949	Alabama-born Hank Williams' recording of "Lovesick Blues" is his first national hit.
1950–1953	Korean War.
1950	Mississippian William Faulkner, creator of the fictional Yoknapatawpha County, wins Nobel Prize.
1952	*Wise Blood*, a novel of religious fanaticism by Georgian writer Flannery O'Connor, appears.
1953	The death of Hank Williams is a major regional and national event.
1954	By its decision in *Brown v. Board of Education of Topeka, Kansas*, the Supreme Court outlaws segregation in public education as inherently unequal.
1955	The murder of Chicago-born African American youth Emmett Till while visiting kin in Money, Mississippi, supposedly for whistling at a white woman, shocks the country.
	The arrest of Rosa Parks for refusing to give up her seat to a white man on a bus in Montgomery, Alabama, leads to a Supreme Court ruling desegregating public transport and becomes one of the most galvanizing events of the civil rights movement.
1956	Elvis Presley, born in Mississippi and raised in Memphis, Tennessee, scores his first major national hit with "Heartbreak Hotel."
1957	Arkansas governor Orval Faubus (who eventually serves six terms in office) draws national attention by using National Guardsmen to bar nine African American students from entering Little Rock Central High School.
	North Carolina-born evangelist Billy Graham conducts a major New York City "crusade."
	Georgia-born Little Richard's debut album, including "Good Golly, Miss Molly," a big hit.
1958	Georgia-born and Florida-raised singer Ray Charles releases "What I Say," a record that took the country by storm and helped usher in a new era of African American popular music—with a large white audience as well—that would come to be known as "soul."
1960	*The Andy Griffith Show* makes its debut on television for the first of eight extraordinarily successful seasons and decades of continuous presence afterwards through reruns. Its depiction of small-town southern (white) life becomes an enduring image of the region.
1962	Appalachian poverty a focus of Michael Harrington's *The Other America*; President Kennedy launches initiative that would become the Appalachian Regional Commission.

1962	Virginia-born singer Patsy Cline wins *Billboard* magazine's Favorite Female Artist award in 1962.
1963	Some 200,000 participate in the Freedom March on Washington, D.C.; Martin Luther King, Jr., among the speakers.
	Bombing of Sixteenth Street Baptist Church in Birmingham, Alabama, causes the deaths of four African American girls.
1964	The Civil Rights Act is the most significant such legislation since Reconstruction.
	The day after passage of the Civil Rights Act, Georgia restaurant owner (and future governor) Lester Maddox wields pistols to keep African Americans out of establishment.
	James Chaney, an African American, and two white fellow activists in the Freedom Summer movement, Michael Schwerner and Andrew Goodman, are murdered by members of the Ku Klux Klan in Mississippi.
1965	President Johnson signs Voting Rights Act to reverse African American disfranchisement.
1968	Rev. Dr. Martin Luther King, Jr., assassinated in Memphis, Tennessee.
	Former Alabama governor George C. Wallace runs strong independent candidacy for the presidency, winning some 13 percent of the ballots nationally and forty-six electoral votes. His unexpected success points the way to the Republicans' future "Southern Strategy."
	Civil Rights Act of 1968 signed into law by President Johnson.
1972	Second-time presidential candidate George Wallace, fresh from a resounding victory in the Florida Democratic primary, is shot and paralyzed while campaigning in Maryland.
	New Orleans native Andrew Young, a veteran of civil rights campaigns with Martin Luther King, Jr., becomes the first southern black elected to Congress since 1898.
1973	Maynard Jackson is elected to the mayoralty of Atlanta, the first African American to hold that position. Jackson serves three terms as mayor.
1976	Jimmy Carter of Georgia, a Democrat, elected president; serves a single term.
1977	The television series *Roots*, based on the book by New York–born, Tennessee-raised writer Alex Haley, becomes a major national phenomenon and one of the most widely

shared cultural experiences in which twentieth-century Americans explore the history of slavery.

Death of Elvis Presley is a major regional, national, and worldwide event.

1979	Virginian evangelical minister Jerry Falwell founds the Moral Majority advocacy group.
1982	George Wallace elected for the fourth time to the Alabama governorship, with unprecedented levels of African American support; his final term in office, 1983–1987, comes to symbolize a new era of racial rapprochement in the South.
	The Color Purple, by Alice Walker of Georgia, is awarded the Pulitzer Prize.
1986	Walmart founder Sam Walton of Arkansas named United States' richest man by *US News & World Report*.
1990	L. Douglas Wilder becomes the first African American elected governor in U.S. history, winning the governorship of Virginia.
1990–2000	At apex of regional trend, North Carolina showed U.S. largest growth in Latino population since previous census, from 77,000 (1 percent of population) to 380,000 (5 percent).
	Textile industry decline becomes precipitous; North Carolina loses over 150,000 jobs.
1992	Bill Clinton of Arkansas, a Democrat, elected president; serves two terms.
1993	Mercedes-Benz opens auto assembly plant in Alabama, heralding a new trend in the South.
2000	In one of the most bitterly contested presidential elections in U.S. history, between Albert Gore, Jr., of Tennessee and George W. Bush of Texas, Florida is the center of disputes over the counting of ballots and effective disfranchisement of African American voters.
	Controversy over the inclusion of the Confederate battle flag motif in Georgia and South Carolina state flags becomes electoral issue, contributing to Democratic governors' defeat.

NOTES

Art

1. For a complete discussion of the styles of Native American tribes in the South and their distinctive artistic considerations, see Christian F. Feest, *Native Arts of North America* (New York: Thames and Hudson, 1992), and Frances K. Pohl, *Framing America: A Social History of American Art* (New York: Thames and Hudson, 2002).

2. Carolyn J. Weekly, "The Early Years, 1564 to 1790," in David S. Bundy et al., *Painting in the South: 1564–1980* (Richmond: Virginia Museum, 1983), 9.

3. Ibid., 25.

4. Ibid., 173.

5. C. Kurt Dewhurst, Betty MacDowell, and Marsha MacDowell, *Artists in Aprons: Folk Art by American Women* (New York: E. P. Dutton, 1979).

6. A complete analysis of the characteristics of American folk art is found in Robert Bishop and Jacqueline Atkins, *Folk Art in American Life* (New York: Viking Studio Books, 1995).

7. Dewhurst, MacDowell, and MacDowell, *Artists in Aprons*.

8. The theory of the use of quilts on the Underground Railroad is found in Jacqueline L. Tobin and Raymond G. Dobard, *Hidden in Plain View: A Secret Story of Quilts and the Underground Railroad* (New York: Anchor Books, 1999).

9. Estill Curtis Pennington, *Look Away: Reality and Sentiment in Southern Art* (Spartanburg, SC: Saraland Press, 1989), 56.

10. Ibid., 18.

11. Ibid., 63–64.

12. Ibid., 91.

13. A complete exploration of outsider art is found in the essays in Gerard Wertkin, ed., *Self-Taught Artists of the Twentieth Century: An American Anthology* (New York: Museum of American Folk Art, 1998), which accompanied the exhibition of the same title.

14. *Clementine Hunter*, Ogden Museum of Southern Art (www.ogdenmuseum.org/exhibitions/featured-artist-hunter.html), accessed June 24, 2004.

15. Barbara Rothermel, "I Paint What I Remember: The Art of Mario Sanchez," in *Folk Art* (New York: Museum of American Folk Art, Fall 1996).

16. Pohl, *Framing America*, 408–410.

17. Ibid., 474–476.

18. Bundy et al., *Painting in the South*, 298–299.

19. Donald Kuspit, *Homeland of the Imagination: The Southern Presence in Twentieth Century Art* (Atlanta: NationsBank, 1996), 12.

20. Rick Stewart, "Toward a New South: The Regionalist Approach, 1900 to 1950," in Bundy et al., *Painting in the South*, 105.

21. Pohl, *Framing America*, 367–368.

22. Ibid., 371–372.

23. Stewart, "Toward a New South," 128–129.

24. Kuspit, *Homeland of the Imagination*, 42.

25. Bundy et al., *Painting in the South*, 320.

Ecology and Environment

1. Mississippi Valley Division, Mississippi River Commission, www.mvd.usace.army. mil/MRC/history.htm, accessed July 6, 2004.

2. U.S. Geological Survey, Center for Coastal Geology, http://coastal.er.usgs.gov/ hurricanes/georges, accessed July 6, 2004.

Ethnicity

1. For an interesting discussion of southern music, see Bill C. Malone's essay "Neither Anglo-Saxon nor Celtic: The Music of the Southern Plain Folk," in *Plain Folk of the South Revisited*, ed. Samuel C. Hyde, 21–45 (Baton Rouge: Louisiana State University Press, 1997); Charles Winston Joyner, *Shared Traditions: Southern History and Folk Culture* (Urbana: University of Illinois Press, 1999); and Alan Lomax's classic *The Folk Songs of North America* (Garden City, NY: Doubleday, 1960).

2. Charles Reagan Wilson, "The Myth of the Biracial South," in *The Southern State of Mind*, ed. Jan Nordby Gretlund (Columbia: University of South Carolina Press, 1999), 3–22.

3. Wilson, "Myth," 16.

4. Charles Winston Joyner, "The South as a Folk Culture: David Potter and the Southern Enigma," in *The Southern Enigma: Essays on Race, Class and Folk Culture*, ed. Walter J. Fraser and Winfred B. Moore (Westport, CT: Greenwood Press, 1983), 163–164.

5. James Cobb, *Redefining Southern Culture: Mind and Identity in the Modern South* (Athens: University of Georgia Press, 1999), 147.

6. See John Shelton Reed, *One South: An Ethnic Approach to Regional Culture* (Baton Rouge: Lousiana State University Press, 1982).

7. Beverly J. Stoelje, "Festival," in *Folklore, Cultural Performances, and Popular Entertainments*, ed. Richard Bauman (Oxford: Oxford University Press), 261–266.

8. Some scholars contest the use of "chiefdoms" in preference to "pre-states." For a good summary of the argument, see Alice Kehoe, *Land of Prehistory: A Critical History of American Archaeology* (New York: Routledge, 1998).

9. Scott Malcolmson, *One Drop of Blood: The American Misadventure of Race* (New York: Farrar Straus Giroux, 2000), 14.

10. See Clyde Ellis, " 'There's a Dance Every Weekend': Powwow Culture in Southeast North Carolina," in *Southern Heritage on Display: Public Ritual and Ethnic Diversity within Southern Regionalism*, ed. Celeste Ray, 79–105 (Tuscaloosa: University of Alabama Press,

2003); Patricia Lerch, "Powwows, Parades and Social Drama among the Waccamaw Sioux," *Museum Anthropology* 16, no. 2 (1993): 27–33.

11. Elizabeth Bird, ed., *Dressing in Feathers: The Construction of the Indian in American Popular Culture* (Boulder, CO: Westview Press, 1996), 9.

12. U.S. Census Office, Eighth Census (1860), *Population* (Washington, DC, 1864).

13. Peter Wood, "Re-Counting the Past: Revolutionary Changes in the Early South," *Southern Exposure* 16, no. 2 (Summer 1988): 31; James Axtell, *The Indians' New South: Cultural Change* (Baton Rouge: Louisiana State University Press, 1997).

14. See John Finger, *Cherokee Americans: The Eastern Band of Cherokees in the Twentieth Century* (Lincoln: University of Nebraska Press, 1984); John Finger, *The Eastern Band of Cherokees, 1819–1900* (Knoxville: University of Tennessee Press, 1991). For an interesting account of métis Cherokee, see Brett Riggs' 1997 essay "The Christie Cabin Site: Historical and Archaeological Evidence of the Life and Times of a Cherokee Metis Household (1835–1838)," in *May We All Remember Well*, ed. Robert Brunk, 228–248 (Asheville, NC: Robert Brunk Auction Services, 1997).

15. John Shelton Reed, "The Cherokee Princess in the Family Tree," *Southern Cultures* 3 (Spring 1997): 112.

16. Theda Perdue and Michael Green, *The Columbia Guide to American Indians of the Southeast* (New York: Columbia University Press, 2001), 141.

17. Ibid., 144–145.

18. See Cecile Carter, *Caddo Indians: Where We Come From* (Norman: University of Oklahoma Press, 1995); Timothy Perttula, *The Caddo Nation* (Austin: University of Texas Press, 1992); George Sabo, "Reordering Their World: A Caddoan Ethnohistory," in *Visions and Revisions: Ethnohistoric Perspectives on Southern Cultures*, ed. G. Sabo and W.M. Schneider, 25–47 (Athens: University of Georgia Press, 1987); Todd Smith, *The Caddos, the Wichitas, and the United States, 1846–1901* (College Station: Texas A&M University Press, 1996); David Lavere, *Contrary Neighbors: Southern Plains and Removed Indians in Indian Territory* (Norman: University of Oklahoma Press, 2000); Ann Early, "The Caddos of the Trans-Mississippi South," in *Indians of the Greater Southeast: Historical Archaeology and Ethnohistory*, ed. Bonnie McEwan, 122–141 (Gainesville: University Press of Florida, 2000). There are also four state-recognized nations: the Adai Caddo (Natchitoches Parish), the Clifton Choctaw (Rapides Parish), the Choctaw-Apache of Ebarb (Sabine Parish), and the Four Winds Cherokee Confederation (Vernon Parish).

19. See Jonathan Hook, *The Alabama-Coushatta Indians* (College Station: Texas A&M University Press, 1997).

20. See Arrell Gibson, *The Chickasaws* (Lincoln: University of Nebraska Press, 1971); Lisa Lefler, "Stress and Coping among Chickasaw Indian Fathers: Lessons for Indian Adolescents and Their Counselors in Treatment or Substance Abuse," in *Southern Indians and Anthropologists: Culture, Politics, and Identity*, ed. Lisa Lefler and Frederic Gleach, 115–123 (Athens: University of Georgia Press, 2002); John Swanton, *The Indians of the Southeastern United States* (Washington, DC: Smithsonian Institution Press, 1998); Muriel Wright, *A Guide to the Indian Tribes of Oklahoma* (Norman: University of Oklahoma Press, 1986). For more on Indians as slaves and as slaveholders, see Malcolmson, *One Drop*.

21. See Robbie Ethridge, *Creek Country: The Creek Indians and Their World* (Chapel Hill: University of North Carolina Press, 2003); Bill Granthan, *Creation Myths and Legends of the Creek Indians* (Gainesville: University of Florida Press, 2002).

22. See Anthony Paredes, "Federal Recognition and the Poarch Creek Indians," in *Indians of the Southeastern United States in the Late Twentieth Century*, ed. J. Anthony Paredes, 120–139 (Tuscaloosa: University of Alabama Press, 1992).

23. See Brent Richards Weisman, *Unconquered People: Florida's Seminole and Miccosukee Indians* (Gainesville: University of Florida Press, 1999).

24. See Helen Rountree, "Indian Virginians on the Move," in Paredes, *Indians of the Southeastern United States*, 9–28. Helen Rountree, *Pocahontas's People: The Powhatan Indians of Virginia Through Four Centuries* (Norman: University of Oklahoma Press, 1990).

25. Samuel Cook, *Monacans and Miners: Native American and Coal Mining Communities in Appalachia* (Lincoln: University of Nebraska Press, 2000).

26. Perdue and Green, *Columbia Guide*; Charles Hudson, *The Catawba Nation* (Athens: University of Georgia Press, 1970).

27. Patricia Lerch, "Powwows, Parades and Social Drama," 82.

28. C. S. Everett and Marvin Richardson, "Ethnicity Affirmed: The Haliwa-Saponi and the Dance, Culture, and Meaning of North Carolina Powwows," in *Signifying Serpents and Mardi Gras Runners: Representing Identity in Selected Souths*, ed. Celeste Ray and Luke Eric Lassiter (Athens: University of Georgia Press, 2003), 56.

29. Perdue and Green, *Columbia Guide*, 132.

30. See Karen Blu, *The Lumbee Problem: The Making of an American Indian People* (Cambridge: Cambridge University Press, 1980); Karen Blu, "Region and Recognition: Southern Indians, Anthropologists, and Presumed Biology," in Paredes, *Indians of the Southeastern United States*, 71–85; Ellis, "There's a Dance."

31. Thomas Ross, *American Indians in North Carolina: Geographic Interpretations* (Southern Pines, NC: Karo Hollow Press, 1999), 214–219.

32. See Jane Landers, *Black Society in Spanish Florida* (Urbana: University of Illinois Press, 1999).

33. See Gilbert Din, *The Canary Islanders of Louisiana* (Baton Rouge: Louisiana State University Press, 1988).

34. Patricia Griffin, *Mullet on the Beach: The Minorcans of Florida, 1768–1788* (Jacksonville: University of North Florida Press, 1991).

35. See Peter Steven Gannon, *Huguenot Refugees in the Settling of Colonial America* (New York: Huguenot Society of America, 1985).

36. George Jones and Renate Wilson, *Detailed Reports on the Salzburger Emigrants Who Settled in America*, vol. 18, *1744–1745* (Camden, MA: Picton Press, 1995), v.

37. On Bethania see Michael Hartley, "Bethania: A Colonial Moravian Adaptation," in *Another's Country: Archaeological and Historical Perspectives on Cultural Interactions in the Southern Colonies*, ed. J. W. Joseph and Martha Zierden, 111–132 (Tuscaloosa: University of Alabama Press, 2002).

38. Ira Sheskin, "American Jews," in *Ethnicity in Contemporary America: A Geographical Appraisal* (Lanham, MD: Rowman and Littlefield, 2000), 238–239.

39. For a bibliography and an excellent introduction to the subject, see David Goldfield, "Sense of Place: Blacks, Jews, and White Gentiles in the American South," *Southern Cultures* 3, no. 1 (1997): 58–79. See also John Reed, "Shalom, Y'All: Jewish Southerners," in *One South: An Ethnic Approach to Regional Culture* (Baton Rouge: Louisiana State University Press, 1982), 103–112, and Robert Rosen, *The Jewish Confederates* (Columbia: University of South Carolina Press, 2000). For more on "foreigners in the Confederacy," see the classic book of that title by Ella Lonn (University of North Carolina Press, [1940] 2002).

40. See Klaus Wust, *The Virginia Germans* (Charlottesville: University Press of Virginia, 1969); Rita Elliott and Daniel Elliott, "Guten Tag Bubba: Germans in the Colonial South," in *Another's Country: Archaeological and Historical Perspectives on Cultural Interactions in the Southern Colonies*, ed. J. W. Joseph and Martha Zierden, 79–92 (Tuscaloosa: University of Alabama Press, 2002).

41. Wust, *Virginia Germans*, ix.

42. David T. Gleeson, *The Irish in the South, 1815–1877* (Chapel Hill: University of North Carolina Press, 2001).

43. Ibid., 35; Earl Niehaus, *The Irish in New Orleans* (Baton Rouge: Louisiana State University Press, 1965).

44. Gleeson, *Irish in the South*, 73.

45. Valentine Belfiglio, *The Italian Experience in Texas: A Closer Look* (Austin: Eakin Press, 1994).

46. Ian Hancock, "Gypsies," in *Encyclopedia of Southern Culture*, ed. Charles Reagan Wilson and William Ferris, 57–58 (Chapel Hill: University of North Carolina Press, 1989).

47. See Tina Bucuvalas, "Epiphany in Tarpon Springs," *Florida Heritage Magazine* 7, no. 4 (Fall 1999).

48. For the story of Hungarians in Texas see James Patrick McGuire, *The Hungarian Texans* (San Antonio: University of Texas at San Antonio, Institute of Texan Cultures, 1994).

49. Celeste Ray, *Highland Heritage: Scottish Americans in the American South* (Chapel Hill: University of North Carolina Press, 2001).

50. Thanks to William A. Steadley-Campbell, a descendant of Daniel Douglas Campbell and a past director of the Walton County Heritage Association, for this information.

51. Lowlanders also came to Georgia in the 1730s, but for economic reasons as farmers and merchants, and were not recruited for strategic purposes to guard the southern frontier against the Spanish, as the Highlanders had been.

52. Although "Scotch-Irish" has been used conventionally, "Scots-Irish" is correct. Scots have not been called Scotch since at least the 1920s; neither should the Scots-Irish be referred to by the name for whiskey.

53. See Landers, *Black Society*.

54. Gary Mills, "Tracing Free People of Color in the Antebellum South: Methods, Sources, and Perspectives," *National Genealogical Society Quarterly* 78, no. 4 (1990): 262; John Thornton, *Africa and Africans in the Making of the Atlantic World, 1400–1800*, 2nd ed. (Cambridge: Cambridge University Press, 1998), 146.

55. Thornton, *Africa*, 310, 317; Wood, "Re-Counting the Past," 37. More than half of all Africans were transported to the Caribbean and another third went to Brazil (Thornton, *Africa*, 317).

56. Jeanette Keith, *The South: A Concise History*, vol. 1 (Upper Saddle River, NJ: Prentice Hall, 2002), 35.

57. Thornton, *Africa and Africans*, 229, 320, 324.

58. John Boles, *The South Through Time: A History of an American Region*, vol. 1 (Upper Saddle River, NJ: Prentice Hall, 1999), 81.

59. Bruce Twyman, *The Black Seminole Legacy and North American Politics, 1693–1845* (Washington, DC: Howard University Press, 1999); Kenneth Porter, *The Black Seminoles: History of a Freedom-Seeking People*, rev. and ed. Alcione Amos and Thomas Senter (Gainesville: University Press of Florida, 1996).

60. See Marina Wikramanayake, *A World in Shadow: The Free Black in Antebellum South Carolina* (Columbia: University of South Carolina Press, 1973).

61. Gary Mills, "Tracing Free People of Color in the Antebellum South: Methods, Sources, and Perspectives," *National Genealogical Society Quarterly* 78, no. 4 (1990): 263.

62. James Dorman, *Creoles of Color of the Gulf South* (Knoxville: University of Tennessee Press, 1996), xi; Gary Mills, *The Forgotten People: Cane River's Creoles of Color* (Baton Rouge: Louisiana State University Press, 1977).

63. See Ellen Shlasko, "Frenchmen and Africans in South Carolina: Cultural Interaction on the Eighteenth-Century Frontier," in Joseph and Zierden, *Another's Country*, 133–144.

64. Gwendolyn Midlo Hall, *Africans in Colonial Louisiana: The Development of Afro-Creole Culture in the Eighteenth Century* (Baton Rouge: Louisiana State University Press, 1995), 29–31, 41.

65. Shana Walton, "Louisiana's Coonasses: Choosing Race and Class over Ethnicity," in Ray and Lassiter, *Signifying Serpents*, 41.

66. See Sybil Kein, ed., *Creole: The History and Legacy of Louisiana's Free People of Color* (Baton Rouge: Louisiana State University Press, 2000).

67. Ibid., xv; G. M. Hall, *Africans in Colonial Louisiana*, 157.

68. Dorman, *Creoles of Color*, x.

69. Jack Forbes, *Africans and Native Americans: The Language of Race and the Evolution of Red-Black Peoples* (Urbana: University of Illinois Press, 1993).

70. Ben Sandmel and Rick Olivier, *Zydeco!* (Jackson: University Press of Mississippi, 1999), 14.

71. Jeff Todd Titon, "Zydeco: A Musical Hybrid," *Journal of American Folklore* 94, no. 373 (July–September 1981): 403.

72. New Orleans' multiethnic history began in the early eighteenth century with French, then Spanish, and eventually American rule. For historical accounts of some of the city's many ethnic groups, see Niehaus, *Irish in New Orleans*; Wallace Bertram Korn, *The Early Jews of New Orleans* (Waltham, MA: American Jewish Historical Society, 1969); and Arnold Hirsch and Joseph Logsdon, *Creole New Orleans: Race and Americanization* (Baton Rouge: Louisiana State University Press, 1992).

73. See Kathryn VanSpanckeren, "The Mardi Gras Indian Song Cycle: A Heroic Tradition," in Ray, *Southern Heritage on Display*, 57–78; Walton, "Louisiana's Coonasses"; Barry Jean Ancelet, Jay Edwards, and Glen Pitre, *Cajun Country* (Jackson: University Press of Mississippi, 1991); Carl Brasseaux, *Acadian to Cajun: Transformation of a People, 1803–1877* (Jackson: University Press of Mississippi, 1992).

74. Shane Bernard, *The Cajuns: Americanization of a People* (Jackson: University of Mississippi Press, 2003), xix.

75. Perdue and Green, *Columbia Guide*, 132.

76. See Max Stanton, "A Remnant Indian Community: The Houma of Southern Louisiana," in *The Not So Solid South: Anthropological Studies in a Regional Subculture*, ed. Kenneth Morland, 82–92 (Athens: University of Georgia Press, 1971).

77. See Virginia Domínguez, *White by Definition: Social Classification in Creole Louisiana* (New Brunswick, NJ: Rutgers University Press, 1986).

78. See Anita Puckett, "The Melungeon Identity Movement and the Construction of Appalachian Whiteness," *Journal of Linguistic Anthropology* 11, no. 1 (2001): 131–146; C. S. Everett, "Melungeon History and Myth," *Appalachian Journal: A Regional Studies Review* 26, no. 4 (1999): 359.

79. Melissa Schrift, "Melungeons and the Politics of Heritage," in Ray, *Southern Heritage on Display*," 106–129.

80. Gary Mills, "Tracing Free People of Color in the Antebellum South: Methods, Sources, and Perspectives," *National Genealogical Society Quarterly* 78, no. 4 (1990): 276, n.6.

81. Susan Greenbaum, *More than Black: Afro-Cubans in Tampa* (Gainesville: University of Florida Press, 2002), 12.

82. Lee Smith, "The Forgotten South: Far from the White Columns and Marble Generals," *Charlotte Observer*, August 4, 1996, Q3.

83. For sources on southern Appalachian mythology, see the early writings of Emma Bell Miles (1879–1919) and Horace Sowers Kephart (1862–1931), and John Charles Campbell's *The Southern Highlander and His Homeland* (published after his death in 1921). For academic studies of Appalachian mythmaking, see Ron Eller, *Miners, Millhands and Mountaineers: Industrialization of the Appalachian South, 1880–1930* (Knoxville: University of Tennessee Press, 1982); Mary Beth Pudup, Dwight B. Billings, and Altina L. Waller, eds., *Appalachia in the Making: The Mountain South in the Nineteenth Century* (Chapel Hill: University of North Carolina Press, 1995); W. K. McNeil, ed., *Appalachian Images in Folk and Popular Culture* (Ann Arbor, MI: University of Michigan Research Press, 1989); Henry Shapiro, *Appalachia on Our Mind: The Southern Mountains and Mountaineers in the American Consciousness, 1870–1920* (Chapel Hill: University of North Carolina Press, 1978); Bruce Ergood and Bruce E. Kuhre, eds., *Appalachia: Social Context Past and Present* (Dubuque, IA: Kendall/Hunt Publishing, 1991); Helen M. Lewis, "Appalshop: Preserving, Participating in, and Creating

Southern Mountain Culture," in *Cultural Heritage Conservation in the American South*, ed. Benita J. Howell, 79–86 (Athens: University of Georgia Press, 1990); Wilma Dunaway, *The First American Frontier: Transition to Capitalism in Southern Appalachia, 1700–1860* (Chapel Hill: University of North Carolina Press, 1996); Helen Lewis, Linda Johnson, and Donald Askins, eds., *Colonialism in Modern America: The Appalachian Case* (Appalachian Consortium Inc., 1978); David Whisnant, *Modernizing the Mountaineer: People, Power and Planning in Appalachia* (Knoxville: University of Tennessee Press, 1981).

84. Patricia Beaver and Helen Lewis, "Uncovering the Trail of Ethnic Denial: Ethnicity in Appalachia," in *Cultural Diversity in the U.S. South*, ed. Carole E. Hill and Patricia Beaver, 51–68 (Athens: University of Georgia Press, 1998).

85. Richard Drake, *A History of Appalachia* (Lexington: University Press of Kentucky, 2001), 86–87.

86. Ibid., 82; see also Wilma Dunaway, *Slavery in the American Mountain South* (Cambridge: Cambridge University Press, 2003); William Turner and Edward Cabbell, eds., *Blacks in Appalachia* (Lexington: University Press of Kentucky, 1985); John Inscoe, *Appalachians and Race: The Mountain South from Slavery to Segregation* (Lexington: University Press of Kentucky, 2001); John Inscoe, *Mountain Masters, Slavery, and the Sectional Crisis in Western North Carolina* (Knoxville: University of Tennessee Press, 1989).

87. Brooks Blevins, *Hill Folks: A History of Arkansas Ozarkers and Their Image* (Chapel Hill: University of North Carolina Press, 2002).

88. Jesse McKee, "Humanity on the Move," in *Ethnicity in Contemporary America: A Geographical Appraisal*, ed. Jesse McKee (Lanham, MD: Rowman and Littlefield, 2000), 28–32.

89. In addition to having a reputation as the Bible Belt or the Sun Belt, the South has also been called the Beauty Pageant belt. South Asian immigrants have even assimilated to the southern emphasis on beauty pageants and annually sponsor an annual "Miss India Georgia" pageant in Atlanta.

90. D. C. Young and Stephen Young, "Ethnic Mississippi 1992," in *Ethnic Heritage in Mississippi*, ed. Barbara Carpenter (Jackson: University Press of Mississippi, 1992), 169.

91. Jessica Barnes and Claudette Bennett, *The Asian Population: 2000* (Washington, DC: U.S. Census Bureau, 2002), 4.

92. Edward Rhoads, "The Chinese in Texas," *Southwestern Historical Quarterly* 81 (July 1977): 1–36.

93. Robert Seto Quan, *Lotus among the Magnolias: The Mississippi Chinese* (Jackson: University Press of Mississippi, 1982); James Loewen, *The Mississippi Chinese: Between Black and White* (Prospect Heights, IL: Waveland Press, 1988); John Willis, *Forgotten Time: The Yazoo-Mississippi Delta after the Civil War* (Charlottesville: University Press of Virginia, 2000).

94. Young and Young, "Ethnic Mississippi," 166–167.

95. For the story of the Japanese in Texas, see Thomas Walls, *The Japanese Texans* (San Antonio: University of Texas at San Antonio, Institute of Texan Cultures, 1996).

96. Allan Burns, "The Newest Indians in the South: The Maya of Florida," in *Anthropologists and Indians in the New South*, ed. Rachel Bonney and Anthony Paredes, 108–125 (Tuscaloosa: University of Alabama Press, 2001); Allan Burns, *Maya in Exile: Guatemalans in Florida* (Philadelphia: Temple University Press, 1993); see also Leon Fink and Alvis E. Dunn, *The Maya of Morganton: Work and Community in the Nuevo New South* (Chapel Hill: University of North Carolina Press, 2003).

97. Although since 1980 Puerto Ricans have established communities in every southern state, Florida is also home to more Puerto Ricans than any other state in the region.

98. Elizabeth Grieco and Rachel Cassidy, "Overview of Race and Hispanic Origin," *Census 2000 Brief* (Washington, DC: U.S. Census Bureau, 2001), 3.

99. Marc J. Perry and Paul J. Mackun, "Population Change and Distribution," *Census 2000 Brief* (Washington, DC: U.S. Census Bureau, 2001), 2, 3. A breakdown of this figure is as follows: 32.6 percent of Mexicans living in the United States live in the South, as do

80 percent of Cubans and 34.6 percent of Central and South Americans. Puerto Ricans are the only Hispanic group to favor settlement in the Northeast (63.9 percent) (Melissa Therrien and Roberto R. Ramirez, "The Hispanic Population in the United States," *Census 2000 Brief*). Recall that the U.S. Census includes Delaware, Maryland, West Virginia, Oklahoma, and the District of Columbia in calculations for the southern region.

100. Marcos McPeek Villatoro, "Latino Southerners: A New Form of *Mestizaje*," in Hill and Beaver, *Cultural Diversity in the U.S. South*.

101. Angela Moore, "Latinos and Southern Religion," paper presented at the annual meeting of the Southern Anthropological Society, Atlanta, Georgia, 2004.

102. Ray, *Southern Heritage on Display*.

103. Fredrik Barth, ed., *Ethnic Groups and Boundaries: The Social Organization of Cultural Differences* (Boston: Little, Brown, 1969).

Fashion

1. Philippe Perrot, *Fashioning the Bourgeoisie: A History of Clothing in the Nineteenth Century*, trans. Richard Bienvenu (Princeton, NJ: Princeton University Press, 1994), 7.

2. Diana De Marley, *Dress in North America: The New World, 1492–1800* (New York: Holmes and Meier, 1991), 57–67.

3. Helen Bradley Foster, *"New Raiments of Self": African American Clothing in the Antebellum South* (New York: Berg, 1997), 18–74.

4. Shane White and Graham White, *Stylin': African American Expressive Culture from Its Beginnings to the Zoot Suit* (Ithaca, NY: Cornell University Press, 1998).

5. John Beardsley, William Arnett, et al., *The Quilts of Gee's Bend* (Atlanta: Tinwood Books, 2002), 18.

6. Reprinted in *New Orleans Times-Picayune*, March 28, 2003.

7. See the discussion of "visual aliveness" and "rhythmized textiles" in Mende culture in Robert Farris Thompson, *Flash of the Spirit: African and Afro-American Art and Philosophy* (New York: Random House, 1983), 208, 209, 217. See also Richard Price and Sally Price, *Maroon Arts: Cultural Vitality in the African Diaspora* (Boston: Beacon Press, 1999); Maude Southwell Wahlman, *Signs and Symbols: African Images in African-American Quilts* (New York: Studio Books, 1993); Gladys-Marie Fry, *Stitched from the Soul: Slave Quilts from the Antebellum South* (Chapel Hill: University of North Carolina Press, 1990); Eli Leon, *Who'd a Thought It: Improvisation in African-American Quiltmaking* (San Francisco: San Francisco Craft and Folk Art Museum, 1987).

8. Leon, *Who'd a Thought It*, 37.

9. Frances Anne Kemble, *Journal of a Residence on a Georgia Plantation in 1838–39* (New York: Harper and Brothers, 1863), 93.

10. Ibid., 35.

11. Ibid., 93.

12. bell hooks, "My Style Ain't No Fashion," *Z Magazine* (May 1992), 28.

13. Robert Tallant, *Gumbo Ya-Ya: A Collection of Louisiana Folk Tales* (Gretna, LA: Pelican Publishing Co., 1998), 19.

14. Elizabeth-Hyde Botume, *First Days among the Contrabands* (New York: Arno Press, 1968), 174–175.

15. Mamie Garvin Fields, *Lemon Swamp and Other Places: A Carolina Memoir* (New York: The Free Press, 1983), 17, 26.

16. Botume, *First Days*, 52, 54, 236–237. For a more recent embroidery of the kind Botume describes, see the photograph of Charles Logan in Wahlman, *Signs and Symbols*, 100.

17. For Louisiana, see Gwendolyn Midlo Hall, *Africans in Colonial Louisiana: The Development of Afro-Creole Culture in the Eighteenth Century* (Baton Rouge: Louisiana University Press, 1992); for South Carolina, see Daniel C. Littlefield, *Rice and Slaves: Ethnicity and Slave*

Trade in Colonial Carolina (Baton Rouge: Louisiana University Press, 1981); on rice production (rice and indigo were grown in the same parts of West Africa, and the targeting of slaves for expert knowledge is similar).

18. Thomas Ashe, *Travels in America*, 3 vols. (London: William Sawyer and Co., 1808), 202–203.

19. Bernard Romans, *A Concise Natural History of East and West Florida* (New York, 1775. Reprint, New Orleans: Pelican Publishing Co., 1961), 97.

20. George Rawick, *The American Slave*, S19: 1641–1642.

21. Ibid., 8: 243–244; 14: 286; 12: 287.

22. Kemble, *Journal*, 93.

23. Quoted in White and White, *Stylin'*, 30.

24. Parthenia Antoinette Hague, *A Blockaded Family: Life in Southern Alabama During the Civil War* (Boston: Houghton Mifflin, 1888), 39.

25. Ibid., 40.

26. Elizabeth Fox-Genovese, *Within the Plantation Household: Black and White Women in the Old South* (Chapel Hill: University of North Carolina Press, 1988), 184.

27. Hague, *Blockaded Family*, 49.

28. Ibid., 46, 58–59.

29. Frederick Law Olmsted, *The Cotton Kingdom: A Traveller's Observations on Cotton and Slavery in the American Slave States* (New York: Alfred A. Knopf, 1953), 206.

30. De Marley, *Dress in North America*, 115. For the dress of poor whites and "crackers," see Shirley Abbott, *Womenfolks: Growing Up Down South* (New York: Ticknor and Fields, 1983). Abbott quotes an itinerant preacher in the Carolina hills in 1766–1972 describing the precursors to Daisy Mae: "the women came to church wearing nothing but 'shifts'; they were barefooted, barelegged, bareheaded." Furthermore, the young women "draw their Shift as tight as possible to the Body, and pin it close, to shew the roundness of their Breasts, and slender Waists . . . and draw their Petticoat close to their hips to shew the fineness of their limbs" (41).

31. Olmsted, *Cotton Kingdom*, 506.

32. Patricia V. Ulrich, "Promoting the South: Rhetoric and Textiles in Columbus, Georgia, 1850–1880," *Dress: The Annual Journal of the Costume Society of America* 11 (1985): 44–56.

33. Solomon Northrup, *Twelve Years a Slave*, ed. Sue Eakin and Joseph Logsdon (Baton Rouge: Louisiana State University Press, 1996), 164.

34. Rawick, *American Slave*, 12: 324–325; 18: 313; S1.5: 298.

35. Foster, *"New Raiments,"* 67–93.

36. Fox-Genovese, *Plantation Household*, 177–181.

37. Foster, *"New Raiments,"* 93–110.

38. Ibid., 104.

39. Botume, *First Days*, 52–53.

40. Olmsted, *Cotton Kingdom*, 480.

41. Frederick Douglass. *Narrative of the Life of Frederick Douglass: An American Slave* (New York: Signet, 1968), 64.

42. Louis Hughes, *Thirty Years a Slave: From Bondage to Freedom* (New York: Negro University Press, 1969), 41–42.

43. Foster, *New Raiments*, 148–149.

44. Douglass, *Narrative*, 28.

45. Foster, *"New Raiments,"* 157.

46. Linda Brent, *Incidents in the Life of a Slave Girl* (New York: Harcourt Brace and Co., 1973), 9.

47. For uniforms see Alexander Warwick and Dani Cavallaro's elaboration of Mikhael Foucault's formulation of modern discipline in the "clothing of the criminal, the pauper and the insane in nineteenth and early twentieth-century institutions. . . . The right to individ-

uality and its self-expression was therefore removed and the right of power to distinguish difference as it saw fit imposed in its place. . . . Dress here nullifies the subject, preventing the establishment of an identity independent of that which the institution wishes to create, reminding him constantly of his relation to that institution" (*Fashioning the Frame: Boundaries, Dress and the Body* [Oxford, Berg, 1998], 75).

48. Quoted in White and White, *Stylin'*, 9.

49. Ibid, 15.

50. Booker Washington, *Up from Slavery* (New York: Penguin Books, 1901), 20–21.

51. Foster, *"New Raiments,"* 11, 224–244.

52. Rawick, *American Slave*, 4: 22.

53. Hague, *Blockaded Family*, 37.

54. Olmsted, *Cotton Kingdom*, 37.

55. Quoted in White and White, *Stylin'*, 15–16.

56. Dominique Cocuzza, "The Dress of Free Women of Color in New Orleans, 1780–1840," *Dress: The Annual Journal of the Costume Society of America* 27 (2000): 82.

57. Quoted in Foster, *"New Raiments,"* 10.

58. Fields, *Lemon Swamp*, 85–86.

59. Fox-Genovese, *Plantation Household*, 213.

60. Fields, *Lemon Swamp*, 20, 155.

61. Perrot, *Fashioning*, 82.

62. The *tignon* has received much attention, being, as one scholar suggests, the first symbol of African American pride on this continent. See Cocuzza, "Dress"; Patricia Hunt, "Swathed in Cloth: The Headwrap of Some African American Women in Georgia and South Carolina During Late Nineteenth and Early Twentieth Century," *Dress: The Annual Journal of the Costume Society of America* 21 (1994): 30–38; Foster, *"New Raiments."*

63. White and White, *Stylin'*, 41–42.

64. Quoted in Michael Cunningham and Craig Marberry, *Crowns: Portraits of Black Women in Church Hats* (New York: Doubleday, 2000), 40–42.

65. Fields, *Lemon Swamp*, 43.

66. Perrot, *Fashioning*, 32.

67. Cocuzza, "Dress," 79.

68. Eliza Ripley, *Social Life in Old New Orleans* (Gretna, LA: Pelican Publishing Co., 1998), 68–69.

69. Fields, *Lemon Swamp*, 61, 63.

70. Ibid., 61.

71. Ripley, *Social Life*, 29.

72. Ibid., 53.

73. Such extreme physical disciplining of the body to become unbending, to be incapable of working, to become what Mikael Bakhtin has aptly named the "classical body," constituted the ideal for the European upper classes from early modern ages. The ideal of such bodies was the classical statue, one that did not engage in a give-and-take with the environment but remained autonomous, without openings that called attention to bodily functions, never seen as sitting or lying down.

74. Anne Hollander, *Sex and Suits: The Evolution of Modern Dress* (New York: Kodansha International, 1995), 139.

75. Ripley, *Social Life*, 53–54.

76. Bell Irvin Wiley, *Plain People of the Confederacy* (Chicago: Quadrangle Books, 1943), 9.

77. Olmsted, *Cotton Kingdom*, 451.

78. Dorothy Downs, *Art of the Florida Seminola and Miccosukee Indians* (Gainesville: University Press of Florida, 1995), 36.

79. Fields, *Lemon Swamp*, 30.

80. Tallant, *Gumbo Ya-Ya*, 72.

81. Jennifer Fleischner, *Mrs. Lincoln and Mrs. Keckly* (New York: Broadway Press, 2003), 10.

82. Hollander, *Sex and Suits*, 89.

83. Perrot, *Fashioning*, 32. Hollander's *Sex and Suits*, John Harvey's *Men in Black* (Chicago: University of Chicago Press, 1995), and Valerie Steele's *Paris Fashion: A Cultural History* all offer interesting readings of the modern suit.

84. Quoted in Perrot, *Fashioning*, 31.

85. Ibid., 32.

86. Hollander, *Sex and Suits*, 90–91.

87. Ibid., 77; Perrot, *Fashioning*, 20.

88. Perrot, *Fashioning*, 106.

89. For clothes care on plantations, see Foster, *"New Raiments,"* 124–130; Fox-Genovese, *Plantation Household*, 185; and Barbara M Starke, "Nineteenth-Century African-American Dress," in *Dress in American Culture*, ed. Patricia A. Cunningham and Susan Voso Lab (Bowling Green, OH: Bowling Green University Popular Press, 1993), 52.

90. Fields, *Lemon Swamp*, 85, 89.

91. Perrot, *Fashioning*, 96.

92. Fields, *Lemon Swamp*, 145, 146.

93. Cunningham and Marberry, *Crowns*, 18.

94. Olmsted, *Cotton Kingdom*, 506.

95. Tallant, *Gumbo Ya-Ya*, 182.

96. Abbott, *Womenfolks*, 155.

97. James Clifford, *The Predicament of Culture: Twentieth-Century Ethnography, Literature, and Art* (Cambridge, MA: Harvard University Press, 1988), 338.

98. William Bartram, *Travels of William Bartram* (New York: Dover Publications, 1955), 393–394.

99. Ibid.

100. Ripley, *Social Life*, 58–59.

101. Dressmaking offered women economic independence throughout the nineteenth century. Therefore, like governesses, they represented liminal experiences that found anxious representations in literature. Portrayed as distressed gentlewomen or ambitious parvenues, they were sometimes associated with prostitution in popular stereotypes not only because of the erotic association with clothing but because woman's business had to be "illegitimate business." Their intimate association with higher classes and daily contact with refinement could in reality create social radicals, personally aware of the "unfairness of things": Abigail Scott Duniway, who had a 1860s millinery shop in Oregon, led the women's suffrage movement on West Coast. Another milliner, Mary Harris from Chicago, became known in American labor radicalism as Mother Jones (Wendy Gamber, *The Female Economy: The Millinery and Dressmaking Trades, 1860–1930* [Urbana and Chicago: University of Illinois Press, 1997], 71).

102. Fields, *Lemon Swamp*, 148–149, 152.

103. Gamber, *Female Economy*, 3.

Folklore

1. Charles Joyner, *Shared Traditions: Southern History and Folk Culture* (Urbana: University of Illinois Press, 1999), 24.

2. John Burrison, *Storytellers: Folktales and Legends from the South* (Athens: University of Georgia Press, 1989), 86.

3. Native American Lore Index, http://www.ilhawaii.net/~stony/loreindx.html.

4. Barry Jean Ancelet, *Cajun and Creole Folktales: The French Oral Tradition of South Louisiana* (New York: Gerald Publishing, 1994), xxxix.

5. Ray Hicks and Luke Borrow, *Jack and the Robbers*, videocassette, Appalachian Storyteller Ray Hicks Series, Part 4 (Derry, NH: Chip Taylor Communications, 1997).

6. Richard M. Dorson, "American Negro Folktales," in Daryl C. Dance, *From My People: 400 Years of African American Folklore* (New York: W. W. Norton, 2002), 44–47.

7. Dance, *From My People*, 23–24. Chandler's tales were first published in *Uncle Remus, His Songs and His Sayings: The Folklore of the Old Plantation* (New York: D. Appleton, 1881).

8. Vance Randolph, *The Talking Turtle and Other Ozark Folk Tales* (New York: Columbia University Press, 1957), 3–5.

9. William Jones, *Personal Reminiscences, Anecdotes, and Letters of Gen. Robert E. Lee* (1876), reprinted in B. A. Botkin, *A Treasury of Southern Folklore* (New York: Crown Publishers, 1949), 174–75.

10. Cecil Sharp in America, http://www.mustrad.org.uk/articles/sharp.htm.

11. Ibid.

12. Uncle Remus Slave Songs, http://whitewolf.newcastle.edu.au/words/authors/H/HarrisJoelChandler/prose/UncleRemus/cornshucking.html.

13. Jon Lohman, fieldwork in Buckingham County, Virginia, 2001.

14. Blue Ridge Institute at Ferrum College, Ferrum, Virginia, www.blueridgeinstitute.org.

15. Jack Solomon, ed., *Ghosts and Goosebumps: Ghost Stories, Tall Tales, and Superstitions from Alabama* (Athens: University of Georgia Press, 1994), 97.

16. Daniel Lindsey Thomas, *Kentucky Superstitions* (Princeton: Princeton University Press, 1920), 9–11.

17. Dance, *From My People*, 560–61.

18. Solomon, *Ghosts and Goosebumps*, 115–16.

19. Ibid., 30.

20. From Thomas E. Barden, ed., *Virginia Folk Legends* (Charlottesville: University of Virginia Press, 1991), 114–15.

21. Bluegrass Banjo, http://bluegrassbanjo.org/banjokes.html.

22. Irma Thomas, *Simply the Best Live!*, Rounder CD 2046.

Food

1. René Laudonnière, *Three Voyages* (Gainesville: University Press of Florida, 1975), 185–207.

2. Betty Fussell, *The Story of Corn* (New York: Farrar, Straus and Giroux, 1999), 194; T. N. Campbell, "Choctaw Subsistence: Ethnographic Notes from the Lincecum Manuscript," *Florida Anthropologist* 12, no. 1 (1959): 17–18.

3. Sam Bowers Hilliard, *Hog Meat and Hoecake: Food Supply in the Old South, 1840–1860* (Carbondale: Southern Illinois University Press, 1972), 41.

4. Harvey Levenstein, *Paradox of Plenty: A Social History of Eating in Modern America* (New York: Oxford University Press, 1993), 54.

5. Kathy Starr, *The Soul of Southern Cooking* (Jackson: University Press of Mississippi, 1989), 8.

6. Vertamae Smart-Grosvenor, *Vibration Cooking or the Travel Notes of a Geechee Girl* (Garden City: Doubleday), 102.

7. Mary Land, Louisiana Cookery (Baton Rouge: Louisiana State University Press, 1954), 73–120.

8. Psyche A. Williams-Forson, "'Suckin' the Chicken Bone Dry': African American Women, Fried Chicken, and the Power of a National Narrative," in *Cooking Lessons: The Politics of Gender and Food*, ed. Sherrie A. Inness (Lanham, MD: Rowman and Littlefield,

2001), 173; LuAnn Jones, Mama *Learned Us to Work: Farm Women in the New South* (Chapel Hill: University of North Carolina Press, 2002), 56–59.

9. National Chicken Council, *Regional Frequency of Eating Chicken* July 10, 2003. http://www.nationalchickencouncil.com/ (accessed October 14, 2003).

10. Louisiana Seafood Promotion Board, *Statistics on Southern Catch* (New Orleans, 2003); Aquaculture Network Information Center, *Crawfish: Overview of the State*, 2003. http://www.agmrc.org/aquaculture/profiles/crawfishprofile.pdf (accessed October 8, 2003).

11. Charles Hudson, *The Southeastern Indians* (Knoxville: University of Tennessee Press, 1976), 285.

12. Raymond Sokolov, *Fading Feast: A Compendium of Disappearing American Regional Foods* (New York: Farrar Straus Giroux, 1981), Karen Hess, *The Carolina Rice Kitchen: The African Connection* (Columbia: University of South Carolina Press, 1992), 99.

13. Edna Lewis, *The Taste of Country Cooking* (New York: Knopf, 1976), 4.

14. Hess, *Carolina Rice Kitchen*, 3–5.

15. Waverly Root and Richard de Rochmont, *Eating in America: A History* (New York: William Morrow, 1976), 38.

16. B. A. Botkin, *A Treasury of Southern Folklore: Stories, Ballads, Traditions, and Folkways of the People of the South* (New York: Crown Publishers, 1949), 550.

Language

1. Charles R. Wilson and William Ferris, eds., *Encyclopedia of Southern Culture* (Chapel Hill: University of North Carolina Press, 1989). See especially the Language section's overview essay. A revised and expanded edition of this section is being planned.

2. See www.ccppcrafts.com/language.

3. Richard Teschner, "Spanish Language," in Wilson and Ferris, *Encyclopedia of Southern Culture*, 782–84.

4. For accounts of its possible origin, see Alexander Hull, "French Language," in Wilson and Ferris, *Encyclopedia of Southern Culture*, 770–71; and Tom Klingler, *If I Could Turn My Tongue Like That: The Creole of Point Coupee Parish, Louisiana* (Baton Rouge: Louisiana State University Press, 2003). The latter work includes a number of texts.

5. Lois Huffines, "German Language," in Wilson and Ferris, *Encyclopedia of Southern Culture*, 771–73; Silke Van Ness, "German," in Jean Haskell and Rudy Abramson, eds., *Encyclopedia of Appalachia* (Knoxville: University of Tennessee Press, forthcoming).

6. For the migration of Celtic languages to the United States and their earlier influence on the English and Scottish and Irish immigrants, see Michael Montgomery, "The Celtic Element in American English," in *Celtic Englishes II*, ed. Hildegard Tristram, 231–64 (Heidelberg: Benjamins, 2000). For an up-to-date survey of bilingualism and languages other than English, see Robert Bayley, and Ruth King, "Languages Other than English in Canada and the United States," in *Needed Research in American English*, ed. Dennis Preston, 163–230 (Durham: Duke University Press, 2004).

7. Michael B. Montgomery and Joseph S. Hall, eds., *Dictionary of Smoky Mountain English* (Knoxville: University of Tennessee Press, forthcoming); Cratis D. Williams, *Southern Mountain Speech*, ed. Loyal Jones and Jim Wayne Miller (Berea, KY: Berea College Press, 1992); Donna Christian, Walt Wolfram, and Nanjo Dube, *Variation and Change in Geographically Isolated Communities: Appalachian English and Ozark English* (Tuscaloosa: University of Alabama Press, 1984); Walt Wolfram and Natalie Schilling-Estes, *Hoi Toide on the Outer Banks: The Story of the Ocracoke Brogue* (Chapel Hill: University of North Carolina Press, 1997); David L. Shores, *Tangier Island: Place, People, and Talk* (Newark: University of Delaware Press, 2000); Patricia Jones-Jackson, *When Roots Die: Endangered Traditions on the Sea Islands* (Athens: University of Georgia Press, 1987).

8. Michael Montgomery, "The Scotch-Irish Influence on Appalachian English: How

Broad? How Deep?," in *Ulster and North America: Transatlantic Perspectives on the Scotch-Irish*, ed. Curtis Wood and Tyler Blethen, 189–212 (Tuscaloosa: University of Alabama Press, 1997); Montgomery forthcoming?

9. Mitford McLeod Mathews, ed., *The Beginnings of American English: Essays and Comments* (Chicago: University of Chicago Press, 1931).

10. Guy Bailey, "When Did Southern American English Begin?," in *Englishes around the World I*, ed. Edgar W. Schneider, 255–75 (Amsterdam: Benjamins, 1997); Guy Bailey, "Digging Up the Roots of Southern American English," in *Studies in the English Language II: Conversations Between Past and Present*, ed. Anne Curzan and Kim Emmons, 450–60 (Berlin: Mouton de Gruyter, 2004).

11. Ellen Johnson, *Lexical Change and Variation in the Southeastern United States, 1930–1990* (Tuscaloosa: University of Alabama Press, 1993).

12. For a survey, see Michael Montgomery and Guy Bailey, Introduction to *Language Variety in the South: Perspectives in Black and White*, 1–29 (University: University of Alabama Press, 1986), and essays in Sonja Lanehart, ed., *Sociocultural and Historical Contexts of African American English* (Amsterdam: Benjamins, 2001).

13. David Dalby, "The African Element in American English," in *Rappin' and Stylin' Out: Communication in Urban Black America*, ed. Thomas Kochman, 170–86 (Urbana: University of Illinois Press, 1972).

14. Much of this discussion is accessible at www.fsweb.berry.edu/academic/hass/ejohnson/ebonics.htm, which has sections on official positions on the Ebonics issue, public statements, journalistic commentary, and other topics.

15. For a survey, see Lisa Green, *African American English: A Linguistic Introduction* (Cambridge: Cambridge University Press, 2002).

16. Lorenzo Dow Turner, *Africanisms in the Gullah Dialect* (Chicago: University of Chicago Press, 1949). Reprinted in 2002 by the University of South Carolina Press with a new introduction by Katherine W. Mille and Michael Montgomery.

17. See www.seaislandcreole.org.

18. James B. McMillan and Michael Montgomery, *Annotated Bibliography of Southern American English* (Tuscaloosa: University of Alabama Press, 1989).

19. Hans Kurath, *Word Geography of the Eastern United States* (Ann Arbor: University of Michigan Press, 1949).

20. E. Bagby Atwood, *A Survey of Verb Forms in the Eastern United States* (Ann Arbor: University of Michigan Press, 1953); Hans Kurath, and Raven I. McDavid, Jr., *The Pronunciation of English in the Atlantic States* (Ann Arbor: University of Michigan Press, 1961).

21. Raven I. McDavid, Jr., "The Dialects of American English," in W. Nelson Francis, *The Structure of American English*, 480–543 (New York: Ronald Press, 1958).

22. Lee Pederson, Susan Leas McDaniel, et al., eds., *The Linguistic Atlas of the Gulf States*, 7 vols. (Athens: University of Georgia Press, 1986–92). Research for this project was conducted from 1968 to 1992.

23. For a current survey of Linguistic Atlas projects, see William Kretzschmar, "Linguistic Atlases of the United States and Canada," in Preston, *Needed Research*, 25–48.

Music

1. Bill C. Malone and David Stricklin, *Southern Music/American Music*, rev. and expanded ed. (Lexington: University Press of Kentucky, 2003), 1.

2. Tony Russell, *Blacks, Whites and Blues* (New York: Stein and Day, 1970), 30.

3. Ibid., 31.

4. Eric Lott, *Love and Theft: Blackface Minstrelsy and the American Working Class* (New York: Oxford University Press, 1995), 6.

5. Ibid.

6. Benjamin Filene, *Romancing the Folk: Public Memory and American Roots Music* (Chapel Hill: University of North Carolina Press, 2000), 26.

7. James C. Cobb, *Redefining Southern Culture: Mind and Identity in the Modern South* (Athens: University of Georgia Press, 1999), 95.

8. Albert Murray, *Stomping the Blues*. Twenty-fifth anniversary ed. (New York: Da Capo Press, 2000).

9. Malone and Stricklin, *Southern Music*, 65.

10. Russell, *Blacks, Whites and Blues*, 26.

11. Ibid.

12. Allen Lowe, *American Pop from Minstrel to Mojo: On Record 1893–1956* (Redwood, NY: Cadence Jazz Books, 1997), 158.

13. Mark Zwonitzer with Charles Hirshberg, *Will You Miss Me When I'm Gone? The Carter Family and Their Legacy in American Music* (New York: Simon and Schuster, 2002), 5.

14. Malone and Stricklin, *Southern Music*, 67.

15. Filene, *Romancing the Folk*, 64.

16. Quoted in Robert Palmer, *Rock and Roll: An Unruly History* (New York: Harmony Books, 1995), 25.

17. Peter Guralnick, *Sweet Soul Music: Rhythm and Blues and the Southern Dream of Freedom* (New York: Harper and Row, 1986), 403.

18. Bill C. Malone, *Country Music U.S.A.*, rev. ed. (Austin: University of Texas Press, 1985), 240.

19. Peter Guralnick, *Searching for Robert Johnson* (New York: Dutton, 1989).

20. Greil Marcus. *Mystery Train. Images of America in Rock 'n' Roll Music*, 3rd rev. ed. (New York: Plume, 1990), 174–175.

BIBLIOGRAPHY

Agee, James, and Walker Evans. *Let Us Now Praise Famous Men*. Boston: Houghton Mifflin, 1941.

Ayers, Edward L. *The Promise of the New South: Life after Reconstruction*. New York: Oxford University Press, 1992.

Ayers, Edward L., and Bradley Mittendorf, eds. *The Oxford Book of the American South: Testimony, Memory, and Fiction*. New York: Oxford University Press, 1997.

Barrows, William. *The General; or, Twelve Nights in the Hunters' Camp*. Boston: Lee and Shepard, 1869.

Bartley, Numan V. *The New South, 1945–1980*. Baton Rouge: Louisiana State University Press, 1995.

Berlin, Ira. *Generations of Captivity: A History of African-American Slaves*. Cambridge: Harvard University Press, 2003.

Bodenhamer, David J., and James W. Ely, Jr., eds. *Ambivalent Legacy: A Legal History of the South*. Jackson: University Press of Mississippi, 1984.

Boles, John B., ed. *A Companion to the American South*. Malden, MA: Blackwell, 2002.

Cash, Wilbur Joseph. *The Mind of the South*. 1941. Reprint, New York: Vintage Books, 1969.

Clark, Thomas D., ed. *The South since Reconstruction*. Indianapolis: Bobbs-Merrill, 1973.

Cobb, James C. *The Most Southern Place on Earth: The Mississippi Delta and the Roots of Regional Identity*. New York: Oxford University Press, 1992.

Daniel, Pete. *Lost Revolutions: The South in the 1950s*. Chapel Hill: University of North Carolina Press for Smithsonian National Museum of American History, 2000.

———. *Standing at the Crossroads: Southern Life since 1900*. 1986. Reprint, Baltimore: Johns Hopkins University Press, 1996.

DuBois, W.E.B. *The Souls of Black Folk*. Chicago: A. C. McClurg & Co., 1903. Henry Louis Gates, Jr. and Terri Hume Oliver, eds. New York: W. W. Norton, 1999.

Eaton, Clement. *The Growth of Southern Civilization, 1790–1860*. New York: Harper, 1961.

———. *A History of the Old South: The Emergence of a Reluctant Nation*. 1949. Reprint, Prospect Heights, IL: Waveland Press, 1987.

Egerton, John. *Speak Now Against the Day: The Generation Before the Civil Rights Movement in the South*. New York: Alfred A. Knopf, 1994.

Bibliography

Ellison, Ralph. *Invisible Man*. New York: Random House, 1952.

Faulkner, William. *Absalom, Absalom!* New York: Random House, 1936.

Foner, Eric. *Reconstruction: America's Unfinished Revolution, 1863–1877*. New York: Harper and Row, 1988.

Fox-Genovese, Elizabeth. *Within the Plantation Household: Black and White Women of the Old South*. Chapel Hill: University of North Carolina Press, 1988.

Freehling, William W. *The Road to Disunion: Secessionists at Bay, 1776–1854*. Vol. 1. New York: Oxford University Press, 1990.

Glasgow, Ellen. *The Sheltered Life*. New York: Scribner, 1938.

Goldfield, David R. *Black, White, and Southern: Race Relations and Southern Culture, 1940 to the Present*. Baton Rouge: Louisiana State University Press, 1990.

Hall, Kermit L., and James W. Ely, Jr., eds. *An Uncertain Tradition: Constitutionalism and the History of the South*. Athens: University of Georgia Press, 1988.

Hurston, Zora Neale. *Their Eyes Were Watching God*. 1937. Reprinted with foreword by Edwidge Danticat. New York: HarperCollins, 2000.

Jones, Suzanne W., ed. *Growing Up in the South: An Anthology of Modern Southern Literature*. New York: Penguin Group, 2003.

Key, V. O. *Southern Politics in State and Nation*. 1949. Reprint, Knoxville: University of Tennessee Press, 1984.

Klarman, Michael J. *From Jim Crow to Civil Rights: The Supreme Court and the Struggle for Racial Equality*. New York: Oxford University Press, 2004.

Little, Priscilla Cortelyou, and Robert C. Vaughan, eds. *A New Perspective: Southern Women's Cultural History from the Civil War to Civil Rights*. Charlottesville: Virginia Foundation for the Humanities, 1989.

Malone, Bill C. *Country Music U.S.A.: A Fifty-Year History*. 2nd rev. ed. Austin: University of Texas Press, 2002.

McPherson, James M. *The Battle Cry of Freedom: The Civil War Era*. New York: Oxford University Press, 1988.

———. *The Illustrated Battle Cry of Freedom: The Civil War Era*. New York: Oxford University Press, 2003.

Morgan, Philip D. *Slave Counterpoint: Black Culture in the Eighteenth-Century Chesapeake and Lowcountry*. Chapel Hill: University of North Carolina Press, 1998.

Myrdal, Gunnar. *An American Dilemma: The Negro Problem and Modern Democracy*. New York: Harper and Brothers, 1944.

Norman, Gurney. *Kinfolks: The Wilgus Stories*. Frankfort, KY: Gnomon, 1977.

O'Brien, Michael. *Conjectures of Order: Intellectual Life and the American South, 1810–1860*. Chapel Hill: University of North Carolina Press, 2004.

O'Connor, Flannery. *Wise Blood*. New York: Harcourt, Brace, 1952.

Paredes, J. Anthony, ed. *Indians of the Southeastern United States in the Late Twentieth Century*. Tuscaloosa: University of Alabama Press, 1992.

Rawlings, Marjorie Kinnan. *The Yearling*. New York: C. Scribner's Sons, 1940.

Scott, Anne Firor. *The Southern Lady: From Pedestal to Politics, 1830–1930*. 1970. Reprint, Charlottesville: University Press of Virginia, 1995.

Tindall, George. *The Emergence of the New South, 1913–1945*. Baton Rouge: Louisiana State University Press, 1967.

Walker, Alice. *The Color Purple*. New York: Harcourt Brace Jovanovich, 1982.

Welty, Eudora. *Thirteen Stories*. New York: Harcourt, Brace and World, 1965.

Williams, Tennessee. *A Streetcar Named Desire*. New York: New Directions, 1947.

Williamson, Joel. *The Crucible of Race: Black/White Relations in the American South since Emancipation*. New York: Oxford University Press, 1984.

Wilson, Charles Reagan, and William Ferris, eds. *Encyclopedia of Southern Culture*. Chapel Hill: University of North Carolina Press, 1989.

Woodward, C. Vann. *Origins of the New South, 1877–1913.* 1951. Reprinted with critical essay by Charles B. Dew. Baton Rouge: Louisiana State University Press, 1971.

———. *The Strange Career of Jim Crow.* 3rd rev. ed. New York: Oxford University Press, 1974.

Wright, Gavin. *Old South, New South: Revolutions in the Southern Economy since the Civil War.* New York: Basic Books, 1986.

Wright, Richard. *Native Son.* New York: Harper and Brothers, 1940.

Wyatt-Brown, Bertram. *Southern Honor: Ethics and Behavior in the Old South.* New York: Oxford University Press, 1982.

INDEX

Aaron, Hank, 448

Abbot, Scaisbrooke Langhorne, 58

Abbott, Shirley, 184

abolition, 331; art, 48; Emancipation, 48, 331; literature, 336–341; religious support for, 338; women's role in, 338. *See also* Civil War; slavery

Abrahams, Roger D., 242

Absalom, Absalom!, 351, 353

Acadians. *See* Cajuns

ACC (Atlantic Coast Conference), 452

accessories. *See* fashion and clothing

"Achy Breaky Heart," 398

acid rain, 96, 107

Adams, Henry, 329

Adams, James Taylor, 248

Adams, Shelby Lee, 60

Adelson, Bruce, xxii

Adventures of Huckleberry Finn, 345

Affrilachians, 142

African American English (language), 312

African Americans: Affrilachians, 141; architects, 22; art, 12, 42, 48, 52–57; civil rights movement, 56–57, 209–211, 356–358, 414–416, 424; educational institutions, 22, 454–455; fashion and clothing, 179; film characters, 206–209; folklore and folklife, 232–235, 241–243, 246–247, 349, 434–435; free blacks, 176; language and linguistics, 134, 311–314; literature, 331, 340, 344, 346; middle class, 172–173; music, 241–243, 376–383, 386–390, 393–395; quilting, 46, 164; religion and spirituality, 377, 417, 423, 430–435; sports and recreation, 442–449, 451, 453, 455–457, 459–460; textile production, 166–167. *See also* abolition; slavery

African immigration: influence in southern art, 57; slavery and, 133–140

African Methodist Episcopal Church (AME), 413

Africanisms in the Gullah Dialect, 313

AFS (American Folklore Society), 223, 225

Agee, James, 350

agriculture and farming, 3, 18, 23, 89, 96; climate, effect on, 81, 270–271; dried beans and peanuts, 284; dyeing, 166–168, 175; Farm Security Administration photography project, 50; Farmland Protection Policy Act, 106; federal programs, 50, 106, 147, 268; fertilizers and pesticides, 93, 104–105; genetically engineered seeds, 93; George Washington Carver and, 284; Great Depression, impact on, 50; literature and the agrarian tradition, 348–352; livestock practices, 92, 105–106; Mississippi River ecosystem, effect on, 83–84; plant diseases and

agriculture and farming (*continued*)
infestation, 93, 96, 104–105, 107;
plantation era, 91–94; pollution by,
104–105; sugar cane and refinement,
93–94, 294–295; Thomas Jefferson and,
266, 331; vegetables, 281–284; weather-
related folk beliefs, 247. *See also* food;
specific crop by name
Aiken-Rhett House, 17
air conditioning, 4, 18–19
air pollution, 107
air travel, development of, 25
Airborne Topographic Mapper (NASA),
102
Alabama, 212
Alabama Art League, 58
Alabama-Mississippi All-Star Classic, 462
Albers, Josef, 59
Album quilts, 45
alcoholic drinks, 289–291, 456
Algonquian language, 118, 307
Ali, Muhammad, 450
All God's Chillun Got Wings, 208
All the King's Men, 205, 352
Allegheny Mountains, 79–85
Allen, Lee, 389
Allen, William Francis, 241, 378
alligators, 80
Allison, Dorothy, 358, 359
Allman Brothers Band, 396
Alston Records, 397
Altman, Robert, 202–203
amateur sports. *See* sports and recreation
ambrosia, 269
American Council of Learned Societies,
314
American Dialect Society, 314
American Farmland Trust, 106
American Folklore Society (AFS), 223, 225
American Indians. *See* Native Americans
American Institute of Architects, 20
American Religious Identification Survey
(ARIS), 426–427
American Revolution art, 40–42
American Rivers advocacy group, 105
American Slave, The, 163
American Tobacco Company, 18
Amish, 126, 308
Ammons, Elizabeth, 341
amusement and theme parks, 26, 450
Ancelet, Barry Jean, 229
Andrews, Benny, 57

Andrews, Raymond, 355
Andrews, William, 337
Angelou, Maya, 356
Anglican Church, 11–12, 16
animals, 79–83; birds, 41, 79, 80–83, 104;
extinction and endangered animals, 80;
folk tales, 234–236; hunting and fishing,
80, 276, 440–441, 460–461; livestock,
92, 105–106; oil industry and, 97;
panthers, 80, 104. *See also* ecology and
environment; *specific animal by name*
*Annotated Bibliography of Southern American
English*, 314
Another Part of the Forest, 204–205
Antebellum period. *See* segregation
"anti-Tom" novels, 341
antislavery. *See* abolition
Appalachian Mountains: Affrilachians, 142;
Dolly Parton, 27; ecology, 82, 87–88,
106; ethnic populations, 141–142;
folklore and folklife, 230–232;
literature, 359; Native American
population, 36; religion and spirituality,
435
Appalachian National Park Association,
106
Appalachian Trail, 82
Appeal to the Coloured Citizens of the World,
337
aprons, 182
Arab immigrants, 142–143
architecture, 1–31; Antebellum period,
15–18; colonial period, 10–15; early
settlement period, 7–10; ecology, effect
on design, 2, 101; educational programs
for, 22, 28; garden design, 14; historic
preservation, 4, 24, 27–28; plantation
landscape and architecture, 1–2, 11, 13,
21, 92; post–World War II, 25–28; pre-
Columbian period, 5–7; pre–World War
I, 18–23; pre–World War II, 23–25;
public buildings, 11, 16
Arhoolie music label, 387
ARIS (American Religious Identification
Survey), 427
Arlen, Harold, 375
armadillos, 82
Armstrong, Louis, 380
Armstrong, William H., 201
Army Corps of Engineers, U.S., 97
army jackets, 179
Arneach, Lloyd, 227

art, 33–75; African American, 42, 48, 52–57; American Revolution, 40–42; Civil War, 46–49; colonial period, 38; educational institutions, 40, 59; festivals and events, 69–75; folk art, 42–46, 51–55; modern painting, 57–60; Native American, 34–37, 328; photography, 49–51, 60–61; political and social activity of artists, 49, 58; post-Civil War, 46–49; self-taught artists, 51–55; women, 39, 43–46, 53–54, 164. *See also* architecture; film and theater; literature; music
Ashe, Arthur, 455
Ashe, Thomas, 166
Ashkenazi (Jewish) immigration, 124
Asian immigrants, 143–145, 359, 425–426
associations, professional. *See* organizations, list of
Atchafalaya Bay, 87
Atkins, Chet, 391
Atlanta Braves, 448
Atlanta Olympic Games (1996), 28, 459–460
Atlantic Coast Conference (ACC), 452
Atlantic coastline, ecological creation of, 86–87
atom bomb development, 24
Audubon, John James, 41, 84
Auger, Tracy B., 24
Aunt Jemima, 161
autobiographies. *See* literature
automobiles, 25; exhaust and pollution, 82, 107; racing, 456–458; tourism, development of, 25
Awakening, The, 347
Axtell, James, 329
Axton, Estelle, 388

B-52s (band), 398
Baby Doll, 204
badminton, 441
Baer, Clara, 452
bagpipes (Greek), 130
Bailey, Josiah, 420
Bailey, Robert G., 78
bakeries, 287–288
baking, 286–288
Baldwin, James, 209
Baldwin, Joseph Glover, 335
ballads. *See* songs
balseros, 146

Banashak, Joe, 389
bands. *See* music
banjos, 244; related jokes, 249–250. *See also* country music
Bankhead, Tallulah, 202
banking industry, 94
Baptist Church, on slavery, 412
Barbados, slaves from, 134
Barbara Frietchie, 212
barbecue, 274–275
Barber, George, 19
barn design, 23
Barnard, George P., 50
barrier islands, 86–87, 102
Barth, Fredrik, 148
Barth, John, 354
Barthé, Richmond, 56
Bartholomew, Dave, 389
Bartram, William, 185
baseball, 444–449; Jim Crow laws, 445–448; Negro Leagues, 447–448
basketball, 452–453
basketry, indigenous, 36
basquette, 452
Baudrillard, Jean, 180
beadwork, Native American, 36–37
beans, dried, 284
bear as wild game, 276
Bearden, Romare, 56–57
bed coverings as art, 39, 44–46, 164
beef, 275–276
Beginnings of American English, The, 310
Belasco, David, 212
beliefs. *See* folklore and folklife; religion and spirituality
Belle Lamar, 211
Belmead plantation, 17
Belmont Stakes, 442
Beloved, 169
Benedictine sandwiches, 289
Benenhaley, Joseph, 139
Benjamin, Asher, 16
Bennett, Tony, 391
Berkeley, William, 284
Berlin Olympic Games (1936), 459
Bernard, Rod, 387
beverages, 289–292, 456
Beverley, Robert, 330
Beverly Hillbillies, The, 386
Bible Belt, 408–409. *See also* religion and spirituality
Big Sunflower River, 105

Biltmore, 20
biracial classification and Jim Crow laws, 138
Bird, Elizabeth, 115
Birdcage, The, 202
birds, 41, 79, 80–83, 104
Birds of America, The, 41
Birmingham, Alabama, development in, 18
Birmingham church bombing, 417
Birth of a Nation, The, 207–208, 212
Biscayne Bay National Park, 79, 80
biscuits, 286–287
black Catholics, 423
Black Dutch (German) immigration, 125
Black English (language), 312
Black Mountain College, 59
black pride and fashion, 179
Black Reconstruction, 350
Black Seminoles, 135
black spirituals, 241, 378, 431
blackface (minstrelsy), 207, 377
blacks. *See* African Americans
Blackwell, Scrapper, 381
Blethen, Tyler, 133
Blevins, Brooks, 142
blight, chestnut, 84–85
Blue Ridge Mountains, 79–85
Blue Yodeler, 383–385
bluegrass (plant), 85
bluegrass music, 249–250, 385–386
Blues for Mister Charlie, 209
blues music, 380, 391, 434; in literature, 354–355; rhythm and blues, 389–390, 394–395
Bluett, Thomas, 332
BMG-Bertlesman, 380
Boas, Franz, 243
boats and ships: danger to ecosystem, 80; shipbuilding and timber industry, 95; steamboats, 98
Boca Raton, Florida, development of, 21
Bogardus, James, 15
Boggs, Dock, 382
bogs, 79
Boles, John B., 408, 411
boll weevil, 93, 104–105
Bolotosky, Ilya, 59
Bontemps, Arna, 349
Booker T. and the MGs, 388, 395
Boone, Daniel, 91, 237
Botkin, Benjamin A., 163, 233, 237

Botume, Elizabeth, 165, 169
Boucicault, Dion, 207, 211
Boudinot, Elias, 333
bourbon, 290
Bourgeois, Douglas, 60
Bourke-White, Margaret, 350
bousillage entre poteaux construction technique, 9
boxing, 443, 449–450
Boy Scouts, 456
Boyd, Bob "The Rope," 447
Bradford, Perry, 380
Bradley, Owen, 391
Brady, Mathew, 50
Brasington, Harold, 458
Brass Ankles (mulattos) communities, 139
breads, 286–288
Breen, Bobby, 198
Brent, Linda, 170
Brer Rabbit tales, 234–235, 334
Breuer, Marcel, 24–25
Brewster, Herbert, 433
Bride's Quilt, 45
Bridges, Charles, 38
Briefe and True Report of the New Found Land of Virginia, A, 328
Brinkmeyer, Robert, 359
Brockman, Polk, 382
Broderie perse technique, 45
Brook, Richard Norris, 47
Brooklyn Dodgers, 445–446
Brooks, Cleanth, 351
Brooks, Garth, 398
Brown, Allan, 14
Brown, Charlotte V., 20
Brown, James, 395
Brown, Larry, 359
Brown, Sterling, 349
Brown, William Wells, 339, 340
Brown Bomber (Joe Louis), 450
Brown v. Board of Education, 446
Broyles, Frank, 454
Brumbaugh, Rock, 451
Brunswick stew, 276
Bruton Parish Church, 11
Bryan, Lettice, 291
Bryant, Florence, 176
Bryant, Paul "Bear," 454
Buckland, William, 12
building design. *See* architecture
Bullard, Robert, 107
Bureau of Indian Affairs, 116

Burge and Stevens (firm), 23
burgoo, 276
Burnett, Chester (Howlin' Wolf), 111
Burnett, Micajah, 17
Burnett, T. Bone, 399
Burnside, R. L., 398
Butler, Rhett, 168, 177
buttermilk, 291
buttons in fashion, 180–181
Byrd, William, II, 330

Cabell, James Branch, 348
Cabeza de Vaca, Alvar Nunez, 327
Cabildo, 9
Cabin in the Sky, 210
Cable, George Washington, 168–169, 345
Cajun and Creole Folktales, 229
Cajun-Zydeco music, 386–387
Cajuns, 136–138; Cajun French (language), 307; folk tales, 228–230; foods, 271–272; music, 386–387
Caldwell, Erskine, 201, 330, 350
Caldwell, James H., 194
Calhoun, John C., 338, 340
Calusa of the Florida Keys, 35
Calvinists, 123
Cambodian immigrants, 145
Campanella, Roy, 446
Campbell, Colen, 11
Campbell, Luther, 397
Canary Islanders, 122
Cannon, Gus, 381
Canova, Antonio, 12
cantilever barn, 23
Capote, Truman, 203
captivity narratives, 326–328, 332
car racing, 456–458
carbonated drinks, 291–292
Caribbean immigrants, 11, 136. *See also* Creoles
Carmichael, Hoagy, 375
Carnival celebrations, 250
Carr, Leroy, 381
Carrée and Hastings, 20
Carrier Air Conditioning Company, 18–19
cars, 25; exhaust and pollution, 82, 107; racing, 456–458; tourism and, 25
Carson, Fiddlin' John, 382
Carter, Jimmy, 308
Carter, Leonard E., 248
Carter Family (singers), 383–384

Carver, George Washington, 284
carvings, wood, 52
Casey, Harry Wayne, 397
Cash, Johnny, 384
Cash, Wilbur J. (W. J.), 112, 352, 408
cash crops. *See* agriculture and farming; *specific crop by name*
casinos, 116, 441, 451
cast-iron construction, 15, 17–18
Caste and Class in a Southern Town, 408
Catawba Indians, 120
Catesby, Mark, 38
Catholic Church, 422–423
Catholic Irish immigration, 126–127, 133
"cavalier of the South," 17
caveach fish, 278
celebrations. *See* festivals and events
Celie (*The Color Purple*), 201
Celtic immigration, 128, 133
Centers for the Book, list of by state, 372
Central Appalachian broadleaf forest ecosystem, 82
Central Grocery, 289
Chain Gang, 57
Chapman, Conrad Wise, 47
Charles, Ray, 397, 433
Charleston Hotel, 15
Charlie Daniels Band, 396
Chase, Richard, 230
Chavis, Boozoo, 387
Cheek, Joel, 291
cheerleading, 464–465
chemical and occupational hazards, 182, 245
Chenier, Clifton, 387
Chesnut, Mary, 342
Cherokee Indians, 7, 35–37, 115–116, 226–228, 333–334
Chesnutt, Charles W., 345
Chess music label, 393–394
chestnut blight, 84–85
Chicano writers, 357
Chickasaw tribes, 118
chickee building form, 7
chicken dishes, 276–278
Chicora Indians, 120
Child, Francis James, 238, 378–379, 385
Child Ballads, 239
child labor, photographs of, 50
childbirth folk beliefs, 246
Childress, Alice, 356
Childress, Mark, 202

chitlins, 273, 274
Chinese immigrants, 112, 143–144, 272; Chinese Exclusion Act of (1882), 143
Chireau, Yvonne, 434–435
Chitimacha tribes, 117
chitterlings, 273, 274
Choctaw tribal nations, 117–118
Chopin, Kate, 347
Christenberry, William, 60
Christian, Sara, 457
Christian missionaries, 410
Christianity. *See* religion and spirituality
Christmas food traditions, 269–270
chronology of southern events, 469–477
chunkey, 114–115
Church of God in Christ, 432, 433
churches: black, 412–413; design and architecture, 11, 16; hats in, 175; music of, 386, 430–435; suppers, 269. *See also* religion and spirituality
cigar manufacturing, Cuban, 146
cities and urbanization, 106; architectural trends, 25; art, 41, 50; land conservation and urban sprawl, 106; language uniformity, as result of, 312; pollution, 100; rural migration after Civil War, 18; small town development, 27. *See also* architecture
civil rights movement, 57; art, 56; film and theater, 208–211; literature, 356–358; religion and spirituality, 414–416, 424. *See also* class division; segregation; women's movement
Civil War: art, 46–49; cultural isolation of the South, 1; fashion/clothing and, 167–168, 177, 181–183; film and theater depiction of, 211–214; photography, 50; women's movement, 342
Clague, Richard, Jr., 49
Claiborne, Craig, 274
Clark, Keith, 355
Clark, M. Lewis, 443
class division: fashion and clothing, 161–162, 172, 175–178, 180; food, 265–268; language and linguistics, 308; literature, 359–361; portraiture as definition, 40; slavery and clothing allotment, 170; sports and recreation, 440, 455–456. *See also* civil rights movement; slavery
classicism (architecture), 4

Claudel, Calvin, 228
Clay, Cassius, 450
Clay, Maude Schuyler, 60–61
clay eaters, 267
Clean Air Act (1990), 96
Clemson University, 463
climate, 28; agriculture, and, 270–271; architecture, and, 2, 19; change and environmental challenges, 99; fashion, and, 161–162; sports and recreation, 28, 458. *See also* ecology and environment
Cline, Patsy, 391
cloth trade, 163
clothing. *See* fashion and clothing
coaching. *See* sports and recreation
coal and mining, 88, 91, 96–97
coastal regions, 78–81; development and pollution, 100; ecological creation of, 86–87; erosion and wetland loss, 100–104; flooding prevention, 95
Cobb, James C., 112, 381
Coca-Cola, 291, 292
cockfighting, 441, 444
cocktails, 289–291
Coen Brothers, 399
coffee, 291
Coharie Indians, 121
Cold Mountain, 198
Cole, Thomas, 40
College of William and Mary, 11–12, 15
colleges: architecture of buildings, 24–25; black colleges, 22, 454–455; pride and spirit, 463–465; radio and music, 397; sports and recreation, 445, 447, 452–455, 460–465; women's education, 22–23. *See also* educational institutions
collodion art process, 50
Colonel Sanders, 161
colonial period: architecture, 10–15; art, 38; food, 264–265; revival, 4; sports and recreation, 440
Colonial Williamsburg, 4–5, 10, 24, 28, 450
Color Purple, The, 201
colors in fashion, 166–168, 175, 178
Columbia Records, 380
commerce and economy. *See* agriculture and farming; Great Depression; industrial development; plantation era; tourism
commercial ice plant, first, 290
commercially produced bread, 288

communication. *See* language and
  linguistics
Comprehensive Everglades Restoration
  Plan, A, 103–104
Compson, Quentin, 351, 352, 353
Conch populations, 140–141
Confederate artists, 46–49
conferences, literature, list of, 374
coniferous forest ecosystems, 82
Conrack, 201
Conroy, Pat, 2000–201
conservation. *See* historic preservation
  movement
conservation, environmental, 78, 80
conversionist paradigm, 409
cookbooks, 280–281
Cooke, Ebenezer, 330
Cooke, George, 41
Cooke, John Esten, 343
Cooke, Sam, 433
Cookie and the Cupcakes, 387
"Coon in the Box, The," 233
Coonass (Cajuns), 137–138
Cooper, Anna Julia, 346
coral reefs, 80, 86
Corbett, James, 449
corn, 264–265, 282; shucking ceremonies,
  242
cornbread, 286
corridos, 335
corsets and boards, 177, 181–183
cotton, 3, 81, 89; cotton gin, 92–93;
  diseases, agricultural, 93, 104–105;
  water pollution and, 104–105. *See also*
  fashion and clothing
cougars, eastern, 83
country captain dish, 277–278
country hams, 273–274
country music, 25–27, 381–386, 390–391,
  396–399; Grand Old Opry, 383–385;
  jokes, 249–250
Country Music Foundation, 398
Coushatta tribes, 117
Covenanters (Presbyterians), 132
Cowley, Malcolm, 347, 351
cowpea, 283
crabs, 278
cracklin' bread, 286
Craig, Elijah, 290
Cram, Goodhue and Fergusen, 22
Cramer, Stuart, 18
Crazy in Alabama, 202

Creek (Muskogean) Nation, 119
Creole French (language), 307
Creoles, 2, 133–140; architectural design,
  influence on, 2, 9; fashion and clothing
  of Creole servants, 172; folktales,
  228–229; food, 271–272; language and
  linguistics, 136, 307, 312, 313;
  literature, 347; music and culture, 137
creolization, 111, 225
Crescent Hotel, 20
Crews, Harry, 359
Crib, Tom, 443
Crimes of the Heart, 202
crinoline, 182
Criswell, W. A., 416
Crockett, David (councilman), 108
Crockett, Davy, 237, 336
crocodiles, 80
crops. *See* agriculture and farming; food;
  specific crop by name
Crossroads Legend, of Robert Johnson, 239
Cuban cigar manufacturing, 146
Cuban immigration, 139–140, 146; food,
  272; language and linguistics, 307;
  music, 397; writers, 358
Cuban sandwiches, 289
cudgeling, 440
cuisine. *See* food
cult of the Lost Cause, 345–347, 413, 450
cultural captivity thesis and evangelicalism,
  414
cultural distinctions. *See* class division
culture. *See* art; ethnicity
Cumberland Plateau, 88
Cunningham, Michael, 175
Curtis, Austin, 442
cypress trees, 95
Cyrus, Billy Ray, 398
Czech immigration, 129

Daguerre, Louis, 49
Dailey, Jane, 416
Daingerfield, Elliott, 57, 58
Daisy Mae, 161
Daisy, Miss, 161
Dakin, Charles, 15
Dakin, James, 18
Dalby, David, 312
dams, 105. *See also* flooding
Dance, Daryl Cumber, 234
dances and rituals, 115, 118, 244. *See also*
  music

d'Angiera, Pietro Martiere, 326
Daniels, Charlie (band), 396
DARE (Dictionary of American Regional English), 306, 314
Davidson, Donald, 348
Davidson, Olivia A., 22
Davis, Alexander Jackson, 16, 17
Davis, Arthur Kyle, Jr., 240–241
Davis, David B., 332
Davis, Jimmie, 382
Davis, Lorenzo "Piper," 447
Davis, Ossie, 209
Dayan, Joan, 334
days of rest and food, 269–270
Daytona Beach International Speedway, 457–458
de Bienville, Sieur, 271
de Boré, Etienne, 294
de Bry, Theodor, 328
de la Vega, Garcilaso, 327
de Laudonnière, René Goulaine, 327
de Mille, William C., 212
de Soto, Hernando, 7, 90, 273, 294, 327
decentralization (suburbanization), 27
Declaration of Independence, 331
Deep Are the Roots, 208
Delany, Martin, 340
Deliverance, 204
Delta Land photography project, 60–61
Denver, John, 396
department stores, 186
Derby Day food traditions, 270
desegregation, 354
desserts, 292–295
devil in African American folklore, 434
Dial, Thornton, Sr., 52–53
dialects, 308–316; Lower South, 309; South Midland, 309; southern, 314. *See also* language and linguistics
diaries as literature, 342
Diary from Dixie, A, 342
Dictionary of American Regional English (DARE), 306, 314
diet. *See* food
Dillard, J. L., 312
Dinnerstein, Leonard, 133
dirty rice, 285
disco, 396–397
discrimination. *See* civil rights movement; class division; slavery
diseases, agricultural, 93, 96, 104–105
Disney Corporation, 26–27, 450

diversity. *See* ethnicity
"Dixie" (song), 377
Dixie Crystals, 294
Dixie Highway, 25
Dixie nectar, 290
Dixiecrat Revolt (1948), 420
"Dixieland Jazz Band One-Step," 380
Dixon, Thomas, 345
Dobson, David, 131
Dock Street Theatre, 194
documentary films, 205
Dodgers, Brooklyn, 445
dogs as fashion symbols, 176
dogtrot cabins, 2
Dollard, John, 408
Dollywood, 27, 450
Domino, Fats, 389
Donaldson, Susan V., xxi
Dorman, James, 136
Dorsey, Georgia Tom, 381
Dorsey, Joseph, 446
Dorsey, Lee, 389
Dorsey, Thomas, 386
Dorson, Richard, 229
doughnuts, Krispy Kreme, 288
Douglas, Aaron, 56
Douglass, Frederick, 170, 338, 412, 443
Dove, Rita, 356
Downing, Andrew Jackson, 17
Drake, Richard, 141
drawl, southern, 309
dredging, 105
dress. *See* fashion and clothing
dried beans and peanuts, 284
dried corn, 285–286
drinks and beverages, 289–292
Drive-By Truckers (band), 399
Driving Miss Daisy, 161, 211
dry-cleaning business, development of, 182
Drysdale, Alexander, 58
du Pont, William, 20
du Pratz, Le Page, 292
Duany, Andres, 27
DuBois, W.E.B., 346, 349, 378
Dull, S. R., 276
Dunbar-Nelson, Alice, 346
Dutch (German) immigration, 125
Dutch influence on architecture, 11
Dutch Reform Church, 126
Dvorak, Antonin, 378
dyeing, 166–168, 175

Earnhardt, Dale and Dale, Jr., 458
earthenware, art of, 43
East Coast Hockey League, 459
eastern broadleaf forest ecosystems, 84–85
eastern cougars, 83
Easton, Robert, 7
ebonics, 312
eccentricity of southerners as genre, 202
ecology and environment, 77–110;
    colonization period, 90; conservationist
    efforts and current challenges, 99–107;
    ecosystems, 78–85; environmental
    racism, 107; flooding, 95–98, 105–106;
    folk art and, 43; geologic regions
    defined, 78; landscape, geological
    creation of, 86–88; Native Americans,
    89; naturalist painters, 38, 41
economy. See agriculture and farming;
    Great Depression; industrial
    development; plantation era; tourism
ecosystems of the South, 78–85
Edict of Nantes (1598), 123
Edmondson, Edgar William, 52
educational institutions: architecture of,
    15–16, 22, 24–25; architecture, training
    in, 22; art, 40, 59; pride and spirit,
    463–465; radio and music, 397; sports
    and recreation, 445, 447, 452–455,
    460–465; women, 22–23, 39. See also
    colleges
"Edward" (ballad), 239–240
effigy pipes, 36
egalitarianism. See slavery
Egerton, John, 416
eggs, 276
Egyptian Revival style, 17
Eichenseher, Tasha, xix
Eighmy, John Lee, 414
Eisenhower Interstate System, 25
Elder, John Adams, 47
Ellison, Ralph, 112, 354, 355
Ellison, Stewart, 12
Emancipation, 48, 331. See also slavery
Emanuel, David, 124–125
Emmett, Daniel, 377
endangered species of animals, 80
energy production, 91
engineering projects. See architecture
English and Scottish Popular Ballads, The,
    378–379
English architectural influences, 10
English exploration, 7–8, 328–330

English immigration, 130–131
English language, 308–316
engravings, 47
entertainment. See amusement and theme
    parks; art; film and theater; music;
    sports and recreation
entresol house design, 10
environment. See ecology and
    environment
EPCOT, 26
epiphytes, 78–79
equestrian sports, 441–443, 449
Equiano, Olaudah, 332
Equitable Building, 19
Ernest, John, 346
erosion, coastal, 100–102
estates. See plantation era
Estefan, Gloria, 397
ethnicity, 111–160; African and Creole
    populations, 133–140; Civil War and
    decline of ethnic distinctiveness, 128;
    contemporary New Southerners,
    142–148; creolization, 111, 225;
    demographics, contemporary, 426;
    European immigration, 122–133;
    fashion and clothing, 161, 163, 165,
    168, 184–185; festivals, 113–114, 128,
    147–148; food, 270–272; multi-ethnic
    identification, 113; Native Americans,
    114–122; transnationalism, 145. See also
    immigration; language and linguistics;
    religion and spirituality; specific ethnicity
    by name
ethnogenesis, 333
eutrophication, 105
Evangeline, 137
evangelism, 411–421, 430–435. See also
    religion and spirituality; specific
    denomination by name
Evans, Augusta, 342, 343
Evans, Walker, 50, 60, 350
events. See festivals and events
events in South, timeline of, 469–477
Everett, Christopher, 139
Everglades: ecology and environment, 79,
    103–104; Everglades National Park, 79;
    sugar cane crops, 94
Evert, Chris, 456
exploration period narratives, 326–330
expositions, international, 19
extinction and endangered animals, 80
Ezekiel, Moses, 48

fabrics and textiles, 180; African
Americans, 166–168; cotton, 3, 81, 89,
93, 104; decoration, 39; production and
industry, 93, 168, 180, 184, 186;
quilting, 45; silk, 175; Textile Leagues,
452; trade, 163. *See also* fashion and
clothing
fachwerk construction, 2
factory basketball leagues, 452
factory-made fabrics and clothing, 184,
186
Falcon, Joseph and Ceoma Breaux, 387
fall line, creation of, 88
Falwell, Jerry, 419
FAP (Federal Art Project), 23
Farm Book, 266
Farm Security Administration (FSA)
photography project, 50
farming. *See* agriculture and farming
Farmland Protection Policy Act, 106
fashion and clothing, 161–192; black pride
fashion and clothing, 179; class division,
161–162, 180; climate, and, 161–162;
colors in fashion, 166–168, 175, 178;
dressing time and labor, 182; dyeing,
166–168; economy and
commercialization, 163, 184–187;
ethnicity, 163; men, 177–181; slavery,
163–172; social status, 175–177;
uniforms, 178; women, 177, 181–184.
See also fabrics and textiles
Fat Possum music label, 398
Fat Tuesday, 251
Faulkner, William, 351–353
Faust, Drew Gilpin, 342
Federal Art Project (FAP), 23
federal relief programs, 268
Federal Writers' Project (FWP), 163–164,
243, 247
feminism. *See* women
Ferris, Bill, 205
fertilizers, 93
festivals and events: art, 69–75; ethnic,
113–114, 128, 147–148; film, regional,
215–217; folklife, 250–252; folklore and
folklife, 253; food, 298–303; literary,
374; sports and recreation, 467–468;
theater, regional, 217–221
field sports, 459. *See also* sports and
recreation
Fields, Mamie, 166, 173, 175–177, 179,
182–183, 186–187

Filene, Benjamin, 379, 385
film and theater, 193–221; African
Americans as characters, 206–209; civil
rights movement in, 209–211; Civil
War depicted in, 211–214; documentary
films, 205; film, 196–198; Gothic
horror and Gothic decadence genre in
film and theater, 203–206; musicals,
210–211; "New South" theme,
199–201; "Old South" theme, 198;
recession, impact on, 197; Southern
Gothic genre, 201–204; theater,
193–195; theatrical troupes, 193–194.
See also music
films, list of (as reference): architecture,
30–31; ethnicity, 156–158; folklore and
folklife, 252; food, 296–297; language
and linguistics, 320; religion and
spirituality, 438
finance and economy. *See* agriculture and
farming; Great Depression; industrial
development; plantation era; tourism
Finch, Atticus and Scout, 199
Finch, Rick, 397
finger-weaving, 168
Finster, Howard, 53
fires: fire-hunting, 441; fireproof buildings,
12, 13, 15, 18; forest, 82, 85, 96;
hazards and clothing, 182
First Great Awakening, 333
Fish, Jessie, 291
fish and fishing: ecology and environment,
80; fish and seafood, 278–280; sport,
440, 460–461
Fisher, Abby, 281
Fisher, Isaac, 338
Fisk Jubilee Singers, 378
Fitch, Clyde, 212
Fitzhugh, George, 340
Fitzpatrick, John Kelly, 58
Five Civilized Tribes, 35–36
517 Decatur Street (building), 10
fives (game), 441
Flagler, Henry, 20
Flatt, Lester, 386
Fleischner, Jennifer, 177
Flexner, Marion, 276
Flim-Flam Man, The, 203
Flock, Ethel, 457
Flock, Tim, 457
flooding, 95–98, 105–106; Flood Control
Act (1928), 98

floodplains (Mississippi River Delta), 86–87
flora of Everglades, 80
Florida: geological creation of, 86; orange juice, 291; panthers, 80, 104; tourism and, 20
La Florida del Inca, 327
flour, importing, 265
folk art, 42–46, 53–54
folk songs, 238–246. *See also* country music
folklore and folklife, 223–261; African American, 232–235, 241–243, 349, 434–435; beliefs and superstitions, 246–249; holidays and festivals, 250–252; Jack tales, 230–232; jokes, 249–250; legends and legendary figures, 236–238; Native American, 226–228; tall tales, 228–232, 334. *See also* literature
Fontainebleau Hotel, 26
food, 263–303; Cajun, 271–272; cookbooks, 280–281; Creole, 271–272; drinks and beverages, 289–292, 456; ethnicity and, 270–272; hunger and malnutrition issues, 267–268; imports, 267; Native American, 263–264, 281, 289, 292–295; occasions and days of rest, 269–270; signature dishes of the South, 272–295. *See also* agriculture and farming; *specific food by name*
football, 445, 453–454
Foote, Horton, 199
forests, 79–85; acid rain and, 96; fires, 82, 85; protected, 95–96; resources, 94–95; sustainability, 106–107; temperate, 96
Fortier, Alcee, 228–229
Foster, Frances Smith, 332, 337, 346
Foster, Helen Bradley, 163, 170
Foster, Stephen, 377–378
Fountain of Youth, legend of the, 229
4-H Clubs, 456
Four Nations tribes, 117
Fox, John Harrington, 240
Fox, William Henry, 50
Fox-Genovese, Elizabeth, 168, 169
fraktur, 42
France, Big Bill, 457
Frank, Leo, 424
fraternal organizations, 456
Frederick Law Olmsted & Co., 20
free blacks, 176
free people of color (*gens de couleur libre*), 136

French Creoles. *See* Creoles
French exploration and immigration, 7, 9, 123, 327; Huguenots, 39, 123, 327. *See also* Cajuns
French language, 307
French poodles as fashion symbols, 176
freshwater resources, 101, 104–105
fried chicken, 277
Fried Green Tomatoes, 203
Friedman, Alice T., 26
friendship quilts, 46
Frontier Film Group, 205
frosts and agriculture, 81
fruits, 292
Frymire, John, 42
Fugitive poets, 348
Fugitive Slave Act, 341
Fuller, Buckminster, 26
Fuller, Charles, 209
fundamentalism. *See* religion and spirituality
funeral food traditions, 270
FWP (Federal Writers' Project), 163–164, 243, 247

Gabriel's Rebellion, 336
Gaelic language, 133
Gaines, Clarence "Big House," 455
Gaines, Ernest, 356
Gallegina (Elias Boudinot), 333
Gallier, James, 15
Gamber, Wendy, 187
gambling, 116, 441, 451
game hunting, 276, 440–441
games. *See* sports and recreation
gandy dancers, 244
garden clubs, 24
garden design, 14
Gardeners Dictionary, The, 14
garments. *See* fashion and clothing
Garrison, Lucy McKlan, 241, 378
Garrison, William Lloyd, 338
Gary, David Elton, 334
gas and pollution, 105
Gatschet, Albert, 117
gay writers, 358
gazpacho, 283
Geechi islanders, 134
gelatin salads, 283–284
gender. *See* men's fashion and clothing; women
Gendusa, John, 288

General Phonograph Company, 380
genetically engineered seeds, 93
genetically modified organisms (GMOs),
    105
Genovese, Eugene D., 408
gens de couleur libre (free people of color),
    136
"Genteel Acadians" (Cajuns), 137
Gentry, Jane, 239
geologic regions defined, 78, 85
Georgia Classicists, 19
Georgia Tech University, 454, 463–464
Georgian style, 4
geosyncline, 87
German immigrants, 125–126, 141;
    architecture, 2; art, 42; language and
    linguistics, 307
ghost stories, 247–249
Gibson, Althea, 455
Gibson, Clifford, 383
Gillette, William, 212
Gilliland, Henry, 381–382
Gilman, Caroline Howard, 338
Girl Scouts, 456
Gist, George, 333
Glasgow, Ellen, 347
Glassie, Henry, 23
Gleeson, David, 126
global temperatures and warming, 80, 100
GMOs (genetically modified organisms),
    105
Go to Sleep My Girl, 243
Godchaux, Leon, 295
Goddu, Teresa, 334
Going Down to Lynchburg, 58
Gold Wax music label, 389
Goldberger, Joseph, 268
golf, 456
Gondwanaland landmass, 86
Gone with the Wind: architecture, 1; fashion
    in, 168, 177; filming and location of,
    196–197; ideals depicted in, 199, 206,
    212, 325, 352; rewriting from slave
    perspective, 356
Gonzalez, Elian, 146
Gonzalez, Rodolfo "Corky," 357
goobers, 293
Goodwin, D.A.R., 24
Gopnik, Blake, 164
Gordon, Caroline, 352
gospel music, 386, 430–433
Gothic genres (film and theater), 201–206

Gothic Revival style (architecture), 17, 24
gouging, 441
government: architecture of public
    buildings, 11, 16, 23; art policy, 58;
    federal relief programs, 268; housing
    projects, 23; military base design, 23;
    military portraiture, 47–48; national
    parks, 79, 80–81, 107; public buildings,
    11, 16; religion and politics, 418–421,
    429–430; state art commissions, list of,
    67–69; state fairs and sports, 449–451;
    uniforms and fashion, 178
Graceland, 1
Grady, Henry, 18
Grambling University, 455
grammar, southern, 308–309. *See also*
    language and linguistics
Grand Ole Opry, 26–27, 383–385
Grandissimes, The, 168–169, 345
Grapefruit League, 449
Grass Harp, 203
grassroots environmental efforts, 107
Graves, Charlene, 175
gravy, 277
Gray, Richard, 334
Gray, Thomas, 337
Great Awakening, 120, 333
Great Depression, 243; construction
    projects of, 23; literature, 350; music,
    effect on, 385; photography, 50; religion
    and spirituality, 433. *See also* New Deal
Great Smoky Mountains National Park,
    25, 82, 107, 461
Greek immigration, 130, 272
Greek Revival style (architecture), 16
Green, Al, 389
Green, David Gordon, 198
Green, John, 429
Greenbaum, Susan, 140
Griffith, D. W., 197, 207–208, 212
Griggs, Sutton E., 346
Grimes, William, 337
Grimké, Angelina and Sarah, 338
Grimm, Jacob and Wilhelm, 225
grits, 285–286
Grooms, Anthony, 356
Grooms, Red, 60
Gropius, Walter, 24–25
Guatemalan Mayan immigration, 145–146
Gulf Stream, 90
Gullah islanders, 134, 312, 313
Guralnick, Peter, 388, 391

Gwathmey, Robert, 58–59
Gypsy immigration, 129–130

H2A guest worker program, 147
habitation, 79–83; birds, 41, 79, 80–83,
    104; endangered species of animals, 80;
    oil industry and, 97. *See also* ecology
    and environment
Hague, Parthenia Antoniette, 167–168, 177
hair styles and headgear, 173–176
Hairston, Sam, 447
Hakluyt, Richard, 329
Hale, Grace, 199
Haliwa-Saponi Indians, 120
Hall, Drayton, 11
Hall, Gwendolyn Midlo, 136
Hallam, Lewis, 194
Hallelujah, 209
ham, 273–274
Hamm, Mia, 460
Hammerstein, Oscar, 375
Hampton, James, 53
Hampton University, 22
handkerchiefs, 174
hands, condition of, as status symbol, 175
Handy, W. C., 380
Hannah, Barry, 355
Harlem Art Workshop, 56
Harlem Renaissance, 349
Harper, Frances Ellen Watkins, 346
Harper's Magazine (of 1853), 167
Harriot, Thomas, 328
Harris, Jessica, 293
Harris, Joel Chandler, 234, 242, 334, 344
Hart, Bill, 445
harvesting. *See* agriculture and farming
Harvey, Paul, xxii
hats, 175
Hawthorne, Nathaniel, 341
Hay, George D., 383
Hayne, Paul Hamilton, 343
headgear, 173–176
"Headless Ghost of Griffith's Wife, The,"
    248–249
Heart Is a Lonely Hunter, The, 200
Heart of the Maryland, The, 212
Hearts in Dixie, 209
Heisman, John, 453–454
Hellman, Lillian, 204, 350
Hemings, John, 12
Hemings, Sally, 331
hemlines, rise of in fashion, 183

Henley, Beth, 202
Hentz, Caroline Lee, 341
Herkimer, Lawrence "Herkie," 464
Hess, Karen, 283, 285
Heyrman, Christine Leigh, 408, 411
Heyward, Dorothy, 208
Heyward, Dubose, 208, 350
Hi music label, 389
Hibernian Societies, 127–128
Hicks, Ray, 230–232
hierarchy. *See* class division
high school sports, 445, 447, 452–455,
    460–465
Highland Scottish immigrants, 131–133,
    308
Highsmith, Patricia, 358
highway development, 25. *See also*
    automobiles
Hill, Samuel S., Jr., 408, 409, 414
hillbilly music. *See* country music
Hirshberg, Charles, 384
Hischak, Thomas S., xx
Hispanic and Latino culture: churches,
    147; immigration, 146–148, 357;
    language and linguistics, 146–148, 307;
    literature, 357; music, 397; Spanish
    exploration and early immigration, 7,
    122, 326
historic preservation movement, 4–5, 24,
    27–28
historical painting, 46–49
*Historie of Travaile unto Virginia Britannia,
    The*, 328
Hoban, James, 12
Hobson, Fred, 355, 356
hockey, 458–459
hogs, 105–106, 273–275, 283
hogshead cheese, 92, 274
hokum music, 381
holidays and festivals. *See* festivals and
    events
Holiness-Pentecostal movement, 431–435
Hollander, Anne, 178, 180–181
Hollingsworth, William, Jr., 51
Holmes, George Frederick, 341
holy dancing, 432
home baking, 287–288
hominy, 285–286
homosexual writers, 358
Hooper, Johnson Jones, 336
Hopkins, Al, 382
Hoppin' John, 283

horse racing, 441–443, 449
Horton, George Moses, 339
hot breads, 287
Hot Springs National Park, 20, 461
hotels and tourism, 15; architecture, 25–26
Houma populations, 138
house design, 19; low income housing, 23, 27. *See also* architecture
House, Son, 381, 396
"How the Mink Got His Dark Coat," 227
How to Speak Southern, 308
Howard, Ebenezer, 24
Howard, Frank, 463
Howard's Rock, 463
Howell, William Dean, 345, 346
Hudson, Arthur Palmer, 241
Hughes, Langston, 208, 349
Hughes, Louis, 170
Huguenots, 39, 123, 327
Hungarian immigration, 130
hunger and malnutrition, 267–268
Hunt, Alfred, 336
Hunt, Richard Morris, 20, 22
Hunter, Clementine, 53
hunting, 95, 276; as sport, 440–441. *See also* habitation
hurricanes, 101–102
Hurston, Zora Neale, 243, 349
Hurt, Mississippi John, 381, 396
Hush...Hush, Sweet Charlotte, 203–204
hush puppies, 286
Hutcheon, Linda, 360
hybrid cultures and early literature, 334–336
hymnals, 432
hypodescent and race, 138
hypoxia, 105

ice plant, first commercial, 290
iced tea, 291
icons of contemporary music, 391–396
I'll Take My Stand: The South and the Agrarian Tradition, 348
Imes, Birney, 60
immigration: aid organizations, 127–128; European, 122; food, 272; Reform Bill of 1965, 142; religious persecution and, 123–124. *See also* dialects; ethnicity; *specific group by name*
imports, food, 267
In Ole Virginia, 344
Incidents in the Life of a Slave Girl, 340

indentured servants, 133–134. *See also* slavery
Indian moccasins, 171
"Indian Territory," 114
Indians. *See* Native Americans
indigo dye, 166–168
Indochinese immigrants in literature, 359
industrial baseball leagues, 448
industrial development, 44–46, 94; factory-made fabrics and clothing, 184, 186; Industrial Revolution, 44, 93; "New South," 18; pollution, 82, 104–105; waterwheel and energy production, 91
Indy 500 Speedway, 458
infestations and disease, agricultural, 93, 96, 107
International design style, 25
international expositions, 19
Interstate 95, 25
Invisible Man, 354
Iola Leroy; or Shadows Uplifted, 346
IPCC (Intergovernmental Panel on Climate Change), 100, 101
Irish immigration, 126–127; festivals, 128; language and linguistics, 308; work songs, 245
Irish Traveler immigration, 129–130
iron ore, 96. *See also* cast-iron construction
Irving, John Beaufain, 49
Isaac, Rhys, 411
Italian immigration, 112, 128–129
Italian influence on garden design, 14
Italian Renaissance architecture, 10–11
Italianate style, 17

Jack tales, 230–232
Jackson, Andrew: horse racing center, 442; Native Americans, policy on, 114, 410
Jackson, Jesse, 431
Jacobs, Harriet, 340
James, Skip, 381, 395
Jamestown, Virginia, 8, 90, 114, 264, 328
Japanese immigrants, 145
jazz music, 244, 380; in literature, 354–355
Jefferson, Thomas: agriculture and southern food interests, 266, 331; as architect, 4, 15–16, 22; folktales of, 237; Jeffersonianism, rejection of, 340; in literature, 340; literature of, 330, 331; Monticello, 13, 15, 266; Native

American, policy on, 114; religion and spirituality, 409; on slavery, 331
Jekyll Island, 20
Jemima, Aunt, 161
Jennings, Waylon, 396
Jerusalem Evangelical Lutheran Church, 123–124
Jewish immigrants, 124–125; food, 272; military involvement, 48; religion and spirituality, 423–425
Jim Crow laws, 18; biracial classification and, 138; "Jim Crow" persona, 377; Native Americans and, 120; restaurants and segregation laws, 269; sports desegregation, 445–448. *See also* segregation
jockeys, 442–443
"John and Old Master" tales, 232–235
Johns, Jasper, 60
Johnson, Blind Willie, 381
Johnson, Ellen, 311
Johnson, Georgia Douglas, 349
Johnson, James Weldon, 346, 349
Johnson, Lonnie, 381
Johnson, Robert, 239, 381, 391–392, 434
Johnson, Tommy, 381
Johnson, William H., 57
Johnston, Henrietta Deering, 39
Johnston, Mary, 347
jokes in folklore, 249–250
Jones, Bobby, 456
Jones, Charles Colcock, 411
Jones, E. Fay, 22, 27
Jones, Gayle, 356
Jones, Mrs. Francis, 440
Jones, Willie, 442
Jouett, Matthew Harris, 40
Journal of Southern Religion, 409
journalism, photo, 50
Joyner, Charles, 112, 225, 431
Judaism, 423–425. *See also* Jewish immigrants
Jug Band, 381, 383

Kanellos, Nicholás, 358
Karpeles, Maud, 239
karst topography, 88
Kazan, Elia, 205
K.C. and the Sunshine Band, 397
Keckly, Elizabeth, 176–177
Keith, Jeanette, 134
Kelley, Edith, 350

Kelley, Robin D. G., 417
Kemble, Frances, 164, 167, 174
Kenan, Randall, 358
Kennedy, John Pendleton, 337, 341
Kennedy, Roger, 10–11
Kentucky bluegrass, 85
Kentucky Cycle, The, 213
Kentucky Derby, 442–443
Kephart, Horace, 226
Kern, Jerome, 375
Key West, Florida, memory paintings of, 54
Killers of the Dream, 352
Kimball, Fiske, 4
Kimborough, Junior, 398
King, Edward, 343
King, Grace, 341
King, Martin Luther, Jr., 111, 356
King, Mary, 417
Kirby, David, 355
kitchen design of plantations, 3
Koasati tribes, 117
Korean immigrants, 144
Koumenyakaa, Yusef, 356
Krehbiel, Henry Edward, 242
Kreyling, Michael, 353, 354
Krio language, 134
Krispy Kreme doughnuts, 288
Krzyzewski, Mike, 452
Ku Klux Klan, 382, 446; in film, 207–208
Kurath, Hans, 315
Kushner, Tony, 358

Ladd, Barbara, 353
Lafever, Minard, 16
LAGS (Linguistic Atlas of the Gulf States), 315
lakes, oxbow, 83
Land, Mary, 281
landscape and landscaping: art, 41; conservation, 106; design and development, 8–10, 14; geological creation of, 86–88; plantation architecture, 1–2, 11, 13, 21, 92. *See also* architecture; ecology and environment
Langlois, Madame, 265
language and linguistics, 305–324; African American, 134, 311–314; change and innovation, 311; Creole, 136, 312, 313; English language, 308–316; Gaelic, 133; Gullah islanders, 312, 313; Native Americans, 116–118, 120–121, 305–307; non-English, 307. *See also* dialects

Lanier, Sidney, 343
Lankford, George, 334
Lanusse, Armand, 335
lapdogs as fashion symbols, 176
Lapidus, Morris, 26
La Relacion, 327
Latin American Fiesta, 129
Latino and Hispanic culture: churches, 147; immigration, 146–148, 147–148, 357; language and linguistics, 146–148, 307; literature, 357; music, 397; Spanish exploration and early immigration, 7, 122, 326
Latrobe, Benjamin Henry, 12, 13
Laudonnière, Réné, 439
Laurasia landmass, 86
laurel forests, 79
Laveau, Marie, 176
law enforcement and liquor, 456
Law of the Indies, 8
Lawrence, Jacob, 56
Lawrence, Thomas, 40
Lawson, John, 330
Le Grand Derangement, 386
Le Moyne, Jean Baptiste, 271
Le Moyne de Morgues, Jacques, 38, 328
Lebanese immigrants, 142–143
Ledbetter, Huddie (Leadbelly), 385
Lederer, John, 121
Lee, Harper, 199
Lee, Robert E., 48, 237
legends and folklore, 225–236. See also folklore and folklife
legumes, 284
leisure. See sports and recreation; tourism
lemonade, 291
Leoni, Giacomo, 11
Lerch, Patricia, 120
Let It Loose, 397
levees, 83, 97
Levine, Lawrence, 434
Levitt and Sons, 23
Lewis, Carl, 459
Lewis, Edna, 283
Lewis, Oliver, 443
Life of Josiah Henson, The, 341
Life of William Grimes, the Runaway Slave, 337
limestone, 86
Limner, Payne, 42
Limpin' Susan, 282
Lincoln, Mary Todd, 176, 179

Linebaugh, Peter, 333
linen in fashion, 180
lingerie, 177, 181–183
Linguistic Atlas of the Gulf States (LAGS), 315
Linguistic Atlas project, 309, 314
Linguistic Society of America, 314
linguistics. See language and linguistics
lining bar gangs, 244–245
liquor, 289–291, 456
literature, 325–375; African American, 331, 346; African American characters, 344; agrarian tradition as genre, 348–352; cookbooks, 280–281; Creoles as character, 347; cult of the Lost Cause literature, 345–347; exploration period narratives, 326–330; Federal Writers' Project (FWP), 163–164, 243, 247; Hispanic, 357; hybrid cultures and early literature, 334–336; Native Americans, 326–330, 333; poetry, 335, 340, 343, 355; postmodern, 352–361; settler, 329; slavery and captivity, 168, 326–328, 330–333, 336–341; Southern Renaissance in, 347, 354; storytelling, 344; trade, 20; women writers, 341, 347. See also folklore and folklife
Little Colonel, The, 198
Little Foxes, The, 204
Littlest Rebel, The, 198
"Livery Stable Blues," 380
livestock, 92, 105–106
logging and timber, 95–96
Lohman, Jon, xx
Lomax, Alan, 241, 378, 385, 386, 393
Lomax, John, 241, 378, 385
Long, Huey, 205, 276
Longfellow, Henry Wadsworth, 137
Longstreet, Augustus Baldwin, 336
Longwood House, 17
Lorentz, Pare, 205
Los Isleños (Canary Islanders), 122
Lost Cause, cult of the, 345–347, 413, 450
Lott, Eric, 377
Louis, Joe, 450
Louisiana Coastal Wetlands Planning, Protection and Restoration Act (1990), 103–104
Louisiana French (language), 307
Louisiana Purchase, 90
Louisiana Superdome, 28
Louisville Hot Brown sandwiches, 289
Louisville Jug Band, 383

Lounsbury, Carl, 8
"Lovesick Blues," 390
low-income housing design, 27
Lowe, Allen, 384
lower Mississippi Riverine Forest
    ecosystem, 83–84
Lower South dialect, 309
Lowland Scottish immigrants, 131–133
Ludwell, Philip, 440
Lumbee Indians, 121
lumber industry, 95
Lupo, Salvatore, 289
Lyerly, Lynn, 411
Lyotard, Jean François, 356

Mackintosh, John Mohr, 131
Macon, Uncle Dave, 382
"magic animals" tales, 234–236
mail order house plans, 19
Mailer, Norman, 325
major league sports. *See* sports and
    recreation
Malaco music label, 398
malnutrition and hunger issues, 267–268
Malone, Bill C., 375, 382, 385, 391, 432
Mammoth Cave National Park, 88
Mammy (*Gone with the Wind*), 168, 200
manatees, 80, 104
mangrove forests, 80, 103
Manhattan Project, 24
Mann, Earl, 446
Mann, Sally, 61
Manning, Carol S., 347
manor houses. *See* plantation era
Mantz, Johnny, 458
manufacturing centers design, 23
Marberry, Graig, 175
Marcus, Greil, 393
Mardi Gras celebrations, 251
Mardi Gras Indians, fashion of, 165
marine life. *See* habitation
marine parks, 79
Mark, Rebecca, 353
Marling, Jacob, 41
Marrant, John, 332
Marrow of Tradition, the, 345
"Marse Chan," 344
Marshall, Paule, 356
marshes and wetlands, 78–79, 97, 103–104
Martí, José, 139–140
Martí-Maceo Society, 139–140
Martin Luther King Day, 111

Martin, Sara, 382
Martineau, Harriet, 286
Martin's Grocery, 288
Martyr, Peter, 326
masks, Native American, 34–37, 328
Mason, Bobbie Ann, 330, 359
Mason, C. H., 432
mass media and religion, 430–435
Masters Golf Tournament, 456
Matassa, Cosimo, 389
Mathews, Donald G., 408, 411
Mathis, Verdell, 447
Matthews, Uncle Jimmy, 276
Maxwell House Hotel, 291
Mayan immigration, 145–146
Maybeck, Bernard, 20
Mays, Willie, 447
McCauley, Deborah Vansau, 434–435
McClendon, John, 454–455
McCord, Louisa, 341
McCullers, Carson, 199–200, 204, 353
McDavid, Raven, Jr., 315
McGugin, Daniel, 454
McKillop, Alexander, 52
McPhee, John, 105
McPherson, James Alan, 356
meadow ecosystems, 82
meats, 273–276
Melungeon populations, 139
Member of the Wedding, The, 199–200
memory painters, 53–55
Memphis and music, 388
Mencken, H. L., 347, 348, 408
Mennonites, 126, 308
men's fashion and clothing, 177–181
Mercer, Johnny, 375
Mercié, Antonin, 48
mestizos, 147. *See also* Creoles
Mexican immigrants, 147, 272
Miami Beach tourism, 25–26
Miami Sound, 396–397
"Michael, Row Your Boat Ashore," 241
Middle Passage in literature, 332
Middleton Place, 14–15
Midnight in the Garden of Good and Evil, 203
migrant laborers, 147
Miley, Michael, 50
military: base design, 23; portraiture,
    47–48; uniforms and fashion, 178
milk (drink), 291
Miller, Emmett, 390
Miller, Kerby, 133

Miller, Philip, 14
Mills, Gary, 139
Mills, Robert, 13, 18
Mind of the South, The, 352, 408
mineral water and therapeutic resorts, 20
mining, 88, 91, 96–97
Minit music label, 389
minor league baseball. *See* baseball
Minorcans of St. Augustine, 122–123
minorities. *See* African Americans; *specific ethnic group by name*
minstrelsy, 207, 377
mint juleps, 290
missionaries, 410. *See also* religion and spirituality
Mississippi Blues, 205
Mississippi Burning, 211
Mississippi River, 90; architecture of, 9; conservationist efforts and current challenges, 97–100, 103–106; Delta, creation of, 86–87; ecosystem of, 83–84; Embayment, 86–87; Flyway migration route, 83–84; Mississippi River Commission, 97–99; Plateau, 88; riverboat gambling, 451; sediment, 86, 87–88; Valley, 83–84
Mississippian Indian groups, 34–35, 114
Mitchell, Emil and Kelly, 129
Mitchell, Margaret. *See Gone with the Wind*
Mitchell, Steve, 308
Mitchell, Willie, 389
mixed forest ecosystem, 78–81
Mizner, Addison, 20–21
Mockbee, Samuel, 27
modern painting, 57–60
modernism design style, 25
modernized classicism, 23
Moffett, Marian, 23
Mohr, Paula, xviii
molasses, 94, 294–295
Molasses Act (1733), 290
Molineaux, Tom, 443
Monroe, Bill, 385–386, 433
Montgomery, Michael, xxi
Monticello, 13, 15, 266
Montpelier, 20
monumental sculptures, 48
Moody, Anne, 357
Mooney, James, 226
moonshine, 290, 456
Moore, Charles, 26
Moore, Roy, 426

Moravians, 2, 124
Morgan, Georgia, 58
Morgan, Philip, 332
Morgan, Sister Gertrude, 52
Morgan, William, 5
Mormon converts, Native American, 120
Morrison, Toni, 169
Morse, Samuel F. B., 40, 49
Moses, Anna Mary Robertson ("Grandma Moses"), 53–54
Motif-Index of Folk Literature, 225–226
motorboats, danger to ecosystem, 80
mound culture, 6, 34
Mount Vernon, 15
"mountain people," 141
mountain ranges, 78, 82. *See also* Appalachian Mountains, ecology
mountain resources, 94
mountaintop mining, 96, 105
mourning pictures, 43
Mt. Airy, 14
muffulettas, 288–289
mulatto communities, 139, 208
Mulatto, The, 208
Mulberry Row, 13
multi-ethnic identification, 113
Mumford, Lewis, 1
Murphy, Isaac, 443
Murray, Albert, 355, 381
Murray, Pauli, 356
Museum of Early Southern Decorative Arts, 28
Museum of the Cherokee Indian, 7
museums, list of: architecture, 30–31; art, 62–67; ethnicity, 158–160; fashion and clothing, 189–192; folklore and folklife, 253–261; food, 297; religion and spirituality, 438. *See also* special collections, list of
music, 375–405; African American, 241–243, 376–383, 386–390, 393–395; awards, 398–399; bluegrass, 249–250, 385–386; blues, 354–355, 380, 391, 434; church music, 378, 386, 430–435; contemporary music icons, 391–396; country, 25–27, 249–250, 381–386, 390–391, 396–399; disco, 396–397; folk songs, 238–246; Latin, 397; Miami Sound, 396–397; minstrelsy, 377; museums and foundations, 398; musical theater, 210–211; nineteenth-century, 376–379; pop, recent, 396–398; rap,

397; recording industry, 379–383, 388–391; rhythm and blues, 389–390, 394–395; soul, 395; women, 380, 396–397
musicals, 210–211
Muskogean (Creek) Nation, 117–119
Myth of the Cherokee, 227
myths. *See* folklore and folklife

Nabokov, Peter, 7
Naismith, James, 452
Nan-ye-hi (Nancy Ward), 333
Narrative of Arthur Gordon Pym, 334
narratives. *See* literature
NASA (National Aeronautics and Space Administration), 102
NASCAR (National Association of Stock Car Racing), 457–458
Nashville, 202–203
Nashville music, 390–391; Grand Old Opry, 383–385; "Nashville sound," 379, 396
Nat Turner Revolt (1831), 337, 412
Natchez tribes, 118
National Academy of Design, 40
National Aeronautics and Space Administration (NASA), 102
National Association of Stock Car Racing (NASCAR), 457–458
National Baptist Convention, 413
National Estuarine Research Reserve System, 104
National Historic Preservation Act (1966), 27–28
National Hockey League (NHL), 458–459
National Hurricane Center, 102
National Oceanic and Atmospheric Association (NOAA), 101–102
national parks, 79, 80–81, 107. *See also* ecology and environment
National Parks Conservation Association (NPCA), 107
National Weather Service, 102
Native Americans: architecture, 5–7; art, 34–37, 328; Cherokee Indians, 7, 35–37, 115–116, 226–228, 333–334; clan systems, 115; contemporary census figures, 115; contested identity tribes, 121–122; dances and rituals, 115, 118; ecology and environment, 89–90; educational institutions created for, post Civil War, 22; ethnicity, 114–122;

fashion and clothing, 165, 172–177, 179, 184–185; folktales, 226–228; food, 263–264, 281, 289, 292–295; Four Nations, 117; language and linguistics, 116–118, 120–121, 305–307; literature, 326–330, 333; Mississippian groups, 114; Muskogean (Creek) Nation, 119; Pardo communities, 139; Powhatan tribes, 114; powwows, 115, 117, 120; religion and spirituality, 115, 118, 120, 409–410; Removal Act (1830), 90, 114; self-determination via Federal recognition of tribal status, 116; Seminole Indians, 119; sports and recreation, 114–115, 439–440
naturalism in art, 38, 41, 49
nature. *See* ecology and environment; habitation
Naylor, Gloria, 169
needlework (art), 39, 44–46
Negro Act (1735), 170
Negro Leagues, 447–448
Negroes. *See* African Americans
Nelson, Willie, 396
neoclassical motifs in art, 43
Neville Brothers, 389–390
New Critics, 348, 351
New Deal, 23, 243, 420. *See also* Great Depression; WPA
New Empire Theater, 19
New Negro Arts movement, 55
New Orleans, Louisiana, 7, 91; architecture, 9–10; celebrations, 250–251; hairdressers, 176; music, 389–390; restaurants, 271; sinking, threat of, 98, 106. *See also* Creoles
New Orleans Advocate, 415
"New South," 18, 199–201
New Urbanism planning movement, 27
New World, The, 326
New Year's Day food traditions, 269–270
Newcomb College, 22–23
Newman, Frances, 347
newspapers, 335
Newton-John, Olivia, 396
Neyland, Bob, 454
NHL (National Hockey League), 458–459
Nichols, Frederick, 4
Nichols, Roger, 133
Nichols, William, 12, 16
Nicholson, Francis, 10
Nigger, The, 208

nine-banded armadillos, 82
NOAA (National Oceanic and Atmospheric Association), 101–102
Noble, Thomas Satterwhite, 48
Noland, Kenneth, 59
non-Moravian Czech immigration, 129
non-timber forest resources, 95
Nordan, Lewis, 355
Norris, Tennessee, 24
North American Religion Atlas, 427
Northrup, Solomon, 168
Nossiter, Sharon Stallworth, xx–xxi
Notable Historie Containing Foure Voyages Made by Certaine French Captaines unto Florida, A, 328
Notes on the State of Virginia, 330, 331
NPCA (National Parks Conservation Association), 107
Nunez, Victor, 198
Nussbaum, Perry, 424

O Brother, Where Art Thou?, 379, 399
Oak Ridge, 24
Oberteuffer, H. Amiard, 58
Occaneechi Indians, 121
occupational and chemical hazards, 182, 245
oceans, 80, 101. *See also* coastal regions; water
Ocmulgee Mounds, 6
O'Connor, Flannery, 353
Octoroon, The, 207–208
office building design, 19
offshore oil reserves, formation of, 88
O'Hara, Scarlett, 33, 161, 181, 325, 352
oil, 86, 88, 97, 105
Okeh label, 380, 382
Oklahoma Indians, 114
okra, 282
Old Order Amish, 126, 307
Old Order Mennonites, 126, 307
"Old South" as theme in film and theater, 198
Oliver, Joseph "King," 380
Olmstead, Frederick, 168, 170, 179, 184
Olympic Games: Atlanta (1996), 28, 459–460; Berlin (1936), 459
O'Neill, Eugene, 208
Opryland, 26, 450
Orange Bowl, 445, 463
oranges and orange juice, 269, 291, 294
organizations, list of: architecture, 30–31;

art, 62–67; ethnicity, 158–160; fashion and clothing, 189–192; folklore and folklife, 253–261; food, 297; sports and recreation, 468
"Origin of the Earth, The," 227–228
origin tales, 227–228
Original Dixieland Jazz Band, 380
Ouachita Mountains, 78; caverns, 88; ecosystems, 85
Ouachita River mound, 6
outdoor recreation, 460–461; hunting and fishing, 440–441, 460–461. *See also* sports and recreation
outer coastal plain ecosystem, 78–81
Owens, Hubert B., 24
Owens, Jesse, 459
Ownby, Ted, 411
oxbow lakes, 83
Ozark county, 142, 235–236
ozone exposure, 107

Page, Thomas Nelson, 344
Painter, Nell Irvin, 325
paintings: engravings, 47; memory painters, 53–55; modern, 57–60; portraiture, 38, 40, 42, 44, 47; theorem, 44. *See also* art
Palatine immigration, 125
Palladianism architecture, 4, 10–11
Palladio Londinensis, 11
Pangaea, 86–88
pantaloons, 177
panthers, 80, 104
paper manufacturing, 96
parasols, 175–176
Pardo communities, 139
Paredes, Américo, 335, 358
Parker, Antony, 131
Parker, Colonel, 393
parks. *See* garden design
parks conservation movement, 106
Parloa, Mary, 294
parody in literature, 353
Parrish, Robert, 205
Parsons, Elsie Clews, 242–243
Parton, Dolly, 27, 450
Pascal stories, 229
passenger pigeons, 83
patchwork. *See* quilts, art of
Patterson, Paige, 419
Patton, Charley, 381
Payne, Charles, 417

Peabody, Ephraim, 339
Peale, Rembrandt, 40
peanuts and peanut butter, 284
peat, 88
pecans, 293
Peer, Ralph, 379, 380, 382, 383
Peiser, Judy, 205
pelicans, 80–81
pellagra, 268
Penhally, 352
Pentecostalism, 431–435
pepper, 276
Percy, George, 90
Percy, Walker, 354
Percy, William Alexander, 354
Perdue, Thea, 333
Perez, Louisiana Leander, 425
Perrot, Philippe, 162, 173, 176, 180, 182
Perry, Enoch Wood, 47
Perry, Shaw, and Hepburn, 24
Persian embroidery technique, 45
pesticides, 93, 104–105
Peterkin, Julia, 350
petroleum. *See* oil
"petticoat" rebellions, 265
Pettway, Mensie Lee, 164
Pew Oceans Commission, 100
Peychaud, Antoine, 290
Phagan, Mary, 424
Phillips, Sam, 388
Phipps, Susie, 138
photography, 49–51, 60–61
Piazza d'Italia, 26
Pickard, Charles, 378
picnic foods, 269
pidgins (first contact communication), 136
Piedmont Plateau, 81–82
pigeonniers, 3
pigeons, passenger, 83
pigs. *See* hogs
pimento cheese sandwiches, 288
pine borer infestation (1848-1849), 96
Pino, Pedro Bautista, 335
pisè as construction material, 14
Pittman, William Sidney, 22
"Place Congo," 244
Plant, Henry Bradley, 20
plant production for dyes, 166
plantation era, 91; agriculture and farming,
    91–94; architecture and landscaping,
    1–2, 11, 13, 21, 92; art, 38, 41, 42;
    dining, 265–267; literature, 337, 341;

slave-master relationships in folklore,
    233
Plater-Zyberk, Elizabeth, 27
Pleasant Hill, 17
po'boy sandwiches, 288–289
Pocahontas, 237, 329, 410
pocosins, 79
Poe, Edgar Allan, 334
Poesch, Jessie, 1, 11, 14
poetry, 335, 343, 355; African American,
    340. *See also* literature
Poka-Hutchi Art Colony, 58
politics and religion, 418–421, 429–430
pollution: air, 107; automobiles, 82, 107;
    coastal development and, 100; fertilizers
    and pesticides, 93; freshwater resources,
    101, 104–105; indigo, 166–167; power
    plants, 107
Ponce de Léon Hotel, 20
Ponce de Léon, Juan, 7, 90, 229
poodles as fashion symbols, 176
poor. *See* poverty
poor boy (po'boy) sandwiches, 288
pop (drinks), 291
pop music, recent, 396–398
population growth and environmental
    challenges, 99, 100
Porgy and Bess, 208, 350
pork, 273–275, 283
Porter, Katherine Anne, 352
Porter, William T., 335, 336
Portman, John C., 26
portraiture, 38, 40, 42, 44, 47. *See also*
    photography
post–World War II architecture, 25–28
postmodern literature, 352–361
pottery, art of, 43
poultry, 276–278
poverty: diet, 268; immigration to the
    North, 268; pollution, 107
power plant pollution, 107
Powhatan tribes, 114, 329
powwows, 115, 117, 120
pralines, 294
Pratt, Mary Louise, 326
preachers. *See* evangelism
Preakness Stakes, 442
"Precious Lord, Take My Hand," 386
precipitation. *See* ecology and environment
prefabricated housing design, 24
Presbytère, 9
Presbyterian Church Covenanters, 132

Presley, Elvis, 1, 392–393, 433–434
Pressler, Paul, 419
Price of Blood: A Planter Selling His Son, The, 48
Price, Reynolds, 354
Primitive Love, 397
production. *See* agriculture and farming; industrial development
professional organizations. *See* organizations, list of
professional sports. *See* sports and recreation
professional theater companies, 194
pronunciation, 308–316. *See also* language and linguistics
Protestant Church, 147; early settlement period, 123; German, 125; Huguenot, 39, 123, 327; Moravian, 2, 124; Waldensian, 124
Protestant evangelism, 411–412; civil rights movement, 414–416; Civil War, 413–414; music, 430–435; political-right movement, 418–421; progressive movement, 416–418; slavery, 411–413; Southern Baptist Convention (SBC), 419
provinces of the South (ecosystems), 78–85
public buildings, architecture of, 11, 16, 23
public housing projects, 23
public policy and art, 58
Puckett, Riley, 384
Puerto Rican writers, 358
Purdue, F. W., 447
Pure Oil Company, 457
Purlie Victorious, 209–211

quarter racing, 441–442
quill adornment, 36
quilts, art of, 44–46; African Americans, 164; quilting bees, 45, 46

R & B music, 389–390, 394–395
Raboteau, Albert J., 408, 411
race: environmental racism, 107; hypodescent, 138; multiracial groups, 138–139; religion and spirituality, 407, 411–416. *See also* African Americans; ethnicity; segregation; *specific race by name*
racing, car, 456–458
racing, horse, 441–443, 449
radio, 397, 430, 433

railroad: construction and development, 15; immigrant labor, 143; lining bar gangs, 244–245; tourism industry and, 20
Rainey, Ma, 386
rainfall and rainforests, 79
Raleigh, Walter, 292
Randolph, Mary, 277–279, 280
Randolph, Vance, 235–236, 241
Rankin, Tom, 61
Ransom, John Crowe, 348, 351
rap music, 397
Rauschenberg, Robert, 59
Rawick, George, 163
Rawlings, Marjorie Kinnan, 274, 350
Ray, Celeste, xix
RCA Victor music label, 380, 396
ready-made clothing, 184, 186
realism in art, 49
recession, depicted in film, 198
Recollections of a Southern Matron, 338
Reconstruction Period: art, 48; religion and "redemption," 413–414; segregation, 2
recording industry, 388–391. *See also* music
recordings, list of: music, 403–405; religion and spirituality, 438
recreation. *See* folklore and folklife; sports and recreation; tourism
Red, Tampa, 381
red-cockaded woodpecker, 79
red in slavery clothing, 168–169
Red Mountains, 79–85
Redding, Otis, 394–395
Reed, Irving, 229
Reed, Ishmael, 355
Reed, John Shelton, 116, 139
Reed, Ralph, 419
regional dialects. *See* dialects
regional theater, 195–196
Reichardt, Charles, 15
Reimers, David, 133
religion and spirituality, 407–438; abolition, support for, 338; art and, 52, 53; civil rights movement, 414–416, 424; demographics, contemporary, 426–430; evangelism, 408, 411–421, 430–435; festivals, ethnic, 113, 128; Great Awakening, 120, 333; minority religions of the South, 422–426; missionaries, Christian, 410; music,

241–242, 378, 386, 430–435; Native Americans, 115, 118, 120, 409–410; persecution and immigration, 123–124, 132; politics and, 418–421, 429–430; progressive Christianity in the South (post-Civil War), 416–418; race and segregation, 407, 411–416, 423, 431; Reconstruction and "redemption," 413–414; slavery, 408, 411–414, 419; Southern orthodoxy, 409; voodoo, 168–169; women, 411. *See also* churches; *specific religion by name*
R.E.M. (band), 398
Removal Act (1830), 90, 114
Renfro Valley, 25
Reserve refinery, 295
reserves, conservation, 79
resident theater, 195–196
residential architecture, 13
resorts, 20, 26. *See also* tourism
restaurants, 269, 271
restoration projects. *See* Colonial Williamsburg
Reveley, Bryce, xix–xx, 182–183
rhythm and blues, 389–390, 394–395
ribbon appliqué designs, 37
rice, 93, 284–285; plantation design, 3
Rice, Thomas D. "Daddy," 377
Richards, Gary, 358
Richmond, Virginia, development of, 91
Rickey, Branch, 445–446
Riddle, Leslie, 384
Ripley, Eliza, 176–178, 186
river transportation, 9, 91, 98
riverboat gambling, 451
rivers. *See* Mississippi River; water
road development, 25
Roanoke Island settlement, 90, 236
Roberts, Elizabeth Madox, 347
Robertson, Arthur Campbell "Eck," 381–382
Robertson, Pat, 419
Robeson, Paul, 59
Robin, C. C., 285
Robinson, Eddie, 454, 455
Robinson, Jackie, 445–446, 447
Rockefeller, John D., Jr., 24
Rococo style, 38–39
Rodgers, Jimmie, 111, 383–385
Rodriguez, Alva, 243
Rogers, James Gamble, 23
Rolling Stones, 394, 395

Romani (Gypsy) immigration, 129–130
Romans, Bernard, 166
Romantic movement in art, 40
Roosevelt, Franklin D. *See* New Deal
Root, John Wellborn, 19
Rose, Fred, 390
Rosewood, 211
Rothermel, Barbara, xviii–xix
Route 95 (interstate), 25
Rowe, Nellie Mae, 52
Rudolph, Paul, 25
rum, 289–290
Rupp, Adolph, 452
rural conditions recorded in photographs, 50
Rural Studio, 27
Russell, Irwin, 344
Russell, Tony, 376, 382
Rutledge, Sarah, 269
Ryan, Maureen, 359

Sacred Hunger, 361–362
sacred music (church music), 386, 430–435
Saffir-Simpson scale, 102
St. Augustine, Florida, 7, 8
St. Charles Hotel, 15
St. Elmo, 343
St. Joseph Day altars, 128
St. Patrick's Day parades, 113, 128
salads, 283
salamanders, 83
Salmon, William, 11
salt domes, 86
salt production, 276
saltwater intrusion, 101, 103
"saltwater Negroes" (first slaves), 134
San Marcos, Castillo, 8
Sanchez, Mario, 53, 54–55
Sanchez, Sonia, 356
Sancho, Ignatius, 331
sandbars, 86–87
Sanders, Colonel, 161
sandwiches, 288–289
Sanjek, David, xxi–xxii
Sansu Enterprises, 389
Saponi Confederation, 121
Sarasota school, 25
Saucier, Corinne, 229
sausages, 271
Savannah, Georgia, fire devastation of, 18
sawmill, 95
Sawyer, Tom, 98

Sayre, Gordon, 329, 330
SBC (Southern Baptist Convention), 419–420
scam artists, 129–130
Scarborough, Dorothy, 241
scarves, head, 173–176
schools. *See* colleges; educational institutions
Scopes trial, 382
Scots-Irish immigration, 131–133, 141; influence on southern dialects, 309; whiskey, 290
Scott, Evelyn, 347
Scott, Wendell, 457
Scottish Highland Games, 131
Scottish immigration, 131–133, 308
"Scratch, Scratch, Scratch," 247–248
Scruggs, Earl, 386
sculpture, 48, 52–53
Sea Grant, 102
Sea Islands, language of (Gullah), 312–313
sea levels, 86–87, 100, 101, 103–104
Sea World, 26
seafood, 278–279
Sears, Roebuck catalogues, 186
Seaside, Florida, 27
Secret Service, 212
sediment, 86–88
sedimentary plateau formations, 88
segregation: art, 49; desegregation in sports, 445–448; fashion and people of color, 172–177; music, 376–383, 388; Reconstruction period, 2; religion and spirituality, 423, 431; in restaurants, 269; sports and recreation, 445–448, 451, 453–455, 457. *See also* African Americans; civil rights movement; slavery
Sehorn, Marshall, 389
Seminole Indians, 119, 334, 410; Black Seminoles, 135; fashion and clothing, 184–185
Sephardic (Jewish) immigration, 124
Sequoyah (George Gist), 333
Settle, Mary Lee, 357
settlers. *See* colonial period
Severens, Kenneth, 10
Seville Square area, 8–9
Shakers church design, 17
Sharp, Cecil, 238–240, 378–379, 385
shawls, 176
Shawnee tribes, 118

Sheldon, Edward, 208
Shenandoah National Park, 82, 107
Shenandoah Valley campaign (1862), 444
Sheppard, William Ludwell, 47
shipping industry, 94
ships and boats: danger to ecosystem, 80; shipbuilding and timber industry, 95; steamboats, 98
Shoals, Leo "Muscle," 448
shoes, 171, 184
shooting competitions, 450
shorelines. *See* coastal regions
shotgun houses, 2
Show Boat, 210, 375
Shuffle Along, 210
Sider, Gerald, 121
Sidney, Rockin,' 387
Sierra Club, 85
silk in fashion, 175
Simms, William Gilmore, 341
Simpson, Lewis P., 349, 354
Siouan-speaking Indians, 120–121
16th Street Baptist Church, Birmingham, 417
Skidmore, Owings & Merrill, 24
Skynyrd, Lynyrd, 396, 399
skyscrapers, 19
slash and burn farming technique, 92
Slave Songs in the United States, 378
slavery: African immigration and beginnings of slavery, 133–140; architecture, impact on, 1–3, 10–11, 13; clothing, 163–171, 179; cooking traditions, 264–266; corn-shucking ceremonies, 242; denial of heritage, 173; dependence on in agriculture and production, 92, 166–168; education, post-Civil War, 22; first hand account studies, 163; free blacks, 176; hair styles and headgear, 173–176; legislation in support of, 170; literature, 330–334, 336–338; music, 241–242, 376–379, 381; population figures of, 115; religion and spirituality, 408, 411–414, 419; slave-master relationships in folklore, 233; sports and, 443–444; uprisings, 337, 443. *See also* abolition; African Americans; civil rights movement; indentured servants; plantation era; segregation
Sloan, Samuel, 17
smallpox, 89–90

Smart-Grosvenor, Vertamae, 274
Smiddy, "Papa Joe," 250
Smith, Bessie, 380
Smith, Clara, 382
Smith, Dean, 452
Smith, G. E. Kidder, 7
Smith, J. Frazer, 4
Smith, John, 236, 329
Smith, Lee, 141, 359
Smith, Lillian, 352, 407–408
Smith, Louise, 457
Smith, Mamie, 380
Smith, R. T., 359
smoke shops, American Indian, 116
smokehouses, 3
Smoky Mountains. *See* Great Smoky Mountains National Park
SNCC (Student Non-Violent Coordinating Committee), 417, 424–425
soccer, 439–440, 460
social status. *See* class division
societies, professional. *See* organizations, list of
sod games, 463
sodas, 291
soil: conservationist efforts and current challenges, 106; fertilizers and pesticides, 93; slash and burn farming technique, 92. *See also* agriculture and farming; ecology and environment
Sokolov, Raymond, 283
Solbel, Mechal, 411
Soldier's Plan, A (A Soldier's Story), 209
Solomon, Jack, 246
Some Sources of Southernism, 307
Song of the South, 199
songs, 241–243; folk songs, 238–246; "sorrow songs," 378; work songs, 244–246. *See also* music
Sot-Weed Factor, 330
soul music, 395
Sound and the Fury, The, 351–353
Sounder, 201
South Midland dialect, 309
Southern Appalachian Mountains, 82–83
Southern Architect, 20
Southern Baptist Convention (SBC), 419–420
Southern Churches in Crisis, 409
Southern Cross, 411
southern dialect, 314

southern drawl, 309
southern food, signature dishes, 272–295. *See also* food
Southern Gothic genre in film and theater, 201–204
southern hospitality, 267–268. *See also* food
Southern League of Professional Baseball Clubs, 444–445
southern mixed forest ecosystem, 81
southern music. *See* music
Southern orthodoxy, 409
Southern Renaissance in literature, 347, 354
southern rock, 396
Southern Rock Opera, 399
southern spirits, 289–291
Spanish and Latino cultures: churches, 147; immigration, 146–148, 357; language and linguistics, 146–148, 307; literature, 357; music, 397; Spanish exploration and early immigration, 7, 122, 326
Spanish moss, 78–79, 95
Spanish Walloons, 123
Sparks, Randy, 411
special collections, list of: architecture, 30–31; art, 62–67; ethnicity, 158–160; fashion and clothing, 189–192; folklore and folklife, 253–261; food, 297; religion and spirituality, 438. *See also* museums, list of
special occasions and food, 269–270
spectator sports. *See* sports and recreation
speech. *See* language and linguistics
speedways, 457–458
Spelman, Henry, 439
Spencer, Anne, 349
Spencer, Jon, 434
spinning wool, 168
Spiral Group, 56–57
Spirit. *See* Pentecostalism
Spirit of the Times, 335
spirits (drinks), 289–291
spirituality. *See* religion and spirituality
spirituals (music), 241–242, 378, 431
sports and recreation, 439–468; African Americans, 442–443, 455, 457; baseball, 444–448; basketball, 452–453; car racing, 456–458; Civil War era, 444; class division, 440; colonial period, 440; facilities, design of, 28; fashion and clothing, 183–184; football, 445,

sports and recreation (*continued*)
453–454; gambling, 116, 441, 451; golf and tennis, 455–456; high school and college sports, 445, 447, 452–455, 460–465; hockey, 458–459; horse racing, 441–443, 449; hunting and fishing, 80, 276, 440–441, 460–461; Native Americans, 114–115, 439–440; Olympic Games, 28, 459–460; outdoor recreation, 440–441, 460–461; segregation, 443–449, 451, 453–455, 457; slavery and, 443–444; soccer, 460; state fairs, 449–451; track and field, 459; women, 440, 452, 455–457, 460, 464–465; youth sports, 441, 456
spring training, baseball, 449
Sputnik Monroe, 451
standardization of language, 310
Stanley, Ralph, 399
Starr, Kathy, 273
state art commissions, list of, 67–69
State Centers for the Book, list of, 372–373
state fairs and sports, 449–451
Stax music label, 388–389, 399
steam power, 94, 96–97
steamboats, 98
steel, 96–97
Steel Magnolias, 202
Stewart, Jim, 388
Stewart, Maaja A., xix–xx
Stewart, Thomas, 17
stickball, 114
stock car racing, 456–458
Stoeltke, Beverly, 113
stomp dances, 115
Stone, Edward Durell, 21, 22, 25
Stone, Henry, 397
stone crabs, 279
Stoneman, Ernest "Pop," 383
stoneware pottery, art of, 43
stories and storytelling. *See* folklore and folklife; literature
Stovall, Queena, 53
Stowe, Harriet Beecher, 207, 340
Strachey, William, 328
Stribling, T. S., 350
Strickland, William, 16–18
Stricklin, David, 375, 385
Stringfellow, Thornton, 340
strip-mining techniques, 96, 105
stripped classicism, 23
Stroud, T. M., 247–248

Stryker, Roy, 50
Stuart, Gilbert, 40
Student Non-Violent Coordinating Committee (SNCC), 417, 424–425
studios, recording. *See* recording industry
Styron, William, 360
suburbanization, 27
Suddenly Last Summer, 204
Sugar Bowl, 445
sugar cane and refinement, 93–94, 294–295
Sugar King, 295
suits, men's, 179–181
Sullivan, John L., 449
Summitt, Pat, 453
Sun music label, 388
Sunday dinner traditions, 270
Sunday wear for slaves, 163–166
Sundquist, Eric J., 354
Superdome, 28
superstitions, 246–247, 434–435
Survey of Verb Forms in the Eastern United States, A, 315
sustainable forest management, 94
sustainable harvesting, 96
Swallow Barn, 337
Swamp Land Acts (1849–1850), 95–96
Swamp-Pop music, 386–387
swamps, 78–79
Sweet Briar College, 22
sweet milk, 291
"Sweet Potato Queens," 113
sweet potatoes, 293–294
sweet rolls, 288
sweet tea, 291
sweets, 292–295
Swiss immigration, 125
Syrian immigrants, 142–143

T. K. Records, 397
T-shaped houses, 2
Tabasco brand hot sauce, 276
tabby as a building material, 6, 14
tailoring techniques, 179–180. *See also* fashion and clothing
tales and folklore, 225–236. *See also* folklore and folklife
"Talking Too Much" tales, 236
"Talking Turtle, The," 235–236
tall tales, 228–232
Tallant, Robert, 184
Talomico settlement, 6

Tammy and the Bachelor, 198
"Tar Baby, The," 234–235
Tara (*Gone with the Wind*), 1
Tate, Allen, 343, 347, 351
Tavernier, Bertrand, 205
taverns and sports, 440
Tayloe, John, II, 14
Taylor, Alan, 327, 333
Taylor, Peter, 353
Taylor, Robert R., 22
tea, 291
tectonic plates (Pangaea), 86–88
television and religion, 430
temperance movement, 291
temperate forests, 79, 96
Temple, Shirley, 198
Tennessee Centennial Exposition, 19
Tennessee State Capitol, 16, 18
Tennessee State Office Building, 23
Tennessee Valley Authority (TVA), 24
tennis, 455
Tethys Seaway, 86
Textile Leagues, 452
textiles and fabrics, 180; African
    Americans, 166–168; cotton, 3, 81, 89,
    93, 104; decoration, 39; production and
    industry, 93, 168, 180, 184, 186;
    quilting, 45; silk, 175; trade, 163. *See
    also* fashion and clothing
theater, 193–195, 210–211. *See also* film
    and theater
Theatrical Syndicate, 195
theme parks, 26, 450
Theorem painting. *See* portraiture
therapeutic resorts, 20
Theüs, Jeremiah, 38
Thomas, Alma, 56
Thomas, Augustus, 212
Thomas, Daniel, 246
Thomas, Henry "Ragtime Texas," 381
Thomas, Irma, 250
Thompson, E. P., 162
Thompson, Eloise Bibb, 347
Thompson, Robert Farris, 465
Thompson, Stith, 225–226
Thorns, William, 223–224
Thornton, Billy Bob, 202
Thornton, John, 134
Thorpe, Thomas Bangs, 336
threatened species of animals, 80
*Throne of the Third Heaven of the Nations
    Millennium General Assembly, The*, 53

thunderstorms, 101–102
Thurber, John, 284
tignons, 174
timber and logging, 95–96
timeline of southern events, 469–477
Timrod, Henry, 342, 343
Tin Pan Alley, 380
tires, racing, 457
Title IX, 460
Titon, Jeff Todd, 137
To Kill a Mockingbird, 199
tobacco, 3, 18–19, 92, 146, 456
Tobacco Road, 201
"Tobacco Road" basketball, 452
Tolson, Edgar, 52
Tonalist movement, 57
Toomer, Jean, 349
topography, karst, 88
Tourgé, Albion, 345
tourism: amusement and theme parks, 26,
    450; country music attractions, 25–26,
    383–385; Creole culture, 137;
    development of, 20, 25; ethnic sites of
    interest, 126; outdoor recreation,
    440–441, 460–461. *See also* sports and
    recreation
Toussaint, Allen, 389
track and field, 459
trade literature, 20
trade uniforms, 179
tragedy ballads, 245–246
Trail of Tears, 35–36
transcripts published, language and
    linguistics, list of, 323–324
transnationalism, 145
transportation: air travel, 25; automobiles,
    25, 82, 107; boats and ships, 80, 95, 98;
    railroad, 15; travel narratives, 326–330;
    water transportation, 9, 91, 98
Travolta, John, 396
Traylor, Bill, 52
Treasury Department, control of art
    subjects, 58
trees. *See* forests
Trethewey, Natasha, 355
trickster stories, 230–236, 334
Triple Crown, 442
tri-racial isolates, 139
tropical rainforests, 79
tropical region (Everglades ecosystem), 79
tropical storms, 101–102
Trumbauer, Horace, 24

"Try a Little Tenderness," 395
tsabouna (Greek bagpipes), 130
Tucker, Susan, xx–xxi
Turner, Lorenzo Dow, 313
Turner, Nat, 337, 412
Turner, Paul Venable, 16, 24
turnips, 282
Tuscan towers in building design, 17
Tuscarora Indians, 121–122
Tuskegee Indians, 227–228
Tuskegee Institute, 22
TVA (Tennessee Valley Authority), 24
Twain, Mark, 98, 271, 345
Twain, Shania, 398
Tweed, Thomas, 436
twirling (batons), 465
Twitchell, Ralph, 25
2 Live Crew (band), 397
Twombly, Cy, 59
Tyler, Anne, 359

Ulrich, Pamela, 168
Ulster Scottish immigrants, 131–133
Uncle Remus: His Songs and Sayings, 344
Uncle Remus Tales, 234, 242
"Uncle Tom," 207
Uncle Tom's Cabin, 207, 340
Underground Railroad and quilt patterns,
    46
uniforms and fashion, 178
United Nations Intergovernmental Panel
    on Climate Change (IPCC), 100, 101
United States. See entries at U.S.
universities. See colleges
University of Alabama, 16
University of Arkansas, 464
University of Virginia, architecture of,
    15–16, 22
Unsworth, Barry, 361–362
Upton, Dell, 13
Urban League, 56
urban sprawl, 106. See also cities and
    urbanization
U.S. Army Corps of Engineers, 97
U.S. Bureau of Indian Affairs, 116
U.S. Geological Survey, 102
U.S. Post Office and Courthouse, Baton
    Rouge, 23

vacations. See tourism, development of
Valdez, Luis, 358
Vanderbilt, George W., 20

vegetables, 281–284
Veneto, 10–11
Victor Talking Machine Company, 380,
    383
videos. See films, list of
Vietnamese immigrants, 144, 272
Villatoro, Marcos, 147
Virginia American Indian tribes, 119–120
Virginia house building style, 8
Virginia Housewife, The, 277, 278–279, 280
Virginia State Penitentiary, 12
Virginia Writers Project (VWP), 248
Vlach, John Michael, 13
vocabulary. See language and linguistics
Voigt, Ellen Bryant, 355
von Graffenried, Christoph, 126
"voodoo queen" (Marie Laveau), 176
voodoo religion, 168–169
VWP (Virginia Writers Project), 248

Waccamaw-Sioux Indians, 120
waist, small, and fashion, 181
Waldensian Church, 124
Walker, Alice, 201, 356
Walker, David, 337
Walker, Margaret, 356
Walker, William Aiken, 49
Wallace, George, 399
Walloons (Spanish), 123
War on Poverty, 268
Ward, Nancy, 333
Ware, Charles P., 241
Ware, Isaac, 11
Warren, Robert Penn, 205, 351, 352, 354
Warrens of Virginia, The, 212
Washington, Booker T., 22, 171, 172, 346
Washington, George: folktales of,
    236–237; food and drink, 286, 290;
    Mount Vernon, 15
Washington, Martha, 293
Washington, William D., 47
Washington Course, 442
water: coastlines, 86–87; conservationist
    efforts and current challenges, 99–106;
    engineering projects, 91, 105–106; fall
    lines, 88; freshwater resources, 101,
    104–105; landscape design and, 9;
    oceans, 80, 101; pollution, 101,
    104–105; rainfall, 79; transportation, 91,
    98. See also ecology and environment;
    habitation; Mississippi River
Water Is Wide, The, 200–201

waterfalls and energy production, 91
Waterman, Thomas Tileston, 4
watermelons, 293
Waters, Muddy, 393–394
waterwheel, 91
Watson, Tom, 424
Way Down South, 198
weather-related folk beliefs, 247
weaving, finger, 168
Web sites, list of: architecture, 30; ecology
    and environment, 109–110; ethnicity,
    155–156; film and theater, 215; food,
    295–296; language and linguistics,
    321–323; literature, 371–372; religion
    and spirituality, 438; sports and
    recreation, 467
Webb, Clive, 424
Webster, Noah, 310
Weems, Carrie Mae, 61
Weiner, Marli, 341
Wells-Barnett, Ida B., 346
Welty, Eudora, 51, 343, 352
West, Benjamin, 40
West African languages, 313
West Indian manatees, 80
western plateaus, 84–85
wetlands, 97, 103–104
Wheatley, Phillis, 331
whiskey, 290
Whiskey Rebellion (1794), 290
White, Bernice, 435
White, George, 378
White, Graham and Shane, 163, 174
White, John, 38, 328
white supremacy. *See* Ku Klux Klan
Whitefield, George, 332, 333
wild game, 276
wildlife. *See* ecology and environment;
    habitation; hunting
Wiley, Bell Irvin, 178–179
Williams, Hank, 390, 433
Williams, Tennessee, 195, 204, 353
Williamsburg, Virginia, 5, 10, 24, 28, 450
Wilson, Charles Reagan, 111, 413
Wilson, Ellis, 56
winter recreation, 458–459
Wireman, Jaime L., 407
Witherspoon, John, 310
Wodehouse, Lawrence, 23
Wolf, Howlin' (Chester Burnett), 111
Wolfe, Thomas, 350
Wollaston, John, 38–39

women: abolition movement, role in, 338;
    African American, 56, 346; art, 43,
    44–46, 53–54, 60–61; education, 22–23,
    39; fashion and clothing, 177, 181–184,
    187; free women of color, 174; garden
    clubs, 24; music, 380, 396–397;
    photography, 60–61; religion and
    spirituality, 411; social reforms,
    408–409; sports and recreation, 440,
    452, 455–457, 460, 464–465; writers,
    341, 346–347
women's movement, 342, 356–358
Wood, Curtis, 133
Wood, Peter, 115, 134, 328
wood carvings, 52
woodpeckers, 79
Woodward, C. Vann, 342
Woodward, Henry, 284
wool, 168, 180
woolly adelgid, 107
Word Geography, 315
work songs, 244–246
worker programs, H2A guest, 147
working class clothing and fashion, 179
World Heritage Sites, 88
"Wormy Apple" tale, 236
WPA (Works Progress Administration), 51,
    58, 243; Harlem Art Workshop, 56
"Wreck of the Old 97, The," 245
Wren, Christopher, 12
wrestling, 440, 451
Wright, Betty, 396–397
Wright, Frank Lloyd, 21–22, 24
Wright, Richard, 349
Wuthnow, Robert, 420
Wycliffe Bible Translators, 314

Yaeger, Patricia, 353
Yazoo Pumps, 105
Ybor, Vicente Martínez, 146
yeast, 287
YMCAs, 456
yodeling, 384
youth sports and recreation, 441, 456. *See
    also* high school sports
Yuchi tribe, 119

Z. Z. Hill, 398
zippers, 183
Zwonitzer, Mark, 384
Zydeco, Buckwheat, 387
zydeco music, 137, 386–387

ABOUT THE EDITORS AND CONTRIBUTORS

REBECCA MARK is Associate Professor of American Literature at Tulane University and affiliated with the Deep South Regional Humanities Center.

ROB VAUGHAN is President of the Virginia Foundation for the Humanities and founding Director of the South Atlantic Humanities Center. He is also President of the National Humanities Alliance and teaches in the M.B.A. Program at the Darden School of the University of Virginia. Among other publications, Rob is the editor with Merrill D. Peterson of *The Virginia Statute for Religious Freedom: Its Evolution and Consequences in American History* (1988). He received his B.A. from Washington and Lee University and his M.A. and Ph.D. in English from the University of Virginia.

BRUCE ADELSON is the author of thirteen books about sports and American history, some for children, including *William Howe, British General* and *David Farragut, Union Admiral, The Composite Guide to Softball, Grand Slam Trivia and Touchdown Trivia*; and some for adults, including *Brushing Back Jim Crow: The Integration of Minor League Baseball in the American South* and *The Minor League Baseball Book*. He has been a commentator for NPR's *Morning Edition* and CBS Radio's *Major League Baseball Game of the Week* and editor of *The Four Sport Stadium Guide* (1994). Bruce Adelson's work has also been published in the *Washington Post, Atlanta Journal-Constitution, Baseball America, Lingua Franca Magazine*, and *USA Today's Baseball Weekly*.

SUSAN V. DONALDSON teaches American literature at the College of William and Mary, where she has been a member of the English Department faculty since 1985. She is the author of *Competing Voices: The American Novel, 1865–1914* (1998), which won a *Choice* Outstanding Academic Book award, and some thirty articles on southern literature, culture, and art. She is also co-editor, with Anne Goodwyn Jones, of *Haunted Bodies: Gender and Southern Texts* (1997) and has guest-edited two special issues of *The Faulkner Journal*, one on sexuality and the other on masculinity. Currently she is working on two book-length projects, one on the politics of storytelling in the U.S. South and the other on Faulkner, Welty, and the geography of gender.

TASHA EICHENSEHER is a freelance environmental writer. She holds a master's degree in environmental management from Yale University's School of Forestry and Environmental Studies, where she conducted urban wetlands research and investigated the social and economic implications of water resource policy. Her environmental work has also included ecological assessment and communications consulting for local land trusts and open space preservation organizations, as well as a fellowship with the U.S. Environmental Protection Agency. She has done editorial work for *E/The Environmental Magazine, Outside, Vanity Fair, George, Blue*, and *Travel & Leisure*.

PAUL HARVEY is Professor of History at the University of Colorado at Colorado Springs. Most recently, he is the author of *Freedom's Coming: Religious Culture and the Shaping of the South from Civil War Through Civil Rights* (2005), and the co-editor of *Themes in Religion and American Culture* as well as *Religion in America Since 1945: A Columbia Documentary History*.

THOMAS S. HISCHAK is Professor of Theater at the State University of New York College, Cortland. He is the author of *The Tin Pan Alley Encyclopedia; Film It with Music: An Encyclopedic Guide to the American Movie Musical; American Theatre: A Chronicle of Comedy and Drama, 1969–2000; The American Musical Film Song Encyclopedia; The Theatergoer's Almanac; The American Musical Theatre Song Encyclopedia; Stage It with Music: An Encyclopedic Guide to the American Musical Theatre;* and *Word Crazy: Broadway Lyricsts from Cohan to Sondheim*.

JON LOHMAN is the Director of the Virginia Folklife Program at the Virginia Foundation for the Humanities. He graduated from the University of North Carolina and received his M.A. from the University of Chicago and a Ph.D. in folklore and folklife from the University of Pennsylvania. Dr. Lohman's academic work focuses on the public reception of murals and other forms of public art and on the transatlantic celebration of Mardi Gras. He became inspired by Mardi Gras as an elementary school teacher in New Orleans, Louisiana.

PAULA MOHR is a Ph.D. candidate in the Department of Architectural History at the University of Virginia, where she is writing her dissertation on the architecture in Central Park. She received her B.A. from the University of Iowa and an M.A. in museum administration from the Cooperstown Graduate Program in Museum Studies. Ms. Mohr is the former curator of the Department of the Treasury in Washington, D.C., and has also held curatorial positions with the National Trust for Historic Preservation, the National Park Service, and the Old Executive Office Building, Office of the President.

MICHAEL MONTGOMERY is Professor Emeritus of English and Linguistics at the University of South Carolina. He has published widely on many varieties of southern American English, including Appalachian and Gullah, and has researched the transatlantic connections of American English in Ireland and Scotland. His historical dictionary of southern Appalachian speech, *Dictionary of Smoky Mountain English*, was published in 2004.

SHARON STALLWORTH NOSSITER is a former newspaper reporter who has attended culinary classes at home and abroad, and worked variously delivering mushrooms in New Orleans, selling cheese in Manhattan, and prepping food for a busy French Quarter restaurant.

CELESTE RAY is an Associate Professor of Anthropology at the University of the South, where she is department chair. She is the author of *Highland Heritage: Scottish Americans in the American South* (2001), and editor of *Southern Heritage on Display: Public Ritual and Ethnic Diversity Within Southern Regionalism* (2003), *Signifying Serpents and Mardi-Gras Runners: Representing Identity in Selected Souths* (2003), and *Transatlantic Scots* (forthcoming). Ray is President of the Southern Anthropological Society. She completed her Ph.D. in anthropology at the University of North Carolina at Chapel Hill and her master's degree at the University of Edinburgh, Scotland, in archaeology. Her other research interests include ethnoecology.

BRYCE REVELEY is the owner of Gentle Arts Textile Conservation in New Orleans, serves as Textile Consultant at William Doyle Auction Gallery in New York City, and also works as an appraiser of textiles. She has taught human ecology at Louisiana State University and art history at Tulane University, and she has contributed articles to *Southern Accents, Creative Needle, Southern Arts Quarterly*, and other academic publications. Currently, she is working on a book on death and dying in nineteenth-century New Orleans.

BARBARA ROTHERMEL is Director of the Daura Gallery and Instructor of Museum Studies at Lynchburg College. She has taught in Pennsylvania and has served as curator of museums in New York, Pennsylvania, and Florida. She has published frequently in *Folk Art*, the journal of the American Folk Art Museum, and lectures widely on American folk art, nineteenth-century American art, Australian art, and learning from the object in museums. She holds a master of liberal studies/museum emphasis with a concentration in art history from the University of Oklahoma.

DAVID SANJEK is the Director of the BMI Archives. He has a Ph.D. in American literature from Washington University. With his late father, Russell, He co-wrote *Pennies from Heaven: The American Popular Music Business in the Twentieth Century* (Da Capo Press, 1996). He has published widely on popular culture, with music as a primary focus. Recent work includes contributions to *Journal of Popular Music Studies, Quarterly Review of Film and Video*, and *American Studies*, as well as the collections *The Aesthetics of Cultural Studies: Form, Function, Fashion* and *A Boy Named Sue: Gender and Genre in Country Music*. He is completing *Always on My Mind: Music, Memory and Money*.

MAAJA A. STEWART has published *Domestic Realities and Imperial Fictions: Jane Austen's Novels in Eighteenth-Century Contexts* as well as a number of articles on eighteenth-century British literature and culture. Dr. Stewart, who holds a Ph.D. in English literature, is currently doing research on the meeting of different cultures around cloth and color production, a topic she has studied from a variety of perspectives in undergraduate and graduate seminars. Her recent focus has turned to the Deep South, especially New Orleans and the area surrounding it. She is also a textile artist, currently experimenting with dyes, paints, and various other surface manipulations of cloth in quilts and clothes.

SUSAN TUCKER is Curator of Books and Records at the Newcomb College Center for Research on Women, Tulane University. Educated at Tulane and the University of Denver, she is a certified archivist who since the late 1970s has specialized in manuscripts, oral histories, and books related to the lives of women in the nineteenth and twentieth centuries. She is the author of *Telling Memories Among Southern Women* and is a frequent presenter on the history of scrapbooks, photograph albums, and the papers of women. During 1999, she was a Fulbright Scholar to Iceland, where she studied the use of the archives and libraries. Currently she is working with Katherine Ott and Patricia Buckler to edit an anthology of essays on scrapbooks in the United States (forthcoming).

The Greenwood Encyclopedia
of American Regional Cultures

The Great Plains Region, *edited by Amanda Rees*

The Mid-Atlantic Region, *edited by Robert P. Marzec*

The Midwest, *edited by Joseph W. Slade and Judith Yaross Lee*

New England, *edited by Michael Sletcher*

The Pacific Region, *edited by Jan Goggans with Aaron DiFranco*

The Rocky Mountain Region, *edited by Rick Newby*

The South, *edited by Rebecca Mark and Rob Vaughan*

The Southwest, *edited by Mark Busby*